Captain Alex MacLean

I0895597

Don MacGillivray

Captain Alex MacLean
Jack London's Sea Wolf

UBCPress · Vancouver · Toronto

© UBC Press 2008

All rights reserved. No part of this publication may be reproduced, stored in a retrieval system, or transmitted, in any form or by any means, without prior written permission of the publisher, or, in Canada, in the case of photocopying or other reprographic copying, a licence from Access Copyright (Canadian Copyright Licensing Agency), www.accesscopyright.ca.

16 15 14 13 12 11 10 09 08   5 4 3 2 1

Printed in Canada on ancient-forest-free paper (100% post-consumer recycled) that is processed chlorine- and acid-free, with vegetable-based inks.

Library and Archives Canada Cataloguing in Publication

MacGillivray, Don, 1942-
Captain Alex MacLean : Jack London's Sea Wolf / Don MacGillivray.

Includes bibliographical references and index.
ISBN 978-0-7748-1471-3 (bound); 978-0-7748-1472-0 (pbk.)

1. MacLean, Alexander, 1858-1914. 2. Sealing – North Pacific Ocean – History. 3. Sealers (Persons) – Canada – Biography. 4. Sailors – Nova Scotia – Cape Breton Island – Biography. I. Title. .

VK140.M28M27 2008   639.2'9092   C2007-907478-2

Canadä

UBC Press gratefully acknowledges the financial support for our publishing program of the Government of Canada through the Book Publishing Industry Development Program (BPIDP), and of the Canada Council for the Arts, and the British Columbia Arts Council.

This book has been published with the help of grants from Cape Breton University and the Canadian Federation for the Humanities and Social Sciences, the latter through the Aid to Scholarly Publications Programme, using funds provided by the Social Sciences and Humanities Research Council of Canada.

UBC Press
The University of British Columbia
2029 West Mall
Vancouver, BC V6T 1Z2
604-822-5959 / Fax: 604-822-6083
www.ubcpress.ca

To the memory of

Charles "Duffy" MacGillivray

Isabelle Bryson MacGillivray

Gerald Thomas

Contents

Illustrations

Acknowledgments

This book was a long time in the making. One of the positive features is the number of interested and helpful individuals one meets along the way, offering encouragement and valuable information. My colleagues in the History Department at Cape Breton University have been continuously supportive. It is a genuine pleasure to work with them. Cape Breton University, through sabbaticals and research grants, has supported this project over the years. The university library staff has contributed much assistance as this work gradually took shape, and I must single out Cathy Chisholm, Debbie MacInnis, Mary Campbell, Mary Dobson, and especially Laura Sims, Reference Librarian, for many, many hours of their time. Jeff Carre and Lou Duggan smoothed out some computer glitches. Richard MacKinnon took the time to read an early draft of the final chapter. Bruno McInnis, Barry Gabriel, and Chris Reid lent their skills to the illustrations. Gerry Shea in the print shop and John Doue in the mailroom were extremely helpful as I grappled with deadlines on more than one occasion. The staff at the Beaton Institute of Cape Breton Studies was always helpful. A special thanks to Harvey Johnstone, dean of Research and Academic Institutes at Cape Breton University, for his interest and support.

In the wider Cape Breton community, individuals who have read portions or all of the manuscript at various times, and listened to and discussed Alex MacLean with me on countless occasions, include good friends Ellison Robertson, Jim Watson, John Shaw, Jim Kelly, Ian Macintyre, and John MacLean. The interest and assistance of one of Cape Breton's finest genealogists, Father A.J. MacMillan, is deeply appreciated. Former students Dave Fraser and Maureen McDonald were very helpful. Fred Williams from Ingonish kindly shared information. Michael MacPhee, Johnny Macintyre, Donnie MacLellan, the late Donald MacEachern, and the late Ronald J. Beaton generously shared their stories of Alex MacLean. My fourth cousin, Hugh MacPherson, from Big Pond Centre, frequently offered refuge. Stan McLean, the skillful, personable ex-skipper of the *Caritas* who is also from

Big Pond, gave me an opportunity to sail the Bras d'Or Lake on numerous occasions. Marine regulations were strictly followed.

A special note of appreciation is extended to Professor Hugh Laracy, from the Department of History at the University of Auckland, for his generous sharing of information. The recently deceased Briton Cooper "Tony" Busch, who was the former William R. Kenan Jr. Professor of History at Colgate University, shared some of his vast knowledge of the sealing industry in correspondence and in conversation at a conference in San Diego. Neil MacNeil from Bethesda, Maryland, was very helpful in correspondence concerning his father's work. Bruce Nunn from Halifax shared Henry Henderson's work on Robert Henderson. Robert Miller of Coupeville, Washington, shared documents concerning the *Clara Monarch.* Californians Bill Norin and Margaret Reiman, both with distant roots in Cape Breton, have contributed valuable information and demonstrated an ongoing interest in this study.

In Halifax, the hospitality of Susan McLean and Karen Swim added significantly to the enjoyment of my numerous research forays to that seaport. The staff at the Nova Scotia Archives and Records Management, Dalhousie University Library, and the Maritime Museum of the Atlantic was extremely helpful. I would particularly like to acknowledge the assistance and interest of George Dupuis and John MacLeod, of the archives, and David Matthews, who is the former head of the Maritime Museum of the Atlantic. Dr. Allan McDonald, now deceased, who was formerly of Halifax, led me to correspondence from his Cape Breton relatives who were on the west coast in the 1890s. His brother Greg McDonald from Halifax kindly gave permission to cite from this collection.

The individuals at Library and Archives Canada in Ottawa, as every Canadian scholar realizes, were extremely helpful. In Victoria, the staff at the British Columbia Archives, the City of Victoria Archives, and the Maritime Museum were excellent. Professor R.H. Roy also deserves my thanks. My niece, Barb Stewart, tidied up some loose ends in research. Farther up the island, Corinne Stewart in Nanaimo and June and Victor Rushton in Comox were, as always, gracious. In Vancouver, the staff at the University of British Columbia libraries, the Maritime Museum, the Vancouver Public Library, and the City of Vancouver Archives were very helpful. Anthony MacLennan offered accommodations and gathered some valuable research material for me in Vancouver. Murray Lundberg from Carcross, Yukon, tracked down relevant research material on the Klondike period.

I must acknowledge the Oakland Public Library for their assistance on a number of occasions. Sean Folsom and Sharon Devlin were generous hosts in Oakland. Carol Brookman, proprietor of Heinold's First and Last Chance Saloon on the Oakland waterfront, kindly gave permission to use a fine photograph of Alex MacLean. Many people interested in Jack London are indebted to the late Russ Kingman, who was formerly of Glen Ellen, California. I respectfully add my name to the long list. I also owe a note of gratitude to the Western Jewish History Center at the Judiah L. Magnes Museum in Berkeley, California. In San Francisco, the staff at the San Francisco Public Library, the Maritime Museum, the California Academy of Sciences, and the North Baker Research Library of the California Historical Society all contributed valuable information. My hosts in West Hollywood were Belinda and Brian Heron. In San Marino, the Henry E. Huntington Library staff was accommodating. The San Diego Public Library staff also deserves a thank you, as does the staff in the Milton S. Eisenhower Library at Johns Hopkins University in Baltimore. The staff at the National Archives and Records Administration in the Pacific Sierra Region of San Bruno, California, and of the National Archives and Records Administration in the Alaska Region of Anchorage, Alaska, were also extremely helpful. It was a pleasure to carry out research at the Library of Congress in Washington and at the National Archives and Records Management facility in College Park, Maryland. Thanks are also due to the anonymous reviewers at UBC Press and to the Aid to Scholarly Publications Programme.

A special thank you to Robert A.J. McDonald at the University of British Columbia; Geoff Smith at Queen's University; Maurice Smith, curator emeritus at the Maritime Museum of the Great Lakes in Kingston, Ontario; and Brian Osborne at Queen's University. The comments, suggestions, and assistance of Ian McKay in the Department of History at Queen's University were, quite simply, invaluable. Sharise McKeigan came on board early in the voyage, which was admittedly a long one, and kept the crew at their tasks. Her support was essential, and her patience and understanding can only be admired.

A Note on Word Usage

While Alex MacLean and many others used McLean, "Mc" and "Mac" are only preferences. In Gaelic, it is "Mac." The term "Gael" is the only term Gaelic speakers use. The term is ancient. In sources that are cited, the accepted usage, American or Canadian, is continued. Also, while the spelling of "Behring" is retained in contemporary accounts, the commonly accepted "Bering" is used otherwise in the text. The Commander Islands are more correctly the Komandorskiye Islands, but the former was extensively used during the period under study and so was retained. The term "white" is used with absolutely no suggestion of scientific status. It was simply common usage during the period.

Captain Alex MacLean

Introduction

> McLean had an exciting record of adventure and upon his deeds I based my Sea Wolf character. Of course, much of the Sea Wolf is imaginary development, but the basis is Alexander McLean.
>
> – Jack London, 1905

Alex MacLean was a Cape Breton Gael, master mariner, sealer, poacher, adventurer, storyteller, drinking companion, husband, and father. He was an exceptional sailor and a fascinating individual who acquired an enormous reputation in the heel of the age of sail. Although he began sailing the Atlantic in the 1870s, his career centred on the Pacific, and for more than three decades he was one of the best-known waterfront figures on North America's west coast. For a variety of reasons, Alex MacLean's name was recognized in Ottawa, Washington, London, New York, St. Petersburg, and The Hague. His place in Canadian history is sparse and harsh. In Norah Story's *The Oxford Companion to Canadian History and Literature,* MacLean's "career as an international poacher and as a pirate in the Pacific Ocean" began in 1880. She made the connection with London's novel and noted that MacLean "was wanted by many countries, including Canada." Story's sketch did acknowledge that "the testimony of those who knew this outlaw indicates that London maligned him, and that while MacLean ruled his men sternly, he was not harsh or brutal."[1]

Alex MacLean was quite representative of his people, his place, and his time. His grandparents were part of that massive emigration from the Highlands and islands of the west coast of Scotland to North America. More than 20,000 people came to Cape Breton Island, on Canada's east coast, in the early nineteenth century – the single largest group, by far, to settle on the island. Their cultural stamp clearly remains to the present. Alex and his older brother Dan were among the many thousands who departed Cape Breton seeking jobs, opportunities, and adventure. MacLean's career before the mast carried him from the waters of Cape Breton Island and the Atlantic Ocean into the New England fishing fleet and deep-water vessels out of east coast ports during the 1870s. At the end of that decade, he sailed around the Horn and spent the next thirty-five years working the waters of the Pacific. He was on board a seminal sealing voyage into the Bering Sea in 1883, which solidly established and directed Canada's pelagic sealing fleet on the west coast.[2] It was a new, and lucrative, industry for the expanding economy of Victoria, British Columbia. Alex and Dan quickly became two of the most successful sealers, operating out of the capital city throughout the 1880s. But there were problems: "Amphibious is the fur seal, ubiquitous and carnivorous, uniparous, gregarious, and withal polygamous," making it possibly "the most controversial animal in the history of modern diplomacy."[3] The MacLeans could not have targeted a more contentious mammal.

It was a period of expanding empires and changing frontiers. Canada's colonial relationship complicated British-American dealings, and this particular dispute "was the longest-lasting and most intractable dispute of this pivotal period in Anglo-American relations."[4] Russia and Japan were also involved in the sealing industry, so five countries had a direct interest in these mammals, and conflict was close to the surface. Not only national interests but also financial considerations preoccupied the diplomats and politicians. Given this constellation of rival state interests, the fur seal question would tax international amity. There was another significant aspect surrounding the fur seals. The dispute between the United States and Britain, with Canada glaring over Britain's diplomatic shoulder, initially concerned international waters and property rights. Gradually, it evolved into conservation issues and environmental diplomacy, which brought together all five countries and culminated in one of the first "comprehensive wildlife conservation treaties in history" in 1911.[5]

The dispute was an issue that received wide public coverage. As one contemporary writer remarked, "perhaps more printer's ink has been spread over the fur-seal, directly and indirectly, than over any species save man."[6] One of the many personalities involved was Henry Wood Elliott. An outspoken and abrasive American, Elliott was also indefatigable in his quest to save the fur seals, and for more than four decades he strongly criticized the North American Commercial Company, American government administrations, and any expert who disagreed with him. Nor did he forget "Alexander McLean, known as a notorious British pirate" in his public condemnations.[7] Alex MacLean was literally in the front lines of complex and evolving political, diplomatic, financial, and environmental issues – issues that held the rapt attention of governments, special interest groups, and, frequently, the public in all five countries. Russian authorities would confront Canadian, American, and Japanese sealers, and the Americans would seize both Canadian and Japanese vessels.[8] Tracing the voyages, attitudes, and experiences of these seal hunters offers an opportunity to view these international contests of rivalry, expansion, and compromise as well as the political and public debates that accompanied them, from additional, and sometimes individual, perspectives.

On a number of occasions, Alex MacLean's participation in and influence on events ranged far beyond the decks of the vessels under his command. He was the captain of an American vessel, the *James Hamilton Lewis,* which was seized by the Russians near the Commander Islands in 1890. He was a central witness during the Bering Sea Claims Commission hearings in 1896-97. This particular process settled part of the Bering Sea controversy, a major diplomatic difficulty that plagued Canadian-American-British relations for twenty-five years. A few years later, Alex was a leading witness for the *New York Sun* in its defence against a libel suit brought by a rogue adventurer whom MacLean knew all too well. Yet his participation in these legal skirmishes constituted merely some of his more sedentary activities.

Piracy was a term used loosely, sometimes interchangeably, with privateer (operating with the consent of a government through a letter of marque), buccaneer (applied to themselves by Caribbean sea raiders who claimed privateer status), and freebooter (a synonym for buccaneer). The terms were frequently applied carelessly. Piracy, however, is defined as "the practice or crime of robbery and depredation on the sea or navigable river, etc. or by descent from the sea upon the coast, by persons not holding a commission from an established civilized state."[9] Given the severity of the charge, and the penalty for those found guilty, this more restrictive definition should be kept in mind. But piracy was only one of the serious depredations attributed to Alex MacLean, if an account in the *Atlantic Advocate* in 1958 is at all accurate. It states that MacLean "was wanted by at least seven countries for an assortment of crimes ranging from seal poaching and pearl theft to murder and piracy. He was suspected of seventy murders at least, although he was never brought to justice or charged with any of them."[10] The only reference uncovered in the *Canadian Historical Review,* which dismisses MacLean as "the notorious ex-Cape Bretoner," suggests an equally unsavoury character.[11]

Potential biographers of Alex MacLean have not been limited by a meagre amount of material. Newspaper reports, memoirs, articles, memories, and a variety of other recollections of MacLean, many of them based on stories of his exploits on the high seas, circulated widely on the waterfronts of San Francisco, Victoria, Vancouver, and numerous other Pacific seaports. He was not unknown in Yokohama and Hakodate in Japan or in Apia, Samoa, and the Solomon Islands in the southwest Pacific. The stories were retold in the fo'c's'les of sealing schooners and the cycle continued, acquiring changes and embellishments that were part and parcel of the process of popular folk history. He became, for some, a North American folk hero. The tales travelled back across the continent to his birthplace. Alex and his brother Dan were probably the most widely known Cape Bretoners of their generation, and local papers and tellers of tales avidly tracked their activities. They maintained contact with the Gaels in Cape Breton, who interpreted the reported actions and activities of the MacLean brothers through the filter of their rich culture. Alex and Dan did not disappoint them.

The stories have been churning out now for more than a hundred years, and this may partly explain why the extraordinary story of Alex MacLean has not received more comprehensive treatment. According to West Coast journalist Noel Robinson, "there is no doubt that Alexander MacLean – who became known from Alaska to San Francisco as the 'Sea Wolf' – was a born outlaw, and there are more stories told of his hair-raising adventures and brushes with officers of the law up and down the Pacific Coast than are told about any other man who had made his home – if the word 'home' can be used in connection with a man who was hardly ever at home – in Vancouver or Nanaimo."[12] A number of writers and journalists, and a bevy of bureaucrats and other authorities, occasionally attempted to nail him down. One contemporary of MacLean's, an experienced journalist who covered the British Columbia waterfront, warned that "he has been a sort of will o' the wisp ... here, there and everywhere, and chiefly upon the sea."[13] Another astute and long-time observer of the Victoria waterfront scene, Charles Lillard, cautioned: "Almost everyone who has written about MacLean has told a different story ... Personally I believe almost nothing of what I've read about MacLean."[14] One must be careful when wandering through the rich fields of waterfront lore, popular legends, and personal reminiscences.

An additional complication arises from the publication of Jack London's novel *The Sea-Wolf* in 1904. Renewed critical interest in the American novelist in recent years has only reaffirmed his tremendous popularity during his lifetime. Within months of the book's appearance, the fictional character Wolf Larsen was publicly linked with Alex MacLean, who was not only still quite active but was, coincidentally and simultaneously, involved in an illegal and extensively covered seal poaching episode. Thus, the separation between the fictional character and the historical figure tended to blur quite quickly. Stories about Jack London's Wolf Larsen and the Cape Breton mariner were tightly woven together during the last decade of MacLean's life. Increased literacy among the general public, and the appearance of the newly created best-seller list in this period, were part of the backdrop for Alex MacLean and his times. Late in MacLean's career, the modern movie industry was born, and *The Sea-Wolf* was one of the first feature-length films. Alex MacLean literally sailed out of a pre-industrial, pre-cash environment into a turbulent, rapidly changing North American social and cultural scene and, eventually, was transformed into a mass media commodity. The product of a "tenaciously traditional" and pre-capitalist society that was undergoing significant alterations, MacLean thus fits two of the important characteristics that Eric Hobsbawm suggests are required for the emergence of a "social bandit."[15] Others would follow. Herein, perhaps, lies much of the appeal of his story. MacLean was not a western frontiersman, legendary or otherwise, but the American frontier was not the only way of life that was disappearing, being invented, reinvented, or reinterpreted at this time. While MacLean went down to the sea in the early 1870s, thus participating in "the great days of sail," which Gerald Graham dates between 1850 and 1885, he also spent most of his career in the overlapping "dying world of sail," which Robert Foulke holds to be the period from 1870 to 1910.[16] For mariners, as for frontiersmen, it was a period of transition.

In the early 1970s, the editor of the *Alaska Journal,* Robert DeArmond, challenged and cautioned individuals who were interested in MacLean: "The whole career of Alexander MacLean has many tangled threads awaiting for some researcher to untangle."[17] Robert O'Brien was another writer aware of the complications involved in such a project. He was a journalist with the *San Francisco Chronicle* in the 1940s and 1950s. In his column "Riptides" in 1952, he devoted a week to MacLean's exploits and acknowledged: "Now, at this point in time, when so many of the deep-water sailing men are gone, it is all but impossible to separate Alex MacLean and Wolf Larsen, the skipper of the hell-ship Ghost, and to say where the facts end and the legend begins. London himself could not have defined the dividing line."[18] A half-century later, the exact separation remains elusive. Yet, the attraction of this topic also persists. Noel Robinson covered Vancouver extensively for decades and was the only journalist to have had a lengthy interview with Alex. After this session, Robinson confessed: "Only to touch here and there upon the fringe of the remarkable skipper's remarkable career, as I am endeavouring to do, when there is so much matter in that life for a series of thrilling articles, suggests the position of the hungry man looking into the pastry cook's window and only refraining from smashing it and disposing of some of the contents because of what might follow."[19] This interview was published in a Vancouver newspaper in January 1913. It was MacLean's last home port. He was fifty-four at the time and continued to convey a strength of presence. But journalists, conservationists, antiquarians, and academics continued to muddy the waters surrounding the activities and character of Alex MacLean. He remains, in some circles, a name with which to conjure. This book is an attempt to trace his contemporary construction in newspapers, fiction, and memory as well as his evolution, for some, into a legendary figure. It also offers a more complete portrait of one Cape Breton mariner who – because of his maritime career in general and, in particular, his prominent participation in the pelagic sealing industry with all of its successes, conflicts, and economic, environmental, and diplomatic issues – deserves to be more accurately remembered.

1
Cape Breton and Going Down to the Sea, 1858-82

Cape Breton Island, which was barely more than a stone's throw northeast of the Nova Scotia peninsula on Canada's east coast, had a population of around 2,500 in 1801. Then the Gaels arrived. Mostly Gaelic speakers from the Highlands and western islands of Scotland, they formed the dominant ethnic group by the early 1820s. In the late 1820s and early 1830s, more Gaels headed to Cape Breton than to anywhere else in North America. More than 20,000 arrived in Cape Breton between 1802 and 1840, increasing the population to 40,000.[1] Folklorist MacEdward Leach noted they came from "a rich cultural background of story, poetry and song. The beauty, the imaginative power, the dramatic quality, the richness of detail of the old Celtic lore is unsurpassed in Western Europe."[2] The fact that Gaelic is still spoken today in Cape Breton is testimony that they cherished their culture by maintaining "a vital intellectual link" stretching back over two centuries.[3] Scholars attuned to the culture and the language of the Gaels underline that they were hardly in a "constant state of nostalgic mourning for a lost Highland homeland" but, rather, were making "active rational choices to emigrate in order to protect their independence and maintain responsibility for the running of their communities as they saw fit."[4] When John the Hunter MacDonald arrived in Cape Breton in 1834, just in time to experience the "winter of the big snow," he composed a moving and mournful lament about his unhappy exile, *Oran do dh'America/Song for America:* "I am bound, brought low/In the land of snows and sere grasses." He was quickly taken to task by his cousin, Allan the Ridge, who had arrived a couple of decades earlier and who responded with *Chuir thu bòilich sìos 'us bòsd/You have been loud and boastful:*

> Sour to me your idle talk, the speech of your mouth,
> For I was knowledgeable over there
> In cold Scotland; although it is far from me,
> Trifling to me the loss.

He then adds a phrase that, even in English, continues to resonate:

> The land that you left is the land without kindness,
> without humanity for the tenantry.

Allan the Ridge's response directly challenges the content of his cousin's poem and mimics its poetic structure, thus ensuring that his alternative could be sung to any air that suited John the Hunter's lament. Allan the Ridge's version played well.[5] It also puts into context Samuel Johnson and James Boswell's descriptions "of emigrants so happy to leave Scotland that they were not only dancing at the sites of departure but had invented an entirely new dance called 'America.'"[6] The transplanted Gaels in Cape Breton in the second half of the nineteenth century would highlight their cultural characteristics with an outlook that remained Gaelic and was confident and positive. Their Gaelic literary accounts in this period underline "their consistent tone of defiance and optimism, as well as their realism and lack of romanticism."[7]

Their situation in the new world was in striking contrast to the fragmentation of the old Celtic world they had recently left behind. The latter is reflected in the songs composed in the Scottish Highlands and Hebridian Islands by those of their generations who stayed, which were, in Sorley Maclean's description, "naturally depressing and even hopeless in tone."[8] In Cape Breton during this time, it was a different scene. Here the culture of the Gael flourished. It was a far cry from the lamentations emitting from the old country. In John Shaw's assessment, "the dominant tone in Cape Breton seems to emanate from a different world. The direction is outward-looking instead of introspective; the descriptions of nature are clear and unromantic ... there are frequent strains of an underlying healthy cheer and humour, all of which convey an outlook toward the world on the part of Cape Breton Gaels which differed dramatically from that expressed by their relatives and contemporaries in the Highlands." For Shaw, "a strong argument can be brought forth that New World Gaels during this period, for the first time in at least four generations, had the economic means and the freedom from outside pressures and constraints to develop in directions compatible with their cultural potential."[9] This would be the early world of Alex MacLean.

Domhnull (Donald) MacLean emigrated from Scotland in 1803, initially settling on Prince Edward Island. The landlord-tenant situation there, which plagued rural society for much of the nineteenth century, not surprisingly prompted Domhnull (and many other Gaels) to move on. He arrived in Cape Breton around 1810.[10] Various sources suggest that the MacLeans who settled in East Bay were widely known locally for "their fighting and seafaring ability."[11] Domhnull MacLean acquired a grant of 200 acres at the head of East Bay, at the crossroads of the main Post Road from Sydney and the road to Northside East Bay, on 24 October 1822. It was at the location that the Mi'kmaq called Tweednooge – the barrachois that served as the portage from East Bay to Sydney River.[12] The farm was described much later, by a neighbour who grew up on an adjoining farm, as "a dandy piece of land ... one big field, so level you could almost use it as an airfield."[13] In addition, their house was only a few minutes' walk to the shore of the Bras d'Or, a large saltwater lake in the centre of the island with access to the Atlantic Ocean. Their neighbours, almost exclusively other Gaels settling in to begin a new and productive chapter of their ancient heritage, would remember for generations the "great hospitality of the MacLeans."[14]

East Bay was developing into a dynamic community in these years. Father William MacLeod established a "college" in the mid-1820s, and, although it only lasted a few years, it was recognized as an "important pioneering educational effort."[15] His younger brother Neil became the first resident pastor when East Bay became a separate parish in 1838 and, within a few months, had opened a school. Father Neil would remain there for decades.[16] Most of the settlers were Highlanders who had moved on from Prince Edward Island or who had come directly from Morar, on the west coast of Scotland, or the Outer Hebridean Islands of South Uist and Barra. It was a "vigorous Gaelic-speaking community," which took its religion seriously.[17] Yet removal from the old country, "the land without kindness," did not translate into an idyllic situation. Rusty Bittermann's research has solidly established that, while no longer in the precarious position as tenants, a substantial minority was required to work off-farm and off-island for a considerable portion of the year just to maintain their holdings. They would continue to do so for decades. Up to one-third of the households he studied found it necessary to follow this practice for twenty-five to forty years after they had originally settled on the land.[18]

Domhnull MacLean's son Ailean (Allan) and Catrìona (Catherine) MacCormick were married in St. Mary's Catholic Church in East Bay on 26 April 1846 by Father Neil MacLeod.[19] Catrìona was descended from an old Gaelic Catholic family from the Hebrides. The oldest of nine, she had been born in Kildonan, South Uist. Her father was Iain, her mother was Catherine Ross. Tradition has it that these MacCormicks were descended from a Neil MacCormick who had come from Donegal, Ireland, in the 1600s to build and repair galleys for Macdonald of Clanranald.[20] Catrìona's six youngest siblings were born in Cape Breton, in the Upper Leitche's Creek area, between Sydney and North Sydney. The spring of 1846 was the beginning of the most miserable half-decade in the nineteenth century for anyone to settle down and begin to raise a family in rural Cape Breton. The island had just entered a period of distress and suffering that would not be equalled for almost a century. The immigration of the Gaels to Cape Breton came to a shuddering halt.[21]

The main culprit was a potato blight. Secondary factors included a wheat fly infestation, an over-dependence on a single crop, and the fact that Cape Breton was still in a pioneer stage of development. By the spring of 1848, a provincial relief committee reported that "poverty, wretchedness, and misery, have spread through the island of Cape Breton," and the recent refuge of the Gaels would soon earn a description as the "Ireland of Nova Scotia."[22] With a pattern already established whereby people would travel off-island for seasonal wage work, emigration now soared, even though many of the recent Cape Breton Gaels had barely had time to settle down. Not all areas were affected equally nor were all classes of people. But even the East Bay area of Cape Breton County was receiving government aid in the form of barrels of meal by 1847.[23]

Ailean appears to have inherited the initial grant, and his and Catrìona's first child, Catherine (Kate or Ketty), was born in March 1847. Dan was born in the summer of 1848. Catrìona and Ailean would have five more children. The youngest was Alexander, born on 15 May 1858. All would be baptized at St. Mary's Roman Catholic Church in East Bay.[24] Ailean MacLean died on 12 December 1859. He was only forty-three. Dan, the oldest boy, was only eleven, and it is possible that Catrìona then moved the young family closer to her people for a while. One local source has Alex going to school at Upper Leitche's Creek (MacCormick territory) until the age of twelve.[25] These few difficult years would mark the area significantly in numerous ways: "It increased the wealth and power of the island's chief merchants, devastated the new settlers, impoverished established farmers, put a fifty-year halt to immigration to the island, hastened emigration – and forced the diversification of agriculture."[26] For many recent immigrants, their beginning in the new world was a difficult one. Those Gaels who survived, and stayed at least into adulthood, would carry with them a healthy attitude and an abundant cultural heritage when they left Cape Breton. Alex MacLean and his older brother Dan would be adequately packed when they departed.

Little is known about the early years of Dan and Alex MacLean. They may well have sailed the Bras d'Or "almost as soon as they could walk," but their early experiences were not exclusively nautical.[27] Forty years later, Alex reminisced about breaking in horses in Cape Breton as a child.[28] Farm work was strenuous, and Catrìona's struggles with a young, fatherless family would only be partly alleviated by her family's assistance. The second oldest boy, John, would eventually take over the running of the farm, but Dan, and later Alex, followed another traditional pattern for the time and the place – they went down to the sea. According to an acquaintance,

Ronald Gillis, "the MacLeans' early life so near Sydney brought them in contact with men from all parts of the world. And in those far off days the first Atlantic cable landed at North Sydney, so this harbour became first port of call on the North American continent."[29] It was a convenient stop for bunker coal, and ship's captains would receive their next assignment there. In the 1870s, North Sydney was a leading Canadian port in gross tonnage.[30]

Dan began his sailing career in Sydney, leaving Cape Breton in the summer of 1868. He was nineteen. He spent time in the Atlantic coastal trade and later sailed out of New York on deep-water ships.[31] Alex followed a similar pattern. One source has him sailing as a cabin boy with an uncle immediately upon leaving school at the age of twelve. Alex had definitely acquired experience in fishing boats by the age of fifteen.[32] Fishing, of course, was a staple of the Cape Breton economy in the nineteenth century. There was a strong American presence in the industry. There was also a substantial Cape Breton contingent within the American fleet by mid-century. A report from Cape Breton County by G.H. Gesner in 1862 maintained that the American fishing vessels would leave their home port with half a crew and then "land on our southern coast and make up a full crew of our best fishermen, and seamen either for wages or on half their catch, if on half hand (as it is called) they go with the vessel to the States, to dispose of their shairs [sic] where every inducement is used to intice [sic] them to stay, and fish the next season, with them by this means they have drawn away some hundreds of our best fishermen."[33] One estimate from the 1870s had fully one-half of Cape Breton fishermen being employed in American vessels, primarily out of Boston and Gloucester.[34] They were frequently closer. The American mackerel fleet made tumultuous visits to North Sydney on a regular basis during this period, and these occurrences were long remembered in that seaport town. One Northside historian recollects: "It is difficult to imagine the commotion and uproar resulting from such an invasion. Fortified with the beverage of their choice, easily obtainable at the numerous dives and homes where it was openly sold, contrary to the law, they certainly provided lots of excitement. This sort of thing happened every time the schooners entered our harbour," weekly throughout the summer and early fall. "These men made good incomes and they spent it freely, so that their visits, though not without drawbacks, were very much appreciated by the merchants of the town and these were not the vendors of alcoholic beverages only."[35] There were reciprocal visits to American ports. Before the Cape Bretoners in the fleet were paid off, they would return with the vessel to New England, where the catch would be sold and the accounts settled. As maritime historian Captain John Parker notes, "it was then that the wild Cape Bretoners got out of hand and became a legend in Gloucester. Some of these characters were Wild Archie, Big Duncan, John the Weasel and Donald from Bras d'Or. During the sprees that followed the trips the Cape Bretoners paid a very large sum in fines."[36]

Court records in Boston indicate that Alex left Cape Breton in 1873 and arrived in Massachusetts in July, although Alex later remembered leaving Nova Scotia late the following year.[37] The long Depression had commenced, and the expanding coal industry on the island was experiencing serious difficulties as well. The mining labour force in Nova Scotia, for example, increased over 70 percent between 1871 and 1873, prompting many Cape Bretoners to leave their rural communities for the mining districts. Then came the mining collapse in 1875 and a decline in the workforce of almost 60 percent from what it was in 1873. The volatility of this industry offered little guarantee of steady work. It was not a particularly prosperous period throughout the region.[38] It is clear Alex left Cape Breton at a considerably earlier age than his brother Dan. He was one of 5,000 or so Cape Bretoners who departed during that decade, with many heading to New England.[39]

An autumnal leaving was quite in character for the region. The seasonal economic contours of unemployment were characterized by fewer jobs, lower wages, and higher prices during the harshest months, and guaranteed a regular period of hardscrabble for workers every winter. Many left. Most of these migrants, like Dan and Alex, were single and young.[40] Dan was operating out of New York at the time, and a married sister was one of the many "provincials" living in Boston.[41] It was not difficult to get there. One Cape Breton paper in the late 1870s lamented "the weekly leave-taking of so many Cape Bretoners for the United States by every Boston-bound steamer, as well as by Gloucester and Boston sailing vessels."[42] An article in the *Boston Globe* in 1888, entitled "Gloucester Fish Fleet," noted the majority of south shore Nova Scotians who participated in the spring fishery, returned home in the fall, and did "not engage in the hazardous winter fisheries." But "different social conditions" prevailed in northern Nova Scotia and Cape Breton Island for the descendants of the Highland Catholics, necessitating employment in the winter fishery: "These men are the bravest in the fleet, and no idea can be formed of the risks they take and dangers they undergo, unless by personal contact and experience with them."[43] Alex acquired deep-sea experience through the remainder of the decade, operating out of Boston, Philadelphia, and Baltimore. According to Alex, he sailed "all classes of ships" on the east coast, sailing and steam, became well acquainted with the western ocean, and ventured as far as the Mediterranean: "He knew Liverpool like a book ... it was his favourite port."[44] It was an excellent training ground, according to Cicely Fox Smith: "The spirit of Liverpool is the spirit of the Western Ocean ... The Western Ocean, stern, strong, and terrible even in his repose – with his fogs and ice, his storms and hurricanes, praising the Lord – a breaker of strong ships, a maker of strong, resolute, iron men. The Western Ocean is no place for weaklings."[45]

Dan and Alex MacLean were numbered among the many thousands of Nova Scotians who, according to Frederick William Wallace, went to sea, "gaining a name for themselves as splendid seamen, albeit stern disciplinarians, which did more to place their native country before the world than any other thing connected with it."[46] The tingling, blood-surging beginning of Wallace's *Wooden Ships and Iron Men,* with an exchange occurring among the crew on the *Liverpool,* a rolling, plunging barque in the southern latitudes in the mid-1870s, as the *W.D. Lawrence* loomed on the horizon, captured this romanticized reputation: "She was a big ship – a wooden three-master, black-hulled, heavily sparred, and deep-laden – and she was forging through the long green seas with yards almost square and royals and cross-jack furled." The master and mate witnessing this "exhibition of sail-carrying in a heavy breeze, the well-set and well-trimmed sails and yards, the faultlessly stayed masts, and generally spotless appearance of the big ship," comment admiringly: "A down-east Yankee, sure enough. They put the crews through their paces on those packets." What snapped out on the flag halyard, however, was the red ensign of the British Mercantile Marine. "Up on the poop, an old shell-back handling code flags was staring pridefully at the big vessel roaring past them. 'I know that ship, sir,' he vouchsafed to master and mate. 'I sailed in her one time ... A splendid vessel, sir, and the biggest built in Nova Scotia' ... 'Hard packets – these Bluenose ships. Worse than the Yankees,'" notes the captain. "The sailor replied somewhat hesitantly: 'Well, sir, they have that name, but for a man what is a *sailor* an' knows his book there's nothing better nor a Bluenose to sail aboard of. For bums, hoboes, an' sojers, sir, they're a floatin' hell. They stand for no shenanigans aboard them packets, sir. One bit o' slack or a black look an' the mate'll have ye knocked stiff an' looking forty ways for Sunday. They works ye hard, but they feeds you good and treats you good if you does yer work.'" The *W.D. Lawrence* was soon only a speck on the horizon, heading for the Horn: "'There she goes,' observed the old shell-back who had served in her; 'a ramping, stamping, hard-driving Bluenose – wooden ships with iron men commanding them.'"[47]

It was not always a pretty portrait, and, to put many of the characterizations that would be applied to the MacLeans in perspective, it was a highly held belief that Nova Scotians did have a more demanding work culture aboard their vessels. A corrective to Wallace's version is offered in Colin McKay's *Windjammers and Bluenose Sailors*. Ordinary sailors could also harbour the "iron men" characteristics, although the discipline was still direct and frequently brutal. Tellingly, McKay did not distinguish between the Down Easters from New England and the Bluenosers.[48] Nor did mariner and maritime writer Basil Lubbock: "On some of the Yankee hell ships the things that go on are almost incredible ... Legs and arms broken were considered nothing, ribs stamped in by heavy sea-boots had to mend as best they could, faces smashed like rotten apples by iron belaying pins had to get well or fear worse treatment, eyes closed up by a brawny mate's fist had to see ... On board these 'down easters' and 'blue nose' craft, where discipline is enforced by a plentiful use of belaying-pin, knuckle-duster, and boot, the work done is stupendous, and the ship is certainly kept in a wonderfully trim state."[49] Fox Smith also wonders why both practised such rough handling of sailors and thus acquired such notoriety: "What was the reason for the man-handling habits of the Down-east or Blue-nose skippers and mates? It is hard to say. Perhaps the souring effects of successive generations of Puritanical upbringing may have had something to do with it ... Perhaps too the conditions of the Atlantic packet service tended to create a form of discipline enforced by the knuckle-duster and marine-spike form of argument. And the worst of such a tradition is that – once established – you have to go on with it."[50]

There are numerous stories about Bluenose officers in the *San Francisco Coast Seamen's Journal* in the 1880s and 1890s. An editorial entitled "The Old, Old Story" in February 1890, which was prompted by reports of a particularly brutal "tale of murder and mistreatment on the high seas" and featured a Nova Scotia vessel, states: "Nova Scotia vessels have a bad reputation among sailors. The same can be said of New Brunswick vessels. Sailors say that N.B. means 'No Breakfast' and N.S. 'No Supper.' On those vessels the men are fed on the English plan and worked on the American plan. American ships carry smaller crews and work the men harder than other nations. The Nova Scotia man afloat is considered a breed between an American and an Englishman, and a mighty bad breed it is, as many testify."[51] This particular editorial was prompted by an incident involving a Captain Allen and the Nova Scotia bark, the *Argyle*. It was not an isolated one.[52] Another incident involving the *Warrior,* out of Pictou, Nova Scotia, under Captain Kitchen should be noted. Upon their arrival in Boston from Manila, charges of cruelty were brought against the first and second mate and the steward. According to the *San Francisco Coast Seamen's Journal,* what gave the incident significant play in the news was the comment that it was a British craft. The paper was quick to rectify this part of the record: "The plain truth is that the *Warrior* is not a British ship in anything more than a name and a piece of red bunting. She hails from Pictou, N.S., and is what is commonly called a "Bluenose" ... It is well known among seamen that the Nova Scotiamen are as bad as, and in many cases even worse than, the simon-pure American in the treatment of crews."[53] The breath of this reputation, whatever its accuracy, is suggested in Eric Partridge's study on historical slang. During this period, a "Nova Scotia pump" was a bucket with a line attached to draw water; "Nova Scotia soda" for cleaning paintwork was sand; "Nova Scotia sunlight" was moonlight; and "Nova Scotia towing" referred to the practice of using dories to pull out a vessel in order to save the cost of a tug.[54] In addition, during these years, as Eric Sager notes, "the

'Bluenose' master was worthy of his reputation for making unusual demands upon his men. Whatever the size of his vessel, and wherever he might sail, the Canadian master expected fewer men to do the work."[55] While the increase in the ratio of men to tonnage in the last quarter of the century was partly due to changes in the technology, such as the increasing use of double topsails, fewer men were used to move more tonnage for lesser wages, and the "result was the survival of the sailing ship industry."[56] Such was the work world in which Dan and Alex MacLean gained their seafaring experience.

Two of the vessels definitely linked to Alex during this period are fishing boats. He was an able seaman on the *Eddie D. Morrison* and on the *Electric Flash*. The latter was an eighty-two-ton fishing schooner operating out of Gloucester. For part of this period, Alex fished for mackerel out of this Massachusetts port under John McDonald.[57] He also acquired some experience in cable laying. He was in Halifax, Nova Scotia, in January 1879 aboard the 2,000-ton steamer *Minia,* which was owned by the Anglo-American Telegraph Company. (The *Minia* was based in Halifax and had been laying cable since 1874. She would remain in service until 1922 and was one of the vessels that recovered bodies after the *Titanic* disaster.)[58] Alex got into a scrap in Halifax that earned him a charge of assault and jail time. In Alex's version, it was a pretty straightforward sort of affair: "I left the ship and went ashore without liberty, and there were two watches, port and starboard watches, and the watch went ashore that evening that I didn't belong to. I wanted to get ashore that evening for some purpose, and when I was going aboard the ship about 11 o'clock in the evening I happened to get into a row with a man ... Being insulted, of course I had to protect myself ... The principal reason that I was put in jail for was on account of leaving the ship without liberty."[59] A watchman at the Liverpool wharf on the Halifax waterfront was the target of the assault. He was probably the source of the objectionable remarks, although a twenty-year-old seaman returning from a night on the town without permission may have been under the influence and more intolerant of supposed insults. Alex neglected to mention he had help. H.D. MacLean, a twenty-five-year-old Cape Bretoner, assisted him, although it is clear that Alex led the charge. He was fined $10 or ninety days in the Stipendiary Magistrate's Court, while H.D. MacLean received a $5 fine or fifty days. They were released from Halifax City prison five days later, after a cash payment, and sent back on board their vessel.[60] It was not an unusual incident. David McLeod was another Cape Breton seaman. One of Alex's contemporaries, he was born in 1857 and went to sea in 1873, as he explains, in a matter-of-fact way, in his reminiscences: "It was a standing joke to have a run on a Cape Bretoner. Unfortunately, I was always thin-skinned and if you wanted a scrap, I would not go much out of the way to avoid it. Kind of took to it, like an old maid to drinking strong tea."[61] In the next eleven years 1,237 sailors appeared before a Halifax magistrate. Almost 40 percent were natives of the Maritime provinces, and 58 percent of those cases were related to drinking.[62] A few weeks later, on 20 February, a fierce gale sent thirteen schooners and 143 fishermen from the Gloucester fleet to the bottom of Georges Bank. As the fleet limped back to port late that month, the survivors agreed: "It was the toughest gale they ever encountered." The Gloucester fleet lost twenty-nine schooners, almost one-tenth of her entire tonnage, and 249 men that season.[63] If Alex was looking for reasons to move on, both the dust-up in Halifax and the February gale may have soured him somewhat on the east coast.

By heading west, Alex would also have been following a fairly familiar path trod by Cape Bretoners over the previous few decades. People had been leaving Cape Breton since the 1830s, initially pushed by local conditions and pulled by perceived opportunities in the "Boston states." The California gold rush in the late 1840s added an additional attraction. The frontier and other opportunities kept moving west.[64] In 1879, at the age of twenty-one and with over seven years of sailing experience, Alex headed out to San Francisco. The boom years of the California grain trade had begun, and he worked his passage as an able seaman on the 1,535-ton *Santa Clara,* out of Philadelphia, "a first class ship in all respects and for many years one of the best known vessels engaged in the California trade."[65] The *Santa Clara* was a Down Easter, built in Bath, Maine, in 1876. Designed specifically for the Cape Horn passage, the Down Easters had "a good turn of speed, very strongly put together and economical to work, yet requiring only half the men needed by an out-and-out flyer."[66] The designers and builders evolved "a magnificent type of a wooded full-rig ship, which soon became known the world over for her smart, spic and span appearance, and fierce discipline."[67] The *Santa Clara* was commanded in these years by Captain William Tobey Jr., "one of the best known and most highly esteemed shipmasters engaged in the California trade."[68] It is likely that the experience on the *Santa Clara* was a valuable one for Alex. His later reputation, when he acquired command of his own vessels, suggests he could easily have fit in with the American Cape Horn fleet. Dan MacLean arrived in California around the same time, possibly on the same ship.[69] The west coast waterfront scene would never be quite the same again.

After his voyage around Cape Horn in the *Santa Clara,* Alex MacLean checked out the San Francisco scene "for a few months."[70] In the spring of 1880, he headed north to British Columbia. Alex and Dan are two of the 777 – out of 50,387 British Columbians – enumerated as being from the Maritimes in the 1881 census. Alex is registered as a twenty-two-year-old navigating officer. Both he and Dan were residing in Victoria at different addresses.[71] Cole Harris has cultivated this statistical field extensively, noting that "social spaces were changing" at the time and "society and space were recalibrating each other, and something like a larger British Columbian society ... was beginning to emerge."[72] In this western colony, "whites could find many landmarks of a familiar world." Victoria, with a population of 6,000, had the largest middle-class component, the largest urban centre, and was "the most English." For Harris, "class identity was most developed among the elite" in the British Columbia of 1881. Neither Alex nor Dan would have been eligible for membership in this group because of their occupation, financial status, and religion.[73]

Alex's initial role was as an active participant in the transportation and communication links in this emerging society. Steamboats were an important element of this system at the time, and Alex spent the next couple of years on the rivers and lakes, initially serving on the sternwheeler *Gertrude,* working for doughty Captain William Moore, and travelling from Vancouver up the Fraser River.[74] In 1881, he began a stint on the steamer *Sir James Douglas,* a revenue boat in the Canadian customs department. The Canadian government had recently purchased the telegraph lines in British Columbia from the Western Union Telegraph Company and was busy connecting Vancouver Island and the mainland via Nanaimo, Gabriola Island, and Point Grey. The project would be completed by 1882.[75] Alex's sea time and his east coast experience with cable laying would have been attractive to his employer. He served as an able seaman for five months and then as mate for a year on the *Douglas,* a flexible vessel that was "pressed into service for all kinds of work," including cable laying.[76] Alex mentioned that they "had a boat at the time specially built for the purpose ... called the *Electric*." Possibly, he served on both.[77] While the project was still underway, the federal minister of railways and canals, Sir Charles Tupper, a Nova Scotian, went west in August 1881, primarily to further the interests of the Canadian Pacific Railway. While in Victoria, the *Douglas,* with Alex among the crew, was placed at Tupper's disposal, and the prominent politician boarded the vessel for a jaunt up to Nanaimo. History is mute as to whether or not the two Nova Scotia natives exchanged words, but Alex remembered the trip and made reference to it more than thirty years later.[78] However, the main purpose for the *Douglas'* voyage at this time was cable laying, and, for this, Alex soon drew attention to himself. The story from this early part of Alex's career on the Pacific is suggestive and came from another individual who was involved in the project on the *Douglas:* "The cable, being unwound from a drum placed in a large tank, kinked and began flying in all directions. In such circumstances the only way to save the situation was for a man with sufficient nerve to run around inside the tank at the risk of his life, endeavouring to fix the cable in position hand over hand. The two men in the tank had jumped out, but MacLean jumped in and accomplished this feat." Much later, when asked about this incident, Alex made light of it but acknowledged that it was true.[79]

While Alex was laying cable and gaining experience in steam vessels, his older brother Dan was sailing British Columbia and Alaskan waters in the seven-ton sloop *Flyaway*. He was questionably linked with discoveries of both gold and coal.[80] Alex was also lured north. In 1882, he left Victoria and took a steamer to Juneau, Alaska, where he tried his hand at mining in partnership with one Archie McCulligan, remaining there for about seven months. Juneau, founded in 1880-81, was the first boom town connected to the discovery of gold in Alaska. Occupationally, mining was far removed from the sea, and it comes as little surprise to learn that Alex disliked it.[81] He met up with Dan again in Juneau, although he did not join his older brother on his jaunts in the *Flyaway*.[82] He would hardly have had time. Other vessels that Alex has been linked with in these early years in British Columbia waters, primarily the Fraser River, include the *Western Slope*, the *Pacific Slope*, and the legendary *Beaver*. The former two were also associated with Captain Moore. The latter was the first steamship on the northwest coast, which operated between 1836 and 1888, although Alex's links with her are tenuous.[83]

For about three years, Alex and Dan MacLean would survey the wider picture on the Pacific coast, separately working on various vessels and at varied occupations. It seems as if they were searching for an opportunity that had so far been overlooked, some activity to which they could direct their considerable energies and talents. Dan appears to have done most of the exploring in his sloop *Flyaway*, and, in his travels along the Alaskan coast and in the Bering Sea, he noted the large number of fur seals in the area.[84] This period spent along the coast and in the northern Pacific also enabled both MacLeans to learn "a great deal about the uncharted waters which served them well later on."[85] Indeed it did.

Late in 1882, they returned to the east coast. As Alex later explained, "I just wanted to take a trip down east."[86] However, this response is more indicative of a character trait – never volunteer information – than an explanation. During that trip, they made a number of significant moves. On 1 December 1882, Alex and Dan became American citizens in Boston. It is unclear why they made the switch. It is possible that they had already made arrangements to ship out on a San Francisco-based vessel in March of the following year, and maybe they were intending to use the California city as homeport.[87] If they had already decided to concentrate on the North Pacific and Alaskan waters by shipping out of San Francisco (which would happen the following year), maybe they felt becoming American citizens made sense. Besides, Alex and Dan may have been British subjects in a legal and political sense, but culturally they were Gaels – the most "English" aspect about them would have been their second language.[88]

While discarding their status as British subjects, they do not seem to have been clearing the decks of their Cape Breton connections. After their business in New England, they continued home, visiting for a month. In East Bay, the original two hundred acres acquired by their grandfather Domhnull were now divided, with Alex and Dan each acquiring fifty acres of the eastern portion of the land, along with small house plots on the main road. Their brother John, who had remained in Cape Breton on the farm, acquired the remaining 100 acres.[89] Alex and Dan were still in their prime, and the land division suggests that they were continuing their ties to their Cape Breton Gaelic community. Neither of them would ever build on, or plough, their grandfather's land. They continued to look to the sea and soon headed out west again.

It was now time for the MacLeans to go sealing. A new industry was about to expand significantly. Seal hunting was hardly a new activity on the west coast. The Russian rookeries in the Bering Sea were on the Commander Islands, Bering and Copper, which had been discovered in 1741. The American rookeries for the Pacific fur seals were located in the Pribilof Islands, on the Alaskan side of the Bering Sea. St. George and St. Paul had been discovered in the 1780s.[90] These were the breeding grounds of the North Pacific fur seal or *Callorhinus ursinus*. The Pribilof Islands, 160 miles from the nearest land, attracted around 80 percent of the seals from the Pacific Ocean. Two smaller breeding grounds on the Asiatic side of the Pacific – the Commander Islands and Robben Island in the Sea of Okhotsk – accounted for most of the remainder.[91] From Attu, the easternmost point of Alaska's Aleutian Islands, it is only 180 miles to the Commander Islands and from there it is less than 100 miles to Russia's Kamchatka Peninsula. The Pribilofs, which are of volcanic origin, treeless, and usually submerged in mist, were 220 miles northwest of Unalaska and the port of Dutch Harbor in the Aleutians.[92] The discovery of these rookeries led to a tremendous slaughter, which continued when the islands came under the control of the Russian-American Company in 1799. Eventually, the killing was brought under control, and by the early 1860s there was an annual harvest from the rookeries of 70,000 seals.[93]

Captain William Spring of Victoria, "the pioneer of modern sealers," began trading along the coast, in association with Captain Hugh McKay, in the 1850s. Occasionally Aboriginal hunters would barter sealskins at their trading posts. Customs records at Victoria suggest that the schooner *Kate* went sealing in 1865 and 1866.[94] Early in 1866, prompted by suggestions from Aboriginal hunters, Captain McKay made an attempt at open sea or pelagic sealing in a small trading schooner, the *INO*. Until this time, the Aboriginal hunt was based on land, although they sometimes travelled forty miles offshore. Except for the adult bulls, who wintered in the Gulf of Alaska and the Bering Sea, most of the Pribilof Island fur seals migrated annually from the Channel Islands of southern California northward 7,000 miles along the Pacific coast, usually staying between thirty and seventy miles offshore. The *INO* proved to be too small. The following year, in 1868, the seventy-five-ton *Favorite* was launched.[95] The *Favorite* was primarily intended for cod fishing and trading – sealing was initially an auxiliary occupation – but her sealing successes "more than that of any other vessel demonstrated the possibilities of the industry."[96] The vessel's reputation would be acquired, in part, because of her association with Alex MacLean.

Significant changes came about in 1867 when the United States purchased Alaska from Russia and gained control of much of the area, although there had been a "ruthless slaughter" of seals during the transition period of the late 1860s.[97] American entrepreneurs were quick off the mark. Initially, the US government considered fourteen competing bids, but one group moved faster and was more influential. Hayward Hutchison, representing several San Francisco capitalists, and Captain Ebenezer Morgan, who had the backing of New London, Connecticut, interests, with southern sealing experience, were both in the Pribilofs in 1868. They, along with important San Francisco commercial men, such as Louis Sloss and Lewis Gerstle, eventually combined into the Alaska Commercial Company (ACC).[98] The combined interests of the ACC carried considerable clout. While Hutchison was unsuccessful in his quest for a ninety-nine-year contract, the American Congress did pass legislation on 3 August 1870 giving the ACC a twenty-year lease on the Pribilof Islands to ensure the orderly care of the rookeries. There was a yearly quota (100,000), an annual fee ($55,000), and a royalty ($2.62 per skin).[99] The twenty-year monopoly would prove to be highly lucrative: "A low-investment, low-overhead operation produced net profits of $18,102,140, or just under an average $1,000,000 a year. The risk was small, the labour force immobile, the market assured, and monopoly enforced at law: even in the age of the 'robber barons' this was success to end all successes."[100] It was a deal well worth defending. In 1871, the ACC also secured a lease on Robben Island and the Commander Islands from the Russian czar's government. Since pelagic sealing was almost unknown at this time, these leases "constituted a practical monopoly of the fur-seal industry."[101] During the course of the lease, the American government, through fees and royalties, would recoup the purchase price it had paid Russia for Alaska. But there were also costs involved, and not only for the seals.[102] While the ACC provided a school, medical care, and other provisions for the Aleuts, prompting a later company claim that they had "advantages unequalled by any other group of aborigines employed commercially by a superior race," the real labour practices of the company and the policies of the government were far more devastating. The difficulties experienced by the Aleuts would continue well into the twentieth century.[103]

There were more immediate concerns to the south. As E.W. Wright's *Lewis and Dryden* notes, the grant entailed "ramifications on the international scene. This grant was practically the beginning of the Bering Sea trouble, and in maintaining its policy of protecting the monopoly the United States

Government [had] spent millions of dollars and driven scores of American vessels to the protection of the British flag."[104] The problem was that the seals did not stay around the rookeries. They travelled far and wide, and, while at sea, they were generally considered a common property resource. Only during the summer breeding season were they on or near the rookeries and, thus, a private property resource of the ACC.[105]

The sex ratio of the fur seals at birth was approximately equal. Equality ended there. A mature male could weigh over 600 pounds, while females rarely topped 100 pounds. The males, including the younger bulls and the surplus bachelor bulls, had a relatively short journey, spending their winters just outside the Aleutian Island chain. The strongest males reached the rookeries in late May or early June and began to stake out their territory. Females and immature males returned in late June and early July after migrating maybe, in some cases, 7,000 miles along the continental shelf from south of San Francisco. Others wintered just south of Japan and moved along the Asian coast. They joined two smaller herds with rookeries on the Commander and Robben Islands. The females usually gave birth shortly after arrival and then proceeded to breed again. Then they would be off, sometimes travelling considerable distances, seeking food, before returning to their pups. Meanwhile, the old bulls aggressively and fiercely protected their sites, usually containing forty to fifty cows but sometimes twice that number. Thus, there were a lot of surplus bachelor males on the perimeter. These were the ones that the hunters targeted. For a few weeks in late July and early August, before daybreak, a few men might herd as many as 1,000 males toward the "killing grounds," often at a slow pace as the fur seals tended to overheat on land. Upon arrival, those considered too old, too young, females accidentally included in the herding, and those with damaged pelts were culled, and the "killing gang" methodically struck the selected with a heavy, wooden club. They were followed by young boys who knifed the dead or stunned seals and older boys who ripped the seals open and cut around the head and flippers. The skinners finished the task. The land harvest on the rookeries was bloody, brutal, and efficient. The hunters could harvest up to 5,000 pelts in a day.[106]

Canadian pelagic sealing, with some American involvement, was a gradual development that had evolved out of the coastal trading with Aboriginal villages. Initial efforts out of Victoria in the 1860s and 1870s, with mariners such as Spring, McKay, and James Warren, were tentative forays in the early stages of a potentially significant industry. None of the vessels entered the Bering Sea in their quest for sealskins. The large herds that migrated northward along the coast of California, Oregon, Washington, and British Columbia were enough to keep the few vessels that were involved occupied. They competed with a small fleet of schooners out of Neah Bay, Washington.[107]

There were also occasional thrusts out of San Francisco.[108] Through most of the 1870s, the Victoria sealing fleet consisted of the *Favorite,* the *Thornton,* and the *Anna Beck.* Two other schooners with which the MacLeans would be closely associated, the *Onward* and the *Mary Ellen,* were added to the slowly developing fleet in 1879 and 1880 respectively. These trading vessels were quickly evolving into pelagic sealers.[109] Until then, the cruises were relatively short.

The early 1880s witnessed a significant expansion of both the Victoria fleet and the length of their cruises.[110] While returns in these years are difficult to establish, one estimate reveals that 20,000 skins were acquired "in the immediate neighbourhood of Vancouver Island alone" in 1880, with seven vessels and 186 hunters working out of Victoria. Also, the price of skins more than doubled to $10 in 1881.[111] In that year, there were ten vessels, 292 hunters, and between 13,000 and 14,000 skins harvested, worth between $150,000 and $180,000. By 1882, it was thirteen vessels and 400 hunters, and, for the first time, the London fur market purchased over 20,000 skins from the pelagic sealers.[112] These increased activities, and the fur seals' complete disregard for political and geographic frontiers, ensured political, financial, and diplomatic difficulties for decades. Canada and the United States had a number of major issues to resolve in this period. The fur seal problem would just be the one that "raged the most intensely and the longest."[113] Britain, as Canada's imperial motherland, was intimately involved. The sealing schooners out of Victoria were British vessels. Once out of territorial waters, they became an imperial responsibility. The evolving, sometimes turbulent relationship between Canada and Britain was a complicating factor, as was the British perception of the United States as a potential ally.[114] For their part, the Americans were on the verge of expansion and were adjusting to the relatively recent acquisition of Alaska. Besides, they had to concern themselves with the interests of the ACC. Russia and Japan would eventually be immersed in the mix as well. Alex and Dan MacLean, recently returned from their visit to Boston and Cape Breton, sailed right into the maelstrom. The pelagic sealing industry, and the diplomatic, economic, and political difficulties, would expand significantly throughout the 1880s, partly because of the successes of the MacLean brothers.

2
Pelagic Sealing: Victoria, 1883-87

Alex and Dan MacLean had picked a good time to move to Victoria. The 1870s had been a period of "business stagnation" and there were not many more people in 1881 than there had been twenty years earlier. But Victoria was now on the move, and the expansion of Victoria's sealing fleet in the early 1880s, a new and significant contribution to the economy of the provincial capital, helped to fuel that growth. Alex and Dan joined a population of nearly 6,000, "exclusive of Indians," which had doubled in the past five years.[1] Victoria's "island location, fine harbour, and initial advantage made it the central intermediary point for the regional economy. Control of transportation reinforced the advantage of location; Victoria was a major point on the shipping lanes to San Francisco and London and a focus of regional services to the mainland and the north coast."[2] People and investment began to flow into the area, including a considerable amount of English money. The dry dock in Esquimalt, the island railroad, and the significant increase in manufacturing production all played a part. Only San Francisco had a larger iron works on the west coast. Victoria also featured factories producing boots, shoes, boxes, cigars, and soap.[3]

The town made a variety of impressions. As Ivan Doig phrased it, through the lens of Washington Territory diarist James Swan, "not at all like the dry and dowdy little Queen whose name it wears, this capital of British Columbia. Rather, the city is in the manner of the youngest daughter of some Edwardian country house family, attractive and passionately self-absorbed and more than a little silly."[4] Perhaps a bit risqué as well, considering the openly advertised opium joints and the Johnson Street brothels. Victoria in this period was a major source of opium for the North American market. Opium was one of this city's "legendary attractions," with almost fifty or sixty tons being produced yearly, shipped mostly south and east.[5] Also, at this time, Victoria "had the largest red-light district on the Northwest Coast."[6] Some sources suggest that a section of the waterfront was "a miniature

Barbary Coast full of sailors and gamblers, whores and drunks ... The men were wild and free and the women just as mad."[7]

The emerging sealing industry and its participants would only add to the mix. One Cape Bretoner, seeking a berth for the first time later in the decade, offered a detailed description of the preparations immediately prior to setting out. Tom Brown was chugging into Victoria on a tug one evening: "There was a schooner anchored in James Bay with her sailing flag flying, and the temptation was too much. I was ambitious to be a seal hunter, and was sure I could shoot with the best of them." He was soon on the trail of the sealer's skipper: "That was easy enough to pick up, for when liquor was flowing that's where the gang would be aiding the movement. In those days, no matter which way you went, there were from two to three barrooms in each block." Brown quickly tracked them down at the American Hotel bar on Lower Yates Street by following the source of sundry voices singing "For He Was a Pal of Mine," a popular song of the day: "As I passed through the swinging doors into the barroom, quite a merry party was revealed, the two MacLeans, fine looking fellows both, were in the centre of an admiring crowd, doing the honours. Nobody else could 'treat,' which was apparently satisfactory to everybody present, for there was no quarrelling for the privilege as I noted."[8] Brown went sealing the following morning.

A return in the fall offered another glimpse of the seasonal changes in Victoria. In Robert Nichols' account, "the sealing-crew had gold to spend, and the sooner the better. Top hunters would swagger down the streets, long seal whiskers stuck jauntily in their hatbands. The women of the town, Native and white, blossomed out in silks and geegaws from Hakodate, or gold-trimmed seal-teeth brooches, and bracelets and necklaces of Eskimo and Indian manufacture. Wives hung ornate picture-frames on the walls, and proudly or reluctantly but gingerly placed the huge, polished whale teeth on their fireplace mantels and plate rails."[9] Throughout the decade, the population of Victoria would grow at a steady rate of 1,000 yearly, and "stout brick business blocks were creating a mood of permanence and stability."[10] A New York visitor, arriving in Victoria around the same time as Alex MacLean, was rather impressed with its offerings and its sense of solidity: "Here one has neither the evening winds and disagreeable fogs of San Francisco, nor the rather noxious breezes and mosquitoes of Portland, Oregon. The skies are ever clear, the air is always refreshingly cool, the people look quiet and respectable, and everything is intensely English ... Everything is good, heavy, and substantial – the people, the buildings, the food, the drinks."[11]

After three years on the west coast, Dan and Alex MacLean picked up their pace and became directly involved in the new sealing industry. As *Lewis and Dryden's Marine History of the Pacific Northwest* records, "the year

1883 marked the beginning of an important epoch in the sealing business, with the entrance of the first schooner into Bering Sea. The pioneer craft in this disputed territory was the American *City of San Diego,* in charge of Captain Cathcart and Daniel McLean. She left San Francisco, March 29th, with three hunters, entered Bering Sea and took 900 seals, landed at Hall Island and killed a few polar bears, and arrived at Victoria with her catch October 11th."[12] It was not the first instance of pelagic sealing in the Bering Sea – Captain Cathcart had been there previously and a San Francisco firm, H. Liebes and Company, apparently had two vessels around the seal islands in the Bering Sea in 1880 – but it was possibly the first occasion in which a vessel entered those waters specifically for sealing. Alex had also made it back from the east coast in time to join his brother and Captain James Cathcart on this seminal voyage and, as he later explained, "there had been other vessels in there before, but they didn't go in as a matter of seal hunting." This time they were in the Bering Sea from June to mid-September.[13]

There are some discrepancies in the sources about the roles of the various individuals on this voyage, the size of the catch, and the actual vessel involved.[14] Alex, it seems, was a boat-puller-steerer for a hunter, Warren F. Upson, although he apparently also served as a navigator, as he remembered it later. Double duty on sealers by seamen was not unusual, and it meant an additional wage. In addition, Alex, unlike Dan, usually participated in the hunt when he eventually took command of a sealing vessel.[15] Most references to this voyage echo Lewis and Dryden's version, which has the intrepid sealers on the *City of San Diego,* a forty-nine-ton schooner built in San Francisco in 1881. But Lewis and Dryden also have Alex and Dan MacLean in the smaller and older *San Diego* that year as well. This boat was a thirty-six-ton schooner built in 1850 in Sag Harbor, New York.[16] Charles H. Townsend's exhaustive study, which specifically admonishes readers not to confuse the two vessels, sides with the *City of San Diego,* while Alex MacLean later gave evidence that specified the older, smaller vessel.[17] The detailed write-up in the *Daily Colonist* when the schooner – this contemporary account sided with the *San Diego* – initially returned from the Bering Sea to the port of Victoria on 11 October 1883 is interesting, in part because the catch of 900 seals was mentioned only in passing. Indeed, the captain ("Carthcut" in this version) reported that they had been on a long whaling cruise – San Francisco was just then becoming the world's leading whaling port – and "the crew saw no white men other than themselves" for five months: "Taken together the season may be said to have been stormy and generally unpropitious. No vessels of any description were sighted, and walrus and whales were very scarce." Perhaps the reporter missed the significance of this particular voyage or possibly the captain was downplaying the successful sealing side of it, but much of the *Daily Colonist* article is concerned with a discussion on icebergs, polar bears, and the natural splendour experienced by the crew during the voyage: "The rays of the sun which broke through the clouds are described as having given a most sublime effect to the icebergs (some of them most fanciful in shape) which acted as immense prisms and reflected the most gorgeous hues." A close encounter with a very large polar bear took up even more space in the contemporary newspaper account, but the thirteen men had returned safely to Victoria and were "right glad to once more get ashore after a long and rather tedious cruise." A week later, the newspaper reported that the *(City of) San Diego* had returned to San Francisco.[18]

The significance of the voyage of Captain Cathcart and the MacLeans into the Bering Sea in the summer of 1883 was not lost on others. Within two years, Canadian pelagic sealers operating on the northwest coast and in the Bering Sea would more than triple their average catch to over 1,600 skins per vessel. With dockside prices at Victoria ranging between $6 and $8 per pelt in the 1880s, the average voyage would gross over $11,000. Successful trips could bring a 40 percent return.[19] The Bering Sea voyage of 1883 was doubtless profitable to the MacLeans, but the returns were mostly in the experiences gained. A later estimate that they had made "$200,000 from their first catch" was wildly inaccurate, and it is indicative of just how tall were some of the tales associated with these two men.[20] There was another suggestive side to this trip as well: "It has been said along the waterfront that, with this expedition, they became the first seal poachers to raid the Bering rookeries," but, again, there is little evidence to support the claim that they actually landed on the protected islands on this occasion.[21] In fact, there was a glut in the market at the time that had prompted the Alaska Commercial Company (ACC) to decrease its harvest on the rookeries that season to 75,000.[22] Regardless, the ramifications of this voyage would reverberate for decades. The voyage of the *(City of) San Diego* into the Bering Sea in 1883 initiated what was to become a lengthy and bitter diplomatic dispute over rights to the seal herd. The ACC immediately expressed alarm about the "seal pirates," and pressure was brought to bear on US officials to prevent pelagic sealing in the Bering Sea. The perceived problem would be compounded by the proclivity of the pelagic sealers to trespass on the rookeries. This practice was noticeable the following year.[23]

Pelagic sealing in the Bering Sea was the key to the expansion of Victoria's latest industry – it would become a major resource industry during this period – and the provincial capital was fast becoming aware of this lucrative development.[24] William Spring's son Charles, who became involved in the business the following year, offered a slightly different slant on its initial development and emphasized Dan MacLean's contribution: "Captain Dan McLean ... finally got up to the Bering Sea, and made use of guns on seals there, besides sea otter hunting. From that day the custom grew very rapidly ... [Captain William Spring] promptly started in and secured Captain Dan

McLean himself, who was then with Captain Cathcart in the old schooner the *City of San Diego;* he placed Dan McLean ... in charge of the schooner *Mary Ellen*. That would be in the spring of 1884. They were taking white crews then ... That was the beginning of white crews out of Victoria, with shot guns and rifles ... They were the very best of guns fitted out in San Francisco, under Captain Dan McLean's management."[25] Dan and Alex would remain in the forefront of this industry for the remainder of the decade. Their sealing successes, and the stories that began to swirl around them during the next six years, would provide a sound foundation for the building of the MacLean legend. Their 1883 earnings from the Bering Sea trip were quickly reinvested in sealing. Dan purchased 25 percent, or sixteen shares (a vessel's ownership was divided into sixty-four shares), of the *Mary Ellen* from William Spring in November 1883 for $1,325, and Alex acquired a 25 percent interest in the *Favorite* for $1,837.50. She was the first vessel in which Alex had a financial interest.[26]

With these new developments in the sealing industry firmly established, Dan and Alex MacLean, who were rapidly acquiring sealing knowledge to supplement their considerable sailing experience, now set the pace for pelagic sealing success in the 1880s. They would have more success in acquiring sealskins than any other sealer on the west coast throughout the remainder of the decade. The secondary occupation of walrus hunting essentially disappeared, and sealers began the practice of commencing the season's work off the California coast. Usually the spring hunt had the schooners following the seals along the northwest coast. In the summer, they headed for the Bering Sea. A few of the smaller vessels limited themselves to the coastal hunt. The vessels usually ranged between forty and eighty tons.[27]

Pelagic sealing was completely different from the land harvest. Only the starting time of the hunt, before dawn, was similar. The schooner would lie to and send out the eighteen- to twenty-foot long boats, which were sharp at the bow and stern and called double-enders, with a hunter – the elite of the sealing crew, armed with a rifle or, later, a shotgun – as well as a boat-puller and a steersman. Aboriginals used two-person canoes and spears with a detachable harpoon end. With some rations, a small cask of water, and a couple of gaffs, they would fan out from the schooner. Shot or speared instead of clubbed, these seals were not always retrieved. Once a seal was killed, if there was time, it would be skinned on the small boat and the carcass thrown overboard: "The insides of the boats were slippery with grease and blood, and as the boat tossed in rough seas the men fought to keep their footing as their chilled hands wielded the blubber-coated skinning-knives."[28] Otherwise, skinning was done on the schooner. Jack London describes this scene: "After a good day's killing I have seen our decks covered with hides and bodies, slippery with fat and blood, the scuppers running red; masts, ropes and rails splattered with the sanguinary color; and the men, like butchers plying their trade, naked and red of arm and hand, hard at work with ripping and flensing knives, removing the skins from the pretty sea-creatures they had killed."[29] But such activity only happened if they made it back to the schooner before dark. Sometimes dusk could find them many miles from their vessel, and cold, anxious, hungry hours, or even days, could follow. The schooner had a signal gun to assist their return. Sudden squalls or storms, dense fog, which could settle in quickly and stay for days or weeks, accidents on the boat, attacks by wounded bulls or killer whales, and treacherous reefs and islands were other concerns for the pelagic sealers. The adverse current and prevailing westerlies of North America's west coast made the lee shores particularly treacherous.[30] Over 200 sailors and hunters in the pelagic sealing fleet were lost in 1888-1905. This aspect was reflected in the insurance rates, which were "extremely high by any marine standard."[31] It was a far more difficult process than harvesting on the rookeries. There were a few factors that limited an even greater human toll in this specific industry. One was the short, summer sealing season in the Bering Sea and another was the safety in numbers, since the presence of a considerable fleet meant that there was a good chance that individual boats would be picked up by other vessels, which happened constantly.[32]

Their prey was in demand, fuelled in part by the development in England of a method for removing the coarse, grey guard hairs from the pelt, revealing a rich pile.[33] Sealskins as fashion statements had been evident by the early 1870s. Typically, one of the first purchases of those who were successful in the gold fields of southern California and Nevada was a sealskin coat and muff. The attraction continued into the 1880s. As the *Daily Colonist* one-sidedly explained in the spring of 1884, real and tangible benefits accrued to the wearer: "A seal skin is the most valuable and useful adjunct to domestic comfort and to matrimony that the world knows ... Let her put on a seal skin [coat] and everyone takes a look at her, and even turns back to take another ... It puts the work girl on an absolute equality with the Nob Hill heiress. I have known a whole family of girls comfortably married off by judicious manipulation of a sealskin."[34] Just how many "working girls" would have aspired, or bothered, to acquire a garment that sold for $150-$200 during this period is a moot point. Besides, in the 1880s, sealskin coats were equally popular among men and women.[35]

Although Alex passed an examination in Victoria for the renewal of his Master's ticket on steamers in the coastal trade on 22 January 1884, by the time it was issued a couple of months later he had been on a sealing schooner for more than two months. Alex was on board the *Mary Ellen,* which, under Dan MacLean's command, had outfitted in San Francisco and began sealing on 1 February 1884.[36] At the time, San Francisco was the best location for outfitting a sealing ship, and Alex was probably acquiring additional provisioning and sealing information.[37] The following month, an article in the *Daily Colonist* entitled "Not a Smuggler" became the first of many alleged transgressions and public denials concerning MacLean: "Capt. Alexander McLean ... says that the report about the schooner being engaged in smuggling is all nonsense. The schooner first put into San Francisco for slight repairs, and afterward entered and cleared at the port and was examined by customs officers. She was also compelled to put into Drake's Bay several times during a stress of weather ... Capt. McLean thinks the whole affair has been caused by American sealers and that this will be found to be the case if any investigation is made."[38] The *Mary Ellen* was the "first and properly equipped white sealer sailing out of Victoria," according to sealer Charles Spring.[39] Apparently, it was the only Canadian sealing schooner known to have entered the Bering Sea that year.[40] The last seals were taken on 23 August. Dan returned to Victoria that autumn with 1,954 skins.[41] At some point in the spring, Alex returned to Victoria and took command of the *Favorite*.[42] Carrying on board several Aboriginal hunters and around eighteen to twenty canoes, he did not find it necessary to enter the Bering Sea that year. The coastal hunt was successful, and he returned to his home port of Victoria with 1,754 skins.[43] The *Favorite* was the high boat that spring season for the Victoria fleet. For Alex and Dan, the season was considered a success, and Alex immediately bought a one-third interest in the fifty-five-ton *Kate*. There were twenty pelagic sealing vessels that year, which may help explain why the ACC had difficulty in securing their annual quota. The expansion would continue. By 1892, the fleet would number 124.[44]

By all accounts, Alex MacLean was a fine-looking man. As author and observer Tom MacInnes notes, "he was of the handsome Highland type found among Nova Scotia seamen."[45] Just under six feet, with broad shoulders, trim waist, rosy complexion, fair hair, and striking blue-grey eyes that positively sparkled with good humour, Alex was doubtless already sporting the luxuriant moustache that, along with his eyes, was invariably mentioned whenever his appearance was described. Always well dressed – he was "very particular about his attire" – he was a good dancer to boot.[46] His single status was about to change. Josephine Dauphin was an experienced milliner from New Orleans who arrived in Victoria in 1880, and she was soon numbered among the many independent businesswomen located in the town.[47] She immediately set up in downtown Victoria, on Pandora Street between Blanchard and Quadra, and would remain in Victoria until she died thirty-five years later.[48] Probably she found British Columbia's capital somewhat refreshing, given that New Orleans, with a population of around 200,000, was "unquestionably the dirtiest and unhealthiest city on the North American continent" at the time.[49] Josephine Dauphin was accompanied by her two daughters, Marie, twenty-one, and Lucie (later Lucy), eighteen, and her son, Maximilian, ten, who were all born in New Orleans. The

Dauphin family is of particular interest because Alex MacLean soon caught the eye of Lucie Dauphin, or the other way around.

On the morning of 25 November 1884, twenty-one-year-old Lucie Dauphin and twenty-six-year-old Alex MacLean were married by Father J.M. Mandart in the old Saint Andrew's Roman Catholic Cathedral in Victoria. Tommy Burnes, the proprietor of the popular American Hotel, escorted Lucie down the aisle. Bridesmaids were Sarah McDowell and Elizabeth Madigan. Groomsmen were John McDowell, a boilermaker in Victoria, and William Burnes, who worked in his father's hotel.[50] The wedding party appears to have been egalitarian and primarily composed of Irish and Scottish Gaels and the Louisiana Dauphins. Ninety years later, a Victoria journalist rather ungraciously, but not entirely inaccurately, noted that "this affair must be one of the few occasions associated with ... MacLean which a reporter could properly describe as being quiet and impressive."[51] Although Dan MacLean was listed as residing in the American Hotel at the time, he does not appear to have been at his brother's wedding. This fact may help to explain the tone of the affair. The newlyweds settled into a place on Chatham Street, near Quadra Street, in bustling downtown Victoria.[52]

The nuptials of the young couple were also noted in the personal diary of Edgar Crow Baker, who was an entrepreneur and the Conservative member of parliament for Victoria.[53] Baker would have a significant impact on both the economic development of Victoria and on the financial and sealing affairs of Alex and Dan MacLean throughout much of the remaining decade. Cole Harris' description of the British Columbia elite at the time, "the small group of white, Protestant men, most of whom knew each other, who dominated the government, the courts, the churches, and the commercial economy," was a definite fit for Baker.[54] He was an Englishman, a former lieutenant in the Royal Navy. Married to a daughter of Captain Richard Jones of Halifax, Nova Scotia, he arrived in Nova Scotia in 1872 at the age of twenty-six on half pay. Two years later, he and his wife moved to Victoria. His first job was managing a sawmill office for his wife's uncle.[55] His English navy background, his family, in-law, and Freemasonry connections were all advantages. After he had his naval half pay commuted to a lump sum settlement in 1878, he acquired some capital. He then began his steady rise to become "a major figure in the business life of the city."[56] He soon put his $7,285 to work. By 1879, he was secretary to the Board of Trade, a notary public, a real estate agent, a marine surveyor, and a grand secretary of the Masonic Order. The following year, he was involved in the incorporation of the Victoria and Esquimalt Telephone Company. He entered the Canadian House of Commons as the Conservative Party's representative from Victoria in 1882.[57] A man with a variety of financial interests, his diary note of the wedding of Lucie Dauphin and Alex MacLean is neither surprising nor, one suspects, coincidental. Baker viewed most occurrences with an entrepreneurial eye, and the up-and-coming Alex MacLean had also caught his attention.

Aboriginals on Vancouver Island's west coast were experienced seal hunters, and they would play a major role in the developing industry, usually comprising about half of the hunters in the pelagic fleet. They regularly worked in wage labour occupations during this period. In the sealing industry, they hunted, operated canoes, and worked the vessels as seamen. Many of them were Nuu-chah-nulth (formerly referred to as Nootka), which were comprised of Ohiat, Kyuquot, Ucluelet, Clayoquot, Hesquiaht, and Ewlhwillaht. There were numerous Haida, Quatsino, Kwakiutl, Salish, and Tsimshian as well.[58] However, the Aboriginals were not simply wage earners, as Cairn Elizabeth Crockford has demonstrated in an insightful study of Nuu-chah-nulth labour relations in the industry. For Crockford, 1885 marked the end of the "Pioneer Period," which had been characterized by the development of cooperative commodity production involving Nuu-chah-nulth sealers and coastal merchants. During this phase, community leaders, as labour bosses, and not the schooner owner, selected the individuals for the hunt, knowing clearly that there was a set price per skin. In addition, "'boss money' and *cultus potlatch,* which represented a form of remuneration to labour above and beyond traditional capitalist wages" were prominent features. Following this period, "post-production" negotiating was eliminated, primarily because new investors entering the industry, many of whom were also involved in a variety of other enterprises, generally used non-Aboriginal technology and labour.[59] This was part of the backdrop to the 1885 season.

In 1885, everyone with an interest in the Victoria sealing fleet kept a close eye on what would be referred to as the "MacLean experiment." Outfitting the same schooners they had employed the previous year, Dan set out with the *Mary Ellen* and white hunters and Alex had Aboriginals on the *Favorite.* The brothers had a specific purpose, namely to undertake "a direct test of which method of hunting was more profitable."[60] Similar schooners commanded by siblings provided the conditions for as controlled a test as one could expect. Both vessels would complete their hunt that year in the Bering Sea, and the *Favorite* was quite likely "the first vessel to take Indian seal hunters" there.[61] Alex almost did not make it. There was considerable demand for experienced Aboriginal sealers (eight vessels had Nuu-chah-nulth hunters that year), and they were well versed in negotiating with whites. In January, when Alex arrived in Kyuquot, on the west coast of Vancouver Island, offering $2.50 per skin, the villagers declined. They wanted twice that rate. The *Daily Colonist* considered it a strike. Aboriginal councils were held at feasts, and communities compared information and demonstrated a strong sense of solidarity, which was always a part of their negotiation strategy. It worked. By April, the schooners had raised the rate to $4 per skin, and Alex now had seventeen Hesqiats and three Clayoquots to man the ten canoes. Two of the hunters later became separated from the *Favorite* and would not return with the vessel.[62]

A hint of other difficulties to come surfaced with the appearance of the American cutter *Corwin,* which contacted both schooners a number of times while they were sealing. Neither the *Mary Ellen* nor the *Favorite* was distracted from the business at hand.[63] Doubtless the "experiment" appealed to the sense of friendly rivalry between Alex and Dan. It was the type of situation both would relish enormously. Dan acquired his first skins on 26 January, the last on 3 August. Alex, who had to make up for lost time, finished sealing a few weeks later. The MacLean brothers returned to Victoria within a day of each other in mid-September. Financially speaking, it was a dead heat. The *Mary Ellen,* under Dan, acquired a record 2,309 skins. Alex and the Aboriginal hunters in the *Favorite* secured 2,073. The extra harvest on the *Mary Ellen* offset the higher costs of the white sealers. As D.G. Paterson and J. Wilen note in their study of the industry, "the McLean experiment reflects the early ambivalence of the industry over the choice of technology."[64] Part of the financial advantage was that "it costs only about one-half to subsist an Indian crew than it does a white crew, for the Indians live chiefly on the flesh of the seal and hard bread." This particular pecuniary advantage soon changed because, according to Alex's later testimony, the practice quickly altered between 1887 and 1888, and the Aboriginals began to receive more supplies from the ships' stores.[65] The change was also partly attributable to the fact that the whites quickly became experienced. There was, additionally, a difference in attitude. The Aboriginals were far more independently minded. They "do not care about going so far away from home and ... when they are dissatisfied do pretty much as they like," whereas the whites were "in every way ... handier to deal with than the natives."[66] Such a distinction would have undoubtedly been of considerable interest to the new investors. The changing workforce, according to one later commentator, would bring further concerns: "More and more, the seal hunters and boat steerers and handlers were recruited from the rough, lawless flotsam of the seaports, the sea wolves whom Jack London depicted in fiction, men indifferent to hardships and dangerous toil, unafraid to clash with law officers."[67] Eventually, significant changes in sealing regulations in the 1890s would again bring the Aboriginals and their hunting practices to the fore. Such a shift was reflected in the percentage of schooners carrying Aboriginal hunters. It declined to a low of 38 percent in 1891 but rebounded to 88 percent by 1899, a decade after Alex and Dan MacLean had left the Victoria fleet.[68]

The experiences gleaned from the voyages of the *Mary Ellen* and the *Favorite* were instructive. The closely watched sealing voyages of Alex and Dan MacLean in that year were considered a success. One source estimated that the combined catches in the "experiment" were worth $35,000. It was probably close.[69] The two Aboriginal hunters who had become separated from the *Favorite* that season also managed to return safely. Landing on one of the Aleutian Islands, they had made their way to a central trading station with the assistance of some American fishermen, and were then taken to San Francisco on the ACC steamer. The British consul-general paid their passage to Victoria, where they contacted Charles Spring and Alex MacLean. From there, with a canoe, provisions, and a boatload of stories about their experiences, not the least of which were their first impressions of San Francisco, they arrived home in November. It would soon be commonplace for significant numbers of Aboriginal sealers and crewmen to winter over in San Francisco and in various Japanese ports.[70]

Alex probably stayed in Victoria with his wife to spend their second Christmas together. They also had a wedding to attend. They would serve as witnesses for Lucie's mother's civil marriage in Victoria on 16 January 1886. Josephine Licour Dauphin, forty-four, a widow, married forty-year-old John Sewell Bates. A bachelor and farmer, originally from Michigan, Bates was living in Victoria. In the directory that year he was listed as a teamster.[71] This is his only appearance on this historical stage. Josephine would continue to use the Dauphin surname.[72]

Dan took the *Mary Ellen* back to San Francisco late in December 1885. Apparently Dan was not lonely either. On 19 January 1886, "his Scottish friends in San Francisco" held a "Grand Complimentary Party" for him at the Occidental Music Hall on Mission Street, complete with the Clan Pipers and Gregg's Orchestra. Four days later, Dan cleared San Francisco with the *Mary Ellen* for Victoria. Working up along the coast, he picked up his first seal on 3 February.[73] The year 1886 brought excellent sealing weather and additional expansion within the industry. More than 450 men were involved, and the vast majority followed the path blazed by Captain Cathcart and the MacLeans as they entered the Bering Sea.[74] In addition, the completion of the Canadian Pacific Railway meant that sealers could now consign their catches to a London broker in time for the winter sales. This "was the first year that Victoria was directly linked to the main London fur market."[75] These developments underlined the important contribution that the sealing industry was making to the larger economy. Thus began what the *San Francisco Call* referred to as the "annual spring row" between Britain and the United States.[76] For Alaska historian William Hunt, it was national interest, not conservation: "And national interest, fomented by powerful economic concerns, made all the difference. Quite suddenly, the Bering Sea was in the international limelight. Events there had significance. Clamors and alarms sparked by the outraged sensibilities of nationalists raised clouds of war, and it was high time for statesmen to ponder over maps of hitherto neglected regions and wonder how to avert an armed conflict."[77] The pelagic sealing industry was about to enter a serious and difficult phase, and the MacLeans were right in the middle of it.

Part of the problem was the sloppy management of the American monopoly. As Briton Cooper Busch notes, there was in the 1880s "the failure of anyone connected with the islands to report in any meaningful way the decline of the herd" to the ACC. The demands on the resource would continue to increase. During the next five years (1886-90), sealing vessels averaged 1,600 seals per season.[78] The increased harvest of the Canadian pelagic fleet apparently reduced catches, quality, and prices for the ACC, which was a development that the company obviously resented. On the Pribilof Islands, the quantity of marketable seals declined considerably, prompting the ACC to bombard Washington with heated protests and demands for protection.[79] And so, in the assessment of some British Columbia historians, "to protect the interest of the monopoly-holding company [the American government] entered upon a course of illegal, high-handed conduct, altogether opposed to the traditions of that nation."[80]

However, there was also more to it. The ACC's lease was an extremely lucrative one.[81] Mindful as well that a large-scale Canadian enterprise "would seriously threaten the only significant source of revenue from Alaska," Daniel Manning, the American secretary of the treasury, whose "mind seemed to be more fixed upon questions of revenue than upon diplomatic difficulties that might arise from seizures of foreign shipping," moved quickly.[82] The Department of the Treasury did not consult with either the State or Justice Departments before sending instructions to the revenue cutters.[83] The American government sent the armed cutter *Corwin,* the same one that had contacted the schooners captained by the MacLeans the previous year, into the Bering Sea. The *Corwin* seized four sealing vessels, an action that raised the ire of some contemporary, as well as some later, Canadian commentators. Charles Tansill's assessment was succinct: "Canadian vessels had been seized when they were more than sixty miles from the nearest land, and such action was in open defiance of the principles of international law ... Attention was called to the fact that the American government had always made it a point to proclaim in loud tones its adherence to the doctrine of the freedom of the seas."[84] Many people got into the act. Edgar Crow Baker, as the senior member of parliament for Victoria and secretary-treasurer of the British Columbia Board of Trade, forwarded concerns to the secretary of state from Theodore Lubbe, the managing owner of the sealing fleet (and a business associate of Baker's). Lubbe noted the "vital importance to our fishing industry and commercial enterprises generally" and requested the government deal with the conflict "at the very earliest possible moment." Baker considered his "telegram was really the firing of the first shot in the defence of our rights as Canadians to fish anywhere we please on the high seas, including Bering Sea."[85]

The main story in Victoria in 1886 was the seizure by the American revenue cutter *Corwin* of the four sealing vessels. Three of them, the *Thornton,* the *Carolina,* and the *Onward,* were under British registration. The *Carolina* was 139 miles from the coast when she was seized. The other two were sixty-eight miles from land.[86] Sixty-five years earlier, in 1821, when the Russian czar had declared the Bering Sea a closed sea, both the American and British governments had strongly protested, and the czar had backed down. When the British minister in Washington, Sir Lionel Sackville-West, pointed out to Secretary of State Thomas Bayard the earlier American protest against the Russian contention that the Bering Sea was a closed sea, Bayard had replied: "Yes, at that time."[87] When Bayard managed to become more fully informed, he "was absolutely convinced that the seizures by the *Corwin* were wrong from the moment he first heard of them."[88] Tansill has called attention to the "ironic fact" that in this dispute "the United States abandoned its historic stand for the freedom of the seas, and Great Britain defended a doctrine that in practice she had at times openly flouted."[89] Lewis and Dryden add: "This act was the beginning of one of the most disgraceful and unjust policies to which the United States has ever been a party."[90] One American legislator stretched it to the point of calling the seals "domestic animals," prompting a satirical aside from a *Victoria Daily Times* editor: "A seal was shot last week in the river opposite Montreal. It will now be in order for the Alaska Fur Company [sic] to arrest some one, on the ground that the mammal must have wandered away from the Bering Sea."[91] All of the vessels seized were a considerable distance from shore. One contemporary source said "the law should be altered or amended so the public, and not a powerful monopoly, will be benefited. I believe that the same men who are protected on the Atlantic as fishermen should be protected on the Pacific, and not branded as pirates and poachers."[92] One of the four seized was an American ship, the trendsetting *City of San Diego*. This action apparently forced Captain Cathcart out of the business. Even the American flag had "failed to protect the sealing schooners who interfered with the business of the Alaska Commercial Company."[93] The other three schooners, which were all from the Victoria fleet, the *Thornton,* the *Carolina,* and the *Onward,* were registered in Britain. All had been seized beyond Canada's three-mile territorial limit. Since Canada's colonial status meant that it had no authority outside Canadian territorial waters, the seizures were issues for the British government. Since the seizures occurred more than sixty miles from the nearest land, they were "in open defiance of the principles of international law."[94] It was not just the seizures, or the monopoly situation, that antagonized many: "On hearing of these seizures the other Victoria sealers in Bering Sea hurried away, which was doubtless what they were expected to do."[95] The sense of outrage was partially fuelled by the realization that this could be a severe blow to an increasingly lucrative industry in Victoria. For their part, the British had also to factor in America's increasing strength and her potential as an ally.[96] Also, the pelts went to London for processing. The fur industry there employed 10,000 individuals.[97]

There was more to gnaw on for the disenchanted. The *Corwin,* under orders from the Department of the Treasury in Washington, conveyed the seized ships to Sitka, Alaska: "De facto the United States had adopted the policy that the Bering Sea was a *mare clausum.*"[98] Judge Lafayette Dawson in Sitka certainly came close to this interpretation: "The court conceded that all vessels had been more than 60 miles from the nearest landfall; it was sufficient for the vessels to have been within the Bering Sea east of the 1867 Treaty boundary for them to be found guilty."[99] The Canadians and the British considered this closed sea policy and the seizures "a blatant violation of traditional rights on the high seas." An immediate protest from the British government did not prevent fines and a month's imprisonment for the captains and mates. They received $500 and $300 fines respectively. The ships and skins were impounded.[100] The crews of the *Carolina* and the *Thornton* were apparently shipped to San Francisco "and turned adrift, destitute and penniless." The crew of the *Onward* was supposedly turned loose at Unalaska.[101] Another source explains that all of the respective crews were forced to make their own way home from Sitka, and at least one individual, Captain James Ogilvie of the *Carolina,* never made it. Elderly and stressed, he wandered off and died from exposure, prompting Lewis and Dryden to accuse the American government of "indirectly" murdering him.[102] Whatever the travails of these particular sealers, the actions were diplomatically ham-fisted and legally suspect. Further indignation came with the information that the *Onward,* the *Caroline,* and the *Thornton* had been beached on the Alaska shore and the 2,150 skins that had been seized were in an ACC warehouse. Sealers would refer to the final resting point on the Sitka shore for the hapless vessels as "Rotten Row." The *Daily Colonist* now referred to the ACC as "the opulent autocrats who claim jurisdiction over the high seas of the North Pacific ocean" and felt that the action was "an outrage unprecedented in maritime annals."[103] There was something to this perspective. Sackville-West was informed that it was almost impossible "to live or hold public employment in Alaska without keeping on good terms" with the ACC.[104] The American government's "insistence on honoring its commitment to the lease holders" would be a major obstacle to any British-American accord, even though Secretary of State Bayard, with the ACC specifically in mind, was determined "not to allow the interests of any association of Commercial or trading interests to lead [them] into a position not based upon law, justice and consequent National dignity and self-respect."[105] Bayard had his work cut out for him.

The attitude and actions of the American Department of the Treasury had a direct effect on Alex MacLean. On the *Favorite,* with a crew of twenty-six, Alex had sailed from Victoria near the end of May and commenced sealing in the Bering Sea on 9 July. For the remainder of the month, he remained pretty much in the same position, averaging around 75 seals daily. On 28 July, the *Onward,* under Dan Munroe, transferred 507 skins to Alex's schooner.[106] Alex was half owner of both vessels, although the record does not allow a clear distinction between "actual ownership, as distinct from the formal registered ownership."[107] The American cutter *Corwin* seized the *Onward* on 2 August, a day after she had acquired the *Thornton* and the *Carolina*. Then the same cutter came across Alex and the *Favorite* at two in the morning. MacLean was "warned to cease sealing in the Bering Sea and ordered to leave Bering Sea."[108] They were about 115 miles from the nearest land at the time, and the *Favorite* was not boarded.[109] Doubtless the *Corwin* had enough to contend with, as it already had the three Canadian vessels in tow at the time. Alex was not particularly perturbed. He stayed in the Bering Sea another seventeen days, acquiring an additional 675 skins before he departed on 19 August. Dan, on the *Mary Ellen,* eluded the cantankerous *Corwin* entirely. He was too busy sealing. His log has the last seals being taken on 24 August.[110] Given the events in the Bering Sea, however, and with no word from either the *Mary Ellen* or the *Favorite,* the Victoria sealing community was growing anxious about the fate of both vessels by the end of August.[111] The concern was unnecessary. The MacLeans brought both vessels back safely to their home port of Victoria in fine style. Alex brought in a substantial 3,325 skins, the second highest catch of the season. Dan and the *Mary Ellen* returned with a record 4,256 skins, enabling him to "carry the broom" once again. (The most successful schooner would hoist a broom on the main halyard announcing its crew's prowess and signifying a clean sweep.) Dan's record in 1886 would be surpassed only once in the entire history of the Victoria sealing fleet.[112] The combined gross catch of the *Mary Ellen* and the *Favorite* that year was probably worth more than $60,000.[113]

The business partnership between Edgar Crow Baker and the MacLeans intensified. It was not a smooth relationship. Baker was very interested in the financial bottom line, whereas the MacLeans were already exhibiting a free-spending style. Neither Alex nor Dan appeared to have had a strong inclination to save, to budget, or to engage in financial planning. Generous to a fault, profligate, financially irresponsible – whatever phrase one selects to characterize the MacLeans' approach to money management – it seems clearly to have been oriented to the short term. This trait was probably based on occupation, culture, and class. Money was to be used, not accumulated. As Marcus Rediker, and many others, have noted: "A nonaccumulative ethic among seamen ran very deep."[114] Alex and Dan had emerged from a largely pre-capitalist society. Another Cape Breton Gael from this period related that when a neighbour once returned home from the United States with a dollar bill, it was regarded in his community "as a great curiosity."[115] The MacLeans would never be accused of being parsimonious, and their attitude toward, and practice with, their financial gains would be grist for the legend-in-the-making mill. For one distant relative, the way they "scattered money about became a byword in Cape Breton." Another Cape Breton source maintained that they "made and spent several fortunes."[116]

Immediate financial realities had to be dealt with, and the MacLeans' lack of concern with prudent financial management was doubtless one of the topics raised during a number of long sessions held between the far more acquisitive Baker and Alex and Dan in mid-October concerning the *Mary Ellen*.[117] On 18 October, Dan paid $3,000 and became sole owner of the *Mary Ellen*.[118] Although he had just returned with the largest catch in the Victoria fleet, Dan found it necessary to take out a mortgage on the *Mary Ellen* with Baker before the end of the month.[119] Dan also re-naturalized as a British subject at this time, with Edgar Crow Baker serving as justice of the peace during the process.[120] Weeks later, half ownership of the *Onward* was transferred to Dan MacLean as well, and, as Alex later explained, it was "because [he] could not use [his] own name in the ship's register."[121] Baker and the MacLeans may have been looking ahead to the possibility of claims being pressed by the Canadian and British governments for the seizures that season. American citizens would not have fit in this loop. A few months later, Baker would also hold power of attorney for Dan.[122] Whatever else, the successful seasons for Dan and Alex in 1885-86 did not translate into large amounts of readily available cash, and Edgar Crow Baker was well on his way to becoming heavily involved in their sealing ventures. Alex was still part owner of the *Kate*, but he did not send her sealing and sold his interest in her that year.[123] Alex's increased involvement with Baker may explain why the partnership between Charles Spring and Alex MacLean was dissolved in December 1886, with "each retaining his interest in the claims against the U.S. government," for what they were worth.[124] Some interests, it would turn out, were worth considerably more than others, although it would be more than a decade before anyone other than lawyers would see any money. Captain Laughlin MacLean, a native of Prince Edward Island and no relation to Alex and Dan, would take command of the *Favorite* for the next few years.[125]

Victor Jacobson, who was about to begin a long career as a sealer, viewed the changing conditions in the industry in a challenging and competitive light, suggesting, to use Hobsbawm's model, an acceptance of the "social bandit" interpretation: "They were great days. Half the fascination of sealing was in dodging the gunboats."[126] Others were less adventurous. In November, William Munsie, who was heavily involved in the sealing fleet, wrote to George Foster, Canadian minister of marine and fisheries, to inquire anxiously as to the fate of the vessels and also what to expect in 1887: "The industry is of too much importance to Canada to allow the Alaska Commercial Company to dictate who shall or who shall not take seals on the high or Behring's Sea. For the season of 1886 there was brought into Victoria from the Pacific Ocean and Behring's Sea, and shipped from there to England and the United States, 50,000 skins, valued at about 350,000 dollars. It is evident that the business is worth protecting."[127] The seizure of the *Onward* and the other vessels, and the "warning out" of the *Favorite,* would eventually result in tedious diplomatic negotiations and litigation that would drag out for more than a decade. While there was willingness on the part of Britain "to put rapprochement ahead of Canadian desires," American-British conciliation was hampered by the determination of the Canadian, and especially the British Columbian, officials to continue the lucrative pelagic sealing industry.[128]

The difficulties experienced by the Canadian sealing fleet were repeated in 1887. More vessels were involved than in previous years, but the harvest of fur seals decreased, in part because of "boisterous weather" but more because of "the uncertain state of affairs with the United States, and the annoyance caused by the seizures of [their] sealing schooners."[129] These seizures, between 30 June and 2 September, primarily by the American revenue cutters *Bear* and *Rush,* included nine American and six Canadian vessels.[130] Both Dan and Alex were on the British-registered *Mary Ellen* that season. Dan was captain and his brother was "a passenger." The *Mary Ellen* picked up its first seals on 24 January along the California coast. Late in the season, in mid-August, there were reports out of Victoria that included the *Mary Ellen* among those boats seized, but this report proved inaccurate.[131] The MacLeans stopped sealing on 19 August and arrived back in Victoria with 2,457 skins, mostly from the Bering Sea, which proved to be the fourth largest catch of the season. Laughlin MacLean, who had taken command of the *Favorite,* would bring in 1,887 pelts.[132]

Another MacLean also appeared on the scene. Catherine Lucille, a daughter of Lucie and Alex's, was born in Victoria on 3 September.[133] Lucie's presence in this book is minimal. Documentation is sparse. Her husband, like most mariners, was absent for extended periods. Pelagic sealing was not one of those maritime occupations that allowed for wives and sometimes children to accompany their husbands and fathers. Maybe she waited patiently in port for her husband's return, but her role was far from passive. She would bear the major responsibility of raising their daughter and probably of looking after their financial affairs on the home front. The latter would not always be an easy task.

3
Conflict in the North Pacific, 1888-89

It was quite clear that one vessel was not sufficient for the MacLeans. In October 1887, they met with Edgar Crow Baker, entrepreneur, and Conservative member of parliament for Victoria, and proposed that he join them in acquiring a new schooner for sealing. Baker was already bankrolling Dan to an extent and agreed. He also concurred with Dan's suggestion that they follow William Munsie's lead and purchase a schooner in Nova Scotia, rather than having one built in British Columbia.[1] Munsie had recently had the *Pathfinder* brought around the Horn (the first east coast schooner to engage in the Pacific sealing industry), and a few others were involved in similar transactions. It was cheaper than having one built in British Columbia at the time.[2] And so, while Alex was becoming acquainted with his daughter, Dan proceeded east. His arrival in Halifax in mid-November prompted considerable interest within the region "in the comparatively new and rapidly developing Pacific fisheries."[3] The local papers were fascinated with Dan MacLean, with the sealing successes of both brothers, and with the potential for a new maritime industry, even if it was on the other side of the continent. The Halifax waterfront was already abuzz with the knowledge that a number of Nova Scotia schooners had recently departed for the trip around Cape Horn with the intention of sealing in the North Pacific and the Bering Sea. Now they had one of the leading skippers of the Victoria fleet in their midst. Further, he was a local man. Dan was happy to oblige the *Halifax Morning Herald* as it offered a portrait of success: "Captain [Dan] MacLean is a young Cape Bretonian, not over 35. Eleven years ago he was sailing out of Sydney before the mast. Joining an American vessel, he sailed on the Pacific coast, and being a wide awake man, as all Cape Bretonians abroad are, he quickly comprehended the future importance of British Columbia and settled down in Victoria ... Four years ago they engaged in the seal fisheries. This year they own two vessels." The report went on to point out that Dan MacLean had caught 12,000 seals in the previous four years, yielding $85,000. The riches were there for the taking, and the newspaper downplayed the difficult and dangerous aspects: "In the Pacific it is a sure thing, and the fishing is a sporting picnic. The seals float on the water, usually in small groups, and are shot by whitemen and harpooned by Indians from their canoes. The supply is practically inexhaustible. Every shot or spear thrust is worth $8 to $10. Of the seals fired at, 95 per cent are captured." The newspaper was not bothered by its own inaccuracies. The description of the situation was an improbably optimistic one, and there was little mention of the controversy swirling around the seizures by the Americans, although the fate of the *Onward* was mentioned in passing. The article states that this boat "was captured by Yankee pirates in the interests of Alaska fur monopoly for fishing in the high seas and is now rotting on the shores of that barren territory."[4]

The record of the MacLean brothers in pelagic sealing in 1884-87 *was* unrivalled. Dan had commanded the high boat in the Victoria fleet two years running, and Alex was not far behind. Since 1884, they had acquired a combined total of at least 18,128 skins. With an average price in Victoria in the 1880s of $7 per pelt, this number amounted to $126,896.[5] It was enough for the *Halifax Morning Herald:* "There is a great future for this fishery; there is room for almost any number of enterprising men, and there's lots of money in it. Unlike some others, Captain MacLean doesn't want the whole earth and sea, and hopes that Nova Scotians will embrace the opportunity to take the cream of this business. Some one will get it. MacLean prefers that his countrymen should get it rather than Americans. Cape Bretonians are already to the fore – as they always are when opportunities offer."[6] Dan kept both Alex and Edgar Crow Baker abreast of developments as he proceeded to purchase the *Triumph,* an eighty-five-foot, ninety-two-ton two-masted schooner, in mid-November for $5,000.[7] Recently built in Shelburne, Nova Scotia, by Arthur Hood, she was described as "one of the prettiest, fastest and best schooners ever built in Nova Scotia," and the vessel had already acquired a reputation for speed under Captain Lorway, who had highly recommended her to Dan. In her first season, the *Triumph* "showed her heels to every craft in the Canadian and American fleets, except one, the new fishing yacht, *Senator Morgan,* 147 tons, carrying a large area of sail, which beat her half a mile in a 25 mile race."[8] Dan registered as sole owner, although he, Baker, and Walter E. Blackett, a Victoria businessman with Cape Breton connections, each held a third interest. Dan then slipped down to Cape Breton for a brief family visit.[9]

These appeared to be heady times on the Halifax waterfront. Schooner speeds and sailing prowess were in vogue. It was not surprising that Dan MacLean's reputation, and the new but impressive record of the *Triumph,* is linked with a wager. Upon his return from Cape Breton to Halifax to oversee the outfitting of the *Triumph* in preparation for the trip around Cape Horn, a challenge was apparently issued to determine whether Dan and the

Triumph could beat the passage time to Victoria of Captain Sol Jacobs and the Gloucester-based schooner *Mollie Adams*. There is only one source for the wager aspect of the story, and it has proven difficult to establish the exact details. This version has the two vessels in a race, but the issue was the passage time for each vessel.[10] The wager, supposedly $5,000 (which was, coincidentally, the cost of the *Triumph*), involved both Louis Henry Davies (who was, at the time, the member of parliament for Queen's and a former premier of Prince Edward Island) and Colonel James Baker (a retired English army officer and a member of the provincial legislature in Victoria) backing Dan. Dan's wages at the time were $60 a month, and he was about to mortgage his share of the *Triumph* to Baker, so it is unlikely that he was a major money player on this one.[11] Henry Cabot Lodge, who had recently been elected to Congress from Massachusetts and was a staunch defender of fishermen's interests in that state, understandably sided with Jacobs.[12] Dan's opponent was not an ordinary sea captain. Sol Jacobs grew up in Jenkins Cove, Twillingate, Newfoundland. In the 1870s, operating out of Gloucester, he had made an extremely successful career mackerel fishing, acquiring the title "King of the Mackerel Killers" before he was thirty years old.[13] Some people maintained that "no fishing skipper had a more spectacular career, none ever equalled his record for catches and none ever showed more natural talent and courage."[14] The *Mollie Adams,* built in Kennebunk, Maine, in 1884, was the "one-time speed queen of the United States fishing fleet."[15]

Dan was up to the challenge. Crimping was not particularly pronounced in Halifax in those days, and so early one December evening, with the *Triumph* prepared and provisioned for the trip around the Horn, he strengthened his position considerably with a touch of ingenuity, a dash of guile, and a bunch of Cape Bretoners – or so the story goes: "When the *Triumph,* with the sails set, was ready to leave, seven Cape Breton boys nearly all of North Sydney, who happened to be employed in Halifax, were invited aboard to have supper." While dining, the lines were loosened and the schooner drifted out to sea with the wind. When the boys came back on deck, they discovered they were off Point Pleasant: "It was there Captain McLean informed them their landing would be at Victoria, B.C. He had in the meantime written all their relatives that they were sailing. He had also taken the dunnage aboard, and he further informed them that they would be paid good wages and he would guarantee them all good jobs in Victoria for double the wages they had received in Halifax, and he kept his word."[16] This remembrance came fifty years after the event, so a note of caution should be added. Yet, in a general sense, it is believable. Dan's assurances and the favourable picture of western riches and opportunities that had been carried in the Halifax press would have alleviated many of the concerns of the additional Cape Bretoners aboard. Besides, this was the time of year when Halifax port activities slowed down significantly and unemployment rose considerably. The *Triumph*'s double crew may well have given her the ability to carry full sail day and night.[17] The *Triumph* departed Halifax on 14 December.[18] She "was one of the fastest schooners of that time" and made San Francisco in ninety-five days. Slowed down by rains and headwinds, she arrived in Victoria on 24 April after 128 days.[19] As expected, she put on quite a performance: "McLean drove her for all she was worth, and she passed every vessel she sighted on the passage. The *Annie C. Moore* left North Sydney 40 days ahead of the *Triumph,* and the *Maggie Mac* left Halifax 35 days before. The *Moore* got into Victoria at 8 in the morning, the *Triumph* got in at nine at night and the *Maggie Mac* got in half an hour later. The *Triumph*'s crew were composed all of Cape Bretonians."[20] When the *Triumph* arrived in Victoria, the *Daily Colonist* gushed: "She is a beautifully modelled vessel, and is admirably finished, and for beauty and speed has few equals. Capt. MacLean says he passed every vessel *en route* with the greatest ease, and coming up the Straits yesterday his vessel overhauled and passed every craft she met. The Captain is justly proud of his pretty schooner."[21] It should be noted that the *Mollie Adams* departed Gloucester at the end of October, and arrived at Port Townsend on 3 March, for a passage time of 123 days.[22]

Although the time that Dan spent taking the *Triumph* around the Horn was bested by Jacobs, it was still impressive. Yet it is only part of the picture. Almost twice as many people migrated from Cape Breton in the 1880s compared to the previous decade. Vancouver Island was one of the destinations of choice for thousands of Cape Bretoners who were adventurous and anxious to work. Along with seasoned sailors heading for the North Pacific fleet and young men out for adventure as pelagic seal hunters, there were experienced miners heading for the coal fields around Nanaimo (Vancouver Island coal production increased ten-fold between 1875 and 1890), and many others seeking myriad opportunities.[23] Doubtless, the successes of individuals such as Dan and Alex MacLean in the previous few years played a part in some of these decisions. Some people such as Alex MacLean would make the west coast their home. So too would first mate Alf Bissett, another Cape Bretoner, who would have his first sealing trip on the *Mary Ellen* under Alex's command in 1888. Like Dan, Alf Bissett would return east to purchase a vessel – he became part owner of the *Annie E. Paint,* which he purchased in Port Hawkesbury, Cape Breton, in 1890 – and when he married in Victoria a few years later "nearly all the sealing schooners in the harbour were flying their colours" in acknowledgment.[24] Captain Bissett would eventually be described as "one of Vancouver's best known maritime pioneers," and he died there in 1948 in his eighty-seventh year.[25]

The fact that the *Maggie Mac,* under Captain John Dodd, left Halifax on 9 November and the *Annie C. Moore,* under Captain Charles Hackett, departed the same port ten days later suggests the strong participation of both Nova Scotia ships and men in the rapidly expanding Victoria-based pelagic sealing industry. Further, all three vessels arriving in Victoria that day in late April were captained by Cape Bretoners. Charles Hackett was from North Sydney, and, in all likelihood, his brother Fred was also on board, anxious for his first season sealing. They had originally departed from Sydney harbour on 17 November. Charles Dodd was from Sydney and the *Maggie Mac,* a 196-ton three-masted schooner, was one of the largest vessels to join the Canadian fleet.[26] There was one more schooner captained by a Cape Bretoner that sailed into James Bay on 24 April to join the *Triumph,* the *Annie C. Moore,* and the *Maggie Mac*. That evening, the *Mary Ellen,* under Alex MacLean, returned from a nine-week sealing trip along the coast with the largest catch reported to date, entitling the vessel to "carry the broom" as it sailed into the harbour. Not surprisingly, as the local newspapers noted, "the captain and all on board [were] in high spirits over their good luck."[27] For the recently arrived Cape Bretoners, all of the successful sealing stories they had heard appeared to be true. It must have seemed worth the trip around the Horn. There were probably more Cape Bretoners on the Victoria waterfront that evening than ever before. As J. Gordon Smith described, "they are a varied gathering of sailormen these sealers, but for adventure, or for fun and story, the jolly Cape Breton boys, or the hardy men from Nova Scotia or New Brunswick lead them all."[28] When the American consulate in Victoria did a breakdown on the origins of sealers operating out of there a couple of years later, Cape Breton had a separate category from Nova Scotia.[29]

Many Cape Bretoners became well known while in the command of sealing vessels out of Victoria in this period. Northsider Fred Hackett was on the west coast for the first time in the spring of 1888. He and his brother Charles would eventually be considered among "the foremost navigators of the North Pacific."[30] Other Cape Breton master mariners included Melville F. Cutler, Charles Campbell, John MacLeod, Joseph Peppett, Matthew Ryan, Hardy Murray, Charles Le Blanc, and Dan Macaulay. As one young Cape Bretoner in Victoria who was not involved in the sealing industry would write home, "it would but surprise you to know the number of C.B. men here in the sealing business and at other things." The writer was one of three Cape Bretoners who were members of the Victoria Fire Department.[31] On the evening of 24 April 1888, the saloons at Tommy Burnes' American Hotel, at Erickson's Hotel at the foot of Johnson Street, at the Garrick's Head on Bastion Street, and at various other waterfront spots frequented by sailors after successful voyages around the Horn or in the North Pacific surely rang with a variety of Cape Breton dialects.[32]

For those who just wanted to rest after their first trip around the Horn, there was always Mrs. Langley's place. She was formerly from Sydney and, at that time, was "conducting a nice private boarding house on Pandora St., where all Cape Breton folks [would] receive a genuine welcome."[33] Just as welcome as the additions to the workforce were the vessels that the Cape

Bretoners had brought with them. Schooners built in Nova Scotia and New Brunswick for cod and mackerel fishing on the Grand Banks would prove well suited and extremely popular for pelagic sealing. In addition to the vessels taken around the Horn by MacLean, Dodd, and Hackett, at least five others came around in 1888. They included the *Sapphire,* the *Viva,* the *La Houlette,* the *Araunah,* and the *Ariel.*[34] There would eventually be more than thirty schooners built in Nova Scotia and New Brunswick in the industry, a major contribution from the east coast for the Pacific sealing fleet.[35]

While the boatloads of Cape Bretoners and other Maritimers were still on the high seas heading west in the winter of 1887-88, the sealing dispute was continuing apace. On 22 January, Rear-Admiral Algernon Heneage, commander-in-chief of the Royal Navy on the Pacific Station, ordered the captain of HMS *Caroline* to leave Honolulu for Esquimalt and then to "cruize in the Behring Sea for the protection of the British Sealing Fleet that annually assembles in those waters about the middle of July for seal fishing."[36] More detailed orders for Sir William Wiseman, captain of the *Caroline,* followed immediately and were quite clear: "You are to afford these vessels protection from seizure or the exercise of the rights of search on the high seas by the United States Revenue Cruizers, which I understand are stationed at Sitka and Unalaska for such purposes. In the event of your falling in with a sealing schooner in the power of one of these cruizers, you will, on obtaining sufficient evidence of her illegal seizure, claim her release, and, in the event of your request not being complied with you will capture her forthwith."[37]

The situation on the sealing front was warming up considerably. Even Edgar Crow Baker was in a fighting mood. When Dan MacLean had arrived in Victoria with the *Triumph* in late April, his business associate was not at the harbour front to share in the glow. The Conservative member of parliament was in Ottawa describing the issue to his political colleagues. "I do not think there is anyone who occupies a position on the floor of this House who can speak more feelingly on this subject than I can," Baker explained, with disarming frankness, "for the simple reason that I am financially interested in the matter." Baker, ever the ex-Royal Navy officer, could not resist the opportunity to indulge in some sabre-rattling of his own. He argued that every measure should be taken "to induce the Imperial Government to take that step which we would like to see taken yet, and have a reasonable right to demand, namely, to send there an armed vessel, and, if necessary, recapture our vessels, as was done in olden times, with shot and shell, if stern necessity demanded it. That is about the only way to stop such piracy on the high seas and uphold the honour of our flag."[38] As D.G. Paterson and J. Wilen explain, the British diplomats "conveyed the increased irritation and hardening attitude" over the seizures in 1886-87 and, as F.W. Holway, W.H. Sage, H.F. Angus note, the "usual long-spun, diplomatic correspondence commenced and continued, becoming a trifle acrid."[39] It was also "the

Alex MacLean
Vancouver Public Library, Special Collections, VPL 54836

Nova Scotia tow, St. John's, Newfoundland
© Mystic Seaport, Photography Collection, Mystic, CT, No. 73-9-5, http://www.mysticseaport.org/

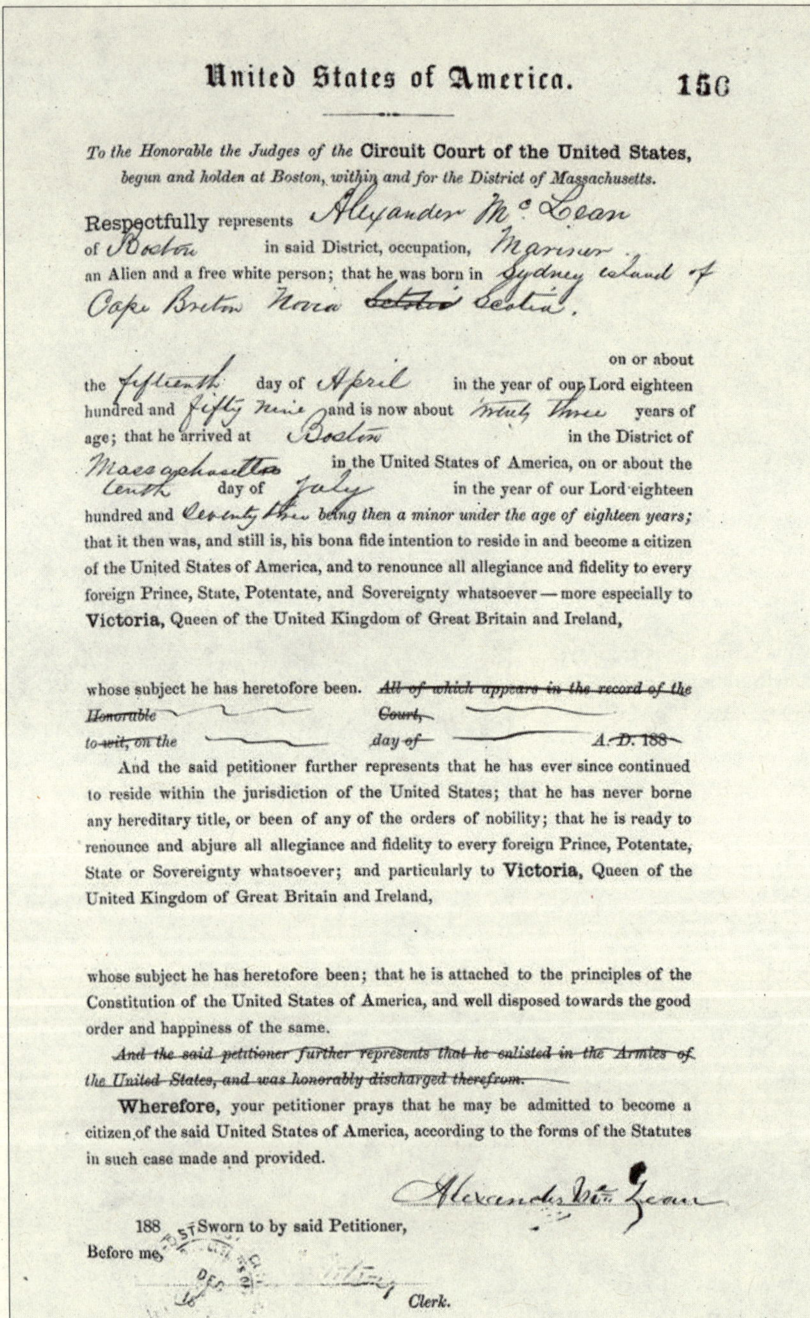

United States of America. 156

To the Honorable the Judges of the **Circuit Court of the United States,**
begun and holden at Boston, within and for the District of Massachusetts.

Respectfully represents Alexander Mc Lean
of Boston in said District, occupation, Mariner
an Alien and a free white person; that he was born in Sydney island of
Cape Breton Nova ~~Scotia~~ Scotia.

on or about the fifteenth day of April in the year of our Lord eighteen hundred and fifty nine and is now about twenty three years of age; that he arrived at Boston in the District of Massachusetts in the United States of America, on or about the tenth day of July in the year of our Lord eighteen hundred and seventy three *being then a minor under the age of eighteen years;* that it then was, and still is, his bona fide intention to reside in and become a citizen of the United States of America, and to renounce all allegiance and fidelity to every foreign Prince, State, Potentate, and Sovereignty whatsoever — more especially to **Victoria,** Queen of the United Kingdom of Great Britain and Ireland,

whose subject he has heretofore been. ~~*All of which appears in the record of the Honorable Court, to wit, on the day of A. D. 188*~~

And the said petitioner further represents that he has ever since continued to reside within the jurisdiction of the United States; that he has never borne any hereditary title, or been of any of the orders of nobility; that he is ready to renounce and abjure all allegiance and fidelity to every foreign Prince, Potentate, State or Sovereignty whatsoever; and particularly to **Victoria,** Queen of the United Kingdom of Great Britain and Ireland,

whose subject he has heretofore been; that he is attached to the principles of the Constitution of the United States of America, and well disposed towards the good order and happiness of the same.

~~*And the said petitioner further represents that he enlisted in the Armies of the United States, and was honorably discharged therefrom.*~~

Wherefore, your petitioner prays that he may be admitted to become a citizen of the said United States of America, according to the forms of the Statutes in such case made and provided.

Alexander Mc Lean

188 Sworn to by said Petitioner,
Before me,

Clerk.

Alex MacLean's American citizenship papers

National Archives and Records Administration, Records of the United States Circuit Court of Boston, petition for naturalization, RG 21, v. 146, 156

Mary Ellen
British Columbia Archives, I-32908

American Hotel; Tommy Burnes second from right
British Columbia Archives, B-01096

Maggie Mac crew, 1891

E.W. Wright, ed., *Lewis and Dryden's Marine History of the Pacific Northwest* (Portland: Lewis and Dryden, 1895), Canadiana Online, produced by http://canadiana.org

most emotional ocean-resource conflict of the late nineteenth century" confronting politicians and diplomats.[40]

The American argument about the closed sea claim was somewhat suspect, not least because when Russia had previously tried this approach in the 1820s the Americans had waged a successful legal battle against it. On this occasion, Russia had initially claimed that her jurisdiction extended "one hundred Italian miles" from the coast, but soon settled for "the reach of cannon shot," which was generally acknowledged to be three miles from the shore. Nor was the American administration unanimous in its present stand. Following the seizures of the previous year, Secretary of State Thomas Bayard "managed to convince President Cleveland and the cabinet that the British were losing patience and that further incidents of a like nature should be avoided."[41] Bayard, "who believed the seizures to be illegal, quietly ordered them stopped in 1888," and he began negotiations with Britain and Russia for a closed season in the Bering Sea.[42] When the Americans opened their orders, "they were found to prohibit the cutters from molesting sealers flying the British flag ... A week or so previously, Admiral Heneage had, somewhat ostentatiously, authorised the announcement that he had detached the sloop-of-war *Caroline* from his squadron" and sent her to the Bering Sea to protect British sealing vessels.[43]

The authorities were doubtless aware that tempers were still testy in Victoria. When one sealing captain was leaving port in March, he mentioned that he "intends to protect himself if molested by American cutter pirates." The Aboriginal hunters, it was reported, were more specific, stating "that they will kill every man who attempts to cross the schooner's rail." Their threat carried additional weight. When the *Alfred Adams* had been seized the previous year, the Aboriginal sealers had forced it to head for Victoria, not Sitka.[44] Others in the front lines noted the militant approach and attitude: "Despairing of any help from British diplomacy or the British navy, the sealers determined to defend themselves and for that purpose arranged to take large crews of armed Indians in their vessels."[45] Rear-Admiral Heneage also put his oar in the turbulent waters, in correspondence with the secretary of the admiralty: "I desire to express my opinion that whatever settlement of this dispute may be come to between the Governments of the United States and Great Britain, it should be stipulated that, besides the restoration to their owners of the vessels seized, full compensation should be awarded for losses incurred by their seizure as well as by the illegal confiscation of their cargoes and other property by the Alaskan authorities."[46] This suggestion, when finally acted upon, would warm lawyers' hearts for years.

The 1888 sealing season was not very successful for the Victoria fleet. As the Canadian government explained, echoing the lamentations and explanations put forward in 1886, "the decrease in the catch in the Bering Sea was very noticeable; it was caused principally by the unsettled state of affairs with the American Government, several of the schooners being afraid to enter these waters at the risk of seizures."[47] Neither Alex, in the *Mary Ellen,* nor Dan, in the newly acquired *Triumph,* seemed particularly perturbed. Less than two weeks after arriving from Halifax, Dan MacLean and the *Triumph* cleared from Victoria for the Bering Sea with, uncharacteristically, Aboriginal hunters on board. The vessel returned on 12 September, having acquired 2,470 skins, all in the Bering Sea, the third best catch in the Victoria fleet for 1888. Alex, with the *Mary Ellen* and an Aboriginal crew, which he usually acquired on the west coast of Vancouver Island, had the highest catch, 3,347, the majority of them also from the Bering Sea. Once again, a MacLean would return to home port "carrying the broom."[48] The value of the combined catch by the MacLeans in 1888 was $58,170. Edgar Crow Baker, who earlier in the year had bought shares in the *Favorite* and would soon acquire a major interest in the *Mary Ellen,* later acknowledged that the *Triumph's* initial voyage to the Bering Sea "yielded a very handsome profit to the owners," and the vessel was paid off in September.[49] The *Mary Ellen* was soon off again on a black cod expedition to the Queen Charlotte Islands, and, when it returned in late December, Alex and Dan MacLean procured additional refinancing with Baker.[50] It appeared that the more successful they were the more they went into debt to Baker.

Alex, possibly spurred on by Dan's exploits and sibling rivalry, was definitely coming into his own. An undated clipping concerning Alex and the *Mary Ellen* from this period, probably from this season, stated: "On one voyage Captain McLean went after the record catch of seals. On returning to Victoria he heard that another boat had a larger catch than his own. Without entering the port he returned again to Alaska for more sealskins."[51] How many Alex acquired personally cannot easily be determined, but he, like many sealing captains, usually set out in the stern boat with the mate and boatswain to join the hunt.[52] This particular story illustrates the competitive nature of the MacLeans, as does a contemporaneous one, related by Ronald Gillis, reminiscent of Jack London's fictional characters. Gillis, another Cape Bretoner on the west coast for the first time, was already acquainted with Dan, having met him in North Sydney. Then he met Alex in Victoria. It was a lasting impression. Once on board the vessel, Alex ordered the crew below and locked the cook in the galley. He "then called his mate, a man by the name of McEachern, a fine specimen of manhood, over six feet tall and would easily weigh 230 pounds, in fact a giant." Alex asked him "if it was true that Captain D. stole some of his best hunters." The mate replied in the affirmative. The visitor had seen prize fighting, "but this was a fight without gloves, without seconds or time and at the end of almost thirty minutes McEachern said, 'I've had enough.'" He could no longer see. "McLean didn't have a scratch and quietly replied that he too had enough. He hooked his arm in McEachern's and led him down the cabin stairs and told me to release the cook and order him to bring hot water. He sponged and bathed the mate's injuries just as gently as a child, using considerable court plaster, then we drank. He asked McEachern whether he would get the men back. His reply was, 'If I don't I won't sail.' Well, the next day they headed up the North Pacific with full crew and McEachern as mate."[53] This source, a close friend of the MacLeans, remembered the event fifty years later. While there is enough evidence to attest to Alex's fighting ability, a thirty-minute scrap with a large adversary without a scratch suggests a fondness for folklore and an acquaintance with literature. In *The Sea-Wolf,* one of Death Larsen's hunters, a "giant" at least 6'8" tall, who weighed in at 240 pounds, was quickly subdued by Wolf. The real-life mate in question was probably John MacEachern, another native of East Bay, Cape Breton.[54]

Added to his burgeoning reputation was MacLean's practice of carrying sail. "Hard driving" or daring seamanship – the question of when to carry sail and just how much their gear would stand – was what many sailors felt able to judge and all could witness. Social visibility was characteristic of seafaring work. As Marcus Rediker explains, "crews were extremely sophisticated in judging the quality of each man's contribution to the sailing of the ship. Everyone knew how to perform the basic tasks, and most men had been on other ships and had seen every chore, from the captain's duties down, executed by others. Consequently even the lowest ordinary seaman considered himself a judge of his officers. Further, work was closely scrutinized since the collective well-being often depended on it."[55] According to two ex-shipmates of Alex's, "we were running down from Cape Cook, Vancouver Island, to Drake's Bay, thirty miles from San Francisco, in the old eighty-five foot *Mary Ellen* ... There was a gale of wind at the time. We were 'winged-out.' Alex would only trust one or two of us with the wheel. We made the run – 750 miles – in sixty hours, which is almost steamer time. Of course, it was a great risk, as any seaman will understand, but Alex was determined to make a record. 'Did you ever know Dan carry such sail as this?' he would say, turning to B___, and the latter would reply: 'No, he wasn't such a damned fool.' But we were all proud of the performance."[56] As Rediker reveals, "a culturally valued notion of defiance, of daring initiative, was built into life at sea by the perilous environment," and Alex obviously relished pushing a situation to the limit.[57] His performance at such times would be long remembered in sailors' lore. And, yes, Wolf Larsen also had "a reputation for reckless carrying on of sail."[58]

The Russians were also watching developments closely. They had established a detachment of soldiers on their island rookeries, Copper and Robben, in 1884. Sealers, to avoid capture within the three-mile limit, would stay farther out and just send the canoes or boats in close to shore. On 1 July, off Copper Island, the Russians grabbed the *Araunah,* which had just arrived from Halifax in March 1888 under the command of Captain Sieward. She was the only sealing vessel seized that year. After the intervention of the British ambassador in St. Petersburg, the crew made their way from Siberia to Japan and eventually back to Victoria.[59] For their part, the Americans held off on their practice of the previous two years, although their lack of seizures that year did not dissipate the ill feelings surrounding the sealing dispute. There had been a decrease in the number of seals that returned to the Pribilof Islands that year. The Alaska Commercial Company renewed its pressure for a ban on pelagic sealing. "In the United States," observed D.G. Paterson, "the Bering Sea issue came to be identified with national integrity in the public mind, but the British diplomats, in deference to Canada, refused to entertain any suggestion of compromise. By the end of 1888 attitudes had hardened." Anglophobia predictably popped up in the presidential campaign that year.[60] The fluctuations within the sealing industry, the vagaries of the weather, and the uncertainty of the status of the Bering Sea in diplomatic circles did not prevent another large fleet sailing out of Victoria in 1889, even though the Cleveland administration approved a bill "requiring the president annually to proclaim U.S. 'domination' over the eastern waters of the Bering Sea and warning pelagic sealers that they were subject to arrest if caught." President Cleveland signed the measure on 2 March 1889, in effect sanctioning the closed sea policy. Incoming president Benjamin Harrison issued the warning on 22 March. Canadian prime minister John A. Macdonald was initially unconcerned. He was misinformed and mistaken.[61] One "old salt" in San Francisco, who had been on an American sealer in the 1820s when a similar but unsuccessful attempt had been made by the Russians, was less than impressed with the closed sea approach. He thought it ridiculous: "The fact is the privileges conferred upon the Alaska Commercial Company by our government are akin to those bestowed by England upon the East India & Hudson [sic] Bay Company ... It would be well for Congress to appoint a commission to investigate and let the public know for whose benefit these fur seals preserves are maintained at the public expense and for what purpose?"[62]

This year would be the last season for Alex and Dan MacLean as members of the Victoria sealing fleet. The reasons were partly pecuniary and partly personal. The financial adroitness of the MacLeans was not as finely tuned as their sailing and sealing abilities. Dan and Edgar Crow Baker were major shareholders in both the *Triumph* and the *Mary Ellen*. Baker was managing owner and ship's husband of both vessels.[63] In the latter roles, Baker received 5 percent commission on disbursements and receipts. At the time, Dan owed Baker a considerable amount of money relating to advances to purchase both the *Triumph* and the *Mary Ellen*. All of Dan's interest in the *Triumph* and the *Mary Ellen* were mortgaged to Baker, who also had power of attorney.[64] Baker was going through a major re-evaluation of his personal and professional life at exactly this time. He had put a lot of energy into seeking a Senate appointment, and when Baker finally realized that this quest had failed, his enthusiasm for a continued political career rapidly ebbed. Even more of his energies were now redirected into his financial situation, which was never far from his mind.[65]

The *Triumph,* one of Baker's major investments in the sealing industry, almost missed the season. Numbered among his many entrepreneurial forays was the Hawaiian Pacific Cable Company, "one of his most ambitious schemes." Baker decided the *Triumph* was suitable as a cable-laying ship, and in December 1888 she went into dry dock to be coppered and to have other conversion work done. As Baker left for Ottawa for his last parliamentary session in January 1889, the work was being completed.[66] While renovations to the *Triumph* to prepare it for one of Baker's non-sealing ventures increased the value of the vessel (and the costs), it also added to the confusion surrounding the role of the vessel and prevented an early start in sealing.[67] While he was in the east "ostensibly attending parliament," Baker's main concerns in Ottawa and Montreal were business-oriented, and he remained there less than two weeks before leaving his parliamentary seat to "come back and look after [his] own interests."[68] It was his last session in Ottawa and would prove to be his last season in the seal fishery business. The cable would not arrive until June, and by then Baker had had to charter another vessel. The cable foray became "his most costly failure."[69] Feeling financially pressured, as usual, Baker, now back in Victoria and licking his wounds from his thwarted political appointment and his delayed and financially unrewarding cable project, finally instructed Dan to get the *Triumph* to sea on 19 March.[70]

Such a task was easier said than done, partly because most of the crew involved with the vessel were doing some serious drinking and it took them a few days to get straightened out. As Baker's biographer noted, "like many a man raised in a cold and rugged climate, not to mention trade, Dan McLean relied on alcohol to ease the more strenuous moments of his existence." Given Baker's state of mind and the *Triumph*'s delay, this period could be considered one of those stressful occasions, and even though the schooner was ready by 23 March both Dan and the cook remained, in Baker's phrase, "tight." On Sunday, 24 March, Baker tracked Dan down at Tommy Burnes' American Hotel, where the captain was having a few. By mid-afternoon, they got away, "drunken crew" and all.[71] With Baker on board, they set out for San Francisco "to get proper sealing boats, and guns, and ammunition, and also to secure the right class of white hunters."[72] Within a day, the "captain and crew [were] gradually getting over their drunks," although the cook's recovery was apparently slower than the others, and the service, with "everything in a mess," was not up to Baker's usual standards.[73] Stress was easily transferred. The ex-English naval officer had to rough it a bit on his sail to San Francisco in the *Triumph,* what with "no table cloth, mugs in place of cups and saucers, only two knives and forks, and only one teaspoon! Fine old picnic on the high seas!"[74] Nevertheless, on 3 April, they arrived at San Francisco and spent the following week acquiring provisions.

Baker also made an agreement with H. Liebes and Company of San Franciso to sell them all of the skins caught by the *Mary Ellen* and the *Triumph* during the 1889 season for $6.25 per skin.[75] This arrangement was made in spite of a statement in a San Francisco publication a few days earlier that "the market for seal-skins is increasing rapidly all over the world." Raw skins worth $9 to $14 last year were now going for $12 to $18.[76] The average price of a pelagic pelt that year would be $9.75, which was considerably more than Baker's agreement.[77] Baker later explained the contract, in part, by saying that the San Francisco company would transship any skins acquired by the *Triumph* and the *Mary Ellen* via the steamer *Elsie* so as to get the skins to market quickly and to minimize the losses if the sealing vessels were seized. The *Elsie* could also replenish the sealers with items such as ammunition, if necessary, in the course of her usual coastal business for H. Liebes and Company.[78] The agreement that Baker, as managing owner of the *Triumph,* made with Herman Liebes in San Francisco on 9 April 1889 is an interesting one, not only because of the low price accepted for the skins and because he made a similar deal at the same time for any catch acquired by Alex MacLean and the *Mary Ellen.* It was also noteworthy because of the men involved. If Dan and Alex MacLean and Herman Liebes had not been closely linked before this date, Baker's arrangement certainly flung them together. Soon, they would be working in concert. Herman Liebes, a long-time player in the fur and sealing business, was a member of the German Jewish "merchantocracy" of San Francisco.[79] He found kindred spirits in the Cape Breton Gaels. As one suspect account later phrased it, "these men were on the lookout for likely, hardy, fit persons to take command of their vessels and push the business of fur seal piracy with secrecy and energy. It was not long before the Cape Breton brothers entered the employment of these American promoters."[80]

None of this emergent alliance was clear as Baker charged around San Francisco that April provisioning the *Triumph.* His sojourn in San Francisco was reasonably successful, although at the end of his stay, after waiting around for six hours, he lamented that Dan went "on a spree after all my care." Baker departed on the morning of 10 April for Victoria by steamer, with Dan still on the missing list.[81] However, Dan was not far from the *Triumph,* and perhaps he just wanted a respite from Baker's complaining. Baker was probably not that pleasant to listen to when dealing with a hangover. Possibly Dan had become reacquainted with San Francisco's famed steam beer or the powerful Pisco punch, with its base of Peruvian brandy, in one or more of the 3,117 licensed establishments and 2,000 illegal pubs that graced the port.[82] Dan found his way back to the *Triumph* and left San Francisco for the return trip to Victoria two days after his business partner, and mortgage holder, had done so. Soon after, on 25 April, Dan set off from Victoria for the North Pacific, with eight boats and a crew of thirty-two.[83] Preparations for the *Triumph* that year were expensive. When Dan had finally departed for the sealing grounds, the costs incurred were more than $15,000. Not much of it had gone into Dan's pocket. He had been drawing wages of $60 a month, and he was now simply on a lay of less than 40 cents per skin.[84] Before entering the Bering Sea, the *Triumph* transshipped her coastal catch of 271 skins to the steamer *Elsie,* and they were taken back to San Francisco. So far, the voyage had been good. The *Triumph* entered the Bering Sea on 4 July.[85]

A week later, early on the evening of 11 July, the *Triumph* was about 100 miles west of St. George's Island. After following her for two hours, the American cutter *Rush* ordered her to heave to and boarded her: "The captain stood at the gangway, and asked the officer his reason for boarding the schooner. The answer was the production of written orders authorizing 'the capture of any vessels illegally sealing in Bering's Sea.' He then asked to be allowed to search the ship, and on permission being accorded him he spent over half-an-hour with his men overhauling the vessel. No find rewarded his search ... the whole of the skins aboard having been dextrously hidden in time to avoid detection." After the search, the American officer expressed "his pleasure at not being under necessity to seize his vessel" and told MacLean that he had seized the *Black Diamond* a few hours earlier and it was now on its way to Sitka, Alaska.[86] Although the *Triumph,* according to a passenger on board the *Rush,* "had been sharp enough to elude the vigilance of our first lieutenant, and had had several hundred skins hidden under the salt," the Americans "were very glad when none were found."[87] How many were not found is a moot point. The estimates ranged from thirty-three to 1,000, but most agree on seventy-two skins. The practice was to put ten to twelve skins in a sack, and six or seven sacks would not have been difficult to hide.[88] Nevertheless, the close call was enough for Dan, and, as he later stated, the American officer "told me that should he again board me and find sealskins on board that he would seize and confiscate the vessel and catch ... therefore, by reasons of his threats and menaces, I was caused to forego my legitimate and peaceful voyage on the high seas and return to the port of my departure, causing serious pecuniary loss to myself, crew and owners."[89]

When the *Triumph* returned to Victoria on 28 July, Baker was not pleased. By his own reports, he was having an extremely difficult time. His failed quest for an appointment to the Canadian Senate still rankled, and there were problems with his various business ventures. These were compounded by family concerns and physical ailments. His diary was his confessional. In early May, his dark mood is suggested when he notes: "Magnificent weather continues – only man is vile." By 20 June, he was "sincerely contemplating leaving B.C. altogether," and the following week brought additional lamentations: "Resignation day – resignation to my fate. Resigned all honorary positions." Then, on 28 July, at least two months earlier than expected: "To add to my discomfort the *Triumph* returns." Dan appeared in Baker's office the following day, "under the weather." For Baker, it was a "pretty busy day for a troubled mind."[90] He would have a few more in the coming months.

Meanwhile, a complaint by some sealing vessel owners, with a summary of the events of 11 July, was immediately conveyed to the British navy.[91] The deputation that went to Esquimalt to interview Commander Sinclair included Captain Cox and William Munsie, and they maintained that "if the acts of the American Government were not speedily put a stop to, the sealing industry of Victoria would be ruined."[92]

Baker, "terribly perplexed" over his financial condition, remained focused on his own problems.[93] Over the next few weeks, Dan MacLean and Edgar Crow Baker would have extensive, sometimes stormy sessions.[94] It remains unclear as to how Baker had expected Dan to respond to the threat issued by the *Rush* on 11 July. Baker's vision was filled with expenses and the loss of potential profits. As he later explained, "I was simply one of the partners managing the affairs of the schooner, and a good deal, necessarily, would be left to McLean's discretion because it was he that got me to go into that venture. Naturally, I would be guided by his report as to the circumstances when he was to return. But it was distinctly understood between him and myself that he would remain there to the very last of the season that he could catch seals, so as to ascertain, if possible, how long that season really did and could last ... he was to remain there until late in September."[95] Risking the wrath of the Americans and the possible seizure of the schooner was apparently not part of Baker's assessment. Baker, a member of Victoria's elite, and Dan MacLean, the freewheeling, not particularly punctual Cape Breton Gael, had little overlap in their attitudes and concerns. They were vastly separated in their financial perspectives. Baker quickly produced a statement of accounts showing that Dan owed him $7,646.06.[96] According to a statement made some years later, "in consequence of the breaking up of the voyage, Baker determined to abandon the sealing business and sold the vessel and equipment at a very large loss to the owners." In early October, Baker, with a minimum amount of dickering, quickly accepted an offer of $9,000 from Captain John G. Cox for the *Triumph*.[97] When Baker was later asked: "You were disgusted with the business?" he responded: "Yes, emphatically ... I looked upon her occupation as gone, and I got what I considered was a fair price, that is compared with what I would get if I waited six months longer. I struck the iron while it was hot ... Knowing that there never should be, and I hope there never would be, friction between Great Britain and the United States. I thought that the United States would get their own way eventually, and I think they will still."[98]

Baker may have given up the fight, but he kept his eye on the spoils. In November, he submitted a claim for $19,674 against the American government.[99] It was also the end for Dan. He cleared out of Victoria in the latter part of August, heading south.[100] He would make one more dramatic appearance in his old home port of Victoria early the following year, with another controversy swirling around him.

The *Triumph* was not the only vessel targeted in 1889. Between 11 July and 6 August, two other vessels besides Dan's were ordered out of the Bering Sea, and six more were seized.[101] They did not, however, remain seized. The *Black Diamond,* under Captain Owen Thomas, had been boarded by the *Rush* on 11 July, a few hours before the *Triumph* had been searched. Thomas' initial response should have been suggestive to Captain L.G. Shepard of the *Rush:* "The *Black Diamond* had refused at first to stop when commanded to do so, and two of the guns were ordered to be run out, on seeing which preparations, she surrendered at once. 'That's the way we make 'em stop, ain't it, papa?' cried our little five-year old, who accompanied his father on that cruise, and jumping up and down, clapping his hands, when on running out the guns the *Black Diamond* 'hove to.'"[102] After their surrender, the ship's papers and seventy-six skins were confiscated, and an American seaman was placed on board with instructions to proceed to Sitka. Ignoring Thomas' contention that he would not comply, the American cutter then steamed away. Thomas simply proceeded to Victoria. The hapless American seaman "offered no resistance, as some of the crew informed him that the Indians would kill him if they saw that he was taking the vessel to Sitka."[103] Mrs. Shepard, who accompanied her husband on the 1889 cruise of the *Rush,* noted it was "a very natural move on their part."[104]

Captain Jacobson, on the *Minnie,* followed the *Black Diamond's* lead a few days later. Late in the season, the *Pathfinder,* under Captain William O'Leary, met a similar fate "and emphasized her contempt for American revenue cutters and their orders" by transshipping 360 skins from the *Kate* (which had also been warned), acquiring fifty additional seals, and then proceeding to Victoria, American prize crew and all. During another pursuit, the American officers aboard the *Bear* were worried about the outcome because "no one wanted to go to Victoria as a prize crew."[105] One San Francisco source thought it was a "farce."[106] Sir Charles Tupper's observations were reflective of this mood on 2 August: "The time is most opportune for sending a British ship of war into Behring Sea with instructions to prevent any further seizure of British vessels in the open waters. I feel sure that if this course be adopted the result will be the promotion of a peaceful settlement of the question." A few days later, Canada's governor general, Lord

Stanley, warned the Colonial Office that the sealers "may be driven to armed resistance."[107]

Not everyone in Victoria followed Baker's lead of washing his hands of the increasingly challenging sealing business. On 27 August, sixteen sealing captains and owners set up the "Victoria shipping owners and masters sealing association" to encourage resistance, demand compensation, and attempt an early meeting with the governor general.[108] The sealers, with both popular and governmental support, had their views conveyed to Britain by the Canadian government.[109] And while the *Halifax Morning Herald* suggested that there would be war if the seizures did not stop, its rival, the *Halifax Chronicle,* had a more realistic observation: "It is talking nonsense. The British people with their hundreds of millions of dollars invested in American enterprises will be very slow to go to war with the United States over the Behring Sea question. We admit that the position is humiliating, but what can be done about it? We can only wait with patience till the good people, the diplomatists, have incubated some better understanding than that at present, and nothing is to be gained by the barking of toothless dogs, bark they ever so bravely."[110]

The management of Baker's business ventures did not initially disrupt Alex MacLean's 1889 season with the *Mary Ellen.* He departed Victoria in plenty of time to participate in the spring hunt along the coast, but this would be one of the few ordinary features of the voyage. One detailed account of the trip on the *Mary Ellen* comes from Tom Brown, a twenty-one-year-old Cape Bretoner, working out of Victoria that winter on a tug and finding it "mighty monotonous." Brown was numbered among the many Cape Bretoners who had arrived in Victoria in late April 1888, having sailed around the Horn on the *Annie C. Moore.* He now had one sealing voyage under his belt as a boatsteerer and was anxious and ambitious to be a hunter.[111] Brown was in luck. Years later, he presented a fine description of waterfront activities in Victoria as the men prepared to leave for the sealing grounds. While chugging back into Victoria one evening on a tug early in the winter of 1888-89 and ruminating on his prosaic life, the scene began to unfold for Brown. He spotted a schooner, the *Mary Ellen,* and soon learned that she was off sealing the next morning and was still short a hunter: "At the time MacLean had the reputation of being 'spectacularly free' with his money in Victoria bars ... I had heard enough about him to provide a glamour; and as he was from the same county of Cape Breton as myself I felt that might help me get the hunter's berth. I had never met him, but was acquainted with Captain Dan, and counted on him to make the introduction." Brown quickly tracked them down to the bar at the American Hotel. He diverted Dan momentarily from "the jollification": "[I] told him that I was after the hunter's berth on the *Mary Ellen.* He said, 'No, my brother wants an experienced hunter.'" Dan eventually relented and told Alex "that I was a 'towny' of theirs and that I should 'make good' because of that ... finally, after a lot of talk, I told him if he would give me the 'chance' and I didn't get an average catch of seals for the season, he would owe me nothing. The proposition appealed to his gambling instinct as well as to his ancestral nature, and he pulled the ship's articles out of his pocket, saying, 'I'll take you at your word; sign here.'" Brown raced back to the tug, stuffed his belongings into a gunny sack, grabbed a "donkey's breakfast" at a store catering to waterfront folk at all hours, and set off sealing.[112]

From the beginning, it was not an ordinary sealing voyage. For one thing, Lucy and eighteen-month-old Catherine were also aboard, an exception to the pattern of the industry. While wives and children frequently accompanied their husbands in merchant vessels, sometimes for years, the sealing pattern was generally different and women were usually not invited on the ship, with the exception of Native women, who occasionally, shipping on the same terms as the men, served as cooks and canoe steerers. While American revenue cutter captains Healy, Shepard, and Evans sometimes had their wives and young children aboard during the Bering Sea patrols in this period, the captains of the sealing ships generally did not have the same allowances. When Victoria Cox accompanied her husband, Captain Clarence Cox, on the sealing schooner *Triumph* to Japan in 1896, she was apparently the first woman to do so.[113]

As soon as the vessel cleared the Strait of Juan de Fuca, the *Mary Ellen* headed to the Queen Charlotte Islands. There, Alex picked up a "rough-looking gang who didn't seem to know much about sealing." He later explained that he had "left them there the previous fall to build a wharf, which was to be used as a fishing base," a tale that may have satisfied young Brown, although a later commentator thought it "sheer whimsy."[114] They then headed down to Drake's Bay, a popular rendezvous spot north of San Francisco frequented by various vessels engaged in assorted pursuits, legal or otherwise. Protected by Point Reyes, it is the closest anchorage north of San Francisco and was a good spot to wait out heavy northwest blows.[115] The weather prevented them from lowering the boats, and so they tucked in. According to Brown, "the suggestion to enter Drake's Bay had been a reasonable one under the circumstances, but when the skipper, after a stay of two days, said we ought to take the vessel into 'Frisco and see the sights, it caused a little comment among the crew, as no one could see any reason why we should go there, having plenty of fresh water and stores aboard."[116] The San Francisco stopover stretched into a month. It is just possible that one of Alex's chores was finding a new place to stay, as the days of him and Dan using Victoria as their home port were rapidly coming to a close – hence, perhaps, the presence of Alex's family. Lucy and Catherine MacLean would return to Victoria in early April via steamship.[117] It is also possible that Alex, himself, may have taken this opportunity to touch base with Herman Liebes.

Eventually, the unexpected and unexplained San Francisco vacation for the seal hunters was over. They were anxious to press on, and, according to Brown, "after shipping a new crew and a friend of McLean's, a Captain Stevens, who McLean informed us wanted to learn the sealing game, we broke out the hook from the harbor mud, and with a fine leading breeze sailed out through the Golden Gate to hunt seals in earnest, which was good business for the hunters, as up until then we had not made our Summer salt, let alone jam for the Winter months to come, although McLean had liberally supplied us with spending money while ashore to sport with."[118] The *Mary Ellen* finally cleared San Francisco in mid-March, just two weeks before the *Triumph,* carrying his brother Dan and Baker, arrived at that port to provision, possibly party, and enter contractual arrangements with Herman Liebes.

The seals were far to the north by this time and initially there was little success. With indifferent sealing and unfavourable weather, the *Mary Ellen* was reported to have acquired only nine seals by late March.[119] From hunter Tom Brown's perspective, the voyage was turning into a disappointing one, although it did have its moments, including "a sailing feat which sailors on this coast regard as among the most remarkable accomplishments on this side of the Pacific."[120] On 8 April, the schooner was hove to 115 miles out in the Pacific, weathering a blow. The sealing schooners usually had a couple of musicians aboard with a fiddle, guitar, or accordion. On this occasion, there were a couple of pipers, and the preparations included a few shots of rum. Alex apparently had a bit of business to transact in Victoria. Two of the crew later related the incident and supplied some backdrop: "Do you mind that wild night in [April] when we were about ninety miles off Flattery and he put off in a boat for Victoria? ... Alex was full of the devil that night. We had two pipers aboard and they played him and Arthur Pennell ... right along the deck before they took to the little 18-foot boat and left the *Mary Ellen* for Victoria. It was a rough night and some of the schooners were hove to. Alex and Pennell had only oars and a sail – and ninety miles to travel." The crew was concerned because of the sea that was running, "but they made Victoria and rejoined us later. It was one of the foolhardiest things I ever remember, but it was just like Alex."[121] And it was just like Wolf Larsen in *The Sea-Wolf.* While waiting for a storm, Larsen "was glad there was an impending struggle, that he was thrilled and upborne with knowledge that one of the great moments of living, when the tide of life surges up in flood, was up on him."[122] Alex and Arthur left at seven in the evening and arrived in Victoria the following afternoon.[123] The *Daily Colonist's* account of their arrival, knowing nothing of the circumstances surrounding their departure, was less dramatic and simply mentioned that Alex "made a quick run up in his small boat" and had reported a meagre 143 skins to date.[124] Whatever his business, it does not appear to have been with Baker.

The latter was surprised when he accidentally met Alex six days later in Victoria.[125]

Alex left Captain Stevens in charge of the schooner: "We had to agree rather than have the schooner go into Victoria and run the chance of losing some, if not all, the crew; for up to that time, being on a 'lay,' they were in debt to the vessel and would welcome the opportunity of deserting if given the opportunity of looking for another berth."[126] At one point, Alex was expected to rejoin his vessel, which was reportedly off the west coast on 25 April, some 125 miles from Victoria.[127] As Tom Brown remembers it, plans were again altered: "At the end of two weeks, instead of going into Neah Bay to pick up McLean, Captain Stevens sailed right by, saying 'We might as well go into Victoria, where we can meet up with the boys for a night's frolic. Arriving at Victoria no one was allowed ashore but the hunters. Here, Bissett and Whitely, two of the hunters, left the ship, and I would have done so too had there been anything else offering."[128] The *Mary Ellen* arrived in Victoria on the evening of 2 May. Baker's diary also makes reference to trouble with the hunters and crew of the *Mary Ellen,* which is not surprising given the curious pattern of the voyage so far and the sparse catch to date.[129]

There was more trouble expected as well. On 26 April, Alex MacLean's signature was one of more than a dozen representing twenty-one schooners on a statement to Rear-Admiral Heneage, commander-in-chief of the Royal Navy on the Pacific Station at Esquimalt. The document referred to the seizures of 1886, the imprisonment, the absence of compensation, the recent proclamation of 22 March by President Benjamin Harrison "warning all persons against entering the waters of the Bering Sea," the presence of American warships, and the fact that some of the sealers had begun the season before the proclamation was issued and were now on their way to the Bering Sea. It was a detailed and reasoned presentation, and it may explain Alex's presence in Victoria and his delayed departure. The letter to Rear-Admiral Heneage noted that several sealing schooners were in port awaiting orders and "having a large amount of property employed in this business, it would be of great advantage to us if some authentic information could be given us as to whether the British Government are advised of the course intended to be pursued by the United States Government in regard to this matter, pending the conclusion of the diplomatic negotiations."[130]

A few days later, with Captain MacLean back on board, the *Mary Ellen* picked up two replacement hunters in Seattle and finally headed into the North Pacific for a four-month sealing cruise. For novice hunter Tom Brown, it continued to be a learning experience in a variety of ways. He gathered additional insight into the character of Alex MacLean: "McLean was a good carrier of canvas and knew just what the hooker would stand. Never did I see the wheel of the *Mary Ellen* in beckets, whether driving ahead or 'hove to' a man was always there. While a driver and a hard master aboard ship,

McLean showed his authority in his own peculiar way, which sailormen more or less admired. 'Growl you may, but go you must,' he would say. When he gave an order, whether necessary or not, the forecastle hand had to jump, or there would be 'hell-a-popping.'"

Their best day sealing was on 15 July with 207 skins. But the weather was generally poor, and they averaged boat launches only four out of every seven days.[131] Then in mid-August, a fog quickly came up and two hunters, George Roberts and Alex's sometime sailing companion Arthur Pennell, failed to return to the schooner. The *Mary Ellen* stayed in the area for the next four days, but their intense search for the missing sealers was unsuccessful.[132]

This misfortune was followed by a few more weeks of lacklustre sealing: "It was the low condition of the larder that gave us warning it was time to be considering the passage homeward; and with the first favorable wind in early September we squared away for 172 Pass, McLean figuring that it wouldn't be advisable to attempt Unimak Pass, where, no doubt, one or more revenue cutters would be waiting for vessels leaving the 'sea.' We all breathed freer when we reached the wide Pacific with our 1,785 skins below decks, for the dread of seizure had more or less worried us."[133] Another check on the larder brought the realization that there were not sufficient supplies to reach Victoria. A few days sailing brought them to Sand Point Bay, in the Shumagin Islands, on the coast of Alaska. Once again, there would be a change of plans. Alex had found out the price for seal skins had increased significantly since he signed an agreement: "The thought of the Victoria dealer getting that additional $3,500 was too much for him, and he evidently made up his mind that no such thing would happen. He wasn't going to 'stand for anything like that.' Furious, he paced the quarterdeck, saying all manner of things, but kept his own counsel."[134] Again the record is hard to unravel. Was MacLean unaware of the contract Baker had made with Liebes in April, a contract that pre-sold the whole catch of the *Mary Ellen* at $6.25 per skin? Was he up to some more complicated scenario of which novice hunter Tom Brown would be unaware? He would hardly have had time to learn of the falling out between his brother and Baker. No papers of Alex MacLean have been uncovered. When Alex wanted to disappear from the view of managing owners, authorities, and historians, he did so.

When the *Mary Ellen* left Sand Point on 5 September, she bypassed Victoria and continued on to San Francisco and to H. Liebes and Company. It was the only catch of the pelagic fleet that came to San Francisco that season. The remainder were landed at Victoria. The absence of the schooner in Victoria by late September prompted some people there to give it up for lost.[135] On 8 October, Edgar Crow Baker had a long discussion about the MacLeans with Morris Moss, a long-time associate of Liebes in Victoria. Baker also got Victoria Customs Collector A.R. Milne to contact his counterpart in San Francisco on the same date.[136] On the following day, by chance, the *Mary Ellen* arrived in San Francisco. Tom Brown's version has the Victoria buyer outguessing MacLean and welcoming him, with appropriate authorities in tow, when the *Mary Ellen* docked in San Francisco. And there was another surprise. Less than an hour after the *Mary Ellen* arrived, the sealer *San Diego* returned as well, and the two hunters missing from the *Mary Ellen* since mid-August, George Roberts and Arthur Pennell, "bobbed up serenely ... to the great surprise and joy of their shipmates." They had managed to make shore – after four days – at Falls Place on Unimak Island in the Bering Sea. Assisted by a Swedish trapper in the area, they had eventually been picked up by the *San Diego*.[137]

For his part, Alex complained to a reporter in San Francisco about the poor state of the sealing industry that year – most of the difficulties he attributed to the weather. He considered the *Mary Ellen's* voyage "the least paying trip she has ever made." The yield was only $10,000. He also maintained that he did not enter the Bering Sea but, as a Victoria newspaper noted wryly, "he probably lost his latitude, for there were some Bering's Sea seals that came his way."[138] As Tom Brown was preparing to return to Victoria via steamer, "feeling none the worse for [his] eight months stretch as shipmate with the most notorious skipper sailing out of the principal sealing port of the North Pacific, [he] paid a visit to the 'Sea Wolf.' While very comfortable, he was not particularly happy over the knot fortune had tied in the string of his affairs."[139] The curious and financially unrewarding voyage of the *Mary Ellen* in 1889 notwithstanding, Tom Brown settled in Victoria and would continue to go seal hunting well into the 1890s.[140] Brown was one of the many Cape Bretoners who on visits home would bring detailed information on the recent activities of the North Pacific sealing fleet, with particular emphasis on the Nova Scotia connections.[141]

Understanding MacLean's actions in regard to the *Mary Ellen* and explaining his almost nonchalant approach to sealing and his mysterious dealings in San Francisco and Victoria that season remain a difficult task. One's frustration is tempered only slightly by the fact that Edgar Crow Baker was also confused. Baker was worried about just what Alex was up to by early October.[142] Nor were his concerns alleviated when the vessel finally arrived in San Francisco. Two weeks after the *Mary Ellen* had returned to port, Baker confessed that he was "much perplexed as to how to proceed against two such anointed scoundrels as Messrs. Dan and Alex." Two days later, this refrain reappeared in his diary: "Full of perplexity re: McLean matters in Frisco."[143] The justifiable concerns doubtless dealt in part with the skins from the *Mary Ellen*. Ten years later, Baker's books still show that no account had been rendered to him for the catch of the *Mary Ellen* that year.[144] There was also the question of Dan MacLean's outstanding mortgages, a bothersome issue to the recently retired politician and still very active businessman. However, in mid-November, Baker was able to record some "good news from Frisco. $2480. mortgage to be paid, Liebes!"[145] Five days later, Baker received the money owed on the *Mary Ellen* from Morris Moss. Herman Liebes and Alex and Dan MacLean were obviously becoming better acquainted. Other issues between Baker and the MacLeans remained unresolved. Baker was by no means finished with the MacLeans, but he would have to wait quite a while for satisfaction. Dan's lack of concern with Baker's financial well-being ensured that the elder MacLean would remain an "s.o.b." in Baker's book for a long time.[146]

For almost a decade, Alex and Dan MacLean had contributed to an industry that had significantly improved Victoria's financial standing. They were prominent in setting the direction and pace of the pelagic sealing fleet. Both were present on the seminal voyage in the *City of San Diego* in 1883. Both were involved in the "experiment" to determine whether the use of Aboriginal or white sealers was the more efficient approach within the industry. Both commanded schooners that returned, "carrying the broom," with the largest catch of the season. Indeed, Dan's record in 1887 would be bested only once, in 1894. They continued to bring in significant catches until 1889. Nonetheless, their declining financial situation, combined with a significant decline in Aboriginal participation, suggested the industry's precarious position. When the role of Aboriginals increased dramatically in the 1890s, Alex and Dan were long gone from the Victoria fleet. They had directly influenced the participation of Cape Bretoners, in particular, and of east coast mariners, in general, in the British Columbia sealing industry. Both were directly involved in the serious conflict that had emerged between the United States and the Canadian and British governments. They had become well known, if not universally well liked, during Victoria's heyday. The mark they made in the 1880s would remain in the collective memory of their home port of Victoria for more than a century. Some of these memories, from Tom Brown and Ronald Gillis, for example, were penned fifty years later, long after the MacLean legend had blossomed, and time and their later reputations coloured these accounts. However, contemporary reports in newspapers on the west and east coasts – including Alex's dash into Victoria in a small boat in April 1889 and Dan's welcome on the Halifax waterfront in November 1887 – as well as the detailed reports of their sealing successes in these years suggest they were more than ordinary sailors and sealers.

4
Home Port San Francisco, 1890

San Francisco, one of the world's great ports, quickly seized the imagination. The Embarcadero "is the street where the city and the hills meet the sea," and waterfront writer Robert O'Brien captured it: "In back of the Embarcadero and looming above it, the city's hills touch the sky, and they and all that space of sky are what lifts your heart when you see San Francisco, not only for the first time, but always. The hills and the sky cast their spell over the dullest of men, stirring him to poetry, inspiring him to liken the city to a beautiful and bewitching woman – an enchantress – with the face and body of a goddess, and a soul that could be as tender as that blue sky and as wistful as the fog that steals gently in from the sea."[1] San Francisco featured a cosmopolitan population approaching 300,000 in 1890 (more than 40 percent were foreign-born) and was becoming the financial and cultural centre of the West. It would be the MacLeans' home port for a decade. Alex and Dan had been acquainted with the California port since 1880, and they had made frequent visits throughout the decade, experiencing "that gay wicked city of the West" during the latter part of its freewheeling days. Another possible attraction, definitely a reality, was that it was also "the world's crimping capital."[2] As marine author Basil Lubbock, who sailed out of there on a barque in 1899, noted, "there is no more dangerous waterfront in the world than that of Frisco; many a mate or apprentice has disappeared never to be seen alive again, and often his body would be found, stripped and mutilated, floating in the Sacramento." Lubbock mentions two "superb Blue-nose sailors" who resisted being shanghaied: "These two fine sailormen had their faces pounded to a jelly with knuckle-dusters and slungshot" by the runners, the crimp's henchmen, in the presence of women and children. That was not unusual. These unfortunates were not the MacLean brothers.[3]

The most notorious section of the port, the black heart of the San Francisco underworld, was known as the "Barbary Coast." The designation had come into general usage in the mid-1860s, and, according to Herbert Asbury, who specialized in portraying the underside of notable American cities, it "was the almost universal synonym for debauchery, [and] its most iniquitous features were confined within the rectangular district limited by Broadway, Washington, Montgomery and Stockton streets." While the area gradually declined in size – by the 1890s it was down to a single block on Pacific Street, also known as "Terrific Street" – it remained a noteworthy section. From 1850 to 1900, "one of the most dangerous areas in San Francisco was the waterfront, along the eastern and northeastern fringes of the Barbary Coast. Murderers, footpads, burglars, hoodlums ... prowled the streets in such numbers and carried on their depredations with such boldness that the police walked their beats in pairs and went in even greater force whenever they found it necessary to enter any of the dives with which the district abounded."[4] Dangerous and disreputable though it was, it may have been the MacLeans' kind of town. According to one Cape Breton source, Alex and Dan "were known to have cleaned up quite a few Barbary Coast saloons."[5]

The Barbary Coast also attracted some notable, or notorious, acquaintances of Alex MacLean. Christian "Charlie" Klengenberg was one of them. He would later recall that the lure of the district was short-lived: "I met a few odd characters along what was the Barbary Coast of San Francisco in those days. And I went the rounds, as a sailor may do when first ashore after so long a time at sea. But in a few weeks the saloons and resorts of San Francisco lost their charm for me."[6] Klengenberg, who would get his start as an Arctic trader during this decade with a line of credit from H. Liebes and Company, was a bit of a case himself.[7] One assessment suggests he was a person who "lived up to the legend of Jack London's Sea Wolf."[8] Klengenberg would later achieve some notoriety for being charged with killing four of his crew on one voyage. He was acquitted, if not completely exonerated, in the historical record in San Francisco.[9] On a later occasion, this northern trader managed to lose overboard a Royal Canadian Mounted Police constable who had been put aboard his vessel to ensure that Canadian regulations were being scrupulously followed, thus ensuring continuing difficulties with the authorities.[10]

Charlie Klengenberg and Alex MacLean would occasionally cross paths in San Francisco and Alaska. And their jaunts in the California port were not always confined to the Barbary Coast. Klengenberg spoke kindly of Alex – "The good man libelled [sic] as the Sea Wolf by Jack London" – and his recollections brought out other aspects of Alex's personality: "I knew him in the passing of having had a drink with him at the Keystone House on Jackson Street, and other saloons on Pacific Street in San Francisco. And once he took me with him very civilly to visit a respectable Scotch family of his acquaintance from Nova Scotia. McLean was a handsome seaman; medium height but very strongly built, especially about the shoulders, and with his long, reddish brown moustache he looked very much the Viking when he was in command on his own ship ... a skilful sailor and a sociable man."[11] Alex was a personable individual who, while meeting new and frequently interesting individuals, also maintained contact with his own people. He, Lucy, and Catherine resided on McAllister Street in San Francisco through much of the 1890s.[12]

If it was a relief to Edgar Crow Baker not to have to deal with "two such anointed scoundrels" as the MacLean brothers any longer, it was likely an emotion shared by both sides. One suspects that, temperamentally, Alex and Dan were considerably more suited to the generous and flexible, if paternal, Herman Liebes than to Baker. Liebes, who was born in Germany in the early 1840s, emigrated to New York in 1862 and, while working in the fur business there, struck up a friendship and partnership with Charles J. Behlow. They soon moved on to San Francisco and established H. Liebes and Company. An English cousin, Isaac Liebes, arrived in San Francisco in 1869. By the early 1870s, their new premises, a four-storey iron building on Montgomery Street, was "one of the sights" of the town, and the Liebes firm was "the 'Glass of Fashion' in the San Francisco fur trade."[13] H. Liebes and Company bought, prepared, and sold furs of all kinds, and most San Francisco fur dealers had acquired training and experience with them. One source noted that the firm's "reputation for fair dealing and quality of merchandise was the very best," and the *San Francisco Chronicle* maintained that it "was rated as the leading fur house in the United States." The company record was a substantial one. By the late 1890s, they advertised as "the largest fur house in the world," and their store would be a retail landmark in San Francisco for a century.[14]

H. Liebes and Company, in its formative years, did not neglect its workers. Carl Rydell, who worked for Herman Liebes in the early 1890s, considered the firm a fair and reasonable outfit: "Liebes and Company were particularly liberal, telling their captains to buy any provisions that they wanted. It was partly on this account that the firm was always able to engage the most experienced hunters and got the best results from its outfits." Rydell remembered Liebes as "an employer who believed in treating his men according to their deserts. He was a friend to his sealing captains and hunters ... When we were broke, the easiest way to get money enough to last us till the next hunting season opened was to ask Herman Liebes for it ... he would pay cheerfully and, into the bargain, take us round the corner for a drink."[15] In the off-season, late autumn and early winter, the company made its vessels available to the hunters if they needed a place to stay. Alex had become closely associated with H. Liebes and Company by the autumn of 1889. Herman and Isaac's interests would acquire the services of both MacLeans, who were two of the most successful sealers in the game to date, for the next few years. Dan would sail under the firm's flag as well as that of another associated San Francisco firm for the remainder of his sealing days.[16] The working relationship between H. Liebes and Company and the sealing captains was clear and open. According to Rydell, "the only orders he had from the owners were to fit out for a year and come back with furs ... No masters of other vessels had such loose orders. The sealer was practically free to go where he pleased and do what he pleased, so long as he came back with a catch of furs. He had, of course, to take into account the laws governing the hunting ... We did take chances with the law at times, and we had many narrow escapes from revenue cutters and warships."[17] It fit with Alex's approach: "The only rule I have found was if they were not in one place to go and hunt for them."[18] Herman Liebes had a markedly different approach to the business than did Edgar Crow Baker. Along with sailing their sealing vessels, Alex also inspected and sometimes bought vessels for H. Liebes and Company. His first purchase was the *James Hamilton Lewis,* which was acquired in Seattle late in 1889.[19]

The MacLeans were already known in the Bay area and their exploits and escapades would soon provide considerable material for the local newspapers and the deep pool of waterfront lore. Whether because of the change between Victoria and San Francisco, the different type of business partners with whom they were associated, their costly clashes with the authorities in the Bering Sea in 1886-89, the changing face of the sealing industry, and the increasing pressures of that occupation, the MacLeans began to take even more chances and to push themselves and their crews into more precarious positions. A definite change can be detected. One distant relative later wrote, perceptively but with some exaggeration, that it was at this point that Alex's "career as an outlaw" started: "From then on he was a marked and hunted man."[20] Since Alex's career in the 1890s, primarily but not exclusively in sealing, reaped fewer financial rewards, his determination to succeed sometimes bordered on desperate, and his activities came more and more to the attention of the authorities and the general public. The MacLeans, and many other sealers, had come to disdain the ever-changing rules and the hindrances placed upon them by the American monopoly and by government regulations. They also began to receive bad press. The pelagic seal hunters could not always resist the temptation to hunt inside the legal boundary and occasionally land on the protected rookeries, and these poachers were now portrayed as pirates and as "despicable predators to American government officials and to most of the public."[21] They seldom received a fair hearing.

To keep such criticisms in perspective, when the American Department of the Treasury later made a comprehensive examination of the practice of raiding and poaching specifically on the American and Russian rookeries, it concluded that the practice was neither common nor numerically significant to the herds. Even the largest combined estimate of seals taken directly from the rookeries in this way from the 1870s until the late 1890s would only equal the catch of one very successful pelagic schooner following regulations in one season.[22] But the raids did occur, and there were dangers, as Henry James Snow, an Englishman who had operated his own schooner out of Japan since the early 1870s, points out: "In the whole course of my experience I have never known an instance ... of a sea-otter hunter or sealer stealing a skin, committing robbery, or assaulting or attacking a native or anyone else, in any of the places visited by him when hunting. On the other hand, scores of men engaged in pelagic hunting have been shot down and murdered while hunting near the land, without even a shot being fired in retaliation by those attacked. Sometimes these victims have been there by inadvertence during thick, foggy weather, and at other times knowingly taking the risk."[23] Snow spoke from experience. In 1888, "while innocently hunting sea otters off Copper Island, Snow's boat was fired on from the shore. Three of his men were killed, and he suffered several wounds before managing to get his boat back to the schooner." In attacks such as these, sealers, especially knowledgeable ones, held important advantages. Fog was an important ally in what Snow called the "cat and mouse game that taxed the skill of navigators."[24] The schooner captains also had the advantage of smaller, more elusive, and often faster vessels. Yet, as Snow also emphasizes, the costs could be staggering.[25]

The reliable *Mary Ellen,* which had been under the command of one or the other of the MacLeans since 1884, would sail under each of them one more time. Both voyages would be memorable, after a fashion, but neither would prove to be particularly illustrious. Alex had returned with her to San Francisco in early October 1889, and Liebes had paid off Dan's mortgage on the boat, which had been held by Baker, that autumn. Late in December, Dan commenced his final run with the *Mary Ellen.* The labour pool available for Dan on the San Francisco waterfront during the Christmas season in 1889 was apparently limited. The legendary and notorious crimps of the San Francisco waterfront were probably involved. As the mate later noted, "the crew was a very poor lot of men, only two of them being sailors."[26] Carl Rydell, a recent member of the Coast Seamen's Union, offered his assessment of the sailors available for the sealing schooners heading out of San Francisco during this period: "They would come back from a nine or ten months' cruise with their accounts overdrawn and would be paid off with a dollar, the minimum that they might be paid under the shipping law. With so little inducement to offer, we had to take whatever men we could get for our crews – generally sots that we found hanging around saloon corners near the waterfront. Some of these had been shoemakers, others bricklayers, and others paperhangers ... With such crews, the officers could not deal softly. The men were in the majority, even with the hunters against them, and they would have taken the upper hand at any show of timidity."[27]

Tom Cummings was one of the unfortunates this time around. He signed on with Dan and the *Mary Ellen* on Christmas Day. Two days later, they set out. That winter, the *Mary Ellen* had to contend with "boisterous" weather, indifferent sealing, and a difficult crew. For Dan, who does not seem to have been a particularly patient man, the conditions were frustrating. When the vessel, after three months at sea, arrived in Victoria on 21 March 1890, she carried only 115 skins. The captain explained that the crew "had received their pay in advance" and then, on 12 March, had refused to work. The lack of success in sealing, a recalcitrant crew, and a frustrated captain probably formed a large part of the backdrop to the ensuing controversy. Dan MacLean responded by refusing rations while he headed for Victoria. The crew talked of "ill treatment" by the captain and being forced to exist on cornmeal and water while the *Mary Ellen* made for port.[28]

Some crew members immediately secured legal advice, and a few days later two provincial police officers served MacLean with a warrant. Dan's supposed callousness concerning cornmeal would soon be magnified to a charge of attempted murder: "When handed the warrant MacLean coolly pocketed it and ordered his men and 12 others that he had hired to help him out, to heave the anchor, get up sail and go to sea." Dan made two unsuccessful attempts to leave, but his sailing prowess failed him this time. A sand bar thwarted him. Provincial Police Sergeant Langley then arrived with reinforcements (having made arrangements for a steam cutter from Esquimalt to act as backup), and Dan was arrested. The crew's ringleader was also served a summons "to show cause why he acted as he did." When the case opened, the provincial police court "was well filled with marine men." There was a lot of local interest in the proceedings. Dan was well known, and the charge was a serious one. It was just the thing to liven up the end of winter in the port. The main object of Dan's wrath was Tom Cummings. While working on the vessel on 12 March, Dan noticed a boom was not made fast:

Captain: Come and make it fast.
Cummings: Yes, sir.
Captain: Never mind your "yes sir"; haul it over quick.

While he was doing as the captain told him he [captain] called him a ___ of a ____, and said "make it fast and don't dictate to me." Captain then drew an iron belaying pin out of the foremast and hit him over the head. Captain told him to go below.

Cummings, who was described as a rancher, denied that he had refused duty a few days before the incident. Another ex-crew member testified that Cummings was following orders when he was hit. For the defence, mate

Arthur Penwell stated: "This is my second season with Captain MacLean and we have always got along splendidly together, and with the men." He went on to point out that "Cummings was very slow, and he was 'cheeky.' He was impudent to me in general."[29] Further, Cummings had apparently made a serious steering mistake the day prior to the incident with the belaying pin. The helmsman's responsibility was a crucial one, and his mistake, as all sailors knew, could prove fatal. Finally, Dan addressed the court: "I did not strike the man to do him any injury. He had been very cheeky aboard ship and refused to do what he was told to. There were three men on the boom and I wanted it fixed. I ordered the mate and two men aft to set the try sail. Told Cummings to make the tail rope fast." Cummings replied there were others who could do it: "I looked around and saw that all the other men were busy; and so I told him again to make the rope fast. He did not do so, so I lowered the boom by the topping lift, so it wouldn't knock the men overboard. Cummings commenced to 'dictate' to me. I had the belaying pin in my hand at the time and I struck him with it. I told him to go below and I made the tail rope fast myself." According to other testimony, Cummings, while clutching a butcher knife, had told Dan: "I will fix you."[30]

A second charge against MacLean was originally delayed because the main witness did not appear. He was eventually found in a saloon, but, as one police officer explained, "he [was] pretty well loaded." Another principal witness left Victoria and possibly the country. A doctor who examined Cummings found him recovered and his scar almost healed. Justice George Walkem soon changed the attempted murder charge, which he considered "hardly warranted," to "assault with intent to do bodily harm." For the judge, "the case as proven was not half as serious as the case charged, although the men on ships should be protected by law as well as on land. The captain of a vessel should always hold his temper." Dan was found guilty of common assault and fined $100, with an additional $20 for costs and $50 to Cummings.[31] The latter presumably went back to the land and work on a ranch.

While Dan's actions were considered excessive by the court, one could point out that, unlike some of the American revenue cutter captains, neither he nor his brother ever made it into the notorious "Red Record" of the *San Francisco Coast Seamen's Journal,* which noted in detail scores of instances of cruelty on American vessels during this period.[32] Following this incident, Dan returned to San Francisco and transferred to the Liebeses' schooner, the *Edward E. Webster,* which was formerly of the Gloucester fleet. He completed that sealing season by bringing the *Webster* back to San Francisco in the autumn with a catch of 1,300. He would command the *Webster* for four more consecutive sealing seasons.[33]

Alex was also in command of two different vessels in 1890. One was the recently purchased *James Hamilton Lewis* and the other was the *Mary Ellen.*

The *Lewis* cleared San Francisco for sealing on 10 January. The mate was George Wester, a former crewman on the *Mary Ellen*.[34] Initially the *Lewis*, and the other sealing schooners, situated themselves off the coast, just north of San Francisco, waiting for the annual migration of the fur seal herd to the northern waters. It was here that Carl Rydell first met Alex MacLean. Rydell, born in Sweden, would later serve as superintendent of the Philippine Nautical School. His autobiography, in which he frequently used aliases, gives a first person account of his initial meeting with Alex MacLean. The incident quickly entered into waterfront lore. In 1890, Rydell was in his first season working on a Liebes' vessel, as a navigator on the fifty-two-ton schooner, the *Alexander*. The fleet had spent much of January and February sealing off the California coast, using Drake's Bay for anchorage at night. There would be twenty to thirty sealing schooners working that area at one time, and there was "a good deal of fraternizing" among them. As Rydell recounts, "one rough day when we all stayed at anchor, there was more visiting and drinking than usual. Wolf Larson [sic] went to visit one of his friends, the skipper of a British vessel, and they drank together till they fell to quarrelling. Then the Britisher clipped one side of Wolf Larson's long red moustache, in which he took great pride, and threw him overboard." Returning to his vessel, he got under way "and sailed about, firing potatoes into the Britisher from his signal gun. The Britisher soon got under way and returned the fire, also using potatoes. This stirred the rest of us, and vessel after vessel joined in the firing till the whole fleet was engaged. Potatoes were flying everywhere. Some men were hit, but none were badly hurt. Finally a truce was made, Wolf Larson invited all hands to a jamboree on his schooner, and peace was declared without any indemnities."[35] Aside from the spectacle of scores of hardened men from the Barbary Coast and elsewhere frolicking in Drake's Bay, the anecdote, which has a ring of truth about it, and its numerous versions offers some insight into MacLean's perspective. He turned a personally embarrassing incident into a barely imaginable food fight that culminated in a céilidh. Doubtless the next morning, MacLean had his vessel cleaned up again: "He had one unusual characteristic among sealing skippers; he always insisted upon his schooners being kept meticulously ship-shape and clean, a most out-of-the-common circumstance in vessels engaged in fishing."[36] The Cockney cook on Wolf Larsen's *Ghost*, with the "decidedly dirty" galley and the woodwork "scummed" with grease, would not have lasted long on MacLean's vessel with her holystoned deck.[37]

MacLean's mention in the historical record that season is suspiciously fleeting. He apparently did not take the *Lewis* into the Bering Sea.[38] Maybe he only took the *Lewis* out for the spring or coastal hunt. (One long-time nemesis would later accuse him of raiding Copper Island with the *Lewis* on 1 August that year.)[39] Other sources state that Alex had one last voyage in the *Mary Ellen* that season, a trip that also remains cloaked in questions. In these versions, Alex had the *Mary Ellen* in close proximity to the Bering Sea early that summer. She was lost on Sand Point Reef in Alaska on 23 July.[40] According to Victor Jacobson, who would spend many years in the Victoria sealing fleet, the vessel was wrecked by Alex MacLean on the rocks in an attempt to collect on insurance, possibly at the prompting of his San Francisco backers: "Captain MacLean ordered the crew ashore, and sold everything to the storekeeper. I believe she belonged to some San Francisco parties at that time. I am not certain, but that is what I believe ... he wanted to do away with the vessel ... to get the insurance, of course. She was insured for some $18,000." This estimate appears high since she had been purchased the previous year for $4,500, and much of this information was told to Jacobson by the local storekeeper at Sand Point.[41] The storekeeper supposedly picked up the *Mary Ellen* from MacLean for $150. He sent it on one trip to the Bering Sea and then resold it to Jacobson for $4,300. At this point, it was not in good shape. According to Jacobson, "she was well run down, both in sails, rigging and gear and everything."[42] Jacobson seems to have purchased the *Mary Ellen* partly out of nostalgia. It had been the first schooner on which he had gone sealing, but he was soon less than impressed with one of the oldest and most successful schooners in the fleet: "She was an awful expensive vessel." Notwithstanding her undoubted hardiness, the *Mary Ellen* may have been, after years of hard usage, a prime candidate for wrecking. There was much rumour, but no conclusive evidence.[43]

The lucrative twenty-year lease for the Pribilof Islands rookeries ceded to the Alaska Commercial Company (ACC) by the US government was set to expire in 1890. It had been quite a profitable arrangement for the ACC. During the previous two decades, "the dividends paid averaged 50% per year on the par value of the stock." As the shareholders had not paid par value for the stock, "the annual return may have been over 500% on the invested capital."[44] Net profits, on a concern that had required little investment and low operating expenses, had averaged almost $1,000,000 yearly over the course of the lease. More than $20,000,000 had been paid as dividends by the ACC, and the government had acquired over $10,000,000. Little wonder there had been no significant stock transfers for years.[45] The activities of the ACC had been subjected to searing, sometimes scurrilous, criticisms since the mid-1870s, and time was now running out. While this was still considered to be the Gilded Age, a period noted for the accumulation of many large fortunes, these years also witnessed a growing movement against trusts and monopolies.[46]

Alaska governor A.P. Swineford had targeted the ACC in 1887, accusing it of various transgressions, and the following year he observed: "It is a great corporate monopoly, created by Congress itself and armed with a monopolistic club in the shape of sole and exclusive possession of a most valuable industry, which it does not scruple to use to beat out, so to speak, the brains of any and all competition for that part of the fur trade not embraced in its lease and contact with the government."[47] When the ACC's Louis Sloss made a public statement in 1889 that his company would not seek a renewal of the lease on the rookeries and that he doubted that anyone else would want it either, he was met with some skepticism. The *San Francisco Coast Seamen's Journal* wryly observed: "We were always under the impression that there was a mint of money in the seal business, and we would have to see figures to convince us to the contrary." And when Sloss explained that the ACC's stated position was partly due to the pelagic sealers, whom he labelled as "a desperate and criminally inclined class of men, sailing in piratical vessels manned by brutal, outlawed sealers," the *San Francisco Coast Seamen's Journal* took specific exception: "Mr. Sloss went a little too far when he made use of such language. He has no facts in his possession to justify such assertions. Those men have never done anything desperate, unless, at times, running the risk of being captured can come under that head. They have simply followed their vocation of seal hunting without permission from the Alaska Commercial Company, and their mode of killing the seals is not as brutal as the means employed by the men of the Commercial Company."[48] Snow, the sealer, would not have disagreed. He compared the directors to "that pirate of the gulls, the skua, amongst the kittiwakes, who, instead of seeking his own food, watches until another bird captures a fish, and then swoops down upon him, compels him to give it up, and swallows it himself. It has always been so."[49]

Others were equally skeptical of Sloss' dour financial analysis. Not surprisingly, the "miraculous production of massive profit from minimal investment," which had flowed from the ACC's lease for two decades, attracted national players as renewal time approached. On 24 December 1889, the government advertised for proposals, and the stipulation that the limit for the following year would be only 60,000 sealskins and not the usual 100,000 did not stop the rush for spoils. Twelve bids were received, including a proposal from the ACC, Sloss' prediction notwithstanding. After an active and bitter struggle, the ACC was unsuccessful. The ACC soon settled its sealing accounts and would continue for many years in the far more competitive Alaskan land fur trade and in the supply of miners and prospectors. Doubtless, the ACC shareholders were mollified somewhat because large dividends continued to flow for a few more years from a $2,000,000 fund that was no longer needed for expenses. The ACC sold their buildings on the Pribilof Islands to the winner for less than $70,000.[50]

The successful bidder for the new twenty-year lease on the Pribilof Islands rookeries was the North American Commercial Company (NACC). This outfit carried strong financial backing and enjoyed solid political clout with President Benjamin Harrison's Republican administration in Washington, which had taken office in March 1889. The NACC received the lease in

March 1890. William Windom, secretary of the Department of the Treasury, approved it. Two of the signatures on the $500,000 bond were those of Darius O. Mills and Stephen B. Elkins.[51] Mills and Elkins had "intimate connections with the Harrison administration." Due to substantial California interests, Mills was "regarded as one of the wealthiest men in the country." His son-in-law was Whitelaw Reid, editor and owner of the *New York Tribune*. Reid would run as Harrison's vice-president the next time out. Reid was also a close friend of the secretary of state, James G. Blaine, who, in turn, was a business and political associate of Elkins. Blaine "had several close political friends who were major stockholders on the NACC."[52] Elkins had been an "adviser and political lieutenant" of Blaine's since the mid-1880s, and he was "on close terms with the Harrison family," having business ventures with Blaine, Blaine's son Emmons, and Harrison's son Russell. Elkins would soon become Harrison's secretary of war.[53] Another participant was Lloyd Tevis, who had been identified with "some of California's greatest business undertakings" over the previous four decades.[54]

There remains some debate over who actually ran the NACC. Initially, there were only a handful of stockholders. The *New York Times* identified Tevis as president in 1891. The *San Francisco Examiner* maintained that it was this California entrepreneur who interested Mills and "Liebes the furrier" in the opportunity and that Tevis "manipulated things so that his company secured the fur seal concession." Charles S. Campbell Jr. suggests that Mills and Elkins were the dominating figures.[55] The initial president of the NACC, however, was Isaac Liebes, another "member of the German Jewish merchantocracy of San Francisco." Isaac was Herman's cousin. It was Isaac Liebes, in his role as president of the NACC, who signed the new lease agreement with Treasury Secretary Windom. According to Briton Cooper Busch, Isaac Liebes was "the man who actually ran the NACC."[56] And it was the interests of the Rothschilds of London, England, that apparently backed the NACC, possibly through Mills' San Francisco connections. Herman Liebes, who for all of his prominence seems to be almost as elusive as Alex MacLean at times, apparently played a fairly considerable role as well.[57] Herman Liebes, in a deposition, noted that he had been, since 1880, "in the habit of buying skins from American and English vessels engaged in what is now known as poaching." He was using the term, as did many others at the time, as a synonym for pelagic sealing.[58] One interpretation has Herman Liebes enticing Elkins into the NACC scheme for his influence and that it was Herman Liebes "who got up the fur company, and showed them millions in sight – so many millions that they bid a tremendous price," according to the *New York Times*. This newspaper described Herman Liebes as "a man concerned in affairs that will do much toward making the history of the Harrison Administration."[59] The NACC was unquestionably a well-positioned, powerful, and persuasive firm for the times, and Isaac and Herman Liebes were very much a part of it. The NACC's close political-financial connections with the Republican Party in Washington would certainly contribute to the early stumbling by the Harrison administration on the delicate sealing issue.

The NACC, like its predecessor the ACC, was predictably hostile to pelagic sealing. The NACC contract with the Department of the Treasury specifically prohibited the lessee from killing seals, other than through the land harvest. During this transitional period in 1889-91, there was a growing realization that the fur seal herd was being depleted to a greater extent than many had realized. This was partly due to "the failure of anyone connected with the islands to report in any meaningful way the decline of the herd" throughout the 1880s. Not until 1889 was the alarm raised by Charles Goff, a recently arrived treasury agent on the islands.[60] This particular issue would add another dimension to the already intense and somewhat convoluted diplomatic debate surrounding the fur seal question. Darius Ogden Mills singled out pelagic sealing as the primary culprit when he expressed the NACC's position in the *North American Review* in 1890: "From the point of view of the interests of commerce, the substantial issue is whether or not this commodity is to be allowed to disappear through the virtual extermination of the seal by the use of methods in the Alaskan waters which have proven fatal to its existence in every other part of the world." Mills brought out the restrictions imposed upon the NACC for the land harvest and contrasted them with "the utter lawlessness and unscrupulousness of the poachers whose appearance on the fishing grounds a few years ago led to the present diplomatic complications ... Their operations are carried on in absolute disregard of the future, their sole thought being of the immediate profit to be made by themselves out of the seals captured."[61]

Briton Cooper Busch estimated that between 1870 and 1910 the pelagic hunt accounted for approximately 1,300,000 skins, the majority in the years 1885-1905, and that at least one out of every two was not recovered. The total decline by this method would raise the loss to close to 4,000,000. However, it should also be noted that, while extensive pelagic practices contributed significantly to the problem, there had been "over-exploitation" of the land harvest in earlier years. During 1870-89, the ACC had actually harvested more than the agreed amount of 100,000 in fifteen of those years, and the ratio of skins acquired between the land and pelagic methods was seven to one. The next twenty years witnessed a dramatic change in the ratio to one to two.[62]

With growing concerns about the declining herd, the slaughter was reduced to 60,000 for the first year of the new NACC lease in 1890. In fact, they would harvest less than 29,000 that year, and in only one other year (1896) would the amount exceed 30,000.[63] What was clear was the incompatibility of the objectives of the rookeries lessee and pelagic sealers. There was also an interesting anomaly at the beginning of the new lease. When it was announced that the NACC was the successful bidder, George R. Tingle, who had served as the chief special agent of the American Department of the Treasury on the Pribilof Islands during 1885-89 inclusive, declared that their bid was ineligible because the "president and stockholders of that company had been and were engaged in pelagic sealing." Secretary Windom apparently informed Isaac Liebes that if such were the case he would have to throw out their bid. Liebes denied the charges, Tingle withdrew them, and the lease was awarded on 12 March 1890. A few weeks later, Tingle joined the NACC as a superintendent.[64]

At this point, Henry Wood Elliott, a frustrated, frustrating, and fascinating conservationist reappeared, with harsh criticisms against the NACC, the Republican Party, Herman Liebes, Issac Liebes, and Alex MacLean. As Elliott later phrased it, Herman and Isaac Liebes "corresponded, combined, confederated with one Alexander McLean, known as a notorious British pirate, for the purpose of committing, and in fact did commit, depredations on the high seas, in American waters, and on the Pribilof Islands by way of unlawfully killing fur seals belonging to the Government of the United States." Elliott would also charge Herman Liebes with perjury for swearing that Alex MacLean was an American citizen.[65] One of the difficulties in all of this is that few of the individuals involved were completely forthright about their activities. For Herman and Isaac Liebes, as Busch perceptively pointed out, "a better response would have been to separate the various branches" of their business interests. It should be noted that a corporation, H. Liebes and Company Incorporated, was organized in July 1890, a few months after the NACC received its lease. In September, the new corporation purchased all of the assets of the former partnership known as H. Liebes and Company. As for the *James Hamilton Lewis,* "without the detailed accounts of that vessel, her precise ownership will never be known, though she certainly was owned by the Liebes interests." The paper trail was complicated, but a connection remained between the Liebeses and pelagic sealing through most of the decade. No formal charges were ever made against Herman and Isaac's interests, although public accusations would periodically pop up for four decades.[66]

Elliott also deserves scrutiny, not least because he was a major source for the alleged transgressions engaged in by the NACC, the Liebeses, and MacLean throughout the period. Elliott had been on the Pribilofs as an assistant special agent for the Department of the Treasury in the early 1870s and had publicly defended the ACC and their lease from as early as 1874.[67] He was financially linked with the ACC from 1876. In 1886, the governor of Alaska described him as "a paid lobbyist of the ACC," and Elliott continued to receive a retainer from the ACC until they lost their lease in 1890. In the 1880s, "he had a reputation as a lobbyist with a wide acquaintance among the lawmakers at Washington, was known as possessing ability with both pen and brush, and had at the time considerable standing as a scientist." Elliott's pervasive influence during this period was in large part because of his Alaska experience, an authoritative manner, and his unequivocal stance. Sometimes Elliott assumed too much. He had a tendency to link himself with the Smithsonian Institute when the link was tenuous or no longer existed.[68] He was nonetheless a persistent individual. In April 1890, he was appointed as special agent of the treasury. There were those in government who would rue that day.

When Elliott returned to the Pribilof Islands that summer, after an absence of fourteen years, he was astonished to learn that the herd was only a fraction of the numbers reported in his earlier census. This was partly a result of his own questionable methodology, which had caused his previous estimate to be about 300 percent too high. As Busch remarked, "his effectiveness was forever handicapped by his arrogant assumption of infallibility in the one aspect that mattered above all – the size of the herd."[69] Elliott blamed the decrease of the herd, up until 1890, on pelagic sealing, but he now veered off in another direction entirely and began to argue "that the North American Commercial Company had, by severe and wanton driving of seals to obtain the quota of 1890, injured the testes of the male seals and rendered them impotent. He therefore recommended a total cessation of killing on the islands at once, as imperative to the safety of the herd."[70] American government officials were not prepared for his findings. For Busch, "this hasty and biologically absurd conclusion brought bewildered astonishment in Washington. In the opinion of his superiors, Elliott clearly had been smitten by some form of insanity – whether temporary or permanent made no difference – as evident in his numbers as in his causal reasoning."[71] By July 1890, Elliott was maintaining that "land killing was the primary cause of the herd's decrease," a position that considerably weakened the American government's position in their dispute with the British and Canadians. His suggested remedy, it was argued, would cause "the ruin of the company that had obtained the lease through competitive bidding, against the company that had subsidised Elliott since 1876."[72] He had made diplomatic life difficult for the American government. The secretary of the Treasury "sent other agents to the islands, all of whom found that there had been no mismanagement, and that Elliott's theory of overdriving and impotence of bulls was not only fallacious, but positively disproved by the existence of a surplus of bulls."[73]

Elliott's "monomaniac conservation efforts" would earn him the sobriquet "Fur Seal Elliott."[74] At times, commentary on his character became particularly nasty: "Rumors that insanity ran in his family and racist comments about his wife's Aleut blood surfaced in conversation and print."[75] Elliott, however, had brought to the fore the fact that over-exploitation of the land harvest could itself lead to the collapse of the herd, thus expanding the issue to include additional concerns. At this point, the question was still about property rights and international waters. Soon, the scientific question of the conservation of the fur seals widened the debate. Given the weakness of the American legal position, underlining the scale of the land killings was another of Elliott's contributions.[76] A talented water-colourist, he also managed to capture, in the wider public debate that ensued, the "attractive, gentle, and intelligent" expressions of the seals in numerous sketches, "which were the sole visual image most people had of the species." He directed a *papier-mâché* exhibition on the fur seals for the Smithsonian, probably for the World's Columbian Exposition in Chicago in 1893. Elliott had his foibles, but he also harboured some formidable strengths. He would prove the foremost defender of the fur seals for the next forty years, while he managed a modest living from occasional government employment, some monies from the ACC, his writings, and gradually selling much of a twenty-two-acre plot acquired by his father in Lakewood, outside Cleveland.[77]

During the spring of 1890, the British authorities had become convinced that some sort of closed season was necessary. They were "determined that any closed season would cover all seal killing," while the Americans wanted to leave land sealing open. The NACC was pressuring Charles Foster, the new secretary of the treasury, and Elkins was leaning directly on Blaine.[78] Although Elliott had "suggested to Blaine that conditions were so critical that only an immediate halt to both land and sea killing would save the fur seal," his reputation and motives were already being questioned. Blaine, as noted, suppressed Elliott's report.[79] From the American government's viewpoint, it was embarrassing and inaccurate. However, the diminishing herd size was becoming a concern. In its first year of operation, the NACC, experiencing difficulties in achieving their decreased quota, was thought to have illegally killed female seals and yearlings. When this was reported to Treasury Secretary Foster on 31 July 1890, the official response was apparently to reassign the agent who had reported it.[80] Elliott had repeated conferences with Secretary of State Blaine over the next few months, aggressively arguing his viewpoint that all land killing should also be stopped. At one point in December, he "went to Mr. Blaine and protested 'in a state of great excitement,' and Mr. Blaine told him to 'keep still.'" Elliott could not do so. He channelled information to the English minister in Washington, Sir Julian Pauncefote, who was quite willing to listen.[81]

Elliott's relationship with the NACC remained adversarial. Still dissatisfied, Elliott made the unforgivable mistake of going public. As the Department of the Treasury later observed, "to force this government's hand, he published in the newspapers the contents of his misleading and biased report, thereby accomplishing the object of its being made public, and at the same time, knowingly, giving to this government's adversary an advantage which practically defeated its case." He was dismissed from the Treasury service the following day. A synopsis of the report was soon published in the newspapers. Members of Harrison's administration doubtless had some empathy with the Alaskan treasury agent who had described the conservationist as "that marplot Elliott."[82]

Having inherited the sealing problem, the Harrison administration managed to compound it. During this period, the controversy was shaped less by legal considerations than by pressure from the NACC, Elliott's interventions, and Britain's decision to use force if necessary.[83] These significant diplomatic, military, and financial issues evolved as the Bering Sea controversy entered its most dangerous and delicate period. The close connection between the NACC and the Harrison administration helps to explain "the decision to send American revenue cutters to the Bering Sea on their provocative mission." This approach, in May 1890, "ushered in the most critical phase of the dispute." Lord Salisbury, the British prime minister, told his confidant, the recently appointed British minister to Washington, Sir Julian Pauncefote, to warn the American secretary of state that a formal protest would be delivered and gave secret orders for two warships in Esquimalt and two in Yokohama to be held in readiness. Salisbury suggested this information be slipped to Blaine as well. Pauncefote did not get these instructions as planned, but the Americans were "aware that London had issued secret orders that naval vessels be held in readiness."[84] The point had been made, and the Department of the Treasury's cutters were detained in Seattle. No Canadian vessels were seized (with the exception of the *Pathfinder,* which, "having been recognized as one which had been seized and escaped during the previous year," was detained in Neah Bay but later ordered released by Washington), and by mid-October, the Victoria pelagic fleet was safely back home.[85] From the Americans' perspective, it was just as well. They were wildly overmatched by the modern battleships and six cruisers that the British Pacific Squadron had stationed at Esquimalt. The antiquated sailing sloops of war manned by the Americans were inefficient, hazardous, and very slow. As one of their captains lamented, "we only overhaul becalmed vessels."[86]

The diminishing size of the fur seal herd and the fact that demand continued to surpass supply helps to explain why vessels in the Canadian pelagic fleet averaged over $20,000 in the 1890 season, even though pelagic skins received a considerably lower market price because of the hole or rent in the pelt ("northwest catch" was the term used by London furriers) and because they could not always be skinned immediately, nor salted as meticulously, as those taken in the land harvest.[87] The determination of the Canadians to continue to engage in the industry was easily explained by the profits as well as by the considerable capital investment that had been funnelled into the Victoria sealing industry. Victoria's sealing fleet now numbered almost seventy schooners and over fifteen hundred men, both Aboriginal and white. Sealskins valued at $750,000 were sent to the London fur auctions.[88] But continuing difficulties with the Americans prompted the sealers to turn to the Russian side of the Bering Sea and to Japan. Other difficulties awaited them there.

5
The *James Hamilton Lewis* and the Russians, 1891

The contentious sealing issue continued in 1891 and included some curious events on the diplomatic scene. On 16 March, American Secretary of State Blaine proposed a *modus vivendi,* or temporary agreement, for the 1891 season that would make sealers immune to seizure so long as they remained outside a twenty-five mile area around the Pribilof Islands. Then, on 3 April, the Americans offered an alternative agreement that would, pending arbitration, prohibit all killing of fur seals on land and sea. The latter was offered in the belief "that Britain was not seriously interested in any prohibition of sealing because of pressures from Canada." The lack of an agreement could then be blamed entirely on Great Britain. The North American Commercial Company (NACC), which was no stranger to the Blaine administration, was also anxious to get up to speed on its slaughter, and, eight days after the second plan was floated, the NACC received a permit to kill 60,000 seals. Then, on 20 April, the British surprised the Americans by agreeing to the alternative temporary agreement.[1] President Harrison and Secretary of State Blaine then had to awkwardly retreat from their arrangement with the NACC. Elliott did not help the Republican administration when he leaked the information to the press in early June, prompting antagonistic editorials from their opponents about clandestine permits. Eventually, an agreement was worked out on 15 June 1891 to prohibit sealing until May 1892. In effect, the Bering Sea would be closed to sealers from July 1891 to May 1892. There would only be a limited kill for food for the Native residents, drastically reducing the NACC's harvest.[2]

This approach did not have the desired effect, nor did it please anyone. The number of seals available for pelagic sealers was increased along the coast because the land harvest on the rookeries had been almost shut down. In addition, the sealers now began to target the Asiatic breeding grounds. By 1892, nine vessels had made it to the Japanese sealing grounds. The following year, there were fifty-three and, in 1894, there were seventy sealing vessels. The Asiatic seal herds would soon be drastically reduced as well.[3]

The agreement was counter-productive for the seals. It also proved extremely unpopular in Victoria, where supporters of the sealing industry argued that the price paid to secure final arbitration, and potential compensation for the earlier illegal seizures, was excessive.[4] It also underlined the sealers' previous concerns about changing regulations after they had sailed for the sealing grounds. It led to additional claims for losses sustained in 1891 because of insufficient notice. Both countries also agreed to establish a commission, with two scientists from each side, to travel to the Bering Sea to collect information. These four individuals, George Baden-Powell, a British member of parliament, George Dawson, assistant director of the Geological Survey of Canada, Thomas C. Mendenhall of the Coast Survey, and C. Hart Merriam from the Smithsonian Institution, visited the Pribilof Islands late that summer. After a few meetings, they were unable to agree on anything other than that the fur seal decline was due to "excessive killing by man," and they disbanded. When Baden-Powell was interviewed a couple of years later, it was noted that the seal population decline was due to poaching and the land harvest and also that many pups were dying "due to 'parasitic uncinaria'" and trampling by older seals, along with "accidental killing by over-driving."[5] What was important, as Kurkpatrick Dorsey notes, was the fact that the commission had been appointed in the first place. More than the Americans, whose legal case was weak, the British were definitely taking a chance in agreeing to a joint study that included scientists. This inclusion would eventually significantly widen the terms of the debate. The tribunal of arbitration would convene in Paris in 1893.[6]

The sealing industry had degenerated into a rough-and-tumble battle of wits between the sealers and the Russian and American coastguards, who set strict territorial limits on the annual hunt. Russia had proclaimed a thirty-mile protective zone around its rookeries.[7] Seemingly overnight, what had been a wide-open race for pelts became a grim struggle. Canadian sealing masters risked seizure and imprisonment in their continuing bids to hunt without restriction.[8] One contemporary Seattle periodical observed that the dispute has not "deterred the sealers from prosecuting their arduous labors, and taking their game wherever it may be found ... To use their own expression, 'they do not scare worth a cent.'"[9]

The Seattle assessment certainly applied to the MacLeans. On 11 February 1891, the *Edward E. Webster,* under Dan MacLean, departed on a "hunting and fishing trip to the north,"[10] and, a month later on 7 March, the *James Hamilton Lewis,* under Alex MacLean, was towed out to sea from San Francisco. The *Lewis* had A. Gyinburg as mate, Joseph McDonald as second mate, a cook, a cabin boy, six hunters, and fourteen able-bodied seamen. She was American-owned, with an American crew. Within two days, the *Lewis* began acquiring seals, and she gradually worked up the coast. They entered Neah Bay for mail on 24 March and continued to work the coastal waters for the next month. Dan, in his second season on the *Webster,* was in contact with Alex, on the *Lewis,* in early May. They discussed their plans for the season and exchanged some crew members. Ten days later, on 15 May, one of the *Lewis'* boats, with three men, failed to return. There was little concern at the time. That season would be long remembered as being a remarkably calm year. MacLean contacted four other vessels and "kept signals going all night." Yet due to the fine weather and the presence of several other vessels in the area, he was not particularly concerned and assumed they ended up on another of the sealers.[11]

It was probably around this time that the "battle of the Aleutians" occurred, an event that is vividly remembered by Captain Ernest F. Jordan. Jordan was a teenager, just beginning a career as a sealer working out of Victoria. He was aboard the recently acquired *Triumph* with his uncle, Captain Clarence Nelson Cox, a native of Maitland, Hants County, Nova Scotia.[12] They were anchored off one of the Aleutians. In close proximity were Alex on the *Lewis* and Captain John Dodd on the *Maggie Mac*. Dodd, a native of Sydney, Cape Breton, had sailed around the Horn in 1888 and was, according to Jordan, "a small but powerfully built man who was generally popular with everyone in the sealing fleet. The same could not be said of McLean. He was well enough liked by many, but was a hard man, much given to using his fists when he was a few 'seas over' ... Broad-shouldered and wiry, he was a born fighter who would dare anything ... the boys used to say that if ever he lost the port light of his schooner he could hang his mustachios in their place." Captain Dodd was already aboard the *Triumph,* and both he and Captain Cox welcomed MacLean on board. Perhaps being on the *Triumph,* Dan's former vessel, which was the one at the centre of the disruption of the partnership between his brother and Edgar Crow Baker, weighed on Alex somewhat. One old timer predicted trouble. "His moustache is bristling," he whispered. "It's a danger signal. There'll be trouble." The captains went below, and the crew could hear them talking and laughing. "At last the three captains came on deck again. They seemed to be jovial enough. All at once McLean gave a shout, jumped off the deck and clicked his heels together. 'I can lick any man on board this boat!' he yelled. 'Come on – I want to fight ...' Off came his broad-brimmed hat and he slammed it down on the deck and jumped upon it ... as he uttered savage war-whoops." Then Captain Dodd, "without hurry or flurry," came on deck. "Little Captain Dodd, who knew how to handle himself as well as the next man, hit out with all the strength of his compact frame. The blow landed squarely on the chin of McLean. He was unprepared for it and was off balance at the time and he reeled back, stunned, and over the bulwark he went – knocked out, and off, with a single punch." Young Jordan snagged Alex's pants with a boathook, but every time he tried to lift him up Alex's head would be forced under the surface. His crew quickly came over in their boat and retrieved their captain. "Captain Alex did not hold any animosity against anyone for the incident. It was all part of the rough and ready life that he and all of us lived. He was often on our vessel again, but he never tried to start anything. He was friendly and soft spoken."[13]

Jordan's reminiscences, printed in 1943, are filtered through more than fifty years of memories. They savour hero-worship and folklore. Another incident, with similar results, came to light thirty years after Jordan's version and was related by Archie Willis, who covered the Victoria waterfront during the declining days of the fleet. It featured Gus Folger, "a ramrod straight New Englander, who stood well over six feet. He spoke softly, using few words. There was a generally observed rule on the waterfront: 'Never tankle with Folger.'" One calm day on the sealing grounds, Alex and Dan were enjoying Folger's hospitality on his schooner. Drinks led to an argument, and Folger supposedly knocked Dan out with a chair, Alex with his fists, and dropped them in their respective dories.[14] But a sore head or a few bruises to the ego were minor hazards in the pelagic sealing fleet. In March 1892, less than a year after MacLean possibly met his match in the Aleutians, Captain John Dodd and his crew of twenty-three went down with the *Maggie Mac* somewhere between Cape Scott and Triangle Island off Vancouver Island. The average age of the crew, which included Dodd's thirteen-year-old son, was twenty-four.[15]

On 28 May 1891, the *Lewis* anchored in the outer harbour at Sitka, Alaska, replenished her fresh water supply, "and smoked the rats out of the vessel." One crew member, Arthur More, took a boat and a gun and deserted. On 1 June, somewhere outside Sitka, Alex and the *Lewis* linked up with Dan MacLean and the *Webster* again. A hunter and a seaman were transferred from the *Webster* to the *Lewis*. By 20 June, the *Lewis* was anchored in Alitak Bay. This was Will Hart's opportunity to desert, and he took it. Dan, on the *Webster*, was experiencing similar difficulties. When a couple of the *Webster's* crew were ashore at Unga, on the Alaska peninsula close to Sand Point, they read notices not to enter the Bering Sea and decided to depart as well. Dan determinedly set out with a couple of the hunters, "chased them with shotguns and rifles" and after one was slightly wounded, persuaded them to return, during which "they were required to man the boat."[16] The MacLeans were obviously up to something more than socializing and exchanging crew members during their meetings at sea. It is likely some of the crew departures were prompted by the suspicion, or conviction, that the MacLeans were preparing to combine forces to raid the Russian rookeries at Copper Island. Dan's response to a warning about American cutters just before the *Webster* entered the Bering Sea, overheard by a crewman, was suggestive: "To hell with the cutters we will go through anyway."[17] The MacLeans had not read, or were little concerned, about the recent article by the NACC's Darius Ogden Mills in the *North American Review* in which he noted that the "Russians make short work, by confiscation and punishment, of vessels found poaching in that quarter."[18]

In preparation for this foray into prohibited waters, the *Lewis* shipped two replacements in late June from near Sand Point. The fact that tensions on the *Lewis* were steadily increasing was soon evident. One of the recent crew additions was stabbed in the chest after he called another on deck to man a pump. Alex responded by making the assailant responsible for the wages and costs of the injured man while he recuperated. This action was not uncommon.[19] When the American gunboat *Thetis* appeared, as Alex noted in his log, she "warned the *J.H. Lewis* from going in the Bering Sea seal hunting, which I abide by."[20] The *Lewis* and the *Webster* then proceeded into Russian waters to prepare for the raid on the Copper Island rookeries. Some of the *Webster's* crew hesitated. Dan's shipboard discipline came into play again, and, according to some reports, "there have been lively times for all hands. A mutiny occurred on board the schooner when she was in the vicinity of the Copper Islands; eight of the crew refused to go to the boats when commanded to do so, and Captain [Dan] MacLean ordered them sent below, where he kept them without anything to eat for a number of hours until they would consent to go out." After the crew reconsidered, Alex and Dan sent twelve boats ashore and they proceeded to slaughter seals "in a fashion that was highly remunerative." Without warning, the Russian guards began shooting, and the crews raced to their boats. The next day they refused Dan's order to repeat the manoeuvre. "The crew state[d] that Captain McLean ha[d] acted in a cruel manner toward them ever since the first boat was lowered, and until the revolt occurred, and ha[d] shown them little mercy." Their refusal was a wise decision. Later, one of the raiders maintained that the crew "would have taken their lives in their hands had they made a second attempt. As it was, he says the bullets played a tune about the heads of the persons in the boats when they were leaving." Another participant later testified that "the bullets began to fall as thick as hail around the boat." One individual, Talbot, fell overboard and drowned in the excitement.[21] One source has Dan being wounded in the affair and successfully escaping from a Russian gunboat.[22] The MacLean vessels parted company at that point. Dan then targeted the rookery at St. Paul Island, arriving there in early September. He was thwarted when the crew, after discussing their options ("we didn't want to do anything against his will, but at the same time we didn't want to risk our lives"), refused to go along with his precarious plan.[23]

The *Webster* arrived back at San Francisco on 2 October, after a twelve-day run from Sand Point, reporting to A.P. Lorentzen of the Pacific Trading Company with 2,100 skins. Dan's severe approach was evident again. According to the *San Francisco Coast Seamen's Journal,* eight of her crew were still in irons because of their refusal to have another go at the Russian rookeries.[24]

Once safely back in a San Francisco boarding house, the *Webster's* crew re-evaluated their recent activities and options, and a few weeks later five of the hunters initiated legal action. They sought $500 damages and $306.66 in wages in the United States district court. They alleged that "Captain McLean made them raid the rookeries at Copper Island, where they were fired upon by Russian soldiers. Captain McLean afterward wanted them to descend upon St. Paul Island, but they again refused, and were thereupon put on a bread-and-water diet for forty-eight hours. [Two] were put in irons for four hours."[25] The case was settled and dismissed without costs to either the claimants or the schooner.[26] A reporter who boarded the *Webster* as soon as it anchored in San Francisco noted that the crew had "a more exciting time than the men of any other of the vessels that have returned to port so far."[27]

One exception would have been the experiences of Alex's crew. The *Lewis* did not make it back to San Francisco on schedule. Some later versions of the events of the summer of 1891 have Alex also making his escape. Supposedly, the Russian cutter *Alexander* was the first to annoy him. "'Lower your boat and send your papers on board,'" ordered the Russian captain. Alex shouted back, and the *Lewis* was soon skipping away. The cutter took ten miles before regaining speaking distance. "'Heave to or I'll fire on you,' yelled the Russian ... McLean turned his megaphone to the cutter and yelled, 'Fire, and be damned!'" With the stars and stripes clearly visible, the Russian prudently declined to engage the *Lewis,* and "there was whisky for all hands that night aboard the Lewis."[28] This report is suspect, however, since it came from a San Francisco newspaper in the summer of 1905, when Alex MacLean was already front-page material for another episode and had recently been linked to Jack London's best-selling novel. There would be little cause for jubilation on board the *Lewis* in 1891.

One coincidence leaps out from the events of the summer of 1891. On 29 July, the ownership of the *Lewis* was transferred from H. Liebes and Company Incorporated to Max Waizman of San Francisco.[29] Two days later, the *Lewis* re-entered Russian waters. There were only 424 skins on board. The weather had been "thick" since 30 July, and there was some dead reckoning going on.[30] The decision was then made to return to San Francisco. Alex MacLean was back on deck at 4:00 a.m. on 2 August. About an hour later, Alex "deemed it necessary to make land in order to test his chronometer, and he accordingly headed for Copper Island." Everything was apparently legitimate: "He had taken no seals since crossing the line that divides Russian and American waters; he had taken none within the limits of Bering Sea. He had not touched land since he left Sand Point, Alaska, on June 27. The seal skins on board the schooner showed that they had been taken from seals shot in the water."[31] At this point, the Russian man-of-war *Aleut* appeared on the port quarter of the *Lewis*. The Russians stated that when they headed for the *Lewis* the latter came about and "crowded on all sail." The Americans later maintained that "having approached sufficiently near to land for his purpose," MacLean's coming about when the *Aleut* began pursuit was "a mere coincidence." MacLean would also assure authorities that the schooner "had never been closer to Copper Island during the entire season" than six miles. While "in pursuit," the Russians saw something thrown overboard, although, according to Alex "there had not been as much as a bucket of water thrown over the side that morning."[32] One source has the *Lewis* drawing away from the attentive and aggressive steam-powered *Aleut,* but this move seems unlikely. The *Lewis* "was probably the slowest of any of the sailing vessels comprising the fleet" and shortly after 5:00 a.m., twelve miles from the southern point of Copper Island, the *Aleut* fired a blank shot. MacLean, "concluding she wished to speak [to] him, hove his vessel to and hoisted the American flag." They awaited the arrival of a boat from the Russian man-of-war.[33]

Lieutenant Lebedeff and six men boarded the *Lewis*. The Russian officer demanded and received the official log and the ship's papers. The logbook that MacLean produced "only contained three entries, two of which related to incidents of life on board." MacLean was adamant in his refusal to present his own log. It would later be argued that the "captain was perfectly aware of his entire innocence of wrong, and, while being a peaceable man, he was willing to waive and dispute as to the right of search on the part of a Russian war ship upon the high sea. He therefore exhibited such documents as served to show his nationality and identity, including his official logbook. He did not deem it necessary to exhibit his private logbook, showing the position of his vessel from day to day. This he was the less disposed to do upon seeing his official logbook promptly confiscated."[34] When asked his business, MacLean supposedly stated "that he had come into those waters to hunt birds and fish."[35] This point was later disputed as well, with the *Lewis'* owners simply pointing out that "it would be a person of exceedingly weak understanding who would offer such an explanation of his presence in those grounds, with seal skins and all the paraphernalia for sealing on board. Whatever may be otherwise affirmed of Captain McLean, he certainly is not such a person."[36] A hasty search of the vessel failed to detect the "easily discoverable" sealskins, although "a tub with reddened water, covered with a shirt" was noted. This discovery, it was later explained, simply "shows that a member of the crew had been employed in washing a red shirt of inferior dye." The Russians then returned to the *Aleut* with the sparsely notated official log.[37]

After a brief consultation, Lieutenant Lebedeff and the six armed Russian seamen returned to the *Lewis* and ordered the captain and most of the schooner's crew to go aboard the Russian ship. It was one thing to be thrown or knocked off someone else's vessel, but Alex obviously drew the line regarding a vessel under his command, and he "did not deem it incumbent on him to accept any order to consider himself under arrest, or to go on board the Russian cruiser and give himself up." Instead, he "made an insolent reply, as did also his mate, McDonald," and they set sail, just as a light fog began to spring up. As the Russian version phrased it, MacLean "peremptorily refused to submit to them, stating that if the commandant of the ship of war needed to see him he could come to him. Thereupon he resumed his course and continued to sail with the wind." Lieutenant Lebedeff and his men headed back to the *Aleut,* shouting: "Fire upon them, they are rascals."[38] Lebedeff signalled his ship by firing his revolver, and the *Aleut* gave chase, firing four or five volleys, and prepared to run the *Lewis* down. The collision carried away the schooner's headgear. Then "the man-of-war made lines fast to the schooner's rigging. As the schooner was being dashed against the war ship and in danger of serious damage, the mate was ordered to cut the lines that held the vessels. This he attempted to do, but the decks of the schooner were immediately crowded with armed men who took possession of the vessel. Captain McLean ... was surrounded by guards."[39] The Russians were learning quickly that when dealing with MacLean one had to act forcefully. "To the verbal summons the captain answered some words, indicating the American flag. To the cannon shot, which pierced the jib, he paid no attention." It was not until the collision, which broke the jib boom and damaged the taffrail of the *Lewis* and the after corner of the poop of the *Aleut,* that the schooner's progress was halted.[40]

There was understandably some confusion during these events. The attempt of the mate on the *Lewis,* Joseph McDonald, to cut the lines was interpreted in a variety of ways, and "some of the man-of-war's men began shouting there was a man with a knife, and [they were] afraid he was going to kill someone. In the meantime the schooner's deck was crowded with Russian guns and bayonets, and all shouting at once." MacLean and his mate apparently did not let up when arrested. As Captain Brandt later reported, "while the attitude of the crew was for the most part apparently passive, next to the captain the most noticeable was the first mate, McDonald, who, according to accounts, not entirely confirmed, however, drew a knife at the moment of arrest."[41] Many of the other versions of the capture that have come down through the years are quite similar to the official record and, thus, if the latter can be believed, are reasonably accurate.[42] What was clear was that the *Lewis* was now in the hands of the Russian authorities, and some of the sealers were understandably concerned. According to one sailor on another of Liebes' schooners at the time, "the Russians showed little mercy to seal poachers. They would confiscate the vessels and put officers and men in the Siberian mines. We took particular care not to be seized by the Russians."[43] Or as Rudyard Kipling would write in the *Rhyme of the Three Sealers* two years later:

> Now this is the Law of the Muscovite, that he proves with shot and steel,
> When you come by his isles in the Smoky Sea you must not take the seal ...
> For life it is that is worse than death, by force of Russian law
> To work in the mines of mercury that loose the teeth in your jaw.[44]

It had been a spirited encounter between the *Lewis* and the *Aleut,* and tempers obviously remained testy on both sides. Twelve hours after the seizure, the Russians "hauled down the American flag, tore said flag in shreds, threw it on the deck, and trampled upon it; that certain members of the crew of said schooner afterwards picked up the pieces of said flag and now hold the remnants of said flag in their possession as a memento of the insult offered to the American flag." The Russian flag flew in its place. As a result of their resistance, MacLean and his crew were placed under arrest. Commandant Brandt drew up an order, and MacLean wrote a protest on the back of the document. The following day, the *Lewis* and her crew were taken to Bering Island, the other main Commander Island. The Russians confiscated the 424 sealskins they had finally uncovered and transferred much of the stores and provisions to the *Aleut.* At this point, the mate and another member of the crew received permission to go aboard the schooner to retrieve their clothes and effects "but everything of value had disappeared." One man lost a gun, rubber boots, a lamb's-wool coat, and shaving outfit; two others lost three guns, gunsmith's tools, and most of their clothing.[45] The seized vessel, under Lieutenant Lebedeff, ten other Russians, and six of the crew, was then taken to Petropaylovski. The captain, mate, and the remainder of the *Lewis'* crew travelled on the Russian vessel. According to Captain Brandt, the district chief in Petropaylovski seized the moment and argued that the people in this area were very much in need of boats. The Russian harvest had been a very poor one that year. Three of the boats carried by the *Lewis* were auctioned off.[46] On 8 August, Alex signed, under duress, some papers in Russian and immediately filed a protest against the seizure.[47] His protest had no immediate impact, but it was the beginning of a long paper trail.

Subsequently, they were all taken to Vladivostok, arriving there on 28 September.[48] During this part of the trip, according to the mate, no berths or hammocks were made available to the *Lewis'* crew on board the *Aleut:* "No rations were served out to me or the members of the crew of *Lewis,* but we were obliged to eat the crew's rations – what they could spare of it – no extra allowance being provided for us. We were treated with indignities generally. This treatment was kept up until our arrival at Vladivostok, at which port we were allowed to go ashore, and for the first two days no provision was made for us, and being without money, were obliged to dispose of what spare effects we had to obtain subsistence." Once ashore at Vladivostok, they were apparently marched through the streets, in a procession headed by a Russian priest and government officials, with MacLean and his men sandwiched between soldiers. Then "they were told that they were under arrest and ordered to report at police headquarters every day." While there, MacLean was informed "repeatedly ... he could gain his liberty by withdrawing his protest, but ... he invariably refused." On numerous occasions, he demanded a trial to straighten everything out but was ignored. Meanwhile, the crew received an allowance of 7.5 cents daily (the captain and mate received 27 cents) for subsistence and ended up sleeping in an old jail "overrun with vermin and breeding pestilence" in Vladivostok. The meagre daily stipend meant that the crew had to sell some of what few clothes they still possessed, and they resorted to begging. They also worked. Albert Leslie Donaldson later stated: "We were obliged and forced to work, handling heavy timbers, loading lighters, scrubbing boots, and general all-round work aboard of a vessel, for which we received a sailor's rations."[49] The ever-active mate even tried to stow away on a Russian steamer, but he was uncovered after a two-day search. Two years later, the owners, captain, and crew would present a petition to the secretary of state asking for the American government's intervention in seeking indemnity from the Russian government. They maintained that "in consequence of the harsh and barbarous treatment received by them at the hands of their captors during their imprisonment, they became and are now emaciated in form, depressed in spirit, undermined in constitution, and permanently injured in health." For a decade, they would maintain this position. They ascribed at least one death to their treatment, although one local historian, probably taking his cue from MacLean's later recollections, would maintain that the crew had been "given the freedom of the city."[50]

Years passed and long after the entire affair was settled, Alex MacLean reflected on his experience in Vladivostok. "I had the finest time I ever had in my life," he observed, noting that not being able to leave the country was the only limitation. "I found the Russians very nice people and very hospitable – especially the naval officers. Almost every day I was aboard one or another of the men-of-war, having a pleasant time, and there was always a horse and saddle at my disposal." They had a lot of time for target practice, and, having some excellent riflemen from California in the crew, the men from the *Lewis* always "came out on top in our matches with the Russians."[51] Apparently, there were different types of contests, and not all of the Russian officers passed muster. Neil MacNeil, a distant cousin of MacLean's, related a version from Vladivostok, still circulating among relatives sixty years later, that suggested a common attitude toward Russian autocracy held by Cape Breton Gaels – and many others. The Russian port was "a mess of mud and dirt," and people, including members of one of the "swank regiments of the Czar," moved about on plank sidewalks. "When the bemedaled, bespurred, and gaudily uniformed officers strutted down the plank sidewalks, ordinary people had to step into the mud to allow them to go by. One afternoon the Sea Wolf was 'doing' the town. As he was strolling along the sidewalk he encountered three officers, walking abreast, in step, and mighty proud of themselves. As the Sea Wolf did not budge, they walked right into him. That started the fight, and the three officers landed on their heads in the ocean of mud, medals, spurs, gaudy uniforms and all."[52] Whether or not it is accurate is a moot point – it is a fine story.

On 10 October, ten weeks after being seized, the *Lewis'* crew was informed they were at liberty to leave Russian territory.[53] A report from a Victoria paper in late October noted, somewhat prematurely, that Lucy MacLean was on her way from Victoria to San Francisco, having received a cable from her husband. The *Victoria Daily Colonist* suggested that MacLean's "proverbial luck" helped him evade "the clutches of the Russian bear" and "a Siberian convict prison," and "there is little doubt, as everyone who knows him will allow, that he has accomplished the feat by cool headed pluck, and a determination to get back home in spite of everything." Few Victorians were surprised. Many apparently predicted from the start of the episode that "Alex would come out on top, no matter how serious the case was."[54] News regarding the seizure was brought to San Francisco by the Russian schooner *Leon* in late October.[55] Another report from San Francisco, which was carried in the newspapers of MacLean's home province, suggested he "escaped" by taking "French leave." There was also a version that popped up years later to the effect that the sealers bribed their way out of Russia with funds from the "MacLean treasury."[56] This scenario seems unlikely, given the proclivity of this "treasury" to frequently run dry.

MacLean and his crew departed Vladivostok just as "it was just closing down for winter" and travelled "in steerage" on a Russian vessel to Nagasaki and then on to Yokohama, where MacLean and four other crew members filed a protest with the American consul-general. They arrived back in San Francisco on 21 December 1891, almost five months after their seizure by the Russians.[57] According to one report from Portland, Oregon, "by habeas corpus or some other hocus pocus method Alexander finally escaped from the Siberian dungeon and when he again struck the Barbary coast in 'dear old 'Frisco,' there was a new swagger in his walk and a fiercer curl in the wonderful moustache."[58] Possible swagger aside, MacLean's return was an inauspicious one for a number of reasons. When the Pacific mail steamer *City of Peking* arrived at San Francisco, after a fifteen-and-a-half-day voyage from Yokohama, she was carrying the *Lewis'* crew and flying the yellow flag.

One report revealed that two steerage passengers, both members of the *Lewis'* crew, had contacted smallpox. It had been discovered immediately after leaving Yokohama. They had been quickly isolated, and few aboard the ship had been aware of the situation. The quarantine officer for San Francisco quickly issued an order that no one was to leave the vessel. The cabin passengers, concerned that they might not be ashore by Christmas, were "highly disgusted" at the turn of events. The two patients, who had apparently contracted the disease in Vladivostok, and the remaining steerage passengers, went to the newly opened quarantine station at Hospital Cove on Angel Island in San Francisco Bay. A.L. Donaldson, one of the vessel's officers and a former member of Dan's crew, was in quarantine until 5 January 1892. The mate on the *Lewis,* the spirited Joseph McDonald, would spend almost three months there. Frederick Grinsted (or Grimsted), the steward, died in quarantine.[59]

The captain, crew, and owners of the *Lewis,* while relieved that the episode with the Russians had not proved even more traumatic, refused to let the matter drop. An exchange of correspondence between the American and the Imperial Russian governments concerning the seizure soon commenced and would continue for a decade. MacLean and other crew members swore depositions in San Francisco early in 1893. In November of that year, the owners, captain, and crew presented a petition to the secretary of state, asking for the American government's intervention in seeking indemnity from the Russian government.[60] The State Department then began proceedings on behalf of the owners and crew of the *Lewis*. The Russians replied that "the complaints of the claimants [were] unfounded," and, in consequence, there was no room "for further action."[61] Later, much was made of MacLean's supposed duplicity in the whole affair. Charles Lillard had Alex pulling a fast one by substituting a new logbook for the one from the *Lewis*. He and Gordon Newell also suggested that MacLean had conned the American State Department by giving the impression that he was an American citizen.[62] But MacLean had been an American citizen since 1882, and within a few months he and Dan would sign documents on a separate sealing matter as American citizens.[63] Besides, there were influential parties aside from MacLean who were involved and determined to extract a price from the Russians. The Russian authorities later questioned the authenticity of MacLean's logbook because it was not submitted until six years and ten months after the seizure. The Americans made light of this argument and explained that a court of admiralty had not been held immediately, in spite of the repeated demand for one from MacLean. Had one been held, then the log would have been produced.[64] The case was serious enough to eventually make it to the Permanent Court of Arbitration at The Hague. At this time, the claimants alleged damages of $101,336.[65] And it was not just MacLean with whom the Russians were concerned. In 1891-92, they seized six British and six American ships just off the Russian coast. The Americans also seized two vessels engaged in raiding the Pribilof Islands in November 1891.[66] With the number of participants increasing, and the seizures, costs, tempers, and legal ramifications all rising, the Bering Sea sealing controversy continued to bedevil personal finances, regional economies, and diplomatic relations.

Alex MacLean had barely made it home to spend Christmas with his wife and daughter. He and Dan wintered in San Francisco. They would have had time to reflect on their move from Victoria to San Francisco. It had not significantly improved their situation. Dan may have been somewhat relieved that he was distanced from Edgar Crow Baker, but it did not seem to have improved his disposition – he experienced serious crew problems that ended up in court in Victoria in 1890 and in San Francisco in 1891. Wright's *Lewis and Dryden* credit Dan with catches of 1,300 and 2,100 sealskins in those years.[67] His results with the *Webster* were respectable but still a far cry from his record with the *Mary Ellen* in 1886. Alex's achievements were even more muted. Aside from the celebrated potato battle and céilidh in Drake's Bay, which quickly entered into waterfront lore, Alex had lost two vessels under his command, the *Mary Ellen* on the rocks in Alaska and the *Lewis* to the Russians. He had also caught the attention of a leading, outspoken conservationist, Henry Wood Elliott. It had not been an auspicious beginning in their new home port, especially with the fur seal dispute still bubbling on high.

6
The Japanese Coast and the North Pacific, 1892-95

In San Francisco on 1 February 1892, Alex and Dan MacLean gave depositions to be used in the upcoming fur seal arbitration proceedings. Speaking as American citizens who had collectively accumulated twenty years of sealing experience, their offerings were knowledgeable, succinct, and remarkably similar. These seasoned sealers agreed that, if the present situation continued, sealing would soon be finished. Alex gave it a decade. Dan, less optimistic, gave the industry only three more years. Alex thought it advisable to protect seals in the Bering Sea "altogether." For him, "I am interested in sealing, and want to protect the seals. I wish to say that I would like to see the seal islands protected from raids, and also the Bering Sea." Dan echoed these sentiments: "I think the seals ought to be protected ... I would like to see the islands protected from raids, and the Bering Sea also."[1] The statements were obviously scripted. These two individuals had been in the forefront of sealing in the Bering Sea for a decade and had probably acquired more seal skins from that area than any other two sealers during this period. This surprising change of attitude would fit comfortably with the perspectives of the North American Commercial Company (NACC), the American government, and even Henry Wood Elliott. Doubtless, Alex and Dan had spent part of January talking with Herman Liebes and his associates. It is possible a decision was made to develop a less confrontational relationship with the American government. The sticky connection between H. Liebes and Company and the NACC lease was a very recent memory. In addition, although an arbitration treaty was only a few weeks away, the situation between Britain and the United States remained tense. Perhaps the brothers were making preparations to bring the American government solidly aboard as they made long-term plans for the case against the seizure of the *James Hamilton Lewis* by the Russians. The depositions, considering the sources, contained some remarkable statements. Even from this distance in time, one can detect a hint of tongue-in-cheek. Within a few weeks, the two San Francisco residents went sealing. Dan, at least, headed for the hunting area off the coast of Japan.[2]

On 29 February, a treaty of arbitration was signed in Washington agreeing to a seven-member tribunal to decide five specific questions concerning exactly what rights the American government had in the Bering Sea. The arbitrators would take a year before they would finally sit down in Paris to discuss the issues.[3] Events almost overtook them. The Americans were prodding the British to renew the temporary agreement, diplomatically and publicly. Their arguments for a continuation included "a greater naval strength in the Pacific than at any period of its history" and the "moral support" of Russia.[4] In the spring of 1892, there were some tense moments in Washington and London with "a crisis of considerable gravity ... seriously jeopardising not only the prospective arbitration but also Anglo-American-Canadian good relations and, perhaps, even peace."[5] By March, President Benjamin Harrison, fighting for his political life, was close to contemplating war. The Canadian sealers remained bitter over the existing modus, and it had just been discovered that the Americans had not lived up to it anyway.[6] On 18 April, less than two weeks before it was to expire, the temporary agreement of the previous year was extended to the end of the arbitration. President Harrison again issued a proclamation prohibiting sealing in the Bering Sea. It caused consternation among the Canadian sealers.[7] For Cecil Clark, "the complicated international rules called for on and off-seasons with local variations which sealers swore were made up on the spot by Americans."[8]

In some ways, the situation was a repeat of the 1891 season. After finishing the coastal hunt, the sealing fleet was already heading for the North Pacific when it was informed of the Bering Sea closure. More than thirty boats then made fast for the Commander Islands. Thus began "the terrible onslaught of pelagic sealers on the seal herd of the Commander Islands."[9] Moreover, as in 1891, the Canadian pelagic fleet catch was quite substantial. Additional vessels came from the east and, as the *Halifax Herald* warned, "it is to be hoped that all will be successful but there may be the possibility of overdoing the thing and so killing the goose that lays the golden egg."[10] The sealers were joined by others operating out of Victoria, San Francisco, and Seattle as well as some from the coast of Japan. One boat was the relatively small forty-two-ton *Rose Sparks*. Her owner was William Sparks and her master was Alex MacLean. It is not known if Sparks had any connection with H. Liebes and Company. Given the sensitivity concerning the possible connections between Herman and Isaac Liebes, the NACC, and American sealing schooners, as well as the publicized events of the previous year with the *Lewis*, it is possible that Herman Liebes and Alex MacLean thought it wise to distance themselves from each other. On 17 March 1892, the *Rose Sparks* departed San Francisco with a crew of fourteen, bound for sealing.[11]

The Russian patrols around the Commander Islands were quite active that season. Many sealing vessels were seized by the hardworking *Zabiaka*. And, as in 1891, some Cape Bretoners were affected. The hapless *Willie McGowan*, owned by several people in North Sydney, Cape Breton, had departed from the east coast on 18 November 1891. She was seized during her first sealing season on 18 July 1892.[12] Two boats and six sailors from Charlie Hackett's *Annie C. Moore* were also caught on one of the rookeries. The Russians picked up at least six vessels that season.[13] Most were Canadian, although one, the *C.H. White*, was out of San Francisco and was associated with the newly formed H. Liebes and Company Incorporated. The Russian authorities were not impressed by their protestations, and the crews were jailed at Petropaylovski. According to J. Gordon Smith, they were "cooped up in what had been hen-houses, they fared badly, their food being a scant supply of black bread. Several died in their far-off jail, and many were treated most severely, the slightest breaches of prison rules being harshly treated."[14] United States navy commander Robley D. Evans, a new player on the scene, noted approvingly that the seized schooners were "condemned and burned. They have a good way of treating such chaps over there; the skins were taken out and sent to San Francisco to be sold for the benefit of the Russian Government, and the prisoners released, to find their way home as best they could."[15]

If the armed might of Russia posed the most pressing challenge for some sealers, many more were menaced by the United States. The NACC lease was in effect, and the rights of a duly approved monopoly had to be protected: "As the 1890's dawned, American martial enthusiasm was in the ascendancy. Crushing the seal pirates might not require sixteen warships and revenue cutters, but the temper of the times doubtless endorsed the action. And so, in 1892, Commander Robley D. Evans found himself directing the largest fleet of American fighting ships, up to that time, in the North Pacific." "Fighting Bob," as Evans was familiarly known, was a "testy character" who relished the task.[16] As he explained in his log, "I am to prepare the fleet, which I am ordered to command, for a six months' cruise in the North Pacific and Bering Sea – the second largest fleet in commission, and the most active and important work of our navy at present." Evans considered all of the possibilities, including those with horrendous ramifications: "At first it looked as if we would surely have a collision with the British navy over the seal question, and I knew, of course, that that meant a bitter and destructive war. The long struggle over the *modus vivendi* was not concluded when my instructions were sent me, and I knew the moment I read them that if I carried them out we would have war on our hands within a week. Hence I was much relieved when the terms of that instrument had been agreed on." He was also prepared for the sealing schooners, each of which, he knew, carried "a good outfit of Winchester rifles for revenue officers or others who interfered with them." His flagship, the USS *Yorkton,* was one of the new steel warships. Due largely to a crisis with Chile in late 1891, all of the new American cruisers were now on the Pacific.[17] As Thomas Bailey wryly observed, "the 'spirited' foreign policy of Blaine caused many an American to experience a pleasant tingling that may have been the rising sap of imperialism. During these years the distinguished American writer Captain A.T. Mahan, the high priest of navalism, began to preach the gospel that naval power and world power are Siamese twins."[18] An Alaskan historian later suggested that it was possible that the "Alaskan waters were an appropriate setting in which to teach John Bull that America had come of age."[19] B.F. Tracy, secretary of the navy, ended his confidential instructions to the commander of United States Naval Forces in the Bering Sea in late April 1892 with forceful directions: "The Department expects you not merely to obstruct, but to prevent the taking of seals in Bering Sea during the coming season and you will adopt such measures, and require of your commanding officers such zeal and energy, as will secure this result."[20] Evans, armed with this wide-ranging mandate, his enhanced naval muscle, and 500 copies of the proclamation, was anxious to get going: "The orders are certainly ironclad, and make me complete boss in the North Pacific and Bering Sea."[21] Captain Evans was obviously unconcerned about his own abilities or his country's aggressive stance. On 9 May, he slipped over to Esquimalt on Vancouver Island and dropped in on Admiral G.B. Hotham. Evans had a "most successful and delightful" visit and "made all arrangements for co-operation during the summer." He had reason to be pleased. As he noted, the commanding officers of the British navy's *Melpomene* and *Daphne* "will be practically under my orders, so I am really to have a big command." For their part, the Canadian sealers suspected Hotham of passing on information to the aggressive and ambitious Evans.[22]

One of Evans' approaches was to locate and seize the supply vessel for the Victoria fleet. His instructions were to warn those vessels not already served notice and to locate the rendezvous for the sealing fleet. Since Evans was responding to a violation of the American customs laws, and thus was outside the terms of the temporary agreement (which had closed the Bering Sea to sealers for another year and limited the land harvest), this latter move would be illegal. It would nonetheless have the advantage of seriously disrupting the Canadian sealing effort. Furthermore, the sealskins that the schooners usually transferred to the supply ship could be used to offset the American costs – if the Americans managed to snag her. However, neither Captain Evans, who was somewhat upset because the secretary of the navy had not advanced him to the rank of commodore to coincide with the importance of his new command, nor his Washington detectives, who haunted the Victoria waterfront, had much initial success.[23] The practice in

Victoria at this time was to send the sealing fleet out to sea with sealed orders that the schooner captains received just prior to departure.[24] In 1891, American treasury agents operating in Victoria had managed to identify the supply ship, but they had been unable to intercept it. Had they done so, it would have proven disastrous for the Canadian fleet. In the descriptive phrase of one sealing captain, the *Danube* "had the blue peter up and hightailed out," and she had returned to Victoria in early July 1891 with almost 18,000 skins from thirty-five sealing vessels.[25] Once Evans arrived in the designated waters, he would also have had to contend with deliberately false information being funnelled to the American navy from Victoria.[26]

Commander Evans steamed out of Port Townsend early on the morning of 13 May on the *Yorkton,* accompanied by the *Adams,* the *Mohican,* and the *Rush*. The *Ranger,* the *Corwin,* the *Bear,* and the *Albatross* would join up with them at Unalaska.[27] The North Pacific was a busy ocean that summer. There were 110 vessels of various registries, and the Americans served 107 notices, warning sealers not to enter the Bering Sea. If they were already there, they would receive a copy of the president's proclamation and a warning to leave immediately. There developed a certain pattern of familiarity, which was based on repetition. According to Evans, "some of them had been boarded so often that their logbooks were veritable collections of autographs of American commanders."[28] A British presence was also evident, but their approach was different. The British would sign the logbook and leave, whereas the Americans would inspect all of the sealskins every boarding. The American practice was time-consuming, bothersome, and disrupted the business at hand. As one sealer on a Liebes vessel that year noted, "taking up so many skins was quite a job, and on a fine day it interfered with our hunting. One search in a day should have been plenty, but two or three hours after one boarding, we were likely enough to be boarded and searched again. We would explain that we had just been searched, as the entry in the logbook showed, but this did no good ... This stupid business disgusted us, and after a time we refused to handle the skins for the boarding officers. Thereafter they had to bring their own men with them for that job."[29]

On 9 June, near Middleton Island, off the Alaskan coast, the USS *Mohican* searched the *Rose Sparks* and warned Alex MacLean that if he went into the Bering Sea for seals his vessel would be seized. Six days later, near one of the passes to the Bering Sea the USS *Corwin* repeated the manoeuvre and gave the message once again to the *Rose Sparks*.[30] In mid-June, Captain Evans was in a lagoon near Alitak, Kodiak Island, waiting out a gale when six sealers tucked in as well. Others followed them the next day. It was here that "Fighting Bob" Evans met Alex MacLean, if Carl Rydell, who was the same age and had a similar appearance to MacLean, can be believed. While the fleet was sheltering in Lazy Harbour, an inlet of Alitak Bay, "all the skippers of the hunting vessels were invited to come aboard the *Yorkton* for a consultation in regard to sealing. 'Fighting Bob' met us at the gangway. My appearance must have struck him unfavourably, for he asked me if I were not Wolf Larson [sic]. I told him that I had not the honour to be so renowned a character." Rydell then apparently introduced "Larson" to Evans, and they all retired to the latter's cabin for cigars and a drink. Evans "remarked that it would be useless for any of us to try to run away from him on the hunting grounds, as he could easily put a hole through our sides. We told him that we knew that very well."[31] For Evans, it was a productive meeting, although he does not mention meeting MacLean in his account.

The constant contact with the pelagic sealers had eventually enabled the Americans to finally identify the supply vessel for the Victoria fleet that season. From one of the sealers, Evans also gleaned the long-sought rendezvous point with the Canadian supply vessel. The *Coquitlam* had cleared Victoria on 8 June, under Captain B.C. McClellin, and had contacted some of the Canadian sealers at Tonki Bay less than two weeks later. The next scheduled "uninhabited bay on the remote frontier" was Port Etches. After the *Mohican's* "inept captain had bumbled the job" of intercepting the *Coquitlam,* Evans turned to the experienced Captain Calvin Hooper of the *Corwin* and ordered him to Port Etches. Hooper expressed concern, but the exchange between him and the commander of the fleet was clear and distinct. Evans stated, "He said to me that the twenty-seven schooners then in port were well armed and would fight to a finish when the time came. I replied that he had several guns of his own, and that he might rely on the *Yorkton* to be somewhere near when the shooting began."[32] Hooper, hardly a novice in these waters, had been in command of the *Corwin* since 1880 and had been the first captain of the Revenue Cutter Service to cruise regularly in the Arctic Ocean. A few days later, on 22 June, the *Corwin* seized the steamer *Coquitlam* in Port Etches. While Captain McClellin tried to argue that he was just there for water and firewood, his case was weakened as the *Coquitlam,* according to Evans, had "received about thirty thousand skins, and at the time of the seizure, in a dense fog, had her hatches open and was transplanting cargo in violation of law."[33] Actually, she had a cargo of 6,190 skins when she was seized. There were about twenty schooners and five warships in the general area at the time. One sealer from Victoria was Oscar Scarf, part owner of the *Agnes Macdonald.* Scarf was on the deck of the *Coquitlam* waiting for his mail when the *Corwin* showed up. He never did receive his correspondence. The supply vessel was towed to Sitka and, in Evans' account, was valued at $600,000.[34] "Fighting Bob" Evans' loose use of legalities ensured that this episode would take up considerable space in a variety of courtrooms for a long time. Twenty-nine years later, the Americans agreed to pay the owners $48,000 for seizing the vessel. But the seizure did disrupt the Canadian sealing season and caused considerable financial distress to a number of individuals.[35] A former associate of Alex MacLean's,

Charles Spring, was one who, as he later testified, "lost everything" in 1892, and he was soon picking up the pieces by retracing his father's earlier occupation as a trader out of Kyuquot.[36]

Another of Evans' high points was the seizure of the schooner *Winifred,* under the command of the legendary Gus Hansen, in late July. He laid charges under the American revenue laws rather than under the temporary agreement and quickly sent the vessel on to Sitka. According to Evans, "the captain of the *Winifred* commanded the *Borealis* last year and raided the rookeries on St. Paul Island, killing four hundred seals. The year before he commanded the *Adele,* raided the island, and killed three hundred and fifty seals. This year he transferred cargo in one of our ports without license ... If I turn him over to the English, nothing will be done to him for raiding, so I determined to send him in and let our courts have a shy at him ... Her captain, the most noted pirate in Bering Sea, will go to Sitka in her."[37] "Fighting Bob's" sense of pride in even getting a hold of the man known as the "Flying Dutchman" was justified. Gus Hansen was "probably the most colorful and certainly the most notorious character of the B.C. waterfront in his day" and was assuredly a thorn in the side of those who regulated the rookeries.[38] He was also not secretive. He frequently boasted of his raids and his ability to outwit the hapless patrols, thus becoming another individual on the folklore stage. He reportedly had a certain flair. On one of his excursions to St. Paul Island, he purportedly gave the guards a choice – lead or rum. They chose the latter.[39] Hansen was quite active in this period, having raided the American rookeries twice in 1890, once in 1891, and, a month before he was finally grabbed by Evans, had managed to bluff his way through a session with the USS *Mohican.*[40] The incident is significant not only for the feeding of Evans' ego and for Hansen, who would spend some time in jail in Sitka, Alaska, but also because a later study would mistakenly identify Alex MacLean as the skipper of the *Winifred.*[41]

"Fighting Bob" Evans considered his stint in the north that season a success: "And so Bering Sea has been freed of seal poachers, for one year anyway, and no war has come of it." Although later, when he was turning another seized sealer over to the senior British officer, he suggested "to keep her out of the sea in future, or we will blow the stuffing out of her." He also admitted that the "Bering Sea is the worst patch of water it has ever been my lot to tackle, and I sincerely hope I may never have it to do again."[42] Aside from the possible chat with Alex and other sealers over drinks and cigars on the *Yorkton,* Evans does not appear to have confronted either of the MacLean brothers that season, although two of the ships under his command had done so. This fact may have been due in part to the fog. As Captain Evans noted in early July, "we have had a fog so thick for two days that it seemed as if we could make a hole in it with the finger and the finger would pop, like a cork out of a bottle, when it came out."[43]

Dan was off once again in the *Edward E. Webster*. The Bering Sea was becoming more dangerous, and he, like many other sealers, headed for the Asiatic coast, acquiring 1,900 skins off Japan. For many sealers, it would be the destination of choice for the next few years.[44] Elliott later noted that Alex MacLean was "in unlawful command" of the *Rose Sparks* that season, and while "no raids [were] reported against him ... he may have been heavily engaged."[45] No other evidence suggests that Alex was involved in raids that season, and later documents confirm that he was the legal captain of the vessel.[46] However, it was not smooth sailing. Alex MacLean had a second poor season in a row. This situation possibly explains some of the difficulties on board the *Rose Sparks*. Late in September, Alex came through the Golden Gate at San Francisco "with a mutinous crew in iron and under hatches, while he worked the craft with only his mate and four boat pullers to help him."[47] It was reminiscent of Dan's return the previous year. Alex returned with only 442 sealskins. Many years later, a crew member on that particular voyage testified that, because of the warnings, they had only hunted as far as the "Pass" and did not enter the Bering Sea. However, according to one San Francisco fur merchant who had inspected the skins at the time and who was attuned to the slight differences among the fur seals of the various rookeries in the Bering Sea, they were from the Pribilof Islands.[48] Wherever they were from, there were not many of them. Financially unsuccessful voyages such as the one experienced by the *Rose Sparks* that year sometimes brought out dissatisfaction and frustration, both during and after the trip. Seamen frequently waited until they returned to the "mainland" to settle a score. This "gave an opportunity to fight a hated officer, or to assault the man when he went up a dark alley."[49] This was obviously one of those times. It may well have been the occasion for the story that has Oakland's famous Heinold's First and Last Chance Saloon as the backdrop. MacLean usually anchored on the Oakland side. He then popped over to Heinold's for a couple of shots of whiskey. Upon leaving the saloon, he was confronted by a "professional prize fighter" hired by two disgruntled crew members. "When they announced their intentions, McLean drew a gun. Eyeing the three would-be assailants, he calmly announced, 'I'll take care of the professional fighter, but if either of you two other bums get into this, I'll kill both of you.'" He then put his pistol away. "Ten minutes, the professional boxer lay prostrate on the ground, beaten to a pulp." Alex brushed himself off, returned for another shot from Johnny Heinold, and rowed back to his vessel.[50]

Masters could push their crew too far. Yet there were also risks in leniency. As Basil Lubbock, a prolific writer of maritime history who was acquainted with the reputation of "down easters" and who had sailed out of San Francisco late in the 1890s, noted, "of course there is also a certain amount to be said on the side of the captains and mates, as nowadays some crews are composed of such villainous scoundrels, that unless you take a high hand with them, and show you are not to be trifled with, they would soon take advantage of what they would call a 'softy,' and a reign of terror would begin, any sort of discipline would be impossible, the men would do just as much work as they felt inclined for, and they would openly sneer and scoff at you if ordered to do anything they did not wish."[51] Dan and Alex MacLean, with their Atlantic Ocean and down easter experience, and having operated for more than a decade out of west coast ports, understood this balance.

It is at this point that the most memorable work on sealing in American literature originates. A custom had developed whereby most of the American sealing fleet wintered in the Oakland estuary. The practice provided the opportunity for one adventurous, and occasionally thirsty, seventeen-year-old to mingle with the sealers and sailors who manned the schooners and frequented the saloons along the Oakland waterfront. That winter, Jack London "practically lived in saloons" and there he met "skippers, mates, hunters, boat-steerers, and boat-pullers." London had never been beyond the Golden Gate, but he had sailed the San Francisco Bay area for the last few years in skiffs and sloops. He was determined, hardworking, and restless. Pete Holt, a seal hunter, "sized him up as a likely young boat-puller and arranged to have him sign on as his helper for the next voyage out."[52] On 20 January 1893, eight days after his seventeenth birthday, Jack London signed on as an able-bodied seaman on the *Sophia Sutherland,* a 150-ton, three-masted schooner built in 1889 and one of the largest in the fleet.[53] Since the temporary agreement that had closed the Bering Sea was still in effect, the *Sophia Sutherland,* when it sailed three days later, headed for the coast of Japan, accompanied by at least half of the entire sealing fleet.[54] The owner, Captain A.C. Sutherland, seemed to young London to be "too old, retiring and ineffectual." London later described him as "a little shrivelled shrimp of a fellow. He didn't know anything about navigation. And he performed no duties whatever on the vessel." The *Sophia Sutherland* was actually run by the sailing master, a Captain Scott.[55] The majority of the crew were Scandinavians. From the east coast, there was only Louis, a "rotund and jovial-faced Nova Scotia Irishman," who retained his name in *The Sea-Wolf.* London had not been served up by the San Francisco crimps. He was on the *Sophia Sutherland* by choice and eager for the experience. He quickly filled in gaps in his nautical knowledge. The following seven-month trip "was smooth, successful, and ... uneventful."[56] According to Charmian, London's second wife, it was possibly "the happiest period of his whole life, that voyage in the *Sophia Sutherland*."[57] It would be London's only sealing voyage, but it would eventually prove to be quite productive. The "run across" from San Francisco to Japan would be the subject of one of London's first publications, in his Oakland high school paper two years later.[58]

London could easily have heard about the MacLeans from stories and conversations in the saloons and along the Oakland-San Francisco waterfront before his departure. At least one report circulating in San Francisco a week before London sailed had MacLean openly preparing for another run at the Russian rookeries.[59] The MacLeans had been operating out of the area for the past couple of years, and Alex's Russian adventure, which had received considerable coverage, had only ended a year earlier. If London was as yet unfamiliar with Alex and Dan, other seaman, as they spun their yarns in the fo'c's'le of the *Sophia Sutherland,* could certainly educate him. London listened. As Robert O'Brien, a waterfront correspondent for the *San Francisco Examiner,* later suggested, "in the long Bering nights, as the forecastle tales spun themselves out in the sickly yellow light of the swinging sea lamps, who knows how the hunters embellished the stories that fired London's imagination? Even then, perhaps, the true image of Alex MacLean was growing blurred, and exaggeration and fancy were at work transforming a man into a tiger."[60] Additional information was probably gleaned during the first stop of the *Sophia Sutherland,* a ten-day stay on the Bonin Islands, which was a sealing fleet rendezvous for the schooners to prepare for the northern hunt in Japanese waters. The Bonin Islands/Ogasawara were 600 miles south of Tokyo and had been annexed by Japan in 1876.[61] There, according to London, "we met old acquaintances from other schooners, fellows we had met in the saloons of San Francisco before we sailed. And each meeting meant a drink; and there was much to talk about; and more drinks; and songs to be sung; and pranks and antics to be performed; until the maggots of imagination began to crawl, and it all seemed great and wonderful to me, these lusty, hard-bitten sea-rovers, of whom I made one, gathered in wassail on a coral strand."[62] London heard lots of stories about the MacLeans that season in the fo'c's'le of the sealer and in the saloons in the Bonin Islands and Yokohama, and the *Sophia Sutherland* frequently crossed paths with the MacLean vessels while sealing in 1893. Perhaps London and his shipmates shared drinks with the crew of the *Webster,* under Dan MacLean's command, during their stay on the Bonin Islands. The *Webster* had cleared San Francisco on 10 January and headed straight there for water. The visits of the two vessels could have overlapped. London's articles in his high school paper on his visit to the Bonin Islands, which came out less than two years later, mentioned fifteen sealing vessels in the small port at one time.[63] For a while, London was apparently on Herman and Isaac Liebes' fifty-two-ton schooner *Alexander*. Alex's acquaintance Carl Rydell was first mate on that vessel that year, and he later recollected in his autobiography that London "got no favors, and he held his own with the rest of the ship's company."[64]

London acquired considerable sailing experience and information about sealing in general, and details about Alex and Dan MacLean in particular, on that trip. The material would provide much of the historical authenticity for *The Sea-Wolf.* London was sealing and sailing and absorbing valuable background material. He returned to San Francisco on the *Sophia Sutherland* in late August and had his first story, "Typhoon Off the Coast of Japan," published a few months later.[65] The stories and tales told by sailors were rich sources of entertainment, of learning, and of solace. Sharing such narratives was a significant part of their work world. The MacLeans, their exploits, escapades, and approach to sailing, sealing, drinking, regulations, and authority in general, were natural grist for this mill.[66] London later publicly acknowledged that he had heard of MacLean's "wild exploits from the men with whom I went seal hunting in 1893. MacLean had an exciting record of adventure and upon his deeds I based my Sea Wolf character."[67] Alex would have been especially hard to miss in 1893 – Stetson, moustache, and reputation aside. He was in command of another *Alexander,* a 294-ton, square-rigged steam bark, which was the largest sealer on the Pacific coast. The *Alexander* was considerably more than three times the average size of the sealing schooners, carrying twelve hunting boats, a stern boat, and a crew of forty-nine, compared with the forty-two-ton *Rose Sparks,* which had a crew of fourteen and which Alex had commanded the previous year. This unique ship was another experiment in sealing.[68] In *The Sea-Wolf,* it would become the *Macedonia,* "the only sealing steamer in the fleet," with fourteen boats and "wild talk of cannon aboard, and of strange raids and expeditions she may make, ranging from opium smuggling into the States and arms smuggling into China, to black-birding and open piracy." It was captained by Wolf's brother, Death Larsen.[69]

The steam bark *Alexander* carried Hawaiian registry that year. It was chartered to and operated by the Pacific Trading Company. This company was incorporated in California on 4 January 1893. Within the week, aside from chartering the *Alexander,* the Pacific Trading Company also came to own and operate the schooners the *Alton,* the *Webster,* the *Herman,* the *Mary H. Thomas,* and the fifty-two-ton *Alexander*. That same month, all of the capital stock of the Pacific Trading Company was issued to H. Liebes and Company Incorporated. Captain Andrew P. Lorentzen was the outdoor manager or ship's husband for the vessels. He did the hiring for the Pacific Trading Company, and seamen signed the articles under this firm. He was "a good friend to Alex MacLean." Lorentzen was also a Pacific Trading Company trustee, as was M.J. Lyon. The latter was, coincidentally, H. Liebes and Company's architect-engineer who "had charge of all their construction work and other interests." Furthermore, the Pacific Trading Company trustees met on the upper floor of the Liebes building on Montgomery Street. Sam Saalburg and Ben Goldsmith looked after Pacific Trading Company's books. Saalburg was bookkeeper and general manager of the office of H. Liebes and Company Incorporated, and Goldsmith was his assistant.[70] The Liebes' interests were still not very far removed from the American sealing fleet.

The stories about the steam bark *Alexander* that season were plentiful, circulated widely, and mainly drew their inspiration from the captain who commanded her. One report from San Francisco, dated 14 January 1893, referred to the latest "bold project" of Captain MacLean. The *Alexander,* under the Hawaiian flag, with sixty armed men and accompanied by the *Webster,* was purportedly preparing to swoop down on the Russian-controlled Copper Island rookeries, clean out the garrison, and slaughter the seals.[71] The *Alexander* cleared San Francisco on 24 January 1893 and engaged in the spring hunt off the coast of Japan.[72] On 8 April, newly re-elected president Grover Cleveland issued a proclamation that continued the temporary agreement and again closed the Bering Sea to seal hunting. Instructions were also issued to the Bering Sea patrol to capture vessels engaged in sealing there as well as those "armed or equipped for that purpose." A list of vessels "to be particularly looked after and apprehended" included those operating under the Pacific Trading Company. Commander Nicoll Ludlow, who was in charge of the United States Naval Force in the Bering Sea that season, sent out to the fleet a specific message concerning the *Alexander* on 26 May: "Enquiries should be made to locate this Steamer. She was reported as going to Japan, which she may do or not. She is also reported as full of men and well armed."[73] These developments were enough to worry some San Francisco interests. Lorentzen hurried across to Hakodate to order the Pacific Trading Company's fleet back to San Francisco. Most of the vessels concerned, including the *Webster* under Dan MacLean, were at Hakodate. Lorentzen was present when the *Alexander* arrived there, probably in early June, to replenish its supplies. Lorentzen, the Pacific Trading Company's agent, informed the *Alexander's* crew of the American proclamation against entering the Bering Sea. Some of the sealers, realizing that their season was effectively over, sought money from the Pacific Trading Company's representative. Their problem was that their initial advance had eaten up their lay, and they had no money forthcoming. The crew of the *Alexander* were particularly determined, and they "almost mobbed" Lorentzen. He had to get a police guard.[74] According to the later recollections of a hunter on board, they then did some sealing in the Russian portion of the Bering Sea, "but things were so bum that we didn't stay," and the vessel eventually returned to San Francisco.[75]

While numerous vessels were boarded by the Americans that season, the *Alexander,* although high on their list, does not seem to have been contacted.[76] Still, the stories of Alex and the *Alexander* kept popping up. A couple of them suggest gun-running. Alex supposedly got involved with "a bunch of dare-devil adventurers. What they were doing history does not relate, but we know they picked up a load of arms and ammunition from the sand dunes of Drake's Bay in California and delivered them somewhere."[77] One of his unidentified San Francisco backers was supposedly "a notorious gunrunner."[78] Yet another scenario came from his younger contemporary, Charlie Klengenberg, who was in the area at the time serving as a cook on the sealing schooner *Hara:* "One day when the men were all out in the boats I was up on deck when a barque sailed by which had just been involved in what might have been an international incident. She was the *Alexander,* and was under command of Captain Alexander MacLean." In passing, "Captain MacLean called out: 'You have not seen me!'" The *Hara's* skipper replied heartily: "No, we haven't seen a sign of you, MacLean!" According to Klengenberg, MacLean had suddenly come upon a Russian revenue cutter in the fog and quickly "fired his two old brass cannons, loaded with scrap iron, across her deck." This account also mentions a clash with an American cutter.[79] It is difficult to authenticate Klengenberg's version. A slightly different account linked both the American and Russian cutters. In this one, the steam bark carried two fourteen-pound guns, and Alex let fly with both guns when a steamer he assumed to be Russian poked its nose through the fog. This version has the American cutter *Mohican* as the recipient, and the volley disabled her engines.[80] The *San Francisco Call* later reported that Alex had been chased by an American vessel but that "he fired into and disabled the man-of-war and escaped. Even if there was no truth in the story Alex made a good catch and came back to San Francisco triumphant."[81]

The authorities had initially taken those stories to heart. When the warnings were read in Hakodate, there was specific mention of the *Alexander* being equipped with "heavy armor and guns." One of the ship's hunters later testified that she carried only "a real, regular outfit for a sealing cruise, the best that could be provided" and had no canons, only the regulation "bomb gun" for calling the boats back to the vessel.[82] This was not the general consensus at the time. According to the *San Francisco Call,* "he [MacLean] arrived at this city with the vessel after a cruise that had made him notorious on account of the stories that were circulated about the *Alexander* firing upon the United States warship *Mohican.*" Later, the *San Francisco Call* would refer to this episode as the "famous 'fake' story" that had originated in Seattle.[83] A Portland newspaper, after acknowledging the inaccuracies, continued to suggestively lay some of the blame at MacLean's feet: "Some of the elements of truth were lacking in the story but Alexander never corrected them. Bad enough was good enough for him and he revelled in the belief that he was in a fair way to crowd Capt. Kidd or Sir Henry Morgan for first place in the annals of piratical life on the ocean wave."[84]

The sailing sloop of war USS *Mohican* did not need a renegade sealer to disrupt its progress through the Bering Sea. The flagship of the North Pacific squadron that year was a "slow, deep drafted vessel with limited fuel capacity and antiquated engine," which had difficulty staying off the rocks.

She managed to run aground four times in three years, testimony to the uncharted rocks and reefs and to her unsuitability for the job. On one occasion that year, the *Mohican* became so disabled that she had to be towed 1,100 miles to Sitka.[85] Captain Ludlow, who was in command of the American North Pacific squadron that season aboard the ageing *Mohican,* had received information that Alex MacLean was now in command of the *Alexander* and carrying Hawaiian registry. Further, "MacLean made no secret that he was recruiting a crew of tough sealers and arming his vessel with the avowed intention of conducting his sealing in Bering Sea during the forthcoming season. He had boasted of his intention to resist any attempt by British or American cruisers to board or seize his ship." According to Ludlow, MacLean was expected in Alaskan waters.[86] Elliott's version also has MacLean on the *Alexander* "flying the Hawaiian flag," and although detected by the *Mohican* while attempting to raid at North East Point on St. Paul Island, he escaped in the fog because the latter's propeller was disabled.[87]

The truth was sometimes as elusive as the *Alexander*. There was a report of a raid on the American rookeries on 4 July that year: "Two unknown sealing schooners landed crews on the islands after dark and slaughtered several hundred seals. Watchmen on the islands were overpowered by the raiders, who broke into the salting houses and carried away an immense number of skins belonging to the lessees of the islands. The vessels escaped before the Government cutters could be informed of the occurrence."[88] They were never identified. There were also seizures that year by both American and Russian ships, including the small schooner *Alexander* under the command of Carl Sorenson and first mate Carl Rydell, but both Alex and Dan MacLean made it back to their home port.[89] The same could not be said for all of their crew. Dan headed for Japan with most of the sealing fleet.[90] During this voyage, on 26 July, first mate J. Jacobson, hunter E.J. Sullivan, and carpenter and boat-steerer Dan MacInnis (a Cape Bretoner) "strayed from the vessel during heavy fog and sea" while hunting and were lost.[91] Dan MacLean reported the incident when the *Webster* returned to San Francisco on 11 September with a catch of 1,670 skins worth $25,000.[92] It may not have been the only incident he had to report. The *Webster*'s crew, upon their return, numbered twenty-one, which was ten fewer men than when she departed.[93]

Stories of intimidation, intrigue, and confrontation followed the voyage of the *Alexander* that season right up until the completion of the trip: "When the *Alexander* dropped anchor in the bay MacLean reported that he had a mutineer on board. The man had been ironed and kept in his room for several weeks for an alleged breach of discipline. There was always a mystery connected with his particular case, as some of the *Alexander*'s men said that MacLean had no legal right to detain the fellow." The source of this report, the *San Francisco Call,* also maintained that "six Japanese had been shanghaied from their native land and turned loose to starve in San Francisco." The managing owner of the vessel, Andrew P. Lorentzen, apparently had "his hands full when the steamer *Alexander* came into port trying to pacify the 'kickers.'"[94] Whatever the problems, and whatever Alex MacLean had been up to in 1893, the *Alexander* proved too expensive to operate in the sealing business.[95] The 1893 sealing season, and the stories relayed in the fo'c's'les of the schooners and the waterfront saloons, would pop up in a spectacular way a decade later – to the chagrin of Alex and Lucy MacLean.

In May 1893, a provisional agreement had been reached between Russia and Great Britain, which established a protective zone of thirty miles around the Commander Islands and Robben Island. It would be of little value to the seals.[96] The Paris Tribunal of Arbitration concluded its deliberations in August. It was determined that the Bering Sea was not a closed sea and that the seals could not be protected outside of territorial waters. Essentially, the Americans lost the legal argument. They also "missed an opportunity to acknowledge that the seals were common property in need of international protection" as neither of the scientists on the earlier commission, C. Hart Merriam and Thomas C. Mendenhall, were on the American team that travelled to the tribunal. Their report was tucked away among the sixteen volumes produced by the proceedings. Damages for prior seizures were to be left to the two commissioners.[97] The American Congress balked initially, with some members arguing that if Victoria sealers were to be compensated then American vessels should be treated similarly. The compensation to Canadian sealers would take a few years to resolve. The American sealers' side of it would take decades to be heard.

Nevertheless, an agreement was now in hand, and it included yet another set of regulations. There would be a sixty-mile radius prohibited zone around the Pribilof Islands and a closed season from 1 May to 1 August. Firearms and explosives were also prohibited.[98] While the *New York Times* felt that "the seals are safe at all events" and that the regulations would "ruin the poaching business," others were more doubtful and with good reason. "Nursing females habitually ranged farther than 60 miles from the Pribilof Islands in quest of food where they remained vulnerable to pelagic sealing. A closed season during May, June, and July allowed females to reach the islands and bear their young, only to be killed in August when at sea for food. Pelagic sealers successfully foiled the firearm restriction by employing skilled Indians using spears and canoes." Nor did the award prevent the pursuit of the pregnant seals from January to April along the coast. Also, the regulations did not include American and Canadian ships operating under the Japanese flag from Japanese ports, enabling them to catch seals all year, in all waters beyond the three-mile limit, "and by whatever means they pleased." There remained a lot of work to be done before the various issues would be resolved. The important question of compensation for the earlier illegal seizures would drag on for most of the decade. Nevertheless, the tribunal's decision was in place for five years, so there was a bit of breathing room.[99]

The Americans, having lost the legal approach, now began to gradually move back toward a scientific stance. As Kurkpatrick Dorsey argues, it met with a positive response from the British: "In this shift, Americans received help from British leaders, who for three reasons moved toward compromise. First, they increasingly saw the need to maintain the friendship of the United States in a dangerous world. Second, American scientific evidence suggested that continued pelagic sealing might destroy the species and therefore undermine the London fur industry. Third, believing themselves the most civilized people in the world, the British had difficulty sanctioning the killing of female seals."[100] One "extraordinary and unexpected sequel" to the controversy was that the NACC was now deemed by Attorney General Olney to be liable for the full yearly rental of their lease, regardless of the amount harvested. The amount owed for the 1890-92 period was $290,000. There was also the question of the fees and rent for 1893. The NACC had been limited to 7,500 skins that year, and a protracted legal wrangle began. In March 1893, the Democrats, under Grover Cleveland, were back in office.[101] The new regulations offered little protection to the seals, and did not please the Victoria sealers. As a report out of Victoria, which was carried in the *New York Times,* phrased it, "they bitterly complained of the high-handed manner in which they are being treated in the interest of American speculators and capitalists, for whose benefit their rights and the comity of nations are, they allege, being infringed."[102]

The Bering Sea was now open again, and, at least with the regulations set down clearly, the "sealers departed for the season's cruise with none of the uncertainties regarding their rights which had troubled them in previous years." The year 1894 witnessed the largest pelagic fleet that ever set out, reaping the largest catch ever for the industry. Low prices, however, meant "few of them made any money."[103] Dan MacLean, in his final sealing voyage on the *Webster,* left earlier than usual, departing San Francisco for Japanese waters on 2 November 1893. He began sealing on 29 January 1894. The majority of the Canadian fleet cleared for Japan in early January.[104] Alex MacLean was not far behind, leaving San Francisco on 14 January on another schooner, the 160-ton *Bonanza.* She was owned by the Pacific Trading Company of San Francisco and, like the *Webster,* was linked to H. Liebes and Company Incorporated. The managing owner of the *Bonanza* was Lorentzen, Alex's "good friend."[105] The *Bonanza,* twice the usual size for sealing schooners, carried a considerable number of supplies for the other vessels of the Pacific Trading Company, which she would service in port or on the sea and then transship skins back to San Francisco.[106] Alex departed

San Francisco on a stormy day. It set the tone for the trip, as the account in the *San Francisco Call,* one of the west coast newspapers most critical of the MacLeans, suggested. The mate, one John Parker, protested, "saying that it was dangerous to go outside in such heavy weather. McLean jumped upon Parker, beat him severely and sent him ashore in a boat."[107]

One individual who was out on the sealing grounds that year for the first time was W.G. Emery. "I was enjoying an outing on the Oregon coast, when I chanced to meet an old college classmate who had just returned from a successful sealing cruise; and I heard so much of his experiences and adventures that finally I asked him what chance there would be for me to go with him the next season. He looked thoughtful a moment, then said: 'Well, it is pretty hard for a "greeny" to get a berth, but I will see what I can do for you.'" Emery's college connection worked, and a few weeks later he got the call.[108] This episode is interesting for a number of reasons. College graduates were doubtless a rarity in sealing crews. Little is known about Emery, but he was, in all likelihood, at least middle class. While many members of this segment of society were participating more and more in big game hunting as they sought to call attention to their masculinity – what Tina Loo has portrayed as "bourgeois masculinity" – Emery goes a step further.[109] Not for him the expensive, meticulously planned expedition. He was not looking for a trophy to display in his den, but he was searching for adventure. To slightly paraphrase an observation of Amy Kaplan's, "the [Pacific] figures as the site where you can be what you can no longer be at home – a 'real live man' – where you can recover the autonomy denied by social forces of modernization."[110] Emery would relate his experience in *Outing,* a prosperous American outdoor magazine with a circulation at the time of 90,000.[111]

On 1 January 1894, Emery headed out from Astoria, Oregon, as a hunter on the American sealer *Louis Olsen*. Two weeks later, they skirted the Hawaiian Islands and soon picked up the northeast trades and headed straight for Yokohama. In mid-March, they went to the sealing grounds. Emery presented a detailed and informative picture of sealing activities from a hunter's perspective: "Each boat, lest it should get lost, is provided, before leaving the schooner, with five days' provisions, five gallons of water, one dozen sky-rockets, a 'flare,' and a compass." Sometime in April, heading back to the schooner after a successful day of sealing, two of the *Olsen's* boats, including Emery's, returned to a slight surprise. "About dark we made out the schooner directly ahead and were soon alongside, but to our astonishment and dismay she was not the *Louis Olsen* but the *Edward E. Webster,* of San Francisco, McLean, master ... Captain McLean invited us aboard, telling us we had better not start out again that night as it was beginning to breeze up, but that soon as all his boats came in, he would run down about eight miles to leeward and see if he could find our schooner; if not, he would work in the other direction and probably pick her up the next day." Emery and his mates accepted the offer. When a boat from one schooner was picked up by another, the crew were considered to be part of the host schooner's crew. Any seals acquired during the stay belonged to, in this case, the *Webster*. The skins they had brought with them were packed and a receipt was given. In Jack London's *The Sea-Wolf,* when Larsen was short, he simply took possession of the next boat and crew he came across.

Rough weather followed for three days, cancelling any hunting. One hunter later related what he'd told his crew mates: "If we expected to get back to our schooner soon, we had better take advantage of the first opportunity and make a run for some other vessel, for Captain McLean's brother was somewhere near us in another schooner, the *Bonanza,* which was short-handed, having lost two boats and crews; and it was the intention to find her and put us aboard, when we might as well say good-bye to our schooner, for the other's captain would take particular pains to keep out of the way of the *Louis Olsen*." Forewarned, they boarded a Victoria sealer, the *Geneva,* that evening. The *Geneva,* however, already had a lost crew aboard and so the following day Emery and his colleagues came across yet another schooner, the *Penelope,* out of Victoria under Captain McGrath. One of the hunters with Emery had been on her for the previous two seasons, and, with plenty of room, they remained on the *Penelope* for a month. Finally, after doing more searching than hunting, Emery and his mates were rewarded as they returned at the end of yet another day to the *Penelope*. "When we got almost back, I noticed a boat towing astern of the *Penny,* that someway had a familiar look; but before we had quite made it out, we heard a cheer, and saw Davis and his men in the rigging, waving their hats to us, and we knew we were no longer 'tramps of the sea,' for the *Olsen* could not be far off. A few minutes later we ran down to the *Olsen*. We were met by a ringing cheer, all hands crowding around us, and everything for the moment was forgotten in the joy of our reunion. A very liberal 'splicing of the main-brace' ensued in honor of our return." Emery and the *Louis Olsen* spent the last part of the season in the Bering Sea. "After standing bad weather for nearly five weeks we gave it up in despair, and on the morning of the fourth of September we turned tail to a heavy nor'west gale, and flew, *homeward bound*." The crew had caught 1,372 skins. Emery accounted for 208 of them. The *Louis Olsen* anchored in Victoria harbour on 15 September.[112] The anonymous tipster on the *Webster* had done Emery and his mates a considerable favour. It was not a good year to be on either the *Bonanza* or the *Webster*.

Alex called at the Japanese ports of Hakodate and Yokohama that season. Both were treaty ports. Hakodate hosted several hundred foreign seamen yearly, mostly pelagic sealers. It was a little seaport on the island of Hokkaido, "which Victoria sealers were intermittently taking over or taking apart."[113] The chandler and provisioning merchant firm in the port, T.M. Laffin and

Company, was one of the many attractions that made it a frequent stopping point for the pelagic fleet. Herman and Isaac Liebes had someone, possibly Laffin, looking after their interests there as well. But some schooner skippers viewed Hakodate unfavourably "as it had a bad influence on the crew," given the inclination of some sailors to indulge in a bit of sake after a long voyage.[114] George Cessford remembered being with Alex in a Hakodate bar during this period when "a general free-for-all developed," and one giant sealer purportedly tore out half of MacLean's moustache. "'He was madder'n a bull,' chuckled George, 'but although he always carried a gun, he never drew it.'"[115] Alex's moustache was one of the most commonly mentioned characteristics of his physical appearance and may have been hard to resist in a scuffle.

The situation did not improve in Yokohama. Both Alex and Dan made a questionable impression there. The *San Francisco Call* was quick to remark: "The McLean family seems determined to get itself into trouble no matter what part of the world it takes itself to. The brothers McLean have become notorious in every quarter of this spacious sphere as commanders of 'American' sealing schooners which as a rule are about as un-American in the matter of their management as anything that floats." Dan apparently arrived in Yokohama with a story "that twenty-two of his men, whom he alleged were signed at San Francisco and belonged to the local Sailors' Union, were in mutiny and had threatened his life." There was also an anti-sailors' union spin in the reports. The United States consul-general in Yokohama began to unravel the widely varying versions of events on the *Webster,* and "the longer he listened the madder he got," the *San Francisco Call* reported: "He found that there was not the slightest excuse for charging the men with mutiny and that the stories told about them being 'horrible union men' were exaggerated vastly. Some of the men had shipped at the union's office in San Francisco, but every one of them was working on a 'lay' and could not possibly have any reason for not working to capture as many seals as possible. Several of the crew, it was shown, had refused to go out in a boat when the weather was very foggy and a strong breeze was blowing ... every man was honorably vindicated."[116]

Meanwhile, Alex arrived in Yokohama with ten Japanese in shackles. This "pugnacious skipper's rash act" caused some excitement, according to the authorities: "Imagine the sensation when Alex appeared on the scene with his ten manacled Japs and told a cock-and-bull story about the little brown men refusing to do a stroke of work." As the *San Francisco Call* reported, "Alex told the queer story of having paid his Japs $50 advance money, and alleged that not a man of them would do any hunting. The Japs protested, and declared that they had been most shamefully abused. They were made to remain chained to the decks through all sorts of weather, and suffered untold miseries during their time on board the Bonanza." Little wonder the authorities in Yokohama "thought it rather strange that the two vessels commanded by the McLeans should always be troubled with mutineers."[117] Such proceedings doubtless had an impact on the 1894 sealing harvest, although one report has the *Bonanza* returning with the largest catch of any San Francisco schooner that year.[118] The *Bonanza*'s haul of almost 2,200 skins probably included some of the catch from other schooners connected with the Pacific Trading Company.

Financially, 1894 had not been a particularly good year. Very low prices for the skins severely restricted profits. The difficulties aboard the *Webster* that season disrupted the hunting and ensured that Dan "lost a good deal of time and money."[119] He returned to port with 1,800 skins and did not secure a ship the following year.[120] Yet the continued success of at least some of the pelagic sealers that season prompted an American proposal to simply slaughter the entire Pribilof herd. The reasoning, such as it was, was to pressure the British with the potential loss of jobs in the London fur seal business. The bill passed the House of Representatives in Washington but was tabled in the Senate.[121] It would later reappear.

With the British and Russian fleets mobilizing in eastern waters in 1895 and significantly reducing patrols around the rookeries and in the Bering Sea generally, some reports suggested that "seal poachers [had] been reaping a harvest" on the Russian seal herds on the Commander Islands.[122] For whatever reason, Alex MacLean did not catch any of this action. He took out the *Emma and Louise* in 1895. It was an eighty-nine-ton schooner, built in Little River, California, in 1874, which had joined the sealing fleet in 1891. It proved to be another poor season for Alex. He managed only 350 skins off the coast of Japan and 504 skins in the Bering Sea by the time he finished on 18 September. Clearly, Alex was wide of the mark and had to settle for ninth best out of the thirteen vessels departing San Francisco that year, although the *San Francisco Call* thought "his share [would] keep the wolf from the door for many months to come."[123] Most of the American sealers had not even bothered to get sealing licences. American involvement continued to diminish.[124] The *Emma and Louise* returned to San Francisco on 14 October, minus three men who had been drowned when a thresher shark attacked their boat.[125]

The bad weather, the low prices of the past three seasons, and their difficulties with crews, rookery guards, and cutter patrols all had a financial impact on the MacLeans. Dan did not have a vessel to command that season and was running out of money. He would not embark again on a sealing voyage out of San Francisco. The potential for the 1896 season did not look any better, so Dan prepared to try his luck in Central America with the schooner *Una*. Both MacLeans, but especially Dan, were being hard-pressed by their creditors. Dan's decision to sail to Central America had found its way into the waterfront rumour mill. Soon the rumours also had Alex included in the trip. Anxious creditors of the younger MacLean ran to the sheriff. It was clear that the MacLeans were becoming news whenever there was something just a bit out of the ordinary. The *San Francisco Call* was not one to pass up reporting on the comings and goings of Alex and Dan MacLean, and the newspaper article was titled "After the M'Leans Again," with the subtitle, "Alex and Dan Are in Trouble with the Sheriff's Office This Time." The article read: "Alex and Dan McLean, the two most daring seal-hunters in the United States, are in a peck of trouble. The Sheriff is after one of them, but just which one he wants seems to be the question at issue. The brothers are as alike as two peas, and Dan is frequently taken for Alex, and vice versa." A deputy sheriff spent the morning scouring the waterfront for Alex and, finding Dan, took him to city hall. "There the mistake was explained; but Dan said it was all right, as he would stand responsible for his brother, and that when they had one of the McLeans he was just as good as the other. The Sheriff did not look at it in that light, however, so Dan went out and found his brother." The confusion was soon worked out and the report ended on an optimistic note: "Alex is not going to run away, and will take the *Emma and Louise* out again next season. Dan will also secure a schooner, it is said, and if the rookeries hold out the brothers will probably come back rich men next season."[126] The San Francisco waterfront settled down again. But the *San Francisco Call's* prediction would prove incorrect on most points. Neither Alex nor Dan would go sealing in 1896.

For thirteen years, Alex and Dan had been pathfinders, poachers, and fleetingly profitable partners and competitors in sealing. They were acknowledged as two of the most successful sealers on the west coast. This era had now ended. Aside from a spectacular reappearance by Alex a decade later, the MacLean brothers would no longer directly participate in the sealing industry. It was a good time to depart.

Their timing may have been connected to the shuffle going on in H. Liebes and Company Incorporated. Due to a medical problem, Herman Liebes moved to London, England, in 1895, and, in an interview about the present sealing industry (where he referred to the NACC as "my company"), he explained: "I do not myself believe that any solution can be found which does not include as one of its terms the absolute prohibition of all pelagic sealing. This ought not to be a difficult matter to arrange, having regard to what I assert as an undoubted fact, viz., that pelagic sealing is not, and cannot be, under present conditions, profitable." Herman Liebes died in London on 28 February 1898. He was not quite fifty-six.[127] According to one of their sealers, Isaac Liebes took over the helm of the company around the time Herman moved to London. A more distant style of entrepreneurship meant the dismantlement of the somewhat amiable, if paternal, relationship between the company and the sealers. A replacement for the Liebeses' interests in Hakodate had to be "mobbed and stoned" before he accorded the sealers reasonable treatment. The individual they now had to deal with in San Francisco was, in Carl Rydell's words, "a snob, and he did not like to see a man who worked get more than enough to keep him alive."[128] The next few years would be very poor sealing seasons, and the pelagic fleet would continue to be disrupted. The Americans had seized three Victoria vessels in 1895, and many more were subjected to frequent visitations. American vessels fared no better. Jack London's old vessel, the *Sophia Sutherland,* would face three charges under the sealing regulations that season.[129]

7
The Bering Sea Claims Commission Hearings and Percy Sherwood, 1896

Early in January 1896, a bill was introduced in the American House of Representatives "to prevent the extermination of fur-bearing animals in Alaska." It recommended that a joint commission be established to deal with the problem. The bill stated that "the Alaskan fur-seal herd is being rapidly exterminated by pelagic sealing vessels," primarily Canadian, and that it "is believed by experts that the herd will be so nearly exterminated as to make it very difficult to restore it; and that if pelagic sealing continues, within five years not only the Alaskan herd, but also the Russian and Japanese herds, will be well-nigh extinguished."[1] The following month, one of the major outstanding issues – one that was of immediate and intense interest to the Canadian sealers, namely, the claims for the illegal seizures that dated back to 1886 – was referred to a judicial tribunal.[2] Another legal dispute, the seizure of the *James Hamilton Lewis* by the Russians in 1891, continued its slow march to resolution as well. George R. Tingle, who had earlier been associated with the American Department of the Treasury and then the North American Commercial Company (NACC) and who was presently the attorney for the *Lewis* claimants, now forwarded some new evidence to the American State Department that included additional affidavits and Alex's original logbook. The appearance of the logbook after such an extended period suggested to those of a suspicious mind that it might be less than trustworthy. The Russian government was numbered among such skeptics, but as Tingle assured Secretary of State Richard Olney, "any fair and dispassionate mind" could rest easy as to its authenticity.[3]

Alex MacLean spent the summer of 1896 halibut fishing. In the autumn, he was in San Francisco "looking for business there." One of the main topics along the west coast waterfront that season was the upcoming Bering Sea Claims Commission (BSCC) hearings. Alex later gave assurances that during that time, while "of course [they] used to talk about this commission going to meet" in Victoria, he was not looking up evidence for the hearings: "I swear that I never looked up any evidence in San Francisco."[4] At some point that autumn, Alex MacLean was in Victoria doing a bit of reconnaissance before his appearance at the BSCC hearings. His role would be that of an expert witness on the sealing industry for the American government. His primary contribution would be to assess the value of the vessels and gear impounded in 1886-96.[5] His years working out of San Francisco, his sojourn in Russia, and his trips to Japan had left him no worse for wear. A childhood friend who had relocated to Victoria and who kept in touch with Cape Breton relatives wrote, "I see my old school mate Capt. Alex MacLean every day now. He is here in connection with the sealing commission ... He looks just the same as when I saw him seven years ago."[6] Doubtless, Alex would have looked up his first cousin, Kate MacCormick MacLean, upon his return to Victoria. On these visits, according to family tradition, Alex would announce his arrival by pounding on Kate and Peter MacLean's door and exclaiming in a loud Gaelic voice: "Fosgail an dorust a Cheat! Tha an deamhan ann!" ("Open up the door, Kate! The devil's here!") He invariably arrived with tea and red ribbons for their daughter's black hair. These visits offered an opportunity to converse in Gaelic.[7]

Early one evening in the autumn of 1896, Alex was in the Garrick's Head in Victoria. Also in attendance at the popular watering spot was Tom MacInnes. Tom was a writer, poet, and lawyer attracted to the shadows.[8] He was the newly appointed Canadian secretary to the BSCC. According to Tom, "it was a whiling hour, and between drinks the bartender told me there was a man sitting alone at a table near the window who wanted to speak to me. I sent word for him to join, and he came up. He was slim, trim, medium height, with very broad shoulders, blue eyes and an unusually large reddish brown moustache. He was of the handsome Highland type found among Nova Scotia seamen. I mind he wore grey trousers and a heavy, dark peajacket with brass buttons and cap to match."[9] MacLean was interested in finding out how long it would be before he would be able to give his evidence. He thought MacInnes would be able to give him some sense of the schedule. During "the course of getting to the bottom of that [they] had one drink and another." This led Alex to invite Tom to dinner that evening. The offer was accepted, and they moved on to the Poodle Dog, "a first class eating house."[10] Alex liked to know what was going on, and he generally seemed to be well informed concerning waterfront activities and individuals. Singling out MacInnes suggests that he was aware that the sessions on sealing claims were not their only common thread. Tom, nine years younger, was a native of Ontario. But Tom's father, Senator Thomas Robert MacInnes, was a Gaelic speaker, born in Lake Ainslie, Inverness County, Cape Breton.[11]

That autumn evening in Victoria in 1896 proceeded apace, and Tom MacInnes recounted the night of wining and dining in fine detail. Both he and Alex proved to be excellent storytellers. They were assisted in part by the setting. The Poodle Dog's chef was Louis Marboeuf, who prepared dishes "with the same care one gives to the structure of a sonnet." Having ordered mussels and blue grouse, MacInnes looked around and noticed Vanilla. He "had known her elsewhere as one of the quality; but she was then living quietly and in reduced circumstances at Victoria ... but her troubles had only left her sweeter than in her earlier years; as one may find a ripe hot berry in July sweeter by far than the tart impudence of the berries in early June." She joined them for dinner. Alex's "manner was gentle, and his words carefully chosen. He was evidently much impressed by Vanilla." The wine loosened his tongue, and during the repast Alex produced a small chamois bag. Eleven sizable pearls rolled out on the tablecloth, including "a large, oval, salmon-pink" one. "Vanilla was greatly taken with that one. Naturally she asked him how he had come by them. He answered that he had gotten them honestly and openly as a poacher in the South Seas." Alex had received information from a friend, "indefinitely confined at San Quentin," and sailed a schooner to a French island in the South Pacific. The trick was to get there and away without being noticed by any prowling French gunboat.[12]

Alex's prowess as a storyteller was evident as he continued to relate the uncovering of the pearls and, ultimately, his escape from a French gunboat. It was quite a tale – and quite an evening – and there was a final stanza to the story. "The next time I saw Vanilla," MacInnes remembered, "she showed me the pink pearl. I asked her if she were going to have it set for a ring or a pendant." Later that month, when MacInnes was biding farewell to MacLean, the latter "was rather self-consciously but proudly wearing the pink pearl in his tie, neatly set in five golden claws. For Vanilla was that kind of a girl; she had delight in giving as well as receiving the unexpected gift. And her way was smooth, and her heart was sweet; even as her name."[13] While not casting doubt on Alex's storytelling ability, this vignette is filtered through the lens of poet and romantic Tom MacInnes, which helps explain the archetypical elements.

Alex's reception in his old home port was mixed. By late September 1896, the Canadian government was collecting its legal team for the BSCC. Fred Peters had resigned his position as attorney general of Prince Edward Island and was appointed as senior British counsel. He would be assisted by F.L. Beique of Montreal. E.V. Bodwell of Victoria, a sometime business associate of Edgar Crow Baker, became the local representative and junior counsel.[14] They immediately got to work.[15] Baker carefully watched the proceedings and frequently dined and was otherwise in contact with Peters, Beique, and Bodwell.[16] There was another member of the Canadian team whose participation was not publicly acknowledged at the time. Major Arthur Percy Sherwood, commissioner of the Dominion Police in Ottawa and an officer in the 43rd Ottawa and Carleton Battalion of Rifles, was about to go undercover. He had previously done some investigative work involving sealers in British

Columbia and San Francisco in 1892.[17] As Sherwood confided to a friend in December 1896, immediately before departing for the west coast "where I have some confidential work to attend to," he was going incognito: "I am very anxious that nothing should be said as to my whereabouts while I am away, so please keep it confidential."[18] In Seattle, on his way to the San Francisco waterfront, Sherwood received his instructions and, while not overly optimistic, told Fred Peters: "I can only assure you I will spare no effort to accomplish satisfactory results during my stay in Frisco."[19] The minister of marine and fisheries, L.H. Davies, was in the Victoria area at this time, and he attended one of the early sessions of the commission hearings and visited with his old betting partner, the Honourable James Baker.[20] While Sherwood was making fast for the west, Alex MacLean, who had been subpoenaed by the United States on 8 December, had already begun his testimony. Alex would give evidence and be examined, cross-examined, recalled for re-direct, and subjected to a variety of degrees of scrutiny by legal counsel on at least nine different occasions during the Victoria hearings.[21] Alex was one of the first witnesses called, and he initially gave evidence on 11, 12, and 14 December regarding the value of sealing vessels.[22]

The Americans were at a disadvantage in Victoria. As Don Dickinson, senior American counsel, later explained, "we were brought for the hearing to the principal seat of the pelagic sealing industry of Canada and Great Britain. At that port the complaining British ships were for the most part outfitted for Bering Sea. Among this population from which testimony was to be drawn there was naturally a hostile feeling toward the United States, and toward any person among them having knowledge of the facts who shows any disposition to furnish information in chief on the stand for this Government, or to furnish information on which the statements of the witnesses for Great Britain might be tested on cross-examination."[23] Dickinson led MacLean slowly into his testimony, establishing his experience and his knowledge about west coast sailing vessels. The following morning, Dickinson continued his direct examination of Alex MacLean. Fred Peters then subjected Alex to a rigorous cross-examination.[24] The latter elicited a couple of occasions when Alex had been in jail. One time was in Halifax for six hours seventeen years earlier (actually it had been six days) and the other was in San Francisco for a few hours for fighting. He had been acquitted on the latter occasion.[25] It was also brought out that Alex had attempted to cover up his co-ownership with Charles Spring on two of the vessels that would figure prominently in the commission hearings by some simple scratching and pasting, but the prosecution quickly gave up on this far-too-obvious tack.[26] Dickinson had no reservations about Alex's background: "This witness has been repeatedly attacked as to his credibility and we are willing to have the fullest enquiry as to any act of his life." He stood the test. Since the main issue of these hearings was to fix a "just and proper sum" of compensation, Alex was thoroughly grilled on the value of many of the west coast sealing vessels. When the commissioners took their seats on the morning of 14 December, Peters continued his cross-examination. Doubtless there were times when Alex wished he was with Dan in Mexico.[27] After an exhausting three days on the stand, Alex had a two-week reprieve and returned to San Francisco.

Meanwhile, Percy Sherwood was approaching the problem with all due caution. As he explained to Peters on Christmas Day, "I beg to report for your information that up to the present I have not succeeded in getting hold of anything of consequence or worthy of special note but this is probably due to the fact that I am making haste slowly in order to feel my way and avoid mare's nests if possible." He told Peters: "Those of our old friends of 1892 to whom I have made myself known [are] still disposed favourably and willing to help." Further, "it is rumoured that McLean has been working here for some time for the other side at $5.00 per day." Sherwood placed a considerable amount of emphasis on the $5.00 per day aspect, but the United States counsel, Dickinson, brought it out openly a few days later. And to keep things in perspective, it should be mentioned that the Canadian lawyers Beique and Bodwell, in addition to their retainers and expenses, were receiving $50 per day and $30-$40 per day respectively.[28]

Undercover agents obviously did not take much time off for Christmas festivities. On Boxing Day, Commissioner Sherwood warned his bosses in Victoria that American Secret Service agent Harris and his son were "working up evidence here for a good while" and that N.R. Harris Jr. was probably operating in Victoria under an assumed name. The elder Harris was in charge of the American Secret Service office in San Francisco. His son worked out of there as well. They were acquaintances of Alex MacLean.[29] Sherwood was always on the lookout for anything or anyone to strain the credibility of the Americans' expert witnesses, and he and others placed considerable weight on the fact that Alex was but a common seaman and a boat-puller for Warren F. Upson aboard the *San Diego* in 1883 and that "he lived in the fo'c's'le with the other men." This was hardly shattering news. Alex, who had been twenty-four at the time, had been on his first sealing cruise, and it was common practice for crew members to supplement their pay by assisting the hunters. Sherwood had three people prepared to testify on this irrelevant point. At the same time, Sherwood, trying not to miss a beat, noted that MacLean "is not as bad as I imagined and I am having him sounded."[30] A few days later, he reported that MacLean "is looked upon here as a braggart ... but I have been unable to learn anything which would affect his credibility under oath."[31] The latter observation is a telling one.

After giving evidence on 8 January 1897, Alex MacLean again returned to San Francisco. He unintentionally interrupted the diligent Sherwood hard at work: "I was in one of the saloons along the waterfront having a drink with some of my sealing friends when who should come in but McLean, pretty well loaded up. He joined us and drank, after which I quietly retired. I knew him at once but he didn't me and paid no attention whatever to me. He said he got in at 12:30 today and was full of his experiences of which I shall have a full account tomorrow for I left [Wester?] to pump him dry."[32] Discretion on Sherwood's part was a sensible move. Government officials were not high on Alex's list, and Sherwood's sleuthing could easily have led to an unseemly conflict between the two middle-aged men. It had happened on another occasion. In this instance, according to Alex's sometime shipmate John McConville, the unfortunate official was American. In a saloon behind Meiggs' Wharf in San Francisco, "an argument arose as to the performance of certain horses. A rather blustering Yankee customs officer was there and he told Alex that he (Alex) knew more about driving men than about horses." The discussion quickly heated up, and the customs officer drew his pistol. "Alex, though unarmed, was on the man like a flash, threw him into the air until his head hit the ceiling ... The saloon was full of 'stiffs' and hoboes, for it was a pretty low place." When he recovered, he sought assistance, offering a reward. "Alex just stood with his back against the counter, facing them, his elbows resting on the rail, perfectly calm, with that curious look in those keen blue eyes of his, and defied them to touch him. He was not too well liked there, but not a single man would lay a finger on him. He always had that curious power over other men."[33] Sherwood, of course, had his sources to rely on, and he wisely faded back. The San Francisco waterfront was obviously a talkative spot, if one knew which people to prime and tap.

Two days later, in Victoria, Dan MacLean's declaration of 8 August 1889 was read into the record, and it was mentioned that he would possibly show up for the hearings that were tentatively scheduled for San Francisco. Edgar Crow Baker also gave additional evidence in Victoria and explained why he had entered a partnership with the MacLeans in the first place: "Q: Daniel McLean is looked upon as a very expert master of a vessel? A: Both he and Alexander McLean at that time, and previously, were considered the men best posted in that business."[34]

A great deal of the skulduggery on both sides was used simply to acquire information concerning the value of vessels and the costs of sealing generally. It all had to do with financial compensation. Higher estimates would, of course, work in favour of the Canadian sealers. Many people went to considerable effort to put the correct spin on it all. Some played both sides – for a while. George Dodge was one who supplied detailed costs to Sherwood "before receiving warning from Harris and McLean not to give any information as to outfit." After his place in the dispute had been made clear to him, reported Sherwood, "Dodge is now interesting himself very prominently for the United States."[35] Henry Wood Elliott would later turn MacLean's role upside down, maintaining that he was "in truth working for the highest figures obtainable from the United States Treasury, instead of the lowest." This interpretation portrayed Alex with his eye on the seized vessels in the Canadian fleet in which he had been part owner.[36]

One of Sherwood's best sources was George Wester, a sealer who had sailed with Alex on the *Mary Ellen* in 1889 and as mate and hunter on the *James Hamilton Lewis* in 1890. He would later be suggested as one of the models for Jack London's Wolf Larsen.[37] In 1891, in charge of the *City of San Diego,* Wester had successfully raided the Commander Island rookeries.[38] Now, late in 1896, he was reporting twice daily to Sherwood and was apparently "one of the best men among the sealers, [and] has been working up all possible information." Wester was definitely in the thick of it. One day Sherwood reported that "my man Wester was with Alex McLean, Capt. Scott and another sealer about half an hour ago when young Harris, an operative in the U.S. Secret Service here, came up slapping McLean on the back, took him away from the others saying he had been looking all over for him, they went off together in earnest conversation." Apparently, Wester was unable to listen in on that occasion, but Sherwood's sources were generally quite current. At one point, Sherwood supposedly possessed the text of a message that Secret Service agent Harris had received only an hour earlier.[39] Other sources that Sherwood used included C.D. Ladd, an old-time sealer who "promised to supply [them] with all data," and Donald Ross, of Ross and Hewlett, "who [were] agents for all the British sealers." Ross was described as "one of the best posted men in the port." MacLean had delivered his relatively small catch of sealskins from the *Emma and Louisa* to Ross the previous year. When Sherwood had slipped into San Francisco late in 1896, he set up an office in the back of Ross and Hewlett's store, a location frequented by MacLean and many others, and met some of his informants there.[40]

When reading through Sherwood's constant stream of reports to Victoria, it is obvious that he enjoyed his clandestine role. Sleuthing suited Sherwood. By mid-January, the major was "very busy" and predictably reported that "the plot thickens." He also began to see shadows that did not exist, which was doubtless an occupational hazard. He reported to Peters that they "have begun to be suspicious of my man Wester, and are plainly taking steps to guard against him, but they are totally in ignorance of my being in their midst, and you will continue to be informed of all that is going on." But he was wrong. The Americans themselves approached Wester to give evidence as well.[41] Whatever else Wester was, he was not suspected. Sherwood continued to monitor Alex's every move. He suspected that Alex was trying to locate sealers who had made small catches so as to reduce the overall average and, ultimately, the final awards. He noted that the American sealers would be leaving soon to give evidence in Victoria. Sherwood forwarded their names and an abundance of detail, including suggested lines of questioning. By this point, Sherwood was positively relishing his role: "Not a suspicion of my presence here has been manifested by those most concerned ... I am enjoying the excitement immensely."[42]

All of this information was not free, of course, as Sherwood pointed out. In dealing with the American sealers, Sherwood confronted national loyalties and self-interested plans for cooperation from the US government. Incentives were required: "The money goes like water here ... Since the fun commenced I have been on the go from 8 am always till after 12 and frequently till 2 and 3 but I like it when it goes well." Sherwood not only valued Wester as a source but saw him as playing a larger role in the Victoria hearings: "Wester may be of great use up there if given an opportunity without attracting suspicion." But Sherwood was becoming more and more concerned about dangers lurking around the corner. He suggested to Peters that "if you manage a meeting place with him [Wester] better be a place where there are a number of views and a couple of entrances so that he can go in and out at different doors and thus make shadowing difficult in case of suspicions. Be very cautious." In addition, as Sherwood explained to Peters, Wester "is very nervous lest the other side should ascertain of his connections with us through something which might transpire in cross-examination so I have promised to ask you to be careful." In the end, Wester was not sent to Victoria.[43] All of this intrigue was having an effect on the commissioner of the Dominion Police. Yet Percy Sherwood soldiered on, missing little that was pertinent and gathering and reporting much irrelevant, if sometimes interesting, detail.[44]

By mid-January 1897, the hearings were beginning to wind down, although there were a few waters yet to be muddied. A report from Victoria, also printed in the *Ottawa Evening Journal,* stated that a Canadian witness had been drugged so as to prevent him from giving testimony at the hearing. The report, sent by "some evil disposed person from Victoria," maintained that, as a result, "a marked coldness existed between the American and Canadian counsel."[45] The *Victoria Daily Times* shrugged it off, saying it "emanated from Tory sources," and senior British counsel Fred Peters "with great pleasure bore testimony to the fact that he had never been engaged in any litigation where more peasant relations existed between the counsel on both sides." For his part, Don Dickinson "made a polite little acknowledgement of the British counsel's pleasant words."[46]

Alex's prediction that the hearings would be completed without a stint in San Francisco was coming true. In a way, Sherwood was sad to see the cancellation of the San Francisco hearings. He had made preparations: "I am sorry the Commissioners are not coming here to visit for I had arranged to show 'our people' all that is to be seen in this 'Modern Babylon.'" One can only surmise what Sherwood proposed to expose Peters and his colleagues to in San Francisco – maybe a truncated tour of the remnants of the Barbary Coast, with lashings of steam beer? Sherwood was now beginning to assess the whole situation. He was feeling a bit smug, as he noted in a dispatch to Peters: "Am of course very gratified to learn from you that the work I have been able to do here meets with your approval ... 'Fortune' favoured me as she has so often done before and I was enabled ... to get very close to those whom it was my interest to keep track of, and they of course, all unsuspicious of espionage, could scarcely connect with anyone on this business without my knowing of it, and the rest was easy."[47]

Alex MacLean was back on the stand on 28 and 30 January. The issue of Dan MacLean's constantly changing citizenship occupied the lawyers for some time. The commission held onto Alex until the bitter end. He was recalled in sur-rebuttal, for his last testimony on the last day of the hearings, on 1 February.[48] That evening, the Honourable Don M. Dickinson gave a farewell dinner at the Driard Hotel, the finest in Victoria at the time. It was an affair to remember, with the lieutenant governor, various senators, justices, the honourable Fred Peters, Beique, Bodwell, the Honourable Colonel and Mrs. Baker, and Mr. and Mrs. Edgar Crow Baker, among others, in attendance: "Great taste was shown in the decorations of the tables, the most beautiful roses and other flowers being used in great profusion, and a souvenir for each guest was the menu card, hand-painted, with the provincial arms at the top and a dainty little water color sketch in the centre."[49] Alex MacLean was probably not among the celebrants. Indeed, he may not even have stopped for a jar or two in Tommy Burnes' American Hotel or in the Garrick's Head. As one San Francisco newspaper later reported, "so incensed were the seal hunters of Victoria who attended the trial that Captain McLean's life the day he gave expert testimony could have been purchased for two bits. He escaped through a rear door of the courthouse, hired a boat to row over Puget Sound, was caught in a severe storm and after cruising about in the open sea for two days without food managed to reach the opposite shore and made his escape."[50] The *Daily Colonist* thought that account "sadly overdrawn."[51] But the Americans later complained about the letting down of "the lures of gentility, politeness and entertainment" and the evident hostility displayed by the good people of Victoria, who were "hostile to the case of the United States, by reason of personal and commercial relations with the British sealers and their occupation ... These American sealers ... had to conquer personal safety ... by aggressively fighting for it on the streets." It was later estimated that the testimony of the American sealers saved their government $825,554.50, Sherwood's sleuthing notwithstanding.[52] They were in a paradoxical position. Sherwood later informed

Donald Ross that those sealers such as MacLean who had testified for the Americans had not advanced their cause any "for it is beyond doubt that their evidence will be hurled at them with all possible force when the American cases come up for consideration."[53] Don Dickinson later put it rather more eloquently during prolonged Senate and congressional hearings: "In this emergency counsel requested the American sealers to give their government the benefit of their testimony and knowledge, though aware that it had also seized, destroyed or alienated their ships and property and interfered with their voyages in Behring Sea. The Americans responded to the call of their country ... conspicuous amongst the Americans was Captain Alexander McLean." Dickinson pointed out that "this brave and honest man made oath before the commission to his part ownership" in the two sealing schooners (the *Onward* and the *Favorite*), thus ensuring losing out on any financial compensation because of his American citizenship. "Not only did Capt. McLean lose by his truthfulness, but his activity on behalf of the United States subjected him to many unpleasant experiences and personal risk at the hands of the British claimants and their friends in Victoria. Surely such a man and his countrymen, the American sealers, who joined, deserves the consideration of his government, but has earned the praise of the psalmist given to 'him who sweareth to his own hurt and changeth not.'"[54] These examples of "unselfish patriotism" would be trotted out regularly as the American sealers commenced a long-term campaign to seek compensation for their seizures from the government.[55] Henry Wood Elliott's later assessment of MacLean's motive was more terse: "The rascal is in truth there to serve his sealing associates, and he does serve them well."[56]

The Canadian legal team tucked in to prepare their written argument.[57] Major Sherwood arrived back in Ottawa in mid-February and asked of Donald Ross, "Remember me very kindly to George Wester."[58] Peters, Beique, and Bodwell were very appreciative of Sherwood's services and so informed L.H. Davies as they were completing their written submission.[59] The results of the claims commission (the American government's financial savings notwithstanding), and especially the eventual resolution of the larger issues, including pelagic sealing and the fate of the fur seals, which came with the signing of the convention of 1911, would belie Charles Hibbert Tupper's comment during this period that "Canada's influence with the Great Powers has been exaggerated; we are in international affairs as dumb as the seals."[60] And yet the Canadian government, and not the Canadian sealers, would eventually reap significant financial returns for many decades following the 1911 convention, its limited influence notwithstanding.

The six years that Alex and Dan MacLean had spent in San Francisco had not been particularly auspicious. Both made very public, not always impressive appearances during this period. Some of the incidents associated with them would be remembered, and sometimes altered, for decades. Both had been recognized during the Bering Sea Claims Commission hearings (even by Edgar Crow Baker) as two of the most successful and knowledgeable individuals in the sealing industry. Dan was now finished with sealing. He was somewhere in South America and would only make one more fleeting appearance in the historical record. Alex would take a nine-year break from an industry in decline. It was time to check out other opportunities. He had played a central role during the hearings in Victoria. While he did not receive any substantial economic benefit personally, it is possible he took some satisfaction in a role that helped to limit some inflated Canadian claims to the tune of more than $800,000. Why did he subject himself to this particular ordeal? He was a naturalized American and had been operating out of San Francisco since the autumn of 1889. Maybe he soured somewhat because of his, and his brother's, experiences with Baker in Victoria. Like others who harvest from the sea, he continually sought the "big catch," and other opportunities for significant economic gain would attract him – but only after investing considerable time and effort into the projects. Later events that played out in courtrooms in Montreal and New York indicate his distaste for get-rich-quick scams. Inflating claims while sitting in an office on the waterfront did not appeal to him.

8
The South Pacific Expedition, 1897-98

A sluggish economy lingered from the panic of 1893. This economic malaise dragged out, contributing to a general lack of confidence. Yet in the late 1890s, an exuberant and energetic element could be detected, which began to dissipate the darker clouds. The rapidly approaching *fin de siècle* highlighted, for many, a new beginning or a last chance. The possibilities were many and varied. The sense of "millenarianism" offered additional opportunities for the abundant supply of confidence, men, and swindlers.[1] The last great North American gold rush – the one to the Klondike – began with the strike on Bonanza Creek, a tributary of the Klondike River, on 17 August 1896. It became general knowledge the following summer when the *Excelsior* docked in San Francisco and the *Portland* docked in Seattle. There was a shortage of gold at the time, and within ten days of the *Portland's* arrival, for example, 1,500 people had left Seattle for the north. They were the first of approximately 100,000 who set out for the gold fields. A popular song in Vancouver captured the tone:

> Label your luggage for Klondike,
> For there ain't no luck in the town today,
> There ain't no work down Moodyville way
> Pack up your traps and be off, I say,
> Off and away to the Klondike.[2]

The lure was strong. Some captains experienced difficulty in properly manning their sealing schooners, and those with significant financial investment in Victoria's sealing industry were worried that crews would simply use the sealing ships as transportation to the Yukon. Some did just that. Captain Dan Martin caught "Klondicitis" when he reached Unalaska early in the summer of 1897 and put Luke McGrath in command of the old, reliable *City of San Diego*. As he wrote to his ex-boss, William Munsie, "I took the Gold fever so badly that I could not go sealing." Munsie wanted to charge him with desertion. Some vessels had difficulty raising experienced crews.[3] Victoria sealing captains who did not succumb to the gold fever had other options. It was a good time for treasure hunts. In the spring of 1897, Captain Fred Hackett took time off from sealing and left Victoria for the island of Cocos, off the coast of Costa Rica, in search of buried treasure. Captain J.C. Voss, another Victoria-based sealer, was also approached about the Cocos Island treasure that summer. He made his play for it the following year. According to Voss, the elusive hoard was mostly made up of gold ingots valued at over £7,000,000. The bullion had originally been part of the Peruvian treasury. These were not the first expeditions on this particular quest to originate in Victoria, nor would they be the last (a recent estimate shows over 300 attempts made).[4] Another opportunity floated by Victoria in the summer of 1897. This one, with the Solomon Islands in the southwest Pacific as its destination, would ensnare Alex MacLean.[5]

Niels Peter Sorensen, a Dane of dubious character, had been in Sydney, Australia, in 1896, unsuccessfully trying to interest speculators in a mining venture in the Solomon Islands, when Alex was dealing with the lawyers from the Bering Sea Claims Commission and the high-spirited citizens of Victoria. It was not common knowledge that Sorensen had recently completed an eight-year stint at St. Helena prison in Queensland, Australia, for crimes of robbery and violence.[6] In the summer of 1897, Sorensen appeared in Alex's old home port of Victoria, attempting to entice investors with a prospectus on the South Sea Commercial Company. The heading in the *Daily Colonist,* "A Chance to Be a Millionaire," was suggestive. For one Victoria waterfront source, "it looked altogether too fishy for a straight proposition," and he later expressed his reservations to MacLean.[7] Sorensen soon moved down the coast and blazed into San Francisco. Some sources suggest it was quite an entrance. He "blew into San Francisco wearing the big pearl on his finger and with his wallet filled with quartz so rich that the gold hung from it like congealed molasses."[8] It did not take long for Sorensen and MacLean to connect. Alex later testified: "As near as I can remember it was in San Francisco in 1897 when he was promoting a company to go to the South Sea Islands for mining purposes. He had several samples of minerals that he had brought from the islands, as he said. He said they would assay $5,000 to the ton. The minerals could be found in the islands in great quantities, he said, and he knew where. They were supposed to be in the Solomon Islands." Sorensen played his line out carefully: "It was in 1897, the second day I was in San Francisco. I met [Alex] in a hotel. I had been out and when I came in there was a man sitting there with a great big moustache about eighteen inches long ... and big broad shoulders." Alex related, "I took a liking to this man and got to know him fairly well ... But it was not until I had known him for some time that he told me that his object in coming to this coast was to see if he could get someone to finance an expedition in search of treasure which he knew to be buried on an island in the South Seas. I was not easily taken in ... and at first I suspected a hoax, for I had heard of that sort of expedition before. But I knew the South Seas to some extent and finally I was convinced he was genuine."[9]

Sorensen was a persuasive individual. His information was detailed, the project appeared feasible, and the potential rewards were attractive enough to loosen $16,000 from optimistic investors-participants. Some of them were wage-earning mechanics and clerks; one was an ex-mayor of San Francisco, Edward B. Pond. Alex refused "another good position" and joined the expedition, partly because of the samples he was shown. He dismissed the concerns of his friends in Victoria, assuring one skeptic that "he had better come in anyway and ask no questions – there was money in it." MacLean was probably strapped financially. Having engaged in sealing continually from 1883 to 1895, he had now missed two seasons in a row. His financial record to that time did not suggest a very practical approach to financial matters. Sorensen might have intuited MacLean's pre-modern sensibility. Besides, visions of riches were in the air – the first of the successful "Klondikers" had arrived in San Francisco on the *Excelsior* in mid-July.[10] Financial considerations were likely only a part of MacLean's reasoning. As Hugh Laracy, who has detailed Sorensen's career, noted, "if there was a quarter of the Pacific in which anything might still be possible, it was in Melanesia."[11] The sense of adventure, the thrill of the hunt, and a change of pace continued to strongly attract MacLean and others. There was also a hint of danger. In the previous year, Austrian explorer Baron Foullon Von Norbeck and three others had been killed by locals on Guadalcanal in the Solomon Islands – a story that was widely reported in the press. There had also been the highly publicized departure of the *Percy Edwards* from San Francisco in late February 1897 on its "quixotic and utopian" adventure to the same area.[12]

One aspect of the story, which tells of Sorensen with "a tattered piece of map showing where treasure was buried on some South Seas island," is a bit misleading. He apparently did have a chart, from which he had erased the latitude and longitude, and it supposedly signified the location of extensive gold and copper deposits. He informed MacLean of its existence but, curiously, the skeptical Cape Bretoner would not get a glance at it until they were in the Solomon Islands.[13] One problem, which was unknown to MacLean and others interested in the scheme at the time, was that Sorensen's source was Alexander G. Findlay's *A Directory for the Navigation of the Pacific Ocean,* which he had "carefully studied" during his "enforced seclusion" at the prison in Saint Helena. It purportedly located a rich copper deposit on an island that was completely of coral formation.[14] However, this fact would only be one of the many surprises to come. In effect, the plan was primarily a mining, and not a treasure-hunting, expedition. The South Sea Commercial Company was duly incorporated in California "principally for the purposes of trading and prospecting for minerals in the Solomon Islands," according to the company's secretary, purser, and sometime carpenter, H.C. Grigg.[15] Under MacLean's guidance, the company acquired for the venture the sealing schooner *Sophia Sutherland* for $6,000. MacLean did not contribute financially but was to receive a salary and company stock in return for commanding the vessel. A mining engineer with experience in gold mining was also aboard, as were two expert divers (Sorensen being one of them).[16] One source has MacLean gathering "a cutthroat crew," and the *San Francisco Chronicle* briefly notes in early August that "the irrepressible Captain Alexander McLean is again in command of a vessel and is going to the South Seas ostensibly on a trading cruise."[17] But aside from MacLean, only four able seamen and the mate had sailing experience. The remainder were "fifteen young mechanics and small pay clerks eager for adventure." Sorensen was "general manager."[18] The *Sophia Sutherland,* a substantial schooner of 156 tons, and the same vessel that had introduced Jack London to the adventurous life of sealing in 1893, left San Francisco on 3 September.[19] Her departure caused some comment in the *San Francisco Chronicle:* "While the vessel was preparing for her trip at Hathaway's Wharf, the impression was given out that she was to seek hidden treasures left in some South Sea island by pirates many years ago; but the stores that were put aboard at once disproved the statement made by the promoters of the expedition. Among the stores were a large number of muskets, rifles, and pistols, besides a quantity of mining machinery." The *Sophia Sutherland* loaded provisions for an eighteen-month voyage: "The members of the expedition expect to remain on the islands for three years, and come back with more gold than the luckiest miners of the Klondike region ... While some of the party are engaged in extracting gold from the Solomon Island mountains, others will devote their attention to fishing for pearl oysters."[20]

The scheme, the participants involved, the stories of the extensive amount of firearms on board, and the secrecy surrounding the venture ensured that the waterfront rumour mills were operating at full steam. Various authorities quickly took note. The British consul-general in San Francisco, J.W. Warburton, was instructed by his embassy in Washington to inquire into the company. The British were concerned, in part, because of the recent failure of a colonizing scheme by "utopians-on-the-make called the United Brotherhood of the South Sea Islands," which had departed San Francisco for Fiji earlier in the year.[21] Warburton contacted the South Sea Commercial Company, and the secretary-treasurer H.C. Grigg assured him that the newspaper reports "were either false or exaggerated, and actuated by malice." Grigg explained that it was not a colonizing expedition and that it carried "only sufficient arms for their own protection and nothing else."[22] Warburton passed on to his superiors some general, rather vague impressions that he had acquired about Alex MacLean: "I am informed that Captain McLean, who is a Canadian by birth, but a naturalized American, does not bear a good character. He has, I am told, commanded several sealing vessels, and has been mixed up with questionable transactions." The British authorities were right to be concerned but were so for the wrong reasons. Grigg was not far off the mark in his assessment of the *San Francisco Chronicle's* reliability. The secrecy pledge taken by each member of the expedition accelerated the waterfront talk and helped explain the spin put on the story by the newspaper. The newspaper continued: "Captain Alexander McLean is in charge of the expedition [and] ... he has gathered around him a galaxy of gun-fighters who will shoot at the drop of the hat, and who, in addition to the arms and ammunition carried in the cruiser's outfit, are individually armed to the teeth." Waterfront rumour, MacLean's involvement, and the spirit of the times had thus transformed a group of clerks and mechanics into aggressive adventurers setting off to new frontiers far removed from factories and offices. Grigg properly pointed out that the *San Francisco Chronicle* had only to check its own files to ensure the accuracy of his corrections.[23]

After a five-week uneventful voyage, the *Sophia Sutherland* arrived in Apia, Samoa, on 9 October with a load of lumber.[24] Given the public send-off, and the attention the vessel and crew received from various interested parties, the schooner was not unexpected. Earlier assurances that the vessel only carried "sufficient arms for their own protection" had not dissipated the concerns of the authorities. The word was out: "There was a condition of revolution in Samoa practically all the time, and the Berlin Treaty prohibited the importation of rifles and ammunition. It was reported from San Francisco that the ship was a filibuster and was loaded accordingly. Things were so quiet at Apia that the arrival of such an expedition put the town on the *qui vive*."[25] The Berlin Treaty had been signed by Germany, Great Britain, the United States, and Samoa in June 1889. It had managed to stabilize a difficult situation. Considerable friction nonetheless remained. Samoa did not need adventurers engaged in an unlawful situation at this point. When the *Sophia Sutherland* arrived, William Churchill, the American consul-general in Apia, was right on the heels of the health officer and immediately boarded the vessel. He found no contraband arms on board. He did, however, take notice of Sorensen's presence. Churchill had spent considerable time in the South Seas since 1884 and had first heard of Alex's colleague in 1885. Later that day, Churchill sent for MacLean and filled him in on Sorensen's past.[26] It was a fascinating, mostly factual story that he related to MacLean and doubtless sharpened the captain's canny sense of survival.

Apparently, Sorensen had showed up in Melbourne, Australia, in 1883 "with a story of wonderful pearl ledges he knew of in the Solomons which needed only a solid financial backing to become one of the greatest pearl deposits in the South Pacific ... [and sporting] a pearl as big as a hazel nut."[27]

According to Hugh Laracy, who has unravelled Sorensen's sometimes sordid escapades, the Dane had been a diver on the schooner *Albert* in 1884-85. The vessel was engaged in trading and collecting pearl shells around the Solomon Islands. Reports from this voyage underline Sorensen's harshness and cruelty. A couple of months later, the *Albert* departed Sydney, Australia, with Sorensen as master. The vessel's name was changed to the *Douro,* and the registration was changed from British to Portuguese. "After the formalities had been completed," Laracy recounts, "Sorensen is said to have remarked 'I'm now out of all English law; I'm my own master; I can trade now with what I like – with rifle, cartridge, powder and dynamite.' In fact, as he had already shown, he preferred to trade without giving anything in exchange if that could be managed. Nor would his presumed licence do anything to sweeten his temper. The knavery of the *Albert* voyage was magnified in that of the *Douro."* On this trip, Sorensen's dark side was quickly evident. He physically abused crew members, forced others aboard, and, at Wagina, abducted the chief and successfully demanded a high ransom. He then continued what was essentially an ongoing raid, commandeering canoes, coercing girls on board, and plundering in general. With further depredations planned, some of the crew had had enough and departed, eventually arriving in Cooktown where their story quickly caught the attention of the public and the authorities. Admiral George Tryon, who was in charge of the Royal Navy's Australia station, had the allegations investigated and ordered the *Douro* seized. Sorensen was arrested when he finally docked in Cooktown, Australia, on 24 December 1885. This time around, there was enough crew still in the area to testify. Four months later in Brisbane, Sorensen received a ten-year sentence for robbery and assault under arms. MacLean listened to Churchill's story attentively.[28]

The day after the *Sophia Sutherland* arrived in Apia, Churchill introduced MacLean to another person who happened to be in port. John Strasburg (also known as Captain Hamburg), a trader in the area, shared his recollections of MacLean's present partner. Strasburg was acquainted with Sorensen and had met the refugees from the *Albert/Douro* in 1885. Another individual who was troubled about the expedition was William Lee Chambers, the chief justice of the International Court of Samoa at the time. He expressed concern for the young adventurers: "They told me where they were going, and I tried to stop the expedition. I had been in Samoa for four or five years before and was more or less familiar with such expeditions. I saw the character of these young men and I thought they were not only going off on a wild goose chase but I didn't know what might result. Then I sought out Capt. McLean and had a talk with him along these lines and told him I didn't think these young men should be taken on an expedition of this sort."[29] MacLean was now fully forewarned. Several members of the crew were also involved in the discussions at Churchill's office, and MacLean informed others on board. They remained unmoved by Chambers' concerns. Sorensen was left out of the loop.[30] Determined to proceed, MacLean and the intrepid adventurers aboard the *Sophia Sutherland* set out for Suva, in the Fiji Islands, ten days after reaching Apia. There were ten gallons of liquor on board, located in Sorensen's room, and apparently he was the main consumer.[31] William Churchill soon finished his stint as consul-general and departed Samoa on 3 November. As he passed through Victoria, British Columbia, in December 1897 on his way home, he chatted with local newsmen, mentioned the expedition, and filled them in on Sorensen's background. Churchill's stories about the Dane did not seem improbable to the locals, "particularly as he had as his partner no less well known a person than Capt. Alex McLean."[32]

Meanwhile, MacLean was gradually wading through the bureaucratic barriers in Melanesia. Accompanied by Sorensen, he received a similar reception in Suva to the one he had experienced in Apia on 25 October. He now needed permission from Sir G.T.M. O'Brien, the British high commissioner for the western Pacific, to visit the British Solomon Islands. According to Alex, the high commissioner "did not seem to encourage us in any way to go there. He seemed a little leery about something. It appeared to me from the information I had received in Apia that it was because he was aware of Sorensen. He said nothing to me on this visit, but I called on him again before leaving." The British commissioner consented to a continuation of the expedition only "after Capt. McLean had pleaded that it was composed of many young mechanics who had put all their money into it." The expedition then moved on to Tulagi in the Solomons to apply for mining licences from Charles M. Woodford, the first British resident commissioner. Again, there was a slight hitch. Woodford, after a long personal campaign, had been appointed to the position the previous February, and the British Solomon Islands protectorate was in "a very disturbed state." The commissioner was wary, wanting no disruptions to his linked objectives of pacification and economic development. He "said he would grant a license for every man who would take up a mining claim, but would grant none to Sorensen because it appear[ed] Sorensen was not allowed to do business in the islands." The legal hurdles were finally cleared, albeit with official concern and reservations, and the next few months were spent following Sorensen's directions to various places, seeking gold and copper. According to Commissioner Woodford's later recollections, "having visited the North West end of Rennell Is. where he said that the solid cliff of pure copper too hard to be blasted out by dynamite existed and failing to find it, he told his dupes that he must have mistaken the end of the island and that it was at the South East end. The S.E. end was visited with the same result and he then accounted for its absence by saying that it must have disappeared in an earthquake."[33] Rennell Island was built of coral. There would be no gold or copper found there.

There was a shaft sunk at Maru Bay on San Christoval. Consulting samples that Sorensen had with him, Natives fanned out to seek similar rocks. While traces of gold and silver were found, and examined by the assayer on the vessel, there was nothing of value. Sorensen's contributions at this point were as useful as his maps. They primarily consisted of telling the miners in the crew that they did not know what they were doing. He did not seem to have been burdened with a surplus of common sense. At one point, the mining engineer was all set to shoot Sorensen, but MacLean intervened. They returned to Tulagi in mid-January 1898 with various specimens, and Commissioner Woodford placed a room in his house at the disposal of the assayer. After two days, only one sample had a minute trace of gold. Woodford reported that members of the expedition were disgusted after three months of disappointment.[34]

MacLean and the crew of the *Sophia Sutherland* had certainly given Sorensen an extended benefit of the doubt. A later account noted: "They had given Sorensen a fair chance to make good, McLean said, and when he cruised around and among the islands, bluffing here and failing there, always holding out the lure of the treasure which he had charted on a map from which he had erased the latitude and longitude lines, the party on the *Sophia Sutherland* decided that it was time to pay Sorensen."[35] This decision was timely, and as Commissioner Woodford reported, "by this time the Americans had had enough of Sorensen and decided to leave. Sorensen then produced a Power of Attorney from his pocket given to him by the owners in San Francisco empowering him to take possession of the vessel and cargo and to start trading in the Solomons. The faces of the party fell, but one of the office boys produced another Power of Attorney of later date cancelling the one given to Sorensen."[36] Powers of attorney aside, one suspects that MacLean would not have easily given up his command. The experience with the Russians in 1891 quickly comes to mind. Years later, ruminating on this situation during an interview in Vancouver, Alex felt that Sorensen "intended to do to me what he had previously done to another captain in Australian waters. He planned to dispose of me and get my crew to let him take command. But he did not realize the sort of man or the sort of crew he was dealing with – though I will say he was a daring fellow."[37] However, enough was enough, and MacLean wanted to leave Sorensen in Tulagi. The commissioner refused. He did not want the Dane either. As a result of his previous record, Sorensen was not allowed on the island. MacLean pressed Woodford, who "wished to know why I could not take Sorensen along and I said I feared trouble on board ship – that Sorensen would be liable to kill somebody, or some of the crew might kill him. I said that if I had to take him I would have to confine him in the hold, and that when crossing the equator it would be so hot the man might die and I would not like to have the responsibility of his death on my hands."[38] There was a possibility that some of the crew would try to lynch him. The following day, the commissioner met again with Alex, but MacLean's message remained firm and quite clear. According to Woodford's recollections, he and MacLean then assured Sorensen, with some understatement, that it would be best if the Dane no longer continued the relationship or the voyage because, as Woodford phrased it, "we thought such a proceeding would be very bad for his health and I gave him the choice of a lodging in the gaol or the coal shed until the departure of the next steamer for Sydney. The Americans generously paid his passage and gave me five pounds to hand to him on his embarkation."[39] Woodford suggested a small island (Gavutu), which was two-and-a-half miles distant and had a small hut on it. He explained to MacLean that, if Sorensen was left there with supplies for two weeks, a steamer, the *Titus,* would call and then continue on to Australia. Alex related, "When I got back to the ship I met Sorensen on deck and showed him the island that the Commissioner had pointed out. I told him I was going to land him on that island, and ordered him to pack up his things and go along with the two men in the boat who were going to take him. He hesitated about packing up, and I told him I would give him fifteen minutes to get ready. I called two men and sent them to his room to get his things out. Then when he saw we were getting them out of his room he gave them a hand, but the men practically did the packing."[40] The two men who deposited Sorensen on Gavutu may have done a bit more, possibly flogging him after they tied him to a coconut tree.[41] Niels Peter Sorensen and the *Titus* arrived in Sydney, Australia, on 5 February, and he recovered from his "very weakened condition." The crew of the *Sophia Sutherland* continued their explorations, unsuccessfully, for two more months.[42] Until now, the Solomon Islands episode, frustrating and unproductive, had bordered on farce. Yet Sorensen's contributions aside, it had had some potential. Resident Commissioner Woodford had submitted a sample to the assayer from another area in the protectorate that was almost 50 percent copper. He lamented the failure of the scheme: "It is to be regretted that an expedition so well equipped for prospecting should have been so much discouraged by their ill success as to abandon the enterprise before making further efforts in other parts of the Protectorate, as I imagine it will be long before persons in such a position to thoroughly test the value of any mineral discovered will again visit the Protectorate." He reiterated this theme the following year.[43]

When Jack London reached the Solomon Islands a decade later, during his ill-fated cruise with the *Snark,* he was told that "the entire crew of his old sealing ship the *Sophie* [sic] *Sutherland* had perished" some years previously. The report was not completely accurate, but it may have been in the back of the novelist's mind when he wrote "The Terrible Solomons," one of his South Sea tales: "There is no gainstaying that the Solomons are a hard-bitten bunch of islands. On the other hand, there are worse places in the world. But to the new chum who has no constitutional understanding of men and life in the rough, the Solomons may indeed prove terrible. It is true that fever and dysentery are perpetually on the walk-about, that loathsome skin diseases abound, that the air is saturated with a poison that bites into every pore, cut, or abrasion and plants malignant ulcers, and that many strong men who escape dying there return as wrecks to their own countries."[44]

The South Sea Commercial Company project, which was now a financial disaster, was about to turn into a tragedy. Up until this time, it had proved to be a relatively healthy voyage. According to Alex, "the crew were all in good health at this time, and I don't believe there had been a man sick from the time we left San Francisco."[45] They continued explorations in the Solomons for the next few months. They called at a trading station at Marau Sound on Guadalcanal to do some work on the *Sophia Sutherland*. Unfortunately, when the vessel was being heaved over for careening it went too far and took on a significant amount of water. That caused a delay. Four adventurers decided to stay in the area longer.[46] Malaria and scurvy would both take their toll on the remainder of the group. One man soon died. There are a number of versions as to what happened next. All underline the stamina of MacLean, who dovetailed smoothly into the popular legend. Alex later explained to Noel Robinson: "I had had no experience with this disease, though I knew it was very serious ... we continued the voyage before a fine breeze and made good sailing. Then a second man died and several others sickened. By this time we were many hundreds of miles from Apia, and I decided to land upon an island and stay for a while, hoping that the more open life on shore would restore the health of the crew." After their health improved, they again put to sea. "This time I determined to take no chances and make for Apia, and, after getting a clean bill of health, continue the voyage to the island."[47] The fever remained, and, eventually, upward of eighteen of the crew died, seventeen buried at sea. "This one survivor also had the fever so badly that he could be of no use to me and lay ill for the rest of the voyage. I contracted it also, but fought very hard against it and it never got a real hold of me. It was terribly hot at the time and almost immediately a man died, it was necessary to bury him. I never expected to reach port – 2,000 miles away – alive, but I determined to make a big effort. I was alone aboard that large three-masted schooner for six weeks, the sick man being of no use at all, and I did my best to navigate her, and finally brought her safely into Apia."[48] Another source has Alex "lashing himself to the helm while he slept" and sailing 1,500 miles.[49] Charles Lillard notes two versions. In one, the distance was 1,500 miles: "As he sailed, his crew, man by man, died of yellow fever. MacLean calmly threw the bodies overboard and continued sailing. Another version has the distance as 2,000 miles and one man surviving along with the captain; since this is MacLean's version it may be worth believing."[50] A decade later, during testimony on a related case, MacLean would offer this account: "A few days after leaving there more of the men took down with the fever and they commenced dying off. When I finally decided to put into Apia the men were dying off so fast that I had no help to handle the ship, and for two weeks I sailed the *Sophia Sutherland* single-handed. I had four men left when I got to Apia but they were all down with the fever. My own health was good until the fever broke out and although it didn't seem to affect me I got practically worn out."[51]

On his return to Apia, Alex saw Chambers again as well as Churchill's replacement, L.W. Osborn. He filled them in on the fever, the failed expedition, and his parting of ways with Sorensen. Finally, on 9 July, Alex cleared Apia for the last time and headed for home port, with only one of his original crew aboard, along with two members of Percy Edwards' expedition. Six of the crew were "beachcombers" that the authorities were pleased to see depart.[52] After a fifty-three-day voyage, the *Sophia Sutherland*, under MacLean's command, returned to San Francisco on 31 August 1898. The expedition/adventure had lasted 362 days. Her reappearance in the west coast port prompted a far more prosaic newspaper report than had surrounded her departure a year earlier. Her cargo of coconuts prodded the *San Francisco Chronicle* to title its piece "Nuts Instead of Nuggets" and conclude that it was all "a wild goose chase ... [and] every man on board has had enough of adventure to satisfy him for the remainder of his life." In this account, Sorensen (referred to as "Pirate Pete") had been seen recently in San Francisco complaining about being "generally ill-treated." He had arrived in the port on 19 June. Sorensen's reappearance in MacLean's home port demonstrated once again the Dane's personal limitations. One report noted that he left a few days before MacLean's return, although MacLean later testified that he ran into Sorensen in San Francisco soon after he returned from the South Pacific.[53]

While MacLean was on his quest in the South Pacific, the United States forbade American citizens from engaging in any pelagic sealing in the Pacific, putting an end to the American pelagic hunt. No American citizen "nor any person belonging to or on board of a vessel of the United States, shall kill, capture, or hunt, at any time or in any manner whatever, any fur seal in the waters of the Pacific Ocean north of the thirty-fifth degree of north latitude and including Bering Sea and the sea of Okhotsk." Even products from pelagic fur seal skins, in any form, were prohibited from importation. Penalties included fines of between $200 and $2,000, six months of imprisonment, and the forfeiture of vessel and equipment.[54] This was, in part, an attempt to strengthen the US position as the Americans tried to convince Russia, Japan, and Great Britain to enter discussions to impose uniform regulations in the North Pacific.[55] The American pelagic fleet had always been relatively small and, as Herman Liebes acknowledged around that time, "pelagic sealing is not, and cannot be, under present conditions, profitable."[56] The additional regulations would have little effect, other than angering and disappointing the disappearing American sealers. The Canadian fleet that year was only half the size it had been three years earlier. Although a growth in the herd over the next few years and a rise in prices attracted vessels back into the industry, the pattern of decline soon reappeared. While American sealers were being shut out by their government, the Japanese government was establishing a subsidy for their sealers, which was effective in 1898, and their presence increased significantly.[57] Changes continued on the wider Pacific as well. In 1898, the United States annexed Hawaii, making the Americans supreme in the eastern Pacific, and followed that up the next year by acquiring the Philippines and thus bolstering their presence in the western Pacific. The American supply lines and zones of control now overlapped the already overlapping interests of Russia and Japan in the Pacific waters.[58]

Meanwhile, the Bering Sea claims made by the Canadian sealers, some of which dated back to 1886, were finally being settled. Part of the reason for the delay, and the refusal of the American Congress to initially approve the agreement, could be found in the following reasoning. If the Canadians received their just due, the American government would then also have to compensate the American pelagic sealers who had suffered similar damages. Hundreds of thousands of additional dollars were at stake. Promoters of the American claims lamented: "It is still due them. No influential nation appeared at Paris to plea their cause, and their claims for damages lie yellow and dusty in the pigeon-holes of the Department at Washington."[59] They would remain there for a while longer.

The Canadians, however, were reasonably successful. Some of them did extremely well. When Fred Peters first received a copy of the schedule of the award in January 1898, he wrote Sir Lewis H. Davies, the minister of marine and fisheries: "I am very happy to be able to report that the parties interested appear to be quite satisfied." Peters was personally in contact with William Munsie and Edgar Crow Baker, "and they [were] fully satisfied with the amount awarded." He went on to underline a number of pertinent points of particular relevance to the MacLean brothers: "Again, the *Triumph* to whom twenty three thousand dollars odd, has been allowed, had no claim whatever except for prospective catch, she was simply warned and immediately left the Sea, and the amount of the award, therefore, proves that prospective catch or something in lieu therefore, must have been given. This example would be sufficient to illustrate this point."[60]

This example belatedly, if silently, acknowledged that Dan MacLean's decision in July 1889 to bring the *Triumph* back to port had been an appropriate one. Summing up the decision, Peters concluded: "We have succeeded in satisfying the claimants, which is practically a great point. Secondly, we have succeeded on the important point of prospective catch, interest, and

American citizenship." The Americans had argued unsuccessfully that an entire claim should fail if an American citizen was even part owner.[61] A cheque from the American secretary of state for $473,151.26 was issued in June 1898.[62] Some claimants were receiving their share by mid-September 1898. Charles Spring, who had been almost ruined in 1886, would receive $15,015.74 for his half ownership of the *Onward,* which was seized that year. The Native hunters who had been on the vessel would split $450. Captain Munroe and the mate of the *Onward* at the time received special personal awards. The co-owner of the *Onward,* Alexander MacLean, received nothing. His claim was disallowed because he was an American citizen. The other vessel co-owned by Charles Spring and Alex MacLean, which had her sealing voyage disrupted in 1886, was the *Favorite.* A claim of $6,202 was submitted. The "claim was based on the fact that she was supposed to have changed her ground on account of the warning."[63] But Alex, who had also been master of the *Favorite* at the time, had not left the Bering Sea until seventeen days after being warned to leave, and this particular award caught in the craw of some influential people in Victoria, even though he was specifically excluded from compensation: "We cannot help thinking that its largeness is due to the fact that the United States authorities were anxious that McLean, whom they will themselves have to pay, and who was their chief witness, should have a chance of establishing a large claim and therefore did not strongly oppose a large award." They worried unnecessarily. Fred Peters, Queen's Counsel, who had led the legal charge for the Canadians at the Bering Sea Claims Commission hearings and who was presently a partner in Tupper, Peters and Potts in Victoria, and E.V. Bodwell, associate counsel for the Canadian government in the Bering Sea litigation,[64] further recommended that the Aboriginal hunters who had been on the *Favorite* that disruptive season only receive $200 compensation for their prospective catch after the warning – "as they really made an excellent season." Charles Spring's creditors were awarded $4,917.08 for his half ownership. Alex received nothing from the *Favorite's* award.[65]

The third claim linked with the MacLeans was that of the *Triumph.* Edgar Crow Baker, ex-managing owner and erstwhile partner of Dan MacLean, had originally put in a claim for $40,950 for the *Triumph's* hassle by the *Rush* in July 1889. It was later revised. Baker owned one-third, as did Dan MacLean, while J.C. Blackett and Rosina Gibson both had a one-sixth interest.[66] The award for the *Triumph's* difficulties and disruption of her sealing season in 1889 was eventually determined to be $23,115.77. However, there was another delay concerning this specific payment. The minister of marine and fisheries had some reservations about just how the *Triumph's* award was to be divided. Davies explained the reason to Peters: "Because you had evidently determined to take into consideration Baker's accounts against McLean which had no connection at all with the *Triumph,* and pay him what he alleged was due him by McLean." Davies then listed the suggested division: among the five hunters, $1,500.00; Edgar Crow Baker, $14,992.45; Daniel McLean, $258.95; J.C. Blackett, $2,991.77; Rosina Gibson, $3,190.85; and E.B. Marvin, $181.75. Davies was particularly concerned "why Daniel McLean, who owned one-third, should receive only $258.95. It may be all right, but I say the explanation does not appear." He felt Baker should square his accounts with Dan MacLean directly.[67] Upon receiving this questioning response from Davies, Peters and Bodwell had a long meeting with Baker to explain the delay and the need for additional statements. Peters immediately wired Davies asking him to reserve action, saying, "You misunderstand whole matter."[68]

Baker, still bemoaning his past foray into sealing, confessed in his diary: "An unaccountable fatality enshrouds this business." What made it worse for Baker was that it seemed as if everyone else in Victoria was already sharing the wealth. "Those interested in Sealing [are] tumbling over one another at Customs House to get their cheques," he noted in his diary a few days later. Due to the specific delay caused by Davies' concerns, Baker was unable to join the throng at the trough. Meanwhile, Peters was assuring Davies: "If there is one claim among the whole lot in which you may be sure that our report is correct, this is the one." Davies' suggestion to separate any unfinished financial business between Baker and Dan MacLean from the *Triumph's* claim did not sit well with Peters. He suggested to Davies that the supplementary report to follow should justify not allowing "Daniel McLean to swindle Baker out of money ... I feel rather strongly on this case, as Baker is a man who took more trouble than almost anyone else, not only in working up this case, but in assisting to work up other cases ... and if you insist on my making any such report, I must respectfully decline, as I think it is on a principle wrong in law, and contrary to all justice and equity."[69] In effect, Baker argued, with the support of Peters and Bodwell, that Dan's portion of the *Triumph's* claim be credited to his various accounts with Baker concerning both the *Triumph* and the *Mary Ellen*. The latter vessel had had no connection with the seizures or the hearings. Peters and the others were powerful voices that could be heard clearly on this issue. Dan was nowhere to be found. Indeed, Baker was his attorney. Only Davies initially questioned the arrangement. For Baker, the suspense continued for a few more weeks. In the decade or so since Baker had washed his hands of the sealing business, he had been busy with other concerns, and he and a variety of partners had incorporated more than ten companies and had to contend with a "severe economic depression" in the middle of it.[70] Baker did not close the books on his most costly failure, the cable concern in the Hawaiian Islands, which had almost ensnared the *Triumph* in 1889, until early 1897. Further, Vancouver was eclipsing Victoria. In the summer of 1898, while waiting for his money from the *Triumph's* claim in the summer of 1898, Baker lamented:

"Everything going on in Vancouver and nothing in Victoria." Baker obviously felt he had lots to worry about, and he immersed himself in it. On 5 October, he noted in his ever-present diary: "No cheque from Ottawa even yet!! More close financing." The phrase "and still no cheque from Ottawa" appeared on a daily basis in his diary, like a mantra.

Eventually, the earnest representations of Peters and Bodwell produced results. Baker, with twenty-one shares, received $14,471.80; Rosine Gibson (eleven shares) got $3,080.03; and John C. Blackett (ten shares) was given $2,287.87. Dan MacLean's award, which for a one-third interest would have been around $7,000, was whittled down to $249.95. He was lucky to get that. Peters and Bodwell had recommended that given that Dan's "whereabouts is not known" even that balance should be paid to Baker, "who is his attorney in fact." A notation by Davies on one of the latter memos, "I don't see any reason for this," squashed that minor detail. Presumably, Dan's account with Baker was finally cleared, although Baker was still noting the absence of any rendered account for the skins taken by Alex to San Francisco in the *Mary Ellen* in 1889. Baker's $14,471.80 share of the award would fit in nicely with the $70,000 profit he received from the sale of his share of the local telephone company around that time.[71] It is not known what ultimately happened to Dan MacLean's cheque for $249.95. Late in 1897, the United States, Russia, and Japan agreed to a closed season in the North Pacific and a pelagic sealing ban in the Bering Sea for the following year – if Britain would go along. The question became entangled in the Alaska boundary dispute, and Canada eventually withdrew. The diplomatic difficulty continued.[72]

9
The Klondike, 1898-1903

The quest for riches, treasure hunts, and sailing to exotic locations all took a back seat to the frenzied search for gold in the late 1890s. San Francisco and Seattle were much like Victoria, caught up "in the turmoil of the Klondike Gold Rush." A very mixed crew, some of whom would acquire legendary status, such as "Swiftwater Bill" Gates and Klondike Kate, passed through the provincial capital.[1] As the chronicler of the Klondike stampede, Edwin Tappan Adney, a special correspondent with *Harper's Weekly* on his way to cover the scene, wrote from Victoria in mid-August 1897: "The streets of leisurely Victoria are thronged with strange men, and there is an earnest look on their faces and firmness in their step. When the sealers return each autumn there is another crowd, but not like this. Victoria has never seen this crowd before." It was a cosmopolitan crowd, and Victoria outlets were steadily selling everything required for the trip north – coats, hats, mittens, boots, shovels, boats, and bacon: "The man who is not going by next boat for the North, or who is not 'waiting till spring,' or who has not decided reasons for not going at all and why every one else should not go, must be a rarity. He does not exist in this town, so far as I have been able to discover in one week's time."[2] This particular rush was one of the few not dominated by mining corporations.[3]

Prior to the rush to the Yukon, Dan MacLean had reportedly been in Mexico and South America, and Alex had been in the South Pacific. Not surprisingly, both were also attracted to the north. Dan was the first to try his luck. He was not successful. On 29 July 1899, the steamer *St. Paul* arrived in San Francisco from St. Michael, Alaska, with a cargo of gold estimated to be worth over $1,500,000. In its regular feature, "Along the Water Front," the *San Francisco Examiner* singled out the return to the city of one of the passengers: "Captain Dan McLean, who was one of the most noted sealers that ever voyaged in the Bering Sea or the Japan and Siberian coast, returned from the Yukon on the *St. Paul* last night, a very sick man. Dan and his brother Alex are known as men who would accept any chance in a sailing boat and as most skilful navigators ... Captain Dan went to the Yukon last year to try his luck at mining. He contracted a cold which settled on his lungs. He returned yesterday almost a wreck from consumption."[4] The *Daily Colonist* picked up the report a few days later, describing Dan as "a well-known navigator, and a brother of Captain Alex McLean of this city ... Both captains are well known sealing men and Captain Dan's illness will be generally regretted." Even though they had not operated out of the port for a decade, and Alex's role in the Bering Sea Claims Commission (BSCC) in 1896-97 had left some lingering mixed feelings, the *Daily Colonist* readily acknowledged Victoria's association with the MacLeans.[5] Reports of Dan's supposed earlier demise (in "early manhood," "after his first seal catch" and "about 1893" are three examples) were obviously misleading.[6] His return to San Francisco on the *St. Paul* in late July 1899 suggests that he may have had the opportunity to cash his $249.95 cheque from the American government and that it may have escaped the grasp of Edgar Crow Baker. Slightly more than two months later, the San Francisco newspapers carried the following obituary: "In Los Gatos, October 5, 1899, Captain Daniel McLean, beloved brother of Captain Alex McLean, a native of Cape Breton, Nova Scotia, aged 49 Years."[7] The phrasing of the notice was doubtless due to Lucy MacLean – Alex was steamboating on the Yukon River, heading for Dawson City at the time – and accurately reflects the sibling relationship. Los Gatos, in Santa Clara County, south of San Francisco, was just becoming an attraction as a summer colony for wealthy San Franciscans because of its weather. Small consolation can, perhaps, be gleaned from knowing that Dan's final days were spent in a location that averaged over 340 sunny days a year.[8] He had been equal to Alex in seamanship and scrapes. According to contemporaries, Dan was hardly in the shadow of his brother. At times, Alex had to push it to keep up with his older brother. Although he was sometimes hard on his crew members, the impression lingers that Dan was at least as hard on himself. No record of a marriage has surfaced.

Alex MacLean managed to avoid the harsh stare of the public eye for a while after his return to San Francisco from the South Pacific in late August 1898. While his wife Lucy and daughter Catherine would remain in the San Francisco Bay area, Alex continued to seek out the action, possibly prodded by his frustrating experience in the South Pacific.[9] It would have been extraordinary had he not also been numbered among those who headed north to participate in "the last great gold rush."[10] It was one of the grand adventures of the time, and Alex had some familiarity with coastal Alaska. There were numerous routes to the Klondike. An expensive all-water one went via St. Michael, Alaska, followed by another 1,700-mile trip upstream to Dawson. This was the one Dan MacLean had used on his return south in the summer of 1899. Weather dictated a narrow travel window. The two most popular routes to the gold fields started at Dyea Inlet, Alaska, and moved through northern British Columbia into the Yukon Territory. The White Pass route started at Skagway, where Alex's ex-employer on the Fraser River, Captain William Moore, had established a homestead ten years previously and had more recently built a much welcomed and utilized wharf.[11] Skagway, at this time, also featured Jefferson Randolph "Soapy" Smith and his gang. His survival skills had been honed in the Denver underworld. This large and imaginative group of con men, thugs, and thieves used scores of scams to fleece the new arrivals. For Samuel Benfield "Sam" Steele of the North West Mounted Police (NWMP), Skagway was "about the roughest place in the world then," where "robbery and murder were daily occurrences."[12] The trail meandered along the Skagway River valley, eventually reaching the summit at 2,865 feet.

The Chilkoot Pass route started at Dyea. Chilkoot was higher, at 3,550 feet, but it was shorter and less rough and was thus more favoured by the stampeders that year. Members of Smith's gang, although not as numerous as they were in Skagway, were also waiting at Dyea for the naive, unsuspecting, and trusting. However, the Chilkoot also featured Sheep Camp, the Alaska staging area for the push to the summit, and, according to Steele, it was a place where "neither law nor order prevailed."[13] The Chilkoot and White Pass routes converged near Lake Bennett, north of Skagway, Alaska, in northern British Columbia, just below the Yukon border. Bennett was a particularly active town at this time and, by the fall of 1897, featured a NWMP station, with the redoubtable Sam Steele in attendance. By the spring of 1898, "the greatest tent city in the world" was springing up until "there was no place left to pitch another tent." Lake Bennett led into the Yukon River system, and all along the shoreline people were building boats and scows as they prepared for the spring thaws. It was almost the only industry in that area that season, and Bennett was a comparatively peaceful place. For Richard Friesen, "the camps at Lindeman and Bennett appeared to be relatively free of the disorder that characterized the settlements of Skagway, Dyea and Sheep Camp. How much of this was due to the sense of relief that the miners experienced upon completing the arduous trek across the passes is difficult to ascertain. Doubtless the obvious presence of the North-West Mounted Police at the major camps north of the summit and their constant patrols between Lake Bennett and the summit contributed to the peacefulness which contrasted so remarkably with the camps of the south slope trails."[14]

Everyone was waiting for the ice to break up that spring. Appropriately, given the settling presence of the NWMP, the Queen of England's holiday was observed in Bennett on 24 May 1898. Organized by the NWMP, the activities began with baseball in the morning, followed by other sports during the day, and a regatta in the evening. The "great event" was a tug-of-war with Scottish, American, Australian, NWMP, and Nova Scotia teams competing. The ethnicity of the participants underlines the international composition of the Klondikers. The presence of a Nova Scotian team is also suggestive.[15] The Nova Scotians on that tug-of-war team were not the first ones in the area. Robert Henderson, sometimes credited as the co-discoverer (with George Carmack) of the gold field, was from Big Island, Pictou County, Nova Scotia, and had been prospecting in various parts of the world since his teens. Robert, as his brother accurately noted, "belonged to that hardy class of miners that first find the gold for the rich."[16] Immediately after George Carmack measured off his two claims on Rabbit Creek, he met four Nova Scotians trudging through the bush. He mentioned his find and pointed them in the right direction, although he did not inform Henderson. As well, Alex MacDonald had been mining and prospecting since 1880 and had been in the district since 1896. He was a native of Antigonish County, Nova Scotia, immediately east of Henderson's Pictou County. MacDonald would quickly develop a leasing or "lay" system on mining properties in the Yukon that would enable him to acquire, for a while, one of the Klondike's largest fortunes. His sobriquet would soon change from "the Big Moose from Antigonish" to "the King of the Klondike," although he was generally called "Big Alex."[17] The Nova Scotians on the tug-of-war team in Bennett in May 1898 were following a path trekked by many of their fellow provincials.

A few days after the festivities, on 29 May, the ice broke and the rush from Bennett began. On that day, Sam Steele counted more than 800 boats under sail on the lake. In the summer of 1898, at the height of the Klondike rush, a dozen or so small steamboats operated between Lake Bennett and Miles Canyon. They connected with others that plied between the foot of White Horse Rapids and Dawson. The local magistrate was Captain W.J. Rant, an ex-British military man. By the early summer of 1898, Bennett, which was now surveyed and divided into lots, was a reasonably orderly community. While "loose characters" abounded – lots of prostitutes, gamblers, and drinkers – the town was balanced by the presence of the NWMP and Presbyterian minister John Sinclair, who "threatened to report one bank clerk to his superiors if he didn't stop racing around town on his dog sled with 'fast women.'"[18] Superintendent Steele, who was now in command of the NWMP in the Yukon and British Columbia, left Bennett in early September 1898 for Dawson, and, according to him, "the gambling houses were left as [they] found them, wide open but closely watched, lest there should be any cheating ... There were worse men in the world than the gamblers of the Klondyke." During his stay in Bennett, Steele had laconically noted that "only three homicides had taken place, none of them preventable."[19]

Alex's turnaround time in San Francisco after his South Pacific ordeal was brief, and he and another San Francisco resident, Charles Brown, soon decided to head toward the Klondike. They were a year behind the earlier

Klondikers. They travelled over either the Chilkoot or White Pass route, heading initially for Bennett. They may have had it a bit easier than the stampeders of 1897. Nonetheless, the railway, which was being constructed between Skagway and Dawson, known as the White Pass and Yukon route, did not reach Bennett until July 1899, after MacLean and Brown had put in an appearance. Henceforth, the long, exhausting, and dangerous trip from Skagway to Bennett would only take four hours.[20] Alex had a contact in Bennett. "Johnny A." MacNeil was from Washabuckt, Cape Breton. He was a childhood acquaintance and distant cousin. Johnny A. was "very much surprised" when his Cape Breton relative first arrived on the scene, and they spent the winter together at Bennett.[21] They had plenty of time to chat: "There in the long Arctic night he told (Johnny A.) much of his experiences and of his troubles and of his ideas of things."[22]

In the *Bennett Sun,* Johnny A. was described as a "contractor and builder," having useful skills to prepare transportation for when the ice broke in the spring of 1899.[23] In the spring of the previous year, ten men had drowned going through Miles Canyon. Steele, who had established his post at Lake Bennett in March of that year, had immediately improvised a system of registration for boats as well as regulations for moving through the canyon. Women had to walk, pilots had to be hired, and names were listed. It was a sensible, if illegal, move, and many lives were saved.[24] Alex MacLean's party passed through the NWMP checkpoint at Lake Bennett on 9 June 1899. He was one of twenty-six individuals registered with this group, which was larger than usual and consisted of four boats and six scows. Scows were usually big open boxes up to forty feet long, with a square sail, and capable of carrying around twenty tons. Alex MacLean and Charles Brown were the two San Francisco residents numbered among the six Californians. Two of Alex's cousins, Johnny A. MacNeil and his brother Michael, were among the seven Cape Bretoners/Nova Scotians in the party. Six individuals from the Pacific Northwest and three from Scotland made up most of the remainder. They were one of the first groups to head out of Bennett that season. They headed for Dawson, a 370-mile trip by lake and river, with "friendly waters" and rapids, whirlpools, and sandbars.[25]

It is not known how many of the twenty-six, if any, found gold. Many went to the Klondike not to dig for gold but to make money by supplying services to others. The few in this group who can be traced fit the pattern. Johnny A. returned to Bennett from Dawson in mid-summer, and the local paper was "pleased to learn that Mr. MacNeil will again engage in business in our city."[26] Bennett, being the end of the rail line that season, would boom for another year.[27] Johnny A. appears to have settled back into Bennett and honed his skills in the service industry. He got involved in the operation of the Palace Hotel, one of the numerous roadhouses that sprang up along all of the various routes to the gold fields. It was a common practice to lease the drinking section of these establishments from the frequently female proprietors. Roadhouses "ranged from dugouts and dirty tents to relatively luxurious 2-storey complexes," and the Palace Hotel was at the high end.[28] It was owned by Mrs. M.J. Taylor and Mrs. Lane and was in operation by May 1899. The reports were favourable: "Mrs. Lane and Mrs. Taylor are making the Palace hotel restaurant very popular. The delicious meals served by them remind one of home. Everything connected with the Palace is first class."[29] In September 1899, these women opened the new Grand Palace Hotel, advertised as the "best equipped hotel in the Yukon district. Everything new and first class." Both establishments were operating in December 1899, and the Palace Hotel Bar, with Johnny A. MacNeil as proprietor, promised "the best of Liquors and Cigars."[30] Next door to the Palace was the Arctic Restaurant and Hotel. This establishment, according to a local journalist, was somewhat more seedy: "I would not advise respectable women to go there to sleep as they are liable to hear that which would be repugnant to their feelings and uttered, too, by the depraved of their own sex." Irving Levin and Fred Trump operated the Arctic.[31] Fred's grandson Donald would make his mark in Atlantic City and New York.

There was a fine dinner at the Palace Hotel that autumn for Captain Rant (he was moving on to be the deputy mining recorder for the Dalton Trail), and the menu was "worthy the efforts of a Windsor chef." On this occasion, feasting and toasting went on until the early morning. The host and hostess were Mr. MacNeil and Mrs. Simpson. By July 1900, Johnny A. was operating the bar of the Grand Palace, the "Best $2 House in the City."[32] But his construction skills were no longer in demand in Bennett. By this time, the White Pass and Yukon route railway line, connecting Skagway and Whitehorse over the White Pass, was completed. It signalled the end of Bennett (only eighty people were still there by the early summer of 1900).[33] Johnny A. MacNeil moved on and continued in the construction business. He would help rebuild San Francisco after the earthquake and fire of 1906. His son Neil spent considerable time during his youth with his grandparents in Washabuckt, Cape Breton, absorbing stories about his relatives and their neighbours. It was grist for his romanticized remembrances in *The Highland Heart of Nova Scotia*. In 1918, Neil would begin a thirty-five-year career at the *New York Times*, eventually occupying the position of managing editor.[34]

Alex MacLean was another Cape Bretoner who was not preoccupied with prospecting for gold. He reverted to his old trade of steamboating, this time on the Yukon River.[35] The *W.S. Stratton* was a seventy-five-foot, 100-ton wooden sternwheeler, built in Seattle in 1898. She arrived in Dawson in June 1899. Big Alex MacDonald acquired a financial interest in her, and Alex MacLean soon took command of the vessel.[36] The Upper Yukon River, between Whitehorse and Dawson, was open for about four months of the year. The ice that year arrived early. Superintendent A. Bowen Perry, who had just relieved Sam Steele as head of the NWMP in the Yukon, first encountered ice on 12 October.[37] Less than two weeks later, two sternwheelers, the *W.S. Stratton* and the *Willie Irving,* were racing against each other, and the freeze-up, as they steamed toward Dawson. Both lost. Steamboat racing was a common and quite competitive tradition in the west, and Alex had probably been introduced to it on the Fraser River by Captain William Moore in the early 1880s.[38] On 24 October, the vessels were caught in ice and crushed on the Yukon River, near Selwyn Creek, 145 miles from Dawson. There were some tense moments. According to one first-hand account, "we found the *Stratton* people all ashore; but they had a narrow escape; the *Stratton* being in mid stream, broadside on, was caught and lifted up on the ice, which broke away on the lower side and the crowding ice on the other turned her clean over, she quickly filled with water and sank. The people had just time to scramble on to the ice and ashore, leaving everything behind; luckily no lives lost. The river was very deep at that spot, she went clean out of sight."[39]

The episode received extensive coverage in the Dawson newspapers. One of the curious aspects was the lack of discipline, or concern, among the crew. The situation was a far cry from the rigid realities on the North Pacific sealing schooners. After members of the *Stratton* crew unsuccessfully attempted to put a line ashore, MacLean called for volunteers to try again, but only the pilot, H. Macbeth, and two passengers, Leroy Pelletier and Henry Quiner, responded. They carried all 800 pounds of cable ashore and made it fast. They then assisted the "more timid" of the passengers ashore. Among those was the individual in charge of the mail. He would be publicly and soundly criticized for abandoning his charge, as there had been plenty of time to fling the sacks on to the ice and walk ashore. Then there were the engineers, who, according to Pelletier, "all along had behaved badly, refusing to obey the full speed bell from the pilot and so handicapping him in his manipulation of the boat in the ice, [and] were among the first to leave the boat." As the situation continued to deteriorate, the fireman, John Reily, assisted by Pelletier and one other volunteer, filled in until the vessel turned over and the big jam caught up to her and ripped the side out. Pelletier, who was experiencing his fourth wreck in five weeks, also provided a few public comments about Alex's performance that were carried in the *Dawson Daily News:* "I have to say that Captain MacLean behaved splendidly throughout. He kept cool, was the last one to leave the boat, and did all that any one man could for the comfort of the passengers afterwards, giving up his bed and eating at the last table always."[40]

Henry Quiner, a passenger who volunteered when the difficulties on the river began, made his comments on the incident in the *Klondike Nugget* a few days later: "He speaks highly of the conduct of Captain MacLean, and says that the latter deprived himself in order to comfort some of the passengers." Quiner, a miner with four years experience in the north country, was quite critical of the NWMP constable in charge at Selwyn, a view shared by the other passengers. Quiner censured Constable Herbert Gregory for a slow response to the distress whistles, which shrieked for an hour with no response from the shore. This had delayed the setting of the lifeline. "Two men, with lanterns on shore, could have rendered to us invaluable assistance, and unquestionably the mail, and much else that was lost, would have been saved," Quiner stated. Around 1,000 pounds of mail and all baggage and freight were lost. In Quiner's words, "after the distressed people had been landed more than half of the men were obliged to pass the remainder of the night around a campfire which had been built near the edge of the river. I do not think that the police treated the stranded passengers and crew in a proper manner. Constable Gregory did not give those who were destitute any food or clothing while I was at Selwyn."[41]

The captain of the *Stratton* also gave a lengthy public statement that was published in Dawson's strongly pro-American *Klondike Nugget*. This was not Alex's usual style. Generally, he avoided reporters and was not one to engage in public criticism of authority in general or officers of the law in particular, regardless what he might say or do privately. But Constable Gregory's apparent incompetence, and lack of compassion, struck a nerve, and Alex responded in a measured, factual fashion. Wolf Larsen's stateroom, it could be noted, had a rack of well-used classics, and "his language was excellent."[42] So was Alex's, and he commenced with a disarming preface and then proceeded to solidly skewer his target, with more than one Victorian turn of phrase:

> I dislike exceedingly to pass reflections upon any member of the N.W.M.P. Until this affair happened, I had never met a constable or officer of the department whom I did not consider efficient and worthy to occupy any position of trust. I do not now attach blame to the department, for I fully realize that what complaints I have only affect the conduct of one or two men.
>
> I wish to state that I saw no men with lights on the shore, and we were obliged to stretch our line as best we could. Immediately after the passengers had been landed, I started to look for the police station. It took me some time to find it. I explained to Constable Gregory the state of affairs, and after considerable parley, he reluctantly consented to give quarters to the eight female passengers.
>
> I returned to the crowd on the shore and notified them of what the police would do, and of the meagre accommodations at the bunkhouse. About 16 people, eight men and eight women, slept at the police station the first night. The bunk house accommodated some others, but at least half the men passed the first night around the camp fires, and many of them were insufficiently clothed.

> The following morning Constable Gregory notified me to get my passengers out of his station. He gave them nothing to eat. In compliance with a telegram from Major Perry, the constable sold me some provisions at noon on the 24th. I distributed them among the passengers and crew. About 15 men, whom I had picked up on the way down the river, were absolutely destitute. They were not employees nor passengers of mine and I thought that it was the duty of the police to care for such as these. But the constable emphatically refused to render them any help whatever; and to save them from starvation I was compelled to render them assistance.
>
> I think that the police at Selwyn treated the stranded people terribly. It is my opinion that Constable Gregory is incapable of filling his present position, and that he should be removed.
>
> I want you to give due credit to Alex MacDonald. He telegraphed me to spare no expense in assisting the shipwrecked people. I did the best I could, and the cost of everything which was furnished to them will be paid by Mr. MacDonald.[43]

Alex MacLean and Alex MacDonald were practising what could be described as a culture of consideration or the "code of the Yukon."[44] Jack London would have understood. Constable Gregory was informed of the allegations and invited an inquiry into his conduct.[45]

MacLean shepherded the rest of the *Stratton's* passengers into Dawson, initially on scows and eventually on dog sleds. MacLean was the last to leave Selwyn, having made arrangements for the ex-crew and passengers of the *Stratton* to receive assistance from the NWMP and the Yukon Field Force. The NWMP supplied the dog teams and drivers.[46] The inquiry into Gregory's conduct, if it was held, did not merit a mention in the annual NWMP report that year, although Superintendent Perry did strike a defensive note.[47] Superintendent P.C.H. Primrose, in charge of "B" Division in Dawson, reported specifically on the incident with the *Stratton* as if he was responding directly to the public accusations of MacLean and others, without acknowledging them: "Everything possible was done to alleviate the hardships of the passengers. Food, blankets, and clothing, &c., supplied."[48] Still, the criticisms targeting the constable could have been close to the mark. Herbert Gregory was from Eden Bridge, England, and had joined the NWMP in 1892. He re-engaged a few times and, while northern postings were admittedly difficult in this period, assessments of his conduct by his superior officers declined from "good" in 1897 to "fair" in 1900 and "indifferent" by 1901. He was discharged at Dawson when his last term of service expired in April 1901. His attempt to re-engage in Regina in 1903 was rejected on medical grounds.[49]

A few of the best-known stories about Alex's sojourn in the north are carried in his cousin's *The Highland Heart*. One of them apparently occurred at the Palace Hotel in Bennett, where a gambler, known both for his cheating and his accuracy with a gun, was operating. "Bullet" Brown had already dispatched one complainer that season, and enough was enough. Some of Brown's victims set up a game between him and Alex. The word travelled fast, and the saloon filled quickly. Alex soon "caught the gambler cheating, slammed his cards on the table, and denounced him for what he was in language that could not be misunderstood. The gambler rose quietly and slowly from the table, simulating what dignity and offended innocence he could, and challenged the Sea Wolf to fight it out with pistols ... MacLean insisted on accepting the challenge on the spot and at once, and named Father (Johnnie A.) for his second." While "they all carried guns," Alex was not an expert. However, he remained unconcerned with the gambler's ensuing display of marksmanship and applauded and congratulated Brown for the exhibition. Then he spoke to the gambler: "'I don't know much about duels. Neither does my second. But I understand it is my privilege to name the distance.' 'That's right,' replied the gambler. 'All right then,' bellowed the Sea Wolf, 'you stand on one side of that table and I will stand on the other side. And you yellow-bellied son of a sea cook, you are not going to shoot first.'" The gambler protested but Alex insisted, and he had the crowd with him. "The strutting braggart turned coward. Captain Alex made him admit that he was a crook, a jail-bird, a wife-deserter and a murderer. He walked up to him and calmly took his two Colts and handed them to (Johnny A). That done, he battered and slammed the gambler about the saloon and finished up by throwing him out the door into the Arctic snow and cold. That was the last Bennett City saw of the gambler."[50] This version reinforces Thomas Stone's findings on the mining community in the Yukon, where "an informal system of popular frontier justice" curtailed and reduced the potential for further violence.[51] Alex's role in this informal and accepted process was just what one would expect from an emerging folk figure. Neil F. MacNeil is the source for this account and his son, Neil MacNeil (Johnny A.'s grandson), later commented: "A large part of my father's knowledge about the Sea Wolf came from word of mouth. Probably most of it from his own father, with whom my father was close. My father's father was in Bennett City with MacLean during the gold rush there ... My father's words in the interview seem to suggest that when he wasn't entirely sure of some facts of the Yukon tale he just went along with what seemed logical."[52]

Unfortunately, situating the incident in Bennett, or in the Yukon Territory, may undermine its credibility. The NWMP presence suggests there would not have been much in the way of gunplay, although the Mounties acknowledged and permitted the "wide open" gambling houses in Bennett. And in Dawson, as NWMP Superintendent Perry noted in 1899, "a man carrying a six shooter exposed on his person would be as great a curiosity in Dawson as in Ottawa."[53] This is not to suggest that Dawson was free of gamblers or that links between cards and gunplay did not exist. Dawson's population at the time was quite cosmopolitan, and the American segment was the largest group, measuring almost 40 percent, although it also included naturalized Americans.[54] Alex had reached Dawson from Selwyn Creek in early November 1899. A brief editorial note in the *Dawson Daily News* at the time noted: "No better evidence of the good times now prevailing in Dawson is to be found than the nightly crowded condition of the various theatres, dance halls, gambling rooms and saloons. They are not mere crowds of idle men, but appear to have money and to spend it freely."[55] Over the next twelve-month period, there were 807 convictions for gambling in the district, along with three for carrying a concealed weapon and two for cheating at cards. One individual, Rattlesnake Pete, was hit over the head with a handgun during a card game.[56] So, while gunfights were not significant in this territory, which was patrolled by the NWMP, gambling was. As Superintendent Primrose noted that month, the NWMP had to deal with the "scum and outlaws of the Coast cities."[57] The incident with gambler Brown could also have occurred somewhere in the north. Another story about Alex from Johnny A.'s son is also suggestive, and sparse: "One spring he teamed up with two Montana miners, named Hustler and Brown, and left Bennett to seek a fortune in the gold fields. Nothing was heard of him for two months and then he returned to the Palace Hotel alone. The absence of Hustler and Brown was noted, but no one asked questions. Finally Father got the Sea Wolf alone and asked the big question. 'Oh, they just got sick and died,' Captain Alex replied. That was that."[58] Records of the Yukon Territory indicate that two people with the surname Brown died in this period, but details are few. Neither one was Charles Brown, Alex's initial travelling companion into the north.[59]

Gold was originally discovered on Anvil Creek, near Cape Nome, in September 1898, and the stampede intensified the following summer when people realized that gold was literally under their feet on the beaches of Nome. That season, about 800 prospectors produced around $2,000,000.[60] The next gold rush was on. Another of Johnnie A. MacNeil's brothers, Captain Alex MacNeil, was in Nome when MacLean apparently put in an appearance there. Nome seemed to be a northern equivalent of the "Barbary Coast." According to Captain MacNeil, "gambling houses, saloons, dancing halls, brothels operated without restraint. Crime and vice were open and profitable. Drunken men battled in the streets with fists or guns. Assault, robbery and murder were daily occurrences. No one felt safe; and in fact no one was. Law enforcement had broken down so badly that no one could be found to serve as sheriff." When Alex arrived, someone suggested that he be made sheriff. He was intrigued: "One after the other the new sheriff visited the scenes of Nome's trouble and gave his orders. That was enough. A deep and beautiful calm descended on the city. Daily the Sea Wolf patrolled the city, greeting everybody cheerfully and occasionally dropping into a saloon for a drink or something to eat. Everywhere he went he was saluted and admired. Nome at last had met its match. The reign of the Sea Wolf did not last long, however, for he moved on and Nome went back to its old ways."[61]

Nome did not have a sheriff and, while there is no reason to suspect that Neil F. MacNeil or his uncle Alex MacNeil toyed with the accuracy of the tale, little collaborative evidence has been discovered to place Alex MacLean in Nome. This gold town had marshals, deputy marshals, and police chiefs, and for a while there was a wild old time around Nome. A similar situation could have occurred somewhere else – the absence of evidence is hardly definitive. In these tales, the actual location was of less significance than the substance of the story. It certainly fits with MacLean and the popular frontier justice theme. In his book, *Klondike Fever*, Pierre Berton cautions: "It is undeniable that the Klondike odyssey has been subject in the past to some fantastic misstatements, errors, half-truths, gerblings, over-romanticizations, and out-and-out fabrications."[62] William Hunt, who has produced considerable scholarly work on the region during this period, offers a pertinent case, which could also be applied to MacLean's sojourn in the north and elsewhere. Hunt uses Jack Kearns' autobiography *The Million Dollar Gate* as a cautionary example: "It is a revelation of the uncertainty of one's reminiscences of events that occurred 60 years past and a warning to historians. In Kearns' memory all the northern gold rushes were one. Stories heard and actual experiences are lumped; geography is confused; time sequences are distorted. Kearns constantly refers to the Klondike, though he did not get within 1,500 miles of that legendary stream." Kearns remembers coming across Soapy Smith in Nome, even though Smith died before Nome existed: "This particular mixup of fact and legend is instructive because it points up the truth that, in a sense, Soapy Smith was at Nome in spirit ... Memory of his colorful infamy kept his image bright. He was the predominant folk anti-hero and in the saloons and in crowded roadhouses on the trail, wherever men gathered to divert themselves, Soapy Smith lived again."[63]

Many people who had found their way to Nome at the time had already experienced failure in the Klondike. They arrived on Alaska's Seward Peninsula disappointed and destitute: "Some were riffraff, disgusted with the strictness of Canadian law. Their bitterness was magnified when they arrived at Nome and found that the entire region had been staked."[64] Two NWMP officers, P.C.H. Primrose and Z.T. Wood, used the term "tough element" and linked the decline in crime in the Yukon Territory at that time with the movement of the crowd toward Nome. Primrose considered the Yukon district to be "well rid of them."[65] Nome had initially been left "to its own resources," although a military force of ten men from St. Michael, under Lieutenant Oliver Spaulding, arrived on 29 June 1899. In September, voters selected W.M. Eddy as police chief. While robberies, assaults, and thefts were numerous, there were only six murders between September 1899 and October 1900, even though it was noted that Butte, Montana, "which is famous as the wickedest city in the United States, is a righteous and law-abiding community" compared to Nome.[66] Eddy's job was made a bit easier in November 1899 when the NWMP from Dawson passed on a list of undesirables, including "the worst criminals ever known on this continent," who were on their way to Nome. The roster included some ex-members of Soapy Smith's gang, and more than one was described as an "all round crook." Many of the known hoods were unceremoniously and illegally dispatched from Nome to Seattle on the revenue cutter *Bear's* last sailing in the autumn. This practice was comparable to the NWMP's practice of giving out a "blue ticket" when they arrested individuals they considered to be "bad characters" and offered them an option to leave the territory, a policy that was also illegal and efficient. Most of Eddy's arrests were for drunkenness. He personally was probably wanted for criminal activities in Colorado and Utah. Eventually, charges of corruption against Eddy included double billing for prisoner expenses, collecting tribute money from prostitutes and gamblers, and other questionable practices.[67] As Thomas Stone notes, the deputy marshals "seldom noted the frequent robberies, burglaries, and assaults that enlivened Nome's streets every night. Most of their duty hours were logged at the Northern Saloon, where harmony and good fellowship prevailed. Perhaps the tender officers already felt too cold to patrol the streets."[68]

By the following March, 837 people in Nome were so disgusted with the lackadaisical approach to law enforcement that they signed a petition for military rule.[69] The first US deputy marshal in the area was Frank Canton, a man with a reputation for law enforcement in Wyoming and Oklahoma, and under his real name, Joe Horner, was wanted as a criminal in Texas. He resigned in 1899.[70] Wyatt Earp arrived in Nome with his wife in 1899 to operate the Dexter Saloon. He behaved generally as "a quiet businessman," although he did get into occasional altercations with patrons and policemen. Cornelius L. Vawter was marshal in 1900-01. He was replaced by one of the corrupt crew known as the "spoilers."[71] Rex Beach captured this affair with his novel *The Spoilers*. Little wonder there were 127 lawyers practising in Nome in 1900. According to Carl Lomen, the son of one of the honest ones, "such was the situation in Nome, Alaska, in the summer of 1900. No law and order. No protection for the honest prospector. No decent living quarters. No food at reasonable prices. No conveniences and comforts of any kind. Weather that would wear the patience of a clergyman. And home thousands of miles away."[72] However, one must be careful not to dichotomize the disciplined Canadian north and its freewheeling American counterpart. There were "deep similarities between the Canadian and the American mining frontiers."[73] In Nome in this period, the individual who probably comes close to fitting Alex MacNeil's story about Alex MacLean is Albert J. Cody, a former Portland, Oregon, policeman. Alex MacLean is not listed among the hoods, rogues, riffraff, marshals, or police chiefs of Nome in the writings dealing with the period, much as one would like to imagine Alex and Wyatt swapping stories in the Dexter Saloon.[74]

There is one other vessel linked with MacLean in the Yukon. In 1901, the boilers, wheel, and other machinery were removed from the steamer *Clara* and installed on the barge *Monarch*.[75] This unwieldy hybrid operated on the Whitehorse-Dawson run.[76] A good friend of Alex's later wrote that around this time Alex purchased the *Clara Monarch* from a Captain Peterson: "From Whitehorse he put a gang of carpenters to work and fitted her up as a passenger boat and sailed for White Horse with a full complement of passengers late in October, everyone predicting that he would not be able to accomplish the trip owing to ice, but he did and came back with passengers and a load of freight and many scows in tow." He paid off the amount outstanding, $6,000, gave the boat back to its previous owner, and left for the south.[77] The records, like the vessel, are confusing. There was a rapid turnover of ownership of the vessel in question in this period. A court case with at least four legal firms and a variety of clients surfaced in the spring of 1902.[78] Yukon River steamboat chronicler W.D. McBride did link the vessel with MacLean and noted that she was known locally as the "Pirate Ship." The reason for the connection is unclear, as London's novel was not yet written. It could have been applied later.[79] A few years later, most of her machinery was removed, and the hull's final resting place was in the Clara Monarch slough, below Whitehorse.[80]

Alex MacLean's sojourn in the north spawned some fine stories and left many unanswered questions. Rex Beach, who wrote the most famous stories regarding the events in Nome at the time, only met Alex in Vancouver a decade later.[81] During this period, Alex was also master of the 1,966-ton *City of Sydney*, a steamer owned by the Pacific Mail Steam Ship Company, and was also employed with the New England Fish Company.[82] When Max Dauphin, a thirty-one-year-old pattern maker with the Albion Iron Works in Victoria, died on 13 July 1902, newspaper reports noted that his sister and brother-in-law, Lucy and Alex MacLean, were living in California.[83] Alex was not listed in the San Francisco directories for 1900-01, but during the next four years he changed residences in the Bay area three times.[84] The almost annual change of address may suggest the family's declining financial position – a reflection of Alex's less-than-successful quests in the South Pacific and the Klondike. What may have made the situation more frustrating was the significant increase in the value of sealskins in this period, a trend that was already evident at the annual auction in London in December 1899.[85]

By this time, another long-standing sealing dispute was working its way toward a resolution. In September 1900, an exchange of notes between the United States and Russia agreed to refer the seizures of the *James Hamilton Lewis* and three other American vessels, which had occurred a decade earlier, to arbitration.[86] The venue was the Permanent Court of Arbitration, which had been developed after the first International Peace Conference at The Hague in 1899. Tobie Michel Charles Asser, counsellor to the Ministry of Foreign Affairs in the Netherlands, would finally resolve the *Lewis* case. The owners, the captain, Alex MacLean, and the crew had initially submitted a claim for $128,189.60. The final damage claim totalled $101,336. Asser conducted the hearings at The Hague from 27 June to 4 July 1902. Herbert H.D. Peirce represented the claimants: "The Government of the United States of America maintains that the said arrests and seizures, as well as all the other acts relating thereto which resulted in injury to citizens of the United States, were contrary to international law and to the treaty rights of the United States, as well as an invasion of the personal rights of its citizens."[87] Their "statement of the facts" noted that the *Lewis* headed toward Copper Island on 2 August 1891 to test the ship's chronometer, then started for its home port. At this point, the Russians arrived: "The vessel with her cargo and equipment and the personal property of the crew was confiscated, and her captain, officers, and crew held as prisoners and subjected to indignity and harsh treatment and the crew put to hard labor. They were miserably lodged in an unwholesome and vermin-infested building and inadequately fed, and in consequence of this treatment they all suffered permanent injury to their health, became emaciated in form, depressed in spirit, and undermined in constitution." They also pointed out that while the female seals travelled distances of up to 200 miles from the rookeries in search of food, the males seldom left the islands during the season. Since between 80-95 percent of the skins seized on the *Lewis* were female, the catch was "predominantly a pelagic one." The statement went on to question the Russian captain's assertion as to how far the vessel had travelled after being sighted, suggesting that the *Lewis* was far too slow to achieve such a rate of speed. It then dealt with the various Russian suspicions that the vessel "had been or intended to be poaching" within the Russian jurisdiction. Much time was then taken up with the question of the logbook: "Had a court of admiralty been held upon the seizure the log book would have been produced in that court. That such a court was not held is no fault of the claimants', whose agent, the captain, repeatedly demanded one." In addition, the Russian government "had arrested and imprisoned the master and crew of this vessel, and after they were released left them to make their way home penniless as best they might."[88]

The American case was persuasive enough for the Dutch counsellor. According to Asser, "the seizure of the schooner took place according to the party claimant at a distance of about 20, and according to the defendant party at a distance of 11 or 12, miles from Russian territory, and that even if the latter version be the true one, the act was accomplished outside Russian territorial waters, which is, moreover, admitted by both parties." Asser decided that "the seizure and confiscation of the *James Hamilton Lewis* and her cargo, as well as the imprisonment of her crew, should ... be regarded as illegal acts," and he proceeded to fix the indemnity. A claim of $25,000 had been entered for the vessel and equipment. He awarded $9,000, pointing out that five months of provisions had already been consumed. That was probably satisfactory to the claimants, considering that MacLean had originally purchased the vessel for Herman Liebes for $4,500. Asser awarded $5,088 for the 424 skins confiscated at $12 per skin. He felt the $36,400 claim for a probable catch of 2,600 skins excessive. (At The Hague, the Americans brought up the case of the *Triumph* before the BSCC as an example of loss of probable catch.) Asser was not totally convinced, and he estimated that a missed catch of 500 seals would be worth $6,000. Finally, for the imprisonment and mental and physical suffering of the seventeen men, he found "evidence in support of these allegations has not been submitted," but because of the "illegal imprisonment" they had right to claim an indemnity, which he fixed at $500 per person. His decision on 29 November 1902 totalled $28,588 with 6 percent interest from 1 January 1892, bringing it to a total of $47,684.78.[89] It is not known how much of this sum Alex MacLean received. A number of sources leave the impression that he received all of it but that seems unlikely. He did not own the vessel, although he would have been eligible for a portion of the probable catch and his individual $500.[90] One source does have Isaac Liebes (as assignee of the owner and assignee and attorney for crew members) receiving $32,547 and Peirce and Tingle picking up $13,940 for legal fees.[91] If correct, this would account for the lion's share of the award.

Controversy continued to swirl around the case for a while longer.[92] A number of contemporary and later sources maintained that MacLean had tricked the American government in the whole affair by pretending to be an American citizen.[93] A few years later, Henry Wood Elliott described the whole process that culminated at The Hague as "a strange and shameful sequel." He claimed that the owners were "determined to recoup themselves even if they suborned perjury and forgery" and that MacLean was a willing participant in the scheme: "McLean, who commanded the *Lewis*, not being an American citizen ... was induced to perjure himself and make oath that he was. This false oath was appended to this bogus claim and a bogus ship's log, made up by this perjured MacLean, was presented to the Department of State as genuine and valid proof that the claim ... was a just and legal one."[94] Elliott was especially adamant on this aspect of citizenship, although numerous depositions and testimony from the 1880s and

1890s state that Alex MacLean was an American citizen throughout the period. It was certainly the reason why he had been specifically cut out of the claims awards a few years earlier. But the Americans had made their point. The Russian seizure had been illegal. The case was closed.

Quick payment of the award by the Russian government prompted the American sealers, who had been seized by their own government cutters, to push their case again as they sought legal redress. The stories about the dangers of Victoria and the unselfish patriotism of the American sealers during the commission hearings in 1896-97 were a prominent part of the argument. As the American Senate Committee on Foreign Relations noted in 1904, the American sealers who had testified at the BSCC hearings "had to conquer personal safety for the witnesses of the United States in Victoria by aggressive fighting for it on the streets."[95] The search for compensation, through various congressional committees, would continue for two more decades. By 1924, there was the additional plaintive and, by then, not inaccurate plea that "the only group left without indemnity, and suffering extreme poverty in their old age from the loss of property is the group composed of our own citizens."[96]

For some, the more pressing question was what could be done about the state of the sealing industry in general. In June 1902, the House Ways and Means Committee in Washington dusted off the suggestion that they solve the problem by killing all of the seals on the rookeries, with the exception of 10,000 adult females and 1,000 young males. Otherwise, "the pelagic hunter [would] continue the ruthless and inhuman destruction of the fur seal in the ocean until their extermination is complete." This drastic solution would "end the business of the pelagic hunter" and the "killing of the surplus female seals ourselves is therefore an act of mercy, since it at once puts an end to the extreme brutality of the pelagic hunter's work."[97] This version was slightly modified from an earlier one by the same committee in the fifty-fourth Congress, which had suggested the species be wiped out entirely. The Americans were apparently serious, believing the herd was rapidly disappearing. The British, while aware of the decline, did not think it was in danger. The American reasoning was partly financial. According to the calculations of the Ways and Means Committee, the costs of the Paris tribunal, the payment to Canadian sealers, the expenses of patrols and treasury agents, and other related costs between 1890 and 1901, when compared with the revenues from the seal islands in the same period, resulted in a deficit of $1,441,331.97.[98] A minority report concurred with the committee in some respects. It strongly disagreed with the drastic measures suggested and went on to quote David Starr Jordan's assessment that "the idea is a monstrous one," which would acknowledge a serious weakness in diplomacy.[99] In Kurkpatrick Dorsey's judgment, the idea was "economically shortsighted, scientifically indefensible, and morally abhorrent."[100]

In the space of a few years, as the nineteenth century was coming to a close, Alex MacLean had become involved in a couple of classic adventures – a year-long, physically taxing expedition to the South Pacific, followed by an arduous venture to the Klondike. He had just turned forty, although blaming his mishaps on a mid-life crisis does not, somehow, seem appropriate. The documentation that has been uncovered from these episodes – in particular, the feat of sailing the *Sophia Sutherland* single-handedly for thousands of miles and eventually returning to the home port of San Francisco, and the publicly collaborating reports of his demeanour during the difficulties with the *W.S. Stratton* – suggest hardiness, resilience, concern for those under his command, and determination. Being initially duped by Sorensen, and racing on the Yukon River late in the season, evokes his questionable judgment, but his ultimate actions when difficulties arose on both occasions underline his strength of character. The awareness of others of these attributes doubtless contributed to the way they perceived him.

10
Poaching with the *Carmencita,* 1904-05

For a few years, from November 1899 to August 1904, west coast newspapers were curiously silent about the activities of Alex MacLean. Listed as living in San Francisco during the 1902-04 period, Alex, Lucy, and Catherine had by 1905 moved across the bay to Oakland and back into the news.[1] Clothing trends and international conflict formed the backdrop to one of Alex's most publicized illegal excursions. Fur coats were back in fashion. In the early Edwardian era, North Pacific sealskins had become, after sable, the most popular of the precious furs. This vogue prompted increased activity in the mid-winter London fur auctions. Sealskins were fetching a high price in this period, averaging $20 per skin.[2] There was also a war to consider. In early February 1904, Japan had severed diplomatic relations with Russia and a conflict had begun. The Russian rookeries located on Robben Island would soon be far less protected.[3] The situation was not unlike 1898 when, because of the Spanish-American War, the American Department of the Treasury had diverted revenue cutters from the Bering Sea. On this occasion, the Japanese sealers, increasingly interested in the industry, had moved in quickly. Sealer Alf Bissett later testified that the Japanese "had drawn from us our best hunters. We had educated them, and they took our best men, and they competed with us ... In 1896 there were a good many desertions from Canadian vessels ... The Japanese carried lots of liquor on board, and I had occasion to know they were bad neighbours."[4] The Japanese had been operating a dozen sealers by 1897 and within a few years had a fleet considerably larger than the Canadian one. In 1904, the Japanese fleet again responded to the changed conditions and engaged in "an unrestricted slaughter such as had never been seen in northern waters."[5]

Nor did the altered situation around the Russian seal rookeries go unnoticed in San Francisco. In the spring of 1904, a young Irishman, Stuart Thompson, having just completed a two-year stint as a freight clerk on an Alaska steamer, was looking for work in the San Francisco area. He acquired what initially seemed to be a rather prosaic task, "finding the owner of an old, partly submerged two-masted schooner in Oakland Creek." This job would evolve into one of the most exciting years of Thompson's life. He completed the search, and the *Jennie Thelin* was purchased for $800 and hurriedly repaired.[6] The ninety-one-foot, 146-ton vessel, which was "the only commercial wooden sailing vessel over 100 tons ever built south of San Francisco," had been built at Davenport Landing, near Santa Cruz, in 1869.[7] The identity of the new owner(s) was somewhat murky. H.C. Groeper of the Shipowners and Merchants Tugboat Company of San Francisco had sold it to Henry Smith who, in turn, had sold it to W.J. Wood. In April, Wood surrendered the American registry, and, on 4 May, E.F. Scott, claiming Mexican citizenship and supposedly being the new owner, applied to the Mexican consul-general in San Francisco for Mexican registry. Provisional papers were granted. Apparently, the schooner was the property of William J. Wood, who owned a sail-making company, R.J. Tyson, a shipping and insurance broker, and William J. Woodside, a shipbroker. They were all based in San Francisco. Scott had become involved only after an unsuccessful attempt to get British registration. Since he held Mexican citizenship, the vessel was technically transferred to him.[8]

During this ownership and registration shuffle, Thompson slipped back into his previous occupation of freight clerk and became responsible for provisioning the vessel. He would work closely with the new captain of the rehabilitated *Jennie Thelin*. Alex MacLean, after a ten-year absence, returned to his previous occupation, even though the Americans had been prohibited from pelagic sealing since 1898. The *Jennie Thelin* was fitted out and quickly transformed into a sealer carrying eight of "the best of boats." Tyson paid for the guns for the voyage, which were selected by MacLean.[9] However, provisioning and preparing the vessel proved to be easier than finding a crew. The purported purpose of "a codfish expedition to Mazatlan, Mexico," as the official version had it, did not attract more than six experienced seamen. The waterfront warning system was operating. The authorities would later allege that the spreading of the vessel's early cod fishing image was "the first deceit" in a process that would witness many more. Nevertheless, as Thompson recollected, Alex did manage to find a crew. It was San Francisco, and, according to Thompson, Captain MacLean "coerced waterfront bums, drunks, jail-birds and others who were brought from boarding-house owners having rent money owed them. Most of these were shanghaied. The ship's 'Doctor' later proved to be an unlicensed quack and was finally arrested at the end of the expedition. Our cook showed his ignorance by making coffee with seawater and was almost thrown overboard. About eight of the crew had never been on the water."[10] A Russian crew member, Oscar Watzschoff, in a contemporary account, described his colleagues as "chiefly composed of men who had been shanghaied – farm hands, donkey drivers, roustabouts and the like."[11] In a private conversation later that year, however, which was tempered by some recent public scrutiny, Watzschoff stated that stories of being shanghaied were "bosh" and several of the crew "were just going up there for the summer and for the fun of it."[12] The "doctor," R.E.S. de Smidt, a British subject and an apparently likeable chap with a vaguely questionable character, was "a jolly good fellow to have on board" who had asked to participate, personally and financially. Predictably known as "Pills" on the trip, he "was along for the fun and excitement."[13] He would prove to be quite useful. Each crew member was asked to become a Mexican citizen. Mexican regulations required a number of citizens of that country to be aboard for registration purposes. Mexico had not signed the Paris award or any of the other agreements that attempted to regulate the industry in these years, and so it was not bound by the numerous provisions that hovered over the sealing industry.[14] On the night of 4 May 1904, hours after the *Jennie Thelin* had acquired provisional Mexican registry and a new name, the *Carmencita* slipped out of San Francisco Bay flying the Mexican flag. It was not an auspicious beginning, according to Thompson. As soon as the sails were hoisted and caught a breeze, the main sail and boom tumbled down on to the deck. Since the vessel was just outside the buoys, the rocks posed an immediate danger, so the small boats were lowered to tow against the breeze, while the first mate spent "an agonizing hour aloft" to repair the rotten ropes.[15] While the new nameplates were being carved and in spite of the fact that she had been cleared for Mazatlan, Mexico, the vessel then headed north.[16] It was soon clear to all on board that they were off to poach seals. This discovery was hardly a surprise to those who were awake, alert, and sober.

Initially, the detailed official preparations made in San Francisco appeared to be paying dividends. At one point, the American cutter *Bear* intercepted the *Carmencita* but found the papers in order. "The officers remarked that the crew looked more Irish than Mexican. McLean passed out cigars and the officers left, marvelling at the command of English our Mexican crew had. Actually there was only one Mexican in our crew, and he was an American citizen."[17] One contemporary account has the *Carmencita* sailing into the Bering Sea under the Mexican flag when she was questioned by another vessel. "There are no cacti nor rattlesnakes in Siberia and it is reported that he was hailed with: 'Where do you hail from?' McLean pointed to his flag. 'What country is that?' was the query. 'Salt Horsia, athwart and along latitude 1, longitude 1 1/2, 2 minutes, 40 seconds,' replied McLean, and the *Carmencita* glided on while the inquirer was trying to locate the country on the map."[18] (The position would locate it in the Gulf of Guinea, off the African coast.) Early in the voyage, a storm and tide beached the *Carmencita* on Attu, near the end of the Aleutians. At this point, Thompson found himself in serious difficulties when he accidentally burned the chief's mother's straw for making mats and baskets. He sought out MacLean, and "we both faced the old grandmother and finally satisfied her with a very generous supply of tea and tobacco." When the *Carmencita* floated off three days later, it leaked badly. "Three pumps had to be manned day and night in 2-hour shifts for the remainder of the trip." Thompson also had a confrontation with a fellow crewman, and they decided to fight it out while MacLean, on the poop deck, pretended not to notice. "I told the lad to take off his oilskin coat and as I ducked under the boom to go to the hatch, a stunning blow on my head knocked me down and I thought the boom hit me; but when I looked up into his infuriated eyes, I knew he had hit me from behind. Boiling over with Irish temper ... I beat him with blows to his head and stomach until he folded up on the deck." Thompson then sat on his opponent's stomach, grabbed his ears and pounded his head on the deck. "He hollered 'quits' and I let him go. The captain called me into his office later. I was afraid he would put me in 'irons' for fighting on the ship; but he said, 'It is best to fight it out.'"[19] It could have been a page out of Jack London's *The Sea-Wolf.*

From the Aleutians they moved into Russian waters and prepared to raid the rookery on Copper Island. There had obviously been some attention to detail, suggesting a certain amount of confidence. MacLean had brought along a large tent to serve as crew quarters once they had settled on the rookery. The first attempt to land occurred in mid-July. The poachers' information about the absence of Russian patrols in the surrounding waters was correct. The land-based guards nonetheless put up a spirited and successful defence. The tent remained stowed aboard the vessel. There would be no camping on the rookery that season.[20] A couple of versions have Alex using a more imaginative approach, telling the Russians that he only landed to fill his water barrels and then producing whiskey to get them drunk. When they awoke, Alex and his crew were long gone.[21] Cecil Clark has Alex using a similar approach and, with goodwill, offering "a case of square-face gin" with a similar result. These canny if somewhat friendlier approaches, if they happened, must be attributed to an earlier occasion and possibly to other sealers such as Gus Hansen.[22]

In late July, the *Carmencita* returned to Copper Island for another go. There were no pleasantries exchanged. Maybe the mate, Russian-born Oscar Watzschoff, was correct when he said: "MacLean had a grudge against the Russians."[23] Alex may have been thinking of the incident a couple of weeks earlier or the episode with the *James Hamilton Lewis* and his visit to Vladivostok in 1891. On 1 August, which was "a thick, muggy morning" and with the *Carmencita* hovering fifteen miles off the Commander Island rookery, the boats, each with three men, set out for shore. The Russian guards, possibly thinking the Japanese were returning (on an earlier occasion that summer and in a similar situation, the Japanese sealers had returned fire), were ready. One participant, Dan Claussen, described the scene to reporters some months later. The haze lifted when the boats were two hundred yards from the beach: "One hundred yards from shore and a volley of rifle shots came from the rocks. Walter York, in the first boat, dropped his rifle and went backward on the bow oar with a bullet through his mouth. The riflemen in the boats returned the fire, but they could see nothing[,] only little puffs of smoke from loopholes in the rocks through which the Cossack guards were firing." The *Carmencita*'s crew, in open boats, were seriously outnumbered: "Some of the boys wanted to make a spurt and charge the works but it would simply have been suicide. I doubt if a man would have reached the shore. The bullets were singing about us like bees. A bucket on which I was sitting was riddled and my compass was shattered by a bullet."[24]

Stuart Thompson's version is quite similar: "One of our boats got lost in the fog and found a clearing near Copper Island. While approaching the island, rifle shots suddenly rang out from behind the rocks and whizzed by, striking the water around them. Walter York, my pal, was rowing frantically to get out of range of the Russians but a bullet hit him, smashing his teeth in and fracturing his lower jawbone ... another man took his oars and rowed into the fog bank to avoid the shower of bullets."[25] Another sealer on the *Carmencita* was wounded but later recovered. Watzschoff credited "Pills" de Smidt with preventing even more casualties: "He was in one of the first boats when the Russians opened fire on us. He stood right up in his boat and took off his coat, stuck it on an oar and began to wave us back. I says to my mates, says I, 'Pills is tryin' to signalize us about something but I can't make it out.'" Then came a hail of bullets from the shore. "But Pills stood up right there in his boat, a fair mark for the Russians, till he had waved us all back, and then got down. With the roarin' of the sea and the barkin' of the seals we hadn't heard the rifles, but when we got a little closer we see the smoke a hangin' in the rocks and the puffs from the loopholes."[26] Walter York was brought back to the *Carmencita,* and his friend Stuart Thompson and Alex MacLean "made him as comfortable as possible."[27] It was difficult. The bullet had smashed his jaw, knocked out several teeth, and lodged in his head. The schooner set sail for Unalaska/Dutch Harbour, reaching there on 17 August. MacLean paid York's passage, and the injured sealer was transferred to the steamer *Senator* and taken to Seattle. The *Senator*'s physician assured the crew that his injuries were not serious.[28] This tragic turn of events was the first loose thread as the *Carmencita* affair slowly began to unravel.

American Press dispatches reporting the incident alerted the North American Commercial Company (NACC). The paper trail commenced with a telegram from the NACC to the Department of Commerce and Labor in Washington on 24 August, suggesting that Walter York be detained, pending an investigation. This communication was followed the same day with a letter from H.H. Taylor, the NACC's president, to F.H. Hitchcock, chief clerk of the Department of Commerce and Labor, supplying additional information, including the facts that the vessel was under the command of Alexander MacLean, "a notorious pelagic sealing captain," and that the venture was financed by Wood, with Tyson paying the bills and acting as business manager. According to Taylor, "we believe a Government official could quietly work up a case against the vessel and the parties who have violated the law." The next day, the *Seattle Post-Intelligencer* carried a statement from York, the twenty-two-year-old eldest of twelve: "I wandered west from my Missouri home and went to sea. Here I am now in a hospital ward. I don't think I deserved such a fate. Anyway, I shall try to get well. What I will do then is hardly worth speculating on now. If I violated any law it was through ignorance on my part. I don't believe in law breaking." The bullet was still lodged in his head, and an operation was scheduled for 26 August. Although weakened, he was "full of hope and courage" heading into the procedure, and the surgeons were optimistic. But the lad from Missouri died on the operating table.[29] The whirl of bureaucratic wheels intensified.

By October, the unsuccessful voyage ended with a characteristic flourish by MacLean in Victoria. According to Stuart Thompson, "his perfect mastery won the admiration of all the sailors and the hundreds of persons at the docks at Victoria when he sailed in a circular path with full sails until the sails 'fell dead' and the anchor was dropped at the end of the voyage."[30] This display would have been of little succour to the family and friends of Walter York. Also unsatisfying was the financial return. The expedition only brought in sixty-five skins and netted a loss of $8,000: "MacLean called each man and gave him one dollar. He had [a] pistol next to him in case anyone might try murder. He was willing to fight it out with anyone. No one challenged him then." The token payment was the minimum required under shipping law. Thompson then signed off, leaving with one final impression of Alex MacLean: "While walking up the street, two swinging doors of a saloon opened up and [Alex] came out with blood on his hands and face but with a smile of victory. I said, 'What happened?' He said, 'Look inside.' I looked and saw two men badly battered flat on the floor in pools of blood and they were still 'out.' Two of his crewmembers decided to 'take him on' and the captain fought both of them at one time." Thompson helped him tidy up. "I said my final good-bye and got a hearty handshake. He was going home to his family."[31] Lucy MacLean and fifteen-year-old Catherine were living in Oakland at the time, and Alex returned there, leaving the *Carmencita* to winter in Victoria.

Even though the *Carmencita* was but one of twenty-one poachers that season around the rookeries – most of the damage inflicted on the herd was at the hands of Japanese sealers – her activities were enough to flag the schooner's name in a number of spheres of authority. The death of Walter York and the pressures of the NACC prodded the American authorities into action. The government assigned Harry M. Moffatt, a detective working under the direction of a Secret Service agent, to the case in September. In mid-October, an operative, who was probably Moffatt, was on the San Francisco waterfront seeking information and relaying it back on a daily basis, ultimately to the Department of Justice in Washington. The agent was instructed to locate Dan Claussen (the chief hunter on the vessel) or any other crew member of the *Carmencita*. He was initially unsuccessful, even though he knew generally where to look, including "the saloons and lodging houses along the waterfront." He met an impressive wall of silence from a host of bartenders as he checked out "every saloon on the water front." He then changed tack and tried the Mexican consul-general, where he received an equally uninformative response until he gave a description of his "brother" who supposedly shipped out on the vessel. The description fitted the recently deceased Walter York. The gambit worked and from the consul-general he received the address of E.F. Scott, "who was, he thought, interested in the vessel." The government operative then returned to the waterfront with his poignant cover. In the City of Stockholm saloon, he came across a well-known "runner" (a crimp's right-hand man) named Eugene Sullivan, and he overheard Sullivan talking about the raid and dropping the name "Russian Oscar." The government agent moved in: "I informed him, as I did the Mexican consul, that I had a brother that had sailed on the *Carmencita* and I was anxious to learn whether or not he was the man that was shot." This ploy broke the informal waterfront barrier erected against outsiders, and Sullivan took him to the Newcastle saloon. Late that evening, Russian Oscar put in an appearance. He was of little assistance to the government agent on that occasion as he "was very drunk and could not talk intelligently." Over the next few days, the agent managed some less than drunken moments with Oscar and finally succeeded in locating Dan Claussen. The latter also agreed to assist the agent in the matter "regarding [his] supposed brother." Without his cover, it is doubtful the agent would even have located these men, let alone talked with them. In the event, they only supplied very basic details about the voyage.[32] Loose waterfront gossip and tales and drunken ramblings only went so far, underlining the waterfront society's interpretations of their activities, which differed from those of the state, and suggest two additional conditions of Hobsbawm's requirements for social bandits.[33] Nevertheless, the undercover effort did underline the specific interest of Washington.

The American government continued their inquiry and informed the Mexican authorities of their concerns. On 4 November, Collector F.S. Stratton of the Port of San Francisco received an official letter from the Mexican consul-general, which stated that the Mexican Department of War and Navy had cancelled the provisional registry of the *Carmencita* because of illegal sealing. Although the vessel had sailed under Mexican registration, however acquired, she had been outfitted in San Francisco and was manned, at least in part, by Americans, who had been specifically prohibited from pelagic sealing since 1898. Russian and American rookeries were also off-limits, and the NACC lease was still in force on the Pribilof Islands.[34] Walter York's death, the significant financial costs, and the loss of the registry did not deter MacLean, or his backers, from their relative safety in San Francisco. Preparations were made for another round of poaching. First, they had to get new papers for the vessel. One report has Woodside and MacLean asking Scott to go with them to the Argentinean consul in San Francisco to get registration for the *Carmencita,* but the consul refused. Scott apparently washed his hands of the whole affair at this point. The *Jennie Thelin/Carmencita,* unregistered, remained moored in Victoria.[35] It was a natural refuge for an American sealer in the off-season. Since the late 1890s, the remains of the American sealing fleet, which were no longer able to openly operate as sealers, had flocked to Victoria.[36] The American consul-general in Victoria doubted whether one-third of the fleet "could get beyond Cape Flattery," and one old schooner had just "keeled over at her moorings, from sheer decrepitude."[37] The *Jennie Thelin/Carmencita* fit right in.

This sealing episode was illegal, tragic, and financially unsuccessful. Hatched on the San Francisco waterfront, it had received little attention, aside from some Russian rookery guards, a few American government officials, and Walter York's family and friends. Then Jack London's newest work of fiction, *The Sea-Wolf,* which was serialized in the *Century Magazine* beginning in January 1904, was published in book form that autumn, with 40,000 copies sold before release. It "shot onto the market like a thunderbolt, became the rage overnight, [and] was on everybody's lips to be praised or cursed."[38] Ambrose Bierce, who was not the sunniest of critics, noted: "The great thing – and it is among the greatest of things – is that tremendous creation, Wolf Larsen. If that is not a permanent addition to literature, it is at least a permanent figure in the memory of the reader. You 'can't lose' Wolf Larsen. He will be with you to the end. So it does not really matter how London has hammered him into you. You may quarrel with the methods, but the result is almost incomparable. The hewing out and setting up of such a figure is enough for a man to do in one life-time. I have hardly words to impart my good judgement of that work."[39] Earle Labor and Jeanne Campbell Reesman write: "*The Sea-Wolf* seems to have all the necessary ingredients for greatness. It pulses with the vitality of its creator; it is structured upon the universal, timeless motif of initiation; its setting is likewise archetypal, with the ship as microcosm and the eternal sea as the most fitting matrix, symbolic as well as literal, for death and rebirth. It also has an excellent cast: convincingly delineated, 'round characters who can stand both as individuals and as representative types – headed by Wolf Larsen, one of the most unforgettable figures in American literature."[40]

Jack London had acquired much experience in the ten years since his return from his sealing voyage on the *Sophia Sutherland* in 1893. He worked in a jute mill and as a coal heaver at a power plant. He enlisted in the west coast contingent of Coxey's industrial army and headed east. Once back in Oakland, he charged through high school and did a brief stint at the University of California in Berkeley before heading to the Klondike and London's East End.[41] He wrote constantly. Aside from articles, and this was the "Golden Age of Magazines," he had ten books published in the 1900-04 period, including the very popular *The Call of the Wild* and *The Sea-Wolf.* Both novels made it to first place on the best-seller list in the United States.[42] For Earle Labor and Jeanne Campbell Reesman, he was "the most flamboyant literary representative" of the era. His name was becoming "a byword for rugged individualism and romantic adventure, and his private life was front-page copy for every major newspaper in the country."[43] London and his latest novel made quite an impact. Initially, no connection was made between the fictional Swede Wolf Larsen and the current poacher Alex MacLean, but that would soon change.

Alex MacLean was a persevering individual who seemed to be spurred on by adversity at times. The conditions that had prompted the ill-fated 1904 expedition were still in place in the spring of 1905. Sealskin prices remained high, and the Russian-Japanese conflict was continuing.[44] By early February, MacLean and his San Francisco colleagues were proceeding with their plans for the coming season. Captain Woodside, in San Francisco, had already contacted some of the hunters for the proposed 1905 voyage. They did not seem to have been particularly secretive, even though a variety of government agencies and organizations were quite interested in what they were up to. Early in the new year, the Department of Commerce and Labor forwarded the information it had gathered, including the reports from the waterfront operative the previous October, to the Department of Justice in Washington, and the latter issued instructions on 16 January "to take such action as may be necessary to secure the arrest and punishment of any one found to have committed an offence within the provisions of the statutes."[45] On 23 February, NACC president Taylor informed Washington that MacLean and six hunters from San Francisco were at Victoria preparing the *Carmencita* for sealing. His information had come from the *Daily Colonist* on 18 February, so it was hardly a clandestine affair.[46] On 26 February, the *Washington Post* carried a report received from Victoria the previous day that noted that "Captain McLean, a San Francisco sealer, was fitting out the schooner *Carmencita* and would sail it under the Norwegian flag. As that country is not a party to the *modus vivendi* regarding pelagic sealing, he is not bound to respect its regulation, and can seal at all seasons."[47]

The difficulty of registration this time around was soon solved through the magic of depositions. The *Jennie Thelin/Carmencita* would again set sail under yet another name. Robert Mullins, a "Master Carpenter of Victoria," certified on 25 February that a schooner, the *Acapulco,* was built in Victoria for a Mexican citizen, Jose Sanchez.[48] Coincidentally, Joseph Sanchez, a "Mexican citizen, residing in the port of Victoria, British Columbia and on the way to that city" made a declaration in San Francisco requesting that the consul-general of Mexico issue provisional clearance papers for a schooner being constructed in Victoria. Sanchez told the authorities that the schooner *Acapulco,* commanded by Captain Alexander Woodside, an American, would transport a cargo of lumber from Victoria to Acapulco. He explained that the request was partly because there was no Mexican consul-general in Victoria.[49] When the San Francisco hunters arrived in Victoria, they signed on as Mexican subjects, just as in 1904. As Captain MacLean, who "was standing by at the time," explained, it was "just a formal matter to facilitate the work of clearing the schooner."[50] The *Carmencita* during this time was, in the phrase of J.C. Newbury, the new customs collector in Victoria, "lying in our harbour ... a nondescript vessel without registry."[51] The specifications of the *Acapulco,* which was supposedly built in Victoria, were surprisingly similar to those of the unregistered *Carmencita.*[52] Yet, as the Mexican consul-general in San Francisco later explained, "all legal formalities were fulfilled at the time and this office had no alternative but to issue the certificate."[53] Washington was also wondering exactly what was going on.[54] Then, on 2 March, Captain Woodside approached Newbury, who later explained the situation to his boss: "I was at first wary of doing business with him in view [of] the bad record of the ship ... I ... told him it was currently reported that another attempt was to be made to go sealing under the Mexican flag in order to avoid the restrictions placed on British and United States vessels. I had several interviews with him and he gave his word of honour to me that such was not the case." Woodside showed Newbury the provisional papers for the *Acapulco* and a letter from the Mexican consul-general in San Francisco. Woodside received clearance for the vessel on 2 March and cleared port with a crew of eight.[55] Newbury, upon reflection, considered "the making of this outward report by Woodside as the most flagrant and premeditated violation of Section 99 of the Customs Act that has ever come under my notice." The shotguns and Winchester rifles that had been stored on shore for safety on 14 October the previous year were placed back on board the same schooner on 2 March, and the *Acapulco/Carmencita/Jennie Thelin* was soon on her way. According to the report outward, she was bound for Acapulco.[56]

The absence of a full crew, or the fact that six of the eight men aboard were not seamen but seal hunters, was of little concern to the captain, who, it transpired, was Alex MacLean and not Alexander Woodside. According to one of the hunters on this voyage, "when MacLean got his clearance ... the *Carmencita* [*Acapulco*] towed out. MacLean said he would ship the crew, boat-pullers, etc. at the quarantine station, but the tug went past there. Then he said he would get them at Sooke, but the tug towed the schooner past Sooke harbour and let go. MacLean said it would be all right; we would get the men at Neah Bay. But we didn't. When we got out of the Straits he said he would pay us seamen's wages if we would work the schooner to Drake's Bay. We did – and arrived there in March."[57] Drake's Bay, which was a short distance north of San Francisco, was still a popular and convenient spot to pursue activities that people considered beyond the ken of the authorities. MacLean was well acquainted with it. Additional guns and stores were loaded, and W.J. Wood arrived from San Francisco with the remainder of the crew. As in the previous year, not all of the crew had solid sailing experience. One of the dissatisfied hunters later stated that "the crew selected was from the riffraff of San Francisco."[58] The *San Francisco Examiner* described the crew as "offscourings and renegades."[59] The new men did, however, have their areas of expertise. If contemporary newspaper reports are to be believed, and it bears repeating that caution is recommended with many of these accounts, MacLean wanted "men who know how to handle a rifle and have smelled gunpowder. He has them now, thirty of them, nearly every man a discharged United States soldier." Many had seen service in the Philippines, and "the thirty soldiers of fortune he has under him, many of whom do not know a buntline from the futtock shrouds but can rest a 30-30 on the lee rail and pick off the weather wheel of a chaser at 500 yards if they are so minded."[60] The crew's makeup gave credence to another suggestion from the *San Francisco Examiner,* which envisioned a Hotchkiss rapid-fire gun being on board to target the Russian rookeries, where, because of the hostilities with Japan, $1,000,000 of sealskins had accumulated.[61]

The American Department of the Treasury warned its revenue cutters to be specifically on the lookout for the *Carmencita* and "if encountered on the high seas flying the American flag to board and search her" and if carrying "any sealing apparatus" to arrest her. If she were flying the flag of another nation, the American authorities would quickly inform that government. "In view of the fact that negotiations are now pending between the United States and Great Britain for a revision of the fur-seal regulations," it was explained to the revenue cutter fleet in early March, "it is particularly important at this time that all possible means should be taken to prevent any illegal sealing by United States citizens."[62] However, the *Carmencita* did not exist anymore. It was the *Acapulco* that left Victoria and that now departed Drake's Bay on 20 March to begin an initially not very successful hunt off the Pacific coast.[63] However, even the crew members could not keep up with the changing names of the vessel, and most continued to refer to it as the *Carmencita*. Numbered among the 1904 crew that had returned for the 1905 season was the not-quite-gregarious "Russian Oscar" Watzschoff. He signed on again as mate. Given the results of the previous voyage and no guarantee of anything more than a $1.00 for four or five months' work, there had to be an obvious incentive. As always, there was the lure of a big catch. Adventure was another powerful attraction. If anything could be guaranteed when sailing with MacLean in this period, it was that the voyage would be interesting. According to one crew member on this trip, "when we left Drake's Bay there was more liquor aboard than the whole thirty of us could have got away with in the season if we had laid off and let the *Carmencita* work her own way about the Bering Sea. And the crew – say there wasn't a sailor in the lot, but I'll admit they were fighters, and with a quantity of fightin' liquor aboard there were lively doings on the *Carmencita*. Sometimes the Captain and the sober ones, if there were any, would have to get in and quell 'em. No, it was not an uneventful voyage."[64] Booze, however, was standard fare in the fleet, according to Carl Rydell: "The sealing vessels always carried large stocks of liquor, and this was dealt out most freely during actual hunting. Then the work was severe and the men had to be humoured to be kept at it."[65] While the authorities would have significant difficulties locating MacLean this season, one individual who did run into Alex MacLean and the *Carmencita* around this time was Max Lohbrunner. It was March 1905, and Lohbrunner was sealing 100 miles off the California coast in a small boat from the schooner *Diana*. He was invited aboard the "strange two-masted schooner" and was surprised to realize the vessel was outfitted for sealing and more surprised to see one of his Victoria acquaintances, Alex MacLean.[66] Numerous individuals in positions of authority would have liked to have been with Lohbrunner on that occasion, with adequate marine backing.

The *Carmencita* worked up the coast during the next month and put into Clayoquot Sound on the west coast of Vancouver Island on 27 April. Alex went ashore with fourteen skins to exchange for provisions and receive mail, giving some credence to the suspicion that he planned to use the area as a base for the 1905 expedition.[67] A San Francisco newspaper would later maintain that he marooned three of his crew there. While it was unquestionably a tumultuous thirty-six-hour visit, the Clayoquot stop was a bit more complicated. When Alex went ashore, Oscar Watzschoff warned his mates: "'Lads, get to work an' scrub up. I know the uncivilizin' influence of Clayoquot liquor, and Alex is liable to come aboard feelin' somewhat barbarous and savage.'" Watzschoff went on to say, "We had everything shipshape an' Bristol fashion when Alex come back, but he was feelin' mussy an' says to ten of the men, says he. 'Here, you lubbers, tumble into boats an' go ashore. I don't want you any longer.'" Watzschoff pointed out that the vessel needed them. "Then he turned on me. 'Who the devil's master of this craft, you or me?' and I says, says I: 'Why, Alex, man, you are, but you can't sail her without men.' 'The ___ I can't,' says he. 'You tumble into that boat. I'll show you whether I can't or not.'" The mate, carpenter, and a boat-puller quickly hopped in a boat. "'Here,' yells Alex, 'you fellers come back here': he had changed his mind that sudden ... I says to Chips, 'Cut that rope, quick,' an' the carpenter whacks it with his knife an' we give way for shore. Alex run for the cabin, but he didn't shoot; I never knowed why."[68] Once ashore, many of the crew proceeded to get "more or less intoxicated," and several were picked up for disorderly conduct.[69] At this point, having doubtless thought a bit more about what the mate had said, Alex ventured off the schooner again and located them at the local drinking hole. "He had three pairs of irons in his hands an' says pleasant-like, 'I've come to take you boys back to the schooner.' About that time we was beginnin' to feel somewhat uncivilized ourselves an' said we see him an' his schooner some place else first." A provincial constable was on the scene "and Alex tried to get him to go away for half an hour an' give him a chance to coax us back with the irons but the constable wouldn't go." He had been given a heads-up about the vessel's suspect papers. "Then Alex, still feelin' barbarous, tried to take us anyway, but we was four to one and we didn't go, but it was some lively an' stirrin' in Clayoquot before it was settled."[70] Eventually, all except Watzschoff and his two companions "went (or were put) aboard the vessel," and the *Carmencita/Acapulco* departed, bringing a sigh of relief from the local constable.[71] Ex-mate Watzschoff, along with "Chips" and a boat-puller, returned to Victoria in early May.

The schooner made two brief visits to Hesquiaht for water and to repair some rigging after running "into a gale off the Vancouver Island coast" and then squared away for Queen Charlotte Sound and sealed there during May. But the captain was cautious, even skittish, and questions began to form among the crew of the *Carmencita,* or so they later maintained. They became suspicious in mid-May when a steamer was spotted in Queen Charlotte Sound: "When she was some distance away we saw that she had a yellow smokestack, like those of government steamers. McLean was considerably frightened. He squared away and ran, but it was soon obvious that it was only a fishing steamer." MacLean also ensured that newspapers were not taken aboard when they occasionally landed for provisions.[72]

Not only a questioning crew and revenue cutters on the high seas worked against MacLean and his backers. In early March, a San Francisco grand jury concluded that MacLean and four of his associates had formed a compact to "wickedly, corruptly, unlawfully, knowingly and feloniously conspire, combine, confederate and agree together among themselves and with divers other persons ... to commit an offense against the United States," namely, "taking part in the unlawful killing, capturing and hunting of fur seals" in the Pacific, north of the thirty-fifth degree latitude. Crew members on the 1904 voyage, including Daniel Claussen, S.E.R. de Smidt, and Stuart Thompson, were among the witnesses who testified before the grand jury, as did E.F. Scott and H.M. Moffatt. The indictment detailed the purchase of the *Jennie Thelin* on 1 February 1904, her registration as a Mexican vessel, the *Carmencita,* on 28 April, her provisioning two days later, and, on 5 May, the surrendering of the American registry and her departure for the Bering Sea.[73] The unravelling of the scheme quickened in mid-June. The interest of the American authorities, which had commenced with the death of Walter York the previous summer, culminated in San Francisco on 13 June 1905, when R.J. Tyson, William J. Woodside, and William J. Wood were arrested. They were not typical waterfront characters. Tyson, a "well known insurance and shipping man," was "reputed to be a millionaire." Woodside was a senior member of his company (Woodside and Company was a ship broker). Wood was president and manager of W.J. Wood Sailmaking Company. While the *Oakland Tribune* reported that the charge was "conspiring to pursue the business of sealing, contrary to the American and Russo-American treaty laws," the *San Francisco Chronicle* noted they were indicted under section 5440 of the Revised Statutes of the United States. The formal charge was that they were "conspiring to commit an offense against the United States," and, as the acting United States district attorney explained, "the fact that these men committed the slightest overt act is all we need to establish the existence of a conspiracy."[74] While the court documents had made reference to supplying and sending the vessel on an illegal sealing voyage into prohibited waters, the conspiracy to defraud the government probably rested on the lease between the government and the NACC. In 1904, for example, the *Carmencita* had returned with sixty-five skins. Under the terms of the lease, at a fee of $9.925 per skin, it would add up to a grand total of $625.62.[75] The bottom line was the NACC sealing monopoly and the missed revenue claimed by the United States Department of the Treasury from the leasing arrangement. The practice of having Americans re-engaged in pelagic sealing would not have done anything to alleviate the long-standing sealing dispute.

It was front-page news in San Francisco but only partly because of the prominence of those arrested. Alex MacLean was also indicted at this time, as was R.E.S. de Smidt, "a very wealthy man who own[ed] large plantations at Tahiti and [was] a British subject," although another source simply described him as "a hooligan." The brave "Pills" de Smidt, who had probably prevented even more casualties during the abortive raid in 1904, turned himself in to the United States marshal's office on the morning of 14 June. Like the other three, he was quickly released on a $3,000 bond. MacLean was a different story. He was now famous for "his inclination to hunt where seals [were] the most numerous," which had "more than once got him into trouble with the authorities." And he was the only one indicted who was at large and at sea.[76] It is at this point that the legend of Sea Wolf MacLean kicks into high gear. As the *San Francisco Chronicle* explained, "McLean's home is on the sea, he knows little of life but that on the deep blue and cannot understand how people can find enjoyment on shore. He is a rover and not a freight carrier; any daredevil enterprise by sea that needs a strong arm can find an adherent in McLean, whether it be a search for pirate's treasure, running a contraband cargo or poaching for seals regardless of any government's protection; he had experience in all."[77] The *Portland Oregonian* suggested that the authorities were arresting all of the wrong people anyway. The "attempt to lock the stable door some twenty years after the horse has been stolen will cause a broad smile all the way from the Golden Gate to 'north of fifty-three.' The wholesale destruction of the seal by the Alaska Commercial Company operating under the patronage of the United States government, ruined the industry in the latter part of the 'eighties' by driving the seals to the Japan coast and to southern latitudes." Those who should be in jail are the San Francisco men "who financed the monopoly that clubbed vast numbers of seal to death on the Pribilofs. It is a poor time to enforce laws for the protection of seal life in a locality from which the seals have long ago been driven."[78] The argument hinted at Hobsbawm's distinction between what the community and the state considered illegal.[79] For the authorities in San Francisco, the *Portland Oregonian*'s observations would not be persuasive. It was reported that customhouse broker (and one-time registered owner of the *Carmencita*) E.F. Scott was the main witness before the federal grand jury, and the government prosecution was relying heavily on his evidence. From the accused, there was a brief bluff, with "talk of countering with a heavy damage suit against the Government" because Mexico had not signed any of the sealing agreements.[80] Tyson and Captain Woodside both denied knowledge of illegalities. Tyson thought the vessel was on a cod-fishing cruise. "It is all a surprise to me," said Captain Woodside. "I have never had anything to do with the sealing schooner either as the *Jennie Thelin* or the *Carmencita*."[81] True to form, de Smidt was standing tall. His initial statement concluded: "For a last word I want to say that everything we did was done openly and above board. We concealed nothing. And you can print it as coming from me that Captain Alex McLean is a jolly good fellow."[82]

Alex MacLean was now positioned front and centre on a far larger stage. Its backdrop is rich and layered. There was the "tumultuous debate" that raged about gender and self-image during this period.[83] Based in part on the cultural insecurity of the *fin de siècle* and on the vigorous response to the advent of the "new woman," middle-class men masked their insecurities with a manly code that re-emphasized "success, aggression, and ruthlessness."[84] The increase in male-only activities, with a particular emphasis on nature, specifically the wilderness, was just the tonic, according to many social commentators. As Tina Loo notes, "in their opinion, 'over-civilization' had resulted in a loss of the very feelings that made a man a man: courage, aggression, mastery. At worst, an over-civilized man was no man at all: He was a woman."[85] Anti-modernism was in full flight, and discussion swirled around secularization, imperialism, and definitions about masculinity and femininity. Jackson Lears has explored the dominant form of American anti-modernism, "the recoil from an 'overcivilized' modern existence to more intensive forms of physical or spiritual experience."[86] He describes anti-modernism's ambivalence, "a complex blend of accommodation and protest," which was rooted in "a crisis of cultural authority" and which, paradoxically, "often looked forward rather than backward."[87] While individual solutions included wilderness treks and big-game hunting, a collective response was militarism. It reached its zenith in the 1890s as "a purgative for overcivilization."[88] Anne-Marie Harvey notes that white middle-class males were "constrained and enervated by the demands of the modern, urban, bureaucratic work place, as well as standardized and feminised by their new roles as consumers in a national market of mass-produced goods."[89] For her, the closing of the frontier "was inseparable from the call for open doors abroad," with the Spanish-American War being "a rescue mission for American manhood from the equally threatening forces of a modern industrial democracy."[90] Not surprisingly, the major best-sellers during the 1895-1902 period were historical romances.[91] As Amy Kaplan argues, "the culture at large was in the process of redefining white middle-class masculinity from a republican quality of character based on self-control and social responsibility to a corporeal essence identified with the vigour and prowess of the individual male body."[92] According to Labor and Reesman, while the main plot of *The Sea-Wolf* was Van Weyden's "growth from effete snobbery into dynamic manhood,"[93] one should also note Jonathan Auerbach's argument that *The Sea-Wolf* "reconfigures masculinity in far more daring, unstable, and dangerous forms than does his previous work."[94] This complex and illuminating backdrop aids in filtering and interpreting the images of Alex MacLean that came flying off the front pages of contemporary newspapers and from the waterfront and government and legal sources.

The *San Francisco Chronicle* immediately responded with the headline "Roams the Sea Like a Pirate of Old." The *Oakland Tribune* also brought up the notion of piracy. Those speculative fires were further fanned when the authorities, prodded by questioning reporters, initially declined to say whether the charge against MacLean was for "conspiracy, or piracy or actual poaching." The warrants that served the others "merely charge conspiracy" but, as the *Oakland Tribune* reminded its readers, death was the punishment for piracy.[95] This "skull and crossbones" twist, which graphically accompanied some of the newspaper reports, was linked to the question of the ship's registration. At this point, the *Carmencita/Acapulco* was operating under a provisional Mexican registration. The *Acapulco*'s papers had not yet been revoked, regardless of how they had been acquired. In addition, the relevant court documents have identical charges against

MacLean and the other four individuals. But technicalities were far less fascinating than pirates, and the newspaper reports from the summer of 1905 would solidly attach the term "pirate" to Alex MacLean.

It was the twentieth century, with one individual under sail sought by many in ships powered by steam. That was all the newspapers needed. As the *Oakland Tribune* noted, "poacher or pirate, Alexander McLean, as bluff and bold a skipper as ever walked the deck of any craft, sails the northern seas."[96] The *San Francisco Chronicle* asked: "'Big Alex McLean' – where is he? Somewhere away up yonder in the heave and settle of the sea, a stanch craft under him and mustering thirty men almost as great daredevils as himself, all armed with repeating rifles." The account quoted Kipling: "There's never a law of God or man/Runs north of Fifty-three" and went on to say: "A devil of a man is Alex McLean, a Nova Scotian, about 40 years old, of Scotch parentage, and, technically, as much a 'jolly rover' as in the days when his Scotch privateering ancestors lay in wait in the hollows of the sea along the pathway of the Spanish galleons before and after the treaty of Utrecht, a matter of 200 years ago."[97] The newspapers were making tremendous leaps of imagination, but, as copy, the MacLean saga proved irresistible. Alex was immediately linked with the best-seller from the previous autumn, Jack London's *The Sea-Wolf,* and no one missed the connection now. It was the subject of an editorial in the *San Francisco Chronicle* entitled "The Strange Story of a Modern North Pacific Rover" because the tale outdid "in many respects the imaginative work of the novelist ... It is remarkable that in these days of steam a sailing vessel should have succeeded so long as the *Carmencita* is represented to have done in following an occupation perilously near to piracy without falling a prey to the vigilant revenue cutters and war vessels patrolling the seas in which she has cruised, and in which she is now cruising, apparently without the shelter of any nation's flag and registry. It will probably be difficult to capture such a resourceful rover as McLean."[98]

The *San Francisco Chronicle* mistakenly noted that charges against MacLean included "selling whisky to Indians." This rumour may have originated with the newspaper's earlier interview with ex-mate Oscar Watzschoff, who had left the vessel in dramatic fashion at Clayoquot a couple of months earlier. The paper noted that the *Carmencita* "carried more liquor than any thirty men could consume in a year's cruise. It is presumed that it was destined for Alaska, but no evidence to that effect has been given out."[99] Meanwhile "he stays at sea, scratches the shrouds and whistles for a wind and laughs in the teeth of the gale when it comes." The *San Francisco Examiner* wanted to know how it would all end or, at least, wanted to keep readers coming back for the next dramatic development: "Will McLean in the flesh prove himself the equal of McLean in the book? Will he fight to the last ditch? Or will he, after all, tumble one more of the heroes of fiction into the dust by tamely

Steam sealer, the *Alexander*

E.W. Wright, ed., *Lewis and Dryden's Marine History of the Pacific Northwest* (Portland: Lewis and Dryden, 1895), Canadiana Online, produced by http://canadiana.org/

Garrick's Head Saloon

British Columbia Archives, A-04661

W.S. Stratton, Yukon River
Stan Cohen, *Yukon River Steamboats* (Missoula: Pictorial Histories Publishing Company, 1982)

Alex MacLean and a skull and crossbones
San Francisco Chronicle, 15 June 1905

Alex MacLean with Stetson hat
Carol Brookman, proprietor of Heinold's First and Last Chance Saloon, Jack London Square, Oakland, CA

surrendering and tamely submitting to the punishment imposed on him?"[100] The *San Francisco Chronicle* knew that the legal intricacies and technicalities about registration and owners and "splitting hairs over the *modus vivendi* is not interesting the public nearly so much as the central figure, the big, rawboned Cape Breton Scotchman, Alexander McLean, captain of the *Carmencita,* and there are many men who are hoping the wind will come strong and free and that his sticks will hold."[101] The social bandit did have his supporters, doubtless including many North American males who were trying to strengthen, or redefine, their masculinity. The west coast newspapers gave their readers plenty of Alex MacLean, authentic and otherwise.

Jack London intensified the interest by solidly linking MacLean and Larsen. The *San Francisco Examiner* carried a statement by the best-selling author on its front page: "I never personally met Alexander McLean, but I heard of his wild exploits from the men with whom I went seal hunting in 1893. McLean had an exciting record of adventure and upon his deeds I based my Sea Wolf character. Of course, much of the Sea Wolf is imaginative development, but the basis is Alexander McLean. Alexander had a brother, Dan McLean, who also was a sealing captain and a petty adventurer of some note."[102] The *Daily Colonist,* which was less impressionable, more contained, and more knowledgeable of many aspects of sealing in general, and of Alex MacLean in particular, noted that the *San Francisco Examiner,* long "a booster of London," had printed the telegram from the novelist about the sealer and "upon this basis the San Francisco paper bases a lengthy glorification of Alex McLean."[103] To prove its point, the *Daily Colonist,* noting MacLean as the inspiration for London's fictional character, reprinted the *San Francisco Examiner's* comments that "will arouse keen interest in the ultimate fate of Captain Alexander McLean in every country where the English language is read. Countless thousands have poured over the history of this man, half monster, half philosopher and all demon, who fought his way through life with scorn for the hearts that were broken or stilled that he might triumph in even the pettiest design. Broad shouldered, deep chested, he is described for us with wonderful eyes and so strong that when he grasps a raw potato in his palm streams of pulp spurt from between his fingers."[104] It was pure fiction. Two days later, the *Daily Colonist,* mindful as well of its main business of selling papers, calmly offered its readers some additional, typical coverage on MacLean from the *San Francisco Examiner,* "which, if it is sadly overdrawn, may be of local interest." Coincidentally, the Victoria paper included a news report the same day about some rather more formidable pirates who had massacred some 150 people in a coastal town on Russia's Kamchatka peninsula.[105]

Jack London's immediate involvement in the public discussion surrounding the MacLean-Larsen connection raises another issue. London was strongly influenced in style and plotting ideas by Rudyard Kipling, and many researchers and reviewers have suggested that London drew extensively from Kipling's *Captains Courageous* in the writing of *The Sea-Wolf.*[106] (It should be noted here that a significant figure in *Captains Courageous* was a Gaelic-speaking Cape Bretoner, but he was not based on Alex MacLean.)[107] Dennis Hensley has argued that London based *The Sea-Wolf* far more on "actual maritime history" than on Kipling's influence and that London had readily acknowledged his debt to MacLean's "exciting record of adventure" in developing the character of Wolf Larsen.[108] Some of Hensley's examples are accurate. The opening scene of the novel portrays "a real ferryboat collision, a real-life model for Wolf Larsen, and a real schooner like *The Ghost.*" The accident did occur in San Francisco Bay on 30 November 1901, and the *Ghost,* while not based on the much larger *Sophia Sutherland* in which the novelist had experienced his sealing adventures, was, at eighty tons, very similar to many of the vessels in the fleet. In the novel, the *Macedonia,* Death Larsen's vessel, was based on the large steam bark *Alexander* that Alex MacLean had commanded in the 1893 season.[109] Hensley is less convincing when dealing with the historical figure of Alex MacLean. He bases his impressions on the wild and woolly newspaper descriptions circulating in the summer of 1905, months after the novel had been serialized in *Century Magazine* and published in book form.[110] Thus, London's use of "actual maritime history" in *The Sea-Wolf* does not include portrayals of Alex MacLean as carried in the *San Francisco Examiner* in the summer of 1905. Hensley leaves a misleading impression: "Captain McLean had a criminal record which included murder, theft, pirating, assault and battery, trespassing and conspiracy. He put a bullet through the head of one of his crewmen and then dumped the corpse in Seattle. He stole the schooner *Jennie Thelin* and made it his own *Carmencita.*"[111]

A few of the lesser charges could be considered accurate. There were minor assault and battery incidents in Halifax and San Francisco, which had been noted during the Bering Sea Claims Commission hearings in Victoria in the autumn of 1896. MacLean's attempts to land on the protected fur seal rookeries could fit under trespassing, and the 1904-05 incidents could be construed as conspiring to defraud the American government under its fee schedule in the NACC lease. No evidence has been uncovered that remotely suggests MacLean was ever charged with murder or piracy, and while he bore some responsibility for Walter York's fate, the bullets were Russian. He was in command of the *Carmencita* with the knowledge of its owners. Most of the more serious accusations do not hold up, other than in the sense that they would continue to be repeated up to the present. London's public statements at the time did not support any of the more outrageous comments, and it appears that the *Daily Colonist's* earlier remarks were not widely off the mark. Secret Service agent N.R. Harris Jr. pointed out to the *San Francisco Examiner* during this informational frenzy in mid-June that

"Captain McLean once rendered the United States Government an incalculable service. He never brags of his conquests nor boasts of any good deeds he may have performed."[112] Harris, an acquaintance of MacLean's from the San Francisco waterfront in the 1890s, maintained that MacLean "may be broad-shouldered enough to stand trial for any reasonable crime on the calendar, but ... scorns the accusation of being a pirate." Apparently, when Alex had lost the Mexican registration in 1904, Harris made a pertinent comment and Alex replied: "Don't you ever believe it. Losing a registration don't feaze [sic] me any, and what's more I'm not a pirate, never was and never will be. Too wise, old man, too wise."[113] But there was more drama when it was reported that the revenue cutter *Bear* had left Honolulu with instructions to capture Alex and the *Carmencita*.[114]

It did not take long for a resourceful reporter for the *San Francisco Examiner* to track down Alex's wife and daughter in Oakland. Lucy MacLean, who was "very much excited," explained to him that she only knew what was in the newspapers, although she was surprisingly candid about her husband in a general way. "I hope he has not got himself into trouble," she said nervously. "He has had notoriety enough. He has been in trouble before for poaching and also for sailing the seas without flying a flag. I wish we could move off in the woods somewhere, so that I would be spared all this new trouble. I know nothing of these charges beyond what I have seen in the papers, and only hope that he will be able to clear himself." The newspapers, with their wild descriptions about pirates, the suggestion of a death sentence, and their almost joyous contemplation of a showdown between one individual under sail and the naval might of two industrialized countries, were doubtless of little succour to Lucy MacLean. Catherine, however, viewed it differently. "Miss McLean, a charming miss of sixteen, seemed rather to enjoy the notoriety attained by her father. She said: 'You know that Jack London took papa for the model of Wolf Larsen in *The Sea-Wolf*. I suppose now that he is about to become famous some more, London will write another book about him.'"[115] The interviews with Lucy and Catherine MacLean shared the page with an excerpt from *The Sea-Wolf*, graphically describing some of Wolf Larsen's harsh activities.[116]

With Alex MacLean and *The Sea-Wolf* definitely linked, the newspapers could scarcely contain themselves. As the *San Francisco Examiner* extolled, "cruising somewhere in the open waters of the Bering Sea, master of a craft armed like a slaver and manned by a crew of offscourings and renegades, Captain Alexander McLean paces the quarterdeck of his trim schooner *Carmencita* in blissful ignorance that the game he plays is near its end ... McLean ... scholar, inventor, athlete, tyrant and poacher, notorious original of Jack London's famous Sea-Wolf, will find a warrant and a cell awaiting him if he ever sails again within the Federal jurisdiction of the United States."[117] It was suggested at the time that the revenue cutters looking for

MacLean would have him picked up by 3 July, the date set for the pleas of the four others who had been charged in San Francisco. This prediction would prove wildly optimistic. In the meantime, as the *Oakland Tribune* noted, "Captain Alexander McLean, the Sea Wolf, still rides the waves a free man, and no one in authority at the Federal building seems to have the remotest idea when he will be overtaken and brought before a court." The paper reported that "there is a great deal of interest in the dashing poacher who is now believed by the officials to be an out and out pirate. The romantically inclined have turned again to London's striking pages and read anew the description of the man who has set the laws and the governments at naught and plowed the deep a very buccaneer ... In the saloons along the waterfront McLean is the hero of the hour; in the swagger down-town clubs his name is the one most discussed. The revival of piracy is a subject that interests all alike." It indelicately suggested that it "may end in the noose for the master of the *Carmencita,*" and San Franciscans, "who knew that the Sea-Wolf would sail the sticks out of her before he would give her up," began to wonder how it would all end.[118] They would have to wait a while. But Jack London, his publishers, and the media had already locked onto the connection noted by Catherine MacLean. "M'Lean is London's Hero," began one story, "roving poacher is Wolf Larsen." The *San Francisco Examiner* wondered: "Will McLean in the flesh prove himself the equal of McLean in the book? Will he fight to the last ditch? ... He has been in many tight places, this buccaneer with blood on his boots, who has so suddenly strode out of the pages of fiction into the limelight of everyday."[119] Little wonder that Lucy MacLean longed to go off into the woods somewhere. After three days of continuous, comprehensive coverage in the San Francisco Bay area newspapers, the story of the "resourceful rover" received a bit of a rest. By late June, the news had trickled back to Canada's east coast, and the local paper repeated London's connection between Cape Bretoners Alex and Dan MacLean, "among the most successful sealers on the Pacific coast," and his new novel. The *Sydney Record* also noted the *San Francisco Examiner*'s "lengthy glorification of Alex MacLean" and its strongly edited version also repeated the "half monster, half philosopher and all demon" description originally carried in the San Francisco newspapers.[120] The connection was one that MacLean would carry for the remainder of his days, and it continues to the present.

11
The *Carmencita* Returns to Victoria, 1905

The extensive newspaper coverage was a major factor in obstructing Alex's illegal objective that season. It is clear that Alex was hardly in "blissful ignorance" of his deteriorating situation, and the crew became suspicious by mid-May. Later they met a whaler, the *Alice Knowles,* "and one of her crew told [them] that revenue cutters were looking for someone on board [their] schooner." At this time, MacLean simply explained to them "someone on board must have done something" and made light of it.[1] The *Carmencita* was not invisible. She was seen at least three times that summer near the three-mile limit around St. Paul Island.[2] Indeed, on 6 August, the British sloop-of-war *Shearwater,* based at Esquimalt, boarded the elusive schooner just off the Pribilof Islands. Between 100 and 250 skins were found.[3] While the ship's papers "did not look just right," the *Shearwater,* being in American waters, was hesitant to act forcibly.[4] One version has someone whose description fit MacLean stating, when asked his name, that he was "Captain Woodside." "Are you a Mexican?" asked the officer of the captain. "Yes," was the prompt reply. "Are your crew all Mexicans?" "Sí, señor!" The officer added: "The crew were the worst looking lot of cut-throats I ever laid my hands on."[5]

Jimmy Newman was a seaman on the *Shearwater* that day and many years later added some rich personal detail. Newman had accompanied Lieutenant Irvine when they boarded the *Carmencita.* The tender was jumping around. The lieutenant "had a job climbing up the side" so MacLean, decked out in a red shirt, with "gumboots up to his thighs, a broad leather belt," bareheaded, with a grin on his face, "leaned down and grabbed our officer with the scruff of the tunic ... and he yanked him up with the roll of the vessel ... and was this lieutenant mad! ... so our officer straightened himself out ... and tried to put on that dignified air." When asked his nationality, MacLean "grinned" and said "Mexican." They then moved on to the captain's cabin to get the papers, and MacLean, demonstrating his natural hospitality, offered the lieutenant a drink. The officer declined: "No, no, no, I never drink on duty!" MacLean turned to Newman: "Well, what about you,

Red?" Newman turned to the lieutenant for permission: "I said: 'It is a bit chilly!' And believe me, I like a shot of rum ... they used to have the Hudson's Bay rum then in the old stone crocks – and he had a cup that I'd bet come out of one of the restaurants on Johnson Street – you know, them thick coffee cups they used to have? It had no handle on it, and the inside of it was as brown as if it had been painted ... So he slung this jug under his arm ... and he slopped it in ... he very near filled that cup." The lieutenant checked the ship's papers, Newman dealt with his chill, and they returned to their vessel. MacLean's demeanour, his open-handedness, courtesy, and sense of humour under the glare of a British warship, while being well within the prohibited sixty-mile limit, to say nothing of the complete exclusion of American citizens from sealing, suggests that the scene could almost be transported back to Sherwood Forest and Robin Hood duping King John's minions. Neither Newman nor the lieutenant had any idea at the time who the sealing captain was, although the young seaman considered him "a hell of a fine fella."[6] There was another twist, according to Mr. Walker, one of the hunters: "Just before the boat came from the *Shearwater,* McLean called to the men about the deck: 'Now, you fellows, understand that Bill Thomas is captain of this schooner: I'm navigator.' That was the first we heard of Bill Thomas being skipper; he shipped as hunter like the rest of us. Bill was an old man – one of the oldest seal hunters on the coast."[7] Walker was probably correct. Thomas had been a crew member on the *San Diego* during the sealing venture into the Bering Sea in 1883.[8] The captain of the *Shearwater* was far more suspicious than Lieutenant Irvine, and the warship was soon making fast for Dutch Harbor to inform the Americans.[9] It was to no avail. The outcome of the contact between the *Carmencita* and the *Shearwater* was particularly frustrating to J.C. Newbury, the customs collector in Victoria: "If the ship's papers had been scrutinized it would have been seen that she had cleared from Victoria for Acapulco direct in ballast and not via Behring Sea on a sealing voyage with hunters using firearms."[10] It was later reported, but unconfirmed, that MacLean's crew raided St. Paul Island in the Pribilof Islands that same day, 6 August, killing as many seals as they could fit in their boats on the beach: "The men were all well armed and warned the natives not to interfere with them."[11]

On 16 August, Captain Pfinger of the *Manning* anxiously sought instructions as to whether or not he could seize the Mexican schooner *Carmencita* or *Acapulco*.[12] He came close. On one occasion, the *Manning* missed the *Carmencita* by just two hours because a US treasury agent had diverted the government vessel from her task in order to carry him from Nome: "When the officers of the *Manning* learned how near they had been to making a seizure they were considerably disappointed."[13] They would remain so. The *Manning* discovered no sealing violations that year and no *Carmencita*.[14] In his report on events that season, Edwin Sims, an American solicitor from the Department of Commerce and Labor, specifically mentioned "a crew of pirates, such as that on the *Carmencita,* which hovered around the islands" and prepared "to land and not only raid the rookeries but plunder the village and salt houses, where are stored valuable furs." He also noted that "the crews of schooners, acting in concert, had effected a landing on the Russian seal islands and had held off the armed guard at least two weeks, during which time both sides suffered many casualties and many seals were killed." But his report also suggests that MacLean's schooner did not land and was not involved in the coordinated raid.[15]

Some maritime writers, such as Joseph Conrad, have suggested that sailors were disdainful of "land entanglements" such as newspapers, especially in the long-distance trade: "We cast such offending rags on one side and rejoiced that we had forgotten the dubious pleasures of civilization."[16] This was not the case aboard the *Carmencita.* On one of their exchanges with the whaler *Alice Knowles* (the two vessels met four times that season), newspapers were received on board the *Acapulco.* MacLean initially cut out the pertinent stories concerning developments in San Francisco. When questioned by the crew, he finally told them about "the fuss they were making at San Francisco over the schooner." One of the newspapers that the crew apparently received was the *Daily Colonist* of 17 June. This issue contained a report about the American cutter *Bear* steaming up from Honolulu, the incitements handed down in San Francisco, and a variety of excerpts from California newspapers. The crew was obviously concerned, and their determination was strengthened by the realization that, if seized, they stood a good chance of losing their wages. Four of them took matters into their own hands and, with one of the boats, headed for the Alaskan shore. The others simply decided that enough was enough: "We decided to quit and come home. There was no scrap. No one would do anything more and we had to come home." On their way back, the temporary captain, Bill Thomas, died and was buried at sea on 23 August.[17]

This decision to return to home port and the way it played out, with Alex no longer in absolute command, is reminiscent of an earlier period. As Marcus Rediker and others have pointed out, eighteenth-century pirate ships operated with a different social order: "Its hallmark was a rough, improvised, but effective egalitarianism that placed authority in the collective hands of the crew." When not engaged "in fighting, chasing, or being chased," the vessel was governed by majority rule.[18] The crew of the *Carmencita* were not pirates. The vessel was registered, regardless of how she had acquired it. It is nonetheless quite reasonable to suggest that all members were aware of their questionable legal position. For some, it had been their second attempt, and sailors were good to talk among themselves. An awareness of sailors' lore may assist in explaining Alex's acceptance of the situation that had developed on the vessel.

On 26 August, the steamer *W.H. Kruger* arrived at San Francisco with a report of the unconfirmed raid in early August.[19] Also in late August, there was talk of fitting out an expedition in San Francisco to sail north to warn MacLean. The plan was to fit out a schooner, manned by Norwegians, ostensibly to carry supplies to Cape Nome. It would seek out the *Carmencita* and take her to South America and sell her at the port of Punta Arenas: "A safe hiding place was to be found for Captain McLean and his crew and all evidence that might incriminate others was to be destroyed." The scheme sounded like just more waterfront talk and was not given much chance to succeed.[20] Once more, the coverage in the newspapers became extensive. While the earlier deadline of 3 July was long passed, many people harboured expectations that the final act of this nautical drama would soon be played out. Many in Victoria awaited the conclusion of the story: "Quite the most interesting topic of discussion amongst seafaring men all along the Pacific coast at the present time is of the exploits of Capt. Alex McLean ... There are several persons in this city who are vitally interested in Captain McLean and his men. It means much to them if the sealer and his piratical crew escape from the clutches of the federal law."[21] But stories would be all the authorities had to gnaw on for a while longer.

Alex MacLean brought the elusive schooner *Carmencita* into Clayoquot on Vancouver Island's west coast on 3 September 1905. He was prompted, in part, by concerns that he could be caught by an American cutter, "as it is pretty generally understood that one at least was out looking for him." The 365 skins that he landed had a market value of around $7,000 in Victoria. It was a slight improvement from the sixty-five acquired in 1904. The skins were quickly transferred, the hunters landed, water and provisions taken aboard, and "she then stood out to sea again for an unknown destination." This reporter felt it safe to add that MacLean "will not run the schooner into any United States port."[22] The landing was soon known about in Victoria and all along the coast.[23] Since Clayoquot was not a port of entry, this manoeuvre of MacLean's also angered Newbury, the customs collector in Victoria. According to a Vancouver newspaper, with Canadian Customs on her trail, and the American squadron in the North Pacific ordered to apprehend her, "the schooner is not likely to get far from Clayoquot."[24] Actually, MacLean was still in Clayoquot three days later. Many people were getting into the act, vying for the role of taking him down. A.E. Smith was the American consul-general at Victoria, and when he heard about the *Carmencita*'s landing he immediately telegraphed Rear-Admiral Caspar Goodrich, who was commanding the Pacific squadron at Port Angeles, Washington. Smith's wire prompted Goodrich to charge north, initially to Esquimalt, with the 5,000-ton cruiser *Chicago*: "Apparently he was going to look for McLean until some one at the dockyard convinced him he was off limits – but not before he made the alternative suggestion that he send the torpedo boat *Manning* up the coast." This action was also discouraged. The "ruffled dignity of the U.S. finally smoothed over with a few quick gins, the *Chicago,* along with the cruiser *Marblehead* and the destroyer *Paul Jones,* returned to Port Angeles."[25] Goodrich would be far more productive the following year in the wake of the San Francisco earthquake.[26]

On 5 September, the same day that the Russian-Japanese War ended with the signing of the Treaty of Portsmouth, six of the *Carmencita's* crew arrived in Victoria from Clayoquot aboard the *Queen City*. The five hunters and the cook immediately attempted to secure their wages by laying a claim on the 365 sealskins that accompanied them. They sought out Newbury for information and advice. The customs officer was ahead of them, detaining the skins upon arrival because they had been landed from a foreign vessel before entry at customs.[27] The *Daily Colonist,* noting the small harvest of skins, quickly dismissed the idea of an August raid. For this paper, the moral of the episode was quite clear: "The so-called pirate had far less skins than the Victoria schooners will have to show for a legitimate cruise."[28] The newspaper stories then began again: "The six sealers who came to Victoria were bound to a pact of secrecy ... Finally they admitted they were sealers – and also admitted they were thirsty for beer. They insist there was no raid. The small number of skins they brought home confirms this." They maintained that Captain Thomas was the vessel's master and that he was buried at sea in late August. "Was Thomas made captain because he died?" asked a bystander. "He was captain," replied the sealer, "McLean was navigator. I don't say we took orders from Thomas. There were blamed few orders given on the *Carmen* – I mean *Acapulco.* When we wanted to go hunting, why we went, that's all." They then began to strain credulity considerably, although one seaman made a nice attempt. "As a matter of fact," said one of the men, "the stories published in San Francisco of the 'fierce' McLean being a raider and pirate are enough to make anyone who knows the man laugh. McLean hasn't sand enough to fight a mouse, and if Jack London founded his character of 'The Sea Wolf' upon that of Alex McLean, it's a poor copy. Dan McLean, who is dead, was a man willing to take any chance, but Alex isn't. London probably saw a chance for advertisement and took it." The crew appeared to be breaking ranks. At least one of them was quite disenchanted: "He says that Capt. McLean was disliked by all, and that his day of reckoning is coming."[29]

While the Canadian authorities were scrambling to send the fishery protection steamer *Kestrel* to Clayoquot to seize the *Carmencita,* Newbury wired MacLean on 6 September and informed him that the skins sent down had been seized and insisted he come to Victoria immediately. As Newbury explained to his boss in Ottawa, the commissioner of customs John McDougald, "I had telegraphed to McLean at Clayoquot that I was detaining the skins but that he must come up and report at once, as I was doubtful whether he intended to bring the schooner to this port or sail away again." To Newbury's surprise, MacLean replied by mid-afternoon the same day that he would answer the summons to Victoria at once.[30] This seemed suspiciously easy. A week after departing Clayoquot, the *Carmencita* had still not arrived in the provincial capital, prompting additional speculation. While few in Victoria believed that "any raiding was done or contemplated," the local paper continued to pass on what it considered "weird stories" from its counterparts in San Francisco: "It is believed on good authority that the *Acapulco* crew has been unloading skins all along the coast line into boats standing ready and manned by confederates."[31] For Newbury, such an idea was "wild conjecture," and as he later warned Ottawa, "a portion of the matter as given in the newspapers as 'news' will of course have to be liberally discounted as to accuracy." The newspaper report was not sure where the skins had been obtained, but the issue of "an immense quantity of liquor" was brought up again, and it was suggested that it had been used as an article of barter.[32] Whatever MacLean was up to at this point, he had a lot of people wondering for a long time: "British Columbia marine men consider that he accomplished some astonishingly clever manoeuvres with the *Carmencita*. He knew every nook and cranny of that wild and rugged coast like a book."[33]

Unannounced, unescorted, unfettered, and eight days later than a trip between Clayoquot and Victoria would usually take in favourable weather, the *Acapulco* sailed into James Bay in Victoria late on 12 September, flying the Mexican flag. MacLean had arrived after office hours. He would call on Newbury the following morning. Meanwhile, Alex "shook hands with the hunters who had already arrived and were at the wharf to meet him."[34] His reappearance in Victoria seemed almost ordinary. For MacLean, "that barrel-chested figure who has just climbed out of a companionway to step on deck ... [in] his mid-forties, he sports an enormous moustache – to match his bushy eyebrows – and affects the somewhat unseamanlike rig of a black plug hat and the cutaway coat named for Prince Albert. This is the famous Alex McLean, who, after a quick look around the deck, scrambles up a ladder to Store Street and heads for the nearby Lighthouse Saloon and the ministering services of Theodore Fischer, the bartender."[35] His wife and daughter were also waiting for him in Victoria. There had been little peace for Lucy MacLean that summer, and it is likely that she and her daughter had moved up to be with her family for support and to get a bit of a respite from the San Francisco Bay area reporters. Besides, with the outstanding charges hovering over him in San Francisco, it seemed unlikely Alex MacLean would be rushing back there.

After being cautioned by a representative of the owners, Alex initially eluded both the hunters seeking their wages and the reporters hunting for stories. Eventually, he had a brief exchange with a *Daily Colonist* reporter: "'I'll not tell you a thing' said Capt. MacLean. 'You've broken up my voyage

– that's what you've done. Things were printed in the newspapers about me, and when the crew read 'em they wouldn't seal any more. I had to come home. If it hadn't been for the newspapers I'd been sealing yet. Did I raid? No, I did not. I broke no law. We weren't on any rookery, no matter what the papers say, and everything was all right ... The Mexican flag is all right. We can hunt seals within leagues of the islands, and with guns at that. What need had I to be scared of cutters? They can't do anything to me. The *Shearwater* boarded me about ten miles off St. Paul and she found my papers all right."[36] Little additional information was elicited from other crew members at that time, other than that they had been short of food and that the lengthy passage time from Clayoquot was "because of head winds and fog, in which the schooner ran very close to the shore on one occasion when entering the straits. The men tell a similar story regarding the cruise as those who arrived a week ago, and some show they have rehearsed a tale to be told on arrival."[37] They were emphatic that no raids had been made, and there was something to be said for having time to prepare one's story. It did not wash with Newbury: "When asked why he had put in at Clayoquot[,] a place not a port of entry he pleaded shortage of stores and ignorance of our laws. From the list of stores purchased ... it will be seen that nearly everything purchased could have been done without for the three or four extra days which might be required to reach Victoria; with favourable weather the vessel might have made the distance in one day."[38]

Newbury was frustrated. Alex's explanations did not dispel his suspicions. Victoria's customs collector initially and unwisely took out some of his disappointment on P. Ornelas, the Mexican consul-general in San Francisco: "Will you ... please advise me whether the certificate in question was procured from you through misrepresentation or fraud and also whether the shipping of some eighteen men at Drake's Bay was not irregular and whether McLean should really be recognized as Master at all under your consular regulations ... the operations of this schooner or rather those of her Masters and owners for the last two years are open to grave question[.] I wish a statement from you showing that they are contravening the laws and regulations of your country as well as those of Canada." Newbury was not completely satisfied with the prompt reply, which had enclosed copies of the certificates regarding the *Acapulco,* and he wrote to the Mexican official again: "I beg to state that no such persons as Jose Sanchez (reputed owner) and Robt. Mullins (reputed builder) are known here. Neither was any schooner of the dimensions given in Mullin's certificate ever built here." Newbury's outrage prompted him to go a bit too far, as he added: "Capt. Woodside who cleared the vessel from this port assured me that your consulate was aware of the latter fact (that the *Acapulco* was really the *Carmencita*) and that your certificate was granted to allow the *Carmencita* which had got a bad reputation to proceed to Mexico under a new name and there complete Mexican registry in order to be disposed of to advantage." In his cool reply, Ornelas regretted "that [Newbury] should give room and emphasis in [his] seemingly courteous communication to an obnoxious and absurd statement attributed to one Captain Woodside."[39] Newbury was suitably chastised and quickly backtracked in fine bureaucratic fashion: "I hasten to point out that you have quite misunderstood the idea I expressed or intended to express. It was furthermost from my intention to infer that the Mexican Consulate was aware of the fraudulent nature of the transaction ... I have learned by experience that his [Woodside's] statements are not worthy of credence."[40] The provisional Mexican registry for the *Acapulco* would eventually be cancelled on 31 October.[41] According to the *Vancouver Province,* "the whole case seems to have simmered down to one where a number of Americans, not being allowed to go sealing under their own flag, used the Mexican flag to do so."[42] The *Portland Oregonian* took a different tack, which highlighted its disappointment: "Tame and prosaic was the return of Jack London's 'Sea Wolf' ... To assist in shattering the idol which London built, one of the redoubtable Alex's sailors ... stated that the captain bold 'would not fight a cat unless he was full of hootch.'" Accordingly, MacLean was "steadily drifting further away from the reputation which Jack London gave him."[43]

Within hours of their arrival in Victoria, one crew member was charged with being drunk, and Alex, anxious to get his crew out of town, preferably to Seattle, quickly attempted to secure his release. Limiting the sources of the stories presumably could contain the number of versions and questionable details.[44] It was a sensible approach, as one west coast writer noted, "woe to him who forgot that he was with the 'Sea Wolf' to fight and keep his mouth shut" – but not very successful.[45] One of the crew was Bill O'Rourke, an American civil servant who had been working in Manila. O'Rourke had his own story to tell, once he was safely in Seattle. On his way to visit his widowed mother in New York, he decided to take in the sights on the San Francisco waterfront, where he was befriended by a "maritime character." He woke up on the *Carmencita* with a huge hangover and began to argue with MacLean: "The man from Cape Breton with the handlebar moustache promptly handcuffed him and kept him on bread and water for three days. From then on he was worked like a dog, he said, and at Victoria awaiting the ship's registration papers he said he was kept locked below decks." From contemporary descriptions, the crew could well have included a few shanghaied souls, but it is unclear how O'Rourke made it from the San Francisco waterfront to Victoria. One wonders if O'Rourke had had time to read London's latest best-seller during his stopover in San Francisco and thus had come up with the Humphrey Van Weyden-like similarities? Cecil Clark admitted the story "sounded a bit fishy."[46] The *Daily Colonist* remained skeptical about the many and varied accounts linked to the whole affair and continued to downplay the events: "It seems though, from all accounts, both believable and unbelievable – and the captain and his crew tell some weirdly fantastic stories – the voyage has been far from such a buccaneering affair as is made out. Rather it has been a failure ... other than to clear from Victoria for Acapulco under false representations, and to go sealing instead of to his destination, the laws have been treated carefully." In the same report, the *Daily Colonist* carried a fascinating account from a San Francisco newspaper, dated 10 September from Port Townsend, Washington, six days after the *Carmencita* left Clayoquot and two days before she arrived in Victoria. A tugboat and a small fishing vessel crossed paths, and while dickering about tow charges "the mate of the tug, exercising a habit born of long usage, stepped aboard the schooner to get a fine fish. He peered under the hatch and was surprised to see that the fishermen with great care had their catch neatly boxed. Some of the covers were not close fitting, however, and the mate returned to his vessel marvelling over the fact that the halibut being caught these days were covered with a short, soft fur." The mate mentioned it to the tugboat captain, who thought no more of it until he read a few newspaper stories of the *Carmencita's* activities.[47] Newbury considered this tale "pure fabrication," although one long-lasting rumour had the neatly boxed sealskins being sold for $30,000.[48] This particular aspect of the tale, especially its durability for more than fifty years, again suggests the acceptability of social banditry when pitted against opponents such as the North American Commercial Company and the American and Canadian governments.

Back in Cape Breton, the local paper was avidly following the escapades of one of the island's native sons. The *Sydney Record* carried the views of a newspaper correspondent in Victoria: "In an age when romance is passing even from deep sea navigation, there remains to those who revel in tales of adventure, much to stimulate the fancy in the doings of the opium smugglers and the seal poacher. Both of these enterprising free lances [sic] of commerce are found in Victoria, which has long been a base of operations along both lines. Some of the brawling seal hunters who 'whoop it up' in Wharf street saloons after the season's cruise, could, if they would, unfold tales which would make the creations of the writers of fiction seem tame by comparison." The article, not very helpfully, noted that Alex MacLean was "wanted by the authorities on general principles."[49]

Newbury would finally have his day, and on 14 September he levied fines totalling $1,600. The Clayoquot landing would earn MacLean a fine of $800 under section 116 of the Customs Act, "entering at other than a port of entry." This particular charge could have been, but was not, levied twice. The other violations, "departing falsely" (which referred to Woodside's outward report) and "failing to make report at Customs and unloading goods" were good for $400 each. The latter, for Newbury, was "so flagrant a violation of Customs laws that I cannot understand how Capt. McLean can plead ignorance."[50] The *Victoria Daily Times* suggested that Newbury "was disposed to be a little lenient" because the skins had been shipped from Clayoquot in broad daylight "and in no underhand way."[51] Newbury wanted a few more pounds of flesh, but the "complicated and involved" aspects prompted prudence to prevail. While only taking action under the Customs Act, Newbury said, "I feel convinced however that there has been a violation of the Behring Sea Award Act of 1894 (57 Vic. chap. 2) but it will be difficult to make out a case under the Act and as the vessel held a provisional Mexican registry when she cleared from this port I deem it wise for the present at least to give full credence to her documents. I firmly believe and in fact have evidence that they were obtained through misrepresentation and fraud." Newbury felt deeply about the matter, was outraged that people would so deliberately and repeatedly ignore regulations, and realized the wider complications that could result. He poured his outrage out to his boss in Ottawa: "Our own sealing fleet are all operated strictly in accordance with the provisions of the Behring Sea Award Act with its irksome restrictions and it will have a disturbing effect if vessels carrying the flag of a nation which is not a party to the award are operated in the business without the restrictions which apply to our vessels ... what makes the case of this schooner so closely followed is the fact that apparently residents of San Francisco have by fraud and subterfuge procured Mexican registry temporarily in order to make a successful sealing voyage and what makes the case still more pointed is that now it has been done two seasons in succession." Newbury also insisted that "if the Master or owners or their representatives make any statements in defence of their action I would request an opportunity to disprove any what may not be in accordance with the facts of the case."[52] The customs collector was determined to see the incident through to the end.

The fines were paid, under protest, from the proceeds of the sale of the skins that had been consigned to R.P. Rithet and Company.[53] Newbury then released the rest of the skins and the vessel but refused to return the provisional Mexican registry.[54] Immediately, on 15 September, the vessel and remaining skins were seized by a marshal of the admiralty court in an action regarding the crew's wages of $1,094.71. This action was successful, and the schooner was ordered to be sold by the admiralty court. At noon on 23 September, with about twenty people in attendance, including Alex MacLean, the good ship *Jennie Thelin/Carmencita/Acapulco* "was knocked down, together with her sails, anchors, chains, and a complete sealing outfit" to a real estate agent, P.R. Brown, for $1,000. There were no opposing bids, although there was an unconfirmed report that Brown acted for the previous owners.[55] The sum was almost sufficient to meet the wage claims. The old *Jennie Thelin* now had clear title but no registry. Eventually, she would find herself back home, and by the summer of 1906 the *Jennie Thelin* would have a San Diego owner and her original name under the American flag. Six years later, on 10 January 1912, the *Jennie Thelin* was wrecked on the Baja California coast of Mexico.[56]

The same day that the admiralty court proceedings began in Victoria in 1905, H. Moffatt, the Secret Service agent in San Francisco, telegrammed his boss in Washington expressing concern that MacLean and the schooner would soon be off to Mexico and asking whether something could be done because Fred Wilson was arguing that the vessel's papers were good until the following February and she could still be sailed to Acapulco. Also that day, the Department of Justice made a request to its consul-general in Victoria about getting MacLean arrested.[57] The *Daily Colonist,* demonstrating its memory and its sense of irony, noted that the American government, which had relied on MacLean's evidence a decade earlier, was now after him. The following day, there was a conference about Alex MacLean in Washington with the chief of the Secret Service and representatives from the Departments of Justice and Commerce and Labor.[58] British Columbia premier Richard McBride took the American request concerning MacLean under advisement on 17 September. A.E. Smith, the American consul-general in Victoria, was initially under the impression that the government of British Columbia was acting on the request and so informed his government. Hence, there was an Associated Press dispatch out of Washington dated 20 September, which stated that McLean had been arrested in Victoria. This report included the observation that the crew were "as choice a band of robbers and cutthroats as have manned a pirate craft since the days of Capt. Kidd."[59] But the dispatch, as was so often the case with matters regarding Alex MacLean, was premature. He was not arrested. The charge was not an extraditable offence, and a few days later Premier McBride explained to the Americans that "the government of British Columbia cannot act as requested and suggested that application be made to the officers of the imperial navy." The *Shearwater* was expected back from the Bering Sea on 22 September, and "it [was] probable that the United States consul [would] apply to Commander Hunt to act against the alleged poacher." As the *Daily Colonist* explained, "it is questionable, according to those versed in sealing matters, if there is any British or Canadian law which will allow the arrest of the captain or seizure of his vessel under the circumstances. It is the first occasion that the section in question has been applied to such a circumstance. Heretofore any arrests or seizures that have been made under the sealing laws have been made on the high seas."[60] While vessels flying British flags could be (and many were) seized by American authorities, and British warships had the authority to arrest American ones breaking the regulations, Alex MacLean had sailed under neither flag during this period. Nor had he been caught red-handed. He would not make legal history on this occasion. There is also the possibility that the Americans' thirst for justice was tempered by MacLean's supportive role in the Bering Sea Claims Commission hearings in 1896-97.[61]

The charges in San Francisco against MacLean would linger for a decade. MacLean's ability to flit among the various ports along the west coast was now limited considerably. He may have continued to tempt fate. There is a suggestion that he did return to San Francisco briefly in 1907, possibly in command of a lumber schooner.[62] But his days on San Francisco's "Barbary Coast" and hoisting a jar at the First and Last Chance Saloon in Oakland were now over. He had definitely made an impression, and memories of him and stories about him would continue for generations in this area. The MacLean legend was already well on its way to fame when the description of Alex MacLean as pirate graced the front page of the San Francisco-Oakland newspapers in the summer of 1905. The more outrageous suggestions associated with this episode – the theme of piracy and the threat of the death penalty – quickly dissipated under the prosaic and more specific charges under sections 28, 99, and 116 of the Canada Customs Act, and section 5440 of the American revised statutes.[63] The *Portland Oregonian*'s assessment of the recent events could be read in this light: "The career of Alexander MacLean offers strong testimony to the fact that journalistic romance can make a highly sensational piratical hero out of very ordinary material. When Alexander MacLean and 'Brother Dan' came out of the wilds of Cape Breton about twenty-five years ago they were as mild a pair as ever sailed the salty seas."[64] The first statement is worthy of reflection. The second one is more suspect. However, the illegal episode with the *Jennie Thelin* probably was his "most notorious voyage" and certainly was the most publicized. The proliferation of unsubstantiated stories that came out of the *Carmencita* episode would add to the confusion, and to the legend, and would seriously hamper the emergence of a completely accurate picture.

The retrospective, the ambivalence, and the blurredness were not long in coming. The *Vancouver Province* carried the following in early October 1905: "They've got Jack London's Sea Wolf at last. Captain Alex McLean, the federal officers call him; since 1891 scathless [sic] pirate of the protected seal fisheries. Greatly to their surprise they got him without feeling his dirkknife among their ribs. Aboard a revenue cutter, armed to the teeth, before their mind's eye visions of hand-to-hand encounters with ruffians like Morgan's or Capt. Kidd's, while the decks grew slippery with blood, the federal officers sailed northward to take the Sea Wolf, the elusive seal poacher, red-handed. But the Canadians at Victoria had quietly seized him ... As romance it is disappointing, but the federal officers breathed easier." Supposedly, the men on the revenue cutter had "orders to take the Sea Wolf and all on board ... dead or alive." In this account, "it seems marvellous that he should have allowed himself to be taken alive by captors who show no wounds." It continues: "By the federal authorities, by all the skippers of the North Pacific, and by the book-reading public of all the seaports on the western coast of the continent, he was instantly recognised as the terrible hero of *The Sea-*

Wolf." A long excerpt from the novel describing Wolf Larsen follows. Then the fanciful account continues: "And Wolf Larsen of the novel is Captain Alex McLean, terror of the North Pacific, pirate, seal poacher, who had defied and eluded the armed ships of the United States, Great Britain, Russia and Japan for more that twenty years – until a few days ago, when he grew overbold and fell into the clutches of Canadian officers." The newspaper hauled out Kipling's "There's never a law of God or man/Runs north of fifty-three," where MacLean was "pirate king." This account suggests that the myth-making process incorporating specific events began almost immediately after the link was made between the novel and the mariner: "He made his own laws and enforced them by sheer brutality and superior physical strength and daring ... he was absolute monarch." The *Carmencita* was compared to the *Flying Dutchman*.[65] It was a vivid version in the Vancouver paper, and it can be strikingly compared with the more judicious treatment in his old home port of Victoria's *Daily Colonist*.

Reports about all of these developments filtered down to Cape Breton as well. The *Sydney Post* initially relied on a Toronto newspaper correspondent in Victoria and immediately emphasized the romantic-adventurous element. Here also the wilder version was quickly questioned. A week later, the *Sydney Post* did a follow-up, noting the harsh assessments by some newspapers and offering a corrective from a Sydney resident who had sailed with both Dan and Alex: "Alex is not the desperate character that he is painted. He never fired a shot at anything but seals in his life." Nor were the MacLeans "half black as they were painted. They were not angels, but neither were they 'bad men' in the western sense ... If they got a chance to raid a rookery they did so like many of the others ... They were dare-devils but not desperados."[66] The Cape Breton writer who contributed this perspective had left the Pacific six years earlier.

The reports received in Cape Breton of Alex MacLean's recent activities stimulated local memories and probably prompted considerable conversation in the Cape Breton Gaelic communities such as Washabuckt (where his MacNeil relatives lived), the East Bay and French Vale areas, and in the communities situated around Sydney harbour. Sydney, which was incorporated as a city in 1904, and the surrounding coal-mining towns were experiencing massive industrialization. In 1893, a syndicate led by Boston promoter Henry Whitney combined most of the larger coal mines in south Cape Breton into the Dominion Coal Company. Coal production quadrupled by 1902 and was accompanied by the erection of two of Canada's four integrated steel plants, at Sydney and Sydney Mines. Numerous Gaels from the surrounding rural areas flocked to the coal mines and steel plants and many, for the first time, experienced the harsh and unyielding demands of industrial capitalism. The Cape Breton miners, organized since 1880, had entered an intense period of industrial conflict, which would witness numerous appearances by the Canadian army on the coal town streets and which would not slow down until the late 1920s. The steelworkers in Sydney made their first major, and unsuccessful, attempt for union recognition in the summer of 1904. At this time, they would be opposed by most of the representative forces of the dominant culture, the most conspicuous of which were the uniformed and armed militia forces from the mainland.[67] It was the same summer that MacLean was testing the waters of the Bering Sea in close proximity to the Russian rookeries, on his first voyage with the *Carmencita*. For the thousands of steelworkers and miners in the industrial Cape Breton workforce – many recently removed from rural, traditional communities – contemporary accounts of Cape Bretoner Alex MacLean's sailing escapades in the North Pacific must have been viewed as issuing from another time and another world entirely. Many Cape Breton Gaels in particular, adjusting to work in the steel plant, or in "the black pit of misery" in "the country of coal," doubtless cast envious eyes westward to the Pacific and reflected on the spirited adventurer who was one of their own.[68]

12
Setting the Record Straight: Vancouver, 1906-08

According to most sources, Alex's sealing days were finally over after he brought the *Carmencita* into Victoria in September 1905. With the California charges hovering over his head, San Francisco's attractiveness was greatly diminished, and neither he nor his family were anywhere near that city when it was rocked by the earthquake and fire that started on 18 April 1906. He would operate out of Victoria for a while, living on Chatham Street, but Vancouver would become his final home port.[1] While he put his sealing career on the shelf once again, he remained focused on the sea, returning initially to the occupation that had led him from Cape Breton Island to New England in the 1870s. In late November 1905, Alex was in Vancouver trying to buy a vessel for cod and halibut fishing and, mindful of the sealing brouhaha with the *Carmencita* and the ire of American treasury authorities and Canadian customs officials, he must have "spent several weeks recently on the anxious seat at Victoria," or so the *Vancouver Province* delicately reminded everyone.[2] Reports from this period suggest that he "was not financially robust,"[3] which is hardly surprising.

On 20 January 1906, a small fishing vessel, the twenty-ton *Ella G.*, with Captain Fred Forrest in command, departed Victoria for a halibut fishing trip off the coast of Vancouver Island. Alex MacLean was on board and "in charge of the fishing business."[4] Newspaper reports suggest it was not an ordinary fishing trip. She was on "a trip of exploration, which her owner does not at present feel inclined to discuss." The American authorities were apparently watching her movements closely, suspecting smuggling.[5] Initially, according to one version that circulated in Victoria and San Francisco, the vessel tucked into Neah Bay, Washington, but MacLean decided to head into open waters in the face of increasingly difficult weather. Captain Forrest and the crew were strongly opposed to the move. Supposedly the fierce, brutal persona of Wolf Larsen appeared, and "MacLean became again the Sea Wolf. The schooner's master and his mandates were swept aside and with revolver in hand MacLean took active command, the anchor was lifted, and the schooner plunged through the foaming seas, taking a course for the Canadian side." The move was purportedly prompted by the appearance of an American cutter, which signalled the *Ella G.* to heave to. MacLean issued "a scornful burst of laughter" and pressed on. The American vessel then displayed some distress signals, and one of the crew suggested to MacLean that he could now seek safer anchorage. "To this MacLean replied with the grim laugh, well remembered by those who have sailed with him upon his previous adventures, that he was not to be fooled by any d—d Yankee trick, and lay where he was, although in momentary danger of driving ashore."[6] This *San Francisco Examiner* account seems fanciful. The fishing trip continued. So did the stories, not because they were necessarily accurate but because they had been reported. A revised version emerged some weeks later, undermining much of the suspect scenario. There had been no pursuit. MacLean's reported antics on this occasion do not ring clear or true. The "cutter" was the steamer *Queen,* which was in the area in an unsuccessful attempt to assist the 126 passengers aboard the SS *Valencia,* which ran aground near Pachena Point, south of Barkley Sound, on 22 January.[7]

On Saturday, 27 January, rumours circulated that the *Ella G.* might have gone down during a heavy storm.[8] On Sunday evening, a report from Bamfield, on the west coast of Vancouver Island, stated that the schooner had turned bottom up and that all hands had been lost. It prompted an extra edition of a Victoria newspaper, although Lucy MacLean remained confident "that her husband was not born to be drowned in any storm that blows."[9] The *Seattle Post-Intelligencer* put it on the front page with the headline "'Sea Wolf' Goes Down with Ship." The *San Francisco Chronicle* account, in a dispatch from Victoria, noted: "There is an indefiniteness about the news available at Bamfield, but little hope is held out here for the schooner, whose loss was accepted as conclusive by an evening paper." The *San Francisco Examiner's* account sided more with Lucy, although it was hesitant to cast an opinion one way or the other, simply because it involved MacLean: "His career has been such an adventurous one and his luck in escaping danger so remarkable that until his body is recovered from the deep few of those who know his reputation will believe that he has met so prosaic a fate as that of being drowned."[10] Back east, in Nova Scotia's capital, the *Halifax Herald* informed its readers of MacLean's disappearance, describing him as "a notorious sealer ... who won international notoriety as a result of sealing raids and a recent illicit sealing cruise to Bering Sea." The *Halifax Herald* did not forget to mention the Jack London connection, the "Sea Wolf" sobriquet, and the episode with the *James Hamilton Lewis* and the Russians in 1891. His drowning was also duly noted on the front page of the *Sydney Record.*[11] Then, on Monday afternoon, the *Ella G.* arrived safely at Ucluelet, on the other side of Barkley Sound from Bamfield. All six crew members were safe, and the *Ella G.* was "little damaged by her coquetting with the hurricane."[12] The *Daily Colonist* was critical of its competitor, noting the "yarn originated in the anxiety of some people to make a sensational report of a subject they knew nothing of." Lucy MacLean's confidence had not been misplaced, and one front-page report in the *San Francisco Examiner* maintained "the hand of 'Wolf Larsen' has not lost its cunning or the red-moustached Nova Scotian his nerve to challenge fate." Alex quipped that the reports of their demise were "much exaggerated," suggesting an appreciation of Mark Twain and, perhaps, an acceptance of his recent connection with contemporary literature.[13]

While this saga of the *Ella G.* was unfolding, MacLean's American-based associates in the *Carmencita* affair were having their day in court. The trials of William J. Wood, William J. Woodside, S.E.R. de Smidt, and R.J. Tyson were held late in January in the district court in San Francisco. The defence called no witnesses and offered little in the way of cross-examination. Their argument that the *Carmencita's* Mexican registration distanced her from the American statutes was not convincing. Wood, Woodside, and de Smidt were fined $500 each for preparing and sending the *Jennie Thelin* to engage in pelagic sealing in proscribed waters under section 5440 of the American revised statutes. R.J. Tyson was more fortunate, as one juror held steadfast for acquittal. Tyson's second trial late that year found him not guilty.[14] Alex was the only one charged, and absent, from the dock. The charge against him, which was similar to the one against Wood, Woodside, and de Smidt, and presumably carried the same potential penalty, would linger for a decade.[15] It was a long stretch from piracy and the noose. But MacLean remained a bit skittish and constantly kept an eye peeled for American Rear-Admiral Goodrich's minions. Trying to catch halibut, if that is what he was up to, while constantly checking the horizon for American government cutters, was a bit taxing, not to say disruptive, and may partially explain the declining interest of the *Ella G.'s* crew. By early March, Captain Forrest had left the vessel, and the others were not far behind, prompted, in part, by the low catch to date. Alex soon found himself "both master and crew" of the *Ella G.* and still at Ucluelet.[16]

While these events were being played out, MacLean's name popped up in Washington, first in the Senate Committee on Foreign Relations and then in the House Committee on the Judiciary. The occasions were prompted by another attempt to clear the decks for legal action by American sealers for the seizures by the American government. The reports noted their contributions to the American case during the Bering Sea Claims Commission hearings in 1895-96. Conspicuously identified among these American sealers was Captain Alex MacLean, and American legal counsel Don Dickinson's detailed statement of "this brave and honest man" was carried in full in both reports.[17] The next public notice of MacLean's activities came four months later. In early August, the *Daily Colonist* reported that Alex was running a small tug, the *City of Tipella,* out of Vancouver. The owner, Captain Alex Morrison, was "an old shipmate" of MacLean's, and the ex-sealer spent the remainder of the summer on this boat. As in the vast majority of instances in which he would be mentioned from June 1905 onward, this newspaper account immediately associated him with London's novel, and the reporter could not resist offering a description and an assessment of the present tugboat captain who was becoming a folk legend: "Of medium stature, wiry of muscle, with spring-steel nerves and a constitution akin to that of a horse in strength, Captain Alex McLean has in the two and a half decades he has been on the coast had many ups and downs. As a navigator it is admitted that he has no equal."[18]

At this point, the historical record begins to get muddled again. In early August 1906, the *Seattle Post-Intelligencer* reported a costly raid by sealers on the Pribilof Island rookeries earlier that summer, linking it to Alex MacLean. The smear would prove to be almost indelible. The editorial concluded: "The raid of the sealing islands was of such a daring character, and in so much accordance with the known character of the man, that there is some foundation for the belief that it was organized, not by the Japanese, but by a notorious sealer, who has made previous raids on the seal islands on the Russian side of the Bering Sea, and who is the hero of Jack London's *Sea Wolf.*" Anyone on the west coast who followed the sea knew that the editor was targeting MacLean. The *Daily Colonist* came to MacLean's defence, pointing out that he "is now peaceably handling the wheel of a peaceable little tug running out of Vancouver, called the *City of Tipella.* The unfortunate man has had many offences alleged against him and Washington correspondents ... still have a nightmare of raids by him, because he attempted one raid in 1904 at the Copper Island and was believed to have gone to attempt another and did not carry it out. But he did not, as the Seattle paper suggests, organize the fatal raid in Bering Sea."[19] Others were not convinced. One report out of Boston stated that he was "said to be the instigator of the Japanese poaching raid on the seal rookeries," and an article by Robert Dunn, a *Harper's Weekly* special correspondent in Dutch Harbor, Alaska, written in late July, asked: "Was Abe [sic] McLean, Jack London's Sea Wolf, who is as real a being as any of us, back of the raid, we wonder?" Dunn, who had become friends with Jack London during the Russian-Japanese War, noted that MacLean had been "broke" in Victoria last winter and had then headed to the Orient.[20] The blurb from Boston, dated 9 August, was carried on the front page of the *Sydney Record* and described MacLean as a "pirate of the North Pacific, king of pelagic sealing outlaws, and terror of the law-abiding residents" on the Alaska islands: "For nearly twenty years he has violated the law of every nation having to do with any of the sealing grounds, and many bloody deeds are down on his record ... he is the one with whom the revenue officers have had to reckon more than any other man ... He has different times sailed under the Japanese, Mexican, Norwegian and Hawaiian flags, and has been hunted continually. He is the original of Jack London's Wolf Larsen in 'The Sea Wolf' and government authorities state that London's picture of him is not overdrawn."[21]

Henry Wood Elliott was also not dissuaded by the assurances of the *Daily Colonist.* Alex MacLean was back in his crosshairs. In early September, Elliott informed the American State Department that a tragic raid, which had been carried out on St. Paul Island in mid-July, had been planned in Victoria and San Francisco the previous spring. Later, he would be more specific, maintaining that MacLean was in charge and had directed the raid.[22] Admittedly, there is a gap in MacLean's whereabouts between his reported difficulties on the *Ella G.* in early March and his tugboating stint out of Vancouver in early August, but the latter item was carried in the *Daily Colonist* and this paper was adamant that MacLean had not been involved in sealing in 1906.[23] Elliott was not wildly off the mark in a general sense. There was a lot of poaching activity during this period. The Japanese pelagic sealers were extremely active, constantly raiding the rookeries during this time. Prohibited from using firearms at any time, Canadians were compelled to observe a closed season between 1 May and 31 July and were forbidden to operate within a sixty-mile radius of the Pribilof Islands. Bound only by the traditional three-mile limit, the Japanese were not restricted by the Paris award and were able to use guns.[24] There were about fifteen Canadian and thirty Japanese vessels in the pelagic fleet in 1906, and Fredericka Martin knew who to blame for the recent decline of the herd: "It was the sweep of schooners flying the Japanese flag from one migration to another, from the Commander Islands to the Pribilofs and onto their shores, that drove most Canadian sealers out of business. Murderous gangs landed on St. George beaches ... Protected by overhanging cliffs, they secretly killed their helpless prey and were gone. A broken club, skinned carcasses, or blood-splashed rocks betrayed their visits too late."[25] This "reign of terror" would continue for a few years. According to Gerald O. Williams, "not a summer passed without Japanese schooners being seized for poaching even within the 3-mile limit, and an increasing number of Canadians and Americans, the freebooters of the former pelagic sealing fleets of these two nations, now began to secure employment on the Japanese vessels or operate sealers under the Japanese flag and registry."[26] That year, the usual summer count of seals on St. Paul Island, where four-fifths of the Pribilof herd was located, was disrupted in mid-July by the close presence of a number of Japanese sealers around the rookery. Continued enumeration would have driven more seals into the range of the hunters.[27] These sealers were frequently within the three-mile limit and sometimes closer. There had been a couple of raids at St. Paul Island on 17 July 1906, during which five Japanese sealers were killed, two were wounded, and ten others were taken prisoner. After three months' imprisonment in Valdez, Alaska, the surviving raiders were deported to Japan.[28]

Such tragedies did not deter many sealers. In late August, seven schooners could be seen simultaneously from St. Paul Island. On clear days, they hovered just outside the territorial limit. When the fog moved in, so did the sealers, resulting in "an immense loss of seal life."[29] American treasury agent Walter Lembkey, who was on the Pribilof Islands at the time, had no doubt that "in a comparatively short time such reckless slaughter will accomplish the commercial extinction of the species." In his annual report, he noted: "Probably never in the history of the seal islands has the fur-seal herd suffered such a heavy blow as that which resulted from the operations of the pelagic fleet during the past summer."[30] A low American estimate had the pelagic fleet acquiring twice as many sealskins (27,216) from the Pribilof herd as the North American Commercial Company (NACC) had done in 1906 (14,476).[31] The various regulations, stipulations, agreements, awards and the exclusion of American sealers notwithstanding, the competition, and the almost constant conflict that had been a feature of the industry since the mid-1880s, continued. The activity around the rookeries in the summer of 1906 prompted one of the treasury agents to report that the recent actions of these pelagic sealers had surpassed "all the brazen effrontery of the Canadians during their entire sealing history." It is noteworthy that the agent in charge of the seal fisheries that season makes no mention of Alex MacLean in his reports.[32]

Pelagic sealing had always been a dangerous and costly business. Around the protected rookeries, it now became a particularly deadly affair. The loss of Japanese lives in mid-July, and the realization that at least some Americans had been involved in the previous two seasons, ensured that Elliott would again receive a hearing. His claim that the raids had been planned in San Francisco and Victoria the previous spring prodded the Department of Commerce and Labor, which was now responsible for the seal rookeries, to attempt to establish whether these charges were true. When asked for proof, Elliott wrote a somewhat arrogant reply to American President Theodore Roosevelt, which, while offering little in the way of substance, zeroed in on MacLean: "The fact that a notorious Canadian fur-seal pirate has successfully passed himself off upon the agents of the Department of State and of Commerce and Labour, as an excellent and worthy American citizen from 1892 down to October, 1905, does not warrant me in putting the data which I hold into such hands at this hour. I can place that raid of last July where it belongs if I have the opportunity, but no ignorant or inexperienced investigator can properly and effectively handle my data." One can sense an increasing degree of frustration and stridency on Elliott's part, due in large measure to the fact that not everyone would listen to him. Elliott did say he would give the Department of Commerce and Labor the information once he had an opportunity to visit San Francisco and Victoria. However, he urged caution. Not just anyone could get to the bottom of this nefarious scheme and, as he explained to the secretary of commerce and labor, V.H. Metcalf, "those men who have planned that raid are old in this illicit business; they have employed Japanese hunters in doing this work on the Pribilof Islands ever since 1882-1884; they are crafty and wary, and until I am able to get certain written statements from the hands of certain persons associated with them no end of justice or good for the public interests will be secured by publishing to your agents those facts bearing on them now in my possession."[33]

Edwin W. Sims, a solicitor for the Department of Commerce and Labor with experience in the sealing business, was asked to comment on Elliott's charges. Sims had been in Alaska during the 1906 season and had been further briefed by Lembkey when the latter was on his way back to Washington that autumn. Sims noted that he had heard similar suggestions about a planned raid at both Seattle and San Francisco, "but it seemed to be so vague and indefinite and to have so little foundation" that he did not bother to mention it earlier, nor did he deem it necessary to alter his original impression now. Sims also noted a number of inaccuracies in Elliott's claims.[34] Lembkey also responded to Elliott's accusations. As a result of the "intimation expressed" by Elliott that he would disclose the facts "provided he [was] given employment by the Government," Lembkey cautioned the senior officials that they should be aware of Elliott's track record in the seal industry. He then presented a devastating critique of the crusading conservationist's checkered career. He pointed out that Elliott stood "convicted" of a number of charges that seriously damaged his credibility.[35] The American authorities ultimately responsible for the Alaskan rookeries, including the agents on location, were less than convinced of Elliott's accuracy or motives. The *Daily Colonist,* which had followed MacLean's career as closely as any newspaper and usually reported his feats and shenanigans while expressing a healthy skepticism, offered comments on Elliott's accusations: "The above may read well in places where the truth is not known; but in Victoria it will provoke much amusement among those conversant with the facts. Whatever he did in other years, in 1906 Capt. MacLean did not engage or have any connection whatever in pelagic sealing or other industry than the operation of a small tug, the *City of Tipella.*" The newspaper also pointedly noted: "If the business is as profitable as the professor states, Capt. McLean is probably sorry the accounts of his daring deeds in the north are untrue."[36] Only Elliott, and later writers such as Gordon Newell and Gerald Williams, has Alex around the Pribilof Islands in 1906.[37]

Elliott was unrepentant, repeating his host of charges against the NACC and others to the Committee on Ways and Means in Washington in January 1907. This particular body was unimpressed and "practically suppressed the entire hearings."[38] The Committee on Ways and Means "became so disgusted with his baseless complaints and with his vituperation of public men of high standing, then dead, that they ... virtually hooted him out of the committee room."[39] Elliott, however, could not easily be silenced, and he continued to beat one of his favourite drums – the reason for the destruction of the fur seals – in an article of the *North American Review* in 1907: "It is due entirely to the greed, cruelty and avarice of certain men – unspeakable men, who, shielded and panoplied by imperfect law and regulations, have wrought this loot and ruin of our fur-seal herd of Alaska."[40] In yet another piece that year, he publicly targeted Alex MacLean, listing a series of depredations going back to the early 1880s. This article first appeared in the *New York Herald* on 8 September 1907 and was reprinted in various North American newspapers.[41]

It was the most comprehensive public attack upon MacLean to date. The accusations were widely circulated. As the *Daily Colonist* wryly noted, "while Capt. Alex McLean has been living quietly in Victoria and vicinity, peacefully engaged in his avocation of towing logs and tugboating generally on the British Columbia coast, he has been acclaimed through the United States as a 'seal pirate.'" Elliott, "an alleged expert regarding pelagic sealing, says that Capt. Alex McLean has been directing pirate raids on the rookeries of Bering Sea, organizing the Japanese boats which are hunting in that water, and otherwise engaging in adventures in the northern seas, all of which is news to Capt. McLean." The *Daily Colonist* concluded that Elliott's latest volley "contains a slight amount of truth embroidered with much more untruth."[42] This particular account of Elliott's is of some interest because of the serious allegations, the wide coverage, and the obvious reliance on this source by later accounts and assessments of MacLean. In this summary, Elliott offers up some background, going back to the early 1880s and "an old San Francisco firm." He explains that it was at this time that the MacLeans appeared on the Pacific coast. Apparently, the labour pool on the west coast for this emerging trade was small, and the two Cape Bretoners arrived just as "the business of raiding the Russian and Alaskan seal islands had been fairly started by this San Francisco fur trading house and its agents in Victoria ... These men were on the lookout for likely, hardy, fit persons to take command of their vessels and push the business of fur seal piracy with secrecy and energy. It was not long before the Cape Breton brothers entered the employment of these American promoters." In Elliott's scenario, Dan specialized in raiding the American islands and Alex "devoted his wit and seamanship" to their Russian counterparts: "From the date of their entry into the business of fur seal piracy in 1883, up to the close of the season in

1891, the McLean brothers made a great record for themselves and their employers." Elliott continued: "As the career of Alexander McLean happens to be the one most spectacular and notorious we will confine our review to his chief and salient transgressions. They certainly put up a great show of rascality both on his own part and that of his associates." In Elliott's account, Alex MacLean raided Copper Island with the *James Hamilton Lewis* and came back with 2,612 skins worth more than $25 each. The "pure velvet," as Elliott called the net profit, was $17 per skin: "How the division between them was made we will never know. Pirates do not keep books."[43]

Elliott then described the events of 1891, which "shows the spirit of a true pirate on his part and the energetic backing of his owners." MacLean cleared from San Francisco in March 1891: "The next heard from this British pirate (for he was and is not an American citizen and never has tried to be one)" was his seizure by the Russians in August of that year and his eventual return to San Francisco without his vessel. Both the seizure and the empty return were accurately described. This brought him to a "strange and shameful sequel" in which the owners and MacLean committed perjury and submitted a bogus claim, supported by bogus documents, to the State Department, which were "exploited at The Hague." Elliott repeated his claim that MacLean was in charge of and directed two of the Japanese schooners involved in the raids in July 1906 "but he keeps out of sight" and he "never has been an American citizen."[44]

The question of MacLean's citizenship was, in a sense, pivotal. Elliott's criticism of Herman and Isaac Liebes and the NACC regarding sealing practices, and their misleading of the American State Department, would be strengthened considerably if his accusations regarding MacLean's citizenship status were correct. Herman and Isaac Liebes were aware of this argument and tried to protect themselves later by explaining that MacLean's affidavits, which stated his American status, had not been taken by them but, rather, by a subordinate. They were also based on earlier affidavits and relied on the prevailing consensus within the fur trade – namely, that MacLean had become an American. They argued that if Alex MacLean had misled the Liebeses they were unaware of it and should not be held responsible. Herman Liebes was long gone by this time. Others connected to the firm were just trying to hedge their bets.[45]

Due consideration must be given to the records of the Circuit Court in Boston from 1 December 1882 and the document, signed by Alex MacLean at that time, which affirmed that he was "ready to renounce and abjure all allegiances and fidelity to every foreign Prince, Potentate, State or Sovereignty whatsoever; and particularly to Victoria, Queen of the United Kingdom of Great Britain and Ireland."[46] Whatever else Alex MacLean was, in December 1882 he became an American citizen. Then there are the affidavits given in San Francisco in the early 1890s as well as the presentation of

Alex MacLean's naturalization papers by senior American counsel Don Dickinson to the Claims Commission in late December 1896. San Francisco-based Secret Service agent N.R. Harris Jr. was another well-posted individual who was convinced that MacLean was "a full-fledged American citizen," a view he shared with Victoria customs collector J.C. Newbury. The latter's lengthy reports to Ottawa do not make an issue of his citizenship, other than to report the subterfuge surrounding the Mexican connection, which was quickly uncovered. Since Newbury was a bureaucrat at heart, such an irregularity would have upset him.[47] Finally, there is common sense. Alex MacLean had been part owner of two vessels that resulted in significant compensation after the Bering Sea Claims Commission hearings, and he had been specifically excluded from sharing in this largess because of his American status. If there were ever a time throughout his career when it would have been to his financial advantage to be a British subject, it was then. But he did not play that card.[48]

American seizures of Canadian vessels continued. On 29 May 1907, the sealing schooner *Carlotta G. Cox,* out of Victoria, was seized by the *Rush.* The Victoria Sealing Company protested, pointing out that when she was seized several Japanese schooners, using firearms, were in the immediate area and were completely ignored.[49] Patrols by the American revenue cutters around the Pribilof Islands in 1907 were "active and zealous." They had to be: "In dense fog, which prevails largely in summer, navigation among the reefs and currents about the islands is dangerous in the extreme and patrol vessels must proceed cautiously, while a sealing schooner with light tonnage and wooden bottom may come in close with little danger." The pelagic hunters "watch closely the movements of the vessels on patrol and are quick to take advantage of every move on their part."[50] Pelagic sealers were more active around the American rookeries than during the previous year, as were the patrols of the revenue cutters, assisted by the appearance of the cruiser *Buffalo* in late August. The assistance may have been needed. The industry, like the waterfront, was rife with rumours. The latest, according to the captain of the sealer *Vera,* was that the Tokyo-based *Kensai Maru* had recently returned from the North Pacific and her skipper had stated "that thirty-three Japanese sealing schooners which carry machine guns have arranged for a concentrated raid this winter on the Pribilof Island rookeries, planning to club the seals on St. Paul and St. George islands and rob the salt houses." The *Kensai Maru's* captain had declined participation.[51] Maybe he simply realized that seals were not present on the Pribilofs in winter.

There were no raids reported on the American rookeries that season or arrests made on shore. The Americans did seize a couple of Japanese schooners on 3 July 1907. The captains were both Japanese.[52] While Elliott had maintained that the Japanese vessels that were heavily involved in the rookery raids were primarily owned by Victoria and San Francisco partners, such a claim does not appear to have been the case. There was some involvement by Americans and Canadians, but it was nowhere near the extent suggested.[53] Nevertheless, the rumour implicating Canadians was still circulating. As the *New York Times* explained, "as a matter of fact, the meanest and most ruthless slaughterers of seals are the Canadians, whose cause was adopted by their Government. It is quite possible that just as the Gloucester fishermen on our own coast are in large part 'Bluenoses,' registered as Americans for the purpose of having their catch admitted as the 'product of American industry,' Canadians may have chosen to register themselves as Japanese, when they were caught, in the hope of mitigating their punishment."[54] Late in the year, participants in the Victoria fleet were thinking about putting some of their vessels under Japanese registry, and at least one owner did so.[55] For their part, the Americans brought in three Gatling and five Hotchkiss guns late in the season for the defence of the Pribilof Islands and began target practice. Until this time, aside from a small brass cannon for signalling and a few rifles belonging to the Natives, there had been only twelve rifles on St. Paul Island and six on St. George Island for protecting the rookeries, villages, and salt houses.[56] The Russian rookeries also received their share of attention. Three Japanese schooners raided those rookeries in 1907, and the Russians captured twelve Japanese. They were later released.[57]

Alex MacLean was supposedly up to his old tricks in 1907, raiding the Russian rookeries as captain of the Japanese schooner *Kensai*. According to Williams, Alex and his crew allegedly "captured the fur seal salting house with its store of land-killed seals. He and his crew had held the Russian guards at bay by small arms fire and succeeded in looting the warehouses and returning the cargo to their schooner without being impeded."[58] One problem with this scenario is that Alex MacLean was also in command of another vessel, the thirty-nine-ton *Chieftain,* around the same time, although he was not going anywhere with her. The *Chieftain* had caught fire in early June 1907, when she was anchored off Port Essington on the Skeena River. Robert Cunningham owned the vessel. Port Essington was the headquarters of the northern British Columbia salmon industry, and Robert Cunningham and Sons had a large cannery there. In this incident, the upper works and deck of the *Chieftain* were destroyed. The crew of the river steamer *Northwest,* claiming that the *Chieftain* was abandoned, made an attempt to take possession of the vessel. MacLean, who conjured up a touch of indignation while doubtless savouring the irony, exclaimed: "'Why, they were regular pirates.'" The *Daily Colonist* reported: "Captain McLean whistled five times, the signal for assistance, and the *Northwest,* Capt. Bonsar, bore over toward the burning vessel. In the meantime the captain and boat's crew went to the government steamer *Vulcan* and landed ashore seeking assistance ... Before he reached the vessel again he found two men from the *Northwest* on board and the steamer playing a hose on the burning tug." MacLean reacted in good fashion. "'What do you want aboard here?' said Capt. McLean, when he saw men on board. 'We've taken possession of this vessel; found her abandoned,' replied the invaders. 'You did, did you?' said the Sea Wolf. 'You've got another guess coming; I'm in charge here' ... The owners of the *Northwest* made a salvage claim against the *Chieftain* and the two men of her crew remained on board. They were not interfered with by the *Chieftain's* crew and were told not to interfere with the work on board the vessel unless, as Capt. McLean put it, they happened to be good swimmers." Eventually, the two men returned to the *Northwest,* with the owners of this vessel threatening a legal battle. MacLean ended up bringing the *Chieftain* down from Port Essington for repairs.[59] Again, it would be difficult even for the Sea Wolf to be in two places at once. MacLean's well-known poaching attempts with the *Carmencita* in 1904-05, his reputation, his association with London's novel, and Elliott's widely publicized pronouncements, help explain why some writers were reluctant to let MacLean leave the sealing grounds. MacLean made good copy, and unbelievable stories became less so when he was inserted into them.

The next year, 1908, was supposedly a repeat of the previous season: MacLean was in charge of a Japanese vessel and terrorizing the Native people on the Pribilof Islands. This scenario has MacLean's luck running out, another capture, and yet another end to his sealing career.[60] These accounts should also be looked at because of their specific accusations, their extensive coverage, and the fact that they remain solidly entrenched in the historical record. The backdrop for the strained and tension-filled 1908 sealing season was the aggressiveness of the Japanese pelagic fleet. Japan had secured the Robben Island rookery from Russia as a result of the Japanese victory in the Russian-Japanese conflict. Now, Japanese sealers became even more active around the other rookeries. Initial reports from Russia's Copper Island detailed a number of confrontations, gunfire exchanges, and the looting of a village. A number of Japanese were killed during these raids and others were reportedly summarily executed by Russian guards. Some seem to have had their sentences commuted. It was clear that there had been some serious conflict.[61] The Americans were concerned that it could happen in their area as well: "The Commander Islands are, in fact, the scene of frequent violence and bloodshed from the lawless incursions of Japanese vessels."[62]

There were thirty-eight Japanese sealers in the Bering Sea that season. While the Canadians did not have experienced crews to man many vessels, the small size of the Canadian fleet – numbering eight boats – was due, it was argued, to the fact that the Canadian sealers were "dispirited" because they could not compete due to the sixty-mile limit and a prohibition on firearms. The Japanese had guns and could operate to within a three-mile range of the rookeries.[63] The 1908 sealing fleet was also more intrusive, according to Lembkey, the treasury agent: "If anything, the sealers have been more aggressive than before." In the Pribilof Islands, the fleet concentrated on St. Paul Island, specifically at the northeast and west points. At the northeast point, which had the largest rookery and a salt house containing thousands of skins, the Native guards were now more impressively armed. The Hotchkiss guns proved to be quite successful in convincing the approaching boats to "hurriedly" come about and head back to their schooners, which were usually just outside the three-mile limit.[64]

The Americans also continued to be concerned about the presence of Canadian sealers sailing under the Japanese flag. This prompted the American authorities to start making lists that year. In June, Captain F.M. Munger, who was commanding the revenue cutter fleet in the Bering Sea that season, reported that five of the Japanese vessels were known to have "white" masters or navigators aboard. For Munger, the *Kensai Maru,* which is of particular interest here, had a Captain Ritchie, identified as a Canadian, and two hunters from Victoria, Ned Burke and Bill Williams. A list compiled later in the season by Lembkey was quite similar. Alex MacLean does not appear on either list.[65] Late in June, a number of these vessels paid a brief visit to the port of Unalaska and were scrutinized by the American authorities. When the *Kensai Maru* arrived there, she was reportedly carrying a Canadian captain, six Canadian hunters, and a crew of thirty made up of mixed nationalities. The Canadians were not specifically identified in this report. In mid-July, Captain Munger "sent word to the islands that the crew of this vessel was composed of desperate men, and for the native guard to keep a sharp outlook and not mistake this vessel for a cutter." The crew had altered her rigging and painted her hull white. A few days later, on 22 July, the *Kensai Maru No. 2* and the *Saikai Maru,* without the assistance of a breeze to slip them back over the line, were seized by the USS *Bear* for sealing within three miles of St. Paul Island. The captain of the *Bear* reported that the *Kensai Maru* did not heave to until a warning shot was fired. The schooner, which had acquired the reputation "of being a terror to all defenceless people," was now in tow.[66] And some suspected, reminding one again of Kipling, that the Japanese vessel was designed to deceive. With the *Kensai Maru's* altered appearance and her "quaker smokestack," she could easily be mistaken for either of the American revenue cutters, the *Rush* or the *Perry,* in a fog. In addition, Captain Munger thought that this particular vessel had become a leader "in trespassing on territorial waters." Lembkey, while still unsure of her captain's correct identity, was clear about her reputation: "The *Kensai Maru,* Capt. Richardson, [Ritchie] probably has been more aggressive in approaching shore this summer than any other vessel in the fleet, and her master has been known to express contempt for the shore guard as well as for the cutter patrol. It is believed that no vessel in the fleet deserved capture more than the two taken by the *Bear,* and that their apprehension had a restraining effect upon the remainder of the fleet."[67]

The crews of the two vessels seized on 22 July would eventually have their day in court in November in Valdez, Alaska. In later legal manoeuvres, the American authorities argued that the "*Kensai Maru* has gained among the natives of Alaska the name of 'Terror.' She changed her rig and painted her hull white to simulate a revenue cutter. Her crew, as is well known, is composed of desperate characters. She makes an American port the base of her lawless operations. She is a lawless rover of the sea and goes out to maraud and prey. She is far from engaging honestly in lawful business." There was another dimension to it, which was brought out during an application to halt the forfeiture of the vessel and her cargo (the 416 sealskins seized were valued at $9,000). The defence action was strongly opposed by the United States Department of Commerce and Labor. The latter argued: "The real culprits in all violations of the fur-seal laws in Bering Sea are the owners of the vessels and the captains thereof ... While the men caught violating our laws must be punished, it is evident that if the ship goes free the principal culprit has not suffered, and that nothing has been accomplished toward deterring the same or other vessels setting our laws at defiance in the future."[68]

However, none of the contemporary reports from Alaska or Washington concerning the *Kensai Maru* that this researcher has consulted link the boat with Alex MacLean. It seems remarkable that such a high-profile sealer and poacher as Alex MacLean, whose existence was well known to those charged with keeping order in the Bering Sea, would not be mentioned in the various dispatches, reports, and memorandums of the Department of the Treasury concerning the events in 1906-08 if he had actually been involved. Yet one fairly recent study insists that he was present. According to Gerald Williams, MacLean's depredations did not cease until the latter year: "The *Kensai Maru,* captained by the infamous Captain McLean of *Winifred* fame and carrying a predominantly Anglo-Saxon crew was one of the more notorious sealers during this period ... Under Captain McLean the ship had raided not only in the Pribilofs but all along the Aleutian Chain trading liquor for the few remaining otter pelts and taking by force, those that were not freely offered in commerce. McLean had even altered the *Kensai Maru* by erecting a false smokestack to make her resemble the cutters *Rush* and *Perry* from a distance in a fog."[69] Most of the statements in this account regarding the *Kensai Maru* appear to be correct and are taken primarily from Captain Munger's and Treasury Agent Lembkey's accounts in government documents concerning the Alaskan seal rookeries. They do not mention MacLean.[70] It is Williams, in his 1983 study, who inserts MacLean's name.[71] The *Daily Colonist,* ever vigilant on sealing events in the North Pacific and the Bering Sea and on the exploits and escapades of MacLean, closely followed the developments of the seized Japanese schooners and their crews. In these reports, the only non-Japanese person to be identified was a "Captain Ritchie, a former Victoria sealer who was on the *Kensei Maru* as navigating officer."[72] Alex MacLean's name has stubbornly refused to pop up in the historical record where some have insisted it should.

There are also the district court records for the Third Judicial Division in Valdez, Alaska, and the special term that was held in the fall of 1908 to deal with the sealers seized in July. The *Kensai Maru No. 2* was a 139-ton schooner out of Tokyo with a Japanese captain at the helm by the name of Minami. The vessel was owned by the Dai Nippon Deep Sea Fishing Company of Tokyo, and it had left Japan on 1 April. The navigator, or sailing master, was identified as J. Ritchie, who had been on the vessel for the past four years. Most of the other defendants identified during the legal proceedings were born or living on the Bonin Islands, which were a Japanese possession. Although pleas of not guilty were entered, the jury trial only took two days in early November and resulted in convictions. Each defendant was fined $600.[73] For the *Daily Colonist,* "this was the first conviction in the history of Alaska where pelagic poachers have been arrested and there has been a conviction."[74] Alex MacLean is not listed in the Alaska court records for this action.

In addition, the newspaper reports place Alex MacLean back on the Skeena River in April 1908. Predictably, the Skeena contract was no ordinary river job. According to the Vancouver and Victoria newspapers, "where there is no danger or excitement is not the place to look for Alex McLean ... Grand Trunk Pacific contractors came along looking for a man who would eat, sleep and work on a floating mine bigger than any staked out for the protection of Port Arthur." The "contract looked dangerous enough to tempt McLean out of his lair; he sniffed the job and its price, thought of the chances of hitting drifting cottonwood logs with his floating mine in piloting it up the narrow channels of the rushing Skeena in the night watches – reckoned the cost – flip[ped] a coin and signed." The job entailed running cargoes of gelignite and black powder from Prince Rupert up the Skeena to the Grand Trunk Pacific railway construction camps.[75] These public accounts note that MacLean had been more or less idle in Vancouver since the *Carmencita* affair.[76] Five weeks later, in late May 1908, he was reported as taking command of the 376-ton *Strathcona,* registered in Vancouver, for service on the Skeena.[77] He was back working the British Columbia rivers as he had done in the early 1880s. Thus, it seems unlikely that the notorious Alex MacLean was, in 1908, attempting to cash in on one of the biggest sealskins sales in years, with an estimated selling price of $22 per pelt at the London auctions.[78] The main problem for those historical accounts that continued to place MacLean in the sealing industry after 1905 concern their references. The two sources that Williams recommended for "an interesting discussion" of the MacLeans are confusing and unreliable. Williams is also following Gordon Newell's lead. While readily acknowledging Newell's significant contributions to the field – he authored a dozen books on west coast maritime topics and edited the indispensable *H.W. McCurdy Marine History of the Pacific Northwest* – it must be acknowledged that when Newell ventures into MacLean terrain he tends to lose his way and appears to rely excessively on Henry Wood Elliott's version of events. Newell's statement that MacLean "wasn't an American citizen, never had been and had never made any effort to become one" has a familiar ring, and his material on MacLean shows a definite acquaintance with Elliott's article, "Thirty Years of Japanese Seal-Piracy in Alaskan Waters."[79] It is reasonable to suggest that Alex MacLean's sealing career did end in Victoria in September 1905 with the *Carmencita,* other versions notwithstanding.

Some contemporary versions of MacLean's activities in these years border on bizarre. Late in October 1908, another "weird tale" made it into the local papers on the west coast. The *Daily Colonist* prefaced this version by acknowledging that "Capt. Alex McLean has achieved more notoriety than he deserves. While he lives his quiet life as a river steamer captain in British Columbia waters, the readers of many cities still learn that he is a modern pirate." The *Daily Colonist* could not resist passing on the latest story, with a cautionary note that it contained "some slight smattering of truth and more of untruth." According to this account, "Captain McLean and his notorious old schooner ... are famous or 'infamous' from Alaska to Central America, and not a port from San Francisco, Puget Sound and the far north but treasures to this day tales of strange and incredible feats of daring, cunning, deviltry and sheer imprudence, sufficient to build a dozen Jack London tales." The final act "in this drama of the high seas" came a few months ago. "The stage setting fitly supported the culminating tragedy of its lurid shifting program. A night of pitch blackness, the little renegade lying low in a small port north of Vancouver, blockaded by Canadian revenue outside the harbor." The weather was raw, the night black. "Danger lurking without and below in the cabin dark, danger raising a hydra head against the indomitable leader. Mutiny, revolt, hot words, a shot in the gloom from one of his own men, a wounded 'Wolf' hounded by his lesser curs, leaps overboard. There the tale is cut off. McLean has not been seen or heard from since, though some think him still alive, and perhaps operating under another name, a penchant of his." The *Daily Colonist,* which reprinted the piece from *Shipping Illustrated,* thought it amusing. The tale had some vague similarities with the "fake story" of the *Ella G.* early in 1906. The *Shipping Illustrated* report made a reference to the fittings on the *Carmencita,* which doubtless got a rise out of Newbury, the customs collector, considering Alex's cavalier approach to the Canadian Customs Act: "Not only was it a perfect arsenal but unique in many unexpected touches of a cultivated mind, among these being a complete law library."[80] This account suggests that the difficulty in separating Alex MacLean and Wolf Larsen was more than some could, or wanted to, manage. Two days after this lurid tale was reprinted, the *Daily Colonist* had MacLean, "concerning whose sealing exploits so much fiction has been written as fact," back in its pages. He was halibut fishing now, with the *Sea Bird,* out of Prince Rupert. It was late October, the *Sea Bird* was eight days overdue, and the "terrific gales, raging for days with hurricane force," caused enough anxiety to prompt a search by a fishing patrol boat. Alex brought her in safely to Metlakatla, with his crew of six, six tons of fish, and in his own name. The "lesser curs" had not finished him off. For a little while, Alex MacLean, "the bête noire of the patrol fleets of three nations," lived quietly in Vancouver.[81]

It was during this lull that Charles Madsen dropped in on his "old friend." Madsen, a trader and sometime "unofficial leader of the whiskey smugglers" in northern waters, later took pains in his memoirs to distance himself from people like Alex MacLean, "perhaps unjustifiably," he acknowledged. But in Vancouver in the winter of 1908-09, he was simply paying a social call on Alex and filling him in on his latest endeavours, which included building a new vessel: "After telling him about the new ship and my plans, he asked what I would name the schooner. I recalled that the ruthless captain in Jack London's novel *The Sea Wolf* was based upon McLean, and with a laugh, I informed Alex that my vessel would bear the same name." Madsen was one of the few individuals who could carry that off without personal cost. Madsen's *Sea Wolf* was launched in March 1909.[82] MacLean would soon have other opportunities to renew old acquaintances.

13
The Final Years: Vancouver, 1909-14

Alex had made many contacts during his west coast career, which had now spanned thirty years. It is not surprising that he would cross paths, or swords, with some of them again. Charles Madsen's Vancouver visit in the winter of 1908-09 was one of the calmer ones. Shadows of the Solomon Islands and the southwest Pacific now loomed up from the east. Niels Peter Sorensen reappeared in New York during the summer of 1908. The scheme was fronted by the International Salvage Company and was intended to raise the *General Grant* and its supposed cargo of $20,000,000 in gold from its long-time resting place off the west coast of Auckland Isle.[1] A picture of Sorensen accompanied the initial New York newspaper item. A rival paper's associate editor connected the dots. William Churchill, the American consul-general in Samoa when MacLean and Sorensen arrived there in 1897, was, and had been for six years, an editor with the *New York Sun*. He immediately assigned a reporter, armed with some pertinent background information, to the story. The *New York Sun* published its interview with Sorensen on 16 July 1908. When prodded by the reporter, Sorensen acknowledged that he did indeed know "Sandy" MacLean and, as the newspaper noted, "most singular gulp of romance it is too that the knowing one in Victoria, B.C. should be Sandy McLean, seal poacher and pirate, who only once in his lifetime met a man who was his superior in guile, and that man was this same Capt. Sorensen."[2] The article described Sorensen's escapades in the mid-1880s, which earned him his prison sentence in Queensland, and his experience with Alex and the *Sophia Sutherland* in the South Pacific in 1897-98. The article was essentially accurate, although some of the information was second-hand. It was not designed to attract more investors to the scheme. Sorensen immediately demanded a retraction "on the ground that nothing in the story was true." After questioning Churchill again, the *New York Sun* backed its editor and refused Sorensen's demands. He then brought suit for libel, seeking $100,000 damages.[3]

One of defendant Churchill's most important witnesses in the case was William Lee Chambers, the former chief justice of the International Court of Samoa. He was now conveniently practising law in Washington. Another was Alex MacLean. He was contacted in Vancouver and, while declining a trip to the United States, agreed to travel east to give a deposition as a defence witness. The case dragged on for almost three years. Alex appeared early in the final act, delivering his testimony in Montreal on 11 March 1911.[4] MacLean's personality and character, and his past experiences with lawyers and authorities in general, most notably during the sometimes spirited cross-examinations in the hearings in Victoria in 1896-97, assured that he would hardly be overawed by these proceedings. His challenging approach, layered with irony and wit, was evident from the start: "'Are you carrying arms?' asked the judge when Captain McLean entered the witness box. 'Am I what? my lord' asked the astonished captain. 'Are you carrying arms ... firearms?' Captain McLean was hurt. 'Of course I am not, my lord. I thought when I came east I was coming among gentlemen.'"[5] Churchill travelled to Montreal for this part of the legal proceedings and renewed his acquaintance with MacLean. Sorensen's attorney, James F. Egan, explained to Alex that his client, apparently ill and unable to make the journey, was disappointed in not being able to come up and meet him again. MacLean shot back: "You tell Sorensen that a bucket of hot water and plenty of mustard is the best thing I know of for cold feet."[6] This rebuttal helped set the tone for the Montreal proceedings. During a cross-examination, Egan brought up MacLean's refusal to enter the United States:

Q. Do you intend to go to the United States?
A. No, sir.
Q. In the near future?
A. I may in the near future.
Q. When?
A. I could not say exactly.
Q. Do you intend to go say within the next month or so?
A. I might.[7]

Alex was less than intimidated: "McLean said he is now wanted in the United States for taking a ship called the *Carmencita* out of San Francisco under the Mexican flag and going seal hunting in the Bering Sea instead of to the place he had cleared for. He had been indicted for that, but the offence is punishable only by a fine. He said he didn't want to stand trial until he was ready although he expected to be ready soon."[8] MacLean viewed these charges as being akin to an inconvenience:

Q. Are you wanted for any crime in the United States?
A. I am.
Q. You are?
A. I don't know if it is a crime or not.
Q. What is it you are wanted for?
A. For taking a ship out from San Francisco, some four or five years ago ... It appeared afterwards that in doing so I had broken the United States laws.[9]

As Alex explained, "there is no telling what time I may go to the United States." His position received support from Chambers when the latter was being cross-examined: "'If you knew that McLean did not dare to come into the State of New York and take the stand in this case because he is wanted here for a crime, would that have any bearing upon the credit you would give to his statement?' asked ... counsel for the plaintiff. 'No. I think he ought to keep away. He has not been convicted, and it is his business to keep out of the jurisdiction that might convict him. I do not think any less of a man for keeping out of the way of the court.'"[10]

The main thrust from Sorensen's camp was the association with London's novel. It was not long in coming. When MacLean was pointedly asked: "You were the character who was portrayed in that book as Wolf Larsen?" he replied: "I could not say I was."[11] Sorensen's counsel would hammer repeatedly on this connection. If Egan's aggressive questioning during this part of the proceedings was designed to bring MacLean's temper to the surface, it was unsuccessful. MacLean maintained a measured response:

Q. Are you an implacable hater?
A. No sir ...
Q. Captain MacLean, are you a man-driving adventurer, and known as such along the Pacific coast from Mazatlan to Copper Island?
A. No, I do not believe I am, particularly.
Q. Particularly; do you think you are at all?
A. No, not any more than others.[12]

Counsellor Egan cross-examined MacLean extensively as to whether or not a number of incidents from London's novel were taken directly from MacLean's experiences:

Q. Can you remember any one thing in that book which resembles your life?
A. No. Of course, the sealing part in it resembles some of the work of catching seals.

Q. But you know that he pictured Wolf Larsen as a most brutal violent man? Doesn't he?
A. Yes, sir.
Q. Does that agree with what you know of yourself?
A. No, I don't think it does. Nor anyone else that knows me.[13]

Egan then cited from the novel:

> He left the chair, just as he sat in it, squarely, springing from the sitting posture like a wild animal ... and like a tiger covered the intervening space. It was an avalanche of fury that Johnson strove vainly to fend off. He drew [threw] one arm down to protect the stomach, the other arm up to protect the head; but Wolf Larsen's fist drove midway between, on the chest, with a crushing, resounding impact. Johnson's breath, suddenly expelled, shot from his mouth as suddenly checked, with the forced, audible expiration of a man wielding an axe. He almost fell backward, and swayed from side to side in an effort to recover his balance.

Q. Did you ever jump on any man that way?
A. No, sir, not that I remember.
Q. That incident is not taken from your life?
A. No, sir ...
Q. Well, was it true that Jack London wrote of you when he pictured this man that I have read to you of?
A. I have no proof that he wrote of me.
Q. Now, listen to me, Captain, is it true that Jack London wrote of you when he wrote this passage that I have here read to you of Wolf Larsen in this book?
A. No, that has never taken place in my life.
Q. At any time in your life, did you recover a broken boat, and in doing it you lost the life of a sailor, and you said to some one 'Kelly didn't amount to much.'
A. No, sir.[14]

Undeterred, Egan pressed on to a couple of other incidents from *The Sea-Wolf*:

Q. Now, was there a time when two of your crew against whom you had great enmity were out in a boat, and you brought your vessel about in front of them on several occasions seeking to bring them aboard but luring them on, a storm was raging at the time, and deliberately let them drown, and then did you ever turn to anyone and say 'I kept my promise. I did not lay hands on them.' Did that ever occur in your life?

A. No, sir ...
Q. Did you ever have any trouble with a cook and to punish him for it, did you put a rope around his waist and drag him after the vessel?
A. No, sir.
Q. Then that incident in *The Sea-Wolf* is not from your life?
A. No, sir.
Q. And did you ever, on such an occasion, when the cook was being dragged, permit him to stay in the water long enough to have a shark snap off his right foot?
A. No, sir.
Q. That incident in this book is not taken from your life, is it?
A. No, sir.[15]

Egan's determined attempt to commit that common biographical fallacy whereby a novelist's writings were treated as straightforward reporting about reality did not carry the day. His theatrical performance in the Montreal courtroom was probably impressive. From a legal perspective, and when subjected to a reality check, it did not come close to a passing grade. Nor did it appear to have had much impact on Alex MacLean. He remained calm and collected throughout the cross-examination. He probably earned the $500 he received for his expenses and time going east to Montreal.[16] A few years later, in November 1916, during a legal dispute between Jack London and some neighbours concerning riparian rights, his opponents cited a character from another novel, *The Valley of the Moon,* in their presentation and the judge forbade using London's fiction as evidence.[17] Had this interpretation been used in Montreal, Egan would have had even less material to present.

The libel case went to the New York City jury later that month, and the *New York Sun* ensured its readers that they would be informed about Sorensen and MacLean: "Twelve New York jurors sitting in the old Tweed court house have been listening for five days to stories from the South Seas ... No jury in New York probably was ever so entertained with proven incidents of wild life in wild lands, and the twelve listened with all their souls and came back gladly day after day to hear more." Entertaining though it was, they could not come to an agreement, and they were discharged. Six of the jurors had apparently agreed totally with Churchill and the *New York Sun* while the others had held out for a nominal award of six cents because the newspaper had not furnished "technical proof of all the published statements."[18] The following September, both parties agreed to a discontinuation, and there were no additional costs for either side.[19]

When Alex departed Montreal by train for his return trip to Vancouver, he ran into his legend again:

> I was travelling back from Montreal last year and sitting quietly in the smoking compartment one day when a young man, who looked like a rancher, began "blowing" a bit and, among other things, said he had lived in British Columbia. "Jack London's Sea Wolf lives somewhere on the coast there, doesn't he?" someone asked, and at once the young man said he knew him, and then proceeded to describe him. I was sitting just facing this young man and every now and then asked him for some further particular. It was a fearsome picture he painted, and the skipper chuckled at the recollection, and when he had finished I had a picture of myself nearly seven feet high and with a sort of wild-man-of-the-woods appearance. That young man had told me he was leaving the train early the following morning. His berth happened to be next mine, so, just as he was turning in that night, I said rather gruffly, "It may interest you to know that the Sea Wolf from British Columbia has been sitting facing you all the evening and he won't forget your description of him in a hurry." I kept that young man in sight until he left the train next morning and saw that he did not repeat what I had told him, as it would have made the rest of my journey uncomfortable if the story had got about, but I could not resist having my little joke at his expense.[20]

Fame and boasting both had their price. After Alex returned to Vancouver, Churchill kept him informed as the trial finished up in New York. MacLean penned a reply from his residence on Burrard Street on 23 April, addressing Churchill as "Dear friend." It was brief, two pages, and soon cut to the quick: "I do not suppose that Sorensen will try again to recover any damages from the *Sun* for his unblemished character, and that the case is closed, and the public should be thankful to you for exposing him in time." Alex was also "pleased" that Justice Chambers assisted at the trial, saying, "and I am very sorry I was unable to appear there in person."[21] There is a certain Victorian propriety in some of the phrasing, but what also shines through is his wit and his pleasure at the outcome. The Vancouver-based master mariner, along with the New York newspaper editor and the ex-chief justice of the International Court of Samoa, seem to have thoroughly enjoyed disrupting another of Sorensen's exploitative scams.

In the last few years before the First World War, Alex and "his kindly, gentle wife" Lucy were living in downtown Vancouver on Burrard Street, a short walk from False Creek, where the last vessel under his command was berthed. He was "plying a reasonably prosperous, respectable trade" with the *Favorite,* "a small, prosaic harbor tugboat."[22] She carried the same name as the sealing schooner that Alex had first acquired an interest in back in 1883. Their daughter Catherine, in her mid-twenties and single, was also in the city for most of this period, working variously at the Hotel Vancouver and the *Vancouver News-Advertiser*.[23] Noel Robinson, an experienced journalist working in Vancouver, had a long interview with Alex MacLean at the captain's residence in December 1912.[24] Alex, who was fifty-four at the time, was described by Robinson as "a man of very striking appearance, of middle height, but powerfully, though sparsely built. The physical features I remember most clearly about him were his flowing moustache and his clear, cold, light blue eyes. He did not look at all like the typical sailor for he wore a Stetson hat and dressed smartly."[25] It may have been the only interview given by MacLean that was not confrontational or linked to a legal case. The captain was taking it easy and was prepared to chat: "He was enjoying one of those brief periods of home life that he allowed himself now and again with his wife and daughter. But even in that quiet home he was surrounded by many a relic of his adventurous career." Robinson remembered "that spears, criss-crossed, decorated the walls; a carefully finished wooden trough in which the cannibals of the South Sea Islands had been in the habit of placing portions of their unsavoury human feasts reposed in one corner of the room; a huge club of hard wood, one edge as sharp as a razor and once the property of a South Sea Islander, stood in another. A paddle, beautifully inlaid with mother of pearl, also attracted my attention."[26]

This interview is the basis for one of the many aspects of his career where the evidence remains confusing. MacLean started it by relating an incident, purportedly from the San Francisco waterfront around 1905, to Robinson. In this version, he explains: "One morning ... a well-set-up, rough-and-tumble type of man – open-faced and cleareyed – wended his way down to one of the marine stores on the San Francisco waterfront." MacLean, "a spare, broad-shouldered, blue-eyed man with tremendous brown mustachios, the ends of which almost reached the lapels of his coat and seemed quite in keeping with his exceptionally shaggy brown eyebrows" was in the store, which was "full of a hotch-potch of seafaring flotsam and jetsam, constituted just the right setting for these two men." The other individual gave the skipper a box of cigars:

> "Good luck and a good catch. Can't wait – got to hustle this morning," breezed the visitor as they gripped hands ... "By the way, there's a book in with the cigars. Don't open the box till you're way up on the sealing grounds – I've got a reason." "Right y'are, Jack." And Jack London – for the visitor was the famous novelist – disappeared. Weeks later, while another sealing captain was visiting his vessel, MacLean opened the box and "comfortably ensconced amongst the Havanas, a volume entitled *The Sea-Wolf*. The title conveyed nothing to him at the time and he put the book aside for future perusal. A week later he picked it up and, as it was a novel about sealing, he

> read it through at one sitting ... "I read the book with such mixed feelings that perhaps it was as well Jack wasn't there when I finished it," McLean commented.[27]

According to Robinson, this "trick" of London's "came very near to breaking their friendship." The story Alex told to Robinson that December day would be repeated and embellished, not least by Robinson, in a number of pieces over the years. The version recounted here is a later construction by Robinson that was first published in *Maclean's* ten years after the interview.[28] It is a good story, one that people would want to believe. The initial interview in the *Vancouver News-Advertiser* ran when London and MacLean were still active. The time frame supported it. When the novel was published in October 1904, Alex's family was in Oakland. London was also in the San Francisco Bay area in the months following the publication of *The Sea-Wolf.*[29] The source was an excellent one. As Robinson wrote in early January 1913, "it was not easy to persuade the redoubtable skipper to let the above interesting anecdote appear in print. Indeed, it was not easy to get him to talk about himself at all."[30] But Robinson was persuasive and so was MacLean, and decades later the experienced journalist was still maintaining that London knew MacLean well.[31] As MacLean told Robinson in the interview, "it is six years since then and time heals most things and Jack and I are good friends enough now."[32]

Tom MacInnes, who had two extended conversations with MacLean in 1896 and 1907, has another, far less likely version: "Some years later [after 1896] McLean fell in with Jack London at San Francisco, and of a night would spin for him a mix of many things about his experiences and escapades in the Pacific. London took the rough stuff of the yarn, and worsened it until it was worsted as novel material for the public which had a taste for that sort of thing, if it can be read comfortably at home. But doing so he published McLean to the world as the bestial Sea Wolf."[33] In Montreal during the Sorensen libel case in 1911, in response to the question of when he had met Jack London, MacLean had replied: "It would be some years ago before he ever wrote that book ... I saw him in San Francisco."[34] One writer had MacLean and London meeting at Heinold's First and Last Chance Saloon on the Oakland waterfront, with Alex numbered "among London's many real friends."[35] Ronald Gillis took this episode further, contending that the "Sea Wolf" tag was "a poor reward for Captain Alex's kindness in rescuing Jack London from the slums of San Francisco and taking him on a sailing trip to Alaska."[36] So are stories, and relationships, stretched.

The story of the relationship between Alex MacLean and Jack London persisted. In Vancouver years later, A.M. Donaldson showed a copy of *The Sea-Wolf* to George McInnis "and on the fly leaf was written in a bold hand, 'this is not true' etc. It might be the one London gave to Alex in Frisco."[37] In Montreal in 1911, MacLean acknowledged: "A copy was sent to me by a party when I was leaving San Francisco, in fact I did not know what book it was when it was presented to me. I was just leaving on the ship." At that time, he testified that he "believed he got the copy of the 'Sea Wolf' indirectly from Jack London."[38] The latter statements seem reasonable. What is clear is that Alex did read the novel soon after it was published.[39] In 1907, he had complained bitterly to Tom MacInnes "about the way Jack London had maligned him. He expressed a hot desire to be in a position some day to shanghai him; and having him at sea to put him through his paces in a way that he had never treated any man." MacInnes suggested to him that "London might have taken all the proven valor and skill of the McLean and blended it with what he knew of Bloody Fritz Hansen, the German captain, and Sapinza, the half Chinese half Filipino smuggler ... I said it was London's right as a writer to try and make a new character out of them all, however beastly and unlikely a mix he made of it." To this literary lesson, Alex "only scowled."[40] MacLean was little bothered by the "nautical Nietzsche" characterization or by the "naturalistic theme of atavism, the notion that civilization is but a thin veneer which, when stripped away, permits man's reversion to his intrinsically savage nature."[41] A relative of MacLean's, who had been in contact with him during this period, maintained that Alex had two main objections to the novel: "First he objected to being made a 'Swede' and secondly he objected to being killed off in the final chapters after a sound licking."[42]

The main problem with some aspects of Alex's version is that London had no recollection of ever meeting MacLean. It is clear that he did not keep abreast of MacLean's career after the brouhaha with the *Carmencita* in the summer of 1905. When a relative of Alex's wrote to London late in 1914 requesting information on the mariner, London replied: "I never personally laid eyes on Capt. Alex McLean in my life but I was sealhunting off the coast of Japan and crossed the trail of his schooner many times in 1893."[43] Whoever gave a copy of *The Sea-Wolf* to MacLean on the San Francisco waterfront could, however, have left the impression that it was from the novelist. Alex was an imaginative and flexible individual. He was a storyteller, the tale fit, it was believable, and Robinson was a bit of a romantic. Why not? Also, being forced to carry the "Sea Wolf" sobriquet constantly from the summer of 1905 had not proved particularly advantageous to MacLean. According to Robinson, "I have it on the good authority of his personal friends who esteemed him highly, that, from the year when the book was published until the day of his death, he suffered severely financially from having his name linked with that of Wolf Larsen – for obvious reasons. There was hesitation in employing a man whose reputation for devilty and sealing piracy, after the publication of the book, became a byword on this Pacific coast."[44]

Being constantly tarred with the same brush for so long from so many sources may have prompted MacLean to add to it all. Maybe he did it out of deviltry. Robinson was an experienced journalist and this meeting was not their only one.[45] Fact and fiction continued to combine and create real-world consequences. On 11 August 1914, the federal royal commission on Canadian pelagic sealers claims was holding hearings in Victoria. The government's counsel, Frank J. Curran, had obviously not kept up with popular literary works after acquiring his bachelor of arts. Certainly, he was no James Egan. In 1911, Sorensen's counsel had attempted to shoehorn MacLean into London's fictional work in specific detail. Three years later, Curran had MacLean writing the novel. The brief exchange came about when Curran was questioning long-time competitor and sealer Lachlan MacLean:

Q. Are you any relation to the MacLean who wrote a book called *The Sea-Wolf* about sealing?
A. I never knew he had sense enough to write a book.
Q. He is not the MacLean mentioned in the book?
A. No.
Q. Or that wrote the book?
A. No, sir.[46]

The line between fiction and reality sometimes meshed completely. When a long-time member of the American coast guard died in Seattle in 1958, the *Marine Digest* noted he first went to sea from San Francisco in 1883 at the age of thirteen. This account then continued, in a matter of fact way: "After that he sailed in a schooner in the Bering Sea. The skipper was Wolf Larsen, principal character in Jack London's famous novel, *The Sea-Wolf.*"[47]

Biographical fallacies and literary creations as real life characters notwithstanding, significant changes on the international diplomatic stage in these years would ultimately resolve the sealing dispute. The Alaska boundary had been settled by 1903, and in the next few years it became clear to the Americans that the main threat to their seals came from the expanding and quite aggressive Japanese fleet. The Canadian government, which Secretary of State John Hay memorably characterized as "a married flirt, ready to betray John Bull on any occasion, but holding him responsible for all her follies," was coming to the realization that pelagic sealing was no longer profitable. In addition, in mid-1905, Elihu Root, whose background suggested conservation, became secretary of state. Governor General Lord Grey and British Ambassador Sir James Bryce appeared on the scene as well. The seed planted by the volatile Henry Wood Elliott, that the Americans should share the herd with the Canadians, had sprouted.[48] Early in 1909, the American government set up a fur seal advisory board, with Dr. David Starr Jordan, an eminent biologist and president of Leland Stanford University, as chair. Jordan found Elliott's work "marred by unbalanced assertions, many of which seem to show a lack of both honesty and sanity," which helps explain why Elliott was not included on the board.[49]

The pelagic sealing industry in the North Pacific had declined quickly after MacLean retired from the hunt in 1905. In 1906, only seventeen sealing vessels sailed from Victoria, half the number there had been four years previously. The following year saw the lowest catch in years, 50 percent of the amount acquired in 1906. The decline continued. The year 1908 witnessed the smallest fleet out of Victoria in twenty-five years. It bottomed out at five vessels in 1909, and only high prices in London ($28.50 per skin) enticed that number of sealers to continue for the last two years of pelagic sealing in the North Pacific. In the latter year, the entire Victoria fleet acquired only 2,748 skins, considerably less than the yield from a single vessel during the high-riding 1880s.[50] Japanese pelagic sealing vessels increased, going from thirteen in 1897 to twenty-five in 1910, "but this only hastened the destruction of the herd." As American commissioner of fisheries George Bowers noted, the failure to maintain the resource was quite unfortunate: "This chapter in our history is a most serious indictment of our business capacity."[51]

The twenty-year lease held by the North American Commercial Company (NACC) was scheduled to expire on 1 May 1910. The government prepared a draft for a new twenty-year lease. There was concern expressed by interested parties in San Francisco that the NACC would seek renewal without opening the bidding process.[52] However, the bidding process was not reopened nor was the NACC's lease renewed. American secretary of state Elihu Root proposed that Russia, Britain, and Japan confer in an attempt to settle the issue. All agreed. Canada refused to participate then because a plan to compensate the Canadian sealers for the end of the industry had not been put in place.[53] In February 1910, the Americans agreed to advance $200,000 to the Canadians as compensation for ending the pelagic hunt, but protracted and difficult negotiations continued a bit longer. On 7 July 1911, a final agreement was reached. Britain, the United States, Japan, and Russia signed the North Pacific Fur Seal Convention, prohibiting all pelagic sealing. The fur seal herd would gradually recover, increasing an average 11 percent over the next few decades. All that remained was a supervised land harvest of surplus bachelor males from which Canada, Japan, and Russia would be guaranteed a percentage of the harvest.[54]

The sealing vessels were easily reconverted to halibut fishing, and this industry continued to expand.[55] Not all of the sealing schooners made the dignified transition. C. Fox Smith explains: "Some simply disintegrated on

Sitka's aptly named 'Rotten Row.' Others became sodden hulks in 'the Arm,' a neglected corner of Victoria's inner harbour: a dismal, stagnant sort of spot, dedicated to garbage, and dead cats, and snags, and sawmill refuse, and mouldery slipways, and sinister leaning boathouses that seemed waiting for murders to be committed in them." They were still there before the war, "poor melancholy-looking relics of what had been in their day among the most sea-worthy and staunch of small seagoing craft. I believe one or two of them were taken to serve as some kind of bonfire at one of those peculiar carnivals or similar festive occasions of which the Pacific coast is so inordinately fond. But they refused either to burn or sink."[56] One of the three vessels that was ungraciously torched in 1913 but stubbornly refused to burn was the *Mary Ellen,* Dan MacLean's schooner through much of the 1880s.[57]

As of May 1909, Canada had its own Department of External Affairs. The country was maturing as it entered more fully into the wider diplomatic world. Canada's agreement with the sealing convention removed a long-standing thorn in Canadian-American, Canadian-British, and British-American relations. Also, Japan and the United States were working on a trade agreement, and the convention ensured that it would not be compromised. As well, Russia and Japan were anxious not to have the issue escalate into a more serious crisis.[58] The North Pacific Fur Seal Convention of 1911, along with the Inland Fisheries Treaty in 1908 and the Migratory Bird Treaty of 1916, were "the first three comprehensive wildlife conservation treaties in history." As Kurkpatrick Dorsey notes, the irony was that "these cooperative agreements came from one of the most power-orientated periods in Great Power relations." Boiled down, it was "the interaction of science, sentiment, and economics."[59]

The North Pacific Fur Seal Convention of 1911 did provide all parties with a measure of diplomatic satisfaction. This is not to suggest that everyone was happy about the outcome. Since Canada, unlike Russia, Japan, and the United States, possessed no rookeries, it was "the main beneficiary of the pelagic-sealing industry," and the agreement, which would have Canada receiving 15 percent of the American and Russian harvests, was described as a "splendid bargain" for Canada. As Alvin Gluek notes, it was "an annuity that no sensible actuary would ever have written," although some people in Victoria and elsewhere remained less than satisfied.[60] The Canadian Pelagic Sealing Commission was appointed on 10 June 1913 to investigate "the claims of certain Canadian pelagic sealers" relating to the Pelagic Sealing Treaty of 7 July 1911 and the Paris Award Regulations of 1893.[61] Under the assistant judge of the Exchequer Court, Louis Arthur Audette, hearings were held in Victoria, Halifax, Sydney, and Ottawa. Many people took a run at it, which was somewhat reminiscent of the situation captured, and bemoaned, by Edgar Crow Baker during and after the hearings in Victoria in the late

1890s. The commission dealt with 1,605 claims totalling over $9,200,000. It should be mentioned that Alex MacLean was not numbered among the petitioners, not surprisingly, given his American citizenship.[62] For a variety of reasons, most of the claims would be disallowed. Only $60,000 of the $200,000 initially presented by the American authorities to the Canadian government had been awarded by 1916. By 1910, the Canadian pelagic sealing fleet had almost disappeared. Holding on to the principle of freedom of the seas over financial concerns had carried a cost, and arguments and disputes regarding compensation for the Canadian pelagic sealers would continue for decades. During the depression of the 1930s, the "question of compensation has been brought up by our British Columbia members at Ottawa ... A share of it rightly belongs to the Victoria people who carried on the business, and lost heavily when it was so summarily closed." Their interest in this issue was probably prompted by the knowledge that in 1934 the Canadian government received more than $1,000,000 as its share of the treaty arrangements.[63] As late as November 1947, the *Daily Colonist* was observing that the descendants of the sealers had not entirely given up hope for compensation. They were apparently seeking a share in the latest proceeds the Canadian government had received from the convention of 1911.[64]

The four-nation agreement of 1911 was not enough for Henry Wood Elliott, even though when the bill passed Congress it had been altered to include a five-year suspension on land kills as well.[65] He enlisted the assistance of William T. Hornaday, the director of the Bronx Zoological Park and the driving force behind the Permanent Wild Life Protection Fund. They were kindred spirits. Hornaday was a zealot who always had an eye out for conspiracies and a disdain for "careful, specialized studies." Elliott, Hornaday, and other officials of the Camp Fire Club of America targeted the public and the politicians through publications such as *Field and Stream*.[66] The Senate and congressional hearings that followed, featuring a barrage of accusations concerning a host of transgressions, real and imagined, over the previous thirty years, dragged out in Washington for the next several years and provided Elliott with an excellent stage.[67] The various reports were published, sometimes on the front page of the *New York Times*.[68] Elliott's usual targets were strongly criticized, and he invariably included Alex MacLean, the "notorious pirate," in his condemnations. Elliott's numerous opponents frequently responded with a comparable degree of energy and vitriol. Elliott last appeared before a Senate committee concerning sealing in 1926, at the age of seventy-six.[69]

Late in August 1914, with his wife Lucy in a Victoria hospital, Alex was staying alone on the forty-foot, seventeen-ton tug *Favorite,* built in Chinook, Oregon, in 1881. It was tied up alongside three other boats in False Creek on the Vancouver waterfront.[70] On the afternoon of 26 August, Albert Foote entered the Clarence Hotel in downtown Vancouver. The manager of the hotel was Jake Hildebrand, a well-known figure in the port. Jake "was entertaining a visitor and in his usual lavish manner saw that his guest's glass was never empty." Jake's crony that day was Alex MacLean. Foote was acquainted with both men, and he joined them: "I knew Captain McLean pretty well. I never could understand just how Jack London ever got anything out of him about his seal poaching adventures. The captain was a big boned, husky Scot. He had an enormous reddish moustache. He looked the part of the 'Sea Wolf' all right, but I had always found him soft spoken, mild mannered and never knew him to allude in any way to his sanguinary adventures."[71] Jake and Albert saw Alex leave the hotel, heading back to his tug. He disappeared that evening. Rumours immediately circulated, fuelled in part because of a liquor-related altercation earlier that day aboard one of the other boats tied up alongside the *Favorite*. MacLean had not been involved in that incident. The *Vancouver Province* reported: "When last seen alive ... McLean was drinking heavily, it is said."[72] Captain Charles Betts saw him around five or six o'clock that evening: "He was sober. I gave him a check." Betts, a friend of MacLean's and manager of the Metropole Transportation Company that had chartered the *Favorite,* went to check on Alex after he failed to show up the following morning. According to Betts, "the captain was very punctual in coming around and [Betts] went to see if he was sleeping. Someone went aboard and said he wasn't there but that his hat was on board ... I knew he prized a hat of that kind."[73]

Catherine first learned of her father's disappearance from Captain Betts who "called up and asked me of any trips my father might have taken – any place he might have gone ... he told me the last he had been seen was about eleven o'clock on Wednesday night in the London Hotel. He had a few drinks I believe, either beer or mixed – I am not positive of that, but he could walk perfectly straight – he was not what you would call intoxicated." At the time, Catherine had not known about finding the hat, but "as soon as I found that out, I jumped to the conclusion something must be really wrong."[74] This minor detail alerted MacLean's acquaintances and friends. Police Constable Carl Anderson was acquainted with Alex and his headgear, and remembered it was "a big black Stetson hat with a white rim – [and] it was on the *Favorite*. That was the kind of hat he took pride in." Aside from the hat, there was nothing for more than a week. On Sunday, Catherine went down to the *Favorite* and "took away the papers there were around there." When Captain Betts was asked about MacLean's habits, he replied that Alex "was always strict with anything there was to do." He added: "Even if he was sober he might fall – stumble at night."[75] By 3 September, the *Vancouver Province* was reporting that the harbour police "have prosecuted a most thorough search of the waterfront and have again dragged the water without discovering anything which might tend to throw any light upon his movements. The discovery of his hat is the only tangible evidence that the police have been able to discover." The next day, as Daniel Snell, an engineer with the BC electric steam plant, was beginning his morning shift he noticed something along the shore. Snell had spoken with Alex on a number of occasions, and he and his co-workers immediately identified Alex MacLean's body in False Creek.[76] It was the day after Catherine MacLean's twenty-seventh birthday. For the *Vancouver News-Advertiser,* "whether the well-known skipper met his death by foul play or by losing his balance ... is not known."[77]

An inquest was held the next day. Doubtless aware of the rumours swirling around the well-known mariner's disappearance, George Frederick Curtis was diligent in his post mortem: "I examined carefully for any fracture of the skull or long bones and discovered none, nor could [I] find any marks of violence at all." With the chest, stomach, and intestinal canal all filled with seawater, Alex MacLean, the coroner deduced, had died by accidental drowning. The *Favorite* was the third of four vessels moored alongside, and Alex had apparently stumbled going aboard the tug.[78] The west coast newspapers, although filled with events in Europe, were quick to briefly acknowledge his career. The *San Francisco Chronicle* headlined "German Armies at the Gates of Paris" but also found room on the front page for "Captain McLean, the 'Sea Wolf,' Is Dead," because "his name was remembered in every port from Alaska south to the Golden Gate."[79] The *Vancouver News-Advertiser* stated: "The untoward end which has befallen him recalls once more to public notice one of the most remarkable seafaring men on this Pacific Coast and one of the most singular and adventurous careers." This report, probably written by Noel Robinson, went on to point out that "Captain MacLean was, as nearly everyone acquainted with Pacific Coast history is aware, the original of Wolf Larsen, the principal character in Jack London's famous novel, *The Sea-Wolf,* though it is only fair to state that no one attributed to him all the brutal actions which the novelist made that strange skipper responsible for." The piece carried a physical description, "medium height, but powerfully built, the two characteristics about the personal appearance of this remarkable man were his huge, red mustachios, heavy eyebrows and steel-blue eyes," and offered a sampler of the previous four decades, highlighting the Sorensen saga and the *James Hamilton Lewis* affair with the Russians. The reporter was just warming up: "Then there was his famous *Carmencita* expedition and – but space forbids further references to the adventurous career of this rover whose untimely death while still in middle life will come as something of a shock not only to Vancouver mariners but to mariners in many other ports, including San Francisco, where he spent many years and where he became acquainted with Jack London."[80] One suspects that Alex MacLean would have relished the stories that rolled out after his body was found. The *Vancouver News-Advertiser* reported: "The death of Captain Alexander McLean was accidental. This was made clear at the inquest ... There was no direct evidence to throw light upon the final scene in the life drama of the adventurous 'Sea Wolf,' but it is pretty certain that, upon arrival somewhere about midnight at the waterfront on False Creek, where the *Favorite,* the tugboat of which he was skipper, was moored, the unfortunate mariner, having to pass over two other small vessels to reach his own, missed his footing and fell into the dark water."[81]

Cape Breton newspapers also had far less coverage of his demise than of some of his earlier exploits. As writer-acquaintance Tom MacInnes later noted, the guns of August were reverberating "and so it is scarce to be wondered that the passing at Vancouver of as picturesque a picaroon and master of little ships with sails as ever figured in a story book was barely noticed in the local press." He wrote, "I thought what a shabby trick of fate that so excellent a sailorman should meet with so paltry a death in a puddle of False Creek; a sailorman who had such an acquaintance with the wildest winds and most swinging great waves and shark-infested depths of the Pacific; a sailorman who skilfully raided the Russian and American seal rookeries in Bering Sea, and almost as successfully robbed the French pearl fisheries of the Polynesian islands to the south."[82] Journalist Noel Robinson followed through to the end: "I attended the inquest into his death, in company with an old friend, the late Captain Charles Eddie, a very fine seafarer all over the world in sail and steam who hailed from the Highlands of Scotland and who was then examiner of masters and mates at Vancouver." According to Robinson, "despite the 'Sea Wolf's' nefarious career – perhaps because of it, and his courage – Captain Eddie, who was a great lover of adventure and romance, had a warm corner in his heart for him and, when he heard that Alex had met his end one dark night by striking his head against a log after falling in attempting to board his boat on False Creek, he 'phoned me up to ask me to attend with him the inquest and the funeral." As they paid their final respects to MacLean, "Captain Eddie remarked, 'Well, some of the bad things they have said about him may be true, but he was a real man with lots of guts. What a fine naval officer he would have made if his life had fallen along different lines.' That tribute from the lips of the old Highlander is not an unfitting epitaph."[83] Alex MacLean was buried on 8 September 1914 in Mountain View Cemetery, Vancouver. He was fifty-six. His grave remains unmarked.[84]

One contemporary assessment of his career appeared in another of his old home ports, San Francisco, in early October 1914: "Death Downs the 'Sea Wolf.'" The author of this detailed account was struck by the manner in which he died. It was "startling in its prosaicness. From the South Seas to Kamchatka the 'Sea Wolf' was known as the most fearless poacher of his generation." The *San Francisco Chronicle* article touched most of the high and low points of his west coast activities and could not get over the fact that he was "swallowed up in six feet of water in unromantic little False

Creek."[85] Like so many other aspects surrounding MacLean, not everyone accepted the verdict at face value. Decades later, an article in a Halifax, Nova Scotia, newspaper still declined to accept the inquest's findings and concluded: "It was a violent end to a violent life and although officially called accidental death, the truth will never really be known."[86]

Lucy MacLean recovered from her hospital stay in Victoria, and she apparently remained in the provincial capital, where her mother, sister, nephews, and nieces resided. Josephine Dauphin, Alex's mother-in-law, who had arrived in Victoria with her three children thirty-five years earlier, died in Victoria on 1 April 1915 at the age of seventy-five. She left "a very large number of friends," two daughters, both living in Victoria, seven grandchildren, and four great-grandchildren.[87] Her younger daughter Lucy, Alex's wife, died in Victoria on 17 January 1926.[88] She was sixty-four. What little is known about Lucy Dauphin MacLean is primarily gleaned from newspapers. Within a few years of the arrival in Victoria of the Dauphin family, there was a quiet, gracious Roman Catholic wedding, followed a few years later by the birth of their daughter, Catherine. Given Alex's primary occupation, sealing, Lucy was seldom on board his vessels, although she and eighteen-month-old Catherine were on the first leg (from Victoria to San Francisco) of the somewhat mysterious voyage of the *Mary Ellen* in the winter of 1889, which is so vividly remembered by Tom Brown. She was present in San Francisco when he returned from Russia in 1891 and from other trips to the Bering Sea, the North Pacific, the southwest Pacific, and the Klondike. Aside from one brief, intrusive moment with a *San Francisco Examiner* reporter in Oakland in June 1905, and a quote from her in January 1906, her voice is unheard. After thirty years of marriage, she had remained, in Noel Robertson's phrase when he visited their apartment in Vancouver in 1912, Alex's "kind and gentle wife."[89]

She must have had to do more than manage the household accounts, however. On more than one occasion, her husband returned from an extended sojourn with little enough to stock the larder or pay the bills. In the first years of their marriage, Alex returned to Victoria, year after year, with sizeable catches. But there were many lean years. In 1891, Alex returned from Russia minus a vessel, and his 1892-95 San Francisco-based seasons were not particularly prosperous. When he returned from his exhaustive trip to the South Pacific in 1898, he had only a cargo of coconuts. He did not strike it rich in the Klondike, and he saw little profit from the ill-fated *Carmencita* expeditions in 1904-05. Like the women in the American whaling industry, Lucy could not afford to be dependent.[90] She had probably picked up expert millinery skills from her mother, which may have been one of their survival strategies. One suspects that Lucy Dauphin MacLean, like her mother Josephine and her daughter Catherine, was an independent and capable woman. In a quiet testimony to Lucy, and possibly to Alex as well and to the culture of the people who follow the sea, the majority of her pallbearers were old sea captains and included a Cape Bretoner. Lucy would be buried alongside her mother in the Dauphin family plot in Ross Bay Cemetery in Victoria.[91] It is not known what happened to Catherine MacLean after her father died in 1914, although she was listed as living in Victoria when her grandmother died in April 1915. There was no mention of her in the brief obituaries in the newspapers when her mother died a decade later, and neither a marriage nor a death certificate has been located.[92] Catherine's later years, and her death, remain elusive. There is only Noel Robinson's tantalizing snippet of information he related to another journalist many years later. Robinson had joined the Canadian army and participated in the storming of Vimy Ridge in April 1917: "Just before the final action he was talking to a soldier who had been a bartender in Nanaimo and the man mentioned Alex McLean. 'I met his daughter in the Yukon,' he said. 'It's a long tale and I'll tell you later.' Ten minutes later the man was dead."[93]

Years after Catherine disappeared, and more than a decade after her father was buried, what could be considered the final chapter in the Bering Sea pelagic sealing saga took shape. Measures to compensate the American sealers for what they considered their legitimate claims against the United States government had periodically made it on to the floor of Congress, invariably with a reference to their role in the Bering Sea Claims Commission hearings in Victoria in 1896-97. According to a 1904 report, "the only group left without indemnity and suffering poverty from the loss of their property is that from which came the witnesses whose testimony protected the Government at Victoria."[94] Eventually, the American government had compensated the Canadian sealers, the Russian government had reimbursed some American sealers, and the British government was negotiating with the Russians for an arrangement for the Canadians affected. The only ones outside the loop were the American sealers, seeking restitution from their own government. They were simply looking for their day in court, which they felt should be held in the district court for the northern district of California, "the nearest court of competent jurisdiction to the localities where the seizures were made, and is most accessible to the witnesses, who, for the most part, are seafaring men residing in that vicinity."[95] Similar requests were made in 1908 and 1910, but, as one Alaskan chronicler noted in 1913, "broken in fortune, shaken of nerve, dim of eye, aged and heart-sick, many of them facing a grave in Potter's Field ... their pleadings [had] been in vain."[96] Some of the seizures and interruptions of sealing voyages dated back to 1886.

Finally, in 1924, the American Congress approved an act for the district court in northern California "to adjudicate claims of American citizens (who suffered damages or loss resulting from seizure, detention, sale, or interference by United States of vessels charged with unlawful sealing in Bering Sea during years 1886-96)." It had been a long haul. The American sealing vessels seized or thwarted by the American authorities in 1886-96 inclusive, and the sealers involved, would have an opportunity to put forward their case over the next two years.[97] Thirty-five legal suits, initiated by "American citizens or their heirs or legal representatives," followed in the California court system. The amount of money awarded in some of these cases suggests that the prolonged campaign had proved worthwhile, at least for those who survived, remembered, and had the resources to continue the struggle. The generous financial settlements help explain why so many of these legal decisions were appealed by the government.[98] The benchmark case, commonly cited, is *Whitelaw v. United States*. District Judge Frank H. Kerrigan rendered the judgment on 16 September 1925. He thought it an "unusual and highly interesting case." The 120-ton *La Ninfa* was initially seized by the revenue cutter *Corwin* in July 1891, while on a sealing and whaling cruise, and taken to Sitka, Alaska. She was released on bond in November 1891. In 1892, Commander Evans on the American flagship *Yorkton* warned *La Ninfa's* captain "not to hunt for seals in the (Bering) Sea," and the vessel "was peremptorily ordered to go to Sand Point and land all her sealing gear there." The 1891 case was initially dismissed by the Circuit Court of Appeals of the Ninth Circuit in June 1896. The claimant, finally given the chance in 1924, now sought damages of $99,000 for disruptions of the two voyages. The judge dismissed the government argument that "the question of probable catch is not one to be allowed." The American authorities had previously argued this point unsuccessfully during the Bering Sea Claims Commission. They had had more success when they advanced the opposite argument at The Hague in 1902. In September 1925, Judge Kerrigan felt that there was a strong case for damages for "the wrongful exclusion from the sealing grounds." Further, he stated, "American and British subjects have been compensated for similar losses, the United States even acting on behalf of the former in claiming damages from Russia. It is hardly reasonable to believe that Congress intended to deny similar relief to other American citizens, in enacting law which purported to grant them compensation for exactly similar wrongful acts." Judge Kerrigan then turned to the question of "prospective catch" in an average season and also established average prices for the specific seasons. Along with expenses due to the seizure in 1891, estimated at $7,000, and whaling losses of $16,218, the total award in this specific instance came to $75,770.[99]

The vast majority of cases went on to appeal court. The other commonly cited case, *Bird et al. v. United States,* dealt with twenty-four of them. Since "only American citizens or their heirs or legal representatives" could maintain the action, there were difficulties with two cases in which the claimants were not Americans. Neither of these cases, it must be noted, was connected to Alex MacLean.[100] Most of the cases rested upon the charge of "interference" only, and the court ruled that it was not essential that physical force be actually employed.[101] Some claims connected with H. Liebes and Company Incorporated proved lucrative. In one relevant suit, the Pacific Trading Company owned eleven-sixteenths of a vessel that was interfered with in 1893. The vessel was the steam bark *Alexander*. That year, she was under the command of Alex MacLean. In another suit, M.J. Lyon (the only surviving trustee of the Pacific Trading Company) claimed damage for vessels owned by H. Liebes and Company in 1893, including the *Edward E. Webster,* which had been under Dan MacLean's command at the time. The decision came down on these two suits on 23 May 1927, with awards of $140,353.45 and $13,491.19. The government appealed, but this action was dismissed in June 1928. According to a Department of the Treasury memo dated 22 August 1928, the American government paid a total of over $492,922 to settle twelve cases on 20 August, including the $153,844.64 awarded to M.J. Lyon. This total was fairly close to what the United States had paid the Canadian sealers ($473,151) in 1898. Luckily for the American authorities, the 1924 legislation had contained no provision for payment of interest.[102] There is nothing uncovered in the historical record to indicate that any MacLean sought, or touched, a penny of this belated financial award. Dan, Alex, and Lucy were in their graves before any payments were made, and Catherine had seemingly disappeared.

During his stint in Vancouver, which was his last home port, Alex had remained on the water, commanding fishing vessels, river steamboats, and tugboats. His more dramatic experiences, clashing with a Russian warship, severe sailing in the South Pacific, dashing off to the Klondike, and raiding rookeries and illegal sealing in the Bering Sea were all behind him. His activities in his later years, running explosives up the Skeena River and riding out serious weather on the *Ella G.* and the *Sea Bird,* suggest his sense of adventure and survival remained. He had made an impression on Vancouver's collective maritime memory. He did not try to avoid his past – not that he had a choice – but he arrived in Vancouver carrying a substantial, somewhat suspect reputation. In Montreal, he dealt directly with Sorensen's lawyers concerning his connection with London's novel. On his return trip to Vancouver, and in his later interview with Noel Robinson, he demonstrated that his broad shoulders were adequate for the load.

Newspaper accounts of the period and the assessments of contemporaries, with a few exceptions, leave an impression of an individual who was not plagued by doubt, carried through with his responsibilities, whatever they may have been, continued with his social and storytelling skills, and earned considerable respect from many of those Vancouverites who crossed paths with him in those years. Captain Charles Eddie's comment to Noel Robinson at Alex's wake, "a real man with lots of guts," captures this aspect.

Alex MacLean and Lucy Dauphin were married for thirty years, but little can be gleaned about their private life. Robinson's visit in December 1912 offers a fleeting glance, suggesting a comfortable, strong relationship between the Cape Bretoner and the New Orleans-born woman. Her ties with her family appear to have remained close after the Dauphins moved to Victoria in 1880. Catherine MacLean was obviously proud of her father, and she remained in close proximity to her parents during their years in Vancouver. She was apparently staying with them when Robinson visited in 1912. She was twenty-five. That was not an uncommon pattern at that time. When her father drowned, she was staying in the Stanley Rooms on Pender Street, but she was close at hand and, according to evidence at the inquest, knowledgeable about his activities.[103] Alex MacLean did have his moments. He also had strong family ties. Able, experienced individuals accorded him considerable respect. Vancouver also has good reason to remember him.

14
The Legend of Alex MacLean

Alex MacLean was an exceptional mariner and a memorable individual who made quite an impression on many of his contemporaries. Stories were told. Over time, distance, and retelling, alterations and additions can be noted and sometimes traced. The tone and scale of the oft-repeated waterfront stories as well as the fo'c's'le tales and contemporary newspaper accounts, the adjectives used to describe MacLean and his deeds, the situations in which he purportedly placed himself, and, significantly, the longevity of many of the accounts can lead one to view MacLean as a popular legendary hero. These factors would help explain why there were so many stories that have endured for more than one hundred years.

Folk Legend Process

Folklorists offer some specific criteria for determining whether or not someone is a popular legendary hero. The construction of a folk hero begins with the individual's own constituency, whose viewpoint he expresses. Although personalized and historical, MacLean's folk-hero quality lay in his role as a master mariner, who happened to be a Cape Breton Gael, operating out of North American west coast ports in the declining days of sail. The portrayal is then broadened. Legendary heroes were not in control of the recreation of their past, although in MacLean's case he gave it a little shove in particular directions now and then. In folklore, the heroes are the inspiration for tales. They do not relate them.[1] One could note MacLean's reticence with Noel Robinson in Vancouver in 1912, when the journalist had difficulty prying out information on the captain's adventures, and contrast this reluctance with the almost constant stream of stories about MacLean from west coast waterfront sources. Further, the "feats, escapades, and mannerisms" of these legendary individuals "appealed to ever-widening audiences," and they "attracted attention not because of their uniqueness, but because of their representativeness."[2] Appeal was based on approved traits and values.

Legendary American figures "sprang to eminence from the people," and it was "only the folk who spin legends, relate anecdotes, and sing ballads about a figure that has captured their imagination [who] can provide the evidence."[3] Group awareness and acceptance is a key component, with the process providing "a sort of automatic random sampling."[4] The legend, by definition, is a communal possession and is constructed from the anecdotal observations of participants in the subculture. A body of legends evolves in a nonlinear, often discontinuous way. It is "relatively unstructured."[5] The tales are repeated, and then a separate body of legends can be told about and attributed to the colourful figure. As Richard Dorson remarks, "legends alter and reshape the personage from history to suit the folk imagination."[6] In Alex MacLean's case, the reshaping was projected back into his early years – his experiences and feats in cable laying off both the Atlantic and Pacific coasts in the late 1870s and early 1880s – and his remarkable sealing successes out of Victoria in the latter decade. One could, and many did, also borrow from the deep, frequently romanticized history of the Gaels and sailors' lore.

Oral history was an integral part of the process: "Folklorists will agree that legend as one outcropping of folk narrative must enter at some point into word-of-mouth circulation. They recognize that legends, while frequently hard to believe, are nevertheless believed."[7] Sometimes the stories were told to begin a discussion of belief. Sometimes the tellers told them as true stories. These feats may or may not have actually happened, but belief is an essential component. Some sources were more questioning, especially those who were attempting to unravel the folk fabric and separate the historical and the legendary. As Charles Lillard stated, "personally I believe almost nothing of what I've read about McLean ... Almost everyone who has written about McLean has told a different story. A certain number are obviously based on confusion." While Lillard himself slipped into this difficulty on occasion ("If anything McLean was deadlier than the fictional Larsen"), he was aware of the pitfalls and fared far better than a host of other writers when it came to accuracy regarding Alex MacLean.[8]

Historians have a particular problem when confronting a popular legendary figure. In the world of folklore and social history, local tradition "tends to transmute legend into fact," and the legend becomes "one of the chief devices used by the folk to transmit history."[9] The process has certain requirements: "For an item to survive – particularly orally, it must have significance larger than others. In legends, this usually is embodied in a protagonist, be it a person or an object, a saint or a sinner. To the Anglo-American folk, the hero must demonstrate great strength, must endure great hardship, must have great courage. When he wins he may boast about it, but when he goes down he must go down bravely, overcome by a sea of troubles."[10] Few questioned MacLean's strength or courage, although some might suggest bravado on occasion, and his experience in the South Pacific in 1898 demonstrated his endurance. On this occasion, MacLean almost single-handedly faced the challenge of fever, crew loss, and a long, arduous voyage. It fits comfortably with the mythical pattern – the call to adventure, crossing over into an unfamiliar world, dealing with a serious ordeal, and returning to the ordinary world.[11] The premature reports of MacLean's demise, especially the account carried in the *Daily Colonist* in 1908, fit the bill for the last requirement: "Danger lurking without and below in the cabin dark, danger raising a hydra head against the indomitable leader. Mutiny, revolt, hot words, a shot in the gloom from one of his own men, a wounded 'Wolf,' hounded by his lesser curs, leaps overboard. There the tale is cut off. MacLean has not been seen or heard from since."[12] This account, which is "pure fabrication," to use Victoria customs collector J.C. Newbury's phrase in a reference to another of MacLean's reported manoeuvres, invaluably reveals the folklore process at work. For Eric Sager, who grappled with seamen's oral history in a later period, "memory distils the past. It is an act of selection, but this does not negate its value. The very process of selection provides in itself important historical data, because what somebody remembers offers an indication of what has been important to them over time."[13] The process was in operation in the fo'c's'les of the sealing schooners, in the saloons in San Francisco, Victoria, Vancouver, the Bonin Islands, Hakodate, and the Klondike, and in Cape Breton kitchens. Even if some, or many, of the stories about Alex MacLean were not true, they were stories told about him by people who had known him, or known of him, and they were remembering him in their own way. One should also keep in mind Keith Walden's suggestion that "what many people want from history itself is not an understanding of the Truth – of what actually happened – but, rather, contact with familiar patterns which provide some sort of fundamental reassurance about man's fate, the meaning of life, and the nature of things, patterns which, in themselves, are sometimes felt to constitute Truth."[14] Folklore scholar William Wilson reminds us: "What actually happened is often less important than what we think happened. We are motivated not by actual fact but by what we believe to be fact."[15] There is a judicious mixture of fact, remembrances, and imaginative recreation by those who knew, or knew of, Alex MacLean. As an old shellback in Victoria phrased it: "I knew him slightly by acquaintance and widely by reputation."[16] There were numerous Alex MacLeans in the public imagination.

Mariners and Legends

Sailors were a breed apart. Sager notes that sailors' yarns are "imaginative constructions of character and circumstance, containing metaphor and allegory. The oral testimony reflects not so much events, as the values or needs that caused events to be put into very fallible memories, retained there, and brought forth in the present."[17] Those who follow the sea have an immense resource upon which to draw. During the last days of sail, they needed all the help they could get. Robert D. Foulke refers to the 1870-1910 period as the "dying world of sail." It was MacLean's sea generation, and it was characterized by smaller crews, lower wages, more work, and additional accidents – in effect, a general decline in conditions. The immoderately romanticized and glorified days of sail had, in actuality, an unseemly, difficult, and prolonged closing.[18] It was during this period that MacLean operated. Sailors' options had declined. The fact that they still existed, however, as Sager reminds us, was because sailing ships continued to move more tonnage with fewer men in the final period of sail.[19] As well, they contained a significantly different work world than that of steam vessels, which witnessed a separate rhythm, changed work hierarchy, and increased division and specialization.[20] In addition, they still had the work culture of the sea to draw on, and, according to Horace Beck, by accepting the whole set of beliefs, "a seaman [had] access to perhaps a couple thousand years of experience and judgement to help him out of trouble." In his book *Folklore and the Sea,* he explains that "a tremendous source of entertainment for seamen was the telling of stories [and] tales ... to a seafaring man, tales, and especially legends, have a significance beyond mere entertainment. As a good Christian reads about the vicissitudes of Job or the exploits of David, so the sailor delights in his yarns. To him they carry almost a religious significance. From them he draws solace and learning."[21]

Such beliefs were not easily discarded. In Halifax, Nova Scotia, in December 1994, as the keel-laying ceremony for the Canadian navy's first maritime coastal defence vessel proceeded at Halifax Shipyard, four D-Day commemorative coins were laid on the keel slipway. This practice is traced back to a Viking ritual in which a coin was dropped below the ship's mast for good luck.[22] Painting with a wide but perceptive brush, Beck points out another pertinent feature. A seaman's life did not permit the luxury of sensitivity, "but if he is crass, crude and cruel, he is also generous; he is tough and he has courage." He underlines this by citing a comment by Herbert Halpert: "When you learn what the fishermen endure and the things they do in their lifetime, courage has no meaning." Thus, for Beck, "as a result of their life, then, seamen tend to paint things large. The details of their dockside excesses must be gargantuan to retain a place in their memory. Living next to danger and sudden death, they recall only those items that are so fraught with peril, so violent or so heinous that they seem unbelievable to a landsman."[23] Understanding this process assists in putting into perspective the tales that Jack London gleaned about Alex MacLean on his voyage to the sealing grounds on the *Sophia Sutherland* in 1893 as well as the talk, tales, and articles from the waterfront over the last 120 years.

Popular Legends

When the literary legend and the folk legend reinforce each other, the popular legend is formed. In this case, part of this process can be accurately dated to mid-June 1905, when MacLean and the *Carmencita* burst onto the front pages of the press, mere months after the publication of Jack London's best-selling novel. This recognition immediately highlighted MacLean as a solitary figure struggling against tremendous odds – indeed, against the inexorable march of progress. London, his publisher, the daily press, and the waterfront wags all had a field day. But those events had merely accelerated and intensified the process. The forming of the legend began years, probably more than two decades, prior to the summer of 1905. The base of the process was MacLean's remarkably successful sealing voyages out of Victoria in the 1880s, aided by his own personality and characteristics. Further, there was immediacy in North American folklore. For Beck, it only took some twenty years or so to turn a story into a legend.[24] The fact that London's *The Sea-Wolf* had become a best-seller a few months before the American and Canadian authorities sought to bring Alex MacLean to justice for the *Carmencita* affair – a quest extensively and gleefully followed in many major North American newspapers – also suggests that the evolution of a myth could be both accelerated and complicated by real-life events. The emergence of the fictional Wolf Larsen into the public realm little more than twenty years after MacLean first appeared on the west coast, and while he was still decidedly active, complicates the job of the empirical historian. The fact-fiction interplay underlines Dorson's observation that the evolution of certain legends "from an oral-folk-local circuit to a print-mass media-national circuit" can be highly complex.[25] Thus, from the summer of 1905 to the present, there were very few mentions of Alex MacLean that did not link him to the character in London's novel. MacLean acquired the "Sea Wolf" sobriquet in 1905, and his contemporaries, acquaintances, and Cape Breton relatives began to use the term, as did many others.[26] From this point on, almost any incident that involved "Sea Wolf" MacLean, no matter how commonplace, had an excellent chance of finding its way into circulation. A fire on board a vessel under his command, a fishing boat overdue, and criticism from a vocal conservationist all ensured that additional information, accurate or otherwise, would enter the public domain and circulate. And the process continued. Once begun, the making of a folk hero had a life of its own.

Legendary Attributes

Folklore studies identify common characteristics shared by popular legendary heroes. Such individuals were known for their courage, temper, endurance, and especially their strength.[27] The actual MacLean, it can be argued, has no difficulty in any of these areas. Indeed, these attributes frequently explain how he managed to get into and out of many troubling situations. Also, most American folk heroes were poor and unlettered in a formal sense. During Alex and Dan's formative years, rural Cape Breton was just emerging from its pioneer stage of development. While Alex was fluent in Gaelic and English, his older sisters could not write English. Public schooling was still relatively sparse in rural Cape Breton during this period, and Alex was, in many ways, quite representative of those Gaels who came of age in the 1860s and 1870s who left Cape Breton seeking jobs, opportunities, and adventure and were little hindered by a lack of formal education. The same could be said about Wolf Larsen. When Wolf was asked: "'Where did you go to school?' 'Never saw the inside of one, worse luck,' was the answer. 'I had to dig it out for myself.'"[28]

A frequently used example in describing the process of a legend in the making is Davy Crockett. It is instructive to compare the Tennessee congressman who died at the Alamo in 1836 and the Cape Breton mariner who drowned in False Creek in 1914. Both men died in their fifties. Crockett started as a backwoods storyteller-politician and was also "a character and a personality in his own right." During his life, and in the following two decades, the organs of popular culture played with the oral yarns told by and about Crockett. Through popular plays and the press, his legend blossomed as a popular and sub-literary hero. It "developed in the oral humor of the frontier and followed a universal heroic pattern common to folk epics."[29] Beck singled out Crockett, who attained "the stature of popular legendary hero" in part because he "had a remarkable way of telling a story, spinning a yarn, and taking a 'social horn.'"[30] Alex MacLean was not dissimilar. One is reminded of the evening in Victoria in 1896 when he enthralled Tom MacInnes and Ms. Vanilla or the crowded scene in the American Hotel saloon in Victoria in 1889, described vividly by Tom Brown, with the MacLean brothers front and centre, doing the honours at the bar, or Alex's conversation with and lasting impression on journalist Noel Robinson in Vancouver in 1912. Personal charm and storytelling were definite attributes for popular heroes. It is clear that Alex had these traits in abundance.

MacLean did not favour a coonskin cap, but he "was very particular about his attire ashore or afloat" with his Prince Albert coat, clerical collar, and, unusual for a waterfront figure, his distinctive black, broad-brimmed Stetson hat.[31] Nor can one forget his long handlebar moustache. MacLean's facial hair, frequently targeted during barroom scuffles, was a source of wonder: "Yet it is almost certain that one moustache that flourished along this coast at the end of last century has not been duplicated. This was an enormous reddish walrus, luxuriant and forbidding, so long that the owner could tie the ends in a bow behind his neck. It was a truly remarkable growth and it belonged to a truly remarkable man."[32] Then there were his eyes.

Noel Robinson, soon after his long interview with MacLean in December 1912, mentioned they were "remarkably keen blue eyes." Ronald Gillis, who also knew him, wrote: "You could hardly tell whether his eyes were blue or grey." It could be noted that Wolf Larsen was similarly sighted: "The eyes themselves were of that baffling protean grey which is never twice the same ... his eyes – blue, clear blue this day ... Ordinarily grey and cold and harsh, they were now warm and soft and golden ... his eyes were clear blue as the sky."[33] One San Francisco writer, in a summary of MacLean's career soon after he died, observed: "London's description of Larsen to one who knew McLean is as nearly a description of the pirate of flesh and blood as if he had sat before the author as he penned his lines."[34] If Jack London did not know Alex MacLean directly, then the novelist's attention to detail from the stories he had acquired was certainly solid.

Legends, Wit, and Style

In the development of the popular legend, according to Beck, "perhaps mostly important is the power of the written word and the publicity agent. Taken together they form a team that is hard to beat."[35] Unlike Crockett, MacLean was not a writer. Aside from interviews and transcribed testimony, notably his appearance before the Bering Sea Claims Commission hearings in 1896-97, his exchanges in the Montreal courtroom during Niels Peter Sorensen's libel suit against the *New York Sun,* and his public statement in the *Klondike Nugget* criticizing North West Mounted Police (NWMP) Constable Gregory, the only writing by Alex MacLean that this researcher has uncovered is a brief note to William Churchill in 1911. But his conversation was frequently interesting and intense. At such times, "he becomes animated and his eyes flash."[36] His wit and sense of irony frequently broke through the historical record. The "much exaggerated" report of his demise in 1906, his comment about the "regular pirates" attempting to take over the *Chieftain* on the Skeena River in 1908, the recipe for "cold feet" that he offered Sorensen's lawyer, and his stringing along the talkative rancher on the train on his return trip from Montreal in 1911 are good examples. His storytelling ability, due in part to his Gaelic culture and its rich oral tradition, was quite evident. Jimmy Newman, who fondly remembered the chilly day in 1905 in the Bering Sea when Alex, posing as a Mexican, gave him a sizable drink of rum, maintained that Alex "was very well liked. I used to meet him in the Clarice quite often, and he used to laugh and tell stories to beat the band. Oh, the man could talk!"[37] On a one-on-one basis, Alex was a match for some fine writers and journalists. He attracted Jack London. He impressed Tom MacInnes. He fascinated Noel Robinson. He made good contacts and good copy. The interest did not wane after he died. Journalists, novelists, and even some academics have found him intriguing. This fascination has continued. MacLean was neither shy nor insecure. His self-advertisement was obvious and natural. In this sense, he built on his strengths – his broad shoulders, piercing clear eyes, flowing moustache – and topped it off with his black Stetson hat. The facial hair and the sartorial touches seemed to fit. They were a part of him. Maybe he just became accustomed to a large moustache, felt comfortable with a Stetson, and thought little more about it. He knew who he was, and the opinions of others were not particularly intimidating to him. He made this clear time and again. He was not an individual to be lost in the crowd. For Beck, "personal flamboyance and the ability to talk a good game far outshadows the ability to 'cut the mustard.'"[38] Alex MacLean, it was quite evident, managed all three.

Part of the price for being a popular legendary hero was that the hero's less desirable characteristics were also in full display. Davy Crockett was sometimes portrayed as a "frontier braggart." Other folk characters received criticism as ruffians and fools.[39] Stories about Alex losing his moustache on a variety of occasions or literally being thrown off a sealing vessel (both John Dodd and Gus Folger supposedly managed this feat) fit in here. One might include Carl Rydell's description of the Drake's Bay potato battle of 1890, which culminated in a céilidh, although in this episode MacLean transformed a personal defeat into a festive occasion and a memorable story. One could also refer to Major Sherwood's comments on MacLean as he was sleuthing around the San Francisco waterfront in 1896 or the sealer Lachlan MacLean's disparaging remarks in 1914 about Alex's lack of sense. There is no lack of examples in this area. Some of his escapades bordered on farce. Others were tinged with tragedy.

Viewing Alex MacLean

People saw Alex MacLean through their own eyes, and their visions ranged widely. He may have been "'a sailor of fortune,' eager for adventure – illicit or otherwise,"[40] who was "husky and devil-may-care"[41] and who "won a great reputation for resourcefulness, courage and sheer deviltry,"[42] but everything had its place. For one old sealer, "true, he could bolt his whisky or belt an enemy with the best of them, but he was usually a quiet, well-spoken, well-behaved man, extraordinary neat about his person and his ship."[43] One west coast source noted that "MacLean was no soak. In fact he was an abstemious man, except when he went on an occasional binge of classic proportions."[44] Alex's own assessment of his capacity for booze brings the definition of inebriation, or self-denial, to another level entirely: "'I don't believe I could drink sufficient liquor in one day to get intoxicated,' he said."[45] Such a statement sounds like London's creation: "Wolf Larsen was unaffected by the drink, yet he drank glass for glass, and if anything his glasses were fuller. There was no change in him."[46] A sealing source adds about MacLean: "Oddly, this man of drink and violence was truthful and unblasphemous. He maintained perfect discipline and cleanliness aboard his ship."[47] A distant relative maintained: "At sea he drank and cursed and read philosophy," and a journalist who chatted with him felt he "was a man who thought seriously upon many topics and could converse and argue clearly and interestingly."[48] In addition, "MacLean was always cheerful and, though not naturally humourous, enjoyed a joke and was a past master in dancing the Highland Fling. Though he was, as one of his shipmates remarked, 'full of hellery when drunk,' drink did not make him cruel or savage – it simply added to his desire for dare-deviltry."[49] He was also sentimental.[50]

The seeming contradictions of this complex individual went down well in his homeland: "With few exceptions, the people of Cape Breton who knew the Sea Wolf thought he was greatly maligned. Most of them spoke highly of him. His great strength and daring were admired and extolled, and most of those who had had dealings with him ashore found him gentle and kind ... This mixture of physical prowess and gentleness, of ardor in battle and kindness to the beaten enemy, appealed to the Cape Breton mind."[51] It was also what one expected from a folk hero. The incident in the late 1880s, when John MacEachern from Cape Breton was bested by Alex, his captain, in a fight and then immediately cared for by him, was one of many such stories carried back east. The more cruel and vicious ones received short shift locally. Also, MacLean's concern for and care of all the passengers from the *W.S. Stratton,* which is part of the public record, was quite evident. MacLean sometimes searched for his missing sealers for days, and when Walter York was shot he quickly sought out more adequate medical attention. A relative reported that MacLean would put someone he wanted to get rid of on a remote island or, if that was not convenient, "simply throw him into the Pacific and tell him to swim to shore. 'It was not my fault,' he once told [Johnny A.,] if he could not make it.'"[52] The source notwithstanding, the strong influence of London's novel is evident in this case.

While in the Klondike, Johnny A. MacNeil asked his cousin how many men he had killed up to that time: "He denied that he had ever killed a man, and this is still believed by some of his relatives and friends surviving in Cape Breton. He explained, however, that he had lost fifty-nine of his men, which was probably an understatement."[53] Some of these tragedies can be documented. He lost two boats and probably six men while in command of the *Bonanza* in 1894 and another three men with the *Emma and Louise* the following year. There were also upward of twenty fatalities linked with the South Pacific expedition in 1897-98. He also noted that no one was ever killed on a vessel under him, but one hunter was accidentally shot by his partner in an open boat in the Bering Sea. The latter may be a veiled reference to Walter York. MacLean did bring the *Sophia Sutherland* back in 1898 without his original crew, but he was more successful with the *Ella G.* in 1906 and the *Sea Bird* in 1908, and they should be placed as a counterbalance to his experiences with the *James Hamilton Lewis,* which was seized by a Russian warship, the *W.S. Stratton,* which was smashed by ice on the Yukon River, and possibly the *Mary Ellen,* which was grounded in Alaska. With the *Lewis,* he lost one crew member due to smallpox. There were no fatalities reported on either the *W.S. Stratton* or the *Mary Ellen*. Alex MacLean usually returned to home port with his vessel, crew, and cargo.[54] However, pelagic sealing was dangerous, and when sailing with Alex MacLean one obviously took one's chances. Many did, repeatedly, which is also suggestive. As R.N. DeArmond noted, "the sheer cold-blooded brutality, which Wolf Larsen displayed throughout the novel, was found in neither the MacLeans nor Wester, nor in any other successful sealing skipper, for profitable sealing voyages depended on good hunters, and good hunters were scarce and inclined to be choosy about the captains they sailed with."[55]

Legendary heroes were also frequently less than law-abiding. They were dishonest but mostly in a particular way: "They cheated the cheatable – government ... the landlord and the absentee landowner; they outsharped the sharpie." MacLean's transgressions frequently targeted acceptable foils such as autocratic pre-revolutionary Russian officers, politically powerful monopolistic American companies, or sharpies such as Sorensen and the hapless Klondike gambler "Bullet" Brown, or modern bureaucrats such as Victoria's customs collector J.C. Newbury. As Noel Robinson commented, "whatever else he was, he was veracious – except, perhaps, when he was dealing with his enemy, the law."[56] It was a trait with which many could associate. Stephen Tatum's descriptive phrase about these legendary figures, "an abuser of the law and yet defender of justice," has a particularly resonant ring when one views MacLean's response to NWMP Constable Gregory's actions during the *W.S. Stratton* incident. His strong, and justified, public condemnation after the event was driven by a sense of fairness and compassion for those in his charge.[57] One Cape Bretoner who had sailed with Alex and Dan made a clear distinction between the MacLean brothers and frontier outlaws and maintained that the MacLean brothers were not "'bad men' in the western sense."[58]

Fortuitous Timing and the Media

In the making of a folk hero, MacLean also fulfilled another requirement. His timing was perfect. The publication of London's *The Sea-Wolf* in the midst of MacLean's episode with the seal-poaching *Carmencita* ensured that MacLean's special flair would shine out sufficiently to strengthen the case in various corners of North America. Not many individuals had novels purportedly based on their careers published while they were still active. Fewer still have had these books become best-sellers, with one of the more unforgettable characters in American maritime literature.[59] The appearance of the novel at this particular time accelerated the legend-making process. Alex MacLean paid a price in increased notoriety and job difficulties during his last decade. Understandably, he was upset but soon learned to live with it. He demonstrated his resilience, and his refusal to be baited, during the strident questioning on the possible connection between him and Wolf Larsen in the Montreal courtroom in 1911 and in his relaxed attitude as he strung along the young, fanciful rancher on the train returning home to Vancouver a few days later.

This period witnessed continually increasing literacy among the general population. Best-sellers such as *The Sea-Wolf,* mass circulation periodicals such as *Outing* (when Emery's article on sealing with the MacLeans was published, it had a monthly run of 90,000), and the yellow press spearheaded by William Randolph Hearst ensured a very wide print circulation throughout North America.[60] And it was at a time when middle-class American males were grappling with anti-modernism, American imperialism, and their masculine identity.[61] Many were mesmerized by the front-page adventures of Alex MacLean. Emmett Dalton, a bit of a frontier legend himself, spent more than fourteen years in prison and was released in 1907. In his story, *When the Daltons Rode,* he noted: "Many of the newspapers of the day were not far behind the prolific dime-novel authors and so-called paperback historians in catering to a sensation-hungry populace." Dalton was also perplexed about the "public's seeming love-hate relationship with its outlaws and criminals."[62]

Further, *The Sea-Wolf* quickly and successfully made the transfer to the newest popular media form. At least two films based on the novel were made when MacLean was still working and living in Vancouver. One played in Sydney, Cape Breton, in September 1907, and as the *Sydney Record* reported, "a magnificent specimen of canned melodrama was dished out to the audiences in the Nickel Theatre ... in *The Sea Wolf,* the feature film ... on the present programme. Rugged wanton cruelty intermingled with the most beautiful thing in the world, woman's love, forms the plot and the manner in which the picture-machine delineates the different incidents is almost startling in reality." No association was made in the *Sydney Record* between Cape Bretoner MacLean and Wolf Larsen, even though the local paper had prominently featured Elliott's article from the *New York Herald* and titled it "Cape Breton Seal-Pirates" ten days earlier. Obviously, this short, pirated version did not permit full development of the leading characters, and the connection was missed.[63] Viewers had to wait six more years for a more complete picture. The first authorized movie of *The Sea-Wolf* had its initial public screening at Grauman's Imperial Theatre in San Francisco in early October 1913. General release followed with showings in San Francisco and Los Angeles in early December. It was quite successful and was "the very first American eight reeler." Hobart Bosworth, who considered the novel London's "greatest work," was the producer and set a new standard for the fledgling California film industry.[64] As Jack London wrote at the time, "they are going right on playing it through the second week. It has played beyond capacity and has broken all film records of success in these two cities in which it has been tried out."[65] One wonders when it eventually screened in Vancouver, and if Lucy and Alex attended. A distant cousin suggested he would not have been pleased.[66] The 1930 production, which was the first "talkie," used the barkentine *Bear,* the vessel that Captain "Hell-Roaring Mike" Healy successfully used to hassle the Canadian sealers in the late 1880s, as part of the set. The finest production was made in 1941, with Edward G. Robinson as Wolf Larsen. Other cast members included Ida Lupino, John Garfield, and Barry Fitzgerald. One of the most recent, in 1993, had Charles Bronson cast in Larsen's role. The story continues to excite filmmakers.[67]

Relative Views

Having a popular legend numbered among one's relatives, however distant, appears to have been a mixed blessing. Now, even great-grandnieces and grandnephews find him fascinating. The problem is that their grandparents did not, and their parents could not pass on much family detail on their legendary relative, the Sea Wolf. Relatives Neil MacNeil and his son Neil F. capture this difficulty, and relationship, clearly. Neil F.'s grandfather was kept informed of the activities of Alex and Dan MacLean through two of his brothers: "The Sea Wolf was never discussed openly in Grandfather's family and in fact the relationship was admitted reluctantly ... When they visited Grandfather they would report to him on the Sea Wolf's activities. These reports usually were made at night, after the womenfolk had retired. I happened to eavesdrop on several of them ... my father used to talk at table about the Sea Wolf from time to time – never without a little brag that he was some kind of cousin of ours ... Of course, the MacLeans were rascals of sorts, much in gossip on Cape Breton, and I'm sure a lot of my father's material came from that source too."[68] Another relative, writing in 1966 to his granddaughter, mentioned "an amusing incident" at a school in Dorchester, Massachusetts: "They were showing the film, *The Sea Wolf.* At that time, Sister Agnes Clare, a relative of ours, was supervisor of all the schools in this area run by the Sisters ... When I told her that the pirate was a relative of hers, she almost passed out. Her family had evidently not displayed his picture on the mantle!"[69] The Sea Wolf was not always talked about openly in some Cape Breton circles, but he was discussed, and one detects more than a hint of pride and acceptance in these recollections.

Sometimes Cape Bretoners were quite defensive. William "Billy Senator" MacDonald was a successful accountant in industrial Cape Breton. His father had been in the Canadian Senate. One February day in the 1950s, he was depositing his Old Age Pension cheque. Whatever prompted him, possibly an off-the-cuff remark, he dashed off some comments on the back of the envelope: "Some months ago *Maclean's Magazine* had an article stating that Alexander MacLean had (most brutally, of course) murdered over 40 persons. Trashy magazines like *Maclean's* make a special effort appealing to their moron readers."[70] *Maclean's* had published an article entitled "The Real Sea Wolf," but it was in January 1922. The article was reprinted early in 1953 in the *Cape Breton Mirror,* a local magazine, clearly stating that it was originally printed in *Maclean's*. The piece does not mention any murders. The author was Noel Robinson, who probably had known MacLean better than any journalist and had always attempted to offer a balanced portrait of him. For Robinson, MacLean "was quite unlike Wolf Larsen in type and was certainly never responsible for such villainies as he is made to commit in *The Sea Wolf.*" To be fair to *Maclean's,* "Billy Senator" probably confused the article with an article in the *Atlantic Advocate* by A.W. Roy, which was published in February 1958. This piece maintained that MacLean was accused of seventy murders. "Billy Senator" MacDonald was eighty at the time, and Sydney had just built a junior college, in the face of considerable opposition, and in its early years MacDonald would prove a major benefactor to what eventually evolved into Cape Breton University.[71] MacDonald's brief, defensive outburst, probably misdirected, suggests a heightened sensitivity at the time to criticism of Cape Bretoners from the mainland. Brutal outlaws in the ancestral gene pool were not welcome, especially if they were fictitious.

Independence and Social Bandits

According to London scholars Earle Labor and Jeanne Campbell Reesman, "Larsen is sensitive, intelligent, domineering, arrogant, uninhibited, actively rebellious against conventional social mores, and – above all – alone. He rules alone; he suffers alone."[72] Could this assessment be applied to Alex MacLean? Many thought so. He demonstrated a spirit of independence and a sense of adventure. But he seldom operated independently. In Victoria in the 1880s, he shared ownership of vessels with William Spring and Edgar Crow Baker and was answerable, in part, to them. In the freewheeling 1890s in San Francisco, he had strong employment links with Herman Liebes, who was a major player in the monopolistic North American Commercial Company. Aside from possibly the *Rose Sparks,* each vessel he and his brother captained in this period had close links with H. Liebes and Company, H. Liebes and Company Incorporated, and the associated Pacific Trading Company. Even the supposedly freebooting *Carmencita* episode in 1904-05 had, at its financial base, businessmen on the San Francisco waterfront. In the Klondike, he commanded the *W.S. Stratton*. Big Alex MacDonald, who was one of the main players in the Klondike at the time, owned her. While on the high seas MacLean's decisions were not usually questioned, but the land ties remained. Even though many may have viewed him as operating in an unfettered situation, his reality was far more constricting. Richard McBride, premier of British Columbia from 1901 to 1915, was, according to Allan Smith, "committed in practice to business collectivism, believing in the closest relationship between government and business, and [was] persuaded that the power of the state must be used to create favourable conditions for economic growth," while also maintaining "a public and quite unequivocal enthusiasm for the individualistic creed." For Smith, "language inconsistent with the nature of the reality it claimed to be describing was, in fact, used frequently on the frontier. Developments there which were primarily the result of careful co-ordinated corporate activity were regularly offered as proof of what strong men acting individually could accomplish."[73] Canadians had their own set of myths and, as Smith demonstrated, from the 1850s to 1914, "English Canadians made it very clear indeed that the myth of the self-made man informed no small part of their thinking about society and its nature." It was a particularly useful concept, enabling Canadians in this period to portray their society, as many did, "as one which at once allowed unlimited scope for, and had been shaped by, individual activity," while simultaneously not threatening the standard Canadian code of peace, order, and good government.[74] Baker was quite at home in late-nineteenth-century British Columbia. Larsen, in *The Sea-Wolf,* was not answerable to a fictional version of H. Liebes and Company Incorporated or the Pacific Trading Company, although "Larsen also offers a critique of the system in which he operates. Comparing a wealthy man to a frigate bird 'swooping down upon the bobbies and robbing them of the fish they have caught,' he makes Van Weyden face the notion that the rich prey upon the poor."[75] Henry James Snow's analogy in which he compares the American sealing monopoly on the American rookeries to "that pirate of the gulls, the skua, amongst the kittiwakes, who ... watches until another bird captures a fish, and then swoops down upon him, compels him to give it up, and swallows it himself" is quite appropriate.[76]

For Eric Hobsbawm, the "social bandit" is often a figure who shines a light on exploitation. He lists nine requirements for such an individual to emerge. MacLean, it can be argued, fits into all but two: young and single, with a short career. Alex went down to the sea and stayed there for forty years. He was also married for thirty years. However, the rest of the pattern fits snugly. His poaching activities were not considered in a harsh light by other sealers, west coast waterfront communities, and many within the wider society back home. His courtesy and sense of humour were evident during such incidents as the visit by two members of the *Shearwater* crew in the Bering Sea in 1905 and in numerous waterfront saloon situations. He came from a humble financial background and, in the eyes of many, achieved prominence. Finally, he came from a very traditional, definitely pre-capitalist society, and his chosen occupation, sailing, was under siege and being transformed during his working life.[77] Perhaps MacLean, like many, bought into the popular myth of the self-made man. Consider the treatment accorded Dan MacLean by the Halifax newspapers when he was in town to purchase the *Triumph* in 1887. The *Halifax Herald* celebrated him and noted that he and his brother were now the owners of two vessels four short years after they started sealing. There are also the newspaper reports in the summer of 1905 about Alex that cited Kipling's "There's never a law of God or man/ Runs north of fifty-three" and assured their readers that many individuals "are hoping the wind will come strong and free and that his sticks will hold."[78] Here, the historical, literary, and social bandit/legendary figures are all in play.

The 1950s in North America did not constitute a period that emphasized and promoted individuals swimming against the tide or questioning or ignoring authorities. The Disney-engineered Crockett revival that decade thus presented the frontiersman as "an all-American boy scout type."[79] While modern middle-class North American society positioned MacLean on the periphery, it can be argued that he was but a cog in the wider financial plans of Edgar Crow Baker in Victoria and of Herman Liebes in San Francisco. Yet he would continue to appeal to those who felt unfulfilled or constrained by society. As Tatum suggests, "we seemingly desire to know all about the outlaw hero because he is, for a brief moment, imagined to be more alive and more vivid than the common man."[80] And, as Dorson notes, "the legends of a given period in American history reflect the main concerns and values, tensions and anxieties, goals and drives of the period."[81] In the late 1990s, another writer returned to the Baja peninsula seeking the wreck of the *Sophia Sutherland,* "an artefact from the foundation of the American psyche."[82] If one did a textual analysis of all of the period pieces about MacLean, and if one filtered the various interpretations of him through certain sociological and psychological preoccupations of society, such as was done by Tatum on Billy the Kid, is it possible to detect patterns and construct theories? Could Alex MacLean also be interpreted as an extended metaphor, whose changing shape provides a key to understanding society's specific needs of the moment? MacLean, however, unlike Davy Crockett or Billy the Kid, was not the subject of even one substantial article, book, or film in any of the periods that followed. The necessary reliance on a score of brief articles, mostly by journalists (a number of them simply reworking their original piece), cameo appearances in a few memoirs, an occasional letter to the editor, short oral reminiscences, and contemporary newspaper reports would significantly hamper a literary analysis of MacLean through the years because of their narrow base. What was reinterpreted, on a regular basis, was London's life and, to a lesser extent, his writings. *The Sea-Wolf* remains popular and in print, and London "remains today the most widely read American author in the world."[83] This work, however, is the first comprehensive study of Alex MacLean – hence, the biographical route. The historical MacLean and the legendary MacLean can be best understood in the political, economic, social, and cultural context of his time.

Breaking the Surface

Perhaps remembrance and forgetting in this case is a more happenstance process. Ronald Gillis' recollections in a Cape Breton newspaper in November 1936 were carried and commented on in the *Vancouver Province* shortly afterward. B.A. McKelvie's reminiscences of sealer Captain E.F. Jordan in that newspaper in 1943 prompted Noel Robinson to dust off his version a few weeks later.[84] The decades-long determination of some sealers, American and Canadian, and their descendants, to seek reimbursement also ensured that the distant days of the North Pacific sealing fleet would regularly break the surface for another round of stories and recollections.[85] When Victor Jacobson died in Vancouver in 1949 at the age of ninety-seven, the report noted that he "was a contemporary of Jack London's legendary Sea Wolf."[86] And when Thaddeus Jones stumbled across the remains of the *Jennie Thelin* on an isolated beach on the Baja California coast of Mexico in the early 1970s, there was another flurry of information about MacLean and the *Jennie Thelin/Carmencita/Acapulco* in the *Marine Digest* from such notable marine researchers as John Lyman and R.N. DeArmond.[87] It is evident that some concerns and values that can be lifted from the Sea Wolf MacLean legend were common to all of the generations that followed. A spirited, skilled individual, disdainful of a suffocating conformity, is always refreshing. People continued to share what they knew or believed about Alex MacLean, and it did not take much prompting.

The lament of those who note that Canadian history is far duller than the American version because of the absence of colourful figures is well known. George Bowering captures this spirit in his novel *Shoot!* which is based on the four members of the McLean Gang (the youngest was fifteen) who were hanged in British Columbia in 1881. They were not related to Dan and Alex. Consider this excerpt:

> In 1881 Billy Bonney was found guilty of murder, but he killed two guards and got away. Pat Garrett knew where to get him, and told Billy who he was in the dark by plugging him.
>
> In 1882 Jesse James got shot in the back of the head by a gun in the hand of a Mr. Ford.
>
> Alex Hare and the McLean brothers died six months before Billy did, and a year and a half before Jesse did.
>
> Canadian history is mainly written by schoolteachers who know a lot about the Government. If an individual with a gun shows up, he had better be an American or else.

> In the Kamloops museum there's a display including pistols about Bill Miner the train robber. He was an American who snuck into Canadian history with a gun in his hand.
>
> People dont want to know about the McLeans. They werent Americans. They werent white people and they werent Indians.
>
> They might as well have been dead all along.[88]

It is a fine novel and a perceptive point. Bowering's McLeans do make it into the *Canadian Encyclopaedia* but only as a gang and with the shortest write-up. The other McLeans mentioned include two politicians, two publishers, a fur trader, and a meat packer.[89] There was no room for the "notorious ex-Cape Bretoner" Alex MacLean in this source or, surprisingly, in Bowering's next work, *Bowering's B.C.: A Swashbuckling History*.[90]

Also on the periphery of Canada's collective memory was another contemporary Gael, the outlaw Donald Morrison (ca. 1858-94). Having lost the family farm near Megantic, Quebec, through what he considered unjust dealings, he killed a special constable and evaded capture for a considerable period through the assistance of his sympathetic neighbours. Jack Little's excellent study of this Gael suggests some striking similarities to MacLean, including their year of birth and Morrison's departure as a young man for the far west for an extended period. Little attributes the story of Morrison's widespread attention and sympathy to the "unusual combination of two powerful myths," the declining western frontier and "the proud Highland warrior and his faithful clan." Donald Morrison and Alex MacLean would have understood each other in Gaelic and in English. Morrison's literary epitaph was a poem, *Donald Morrison, the Canadian Outlaw,* written by Angus Dhu in 1892.[91]

Neither Donald Morrison, the British Columbia McLeans, nor the Cape Breton MacLeans occupy the historical stage with the same prominence as their American counterparts. This fact obviously bothered one old-timer in British Columbia who, in September 1966, looking ahead to Canada's fast-approaching centennial, was prompted to write to the *Vancouver Sun*. It was his concern that Canada should acknowledge "some of the men who put color and romance into the grey, pioneer days," and he had a particular individual in mind: "The United States had its Davy Crockett and other heroes, mythical and otherwise, but Canada had a great natural athlete and adventurer, although his name is almost unknown today." It was Alex MacLean. "While still in my teens I met him on Johnson Street, at that time a mecca for shellbacks from every point on the compass. They sailed the seal hunting schooners and when ashore they fought among themselves, but quit when 'Bully' MacLean appeared." For this British Columbian, MacLean's "feats of strength and fighting ability were discussed and admired by sailors in foc'sles from Panama to Nome. He fought a number of fights in the ring across the line, and many experts tried to get him to quit the sea but his turbulent spirit belonged to far away places."[92] The letter writer's vision was steeped in the brew of the popular legendary hero. Charles Lillard agreed that the Canadian historical stage "offered a wealth of material," and, as he wrote twenty years later, "our past was as colourful as anything south of the border. We didn't have cowboys, but Canada had the sealing fleet. Jack London's Sea Wolf sailed out of Victoria, not San Francisco; Wolf Larsen's real name was Alex MacLean, by birth a Cape Bretoner."[93] The claim of proprietorship was, however, too narrow. Alex MacLean did not belong exclusively to Cape Breton, British Columbia, or Canada. MacLean played on a wider stage – North American and the Pacific – the popular history of those who go down to the sea.

Images of Seals and Sealers

MacLean's popularity in the public mind was hindered in part because his target for much of his career was the fur seal. Henry Wood Elliott's formidable voice against the seal harvest was considerably enhanced in the public debate because of his talents as an artist. His drawings and watercolours of seals were difficult to counter, especially when the ultimate result was a fashionable coat. For many, the primary, frequently only, introduction to MacLean was through the novel. London wrote, "North we travelled ... ravaging and destroying, flinging the naked carcasses to the shark and salting down the skins so that they might adorn the fair shoulders of the women of the cities."[94] Some attitudes and practices have not changed noticeably over the years. In an article entitled "The Fur Seal Killers" published in 1975, Raymond Davis describes a trip to the killing grounds on St. Paul Island in the Pribilof Islands. One of the few differences from sixty-five years earlier was that the Aleut "seal killers" now arrive on location in trucks. The fur seals are still dispatched by clubbing. Davis quotes John Walsh of the International Society for the Protection of Animals who, while acknowledging "nothing works as well as the club," states: "Aesthetically, the public will never accept the clubbing of seals. It's caveman stuff." For his part, demonstrating a continuing inclination by some animal-rights activists to egregious comparisons, Davis drew attention to a release by the United States Department of the Interior, underlining carcass-handling improvements in the sealing industry in 1965, noting that this "tribute to man's mechanical genius compares favourably with any progress report submitted by an SS functionary on the guard staff at Auschwitz or Dachau."[95]

Images would play a significant role this time around as well. The campaign in the late 1970s and early 1980s, spearheaded by the International Fund for Animal Welfare, Greenpeace, Brigitte Bardot, and others, utilized posters of whitecoats – "that endearing whiskered visage with the ebony eyes" – so effectively that in 1983 the European Economic Community prohibited the importation of sealskin products. The objects of scorn this time were the club-wielding sealers, primarily from Newfoundland, who sought the harp seals and were portrayed as "baby-killers." Their position that "we are farmers and seals are one of the crops we harvest from the sea" received short shift. Many Inuit along the Arctic coast, primarily dealing with ringed seals, would also be seriously affected, although "professional animal-rights activists" were little concerned with that collateral damage.[96] Fashions and regulations would continue to change, and in 2004 the International Fund for Animal Welfare, in a coalition with the Humane Society of the United States, was outraged because of the increased harvest allowed by the Canadian government.[97] Contrary views continue. Beyond their own ranks and communities, seal hunters have not been accorded a particularly high standing in the public mind for the past 120 years.

Nationality and Remembering

MacLean's relative obscurity in the United States may also be partially explained by his place of birth. From the 1880s, newspapers, observers, writers, and waterfront commentators constantly made reference to Alex's Cape Breton/Nova Scotia origins. A barrage of public statements, spearheaded by Henry Wood Elliott in letters and articles in major newspapers and in congressional hearings over more than thirty years, consistently emphasized MacLean's status as a British subject. Eventually, this understanding made its way into the historical record. While the mythical Paul Bunyan boasted of French-Canadian roots that did not prevent four American towns, in Minnesota, Washington, and California, from claiming the lumberjack as their own, such claims are easier to make, promote, and defend when the individual in question never existed.[98] Alex's actual roots were a factor in the somewhat complicated process of determining who was an American folk hero. Besides, during his most successful sealing years, the 1880s, he operated out of Victoria, British Columbia, and his last decade was spent in Vancouver. Thus, as an American folk hero, he was overlooked. Not by all Americans, of course, as contemporary accounts in San Francisco and Oakland newspapers from the 1890s until his death in 1914 demonstrate. Note could also be made of Robert O'Brien's week-long series on MacLean in the *San Francisco Chronicle* in 1952 and the recording made with Stuart Thompson in that port around the same time, which remembered the 1904 *Carmencita* voyage. MacLean may not have made the initial American folk hero cut, but if one peeled away a few layers of the San Francisco/Oakland waterfront memory bank he was, for some, still on the roster. Johnny Heinold's First and Last Chance Saloon opened in 1883, and it is still operating on the Oakland waterfront. In recent years, it has been designated as a national literary landmark and is listed on the National Register of Historic Places.[99] A photograph of Alex, wearing his Stetson hat, is on the inside wall. Alex MacLean is definitely a part of the marine history and folklore of California and the Pacific. As one San Francisco assessment of MacLean noted, a month after he died, he was "one of the most picturesque characters the Pacific Coast ever has seen."[100] Canada's east and west coasts must share this mariner with their American neighbour.

In 1977, Allan Marble's *Nova Scotians at Home and Abroad* was published because, as the author explained, many Nova Scotians "have not been accorded their just place in the artistic, scientific and social development of Canada, the United States, and indeed, the World." The criteria were, in some ways, quite specific. One had to have been born in Nova Scotia, spent at least five years there, and "excelled in some field of endeavour," usually by occupying some senior position in government, military, religion, academics, literature, or sports or receiving some significant award. His final tally was 625 Nova Scotians, living and deceased. Alex MacLean made the cut, under the category of "adventurer." One would like to think Alex would have been amused, but not surprised, to be lumped in with lieutenant governors, university presidents, Supreme Court judges, archbishops, and others of that ilk. Marble's inclusion of MacLean, and prospector Robert Henderson, underlines the significant roles sometimes played by "ordinary" people, and suggests that their contributions and attributes have not entirely been forgotten. Implicit, as well, is the acknowledgment of the contributions made by many Cape Bretoners and Nova Scotians in their far-flung new communities.[101]

These two East Bay-born mariners have not been completely forgotten in their homeland. Alex and Dan MacLean are still remembered in Cape Breton among older, informed, and interested individuals. Johnny Macintyre, Donald MacEachern, and Michael MacPhee all had some knowledge of Alex and Dan, and their recollections, which were fairly similar, suggest a sense of pride and association. Johnny Macintyre grew up on land adjoining Domhnull MacLean's grant, and he continues to reside in the area. Donald MacEachern was from Northside East Bay, and it is highly probable that it was his relative who struggled, and eventually sailed, with Alex out of Victoria. The three informants also shared an appreciation of Gaelic.[102] A few years back, while making arrangements for one of my research trips out west, the travel agent, aware of my interest, casually mentioned that his people, some of whom also apparently sailed with MacLean, had the tag "they sailed with the Sea Wolf crowd" hurled at them many years ago. Judging from his demeanour during our exchange, he does not consider the link an insult.[103] Researching MacLean out west was actually facilitated slightly because, for decades, in archives, libraries, and museums in Victoria, Vancouver, Oakland, and San Francisco staff members regularly clipped letters and articles from local newspapers that dealt with MacLean's career. These indexes and vertical files also suggest an ongoing interest with the mariner in those ports.

This researcher was unable to fill in a few serious gaps. Catherine MacLean's story after 1915 is still untold. Numerous leads were followed to dead ends.

Catherine's fading from history is especially frustrating. This feeling is tempered only slightly by the realization that experienced journalist Noel Robinson, who knew Alex MacLean and wrote about him, off and on, for over forty years, also remained in the dark about her. There was also that tantalizing and unguarded phrase of Lucy MacLean's to a reporter from the *San Francisco Examiner* in the summer of 1905 about Alex "sailing the seas without flying a flag." Maybe it was a vague reference to another very faint episode mentioned primarily by Tom MacInnes that centred on Alex poaching pearls in the South Seas. These failures in research are acknowledged. The historical footprints of an individual and his closest relatives, which were so prominently in the public limelight, are sometimes surprisingly faint.

MacLean and His Times

West coast newspapers, local histories, and brief marine-related articles continue to refer to Alex and Dan MacLean on occasion. A fairly recent one, from T.W. Paterson, appeared in the *Nanaimo Daily News* in 1999 and noted: "Of all the rollicking, rip-roaring mariners to set course in B.C. waters in days gone, Capt. Alex McLean is without equal."[104] Paterson's vignette captures many of the high and low points of his career. This study, although historical, is not preoccupied with viewing history and legend as two mutually exclusive spheres, and it has tried to avoid what Tatum calls "the inherent problems of this rigidly dualistic separation of mind and reality."[105] Of great importance in this study were the anonymous storytellers on the waterfronts and sealing vessels who preserved the tales, remembering Alex MacLean in their own way. But one should not lose sight of Alex MacLean as a historical figure. A Cape Breton Gael, he travelled to New England and then sailed around the Horn in the declining days of sail to the pelagic sealing frontier of the Bering Sea. His decision to migrate was one that he shared with thousands of Cape Bretoners of his generation. Scores of them followed the path of Alex and Dan exactly and engaged in pelagic sealing in the North Pacific. Seeking riches in the South Pacific and the Klondike at the *fin de siècle* were also activities shared by many others. Alex MacLean was an active participant in a host of significant and important events. His sense of pride, dignity, and compassion, with occasional lapses, and his apparent delight in retaining his first language, Gaelic, were portions of his cultural baggage that he found no burden to carry. In many ways, he was representative of his generation and his place.

The maritime economy of Cape Breton and Atlantic Canada did not make the transition from sail to steam. Investors went elsewhere.[106] MacLean's culture, the culture of the Cape Breton Gaels, took longer to decline, but eventually the social and institutional attacks by the dominant culture proved overpowering. The proud and rich Gaelic tradition would be almost destroyed. Remnants would be salvaged and promoted as a tourist attraction rather than approached as a valuable resource.[107] The fact that this process is not entirely completed in the early years of the twenty-first century is a testimony to the resilience and tenacity of the culture of the Cape Breton Gaels. Alex MacLean was a product of it. The mark he left on the collective Cape Breton consciousness and on the waterfronts of Victoria, Vancouver, Oakland, and San Francisco is an enduring one. He was unquestionably a superb sailor, sealer, and scrapper. He did not always win – who did? – but many of his reversals and mistakes simply fuelled his determination. He deserves a more comprehensive and accurate place in our history and in our memories.

This book is unabashedly a biography. David Frank, in an insightful study of another Cape Bretoner, reminds us: "All history, social or otherwise, ultimately reduces itself to the story of individuals and their times."[108] Thus, context is necessary. The story of Alex MacLean and his times offers an antidote to some post-modernist critical approaches. His period, featuring another disappearing frontier, hosted a variety of fascinating trends: antimodernism, imperialism, environmentalism, masculinity and gender issues generally, increased literacy, and best-sellers. They were all part of the changing North American social fabric. These factors assist in understanding and explaining how he was viewed and portrayed by others. Hopefully, this study will prompt additional investigation in these areas. Alex MacLean could serve as a useful guide.

Some areas remain depressingly similar. One of the rites of spring recently is the continuing clamour over the seal hunt. The ruckus went up a notch in March 2006 with appearances on CNN's *Larry King Live* by Newfoundland premier Danny Williams and Paul and Heather McCartney. Rex Murphy, the Newfoundland-born *Globe and Mail* columnist, termed the latter episode "the pompous in full communion with the vacuous."[109] McCartney compared "the seal hunt to the ancient slave trade."[110] In the hundred years since Henry Wood Elliott published his article on seal piracy in Alaskan waters, featuring the damning accusations against MacLean, the tone, in some circles, is unchanged. Boycotts are the weapon of choice for the seal hunt protestors now, aimed at ending the harvest of harp, hooded, and grey seals.[111] In March 2007, the European Economic Commission declined to impose an immediate ban on the importation of Canadian seal products but did decide to proceed with a study on the industry. At the same time, an Inuk, Aaju Peter, from Nunavut, travelled to Europe to counter "misinformation." It is unclear if her explanation: "We were telling them we hunt it and we eat it because we cannot grow potatoes, we cannot grow vegetation," will have any impact.[112]

The contemporary strident squabble – one can hardly call it a debate – does not involve the northern fur seal. They have survived. By the 1950s, the population of the eastern Pacific stock was estimated at 2,000,000. While the most recent estimate is down to around 722,000, with a significant decline since 1998 (researchers have been unable to identify the factors responsible), and are below their "optimal sustainable population," they are still breeding on the Pribilof Islands, Kurile Islands, Commander Islands, Robben Island, and off the coast of California.[113] This revival is due, in large part, to the North Pacific Fur Seal Convention of 1911, which was signed by four major powers during a period of conflict, expansion, rivalry, and overlapping spheres of influence. Alex MacLean and his times remain richly relevant.

Notes

Introduction

1 Norah Story, *The Oxford Companion to Canadian History and Literature* (Toronto, 1967), 495-96.

2 United States, Congress, Department of the Treasury, Commission on Fur-Seal Investigations, *The Fur Seals and Fur-Seal Islands of the North Pacific Ocean,* compiled by Henry W. Elliott (Washington, 1898), 3 and 224; and Briton Cooper Busch, *The War against the Seals: A History of the North American Seal Fishery* (Montreal and Kingston, 1985), 139-40.

3 Bingham Duncan, "A Letter on the Fur Seal in Canadian-American Diplomacy," *Canadian Historical Review* 43, 1 (1962), 42, citing Samuel F. Bemis, *A Diplomatic History of the United States* (New York, 1942), 413.

4 Paul Gibb, "Selling Out Canada? The Role of Sir Julian Pauncefote in the Bering Sea Dispute, 1889-1902," *International History Review* 24, 4 (2002), 817.

5 Kurkpatrick Dorsey, *The Dawn of Conservation Diplomacy: U.S.-Canadian Wildlife Protection Treaties in the Progressive Era* (Seattle and London, 1998), 4 and 119-24.

6 M.C. Marsh, "Fur Seals and the Fur Seal Question," *Alaska-Yukon Magazine* 3, 6 (1907), 462.

7 United States, House of Representatives, Seal Islands of Alaska, *Letter from the Secretary of Commerce and Labor Transmitting in Response to House Resolution No. 73, Information Relating to Seal Islands of Alaska, 19 July 1911,* House Doc. 93, 62nd Congress, 1st session, 555-56.

8 Terry Glavin, *The Last Great Sea* (Vancouver and Toronto, 2000), 154.

9 Robert Hendrickson, *The Ocean Almanac* (Garden City, 1984), 207. See also *Halifax Chronicle Herald,* 29 July 1997, C17, and the editorial "Sockeye versus the Pirates," *Halifax Chronicle Herald,* 30 July 1997.

10 A.W. Roy, "Life and Death of the Sea Wolf," *Atlantic Advocate* 98 (1958), 77-84. A briefer version, "'Sea Wolf' Was Nova Scotian," was carried in the *Halifax Chronicle Herald,* 8 February 1958, 5. Allan E. Marble, *Nova Scotians at Home and Abroad* (Windsor, 1979), 283, which also includes Roy's assertions, although he qualifies them.

11 Alvin C. Gluek Jr., "Canada's Splendid Bargain: The North Pacific Fur Seal Convention of 1911," *Canadian Historical Review* 63, 2 (1982), 182.

12 Noel Robinson, "The 'Sea Wolf': Story of a Tragic Treasure Hunt," *The Shoulder Strap* 10 (1943), 47.

13 Noel Robinson, "The Story of My Life," *Vancouver News-Advertiser,* 1 January 1913, magazine section, 7.

14 Charles Lillard, "Dining with a Sea Wolf," *Victoria Daily Colonist,* 11 June 1978, 12.

15 Eric Hobsbawm, *Primitive Rebels: Studies in Archaic Forms of Social Movement in the Nineteenth and Twentieth Centuries* (Manchester, 1959), 23-25.

16 Gerald S. Graham, "The Ascendancy of the Sailing Ship 1850-85," *Economic History Review* 9, 1 (1956), 74-88; and Robert D. Foulke, "Life in the Dying World of Sail, 1870-1910," *Journal of British Studies* 3, 1 (1963), 105-36.

17 R.N. DeArmond to Editor, *Marine Digest,* 3 July 1971.
18 Robert O'Brien, "Alex McLean, the Sea Wolf," *San Francisco Chronicle,* 23 June 1952.
19 Robinson, "Story of My Life."

Chapter 1: Cape Breton and Going Down to the Sea, 1858-82

1 Stephen J. Hornsby, *Nineteenth Century Cape Breton: A Historical Geography* (Montreal and Kingston, 1992), 31 and 48.
2 Cited in Michael Kennedy, "'Lochaber no more': A Critical Examination of Highland Emigration Mythology," in Marjory Harper and Michael Vance, eds., *Myth, Migration and the Making of Memory: Scotia and Nova Scotia, ca. 1700-1990* (Halifax, 1999), 276. See "A View from the Ridge," *AmBràighe* (Autumn 1994), 5.
3 Kennedy, "'Lochaber no more,'" 270.
4 Ibid., 279.
5 Ibid., 267–71; and Margaret MacDonnell, *The Emigrant Experience: Songs of Highland Emigrants in North America* (Toronto, 1982), 80-93. Effie Rankin has Allan's version as *Moladh Albainn Nuaidh/In Praise of Nova Scotia.* Effie Rankin, *As a' Bhraighe/Beyond the Braes: The Gaelic Songs of Allan The Ridge MacDonald, 1794-1868* (Sydney, 2004), 76-81 and 159-61.
6 Kennedy, "'Lochaber no more,'" 278, citing L.F. Powell, ed., *James Boswell: The Journal of a Tour to the Hebrides with Samuel Johnson* (London, 1958), 189.
7 Kennedy, "'Lochaber no more,'" 283.
8 Sorley Maclean, "The Poetry of the Clearances," *Transactions of the Gaelic Society of Inverness* 38 (1939), 297, cited in John Shaw, "Observations on the Cape Breton Gàidhealtachd and Its Relevance to Present-Day Celtic Studies," in Gordon MacLennan, ed., *Proceedings of the First North American Congress of Celtic Studies* (Ottawa, 1988), 77.
9 Shaw, "Observations on the Cape Breton Gàidhealtachd," 78. See also John Shaw, "Brief Beginnings: Nova Scotian and Old World Bards Compared," in Donald MacAulay, James Gleasure, and Colm O Baoill, eds., *Festschrift for Professor D.S. Thomson* (Aberdeen, 1966), 342-55.
10 A.J. MacMillan, *A West Wind to East Bay* (Antigonish, 2001), 450-52; and Rusty Bittermann, "Agrarian Protest and Cultural Transfer: Irish Immigrants and the Escheat Movement on Prince Edward Island," in Thomas P. Power, ed., *The Irish in Atlantic Canada* (Fredericton, 1991), 96-106.
11 Ronald Gillis, "The McLeans of Cape Breton and Scotland," *Sydney Post-Record,* 17 November 1936, 4. See also Ian MacDonald, "Pirate of High Seas Ends in False Creek," *Vancouver Sun,* 15 October 1966, clipping in British Columbia Archives (BCA), Captain Alex McLean, vertical file; D'Arcy Marsh, "London's 'Sea Wolf' in Scot's Clothing," *Vancouver Province,* 31 May 1958, 15; and Noel Robinson, "The 'Sea Wolf': Story of a Tragic Treasure Hunt," *The Shoulder Strap* 10 (1943), 47.
12 Sydney, Registry of Deeds, Book D, 92 and Doc. 18134, 207; and C. Bruce Fergusson, *Place-Names and Places of Nova Scotia* (Halifax, 1967), 182.
13 Johnny Macintyre, interview, 27 September 1994.
14 Neil MacNeil, *The Highland Heart of Nova Scotia* (Toronto, 1971), 175.
15 James Cameron, *For the People: A History of St. Francis Xavier University* (Montreal and Kingston, 1996), 13. See also Rev. A.A. Johnston, *A History of the Catholic Church in Eastern Nova Scotia,* vol. 2 (Antigonish, 1971), 88-89.
16 Johnston, *Catholic Church,* v. 2, 117-18.
17 Michael Kennedy, *Gaelic Nova Scotia: An Economic, Cultural, and Social Impact Study* (Halifax, 2002), 75; and Johnston, *Catholic Church,* v. 2, 239.
18 Rusty Bittermann, "Farm Households and Wage Labour in the Northeastern Maritimes in the Early Nineteenth Century," *Labour/Le Travail* 31, 1 (1993), 14-17 and 32.
19 Cape Breton, NS, St. Mary's Church, East Bay, Parish records.
20 A.J. MacMillan, *To the Hill of Boisdale* (Sydney, 1986), 110.
21 R.J. Morgan, "'Poverty, Wretchedness, and Misery': The Great Famine in Cape Breton, 1845-1851," *Nova Scotia Historical Review* 6, 1 (1986), 89. See also Rusty Bittermann, "The Hierarchy of the Soil: Land and Labour in a Nineteenth-Century Cape Breton Community,"

Acadiensis 18, 1 (1988), 33-55; and S.J. Hornsby, "Migration and Settlement: The Scots of Cape Breton," in D. Day, ed., *Geographical Perspectives on the Maritime Provinces* (Halifax, 1988), 15-24.

22 R.J. Morgan, "Poverty, Wretchedness, and Misery," 9. See also Hornsby, *Nineteenth-Century Cape Breton,* 111-20; T.M. Devine, "The Flight of the Poor: Highland Emigration to Canada in the Mid-Nineteenth Century," in Cyril Byrne et al., eds., *Celtic Languages and Celtic Peoples* (Halifax, 1992), 645-60.

23 Bittermann, "Farm Households and Wage Labour," 37; and Morgan, "Poverty, Wretchedness, and Misery," passim.

24 Kate/Ketty married John MacCormick; Donald (Dan) was baptized on 12 November 1848 (sponsored by Duncan Curry and wife); John, born on 27 September 1850; Margaret married Donald MacCormick (John's brother); Sarah married a Mr. Howie; Mary Ann, born 25 May 1856, married Donald Currie. Alex, at four months, was baptized on 16 September 1858, sponsored by a neighbour, Donald Macintyre. Cape Breton, NS, St. Mary's Church, East Bay, Parish records. MacMillan has Sarah marry a Mr. Callaghan, although Registry of Deeds records in 1883 lists her as Sarah Howie. MacMillan, *To the Hill of Boisdale,* 110-22; and Sydney, Registry of Deeds, Book QQ, 204-12. Alex, in passing an exam for competency renewal of Master-steamer in the coastal trade, gave his birthdate as 15 March 1859. BCA, Alex McLean, vertical file, certificate, 22 January 1884. When applying for American citizenship, he lists 15 April 1859. National Archives and Records Administration (NARA), Records of the United States Circuit Court of Boston, petition for naturalization, 1 December 1882, RG 21, sec. 146, file 156.

25 MacNeil, *Highland Heart,* 175; Cape Breton, NS, St. Mary's Church, East Bay, Parish records; MacMillan, *To the Hill of Boisdale,* 119.

26 Morgan, "Poverty, Wretchedness, and Misery," 104. See also Hornsby, *Nineteenth-Century Cape Breton,* 116.

27 Andrew Walter Roy, "Life and Death of the Sea Wolf," *Atlantic Advocate* 98 (1958), 81.

28 City of Vancouver Archives (CVA), George J. McInnis, "Captain Alex McLean: The Sea Wolf," manuscript, 1.

29 Gillis, "MacLeans of Cape Breton and Scotland."

30 John Lovell, *Canadian Dominion Directory, 1871* (Montreal, 1871), 1584; R. Elva Jackson, *Cape Breton and the Jackson Kith and Kin* (Windsor, 1971), 140-41.

31 E.W. Wright, ed., *Lewis and Dryden's Marine History of the Pacific Northwest* (Portland, 1895), 427n4; T.W. Paterson, "Victoria's Own Sea Wolf," *Victoria Daily Colonist,* 25 February 1973, 10.

32 "At 12 years of age he sailed as a cabin boy with his uncle, a sea captain." Letter dated 12 April 1966, in possession of Bill Norin. He had at least seven uncles. United States, Congress, Behring Sea Claims Commission, *Record of Evidence Taken at Victoria, British Columbia by the Commissioners under the Convention of 8 February 1896, between Great Britain and the United States* (Washington, 1897), v. 1, 428; Wright, ed., *Lewis and Dryden,* 428n5, has him sailing on the Atlantic coast in 1873; MacMillan, *To the Hill of Boisdale,* 119, has Alex on the sea as a cabin boy at the age of fifteen; and Charles Lillard, "Dining with a Sea Wolf," *Victoria Daily Colonist,* 11 June 1978, 12, has him going to sea at fourteen. The novel and the film have Wolf Larsen as a cabin boy at age twelve in the English merchant service.

33 Cited in C. Bruce Fergusson, ed., *Uniacke's Sketches of Cape Breton and Other Papers Relating to Cape Breton Island* (Halifax, 1958), 176.

34 Hornsby, *Nineteenth Century Cape Breton,* 152-61. See also Howard I. Chapelle, *The American Fishing Schooners, 1825-1935* (New York, 1973), 119-52.

35 Beaton Institute of Cape Breton Studies, Cape Breton University, G. Fred MacDonald Papers, "Solomon Jacobs," unpublished paper, MG 15, file 41. See also *Halifax Morning Herald,* 16 November 1883.

36 Captain John Parker, *Cape Breton Ships and Men* (Aylesbury, 1967), 130. See also Frederick William Wallace, *Roving Fisherman: An Autobiography* (Gardenvale, PQ, 1955), 139.

37 A petition for naturalization from Boston, dated 1 December 1882, states that Alex arrived there on 10 July 1873. NARA, Records of the United States Circuit Court of Boston, petition for naturalization, sec. 146, file 156.

38 Ian McKay, "The Crisis of Dependent Development: Class Conflict in the Nova Scotia Coalfields, 1872-1876," in Greg Kealey, ed., *Class, Gender, and Region: Essays in Canadian Historical Sociology* (St. John's, 1988), 30-34.
39 In one sample in the 1870-80 period, 52 percent of Cape Bretoners in the United States were in New England. Hornsby, *Nineteenth Century Cape Breton,* 188-94.
40 Judith Fingard, "The Winter's Tale: The Seasonal Contour of Pre-Industrial Poverty in British North America, 1815-1860," Canadian Historical Association, *Historical Papers* (1974), 65-94.
41 Sydney, Registry of Deeds, Book QQ, 204-12; MacMillan, *To the Hill of Boisdale,* 119.
42 Hornsby, *Nineteenth Century Cape Breton,* 188.
43 "Gloucester's Fish Fleet," *Boston Globe,* 13 June 1888, www.lostatsea.ca/gloucns.htm.
44 Congress, Behring Sea Claims Commission, *Record of Evidence,* v. 1, 400; New York Supreme Court Archives, *Nels P. Sorensen v. Sun Printing and Publishing Association,* 1911, Alex McLean's testimony, 3; Noel Robinson, "The Real Sea Wolf," *Maclean's* 35 (1 January 1922), 12.
45 C. Fox Smith, *Sailor Town Days* (Boston, 1923), 103.
46 Frederick William Wallace, *Wooden Ships and Iron Men* (London, 1973), 235.
47 Ibid., 1-4.
48 Ian McKay, "Colin McKay's Alternative Vision of the Age of Sail," in Lewis Jackson and Ian McKay, eds., *Windjammers and Bluenose Sailors: Stories of the Sea by Colin McKay* (Lockeport, 1993), 21-32. See Michael Earle's review in *New Maritimes* (September-October 1994), 23-27; David Sutherland, "Wooden Ships and Iron Men Revisited," *Acadiensis* 8, 1 (1978), 101-6; Robert D. Foulke, "Life in the Dying World of Sail, 1870-1910," *Journal of British Studies* 3, 1 (1963), 105-36.
49 Basil Lubbock, *Round the Horn before the Mast* (Glasgow, 1986), 33-34. .
50 C. Fox Smith, *Sailor Town Days,* 122-23.
51 *San Francisco Coast Seamen's Journal,* 5 February 1890, 1 and 3.
52 Ibid., 13 March 1889, 1; Joshua Slocum, *Sailing Alone around the World,* edited and commentary by Walter Mahnes Teller (New York, 1962), 18-19.
53 *San Francisco Coast Seamen's Journal,* 30 September 1896, 6. Charles Domville-Fife had a different impression: "As in most Nova Scotian ships the crew ... were fed very well, so the sailors had no grounds for complaint on that score." *Epics of the Square-Rigged Ships: Autobiographies of Sail* (London, 1958), 81-82.
54 Eric Partridge, *The Penguin Dictionary of Historical Slang* (Middlesex, 1980), 633.
55 Eric Sager, *Seafaring Labour: The Merchant Marine of Atlantic Canada, 1820-1914* (Montreal and Kingston, 1989), 212.
56 Ibid., 201, 207-9, and 220.
57 William Avery Baker, *A Maritime History of Bath, Maine and the Kennebec River Region* (Bath, 1973), v. 1, 540-44; and v. 2, 628; Congress, Behring Sea Claims Commission, *Record of Evidence,* v. 1, 428, 431 and 463-64.
58 Bill Glover, "The Anglo American Telegraph Company," History of the Atlantic Cable and Undersea Communications, http.//www.atlantic-cable.com/CableCos/AngloAmerican/; George W. Gray, "The Bottom of the Ocean Is 'Main Street' to Him," *American Magazine,* January 1925, History of the Atlantic Cable and Undersea Communications, http://www.atlantic-cable.com/Article/subcable1925.htm.
59 Congress, Behring Sea Claims Commission, *Record of Evidence,* v. 1, 431 and 463-64; *Record of American and Foreign Shipping* (New York, 1878), 724.
60 Nova Scotia Archives and Records Management (NSARM), Stipendiary Magistrate's Court, Halifax, RG 42, Series D, vol. 26; NSARM, City Prison Register, Halifax, RG 35-102, Series 18B, vol. 3; *Halifax Acadian Recorder,* 18 January 1879. Special thanks to George Dupuis, NSARM, for his assistance and interest concerning this incident.
61 David A. McLeod, *Cape Breton Captain: Reminiscences from Fifty Years Afloat and Ashore* (Wreck Cove, NS, 1992), 78.
62 Judith Fingard, *Jack in Port: Sailortowns of Eastern Canada* (Toronto, 1982), 127.
63 Joseph E. Garland, *Down to the Sea: The Fishing Schooners of Gloucester* (Boston, 1983), 2 and 102-4; *Halifax Morning Chronicle,* 10 March 1879, 5; *Halifax Novascotian,* 15 March 1879. For a contemporary account of fishing out of Gloucester in the 1990s, see Sebastian Junger, *The Perfect Storm: A True Story of Men against the Sea* (New York, 1997).

64 Hornsby, *Nineteenth Century Cape Breton,* 196; Bittermann, "Farm Households and Wage Labour," 37. For another perspective on out-migration during this period, see Patricia Thornton, "The Problem of Out-Migration from Atlantic Canada, 1871-1921: A New Look," *Acadiensis* 15, 1 (1985), 3-34.

65 Congress, Behring Sea Claims Commission, *Record of Evidence,* v. 2, 1073. Many sources have Alex down as either second or third mate. See *Vancouver News-Advertiser,* 5 September 1914; Paterson, "Victoria's Own Sea Wolf"; Cecil Clark, "Seawolf McLean Tweaked Russia's Beard," *Victoria Daily Colonist,* 5 April 1959, 8-9; Wright, ed., *Lewis and Dryden,* 428n5; CVA, Herbert Lindsay Cadieux Collection, v. 244; Frederick C. Matthews, *American Merchant Ships, 1850-1900,* series 2 (New York, 1987), 310-12; Baker, *History of Bath,* 544; William Hutchinson Rowe, *The Maritime History of Maine* (Gardiner, 1989), 231.

66 Basil Lubbock, *The Down Easters: American Deep-Water Sailing Ships, 1869-1929* (Glasgow, 1971), 2.

67 Ibid., 2, 16-18, 108, and 226-27.

68 Matthews, *American Merchant Ships,* series 1, 240; series 2, 310-12.

69 Clark, "Seawolf McLean"; Gillis, "McLeans of Cape Breton and Scotland"; *Halifax Morning Herald,* 16 November 1887, 3; Roy, "Life and Death," 79; Wright, ed., *Lewis and Dryden,* 427n4; 428n5.

70 Congress, Behring Sea Claims Commission, *Record of Evidence,* v. 1, 400.

71 Dr. Patrick A. Dunae et al., *Vancouver Island 1881 Census,* http://www.vihistory.ca/content/census/1881 and http://www.familysearch.org/Eng/search/Census/individual_record.

72 Cole Harris, *The Resettlement of British Columbia: Essays on Colonialism and Geographical Change* (Vancouver, 1997), 137 and 140.

73 Ibid., 155 and 158.

74 Congress, Behring Sea Claims Commission, *Record of Evidence,* v. 1, 400 and 430. Norman Hacking, "British Columbia Steamboat Days, 1870-1883," *British Columbia Historical Quarterly* 11, 2 (1947), 82; Art Downs, *British Columbia-Yukon: Sternwheel Days* (Surrey, 1992), 37; Harris, *Resettlement of British Columbia,* 169-72.

75 Canada, Minister of Public Works, *Annual Reports,* 1881, Sessional Paper no. 6, xl-xli and 98; 1882, Sessional Paper no. 7, Appendix 10, 88; 1883, Sessional Paper no. 10, Appendix 28, 7 and 56-61.

76 Wright, ed., *Lewis and Dryden,* 139; Congress, Behring Sea Claims Commission, *Record of Evidence,* v. 1, 400; v. 2, 1073. *Victoria Daily Colonist,* 5 September 1914; *Vancouver News-Advertiser,* 5 September 1914.

77 Noel Robinson, "The Story of My Life," *Vancouver News-Advertiser,* 1 January 1913; Canada, Minister of Public Works, *Annual Reports,* 1881, Sessional Paper no. 6, xli; Canada, Minister of Public Works, *Annual Reports,* 1882, Sessional Paper no. 7, 88.

78 E.M. Saunders, ed., *The Life and Letters of the Rt. Hon. Sir Charles Tupper* (Toronto, 1916), 310-12; Canada, Minister of Public Works, *Annual Reports,* 1883, Sessional Paper no. 10, Appendix 28, 757; Robinson, "Story of My Life."

79 Robinson, "Real Sea Wolf," 13.

80 Clark, "Sea Wolf McLean"; Wright, ed., *Lewis and Dryden,* 427n4; Lillard, "Dining with a Sea Wolf"; John J. Underwood, *Alaska: An Empire in the Making* (London, 1913), 51; William R. Hunt, *North of 53: The Wild Days of the Alaska-Yukon Mining Frontier, 1870-1914* (New York, 1974), 10; Benjamin Franklin Gilbert, "Economic Developments in Alaska, 1867-1910," *Journal of the West* 4 (1965), 509.

81 Congress, Behring Sea Claims Commission, *Record of Evidence,* v. 1, 430; v. 2, 1073; Gillis, "McLeans of Cape Breton and Scotland"; William Hunt, *Distant Justice: Policing the Alaskan Frontier* (Norman, OK, 1987), 12.

82 Gillis, "McLeans of Cape Breton and Scotland"; Congress, Behring Sea Claims Commission, *Record of Evidence,* v. 1, 430-31; Lillard, "Dining with a Sea Wolf"; Wright, ed., *Lewis and Dryden,* 427n4.

83 Wright, ed., *Lewis and Dryden,* 271 and 297. Downs, *Sternwheel Days,* 19, 39, and 43; Edward L. Affleck, comp., *Affleck's List of Sternwheelers Plying the Inland Waters of British Columbia 1858-1980* (Vancouver, 1992), 18, 31, and 41. Wright has Alex in charge of the *Beaver* for a short period of time (at 428n5). *Victoria Daily Colonist,* 5 September 1914, also has Alex in

charge of the *Beaver* in 1884. Derek Pethick, *S.S. BEAVER: The Ship That Saved the West* (Vancouver, 1970), 100-1; Robinson, "Real Sea Wolf," 13.

84 Wright, ed., *Lewis and Dryden,* 427; Ursula Jupp, ed., *Home Port Victoria* (Victoria, 1985), 88.

85 Gillis, "McLeans of Cape Breton and Scotland."

86 Congress, Behring Sea Claims Commission, *Record of Evidence,* v. 1, 430.

87 On their declarations for citizenship, Alex made himself a year younger while Dan knocked off four years. NARA, Records of the United States Circuit Court of Boston, petition for naturalization, 1 December 1882, sec. 146, file 156; Congress, Behring Sea Claims Commission, *Record of Evidence,* v. 2, 1074 and 1955.

88 Alex later testified that "my brother and I became American citizens at the same time," and American naturalization records back him up. Congress, Behring Sea Claims Commission, *Record of Evidence,* v. 1, 430; v. 2, 1074-75 and 1457. But then there is the declaration of 20 October 1886, signed by Dan, which acknowledged that he "took the oath of allegiance to a foreign state, viz., United States, in November 1879." Congress, Behring Sea Claims Commission, *Record of Evidence,* v. 2, 1955.

89 Alex's and Dan's parcels of land later reverted to their brother John. Sydney, Registry of Deeds, Book QQ, 204-12; MacMillan, *A West Wind to East Bay,* 454.

90 Alton Y. Roppel and Stuart P. Davey, "Evolution of Fur Seal Management on the Pribilof Islands," *Journal of Wildlife Management* 29, 3 (1965), 450. An excellent overview is Victor B. Scheffer, Clifford H. Fiscus, and Ethel I. Todd, *History of Scientific Study and Management of the Alaskan Fur Seal, Callorhinus ursinus, 1786-1964* (Washington, 1984).

91 A few fur seals also bred on the Kuriles. Roppel and Davey, "Evolution," 448-50; D.G. Paterson, "The North Pacific Seal Hunt, 1886-1910: Rights and Regulations," in W. Peter Ward and Robert A.J. McDonald, eds., *British Columbia: Historical Readings* (Vancouver, 1981), 344. The Bering Sea was 1,100 miles east to west and 800 miles north to south. F.W. Howay, W.H. Sage, and H.F. Angus, *British Columbia and the United States* (Toronto, 1942), 321; Briton Cooper Busch, *The War against the Seals: A History of the North American Seal Fishery* (Montreal and Kingston, 1985), 114.

92 Terry Glavin, *The Last Great Sea* (Vancouver, 2000), 34; Theodore C. Hinckley, "Rustlers of the North Pacific," *Journal of the West* 2 (1963), 24.

93 D.G. Paterson and J. Wilen, "Depletion and Diplomacy: The North Pacific Seal Hunt, 1886-1910," in P. Uselding, ed., *Research in Economic History,* vol. 2 (Greenwich, CT, 1977), 83-88.

94 Wright, ed., *Lewis and Dryden,* 425; Laurie Jones, *Nootka Sound Explored: A Westcoast History* (Campbell River, BC, 1991), 211.

95 F.W. Howay and E.O.S. Scholefield, *British Columbia from the Earliest Times to the Present,* v. 2 (Vancouver, 1914), 459-60.

96 Wright, ed., *Lewis and Dryden,* 426.

97 Paterson and Wilen, "Depletion," 87-88; Roppel and Davey, "Evolution," 451.

98 See Busch, *War against the Seals,* 103 10, for a good summary. Also, Frank H. Sloss, "Who Owned the Alaska Commercial Company?" *Pacific Northwest Quarterly* 69 (1977), 120-30; L.D. Kitchener, *Flag over the North: The Story of the Northern Commercial Company* (Seattle, 1954), 31-41; Gilbert, "Economic Developments in Alaska," 504-7; Scheffer, Fiscus, and Todd, *History of Scientific Study,* 7.

99 Paterson and Wilen, "Depletion," 88, 132n9; Howay and Scholefield, *British Columbia,* v. 2, 459; Roppel and Davey, "Evolution," 451; James Gay, "Henry W. Elliott: Crusading Conservationist," *Alaska Journal* 3 (1973), 212; George Reiger, "Song of the Seal," *Audubon* 77, 5 (1975), 15.

100 Busch, *War against the Seals,* 114.

101 William R. Hunt, *Arctic Passage: The Turbulent History of the Land and People of the Bering Sea, 1697-1975* (New York, 1975), 228; Busch, *War against the Seals,* 114; Howay and Scholefield, *British Columbia,* v. 2, 459.

102 United States, House of Representatives, Seal Islands of Alaska, *Letter from the Secretary of Commerce and Labor Transmitting in Response to House Resolution No. 73, Information Relating to Seal Islands of Alaska, 19 July 1911,* House Doc. 93, 62nd Congress, 1st session, 343; Underwood, *Alaska,* 260.

103 Samuel P. Johnston, ed., *Alaska Commercial Company, 1868-1940* (San Francisco, 1940), 8; Dorothy Knee Jones, *A Century of Servitude: Pribilof Aleuts under U.S. Rule* (Washington, 1980), passim; Busch, *War against the Seals,* 113-18 and 235-38.
104 Wright, ed., *Lewis and Dryden,* 426.
105 Paterson, "North Pacific Seal Hunt," 343-44; United States, Congress, Department of the Treasury, Commission on Fur-Seal Investigations, *The Fur Seals and Fur Seal Islands of the North Pacific Ocean,* compiled by Henry W. Elliott (Washington, 1898), v. 3, 232; Paterson and Wilen, "Depletion," 83-84.
106 William G. Fitzgerald, "The Romance of Seal Hunting," *Wide World Magazine* 1, 1 (1898), 6; Jeanne Van Nostrand, "The Seals Are about Gone ...," *American Heritage* 14, 4 (1963), 11-13; Harry L. Wells, "Hunting the Fur Seal," *The West Shore* 14, 10 (1888), 548; Jozo Tomasevich, *International Agreements on Conservation of Marine Agreements with Special Reference to the North Pacific* (Stanford, 1943), 68; Busch, *War against the Seals,* 112-13; Lynn T. Sprague, "Exterminating the Fur Seal," *Overland Monthly* 62 (1903), 435-39.
107 Ivan Doig, *Winter Brothers: A Season at the Edge of America* (New York, 1980), 165-66; Ira Chaikin, "James Douglas Warren," *Dictionary of Canadian Biography,* v. 14, 1911-1920 (Toronto, 1998), 1041.
108 *San Francisco Call,* 18 March 1892, 7.
109 Wright, ed., *Lewis and Dryden,* 426; Congress, Department of the Treasury, *Fur Seals and Fur Seal Islands of the North Pacific Ocean,* v. 3, 223-24.
110 Wright, ed., *Lewis and Dryden,* 427.
111 G.O Williams, *The Bering Sea Fur Seal Dispute: A Monograph on the Maritime History of Alaska* (Juneau, 1984), 9.
112 Library and Archives Canada (LAC), Great Britain, Admiralty, Pacific Station Records, RG 8, series 3, vol. 23, 59; Department of the Treasury, *The Fur Seals and Fur Seal Islands of the North Pacific Ocean,* v. 3, 223; LAC, Royal Commission to Investigate and Report upon Claims of Certain Canadian Pelagic Sealers, 1913-15, RG 33, series 107, vol. 3, file 13, pt. 34, 346. Dorsey, *Conservation Diplomacy,* 116.
113 Paterson and Wiley, "Depletion," 82.
114 Robert Craig Brown, *Canada's National Policy, 1883-1900: A Study in Canadian-American Relations* (Princeton, 1964), 46-47; Kurkpatrick Dorsey, *The Dawn of Conservation Diplomacy: U.S.-Canadian Wildlife Protection Treaties in the Progressive Era* (Seattle and London, 1998), 5-6.

Chapter 2: Pelagic Sealing

1 Robert A.J. McDonald, "Victoria, Vancouver, and the Economic Development of British Columbia, 1886-1914," in W. Peter Ward and Robert A.J. McDonald, eds., *British Columbia: Historical Readings* (Vancouver, 1981), 370-71. See also G.W. Taylor, *Builders of British Columbia: An Industrial History* (Victoria, 1982), 126-27; *Victoria City Directory,* 1882-83, 13.
2 McDonald, "Victoria, Vancouver," 373-74.
3 J.M.S. Careless, "The Business Community in the Early Development of Victoria, British Columbia," in D.S. Macmillan, ed., *Canadian Business History: Selected Studies, 1497-1971* (Toronto, 1972), 104-23. Cole Harris, *The Resettlement of British Columbia: Essays on Colonialism and Geographical Change* (Vancouver, 1997), 153-56.
4 Ivan Doig, *Winter Brothers: A Season at the Edge of America* (New York, 1980), 227.
5 Charles Lillard, *Seven Shillings a Year: The History of Vancouver Island* (Ganges, BC, 1986), 173-75; Cecil Clark, "Seawolf McLean Tweaked Russia's Beard," *Victoria Daily Colonist,* 5 April 1959, 8.
6 Lillard, *Seven Shillings a Year,* 171.
7 Norman Hacking, "The Victoria Sealing Fleet," *The Sea Chest* (Spring 1982), 97. See also Patrick Lane, "The Great Pacific Sealhunt," *Raincoast Chronicles* 1, 4 (1974), 47; Patricia E. Roy, *A White Man's Province: British Columbia Politicians and Chinese and Japanese Immigrants, 1858-1914* (Vancouver, 1989), 15-16.
8 Frank Kelley, "Sealing with the Sea Wolf," *Victoria Daily Colonist,* 18 June 1933, magazine section, 1.

9 Robert H. Nichols, "Seal Hunters of the North Pacific," in R.E. Watters, ed., *British Columbia: A Centennial Anthology* (Vancouver, 1958), 128.

10 Taylor, *Builders of British Columbia*, 127; Terry Reksten, *More English Than the English: A Very Social History of Victoria* (Victoria, 1986), 109 and 118.

11 *Victoria Daily Colonist*, 22 September 1880, cited in Reksten, *More English Than the English*, 109.

12 E.W. Wright, ed., *Lewis and Dryden's Marine History of the Pacific Northwest* (Portland, 1895), 427.

13 United States, Congress, Behring Sea Claims Commission, *Record of Evidence Taken at Victoria, British Columbia by the Commissioners under the Convention of 8 February 1896, between Great Britain and the United States* (Washington, 1897), v. 1, 400, 430-32, and 467. See also United States, Congress, Department of the Treasury, *Seal and Salmon Fisheries and General Resources of Alaska* (Washington, 1898), v. 3, 224; v. 4, 731; *Victoria Daily Colonist*, 12 October 1883, 5.

14 British Columbia Archives (BCA), Charles Spring, "Origins of Pelagic Sealing in British Columbia and Its Progress," manuscript; City of Vancouver Archives (CVA), Herbert Lindsay Cadieux Collection, vol. 241; F.W. Howay and E.O.S. Scholefield, *British Columbia from the Earliest Times to the Present* (Vancouver, 1914), v. 2, 461; United States, Congress, Department of the Treasury, *The Fur Seals and Fur Seal Islands*, compiled by Henry W. Elliott (Washington, 1898), v. 3, 224; Congress, Department of the Treasury, *Seal and Salmon Fisheries*, v. 4, 500. BCA, B.A. McKelvie, "Saga of Sealing," manuscript from the recollections of Captain Ernest F. Jordan, Add. MSS. 5, 6; Peter Murray, *The Vagabond Fleet: A Chronicle of the North Pacific Sealing Schooner Trade* (Victoria, 1988), 25 and 144; Congress, Behring Sea Claims Commission, *Record of Evidence*, v. 1, 442; Noel Robinson, "The Story of My Life," *Vancouver News-Advertiser*, 1 January 1913, magazine section, 7; Congress, Department of the Treasury, *Fur Seals and Fur Seal Islands*, v. 1, 142; *Victoria Daily Colonist*, 12 October 1883, 5.

15 Congress, Behring Sea Claims Commission, *Record of Evidence*, v. 1, 400 and 446; Library and Archives Canada (LAC), Department of Marine and Fisheries, Sherwood to Oscar C. Bass, 31 December 1896 and Sherwood to Fred Peters, 19 January 1896, RG 23, vol. 237, file 1433.

16 Wright, ed., *Lewis and Dryden*, 427-28; Howay and Scholefield, *British Columbia*, v. 2, 461; *Marine Digest*, 27 July 1957, 13; 4 January 1958, 18; 14 August 1971, 22-23; CVA, Herbert Lindsay Cadieux Collection, v. 245; Hacking, "Victoria Sealing Fleet," 99. Ursula Jupp, ed., *Home Port: Victoria* (Victoria, 1985), 88.

17 Congress, Behring Sea Claims Commission, *Record of Evidence*, v. 1, 400; New York Supreme Court Archives (NYSCA), *Nels P. Sorensen v. Sun Printing and Publishing Association*, 1911, Alex McLean's testimony, 4, Index 5917; Congress, Department of the Treasury, *Fur Seals and Fur Seal Islands*, v. 3, 224; *Victoria Daily Colonist*, 12 October 1883, 5; Robert N. DeArmond, "The Men behind the Sea Wolf," *Alaska Life* (May 1946), 7; Congress, Department of the Treasury, *Seal and Salmon Fisheries*, v. 4, 500.

18 *Victoria Daily Colonist*, 12 October 1883, 5; 18 October 1883, 5.

19 Congress, Department of the Treasury, *Fur Seals and Fur Seal Islands*, v. 4, 224; Briton Cooper Busch, *The War against the Seals: A History of the North American Seal Fishery* (Montreal and Kingston, 1985), 139-40.

20 D'Arcy Marsh, "London's 'Sea Wolf' in Scot's Clothing," *Vancouver Province*, 31 May 1958, 15.

21 Robert O'Brien, "Alexander McLean, the Sea Wolf," *San Francisco Chronicle*, 23 June 1952.

22 United States, House of Representatives, Seal Islands of Alaska, *Letter from the Secretary of Commerce and Labor Transmitting in Response to House Resolution No. 73, Information Relating to Seal Islands of Alaska, 19 July 1911*, House Doc. 93, 62nd Congress, 1st session, 335.

23 D.G. Paterson and J. Wilen, "Depletion and Diplomacy: The North Pacific Seal Hunt, 1886-1910," in P. Uselding, ed. *Research in Economic History*, vol. 2 (Greenwich, CT, 1977), 90.

24 Cairn Elizabeth Crockford, "Nuu-Chah-Nulth Labour Relations in the Pelagic Sealing Industry, 1868-1911" (MA thesis, University of Victoria, 1996), 7.

25 LAC, Royal Commission to Investigate and Report upon Claims of Certain Canadian Pelagic Sealers, 1913-15, RG 33, series 107, vol. 3, pt. 13, 347. See also *Victoria Daily Colonist*, 26 March 1884; Murray, *Vagabond Fleet*, 24-26.

26 Congress, Behring Sea Claims Commission, *Record of Evidence,* v. 1, 430, 460; NYSCA, *Nels P. Sorensen v. Sun Printing and Publishing Association,* Alex MacLean's testimony, 4; *Victoria Daily Colonist,* 24 December 1896. *Victoria City Directory,* 1884-85, 57; 1887, 68; 1890, 131.
27 The median was fifty to eighty tons. Congress, Department of the Treasury, *Fur Seals and Fur Seal Islands,* v. 3, 224; Paterson and Wilen, "Depletion," 115; *Marine Digest,* 4 May 1957, 34.
28 Nichols, "Seal Hunters of the North Pacific," 126.
29 Jack London, *The Sea-Wolf,* edited and introduced by John Sutherland (Oxford, 1992), 140. All references to the novel are from this edition.
30 Nichols, "Seal Hunters of the North Pacific," 124; Elmer Green, ed., *Adventures of Carl Rydell: The Autobiography of a Seafaring Man* (London, 1924), 72-74; Busch, *War against the Seals,* 131-33; E.M. Sweeney, "Rescue on the Sealing Grounds," *Victoria Daily Colonist,* 1 January 1972, 6; Paterson and Wilen, "Depletion," 107, citing G. Nicholson, *Vancouver Island's West Coast* (Victoria, 1965); J. Gordon Smith, "The Romance of Sealing," *Canadian Magazine* 21 (1903), 393 at 401.
31 Nine sealing schooners were lost in that period, with 231 men. BCA, Eva Marie Sweeney, Add. MSS. 792, v. 2, 25. *Victoria Daily Colonist,* 1 January 1972, has sixteen vessels lost at sea between 1886 and 1900. Congress, Department of the Treasury, *Fur Seals and Fur Seal Islands,* v. 3, 231, lists thirty-three vessels lost between 1889-98.
32 Congress, Department of the Treasury, *Fur Seals and Fur Seal Islands,* v. 3, 231.
33 R. Turner Wilcox, *The Mode in Furs: The History of Furred Costume of the World from the Earliest Times to the Present* (New York, 1951), 122.
34 *Victoria Daily Colonist,* 25 March 1884, citing the *San Francisco Examiner.*
35 Busch, *War against the Seals,* 128; California Academy of Sciences, Anthropology Department Liebes Collection, notes; Wilcox, *Mode in Furs,* 155 and 250.
36 This certificate of competency was issued by the Department of Marine and Fisheries on 9 April 1884. BCA, Alex McLean, vertical file; CVA, Herbert Lindsay Cadieux Collection, v. 241; Wright, ed., *Lewis and Dryden,* 428; NYSCA, *Nels P. Sorensen v. Sun Printing and Publishing Association,* Alex MacLean's testimony, 3.
37 *Victoria Daily Colonist,* 13 December 1896, 6.
38 Cited in T.W. Paterson, "Victoria's Own Sea Wolf," *Victoria Daily Colonist,* 25 February 1973, 10.
39 BCA, Charles Spring, 9; Busch, *War against the Seals,* 130.
40 Canada, House of Commons, *Debates,* 25 April 1888, 975; R.C. Brown, *Canada's National Policy, 1883-1900: A Study in Canadian-American Relations* (Princeton, 1964), 44.
41 Congress, Department of the Treasury, *Fur Seals and Fur Seal Islands,* v. 3, 224-25; BCA, J. Gordon Smith, Add. MSS. 383, v. 2, 37; Wright, ed., *Lewis and Dryden,* 427n4.
42 Wright, ed., *Lewis and Dryden,* 428.
43 Congress, Behring Sea Claims Commission, *Record of Evidence,* v. 1, 401-2; CVA, Herbert Lindsay Cadieux Collection, v. 241; Wright, ed., *Lewis and Dryden,* 428.
44 Wright, ed., *Lewis and Dryden,* 428; Congress, Behring Sea Claims Commission, *Record of Evidence,* v. 1, 460; United States, House of Representatives, Department of Commerce and Labor, *Report from Committee on Expenditures in Department of Commerce and Labor, in Relation to Fur-Seal Industry of Alaska, 31 January 1913,* report prepared by J.H. Rothermel, House Report 1425, 62nd Congress, 3rd session, 2; Busch, *War against the Seals,* 137.
45 Tom MacInnes, *Chinook Days* (Vancouver, 1926), 151.
46 Neil MacNeil, *The Highland Heart of Nova Scotia* (Toronto, 1971), 176-77; Tom MacInnes, *Klengenberg of the Arctic: An Autobiography* (London, 1932), 46-47. See also Marsh, "London's 'Sea Wolf' in Scot's Clothing," 15; Noel Robinson, "The 'Sea Wolf': Story of a Tragic Treasure Hunt," *The Shoulder Strap* 10 (1943), 47; Robinson, "Story of My Life," 7.
47 She was born in Mobile, Alabama, on 13 March 1839 and at the age of nineteen was in the millinery business in New Orleans. Josephine, her twenty-four-year-old bookkeeper-husband William, and their one-year-old daughter Marie were living in the fifth ward of that Louisiana city in 1860. In 1862, another daughter, Lucie (later Lucy), was born. They remained in the central downtown area of New Orleans throughout the 1860s. Their last listing in a New Orleans directory is in 1872. United States Census, New Orleans, 1860-80; *New Orleans City Directory,* 1861-83; Herbert Asbury, *The French Quarter: An Informal History of the*

New Orleans Underworld (New York, 1938), 219 and 229-31; *Victoria City Directory,* 1882-83, 35; http://www.vihistory.ca/content/census/1881.

48 *Victoria City Directory,* 1882-83 to 1914, passim; Victoria, BC, Ross Bay Cemetery Records, Parks Department; City of Victoria Archives, Marriage and Death Registries.

49 Ashbury, *French Quarter,* 290-94.

50 *Victoria City Directory,* 1882-83, 18; *Victoria City Directory,* 1884-85; 1887, 68. *Victoria Daily Times,* 25 November 1884. She signed "Lucie" in the register, but at some point it became Lucy. Victoria, St. Andrew's Parish Records, St. Andrew's Cathedral. See also *Victoria City Directory,* 1882-83 and 1884-85; Reksten, *More English Than the English,* 62; Alexander Begg, *History of British Columbia* (Toronto, 1972), 482.

51 Paterson, "Victoria's Own Sea Wolf."

52 *Victoria Daily Times,* 25 November 1884; *British Columbia Directory,* 1884-85.

53 Baker represented Victoria in the House of Commons from 1882 to 1889. H.J. Morgan, ed., *The Canadian Men and Women of the Time* (Toronto, 1912), 52. BCA, E.C. Baker Diaries, 25 November 1884, Add. MSS. 707, v. 23, which notes "Alex McLean of St. John, N.B. [sic] married to Miss Dauphine [sic] in R.C. Church."

54 Harris, *Resettlement of British Columbia,* 158.

55 G.W.S. Brooks, "Edgar Crow Baker: An Entrepreneur in Early British Columbia," *BC Studies,* 31 (1976), 23-25.

56 Ibid., 24; Harris, *Resettlement of British Columbia,* 158.

57 Brooks, "Edgar Crow Baker," 28; Taylor, *Builders of British Columbia,* 105-7; Morgan, *Canadian Men and Women of the Time,* 51-52; *British Columbia Directory,* 1882-83, 23.

58 Rolf Knight, *Indians at Work: An Informal History of Native Indian Labour in British Columbia, 1858-1930* (Vancouver, 1978), 101-12; Dianne Newell, *Tangled Webs of History: Indians and the Law in Canada's Pacific Coast Fisheries* (Toronto, 1993), 25; John Lutz, "Work, Wages and Welfare in Aboriginal–Non-Aboriginal Relations, British Columbia, 1849-1970" (PhD dissertation, University of Ottawa, 1994), 103-6; John Lutz, "After the Fur Trade: The Aboriginal Labouring Class of British Columbia, 1849-1890," *Journal of the Canadian Historical Association* (1992), 82-85; Clellan S. Ford, *Smoke from Their Fires: The Life of a Kwakiutl Chief* (New Haven, 1941), 135-40.

59 Cairn Elizabeth Crockford, "Nuu-Chah-Nulth Labour Relations in the Pelagic Sealing Industry, 1868-1911" (MA thesis, University of Victoria, 1996), 7, 78-80, 87-89, and 135-36.

60 Paterson and Wilen, "Depletion," 113-15.

61 *Marine Digest,* 7 September 1957, 19.

62 Charles Lillard, *Mission to Nootka, 1874-1900* (Sidney, 1977), 101-2; Knight, *Indians at Work,* 101-12; Murray, *Vagabond Fleet,* 28; *San Francisco Coast Seamen's Journal,* 18 March 1891, 5; Robin Fisher, *Contact and Conflict: Indian-European Relations in British Columbia, 1774-1890* (Vancouver, 1977), passim; Newell, *Tangled Webs of History,* 25; Crockford, "Nuu-Chah-Nulth Labour Relations," 78-79; Archie Willis, "In the Days of Sealing," *Victoria Daily Colonist,* 28 June 1970, magazine section, 4.

63 Brown, *Canada's National Policy, 1883-1900,* 44; Canada, House of Commons, *Debates,* 25 April 1888, 975.

64 Paterson and Wilen, "Depletion," 114. See also Congress, Department of the Treasury, *Seal and Salmon Fisheries,* 4, 501-2; *Victoria Daily Colonist,* 16 September 1885, in CVA, Herbert Lindsay Cadieux Collection, v. 241; Congress, Behring Sea Claims Commission, *Record of Evidence,* v. 2, 1331; Wright, ed., *Lewis and Dryden,* 428; Congress, Department of the Treasury, *Fur Seals and Fur Seal Islands,* v. 3, 226.

65 Congress, Behring Sea Claims Commission, *Record of Evidence,* v. 1, 463.

66 Canada, Department of Marine and Fisheries, *Annual Reports,* 1887, Sessional Paper no. 16, 249.

67 Fredericka Martin, *The Hunting of the Silver Fleece* (New York, 1946), 162.

68 Crockford, "Nuu-Chah-Nulth Labour Relations," 83 and 111.

69 Jupp, ed., *Home Port Victoria,* 88; Busch, *War against the Seals,* 139; *Sydney Post,* 27 September 1905.

70 Lillard, *Mission to Nootka,* 100-1; Knight, *Indians at Work,* 12-13 and 44-45; Murray, *Vagabond Fleet,* 28.

71 BCA, Marriage Registration no. 1886-09-003894; *British Columbia Directory,* 1887, 13.
72 Bates appears to maintain contact with Max Dauphin, Josephine's son. Both of them were working at the Albion Iron Works in the late 1880s and early 1890s and both resided for a while at 24 Caledonia Avenue. Bates' last listing in the directory is in 1894. *British Columbia Directory,* 1889, 81; 1892, 524 and 567; 1894, 268 and 287; *British Columbia Directory,* 1890, 477; 1891, 537.
73 A copy of the Music Hall ticket is in the BCA, R.H. Roy Collection, Add. MSS. 995. Thanks to Ron Filion, San Francisco, for information on the hall. Congress, Department of the Treasury, *Seal and Salmon Fisheries,* v. 4, 502.
74 Department of Marine and Fisheries, *Annual Reports,* 1887, Sessional Paper no. 16, 248; Congress, Department of the Treasury, *Fur Seals and Fur Seal Islands* 1898, v. 3, 224-25; United States, Senate, *Fur Seal Arbitration: Proceedings of the Tribunal of Arbitration at Paris, 1893,* 53rd Congress, 2nd session (Washington, 1895), v. 14, 249.
75 Paterson and Wilen, "Depletion," 95-96; *San Francisco Call,* 18 March 1892, 7.
76 *San Francisco Call,* 18 March 1892, 7.
77 William Hunt, *Arctic Passage: The Turbulent History of the Land and People of the Bering Sea, 1697-1975* (New York, 1975), 224.
78 Busch, *War against the Seals,* 121; Paterson and Wilen, "Depletion," 93.
79 F.W. Howay, W.H. Sage, and H.F. Angus, *British Columbia and the United States* (Toronto, 1942), 321-22; Wright, ed., *Lewis and Dryden,* 428; Theodore C. Hinckley, "Rustlers of the North Pacific," *Journal of the West* 2 (1963), 22-30.
80 Howay, Sage, and Angus, *British Columbia and the United States,* 322.
81 Busch, *War against the Seals,* 111-14; Frank H. Sloss, "Who Owned the Alaska Commercial Company?" *Pacific Northwest Quarterly* 69 (1977), 126.
82 Charles C. Tansill, "The Fur-Seal Fisheries and the Doctrine of the Freedom of the Seas," *Canadian Historical Association Report* (1942), 73.
83 The initiative could have been the result of a misunderstanding. Possibly assuming it was standing policy, a new secretary of the treasury in 1886 forwarded an order written in 1881 (which had been the result of pressure from the Alaska Commercial Company and which had not been acted upon) to the collector of customs in San Francisco. Tansill, "Fur-Seal Fisheries," 73; Busch, *War against the Seals,* 291n56; James Thomas Gay, *Alaska Fur Seal Diplomacy: The Alaskan Fur Seal Controversy* (New York, 1987), 27.
84 Tansill, "Fur-Seal Fisheries," 73.
85 Brooks, "Edgar Crow Baker"; Canada, *Correspondence Relative to the Seizure of British American Vessels in 1886,* Baker to Secretary of State, 9 April 1886 (Ottawa, 1897), 15-16; Canada, House of Commons, *Debates,* 25 April 1888, 975.
86 J.B. Moore, *A Digest of International Law* (Washington, 1906), v. 1, 895 and 917-99; Canada, House of Commons, *Debates,* 25 April 1888, 967.
87 Tansill, "Fur-Seal Fisheries," 74; Hunt, *Arctic Passage,* 230; Howay, Sage, and Angus, *British Columbia and the United States,* 323; Brown, *Canada's National Policy,* 43.
88 Brown, *Canada's National Policy,* 51 (for an overview, see 42-62). See also Tansill, "Fur-Seal Fisheries," 71-81.
89 Tansill, "Fur-Seal Fisheries," 71.
90 Wright, ed., *Lewis and Dryden,* 428.
91 *Victoria Daily Times,* 7 October 1886, cited in Brown, *Canada's National Policy,* 45.
92 Wright, ed., *Lewis and Dryden,* 429.
93 Ibid., 429; Paterson and Wiley, "Depletion," 132-33n12.
94 Brown, *Canada's National Policy,* 47; Tansill, "Fur-Seal Fisheries," 73.
95 Holway, Sage, and Angus, *British Columbia and the United States,* 332.
96 Kurkpatrick Dorsey, *The Dawn of Conservation Diplomacy: U.S.-Canadian Wildlife Protection Treaties in the Progressive Era* (Seattle and London, 1998), 5.
97 Jozo Tomasevich, *International Agreements on Conservation of Marine Resources with Special Reference to the North Pacific* (Stanford, 1943), 67.
98 D.G. Paterson, "The North Pacific Seal Hunt, 1886-1910: Rights and Regulations," in W. Peter Ward and Robert A.J. McDonald, eds., *British Columbia: Historical Readings* (Vancouver, 1981), 345.

99 Howay, Sage, and Angus, *British Columbia and the United States,* 323; Moore, *A Digest of International Law,* v. 1, 895-96; Paterson, "North Pacific Seal Hunt," 345.

100 Paterson and Wilen, "Depletion," 90; Howay, Sage, and Angus, *British Columbia and the United States,* 322; Brown, *Canada's National Policy,* 49.

101 Brown, *Canada's National Policy,* 48.

102 Wright, ed., *Lewis and Dryden,* 429; Smith, "Romance of Sealing," 398; Gerald O. Williams, "Michael J. Healy and the Alaska Maritime Frontier, 1880-1902" (MA thesis, University of Oregon, 1987), 183.

103 *Victoria Daily Colonist,* 9 November 1886; Green, ed., *Adventures of Carl Rydell,* 115.

104 Brown, *Canada's National Policy,* 48-49.

105 Tansill, "Fur-Seal Fisheries," 76. See also Hunt, *Arctic Passage,* 231; Paterson and Walen, "Depletion," 90.

106 Canada, Behring Sea Claims Commission, *Arguments on Behalf of Great Britain,* Claim no. 4, The Favourite, 106; Congress, Behring Sea Claims Commission, *Record of Evidence,* v. 2, 1110 and 1116; *Victoria Daily Colonist,* 24 August 1886.

107 United States, Congress, Fur-Seal Arbitration, *The Counter Case of the United States before the Tribunal of Arbitration to Convene at Paris* (Washington, 1893), 256; Congress, Behring Sea Claims Commission, *Record of Evidence,* v. 2, 1329, 1958-63, and 1987.

108 Behring Sea Claims Commission, *Argument on Behalf of Great Britain,* 106-7; Behring Sea Claims Commission, *Record of Evidence,* v. 2, 1329-30.

109 Behring Sea Claims Commission, *Arguments on Behalf of Great Britain,* 106; LAC, Department of Marine and Fisheries, Peters and Bodwell, Case of the *Favourite,* RG 23, v. 320, file 2691, pt. 1.

110 Congress, Behring Sea Claims Commission, *Record of Evidence,* v. 2, 1330-31; Congress, Department of the Treasury, *Seal and Salmon Fisheries,* 502-3.

111 *Victoria Daily Colonist,* 27 August 1886.

112 Thanks to Brian Young, BCA, and John MacFarlane, Maritime Museum, Victoria, for their assistance and information on this practice. *Victoria Daily Colonist,* 25 April 1888; Gordon Newell, *Pacific Steamboats* (New York, 1958), 42. According to E.M. Sweeney, daughter of sealer Victor Jacobson, there was the "Palm of the Season," which was "the honor of bringing home the largest catch." *Victoria Daily Colonist,* 1 January 1972; BCA, Eva Marie Sweeney, Add. MSS. 792, v. 2, 24; Department of Marine and Fisheries, *Annual Reports,* 1887, Sessional Paper no. 16, 249; *Marine Digest,* 7 September 1957, 19. Clarence Nelson Cox, a Nova Scotian, would beat Dan's record in 1894 with 4,560 skins. Wright, ed., *Lewis and Dryden,* 435n19. Leonard McCann, "Clarence Nelson Cox," *Dictionary of Canadian Biography,* v. 13 (Toronto, 1994), 228, has Dan MacLean's catch that year at 4,268.

113 Using a Victoria dockside price of $8 per skin. *Halifax Morning Herald,* 16 November 1887; Busch, *War against the Seals,* 139-41.

114 Marcus Rediker, *Between the Devil and the Deep Blue Sea: Merchant Seamen, Pirates, and the Anglo-American Maritime World, 1700-1750* (New York, 1993), 147.

115 Aeneas McCharles, *Bemocked of Destiny* (Toronto, 1908), 11.

116 MacNeil, *Highland Heart,* 35 and 176; Beaton Institute of Cape Breton Studies, Cape Breton University, Captain John Parker Collection, J.H.L. Gillis to Capt. J. Parker, 11 May 1976, MG 50, 12; *Sydney Post,* 27 September 1905.

117 BCA, E.C. Baker Diary, 20 October 1886, Add. MSS. 707, v. 25, 18.

118 Congress, Behring Sea Claims Commission, *Record of Evidence,* v. 2, 1952-55.

119 Brooks, "Edgar Crow Baker," thesis, 244. See Baker's financial statements in LAC, Department of Marine and Fisheries, v. 320, file 2691.

120 Congress, Behring Sea Claims Commission, *Record of Evidence,* v. 2, 1952-56.

121 The transfer, from the estate of William Spring, was on 3 January 1887. Congress, Behring Sea Claims Commission, *Record of Evidence,* v. 2, 1952-62; LAC, Department of Marine and Fisheries, v. 320, file 2691.

122 Baker acquired power of attorney on 17 January 1887. Report of Messrs. Peters and Bodwell in the case of the Triumph 1889, LAC, Department of Marine and Fisheries, v. 320, file 2691.

123 Congress, Behring Sea Claims Commission, *Record of Evidence,* v. 1, 407 and 460.

124 *Victoria Daily Colonist,* 29 December 1896.
125 Laughlin MacLean arrived in Victoria in 1886. Wright, ed., *Lewis and Dryden,* 432.
126 N. de Bertrand Lugrin, "Epic of the Seal Hunters," *Canadian Geographical Journal* 4, 5 (1932), 301. In a reply to a telegram from E.V. Bodwell to Theodore Lubbe on 20 August 1897, inquiring who owned the ship in 1886, why it was sold, and who bought it, Lubbe explained: "We deemed business too risky on account of seizures and dissatisfied with Daniel McLean." LAC, Department of Marine and Fisheries, v. 237, file 1433. See also *Marine Digest,* 7 September 1957, 19; Eric Hobsbawm, *Primitive Rebels* (Manchester, 1959), 15.
127 Cited in Brown, *Canada's National Policy,* 51.
128 Dorsey, *Conservation Diplomacy,* 6; Tansill, "Fur-Seal Fisheries," 78-79.
129 Department of Marine and Fisheries, *Annual Reports,* 1888, Sessional Paper no. 6, 248.
130 Senate, *Fur Seal Arbitration: Counter Case of the United States,* v. 2; Hacking, "Victoria Sealing Fleet," 101.
131 Congress, Behring Sea Claims Commission, *Record of Evidence,* v. 1, 402-3; Congress, Department of the Treasury, *Seal and Salmon Fisheries,* v. 4, 502; *Victoria Daily Colonist,* 19 August 1887, in CVA, Herbert Lindsay Cadieux Collection, v. 241.
132 Congress, Behring Sea Claims Commission, *Record of Evidence,* v. 1, 402-3; v. 2, 1330-31; Congress, Department of the Treasury, *Seal and Salmon Fisheries,* v. 4, 503 and 1898; Department of Marine and Fisheries, *Annual Reports,* 1888, Sessional Paper no. 6, 248; Wright, ed., *Lewis and Dryden,* 432.
133 *Victoria Daily Colonist,* 6 September 1887.

Chapter 3: Conflict in the North Pacific, 1888-89

1 Baker "drew up an agreement for a $6,000 investment; divided into three equal shares between himself, Dan McLean and Victoria businessman, W.E. Blackett." Early in 1888, Baker bought shares in the *Favorite* and later that year bought a major interest in the *Mary Ellen.* G.W.S. Brooks, "Edgar Crow Baker: An Entrepreneur in Early British Columbia" (MA thesis, University of British Columbia, 1976), 245-46.
2 The *Pathfinder* was brought around the Horn by Captain William O'Leary of West Quoddy, NS, leaving Halifax on 20 November and arriving in Victoria on 17 April 1886. F.W. Wallace, "B.C. Sealers Claims Revive Memories of Old Days," *Canadian Fisherman* 21, 8 (1934), 19; W.E. Wright, ed., *Lewis and Dryden's Marine History of the Pacific Northwest* (Portland, 1895), 428; *Halifax Morning Herald,* 16 November 1887; Library and Archives Canada (LAC), Royal Commission to Investigate and Report upon Claims of Certain Canadian Pelagic Sealers, 1913-1915, RG 33, series 107, v. 2, pt. 7, 302; and v. 4, pt. 17, 267.
3 *Halifax Morning Herald,* 16 November 1887.
4 Ibid.
5 Briton Cooper Busch, *The War against the Seals: A History of the North American Seal Fishery* (Montreal and Kingston, 1985), 139.
6 *Halifax Morning Herald,* 16 November 1887.
7 British Columbia Archives (BCA), E.C. Baker Diaries, 16 November 1887, Add. MSS. 707; United States, Congress, Behring Sea Claims Commission, *Record of Evidence Taken at Victoria, British Columbia by the Commissioners under the Convention of 8 February 1896, between Great Britain and the United States* (Washington, 1897), v. 2, 1419-23.
8 The *Triumph* was originally registered on 2 April 1887. BCA, R.H. Roy Collection, Add. MSS. 995, declaration by Mary Blackett, 13 August 1889; City of Vancouver Archives (CVA), Herbert Lindsay Cadieux Collection, v. 243.
9 Dan declared at Shelburne on 16 November 1887 with respect to the *Triumph,* "never taken the oath of allegiance to any foreign state," and so on, and is registered as owner of sixty-four shares. Congress, Behring Sea Claims Commission, *Record of Evidence,* v. 2, 1424 and 1956; *Halifax Morning Herald,* 16 November 1887; Brooks, "Edgar Crow Baker," thesis, 246.
10 Ronald Gillis, "The McLeans of Cape Breton and Scotland," *Sydney Post-Record,* 17 November 1936, 4, has the challenge coming from Sol Jacobs. See also Beaton Institute of Cape Breton Studies (BI), Cape Breton University, G. Fred MacDonald Collection, "Solomon Jacobs," MG 15, file 41; Wright, ed., *Lewis and Dryden,* 431-32; Congress, *Fur Seal Arbitration:*

The Counter Case of the United States before the Tribunal of Arbitration to Convene at Paris (Washington, 1893), 257; Peter Murray, *The Vagabond Fleet: A Chronicle of the North Pacific Sealing Schooner Trade* (Victoria, 1988), 157; Down to the Sea in Ships, http://www.downtosea.com/1876-1900/1888.htm.

11 C.W. Parker, ed., *Who's Who and Why, 1917-18* (Toronto, 1918), 773; *Victoria Daily Colonist,* 7 August 1906; "Lt.-Col., the Honourable James Baker," *Western World* 5, 58 (1894), 254-56; BCA, James Baker, vertical file; Congress, Behring Sea Claims Commission, *Record of Evidence,* v. 2, 1424; LAC, Department of Marine and Fisheries, Baker's accounts, RG 23, v. 320, file 2691; BCA, E.C. Baker Diaries, 16 December 1887.

12 John A. Garraty, *Henry Cabot Lodge: A Biography* (New York, 1953), 235; Gillis, "The McLeans of Cape Breton and Scotland."

13 Joseph E. Garland, *Down to the Sea: The Fishing Schooners of Gloucester* (Boston, 1983), 133.

14 BI, G. Fred MacDonald Collection, "Solomon Jacobs." See also Garland, *Down to the Sea,* 51 and 161; *Victoria Daily Colonist,* 10 April 1889; *Bath Times,* 10 April 1902; Joseph E. Garland, *Gloucester on the Wind: America's Greatest Fishing Port in the Days of Sail* (Dover, 1995), 122. The *Boston Globe,* 13 June 1888, has Jacobs as a native of England who went to Newfoundland when quite young. Down to the Sea in Ships, http://www.downtosea.com/1876-1900/1888.htm.

15 Ursula Jupp, ed., *Home Port: Victoria* (Victoria, 1985), 117; Down to the Sea in Ships, http://www.downtosea.com/1876-1900/1888.htm.

16 Gillis, "McLeans of Cape Breton and Scotland."

17 Ibid.; D.G. Paterson and J. Wilen, "Depletion and Diplomacy: The North Pacific Seal Hunt, 1886-1910," in P. Uselding, ed., *Research in Economic History,* vol. 2 (Greenwich, CT, 1977), 104; Judith Fingard, *Jack in Port: Sailortowns of Eastern Canada* (Toronto, 1982), 6 and 11-13; Judith Fingard, "The Winter's Tale: The Seasonal Contour of Pre-Industrial Poverty in British North America, 1815-1860," Canadian Historical Association *Historical Papers* (1974), 65-94. Alfred Bissett of River Bourgeois, Richmond County, Cape Breton was first mate on this trip. Other Cape Breton crew members included Richard Gibbons of Sydney, Tom Moore and Tom Lovell of North Sydney, Harry Helford, John McCormick, Daniel McVicar, Peter McLean, and Lawrence Burke. LAC, Royal Commission to Investigate, v. 1, file 2, pt. 2, 1330; *Sydney Post,* 27 September 1905; *Daily Colonist,* 23 December 1887.

18 *Halifax Morning Herald,* 14 December 1887.

19 *Sydney Post,* 27 September 1905; Wright, ed., *Lewis and Dryden,* 443.

20 *Sydney Post,* 27 September 1905; *Victoria Daily Times,* 24 April, 1888; *Victoria Daily Colonist,* 25 April 1888; *Halifax Morning Herald,* 9 November 1887.

21 *Victoria Daily Colonist,* 25 April 1888.

22 Down to the Sea in Ships, http://www.downtosea.com/1876-1900/1888.htm.

23 Stephen J. Hornsby, *Nineteenth Century Cape Breton: An Historical Geography* (Montreal and Kingston, 1992), 188-200; Allen Seager, "The Resource Economy, 1871-1921," in Hugh Johnson, ed., *The Pacific Province: A History of British Columbia* (Vancouver, 1996), 217; Hugh Johnson, "Native People, Settlers and Sojourners, 1871-1916," in Johnson, ed., *Pacific Province,* 184.

24 *Sydney Post,* 27 September 1905; LAC, Royal Commission to Investigate, v. 1, pt. 2, file 1330-63; *Victoria Daily Colonist,* 22 November 1892; BCA, R.H. Roy Collection; Captain John Parker, *Cape Breton Ships and Men* (Aylesbury, 1967), 129.

25 *Vancouver Sun,* 6 May 1948; BCA, Alf Bissett, vertical file.

26 The record passage of any Nova Scotia schooner to round the Horn in that period would be achieved by Captain H.F. Sieward in the *Geneva* in 1891. It took only 108 days from Halifax to Victoria, "a passage which equals that of the best of the great California clipper ships of the 'fifties." Wallace, "B.C. Sealers Claim Revive Memories of Old Days," 19; *Victoria Daily Times,* 24 April 1888; LAC, Royal Commission to Investigate, v. 2, pt. 7, file 481; Busch, *War against the Seals,* 138.

27 *Victoria Daily Colonist,* 25 April 1888; *Victoria Daily Times,* 25 April 1888.

28 J. Gordon Smith, "The Romance of Sealing," *Canadian Magazine* 21 (1903), 393.

29 BCA, American Consulate Records, Victoria, L.W. Myers to State, 19 September 1892, A-735.

30 BCA, B.A. McKelvie, "Saga of Sealing," manuscript from the recollections of Captain Ernest F. Jordan, Add. MSS 5, 10-11. See also Parker, *Cape Breton Ships and Men,* 58, 82, and 89; Elva E. Jackson, *North Sydney, Nova Scotia: Windows on the Past* (Belleville, 1982), 39 and 46.

31 Halifax, Nova Scotia, Greg Mcdonald Private Collection, James McNeil correspondence, John McNeil to James McNeil, Victoria, 4 August 1891 and 2 October 1892; Jackson, *North Sydney,* 13, 39, and 119.

32 D'Arcy Marsh noted that the Erickson was a favourite haunt of Alex's. "London's Sea Wolf in Scot's Clothing," *Vancouver Province,* 31 May 1958, 15.

33 *North Sydney Herald,* 21 March 1888, cited in Hornsby, *Cape Breton,* 199.

34 *Marine Digest,* 4 May 1957, 22; 29 June 1957; 11 January 1958; 8 February 1958; BI, Captain John Parker Collection, MG 12, file 50.

35 Throughout the duration of the pelagic sealing industry, around 270 vessels were used; the origins are known for 225 of these vessels: California, sixty-five; Washington, forty-nine; Atlantic, forty-eight (sixteen from the American east coast and thirty-two from Nova Scotia and New Brunswick); British Columbia, thirty-two; Oregon, sixteen; Japan, eight; and Alaska, five. The median was fifty to eighty tons. *Marine Digest,* 4 May 1957, 34. The practice of Victorians purchasing eastern schooners for use in the Pacific continued until at least 1905. *Victoria Daily Colonist,* 17 October 1905.

36 LAC, Great Britain, Admiralty, Pacific Station Records, Heneage to Sir William Wiseman, captain of the *Caroline,* 22 January 1888, RG 8, series 3B, v. 25, Sailing Order no. 1.

37 Ibid., Sailing Order no. 2.

38 Canada, House of Commons, *Debates,* 25 April 1888, 973-77.

39 Paterson and Wilen, "Depletion," 90; F.W. Howay, W.H. Sage, and H.F. Angus, *British Columbia and the United States* (Toronto, 1942), 323.

40 John Herd Thompson and Stephen J. Randall, *Canada and the United States: Ambivalent Allies* (Montreal and Kingston, 1994), 62.

41 D.G. Paterson, "North Pacific Seal Hunt 1886-1910: Rights and Regulations," in W. Peter Ward and Robert A.J. McDonald, eds., *British Columbia: Historical Readings* (Vancouver, 1981), 346; LexisNexis® Academic, *La Ninfa; Whitelaw v. United States,* No. 24, 75 F. 513 (29 June 1896) (Circuit Court of Appeals, Ninth Circuit).

42 Busch, *War against the Seals,* 148.

43 "Our American East India Company," *The Argonaut* (San Francisco), 1 April 1889, clipping in LAC, Great Britain, Admiralty, Pacific Station Records.

44 *Victoria Daily Colonist,* 17 March 1888; Wright, ed., *Lewis and Dryden,* 430-32.

45 Up to March 1888, "no effective or even earnest step had been taken by the Foreign Office." John S. Ewart, *British Protection, Bering Sea Seizures* (Ottawa, 1913), 68.

46 LAC, Great Britain, Admiralty, Pacific Station Records, Heneage to Secretary, 9 June 1888, no. 119. See also Barry M. Gough, *The Royal Navy and the Northwest Coast of North America, 1810-1914* (Vancouver, 1971), 236n67.

47 Canada, Department of Marine and Fisheries, *Annual Reports,* 1889, Sessional Paper no. 8, 240.

48 LAC, Great Britain, Admiralty, Pacific Station Records, includes Baker's declaration, dated November 1889, v. 24E, with 2,491 skins. Congress, Behring Sea Claims Comission, *Record of Evidence,* v. 2, 1420, has Dan returning on 10 September 1888. Department of Marine and Fisheries, *Annual Reports,* 1889, Sessional Paper no. 8, 240. Alex stopped sealing on 19 August. Congress, Behring Sea Claims Commission, *Record of Evidence,* v. 1, 403 and 462; v. 2, 1331.

49 LAC, Great Britain, Admiralty, Pacific Station Records, v. 23-24, has the *Triumph*'s catch of 2,470 skins worth $24,700. A later declaration by E.C. Baker has the catch sold in Victoria for $14,219.75. Registered owners at the time were Baker (twenty-one shares); Walter E. Blackett (twenty-one shares); and Dan MacLean (twenty-two shares). Department of Marine and Fisheries, *Annual Reports,* 1889, Sessional Paper no. 8,240, has Alex's catch worth $33,470 and Dan's at $24,700. Brooks, "Edgar Crow Baker," thesis, 246-47.

50 It was a chattel mortgage for an additional $500. BCA, E.C. Baker Diaries, 21-22 December 1888; Brooks, "Edgar Crow Baker," thesis, 249.

51 "On the second trip he is said to have brought the largest catch of sealskins ever taken to Victoria." This was incorrect. LAC, Department of Marine and Fisheries, v. 425, file 14.
52 National Archives and Records Administration, *Rose Sparks Martinez v. United States,* United States District Court, Northern District of California, Court of Criminal Appeal, Ninth Circuit, Transcript of Record, 11 April 1927, RG 276, No. 5083, 15-17.
53 Gillis, "McLeans of Cape Breton and Scotland."
54 Ibid.; Neil MacNeil, *The Highland Heart of Nova Scotia* (Toronto, 1971), 176; BI, Joseph Lawrence MacDonald, Tape no. 326; Michael MacKenzie, *Memories Recalled* (Sydney, 1992), 2-3; A.J. MacMillan, *A West Wind to East Bay* (Antigonish, 2001), 301; Jack London, *The Sea-Wolf,* edited and introduced by John Sutherland (Oxford, 1992), 109 and 208.
55 Marcus Rediker, *Between the Devil and the Deep Blue Sea: Merchant Seamen, Pirates, and the Anglo-American Maritime World, 1700-1750* (New York, 1993), 95.
56 Noel Robinson, "The Real Sea Wolf," *Maclean's* 35 (1 January 1922), 12. See also LAC, Royal Commission to Investigate, v. 4, pt. 16, file 22; Robert D. Foulke, "Life in the Dying World of Sail, 1870-1910," *Journal of British Studies* 3, 1 (1963), 120-21.
57 Rediker, *Between the Devil and the Deep Blue Sea,* 250.
58 London, *The Sea-Wolf,* 50.
59 J.B. Moore, *A Digest of International Law* (Washington, 1906), 1, 908; Wright, ed., *Lewis and Dryden,* 432; United States, Congress, Department of the Treasury, *Seal and Salmon Fisheries and General Resources of Alaska* (Washington, 1898), v. 4, 734.
60 Paterson, "North Pacific Seal Hunt," 346; Thomas Bailey, *A Diplomatic History of the American People* (New York, 1964), 403-4.
61 Paterson, "North Pacific Seal Hunt," 346-47; Charles Campbell, "The Anglo-American Crisis in the Bering Sea, 1890-1891," *Mississippi Valley Historical Review* 48 (1961-62), 393-94; Canada, House of Commons, *Debates,* 26-27 March 1889, 811 and 871.
62 *San Francisco Coast Seamen's Journal,* 3 April 1889, 11 February 1891.
63 Baker, managing owner, had twenty-one shares of the *Triumph,* Dan had twenty-two, Rosine Gibson had eleven, and John C. Blackett had ten. United States, Senate, *Fur Seal Arbitration: Proceedings of the Tribunal of Arbitration at Paris, 1893,* 53rd Congress, 2nd session (Washington, 1895), v. 5, 422; LAC, Department of Marine and Fisheries, v. 320, file 2691, pt. 1.
64 LAC, Department of Marine and Fisheries, copy of Mr Peters and Mr Bodwell's report regarding the schooner *Triumph,* v. 320, file 2691.
65 Brooks, "Edgar Crow Baker," thesis, 210-14; Henry James Morgan, *The Canadian Men and Women of the Time* (Toronto, 1912), 51-52.
66 Congress, Behring Sea Claims Commission, *Record of Evidence,* v. 2, 1457; G.W.S. Brooks, "Edgar Crow Baker: An Entrepreneur in Early British Columbia," *BC Studies* 31 (1976), 38-40.
67 LAC, Great Britain, Admiralty, Pacific Station Records, E.C. Baker's declaration, November 1889, v. 24.
68 Congress, Behring Sea Claims Commission, *Record of Evidence,* v. 2, 1456; Brooks, "Edgar Crow Baker," thesis, 255.
69 Brooks, "Edgar Crow Baker," *BC Studies,* 39-42. Later Baker noted: "I have forgotten all about that cable business, and it is one of the things I wish to forget. I dropped about $17,000 on it, and I do not want to remember it." Congress, Behring Sea Claims Commission, *Record of Evidence,* v. 2, 1429-30.
70 BCA, E.C. Baker Diaries, 19 March 1889.
71 Brooks, "Edgar Crow Baker," thesis, 256; BCA, E.C. Baker Diaries, 23-24 March 1889.
72 Congress, Behring Sea Claims Commission, *Record of Evidence,* v. 2, 1422.
73 BCA, E.C. Baker Diaries, 25 and 28 March 1889.
74 Ibid., 26 March 1889.
75 Congress, Behring Sea Claims Commission, *Record of Evidence,* v. 2, 1426 and 1452-53.
76 "Our American East Indian Company," *The Argonaut* (San Francisco, 1 April 1889), clipping in LAC, Great Britain, Admiralty, Pacific Station Records, v. 25.
77 BCA, J. Gordon Smith, Add. MSS. 383, v. 2, 40.
78 Congress, Behring Sea Claims Commission, *Record of Evidence,* v. 2, 1453-54.

79 Busch, *War against the Seals,* 124; Doris Muscatine, *Old San Francisco: The Biography of a City* (New York, 1975), 217.
80 "Cape Breton Seal-Pirates," *Sydney Record,* 14 September 1907, reprinted from *New York Herald,* 8 September 1907. The writer was Henry Wood Elliott.
81 BCA, E.C. Baker Diaries, 9-10 April 1888.
82 Muscatine, *Old San Francisco,* 213-14 and 231, 421.
83 Congress, Behring Sea Claims Commission, *Record of Evidence,* v. 2, 1420 and 1426; LAC, Department of Marine and Fisheries, copy of Peters and Bodwell's report regarding the schooner *Triumph,* v. 320, file 2691; LAC, Great Britain, Admiralty, Pacific Station Records, declaration of Baker, November 1889, v. 24.
84 Canada, Behring Sea Claims Commission, *Argument on Behalf of Great Britain* (Ottawa, 1896), 146; Congress, Behring Sea Claims Commission, *Record of Evidence,* v. 2, 1419-27.
85 Congress, Behring Sea Claims Commission, *Record of Evidence,* v. 2, 1431 and 1453-54.
86 *Victoria Daily Colonist,* 30 July 1889.
87 Isabel S. Shepard, *The Cruise of the U.S. Steamer "Rush" in Behring Sea* (San Francisco, 1889), 113-14.
88 Congress, Behring Sea Claims Commision, *Record of Evidence,* v. 2, 1421; Behring Sea Claims Commission, *Argument on Behalf of Great Britain,* 147; the *Victoria Daily Colonist,* 30 July 1889, has thirty-three. Fredericka I. Martin, *The Hunting of the Silver Fleece* (New York, 1946), 174-75, has almost 1,000 "hidden deep in the salt bins."
89 Senate, *Fur Seal Arbitration: Proceedings,* v. 5, 342 and 345; LAC, Great Britain, Admiralty, Pacific Station Records, v. 24; *Victoria Daily Colonist,* 10 August 1889.
90 BCA, E.C. Baker Diaries, 9 May 1889; 20 and 27 June 1889; and 28-29 July 1889; Senate, *Fur Seal Arbitration: Proceedings,* v. 5, 342.
91 LAC, Great Britain, Admiralty, Pacific Station Records, Wm. Munsie et al., 29 July 1889; [enclosure] to Heneage, 30 July 1889, v. 25.
92 *Victoria Daily Colonist,* 30 July 1889.
93 BCA, E.C. Baker Diaries, 5 August 1889.
94 Baker had difficulties with some of Dan's accounts since San Francisco. On 15 April, he noted "Dan MacLean's San Francisco drafts bothering [him]." BCA, E.C. Baker Diaries, 15 April 1889 and 16-17 August 1889.
95 Behring Sea Claims Commission, *Arguments on Behalf of Great Britain,* 146; Congress, Behring Sea Claims Commission, *Record of Evidence,* v. 2, 1420.
96 By this time, Baker had twenty-one shares, Dan had twenty-two, and Blackett's had been divided between John C. Blackett (father of Walter) with ten shares and Rosina Gibson with eleven. LAC, Department of Marine and Fisheries, copy of Peters and Bodwell's report regarding the schooner *Triumph,* v. 320, file 2691.
97 Behring Sea Claims Commission, *Arguments on Behalf of Great Britain,* 148; Congress, Bering Sea Claims Commission, *Record of Evidence,* v. 2, 1431-33; BCA, E.C. Baker Diaries, 10-12 October 1889. Five years later, Captain John G. Cox, in the *Triumph,* would return to port with 4,560 skins; it was the only time that Dan's record catch in 1886 was surpassed. CVA, Herbert Lindsay Cadieux Collection, v. 243.
98 Brooks, "Edgar Crow Baker," thesis, 261-62, leaves the impression that Baker became more involved: "His involvement in sealing continued throughout the 1890s until the hearings of the Sealing Claims Court in 1897." Although Baker did prepare his own claim, and assisted in preparing others for the commission hearings, the selling of the *Triumph* and receiving Dan's outstanding mortgage on the *Mary Ellen* in the fall of 1889 seems to end Baker's involvement as a participant in the industry. Congress, Behring Sea Claims Commission *Record of Evidence,* v. 2, 1433. Mary Blackett was the wife of J.C. Blackett of Victoria, who was presently living in Oakland, California, and was born in Sydney, Cape Breton. BCA, R.H. Roy Collection.
99 Baker calculated a balance of 2,428 skins at $8 per skin and $250 for legal and other expenses. LAC, Great Britain, Admiralty, Pacific Station Records, v. 24.
100 BCA, E.C. Baker Diaries, 20 August 1889.
101 Those seized were the *Black Diamond,* the *Minnie,* the *Pathfinder,* the *James G. Swan,* the *Juanita,* and the *Lily*. Those warned included the *Triumph,* the *Ariel,* and the *Kate*. Senate,

Fur Seal Arbitration: Proceedings, v. 2, 109; Howay, Sage, and Angus, *British Columbia and the United States,* 461.

102 Shepard, *Cruise of the U.S. Steamer,* 112.

103 Wright, ed., *Lewis and Dryden,* 434. See also LAC, Great Britain, Admiralty, Pacific Station Records v. 23, enclosure 5 in no. 92.

104 Shepard, *Cruise of the U.S. Steamer,* 112-13. In 1892, Captain Mike Healy's wife accompanied him on the *Bear* cruise to the north. It was his thirteenth and her fourth trip. *San Francisco Call,* 27 April 1892, 2.

105 Wright, ed., *Lewis and Dryden,* 434; *Victoria Daily Colonist,* 30 August 1889; Robert Craig Brown, *Canada's National Policy, 1883-1900: A Study in Canadian-American Relations* (Princeton, 1964), 102; Gerald O. Williams, "Michael J. Healy and the Alaska Maritime Frontier, 1880-1902" (MA thesis, University of Oregon, 1987), 188.

106 *San Francisco Coast Seamen's Journal,* 19 February 1890.

107 Wright, ed., *Lewis and Dryden,* 434; *Victoria Daily Colonist,* 30 August 1889; Brown, *Canada's National Policy,* 102.

108 *Victoria Daily Colonist,* 28 August 1889; BCA, Victoria Sealing Company, Minute Book, Add. MSS. 16.

109 Paterson, "North Pacific Seal Hunt," 347.

110 *Halifax Morning Chronicle,* 28 August 1889.

111 Brown, who was interviewed by Kelley four decades later, gives the date as February 1891, but an internal record of evidence suggests 1889. One of the hunters, Alf Bissett, later said they departed Victoria in December 1888. F.M. Kelley, "Sealing with the Sea Wolf," *Victoria Daily Colonist;* 18 June 1933, magazine section, 1; LAC, Royal Commission to Investigate, v. 2, 1139 and 1331-32; Jackson, *North Sydney,* 39.

112 Kelley, "Sealing with the Sea Wolf." See Thomas Brown's testimony as a boat-puller in Senate, *Fur Seal Arbitration: Proceedings,* 1892, depositions, v. 3, 318-26; Jackson, *North Sydney,* 39; Busch, *War against the Seals,* 291n55. This was the era of the workingman's saloon. See Madelon Powers, *Faces along the Bar: Lore and Order in the Workingman's Saloon, 1870-1920* (Chicago, 1998), especially "Clubbing by Treat," 93-118, and "Songs and Singing," 180-206.

113 Rolf Knight, *Indians at Work: An Informal History of Native Indian Labour in British Columbia, 1858-1930* (Vancouver, 1978), 112 and 216; Shepard, *Cruise of the U.S. Steamer,* 112-13; *San Francisco Call,* 27 April 1892, 2; Leonard McCann, "Clarence Nelson Cox," *Dictionary of Canadian Biography,* v. 13 (Toronto, 1994), 228.

114 Kelley, "Sealing with the Sea Wolf"; Cecil Clark, "Victoria Was a Smuggler's Hide-Away," *Victoria Daily Colonist,* 5 April 1959, 8-9; and 15 January 1961, 8-9.

115 Kelley, "Sealing with the Sea Wolf"; Clark, "Victoria"; Don B. Marshall, *California Shipwrecks* (Seattle 1978), 119.

116 Kelley, "Sealing with the Sea Wolf."

117 They returned on the *City of Puebla* on 7 April. *Victoria Daily Colonist,* 9 April 1889, 6.

118 *Victoria Daily Colonist,* 19-20 March, 6 April 1889; Kelley, "Sealing with the Sea Wolf."

119 *Victoria Daily Colonist,* 2 April 1889; Kelley, "Sealing with the Sea Wolf."

120 Robinson, "Real Sea Wolf," 12.

121 Ibid. See also A.W. Roy, "The Life and Death of the Sea Wolf," *Atlantic Advocate* 48, 6 (1958), 79; Robert H. Nichols, "Seal Hunters of the North Pacific," in R.E. Watters, ed., *British Columbia: A Centennial Anthology* (Vancouver, 1958), 127. According to Victor Jacobson, "all our schooners carried a musician or two." N. de Bertrand Lugrin, "Epic of the Seal Hunters," *Canadian Geographical Journal* 4 (1932), 301, cited in Busch, *War against the Seals,* 134.

122 London, *The Sea-Wolf,* 143.

123 *Victoria Daily Colonist,* 10 April 1889.

124 Ibid.; T.W. Paterson, "Victoria's Own Sea Wolf," *Victoria Daily Colonist,* 25 February 1973, 10. In 1889, Alex had a white crew of about twenty-three. Congress, Behring Sea Claims Commission, *Record of Evidence,* v. 1, 403.

125 BCA, E.C. Baker Diaries, 15 April 1889.

126 Kelley, "Sealing with the Sea Wolf."

127 *Victoria Daily Colonist,* 25 April 1889.
128 Kelley, "Sealing with the Sea Wolf."
129 BCA, E.C. Baker Diaries, 3-4 May 1889.
130 Alex's signature is beside the *Mary Ellen* and the *Triumph.* LAC, Great Britain, Admiralty, Pacific Station Records, R.P. Rithet et al. to Heneage, 26 April 1889, v. 25.
131 Kelley, "Sealing with the Sea Wolf."
132 *Victoria Daily Colonist,* 17 October 1889; BCA, B.A. McKelvie, "Saga of Sealing," manuscript from the recollections of Captain Ernest F. Jordan, Add. MSS 5, 2-3.
133 Kelley, "Sealing with the Sea Wolf."
134 Ibid.
135 A total of 39,538 skins were landed at Victoria by Canadian and American sealers in 1889 and 1,800 at San Francisco. United States, Congress, *Report on the Condition of the Fur-Seal Fisheries of the Pribilof Islands in 1890,* compiled by H. Elliott (Paris, 1893), 335; *Victoria Daily Colonist,* 17 October 1889.
136 BCA, E.C. Baker Diaries, 8 October 1889.
137 *Victoria Daily Colonist,* 17 October 1889.
138 Ibid.
139 Kelley, "Sealing with the Sea Wolf"; Clark, "Victoria."
140 Wright, ed., *Lewis and Dryden,* 453-54; Jackson, *North Sydney,* 39.
141 In October 1891, for example, the *North Sydney Herald* commenced a piece prompted by Brown's visit with "half the Fleet are from this Province and they Succeed Best." *Halifax Morning Herald,* 24 October 1891, 1.
142 BCA, E.C. Baker Diaries, 8 October 1889; Murray, *Vagabond Fleet,* 173-74.
143 BCA, E.C. Baker Diaries, 23 and 25 October 1889.
144 LAC, Department of Marine and Fisheries, copy of Peters and Bodwell's report regarding the schooner *Triumph,* v. 320, file 2691.
145 In mid-August, Baker's statement on the *Mary Ellen* included a mortgage of $2,000 and interest of $440 since 27 October 1887. BCA, E.C. Baker Diaries, 14 and 19 November 1889; LAC, Department of Marine and Fisheries, copy of Peters and Bodwell's report regarding the schooner *Triumph,* v. 320, file 2691, pt. 1.
146 BCA, E.C. Baker Diaries, 18-19 October 1889.

Chapter 4: Home Port San Francisco, 1890

1 Robert O'Brien, *This Is San Francisco* (New York, 1948), 4.
2 University of San Francisco, www.usfca.edu/150years/vignette/vign8; United States, Congress, Behring Sea Claims Commission, *Record of Evidence Taken at Victoria, British Columbia by the Commissioners under the Convention of 8 February 1896, between Great Britain and the United States* (Washington, 1897), v. 1, 430.
3 Basil Lubbock, *Round the Horn before the Mast* (Glasgow, 1986), 21, 74, and 135 (the sailors in question were Steve Brodie of Yarmouth, Nova Scotia, and Charlie McDonald from Prince Edward Island). See also C.I. Hamilton, "Seamen and Crime at the Cape, ca. 1860-1880," *International Journal of Maritime History* 1, 2 (1989), 10; Ursula Jupp, ed., *Deep Sea Stories from the Thermopylae Club* (Victoria, 1986), 22-23; Bill Pickelhaupt, *Shanghaied in San Francisco* (San Francisco, 1996).
4 Herbert Asbury, *The Barbary Coast: An Informal History of the San Francisco Underworld* (New York, 1933), 49-50, 98-101, and 198-231.
5 Beaton Institute of Cape Breton Studies (BI), Cape Breton University, William "Billy Senator" MacDonald Papers, MG 12, file 88, viii.
6 Cited in Tom MacInnes, ed., *Klengenberg of the Arctic: An Autobiography* (London, 1932), 9-11 and 40-41.
7 John Burnham, *The Rim of Mystery: A Hunter's Wanderings in Unknown Siberian Asia* (New York, 1929), 23.
8 William R. Hunt, *STEF: A Biography of Vilhjalmur Stefansson, Canadian Arctic Explorer* (Vancouver, 1986), 21.
9 William R. Hunt, *Distant Justice: Policing the Alaskan Frontier* ((Norman, 1987), 24-25.

10 Robert Knuckle, *In the Line of Duty* (Burnstown, ON, 1994), 135-37; Allan Marble, *Nova Scotians at Home and Abroad* (Windsor, 1977), 256-57.

11 MacInnes, ed., *Klengenberg,* 46-47.

12 In the early 1890s, Alex and Dan operated out of an office at 11 1/2 Steuart. In 1894, Alex resided at 903 McAllister; from 1895 to 1899, he was at 1053 McAllister. *San Francisco City Directories, 1892-1903,* passim.

13 "The Liebes Company," *Jewish Bulletin,* 20 February 1981 (copy in San Francisco Public Library, Civic Center, San Francisco History Room, San Francisco); California Academy of Sciences, Anthropology Department, Liebes Collection, notes. See also the *Buyers' Manual and Business Guide* (San Francisco, 1872), 52-55; United States, Congress, Department of Foreign Relations, *Whaling and Sealing Claims against Russia,* report prepared by Herbert H.D. Peirce, Appendix 1, 1902, 57th Congress, 2nd session, Doc. 1 (Washington, 1903), 153-55; Peter R. Decker, "Jewish Merchants in San Francisco: Social Mobility on the Urban Frontier," in Moses Rischin, ed., *The Jews of the West: The Metropolitan Years* (Berkeley, 1979), 11-29; *San Francisco Chronicle,* 30 May 1920, 5; Great Register of Foreign-Born Voters in California, 1872, http://feefhs.org/fbvca/1872.html. The *San Francisco Chronicle,* 2 March 1898, 8, has Herman Liebes born in Rawicz, Prussia, in 1842.

14 LexisNexis® Academic, *H. Liebes and Co. v. Commissioner of Internal Revenue,* No. 14501, 15 B.T.A. 149 (30 January 1929) (U.S. Board of Tax Appeals); *San Francisco Chronicle,* 2 March 1898, 8; *San Francisco Examiner,* 10 September 1899, 5.

15 Elmer Green, ed., *Adventures of Carl Rydell: The Autobiography of a Seafaring Man* (London, 1924), 70-71 and 106.

16 Congress, Behring Sea Claims Commission, *Record of Evidence,* v. 1, 431-32 and 459; v. 2, 1952; Gordon Newell, ed., *The H.W. McCurdy Marine History of the Pacific Northwest* (Seattle, 1966), 31.

17 Green, ed., *Adventures of Carl Rydell,* 71.

18 United States, Senate, *Fur Seal Arbitration: Proceedings of the Tribunal of Arbitration at Paris, 1893,* 53rd Congress, 2nd session (Washington, 1895), v. 3, 427-30.

19 Congress, Behring Sea Claims Commission, *Record of Evidence,* v. 2, 1264. See also Congress, Department of Foreign Relations, *Whaling and Sealing Claims,* 104 and 120; United States, House of Representatives, Department of Commerce and Labor, *Report from Committee on Expenditures in Department of Commerce and Labor, in Relation to Fur-Seal Industry of Alaska, 31 January 1913,* report prepared by J.H. Rothermel, House Report 1425, 62nd Congress, 3rd session, 4; E.W. Wright, ed., *Lewis and Dryden's Marine History of the Pacific Northwest* (Portland, 1895), 434; Norman Hacking, "The Victoria Sealing Fleet," *The Sea Chest* (Spring 1982), 101; United States, Congress, Department of the Treasury, *Seal and Salmon Fisheries and General Resources of Alaska* (Washington, 1898), v. 4, 735.

20 Neil MacNeil, *The Highland Heart of Nova Scotia* (Toronto, 1971), 184.

21 William R. Hunt, *Arctic Passage: The Turbulent History of the Land and People of the Bering Sea, 1697-1975* (New York, 1975), 231.

22 Congress, Department of the Treasury, *Seal and Salmon Fisheries,* v. 2, 195-99; v. 4, 731-39.

23 H.J. Snow, *In Forbidden Seas: Recollections of Sea-Otter Hunting in the Kurils* (London, 1910), 264.

24 Hunt, *Arctic Passage,* 253.

25 Snow, *In Forbidden Seas,* 264.

26 *Victoria Daily Colonist,* 28 March 1890. For a sensational treatment of the general crimping scene, see Ashbury, *Barbary Coast,* 198-231; O'Brien, *This Is San Francisco,* 13-17; Pickelhaupt, *Shanghaied in San Francisco.* For Robert Henderson's experience, see Captain Henry Henderson, *Robert Henderson's Discovery of the Klondike* (Pictou County, NS, 1998), 23-24.

27 Cited in Green, ed., *Adventures of Carl Rydell,* 55 and 69-70.

28 *Victoria Daily Colonist,* 22 March 1890.

29 Ibid., 25 and 28 March 1890.

30 Ibid., 3 April 1890.

31 Ibid., 3 April 1890; Congress, Behring Sea Claims Commission, *Record of Evidence,* v. 2, 1952.

32 *San Francisco Coast Seamen's Journal,* 11 September 1889; 21 and 28 February 1894; and 6 November 1895. See also Dennis L. Noble and Truman R. Strobridge, "Early Cuttermen in Alaskan Waters," *Pacific Northwest Quarterly* 78, 3 (1987), 74-82; Basil Lubbock, *The Down Easters: American Deep-Water Sailing Ships, 1869-1929* (Glasgow, 1971), 18; Mary and Albert Cocke, "Hell Roaring Mike: A Fall from Grace in the Frozen North," *Smithsonian* 13, 11 (1983), 119-37.

33 Wright, ed., *Lewis and Dryden,* 435-36 and 427n4; *Marine Digest,* 31 August 1957, 14.

34 House of Representatives, Department of Commerce and Labor, *Report from Committee on Expenditures,* 3; Wright, ed., *Lewis and Dryden,* 436n20.

35 Green, ed., *Adventures of Carl Rydell,* 75-77 and 114. See also Charles Lillard, "Dining with a Sea Wolf," *Victoria Daily Colonist,* 11 June 1978, 12.

36 Noel Robinson, "The 'Sea Wolf': Story of a Tragic Treasure Hunt," *The Shoulder Strap* 10 (1943), 47.

37 Jack London, *The Sea-Wolf,* edited and introduced by John Sutherland (Oxford, 1992), 11; British Columbia Archives (BCA), Imbert Orchard, "Days of the Sealing Fleet: People in Landscape," interview with Jimmy Newman, Max Lohbrunner, Noel Robinson, 1970, No. 2466.

38 Congress, Behring Sea Claims Commission, *Record of Evidence,* v. 1, 404.

39 Elliott later maintained that MacLean and the *Lewis* brought 2,612 skins back to San Francisco in 1890. Henry Elliott, "Thirty Years of Japanese-Seal-Piracy in Alaskan Waters," *New York Herald,* 8 September 1907, magazine section, 5.

40 Wright, ed., *Lewis and Dryden,* 435. The same source lists 1,066 skins for the *Mary Ellen* in 1890.

41 Library and Archives Canada (LAC), Royal Commission to Investigate and Report upon Claims of Certain Canadian Pelagic Sealers, 1913-15, RG 33, series 107, v. 1, pt. 4, 639; BCA, Eva Marie Sweeney, Add. MSS. 792, v. 1, 4-5.

42 LAC, Royal Commission to Investigate, v. 1, pt. 4, 639-40; v. 3, pt. 14, 929; BCA, Eva Marie Sweeney Add. MSS. 792, v. 1, 5; Wright, ed., *Lewis and Dryden,* 435.

43 BCA, Eva Marie Sweeney, 5; LAC, Royal Commission to Investigate, v. 1, pt. 4, 217.

44 Frank H. Sloss, "Who Owned the Alaska Commercial Company?" *Pacific Northwest Quarterly* 69 (1977), 126.

45 See L.D. Kitchener, *Flag over the North: The Story of the Northern Commercial Company* (Seattle, 1954), 78-80; Briton Cooper Busch, *The War against the Seals: A History of the North American Seal Fishery* (Montreal and Kingston, 1985), 110-14; Morgan B. Sherwood, *Exploration of Alaska, 1865-1900* (New Haven, 1965), 44-49 and 89; Roland L. DeLorme, "The Alaska Commercial Company and the U.S. Customs Bureau," in *The Sea in Alaska's Past: Conference Proceedings* (Anchorage, 1974), 156-57 and 171-72; Dorothy Knee Jones, *A Century of Servitude: Pribilof Aleuts under U.S. Rule* (Washington, 1980), 35-36.

46 H. Wayne Morgan, ed., *The Gilded Age* (Syracuse, 1970); Matthew Josephson, *The Robber Barons* (New York, 1934).

47 Kitchener, *Flag over the North,* 79-80.

48 *San Francisco Coast Seamen's Journal,* 23 October 1889.

49 Snow, *In Forbidden Seas,* 264.

50 Busch, *War against the Seals,* 122-23; Sloss, "Who Owned the Alaska Commercial Company?" 127; Kitchener, *Flag over the North,* 45 and 81; Jean Rhoda, "Fur Seal in Alaskan Waters," *Overland* 62, 3 (1913), 225-32; Gerstle Mack, *Lewis and Hannah Gerstle* (New York, 1953), 41 and 56; Irene Narell, *Our City: The Jews of San Francisco* (San Diego, 1981), 90; Charles Campbell, "The Anglo-American Crisis in the Bering Sea, 1890-1891," *Mississippi Valley Historical Review* 48 (1961-62), reprinted in W. Peter Ward and Robert A.J. McDonald, eds., *British Columbia: Historical Readings* (Vancouver, 1981), 332.

51 The North American Commercial Company (NACC) submitted three of the twelve bids. The annual rental was increased to $60,000 (from $55,000) and the tax/skin to $9.625 (from $2.62). National Archives and Records Administration (NARA), Records of the U.S. Fish and Wildlife Service, RG 22, sec. 91, file 311; Mack, *Gerstle,* 56, has Isaac Liebes as president, D.O. Mills as vice-president, and Ernest A. Cox as secretary; House of Representatives, Department of Commerce and Labor, *Report from Committee on Expenditures,* v.

1, 3; Busch, *War against the Seals,* 124; A.Y. Roppel and S.P. Davey, "Evolution of Fur Seal Management on the Pribilof Islands," *Journal of Wildlife Management* 29, 3 (1965), 451. A later congressional committee identified Mills, Elkins (Senator from West Virginia), Tevis, and Herman and Isaac Liebes associated with the NACC. United States, House of Representatives, Department of Commerce and Labor, *Expenditures in Commerce Department Committee, Fur Seal Industry ... submitted by Mr. Rothermel, 4 April 1914,* House Report 500, 63d Congress, 2nd session, 7.

52 James T. Gay, "Henry W. Elliott: Crusading Conservationist," *Alaska Journal* 3 (1973), 214; Busch, *War against the Seals,* 123; *Dictionary of American Biography (DAB)* (1935), v. 15, 482-86.

53 *DAB* (1936), v. 6, 83-84; James T. Gay, "Bering Sea Controversy: Harrison, Blaine and Cronyism," *Alaska Journal* 3 (1973), 13; Campbell, "Anglo-American Crisis, 1890-1891," 320.

54 *DAB* (1936), v. 18, 384-85; *New York Times,* 13 December 1891, 1; *San Francisco Examiner,* 26 July 1899, 14.

55 *New York Times,* 13 December 1891, 1; Campbell, "Anglo-American Crisis, 1890-1891," 319-20. See also *San Francisco Examiner,* 26 July 1899, 14.

56 Busch, *War against the Seals,* 124.

57 Congress, Department of the Treasury, *Seal and Salmon Fisheries,* v. 4, 731; Peter Murray, *The Vagabond Fleet: A Chronicle of the North Pacific Sealing Schooner Trade* (Victoria, 1988), 23.

58 Congress, Department of Foreign Relations, *Whaling and Sealing Claims,* 154.

59 *New York Times,* 13 December 1891, 1; 30 January 1913, 1. See also Busch, *War against the Seals,* 124; "The Liebes Company," *Jewish Bulletin* (20 February 1981); Rudolf Glanz, "From Fur Rush to Gold Rushes: Alaskan Jewry from the Late Nineteenth to the Early Twentieth Centuries," *Western States Jewish Historical Quarterly* (January 1975), 98; California Academy of Sciences, Liebes Collection, notes.

60 Busch, *War against the Seals,* 121; Mack, *Gerstle,* 55.

61 D.O. Mills, "Our Fur-Seal Fisheries," *North American Review* 151 (1890), 301-2; Busch, *War against the Seals,* 154.

62 In the 1870-89 period, the land harvest accounted for 1,977,337 skins, while pelagic sealing acquired 277,982. From 1890 to 1909, skins from the rookeries numbered 342,300, while the pelagic total was 621,989. Busch, *War against the Seals,* 110 and 145; Jomo Tomasevich, *International Agreements on Conservation of Marine Resources with Special Reference to the North Pacific* (Stanford, 1943), 76 and 89.

63 On a relatively small investment, the NACC, over the life of the lease, received an estimated profit of 45 percent on income. Mills, "Our Fur Seal Fisheries," 304; Busch, *War against the Seals,* 110, 120-21, and 127-32.

64 Tingle was an agent from 1 July 1885 to 30 April 1889. United States, House of Representatives, Seal Islands of Alaska, *Letter from the Secretary of Commerce and Labor Transmitting in Response to House Resolution No. 73, Information Relating to Seal Islands of Alaska, 19 July 1911,* House Doc. 93, 62nd Congress, 1st session, 555; Busch, *War against the Seals,* 144, NARA, Records of the U.S. Fish and Wildlife Service, file 132; United States, Congress, *Report on the Condition of the Fur-Seal Fisheries of the Pribilof Islands in 1890,* compiled by H. Elliott (Paris, 1893), 308; House of Representatives, Department of Commerce and Labor, *Report from Committee on Expenditures,* 60.

65 House of Representatives, Department of Commerce and Labor, *Report from Committee on Expenditures,* 3.

66 According to the certificate of ownership in the collector of customs files in San Francisco, the *Lewis* was registered on 10 January 1890 with Herman Liebes as sole owner. She was transferred to H. Liebes and Company, Incorporated on 17 September 1890 and on 29 July 1891 to Max Waizman. Congress, Department of Foreign Relations, *Whaling and Sealing Claims,* 120; *San Francisco Chronicle,* 30 May 1920, 5; Busch, *War against the Seals,* 154-56.

67 Elliott was an assistant special agent on the Pribilof Islands in 1872-73. NARA, Records of the U.S. Fish and Wildlife Service, file 132; Sherwood, *Exploration of Alaska,* 46-51; Henry Elliott, "The Fur Seal Millions on the Pribilof Islands," *Harper's New Monthly Magazine* 48 (May 1874), 797, cited in B.F. Gilbert, "Economic Developments in Alaska, 1867-1910," *Journal of the West* 4 (1965), 504 at 506.

68 House of Representatives, Seal Islands of Alaska, *Response to House Resolution No. 73,* 1157-58. Campbell, "Anglo-American Crisis," 332.

69 Busch, *War against the Seals,* 119; David Starr Jordan, *The Days of a Man* (New York, 1922), 550-51.

70 House of Representatives, Seal Islands of Alaska, *Response to House Resolution No. 73,* 449-50.

71 Busch, *War against the Seals,* 120-21.

72 House of Representatives, Seal Islands of Alaska, *Response to House Resolution No. 73,* 1154-55.

73 Ibid., 449-50.

74 Ted C. Hinckley also noted that Elliott's "artistic fervor outran his reportorial veracity." *The Americanization of Alaska, 1867-1897* (Palo Alto, 1972), 112 and 184.

75 Elliott had married Alexandra Melovidov (Melovidoff) in 1872. Glenn A. Geiger, "The Saga of the Alaskan Fur Seals," *The Explorer* 17 (1975), 5 at 11. Geiger is Elliott's great-grandson.

76 Busch, *War against the Seals,* 121; Dorsey, *Conservation Diplomacy,* 108 and 119-20.

77 He had also served as an artist on the U.S. Geological Survey for Colorado, New Mexico, and Wyoming territories in 1869-71. Dorsey, *Conservation Diplomacy,* 112; "A Novel Exhibition," *San Francisco Coast Seamen's Journal,* 11 November 1891; Robert L. Shalkop, *Henry Wood Elliott, 1846-1930: A Retrospective Exhibition* (Anchorage, 1982), 9 and 15. The University of Alaska Museum in Fairbanks has seventy-three of his works.

78 Gay, "Bering Sea Controversy," 14; Campbell, "Anglo-American Crisis," 332.

79 See correspondence to Secretary of State John Foster, 23 February 1893 in NARA, Records of the U.S. Fish and Wildlife Service, file 430; Gay, "Bering Sea Controversy," 15; Busch, *War against the Seals,* 119-20. See also Campbell, "Anglo-American Crisis," 328-30.

80 Charles J. Goff was chief agent on the Pribilof Islands in 1890 and had recommended a prohibition on land killings. He was replaced in April 1891. United States, House of Representatives, Department of Commerce and Labor, *A Statement Submitted in Re the Fur-Seal Herd of Alaska to the House Committee on Expenditures in the Department of Commerce,* compiled by H.W. Elliott (Washington, 1913), 136-37; House of Representatives, Department of Commerce and Labor, *Report from Committee on Expenditures,* v. 2; Busch, *War against the Seals,* 127 and 149.

81 House of Representatives, Seal Islands of Alaska, *Response to House Resolution No. 73,* 449-51 and 1156; Paul Gibb, "Selling Out Canada? The Role of Sir Julian Pauncefote in the Bering Sea Dispute, 1889-1902," *International History Review* 24, 4 (2002), 818 and 841. Sir Julian Pauncefote would become ambassador in 1893.

82 Elliott's initial public statement was in the *New York Evening Post* on 24 April 1891. For a concise sample of Elliott's version, see House of Representatives, Department of Commerce and Labor, *A Statement Submitted in Re the Fur-Seal Herd,* 139-49. See also House of Representatives, Seal Islands of Alaska, *Response to House Resolution No. 73,* 450-53; Sherwood, *Explorations of Alaska,* 122. One Alaskan historian has suggested that Elliott's "increasingly bizarre" behaviour stemmed from his irrational response to the "land's brutal, ambivalent beauty." Hinckley, *Americanization of Alaska,* 146.

83 Campbell, "Anglo-American Crisis," 315-16; Busch, *War against the Seals,* 124 and 132; Gay, "Bering Sea Controversy," 12-19; Gay, "Henry W. Elliott," 211-16; William G. Fitzgerald, "The Romance of Seal Hunting," *Wide World Magazine* 1, 1 (1898), 4-11.

84 Campbell, "Anglo-American Crisis," 321-24; Gay, "Bering Sea Controversy," 14; "The Serious Outlook in Bering Sea," *The Nation,* 23 April 1891, 332-33.

85 Canada, Department of Marine and Fisheries, *Annual Reports,* 1891, Sessional Paper no. 8, lxxviii; Campbell, "Anglo-American Crisis," 326.

86 G.O. Williams, *The Bering Sea Fur Seal Dispute: A Monograph on the Maritime History of Alaska* (Juneau, 1984), 4, 17, 19, and 42.

87 Pelagic pelts averaged just over $14 over the 1890-1910 period. D.G. Paterson and J. Wilen, "Depletion and Diplomacy: The North Pacific Seal Hunt, 1886-1910," in P. Uselding, ed., *Research in Economic History,* vol. 2 (Greenwich, CT, 1977), 81; Busch, *War against the Seals,* 127-32; Fredericka I. Martin, *The Hunting of the Silver Fleece* (New York, 1946), 163.

88 *Counter Case of Great Britain* (Washington, 1895), 3, 264, and 499, cited in F.W. Howay, W.H. Sage, and H.F. Angus, *British Columbia and the United States* (Toronto, 1942), 320;

Robert H. Nichols, "Seal-Hunters of the North Pacific," in R.E. Watters, ed., *British Columbia: A Centennial Anthology* (Vancouver, 1958), 123. The top year for vessels was 1892, with 124. Busch, *War against the Seals,* 137.

Chapter 5: The *James Hamilton Lewis* and the Russians, 1891

1 James T. Gay, "Bering Sea Controversy: Harrison, Blaine and Cronyism," *Alaska Journal* 3 (1973), 17.

2 Gordon Ireland, "The North Pacific Fisheries," *American Journal of International Law* 36 (1942), 401-2; Gay, "Bering Sea Controversy," 18-19; G.O. Williams, *The Bering Sea Fur Seal Dispute* (Juneau, 1984), 71n42.

3 Jozo Tomasevich, *International Agreements on Conservation of Marine Resources with Special Reference to the North Pacific* (Stanford, 1943), 83. By 1892, they acquired over 14,000 seals, in 1893, 53,526 seals, and in 1894 over 71,667 seals. United States, Congress, Department of the Treasury, Commission on Fur-Seal Investigations, *The Fur Seals and Fur Seal Islands of the North Pacific Ocean,* compiled by Henry W. Elliott (Washington, 1898), v. 3, 226.

4 D.G. Paterson, "The North Pacific Seal Hunt, 1886-1910: Rights and Regulations," in W. Peter Ward and Robert A.J. McDonald, eds., *British Columbia: Historical Readings* (Vancouver, 1981), 348.

5 William G. Fitzgerald, "The Romance of Seal Hunting," *Wide World Magazine* 1, 1 (1898), 7.

6 Kurkpatrick Dorsey, *The Dawn of Conservation Diplomacy: U.S.-Canadian Wildlife Protection Treaties in the Progressive Era* (Seattle, 1998), 119-20.

7 Both Britain and the United States protested, and agreements, in which Russia was to limit her land catch to less than 30,000 annually, were signed in 1893 and 1894. Tomasevich, *International Agreements,* 86.

8 T.W. Paterson, "Victoria's Own Sea Wolf," *Victoria Daily Colonist,* 25 February 1973, 10.

9 "The Sealing Industry," *Northwestern Review,* Seattle (July-August 1891), copy in City of Victoria Archives.

10 *San Francisco Coast Seamen's Journal,* 18 February 1891.

11 United States, Congress, Department of Foreign Relations, *Whaling and Sealing Claims against Russia,* report prepared by Herbert H.D. Peirce, Appendix 1, 1902, Doc. 1, 57th Congress, 2nd session, 177-82, contains the *Lewis'* log. Joseph McDonald is incorrectly listed as mate at the start of the voyage.

12 Cox had three brothers who were also seamen on the west coast. Leonard G. McCann, "Clarence Nelson Cox," *Dictionary of Canadian Biography,* v. 13 (Toronto, 1994), 228.

13 The quoted passages combine two of Jordan's versions. B.A. McKelvie, "Victoria Mariner Tells Story of 'Sea Wolf" Alex McLean," *Vancouver Province,* 8 May 1943, magazine section, 3; BCA, B.A. McKelvie, "Saga of Sealing," manuscript from the recollections of Captain Ernest F. Jordan, Add. MSS 5, 9-10. See also E.W. Wright, ed., *Lewis and Dryden's Marine History of the Pacific Northwest* (Portland, 1895), 437-38.

14 Archie Willis, "In the Days of Sealing," *Victoria Daily Colonist,* 28 June 1970, 5.

15 Wright, ed., *Lewis and Dryden,* 437-38; Ursula Jupp, ed., *Home Port: Victoria* (Victoria, 1985), 115. The schooners were mostly two-masted, between 60 and 120 tons.

16 The two additions to the *Lewis* in early June were John Bartlett and Frank Little. Congress, Department of Foreign Relations, *Whaling and Sealing Claims,* 180-81; *Victoria Daily Colonist,* 4 October 1891.

17 National Archives and Records Administration (NARA), Pacific Sierra Region, *Stewart Norrie et al v. Schooner Edward Webster,* U.S. District Court-Northern District of California, Admiralty Case Files, 1851-1934, RG 21, Box 520, Case 10264.

18 D.O. Mills, "Our Fur-Seal Fisheries," *North American Review* 151 (1890), 305.

19 Judith Fingard, *Jack in Port: Sailortowns of Eastern Canada* (Toronto, 1982), 102.

20 Congress, Department of Foreign Relations, *Whaling and Sealing Claims,* 181.

21 *Victoria Daily Colonist,* 4 October 1891; William R. Hunt, *Arctic Passage* (New York, 1975), 249; Wright, ed., *Lewis and Dryden,* 437; NARA, *Stewart Norrie et al v. Schooner Edward Webster.*

22 Thomas Seaman, "The Adventures of 'Sea Wolf' McLean," *Victoria Daily Colonist,* 21 June 1953, magazine section, 11; Robert DeArmond, "The Men Behind the Sea Wolf," *Alaska Life* (May 1946), 40.

23 NARA, *Stewart Norrie et al. v. Schooner Edward Webster.* See also *San Francisco Coast Seamen's Journal,* 7 October 1891; *Victoria Daily Colonist,* 4 October 1891; Wright, ed., *Lewis and Dryden,* 427.

24 *San Francisco Coast Seamen's Journal,* 7 October 1891. See also *Victoria Daily Colonist,* 4 October 1891; Wright, ed., *Lewis and Dryden,* 427; NARA, *Stewart Norrie et al. v. Schooner Edward Webster.*

25 The hunters were Edward C. Moore, A. Herbert, Jake Warren, James Golightly, and Stewart Norrie. *San Francisco Coast Seamen's Journal,* 7, 21 October 1891.

26 See the deposition by Norrie in NARA, *Stewart Norrie et al. v. Schooner Edward E. Webster.*

27 *Victoria Daily Colonist,* 4 October 1891.

28 *San Francisco Chronicle,* 15 June 1905. See also Robert O'Brien, "Alex McLean, the Sea Wolf," *San Francisco Chronicle,* 25 June 1952: Neil MacNeil, *The Highland Heart of Nova Scotia* (Toronto, 1971), 185.

29 Congress, Department of Foreign Relations, *Whaling and Sealing Claims,* 204; United States, House of Representatives, Department of Commerce and Labor, *A Statement Submitted in Re the Fur-Seal Herd of Alaska to the House Committee on Expenditures in the Department of Commerce,* compiled by H.W. Elliott (Washington, 1913), 122-23.

30 Congress, Department of Foreign Relations, *Whaling and Sealing Claims,* 102 and 171.

31 The arbitrator, Mr. T.M.C. Asser, demonstrated that the schooner "never in the course of this voyage entered Russian territorial waters." Congress, Department of Foreign Relations, *Whaling and Sealing Claims,* 102, 169, and 172. The assumption here is that the log was correct.

32 Ibid., 102-4, 111-12, 120, 171-72, 176, and 187.

33 Charles Lillard, "Dining with a Sea Wolf," *Victoria Daily Colonist,* 11 June 1978, 12. Russia never argued the *Lewis* was less than five miles from land. Congress, Department of Foreign Relations, *Whaling and Sealing Claims,* 187-90, 206, and 348.

34 Congress, Department of Foreign Relations, *Whaling and Sealing Claims,* 113, 169, 187, and 194.

35 Ibid., 187.

36 Ibid., 190.

37 Ibid., 102 and 114.

38 Ibid., 169, 187, 296, 303, and 353.

39 Ibid., 169-70.

40 Ibid., 169-70, 177-79, 188, and 301.

41 Joseph McDonald moved up from second mate on 5 May. Ibid., 169-70, 177-79, 188, and 301.

42 *San Francisco Chronicle,* 15 June 1905; Robert O'Brien, "Alex McLean, the Sea Wolf," *San Francisco Chronicle,* 25 June 1952; Noel Robinson, "The Real Sea Wolf," *Maclean's* 35 (1 January 1922), 12; "A Never Old Story of the North Pacific," *Canadian Merchant Service Guide* (1923), 44-45; Thomas Seaman, "The Adventures of 'Sea Wolf' McLean," *Victoria Daily Colonist,* 21 June 1953, magazine section, 11; Cecil Clark, "'Seawolf' McLean Tweaked Russia's Beard," *Victoria Daily Colonist,* 5 April 1959, 8; Paterson, "Victoria's Own Sea Wolf," 10; Lillard, "Dining with a Sea Wolf," 12.

43 Elmer Green, ed., *Adventures of Carl Rydell: The Autobiography of a Seafaring Man* (London, 1924), 76.

44 Rudyard Kipling, "Rhyme of the Three Sealers," *Collected Verse of Rudyard Kipling* (London, 1912), 31-41. It was written in 1893. Charles Madsen maintains that Alex MacLean was one of the three sealers. Charles Madsen, with John Scott Douglas, *Arctic Trader* (New York, 1957), 13 124–32, and 185.

45 Congress, Department of Foreign Relations, *Whaling and Sealing Claims,* 170-74 and 187-88.

46 Ibid., 301; Walter A. McDougall, *Let the Sea Make a Noise: A History of the North Pacific from Magellan to MacArthur* (New York, 1993), 371.

47 "I, the undersigned, do hereby protest in behalf of the schooner *James Hamilton Lewis* and owners against the illegal seizure of said vessel, her tacking and cargo, and hunting and

fishing outfit, by the Russian man-of-war *Aleut,* the 2d day of August, 1891, upon the high seas and neutral waters of the ocean. All seal skins on board of said vessel had been killed upon said waters of the ocean with shotguns, and the pup skins on board were taken from the inside of said seal after they were taken on board of the vessel, and no seals were taken on board of the vessel for forty hours previous to the said seizure. I therefore hold the Russian man-of-war *Aleut* and her Government responsible for the detention and losses caused by the illegal seizure of said vessel and outfit and cargo. – Alexander McLean." The protest was given to the commander of the *Aleut* on 12 August 1891. Congress, Department of Foreign Relations, *Whaling and Sealing Claims,* 182.

48 The crew members were Oren Simons and A.C. Simons. Ibid., 170-74.

49 Ibid., 170-74 and 194; *San Francisco Chronicle,* 21 December 1891, 10.

50 The petition was served in November 1893. Congress, Department of Foreign Relations, *Whaling and Sealing Claims,* 103 and 171; Hunt, *Arctic Passage,* 237; *San Francisco Chronicle,* 21 December 1891, 10; Lillard, "Dining with a Sea Wolf."

51 Noel Robinson, "The Story of My Life," *Vancouver News-Advertiser,* 1 January 1913, magazine section, 7.

52 MacNeil, *Highland Heart,* 185-86.

53 Congress, Department of Foreign Relations, *Whaling and Sealing Claims,* 170 and 184.

54 *Victoria Daily Colonist,* 28 October 1891. See also Paterson, "Victoria's Own Sea Wolf."

55 *San Francisco Coast Seamen's Journal,* 4 November 1891.

56 *Halifax Morning Herald,* 3 November 1891; Gordon Newell, *Sea Rogues' Gallery* (Seattle, 1971), 4; Murray, *Vagabond Fleet,* 104.

57 The protest was also signed by Mate Joe McDonald, Oren Simons, A.C. Simons, and A.L. Donaldson and was dated 30 November 1891. Congress, Department of Foreign Relations, *Whaling and Sealing Claims,* 170-77; Robinson, "Story of My Life"; DeArmond, "Men behind the Sea Wolf," 7.

58 *Sydney Record,* 26 September 1905, citing the *Portland Oregonian.*

59 Congress, Department of Foreign Relations, *Whaling and Sealing Claims,* 173-77 and 184; United States, Congress, Behring Sea Claims Commission, *Record of Evidence Taken at Victoria, British Columbia by the Commissioners under the Convention of 8 February 1896, between Great Britain and the United States* (Washington, 1897), v. 1, 464. *San Francisco Chronicle,* 21 December 1891, 10, reported they were the first ones to go to the quarantine station, but according to Luigi F. Lucaccini, U.S. Public Health Service, it opened on 29 April 1891 and dealt with smallpox passengers from the steamship *China.* Thanks to John Soennichsen, historian, Angel Island Association.

60 Joseph McDonald, Albert Leslie Donaldson, Oren Simons, and Andrew C. Simons also signed depositions in San Francisco on 13 January 1893. Congress, Department of Foreign Relations, *Whaling and Sealing Claims,* 171-75.

61 See Congress, Department of Foreign Relations, *Whaling and Sealing Claims,* Lobanow, Ministry for Foreign Affairs, Asiatic Department, to Clifton R. Breckinbridge, Envoy, 18 May 1896, 184; United States, House of Representatives, Department of Commerce and Labor, *Report from Committee on Expenditures in Department of Commerce and Labor, In Relation to Fur-Seal Industry of Alaska, 31 January 1913,* report prepared by J.H. Rothermel, House Report 1425, 62nd Congress, 3rd session, 4.

62 Lillard, "Dining with a Sea Wolf"; Gordon Newell, ed., *The H.W. McCurdy Marine History of the Pacific Northwest* (Seattle, 1966), 248-49.

63 United States, Senate, *Fur Seal Arbitration: Proceedings of the Tribunal of Arbitration at Paris, 1893,* 53rd Congress, 2nd session (Washington, 1895), v. 3, 436-39 and 443-44.

64 Congress, Department of Foreign Relations, *Whaling and Sealing Claims,* 113-16.

65 The claim included interest at 6 percent per annum. J.B. Moore, *A Digest of International Law* (Washington, 1906), v. 1, 928.

66 Ireland, "The North Pacific Fisheries," 402; United States, Congress, Department of the Treasury, *Seal and Salmon Fisheries and General Resources of Alaska* (Washington, 1898), v. 1, 310.

67 Wright, ed., *Lewis and Dryden,* 427.

Chapter 6: The Japanese Coast and the North Pacific, 1892-95

1 Senate, *Fur Seal Arbitration: Proceedings of the Tribunal of Arbitration at Paris, 1893,* 53rd Congress, 2nd session (Washington, 1895), v. 3, 436-39 and 443-44; United States, Congress, *Fur-Seal Arbitration: The Counter Case of the United States before the Tribunal of Arbitrdtion to Convene at Paris* (Washington, 1893), 345-47.

2 Senate, *Fur Seal Arbitration: Proceedings,* v. 3, 436, 443; *San Francisco City Directory,* 1892; *Victoria City Directory,* 1892.

3 Jozo Tomasevich, *International Agreements on Conservation of Marine Resources with Special Reference to the North Pacific* (Stanford, 1943), 81-93.

4 *San Francisco Call,* 6 March 1892, 1; 16 March 1892, 1; 17 March 1892, 1; 18 March 1892, 7; 22 March 1892, 1.

5 Charles Campbell, "The Bering Sea Settlements of 1892," *Pacific Historical Review* 32 (1963), 356.

6 Ibid., 356-57. See also *San Francisco Call,* 16-17 March 1892.

7 G.O. Williams, *The Bering Sea Fur Seal Dispute: A Monograph on the Maritime History of Alaska* (Juneau, 1984), 23 and 27; Gordon Ireland, "The North Pacific Fisheries," *American Journal of International Law* 36 (1942), 402; *San Francisco Call,* 18-19 March 1892, 1; National Archives and Records Administration (NARA), Pacific Sierra Region, *Rose Sparks Martinez v. United States,* United States District Court, Northern District of California, Court of Criminal Appeal, Ninth Circuit, "Opening Brief of Plaintiff in Error," Transcript of Record, 11 April 1927, RG 276, No. 5083.

8 Cecil Clark, "Seawolf McLean Tweaked Russia's Beard," *Victoria Daily Colonist,* 5 April 1959, 8-9.

9 Leonhard Stejneger, "Fur-Seal Industry of the Commander Islands, 1897 to 1922," *Bulletin of the United States Bureau of Fisheries 1925* 41 (1927), 290. See also United States, Congress, Department of the Treasury, *Seal and Salmon Fisheries and General Resources of Alaska* (Washington, 1898), v. 4, 735.

10 D.G. Paterson, "The North Pacific Seal Hunt, 1886-1910: Rights and Regulations," in W. Peter Ward and Robert A.J. McDonald, eds., *British Columbia: Historical Readings* (Vancouver, 1981), 349-50; *Halifax Morning Herald,* 24 October 1891.

11 NARA, *Rose Sparks Martinez v. United States*; E.W. Wright, ed., *Lewis and Dryden's Marine History of the Pacific Northwest* (Portland, 1895), 428n5; United States, Congress, Behring Sea Claims Commission, *Record of Evidence Taken at Victoria, British Columbia by the Commissioners under the Convention of 8 February 1896, between Great Britain and the United States* (Washington, 1897), v. 1, 404; *San Francisco Call,* 18 March 1892, 6; NARA, *Rose Sparks Martinez v. United States;* LexisNexis® Academic, *Bird et al. v. United States and Twenty-three Other Cases,* Nos. 5067-5090 inclusive, 24 F.2d 933 (12 March 1928) (Circuit Court of Appeals, Ninth Circuit); NARA, *M.J. Lyon et al. v. United States,* No. 17543 (United States District Court, Northern District of California), RG 21.

12 Canada, House of Commons, *Debates,* 18 April 1894, 1570-74; *Halifax Morning Herald,* 24 October 1891. Williams has the *Lewis,* under Alex MacLean, captured and burned by the *Aleut* in 1891. He also has the *Lewis,* with Alex MacLean in command, captured and burned by the *Zabraka* in 1892. Williams, *Bering Sea,* 22 and 45.

13 Congress, Department of the Treasury, *Seal and Salmon Fisheries,* v. 4, 737-38; British Columbia Archives (BCA), J. Gordon Smith, Add. MSS. 383, v. 2, 37; Library and Archives Canada (LAC), Department of Marine and Fisheries, RG 23, v. 169, file 647; United States, Congress, Department of Foreign Relations, *Whaling and Sealing Claims against Russia,* report prepared by Herbert H.D. Peirce, Appendix 1, 1902, Doc. 1, 57th Congress, 2nd session, 204.

14 J. Gordon Smith, "The Romance of Sealing," *Canadian Magazine* 21 (1903), 399.

15 Robley D. Evans, *A Sailor's Log: Recollections of Forty Years of Naval Life* (New York, 1901), 355.

16 Ted C. Hinckley, *Americanization of Alaska, 1867-1897* (Palo Alto, 1972), 28; William R. Hunt, *Arctic Passage: The Turbulent History of the Land and People of the Bering Sea* (New York, 1975), 233.

17 Evans, *A Sailor's Log,* 309-10 and 315-16; Williams, *Bering Sea,* 27-28; *San Francisco Call,* 18 March 1892, 7.
18 Thomas A. Bailey, *A Diplomatic History of the American People* (New York, 1964), 421.
19 Theodore C. Hinckley, "Rustlers of the North Pacific," *Journal of the West* 2 (1963), 22.
20 NARA, *Rose Sparks Martinez v. United States,* Tracy to Evans, 25 April 1892.
21 Williams, *Bering Sea,* 40; Evans, *A Sailor's Log,* 310.
22 Williams, *Bering Sea,* 40; Evans, *A Sailor's Log,* 310-13; NARA, *Rose Sparks Martinez v. United States,* Tracy to Evans, 25 April 1892.
23 Williams, *Bering Sea,* 2-3; NARA, *Rose Sparks Martinez v. United States.*
24 Evans, *A Sailor's Log,* 316; Williams, *Bering Sea,* 29.
25 Williams, *Bering Sea,* 20-21; *San Francisco Coast Seamen's Journal,* 14 October 1891; NARA, *Rose Sparks Martinez v. United States.*
26 Evans, *A Sailor's Log,* 323.
27 Ibid., 313.
28 *La Ninfa,* Federal Reporter 75 (September-November 1896), 513-19; Evans, *A Sailor's Log,* 317-18.
29 Elmer Green, ed., *Adventures of Carl Rydell: The Autobiography of a Seafaring Man* (London, 1924), 111-12.
30 Wright, ed., *Lewis and Dryden,* 428n5; Congress, Behring Sea Claims Commission, *Record of Evidence,* v. 1, 404; *San Francisco Call,* 18 March 1892, 6; LexisNexis® Academic, *Bird et al. v. United States and Twenty-three Other Cases;* NARA, *M.J. Lyon et al. v. United States,* No. 17543.
31 Green, ed., *Adventures of Carl Rydell,* v. 1, 110-11. The fictional Larsen would not be created until more than a decade later.
32 LexisNexis® Academic, *United States v. The Coquitlam,* 57 F. 706 (18 September 1893) (District Court, District of Alaska); Dennis Noble and Truman R. Strobridge, "Early Cuttermen on Alaskan Waters," *Pacific Northwest Quarterly* 78, 3 (1987), 74-77; Evans, *A Sailor's Log,* 326-28; Williams, *Bering Sea,* 29-33.
33 Evans, *A Sailor's Log,* 328.
34 Wiliams, *Bering Sea,* 33; Evans, *A Sailor's Log,* 328 and 334-35; Hinckley, *Americanization of Alaska,* 28; Ursula Jupp, ed., *Home Port Victoria* (Victoria, 1985), 118. Wright, *Lewis and Dryden,* 438; *Declaration of Roads Seabrook Verifying Claim re: Seizure of Coquitlam* (Victoria, 1898), 4; LexisNexis® Academic, *The Coquitlam; Earle et al. v. United States,* No. 200, 77 F. 744 (16 November 1896) (Circuit Court of Appeals, Ninth Circuit).
35 Williams, *Bering Sea,* 31-33 and 55-57; LexisNexis® Academic, *Steamer Coquitlam v. United States,* No. 804, 163 U.S. 346; 41 L. Ed. 184; 16S. Ct. 1117 (18 May 1896) (United States Supreme Court); LexisNexis® Academic, *The Coquitlam; Earle et al. v. United States.*
36 LAC, Royal Commission to Investigate, series 107, v. 3, pt. 13, 350-54.
37 Evans, *A Sailor's Log,* 338-39.
38 *Victoria Daily Colonist,* 26 May 1957, in City of Vancouver Archives (CVA), Herbert Lindsay Cadieux Collection, v. 242; Green, ed., *Adventures of Carl Rydell,* 138-39.
39 Smith, "Romance of Sealing," 401; Williams, *Bering Sea,* 37.
40 Williams, *Bering Sea,* 36; BCA, J. Gordon Smith; T.W. Paterson, "Northwest Pirate," *Victoria Daily Colonist,* 19 May 1968, magazine section, 12; Smith, "Romance of Sealing," 393.
41 Williams, *Bering Sea,* 60. The author gets his facts in order at other points (see 36-37 and 41). Williams repeats his assertion regarding Hansen and Larsen in his thesis on Healy. Gerald O. Williams, "Michael J. Healy and the Alaska Maritime Frontier, 1880-1902" (MA thesis, University of Oregon, 1987), 191-92.
42 Evans, *A Sailor's Log,* 356-58, 340. The *Victoria Daily Colonist,* 29 March 1908, found that Evans' book contained "wildly exaggerated statements, the absolute falsehoods and the absurd conclusions written down by Admiral Evans regarding pelagic sealing and the part he played in endeavouring to throttle that industry." Cited in BCA, J. Gordon Smith, file 2, 60. See also Dennis L. Noble, "Fog, Reindeer, and the Bering Sea Patrol, 1867-1964," *The Sea in Alaska's Past: Proceedings* (Anchorage, 1979), 112-55.
43 Evans, *A Sailor's Log,* 329-30.

44 Wright, *Lewis and Dryden,* 427.
45 *Victoria Daily Colonist,* 20 September 1907.
46 NARA, *Rose Sparks Martinez v. United States.*
47 Robert O'Brien, "Alex McLean, the Sea Wolf," *San Francisco Chronicle,* 25 June 1952; Congress, Behring Sea Claims Commission, *Record of Evidence,* v. 1, 404.
48 LexisNexis® Academic, *Bird et al. v. United States and Twenty-three Other Cases;* Congress, *Fur-Seal Arbitration: The Counter Case of the United States,* 356; Tomasevich, *International Agreements,* 67n2.
49 C.I. Hamilton, "Seamen and Crime at the Cape, ca. 1860-1880," *International Journal of Maritime History* 1, 2 (1989), 18-19; Robert Foulke, "Life in the Dying World of Sail, 1870-1910," *Journal of British Studies* 3, 1 (1963), 124-25.
50 Otha Donner Wearin, *Johnny Heinold's First and Last Chance* (no publisher, 1974), 32-33.
51 Basil Lubbock, *Round the Horn Before the Mast* (Glasgow, 1986), 34. See also Hamilton, "Seamen and Crime at the Cape," 1-35.
52 Russ Kingman, *A Pictorial Life of Jack London* (New York, 1979), 41-42.
53 Henry E. Huntington Library, Franklyn Walker Collection, Franklyn Walker, "Jack London: Bibliography," v. 2, 16-17.
54 Wright, *Lewis and Dryden,* 441.
55 Henry E. Huntington Library, Franklyn Walker Collection, vol. 2, 16; Jack London to Roscoe Eames, 11 December 1906, cited in King Hendricks and Irving Shepard, eds., *Letters from Jack London* (New York, 1965), 231.
56 Henry E. Huntington Library, Franklyn Walker Collection, vol. 2, 16-17; Jack London to Roscoe Eames, 11 December 1906, cited in Hendricks and Shepard, eds., *Letters from Jack London,* 231. All references to the novel refer to the Oxford University Press edition in the World's Classics series edited by John Sutherland (Oxford, 1992), 50 and appendix 1, 332-42. In "Chris Farrington: Able Seaman," *Youth's Companion* (23 May 1900), London had an unnamed Nova Scotia man on the sealer *Sophia Sutherland.* Earle Labor, Robert C. Leitz, III, and I. Milo Shepard, eds., *The Complete Short Stories of Jack London* (Stanford, 1993), 3 and 549-55.
57 Charmian London, *The Book of Jack London* (New York, 1921), v. 1, 125.
58 Jack London, "The Run Across," *The High School Ægis,* 2 December 1895, reprinted in James Sissons III, ed., *Jack London's Articles and Short Stories in the Ægis* (Oakland, 1981), 55-58.
59 *New York Times,* 15 January 1893. See also Clarise Stasz, *Jack London's Women* (Amherst, 2001), 29.
60 O'Brien, "Alex McLean, the Sea-Wolf."
61 Kingman, *Pictorial Life,* 45; Jack London, *John Barleycorn* (Santa Cruz, 1981), 146-58.
62 London, *Barleycorn,* 150.
63 NARA, *M.J. Lyon et al. v. United States,* No. 17543, Doc. 16, 74; Jack London, "Bonin Islands: An Incident of the Sealing Fleet of '93," 18 January and 1 February 1895, reprinted in Sissons, ed., *Articles and Short Stories in the Ægis,* 1-10.
64 Rydell remembered being captain that year, but court records indicate he was first mate, with Carl Sorenson in charge of the vessel. Edward Green, ed., *Captain Carl Rydell: On Pacific Frontiers: A Story of Life at Sea and in Outlying Possessions of the United States* (Chicago, 1926), 31 and 77.
65 Jack London, "Story of a Typhoon Off the Coast of Japan," *San Francisco Call,* 11 November 1893; Labor, Leitz, and Shepard, eds., *The Complete Short Stories of Jack London,* v. 1, 1-5.
66 NARA, *M.J. Lyon et al. v. United States,* No. 17540, Doc. 18, Assignment of Errors, 24. See also *San Francisco Examiner,* 15 June 1905; Jack London to *New York Times,* 18 August 1905: "There was no Wolf Larsen aboard 'the Sophie' but there was real action upon which narrative imagination would work." Franklin Walker, *Jack London and the Klondike* (San Marino, 1966), 26; London, *Barleycorn,* 159-61. Foulke, "Life in the Dying World of Sail," 111.
67 *San Francisco Examiner,* 15 June 1905.
68 *Marine Digest,* 8 May 1971, 20; Wright, *Lewis and Dryden,* 442; Congress, Behring Sea Claims Commission, *Record of Evidence,* v. 1, 404; NARA, *M.J. Lyon et al. v. United States,* No. 17543.
69 Jack London, *The Sea-Wolf,* 94. Twenty years later, London had Dan instead of Alex on the *Alexander.* Henry E. Huntington Library, San Marino, CA, Jack London Collection, London to Emma MacLean, 12 December 1914.

70 United States, House of Representatives, Department of Commerce and Labor, *A Statement Submitted in Re the Fur-Seal Herd of Alaska to the House Committee on Expenditures in the Department of Commerce,* compiled by H.W. Elliott (Washington, 1913), 204; Great Register of Foreign-Born Voters in California, 1872, No. 33518; NARA, *M.J. Lyon et al. v. United States,* No. 17540, Doc. 18; LexisNexis® Academic, *H. Liebes & Co. v. Commissioner of Internal Revenue,* Docket no. 68231, 34 B.T.A. 677 (5 June 1936) (United States Board of Tax Appeals); NARA, *M.J. Lyon et al. v. United States,* No. 17543, Doc. 19, 31-34; *San Francisco Call,* 28 May 1894.
71 *New York Times,* 15 January 1893; Wright, eds., *Lewis and Dryden,* 140 and 161; Gordon Newell, ed., *The H.W. McCurdy Marine History of the Pacific Northwest* (Seattle, 1966), 128.
72 NARA, *M.J. Lyon et al. v. United States,* No. 17543, Doc. 19, 13.
73 Ibid., 19-20.
74 Ibid., 29, 43, and 66-72.
75 Ibid., Reporter's Transcript, 42-45.
76 Williams, *Bering Sea,* 4, 34, and 44-47; Evans, *A Sailor's Log,* 327 and 353.
77 Clark, "'Seawolf' McLean;" D'Arcy Marsh, "London's 'Sea Wolf' in Scot's Clothing," *Vancouver Province,* 31 May 1958, 15.
78 Thomas Seaman, "The Adventures of 'Sea Wolf' McLean," *Victoria Daily Colonist,* 21 June 1953, magazine section, 11.
79 Tom MacInnes, *Klegenberg of the Arctic: An Autobiography* (London, 1932), 46-47.
80 Ronald Gillis, "The McLeans of Cape Breton and Scotland," *Sydney Post-Record,* 17 November 1937, 4. In 1937, Gillis wrote to the American assistant secretary of the navy asking if there was any record of MacLean firing on the revenue cutter *Mohican.* That department, in true bureaucratic fashion, passed it on to the coast guard. The response from the latter was that there was no record of a vessel with the name operating by the Revenue Cutter Service in that period. Gillis had phrased it incorrectly. The coast guard and the navy were separate entities. The USS *Mohican* was a sloop of war in the US navy, first commissioned in 1885 and finally decommissioned in 1921. Beaton Institute of Cape Breton Studies, Cape Breton University, Ronald Gillis Papers, W.N. Derby, Commander, United States Coast Guard, Washington, to Ronald Gillis, 1 April 1937, MG 12, file 87. See also *Dictionary of American Naval Fighting Ships,* www.history.navy.mil/danfs/m13/mohican-ii.htm.
81 *San Francisco Call,* 28 May 1894.
82 NARA, *M.J. Lyon et al. v. United States,* No. 17543, Doc. 19, 45-47; and Reporter's Transcript, 42-45.
83 *San Francisco Call,* 28 May 1894 and 2 November 1895.
84 *Portland Oregonian,* cited in *Sydney Record,* 26 September 1905.
85 Williams, *Bering Sea,* 34; Noble, "Fog, Reindeer, and the Bering Sea Patrol, 1867-1964," in *The Sea in Alaska's Past* (Anchorage, 1979), 113-14.
86 Williams, *Bering Sea,* 45 and 77nn119-20.
87 *Victoria Daily Colonist,* 20 September 1907; Peter Murray, *The Vagabond Fleet: A Chronicle of the North Pacific Sealing Schooner Trade* (Victoria, 1988), 103.
88 *New York Times,* 18 August 1893, citing a dispatch from Port Townsend.
89 Wright, ed., *Lewis and Dryden,* 440-41; Smith, "The Romance of Sealing," 399. NARA, *M.J. Lyon et al. v. United States,* No. 17540, Doc. 18, Assignment of Errors, 24; *New York Times,* 2 April 1894. As for rookery raids, "in the ten years of the greatest activity of the pelagic sealers not more than four such attempts were made." John J. Underwood, *Alaska: An Empire in the Making* (London, 1913), 264.
90 Wright, ed., *Lewis and Dryden,* 441-42; NARA, *M.J. Lyon et al. v. United States,* No. 17543, Reporter's Transcript, 16-18.
91 LAC, Department of Marine and Fisheries, Collector of Customs, San Francisco to Wm. Smith, Deputy Minister of Marine and Fisheries, Ottawa, 29 March 1894, RG 23, v. 198, file 926, pt. 1; NARA, *M.J. Lyon et al. v. United States,* No. 17540, Doc. 18, Assignment of Errors, 13.
92 The skins were bringing $15 each. LAC, Department of Marine and Fisheries, Collector of Customs, San Francisco to Wm. Smith, Deputy Minister of Marine and Fisheries, Ottawa, 29 March 1894, v.198, file 926, p. 1.; Wright, ed., *Lewis and Dryden,* 442 and 427n4.

93 George Nidever, a hunter on the *Webster* in 1893, later mentioned that Dan's nephew was lost. NARA, *M.J. Lyon et al. v. United States,* No. 17543, Doc. 19, 72-76.
94 *San Francisco Call,* 28 May 1894; Green, ed., *Adventures of Carl Rydell,* 113.
95 *Marine Digest,* 8 May 1971, 20; Wright, ed., *Lewis and Dryden,* 442; Congress, Behring Sea Claims Commission, *Record of Evidence,* v. 1, 404, 432, and 467.
96 Stejneger, "Fur-Seal Industry of the Commander Islands," 291 and 301; Walker, *Jack London and the Klondike,* 26.
97 Kurkpatrick Dorsey, *The Dawn of Conservation Diplomacy: U.S.-Canadian Wildlife Protection Treaties in the Progressive Era* (Seattle, 1998), 121-22.
98 Right Honourable Viscount Alverstone, *Recollections of Bar and Bench* (London, 1914), 229; LAC, Department of Marine and Fisheries, v. 830; United States, House of Representatives, Seal Islands of Alaska, *Letter from the Secretary of Commerce and Labor Transmitting in Response to House Resolution No. 73, Information Relating to Seal Islands of Alaska, 19 July 1911,* House Doc. 93, 62nd Congress, 1st session, 383; A.Y. Roppel and S.P. Davey, "Evolution of Fur Seal Management on the Pribilof Islands," *Journal of Wildlife Management* 29, 3 (1965), 455.
99 *New York Times,* 17-18 August 1893; Roppel and Davey, "Evolution of Fur Seal Management," 455. From 1894, "Indian hunters were employed on a much more extensive scale than white hunters," and the practice became more profitable. D.G. Paterson and J. Wilen, "Depletion and Diplomacy: The North Pacific Seal Hunt, 1886-1910," in P. Uselding, ed., *Research in Economic History,* vol. 2 (Greenwich, CT, 1977), 113-15; House of Representatives, Seal Islands of Alaska, *Response to House Resolution No. 73,* 857-58; Tomasevich, *International Agreements,* 86-87; Dorsey, *Conservation Diplomacy,* 125.
100 Dorsey, *Conservation Diplomacy,* 108.
101 *New York Times,* 18 August 1893 and 23 July 1897; LexisNexis® Academic, *US v. NACC; NACC v. US,* No. 431, 74 F. 145 (27 April 1896) (United States Supreme Court).
102 *New York Times,* 1 April 1894; Clark, "Seawolf McLean."
103 Wright, *Lewis and Dryden,* 445; Paterson, "North Pacific," 350; Paterson and Wilen, "Depletion," 91-93.
104 LAC, Department of Marine and Fisheries, Collector of Customs, San Francisco to Wm. Smith, Deputy Minister of Marine and Fisheries, Ottawa, 29 March 1894, v. 198, file 926, pt. 1. File is incorrectly labelled "E.D. Webster." Department of the Treasury, *Seals and Salmon Fisheries,* 522; LAC, Department of Marine and Fisheries, Milne to Wm. Smith, 17 January 1894, v. 114, file 117.
105 LAC, Department of Marine and Fisheries, Sherwood to Peters, 18 January 1897, v. 237, file 1433, enclosure 1; Congress, Bering Sea Claims Commission, *Record of Evidence,* v. 1, 467; *San Francisco Call,* 28 May 1894; Congress, Department of Foreign Relations, *Whaling and Sealing Claims,* 204.
106 Congress, Behring Sea Claims Commission, *Record of Evidence,* v. 1, 452-55.
107 *San Francisco Call,* 28 May 1894.
108 W.G. Emery, "Hunting the Fur Seal," *Outing* 31 (1898), 537-48.
109 Tina Loo, "Of Moose and Men: Hunting for Masculinities in British Columbia, 1880-1939," *Western Historical Quarterly* 32, 3 (2001), 296.
110 Amy Kaplan, "Romancing the Empire: The Embodiment of American Masculinity in the Popular Novels of the 1890s," *American Literary History* 2, 4 (1990), 664.
111 Frank Luther Mott, *A History of American Magazines, IV 1885-1905* (Cambridge, 1957), 636.
112 Emery, "Hunting the Fur Seal," 537-48. See also LexisNexis® Academic, *U.S. v. Louis Olsen,* No. 4004, 74 F. 246 (28 April 1896) (District Court, District of Oregon); LexisNexis® Academic, *NACC v. U.S.,* No. 337, 81 F. 748 (7 June 1897) (Circuit Court of Appeals, Ninth Circuit); NARA, *Martinez v. U.S.,* No. 5083, Transcript of Record, RG 276, 48; Green, ed., *Captain Carl Rydell,* 35-36; Jack London, *The Sea-Wolf,* edited and introduced by John Sutherland (Oxford: Penguin, 1992), 155, 190, and 209.
113 Clark, "Seawolf McLean." See also J.E. Hoare, *Japan's Treaty Ports and Foreign Settlements: The Uninvited Guests, 1859-1899* (Folkestone, 1994), 18-21; Paterson and Wilen, "Depletion," 105; Clark, "Seawolf McLean"; Green, ed., *Captain Carl Rydell,* 133.
114 Congress, Behring Sea Claims Commission, *Record of Evidence,* v. 1, 462.
115 Clark, "Seawolf McLean."

116 *San Francisco Call,* 28 May 1894: "There never was a time when there wasn't trouble when you and that brother of yours got together, and I'll lay twenty to one on that." London, *The Sea-Wolf,* 197.
117 *San Francisco Call,* 28 May 1894.
118 Wright, ed., *Lewis and Dryden,* 428n5.
119 *San Francisco Call,* 28 May 1894 and 2 November 1895.
120 Wright, ed., *Lewis and Dryden,* 427n4.
121 Williams, *Bering Sea,* 50-51 and 78nn146-47; James Thomas Gay, *American Fur Seal Diplomacy: The Alaska Fur Seal Controversy* (New York, 1987), 98-99; Henry W. Elliott, "The Loot and Ruin of the Fur-Seal Herd of Alaska," *North American Review* 185 (1907), 431.
122 *San Francisco Coast Seamen's Journal,* 9 October 1895.
123 According to the *San Francisco Call,* 2 November 1895, "as the catch was a fairly good one." See also Congress, Department of the Treasury, *Seal and Salmon Fisheries,* v. 4, 528; CVA, Herbert Lindsay Cadieux Collection, v. 242; Congress, Behring Sea Claims Commission *Record of Evidence,* v. 1, 404; *Marine Digest,* 7 September 1957, 19; Department of the Treasury, *Fur-Seals and Fur Seal Islands,* v. 3, 228.
124 LAC, Department of Marine and Fisheries, Viscount Gough to Marquess of Salisbury, 5 September 1895, v. 301, file 2346.
125 Two victims, Jack Hayden and John McCloskey, were identified. *San Francisco Coast Seamen's Journal,* 9 and 16 October 1895.
126 *San Francisco Call,* 2 November 1895: "All hands went over the side, and there I was, marooned on my own vessel. It was Death's turn, and it's all in the family anyway." London, *The Sea-Wolf,* 275.
127 *Victoria Daily Colonist,* 9 January 1897; *New York Times,* 31 October 1897, 13. See also *San Francisco Call,* 2 March 1898, 7; *San Francisco Chronicle,* 2 March 1898, 8.
128 Green, ed., *Adventures of Carl Rydell,* 133 and 156-61; *New York Times,* 31 October 1897, 13; *San Francisco Chronicle,* 30 May 1920.
129 Charges included sealing in a closed season within a prohibited area, killing without a licence, and using firearms. LAC, Department of Marine and Fisheries, Viscount Gough to Marquess of Salisbury, enclosure, 5 September 1895, v. 301, file 2346.

Chapter 7: The Bering Sea Claims Commission Hearings and Percy Sherwood, 1896

1 Library and Archives Canada (LAC), Department of Marine and Fisheries, RG 23, v. 152, file 425, pt. 9, contains House Report 3206, 54th Congress, 1st session, Report no. 451.
2 F.W. Howay, W.H. Sage, and H.F. Angus, *British Columbia and the United States* (Toronto, 1942), 328.
3 United States, Congress, Department of Foreign Relations, *Whaling and Sealing Claims against Russia,* report prepared by Herbert H.D. Peirce, Appendix 1, 1902, Doc. 1, 57th Congress, 2nd session, 189-97.
4 United States, Congress, Behring Sea Claims Commission, *Record of Evidence Taken at Victoria, British Columbia by the Commissioners under the Convention of 8 February 1896, between Great Britain and the United States* (Washington, 1897), v. 2, 1073-74.
5 Congress, Behring Sea Claims Commission, *Record of Evidence,* v. 1, 419; *Victoria Daily Colonist,* 27 August 1905; T.W. Paterson, "Victoria's Own Sea Wolf," *Victoria Daily Colonist,* 25 February 1973, 10.
6 Halifax, NS, Greg McDonald Private Collection, James McNeil correspondence, John McNeil, Esquimalt, to James McNeil, Cape Breton, 2 December 1896.
7 Margaret Reiman to writer, 15 July 1988 [copy on file with author]. The Gaelic translation was by James Watson, Macintyre Road, Queensville, Cape Breton.
8 Patricia E. Roy, *A White Man's Province: British Columbia Politicians and Chinese and Japanese Immigrants, 1858-1914* (Vancouver, 1989), 199.
9 Tom MacInnes, *Chinook Days* (Vancouver, 1926), 150.
10 Tom MacInnes, *Klengenberg of the Arctic: An Autobiography* (London, 1932), 9-10; *Victoria Daily Colonist,* 20 January 1897.
11 Charles G.D. Roberts and Arthur Tunnell, eds., *A Standard Dictionary of Canadian Biography* (Toronto, 1924), v. 1, 343-46.

12 MacInnes, *Chinook Days,* 149-58.

13 Ibid. MacLean testified in 1911 that he had never been in the South Sea islands prior to 1897. New York Supreme Court Archives, *Nels P. Sorensen v. Sun Printing and Publishing Association,* 1911, MacLean testimony, 90. According to Charles Lillard, "the French government wanted him for piracy (poaching their oyster beds for pearls) and various acts, possibly including murder, in the South Pacific." *Seven Shillings a Year: The History of Vancouver Island* (Ganges, 1986), 177-78.

14 LAC, Department of Marine and Fisheries, Davies to Beique, 29 September 1896, v. 237, file 1433, pt. 2 and pt. 3; and L.H. Davies to F. Gourdeau, n.d., v. 152, file 425, 9; LAC, Sir Arthur Percy Sherwood Papers, MG 29/C/103, 1; G.W.S. Brooks, "Edgar Crow Baker: An Entrepreneur in Early British Columbia," *BC Studies* 31 (1976), 32-33n17.

15 LAC, Department of Marine and Fisheries, v. 237, file 1433, pt. 3.

16 British Columbia Archives (BCA), E.C. Baker Diary, 2 January-2 February 1897, Add. MSS. 707, passim; Brooks, "Edgar Crow Baker," *BC Studies,* 32-33n17.

17 LAC, Sir Arthur Percy Sherwood Papers, Acting Deputy Minister of Marine and Fisheries to Sherwood, 10 August 1894, 1; LAC, Department of Marine and Fisheries, Sherwood to Fred Peters, 25 December 1896, v. 237, file 1433; *Who's Who and Why, 1914* (Toronto, n.d.), 842-43.

18 LAC, Dominion Police Records, Sherwood to S. Carpenter, 10 December 1896, letterbooks, RG 18/E, 3101.

19 LAC, Department of Marine and Fisheries, Sherwood to Peters, 16 December 1896; 26 January 1897, v. 237, file 1433.

20 *Victoria Daily Colonist,* 8 December 1896.

21 Congress, Behring Sea Claims Commission, *Record of Evidence,* v. 2, 1077. The dates were 11, 12, 14 December 1896 and 2, 7, 8, 28, 30 January and 1 February 1897.

22 Congress, Behring Sea Claims Commission, *Record of Evidence,* v. 1, 398-468; *Victoria Daily Colonist,* 12 December 1896.

23 United States, Senate, *Report from Committee on Foreign Relations: Favoring S. 2286, to Confer Jurisdiction upon Circuit Court of United States for 9th Circuit to Determine in Equity Rights of American Citizens under Award of Bering Sea Arbitration of Paris, 21 February 1906,* Senate Report 1201, 59th Congress, 1st session, 3. See also United States, Senate, *Unlawful Seizure of Vessels in Bering Sea, 28 March 1906,* Senate Report 2674, 59th Congress, 1st session, 3.

24 Congress, Behring Sea Claims Commission, *Record of Evidence,* v. 1, 400, 403-6, 414, 419, and 427-30.

25 Ibid., v. 1, 431 and 463-64; *Victoria Daily Colonist,* 13 and 15 December 1896.

26 Congress, Behring Sea Claims Commission, *Record of Evidence,* v. 1, 445-46; v. 2, 1076-77.

27 Ibid., v. 1, 398-468 and 1075; v. 2, 1417-20; *Victoria Daily Times,* 25 January 1910; *Victoria Daily Colonist,* 24 December 1896.

28 LAC, Department of Marine and Fisheries, L.H. Davies to F. Gourdeau, n.d.; and Sherwood to Peters, 25 December 1896, v. 237, file 1433, pt. 3; Congress, Behring Sea Claims Commission, *Record of Evidence,* v. 1, 1076-77.

29 LAC, Department of Marine and Fisheries, Sherwood to O.C. Bass, 26 December 1896; and Sherwood to Peters, 19 January 1897, v. 237, file 1433.

30 LAC, Department of Marine and Fisheries, Sherwood to Peters, 19 January 1897; Sherwood to Bass, 31 December 1896; and Sherwood to Bass, 4 January 1897, v. 237, file 1433. See also LAC, Sir Arthur Percy Sherwood Papers, Letterbooks.

31 LAC, Department of Marine and Fisheries, Sherwood to Bass, 9 January 1897, v. 237, file 1433. On the braggart point, Noel Robinson, who became acquainted with him during his final years in Vancouver, disagreed: "The curious thing about Captain McLean is that in ordinary conversation he is a rather quiet, restrained type of man, not given to talking about himself and his exploits, or to drawing the long bow, but rather the reverse." Noel Robinson, "The 'Sea Wolf': Story of a Tragic Treasure Hunt," *The Shoulder Strap* 10 (1943), 49.

32 LAC, Department of Marine and Fisheries, Sherwood to Bass, 11 January 1897, v. 237, file 1433.

33 Noel Robinson, "The Real Sea Wolf," *Maclean's* 35 (1 January 1922), 12. Sherwood was forty-two at the time; Alex was thirty-eight.

34 Congress, Behring Sea Claims Commission, *Record of Evidence,* v. 2, 1417-20.
35 LAC, Department of Marine and Fisheries, enclosure 1, memo, v. 237, file 1433; Congress, Department of Foreign Relations, *Whaling and Sealing Claims,* 205-7.
36 United States, House of Representatives, Department of Commerce and Labor, *A Statement Submitted in Re the Fur-Seal Herd of Alaska to the House Committee on Expenditures in the Department of Commerce,* compiled by H.W. Elliott (Washington, 1913), 119.
37 LAC, Department of Marine and Fisheries, Sherwood to Peters, 17 and 19 January 1897, v. 237, file 1433; E.W. Wright, ed., *Lewis and Dryden's Marine History of the Pacific Northwest* (Portland, 1895), 436n20; Robert N. DeArmond, "The Men behind the Sea Wolf," *Alaska Life* (May 1946), 44; Basil Lubbock, *The Down Easters: American Deep-Water Sailing Ships, 1869-1929* (Glasgow, 1971), 227-28; Archie Willis, "In the Days of Sealing," *Victoria Daily Colonist,* 28 June 1970.
38 G.O. Williams, *The Bering Sea Fur Seal Dispute: A Monograph on the Maritime History of Alaska* (Juneau, 1984), 22.
39 LAC, Department of Marine and Fisheries, Sherwood to Peters, 18 January 1897; memo, n.d.; Sherwood to Peters, 19 January 1897, v. 237, file 1433, enclosure 1; LAC, Sir Arthur Percy Sherwood Papers, Sherwood to Peters, [?] January 1897.
40 *Victoria Daily Colonist,* 6 April 1889; LAC, Department of Marine and Fisheries, memo, n.d., v. 237, file 1433, enclosure 1; *San Francisco Coast Seamen's Journal,* 16 October 1895.
41 LAC, Department of Marine and Fisheries, Sherwood to Peters, 15 January 1897, v. 237, file 1433.
42 LAC, Department of Marine and Fisheries, Sherwood to Peters, 16 January 1897; Sherwood to Bass, 16 January 1897; and Sherwood to Peters, 17 January 1897, v. 237, file 1433; LAC, Sir Arthur Percy Sherwood Papers, Sherwood to Newcombe, 19 January 1897.
43 LAC, Department of Marine and Fisheries, Sherwood to Peters, 17 and 19 January 1897, v. 237, file 1433, enclosure 1, memo. In the same note, one detects a bit of testiness: "What's the matter with acknowledging my reports. I don't know if you get them all."
44 "As expected McLean and Scott left for there [Victoria] last night, both were very drunk when they boarded the train." LAC, Department of Marine and Fisheries, Sherwood to Bass, 19 and 26 January 1897; memo, Sherwood to Peters, 17 and 19 January 1897, v. 237, file 1433, enclosure 1.
45 *Victoria Daily Colonist,* 23 January 1897.
46 *Victoria Daily Times,* 22 January 1897; *Victoria Daily Colonist,* 23 January 1897.
47 LAC, Department of Marine and Fisheries, Sherwood to Bass, 26 January 1897; Sherwood to Peters, 26 January 1897, v. 237, file 1433, enclosure 1.
48 Dan MacLean, it was noted, was naturalized as an American in 1882 but re-naturalized as a British subject in 1887. He also gave legal depositions as an American in 1892. Congress, Bering Sea Claims Commission, *Record of Evidence,* v. 2, 1987-89; Canada, Behring Sea Claims Commission, *Arguments on Behalf of Great Britain* (Ottawa, 1896), 147.
49 *Victoria Daily Colonist,* 2 February 1897.
50 *San Francisco Examiner,* 16 June 1905.
51 *Victoria Daily Colonist,* 20 June 1905.
52 United States, Senate, *Report from Committee on Foreign Relations, on S. 390, to Confer Jurisdiction upon Circuit Court of United States for 9th Circuit to Determine in Equity Rights of American Citizens under Award of Bering Sea Arbitration of Paris; with Views of Minority, 29 January 1908,* report prepared by J.B. McCreary, Senate Report 140, 60th Congress, 1st session, 29 January 1908, 2.
53 LAC, Sir Arthur Percy Sherwood Papers, Sherwood to Donald Ross, San Francisco, 9 March 1897.
54 Senate, *Report from Committee on Foreign Relations, on S. 390,* 3.
55 Ibid., 5-6; *Victoria Daily Times,* 25 January 1910, 20.
56 *Victoria Daily Colonist,* 20 September 1907.
57 Ibid., 2 February 1897.
58 LAC, Department of Marine and Fisheries, Sherwood to Peters, 26 January 1897, v. 237, file 1433, enclosure 1; LAC, Sir Arthur Percy Sherwood Papers, Sherwood to Ross, 23 February 1897 and 9 March 1897.

59 LAC, Sir Arthur Percy Sherwood Papers, F. Peters, F.L. Beique, E.V. Bodwell to L.H. Davies, 30 March 1897, 1.

60 C.H. Tupper, "Crocodile Tears and Fur Seals," *National Review* 28 (1896-97), 88.

Chapter 8: The South Pacific Expedition, 1897-98

1 Douglas Fetherling, *The Gold Crusades: A Social History of Gold Rushes, 1849-1929* (Toronto, 1997), 124 and 136.

2 L.H. Carlson, "The Discovery of Gold at Nome, Alaska," in Morgan B. Sherwood, ed., *Alaska and Its History* (Seattle, 1967), 354-55. See also Morris Zaslow, *The Opening of the Canadian North, 1870-1914* (Toronto, 1971), 103; Richard J. Friesen, *The Chilkoot Pass and the Great Gold Rush of 1898* (Ottawa, 1981), 32-33; Pierre Berton, *The Klondike Quest: A Photographic Essay, 1897-1899* (Toronto, 1983), 9-10; David Neufeld and Frank Norris, *Chilkoot Trail: Heritage Route to the Klondike* (Whitehorse, 1996), 50; Fetherling, *Gold Crusades,* 124 and 136. A frequently cited estimate has 100,000 setting out for the gold fields, 40,000 reaching Dawson City, and 20,000 actually searching for it. About 4,000 discovered gold, 300 of them finding enough to be considered rich, and fifty managing to keep their wealth. See Klondike Gold Rush National Historical Park, http://www.nps.gov/archive/kigo/history.htm.

3 While thirty-seven schooners cleared from Victoria in 1900, good crews could only be obtained for thirty vessels. Library and Archives Canada (LAC), Department of Marine and Fisheries, Pelagic Fleet 1900, RG 23, v. 262, file 1750. "Klondicitis" was coined by the governor of Alaska, John G. Brady, to describe the universal desire to go to the gold fields. L.H. Carlson, "The Discovery of Gold at Nome," 355n5.

4 *Victoria Daily Colonist,* 6 November 1908, 9 October 1910, and 22 August 1976; *San Francisco Coast Seamen's Journal,* 14 February 1894; Ursula Jupp, ed., *Home Port Victoria* (Victoria, 1985), 137-54; J.C. Voss, *Venturesome Voyages* (London, 1989), 17-56; *Seattle Post-Intelligencer,* 17 September 1905, 3; "Finding Pirate Gold on the Real Treasure Island," *San Francisco Examiner,* 11 February 1906, magazine section.

5 Cecil Clark, "Victoria Was a Smuggler's Hide-Away," *Victoria Daily Colonist,* 15 January 1961, 8; Noel Robinson, "The 'Sea Wolf': Story of a Tragic Treasure Hunt," *The Shoulder Strap* 10 (1943), 47-48.

6 Hugh Laracy, "Niels Peter Sorensen: The Story of a Criminal Adventurer," *Journal of Pacific History* 35, 2 (2000), 147-62; Hugh Laracy, "'Quixotic and Utopian': American Adventures in the Southwest Pacific, 1897-98," *Pacific Studies* 24, 1-2 (2001), 39-62. For some Victoria, BC, versions, see Thomas Seaman, "The Adventures of 'Sea Wolf' McLean," *Victoria Daily Colonist,* 21 June, 1953, magazine section, 11; Clark, "Victoria Was a Smuggler's Hide-Away"; and Cecil Clark, "Seawolf McLean Tweaked Russia's Beard," *Victoria Daily Colonist,* 5 April 1959, 8-9.

7 Article ends: "I told you so." *Victoria Daily Colonist,* 8 December 1897. See also Neil MacNeil, *The Highland Heart of Nova Scotia* (Toronto, 1971), 179; Laracy, "Niels Peter Sorensen," 155.

8 *New York Sun,* 16 July 1908. Laracy suggests Sorensen's scheme originally centred on pearls but sensing the gold fever he turned the emphasis to minerals. Laracy, "Quixotic," 51.

9 Ian Macdonald has them teaming up in Vancouver, *Vancouver Sun,* 15 October 1966, clipping in British Columbia Archives (BCA), Alex McLean, vertical file, as does Robinson, "The 'Sea Wolf,'" 47-48.

10 Zaslow, *Opening of the Canadian North,* 103; *Victoria Daily Colonist,* 8 December 1897; New York Supreme Court Archives (NYSCA), *Nels P. Sorensen v. Sun Printing and Publishing Association,* 1911, Alex McLean's testimony, 8, 10-11, 30, and 117-19; Laracy, "Niels Peter Sorensen," 155. Pond was mayor from 1887 to 1891, Mayor of San Francisco, http://www.nndb.com/gov/867/000047726/.

11 Laracy, "Quixotic," 41.

12 Ibid., 40-43.

13 Clark, "Victoria Was a Smuggler's Hide-Away"; NYSCA, *Nels P. Sorenson v. Sun Printing and Publishing Association,* Alex MacLean's testimony, 8, 10-11, and 30; Great Britain, Colonial Office, Original Correspondence, Western Pacific, 1878-1914, Charles Woodford [resident commissioner in the Solomons] to Escott, 2 September 1912, enclosed in Escott to Colonial

Office, 22 November 1912, CO 225/106(2). It contains a full account of the expedition to the Solomons in 1897. See also Woodford to High Commissioner, 14 July 1913, CO 225/106(2).

14 Findlay's first edition (London 1851) did not include that specific reference, but four subsequent ones (1863-84) did so. Laracy, "Niels Peter Sorensen," 155n30; Great Britain, Original Correspondence, Western Pacific, C. Woodford to A. Hunt, 2 September 1912, 106(2).

15 Andrew Walker Roy, "Life and Death of the Sea Wolf," *Atlantic Advocate* 98 (1958), 77; Great Britain, Original Correspondence, Western Pacific, H.C. Gingg to J.W. Warburton, 11 September 1897, enclosure 1 in Warburton to Colonial Office, 14 September 1897, 54(1); *New York Sun,* 29 March 1911; NYSCA, *Nels P. Sorenson v. Sun Printing and Publishing Association,* Alex MacLean's testimony, 11.

16 *New York Sun,* 16 July 1908, 29 March 1911; *San Francisco Chronicle,* 5 September 1897, extract in enclosure 2 in Great Britain, Original Correspondence, Western Pacific, Warburton to the Colonial Office, 14 September 1897, 54(1); Robinson, "The 'Sea Wolf,'" 47-48; NYSCA, *Nels P. Sorenson v. Sun Printing and Publishing Association,* Alex MacLean's testimony, 9 and 136.

17 Clark, "Victoria Was a Smuggler's Hide-Away"; *San Francisco Chronicle,* 7 August 1897.

18 A later story also had Jack London travelling to Samoa with him, but London left San Francisco for the Klondike in late July 1897. NYSCA, *Nels P. Sorenson v. Sun Printing and Publishing Association,* Alex MacLean's testimony, 11, 13, and 66; Russ Kingman, *A Pictorial Life of Jack London* (New York, 1979), 71. The list of the *Sophia Sutherland* included Berge (or Borge), E. Cunath (Kunath, Kinath), Arthur DeWitt, H.C. Gingg, J. Goldsmith, Greenwood, Headburg, Higgins, Al Kohn (Cohen), Lampe, Alex MacLean, Joseph Nicholson, Olsen, Smadeke, N.P. Sorensen. *San Francisco Chronicle,* 28 July 1898, 12, cited in Laracy, "Quixotic," 19.

19 *New York Sun,* 16 July 1908 and 29 March 1911; MacNeil, *Highland Heart,* 179; *Marine Digest,* 18 January 1958, 12; Clark, "Victoria Was a Smuggler's Hide-Away."

20 *San Francisco Chronicle,* 5 September 1897, extract in enclosure 2 in Great Britain, Original Correspondence, Western Pacific, Warburton to the Colonial Office, 14 September 1897, 54(1).

21 Laracy, "Niels Peter Sorensen," 156.

22 Ibid., 156-57; Great Britain, Original Correspondence, Western Pacific, Warburton to the Colonial Office, 14 September 1897, 54(1). The vessel was the *Percy Edwards.* See *San Francisco Chronicle,* 7 August 1897; H.C. Gingg to J.W. Warburton, 11 September 1897, enclosure 1 in Great Britain, Original Correspondence, Western Pacific, Warburton to the Colonial Office, 14 September 1897.

23 The *San Francisco Chronicle* report was included in enclosure 1 in Great Britain, Original Correspondence, Western Pacific, Warburton to Marquess of Salisbury, 14 September 1897, 54(1).

24 *New York Sun,* 29 March 1911.

25 The term "filibuster" is used in the sense of an unlawful military expedition. Judge Chambers' testimony, *New York Sun,* 29 March 1911.

26 MacNeil, *Highland Heart,* 179; NYSCA, *Nels P. Sorenson v. Sun Printing and Publishing Association,* Alex MacLean's testimony, 14; Joseph Theroux, "William Churchill: A Fractured Life," *Hawaiian Journal of History* 29 (1995), 101 and 104.

27 *New York Sun,* 16 July 1908.

28 Laracy, "Niels Peter Sorensen," 151-55; *New York Sun,* 16 July 1908; NYSCA, *Nels P. Sorenson v. Sun Printing and Publishing Association,* Alex MacLean's testimony, 14-19.

29 Laracy, "Niels Peter Sorensen," 9; *New York Sun,* 29 March 1911. Jack London was in the Klondike at this time. Kingman, *Pictorial Life,* 71-82.

30 NYSCA, *Nels P. Sorenson v. Sun Printing and Publishing Association,* Alex MacLean's testimony, 18 and 121.

31 Alex stated: "In fact, I had no liquor of my own on board the ship." NYSCA, *Nels P. Sorenson v. Sun Printing and Publishing Association,* Alex MacLean's testimony, 19, 52, and 83; Voss, *Venturesome Voyages,* 102-3; *New York Sun,* 29 March 1911.

32 *Victoria Daily Colonist,* 8 December 1897; Theroux, "William Churchill," 107. See also Clark, "Seawolf McLean."

33 The Solomons were part of Melanesia; Samoa was included in Polynesia. *New York Sun,* 29 March 1911; NYSCA, *Nels P. Sorenson v. Sun Printing and Publishing Association,* Alex MacLean's testimony, 24-28. According to Woodford, the first resident commissioner in the Solomons, "the hopes of the expedition were based upon some fabulous accounts of the existence of gold and copper reported to have been seen on San Christoval, by a man of notorious character, who induced the members of the expedition to embark their capital in the undertaking." Great Britain, British Solomon Islands, Colonial Reports, *Annual Report for 1897-98* (London, 1898), v. 251, 8; Ian Heath, "Charles Morris Woodford: Adventurer, Naturalist, Administrator," in Deryck Scarr, ed., *More Pacific Island Portraits* (Canberra, 1978), 202-5.

34 Great Britain, Original Correspondence, Western Pacific, Woodford's annual report for 1897-98, 8, 106(2); *New York Sun,* 29 March 1911; NYSCA, *Nels P. Sorenson v. Sun Printing and Publishing Association,* Alex MacLean's testimony, 125; Laracy, "Niels Peter Sorenson," 157-58; Laracy, "Quixotic," 52-53.

35 *New York Sun,* 29 March 1911.

36 *Ibid.;* Great Britain, Original Correspondence, Western Pacific, Woodford's annual report for 1897-98, 106(2).

37 "After we reached the islands where Sorensen said the treasure was to be found, I found out – I need not tell you how – that Sorensen had deceived me ... He had entirely misrepresented the conditions." Robinson, "The Real Sea Wolf," *Maclean's* 35 (1 January 1922), 12-13.

38 *New York Sun,* 29 March 1911; NYSCA, *Nels P. Sorenson v. Sun Printing and Publishing Association,* Alex MacLean's testimony, 34-35.

39 Great Britain, Original Correspondence, Western Pacific, Escott to Colonial Office, 22 November 1912, Enclosing Charles Woodford to Escott, 2 September 1912, CO 225/106(2); Laracy, "Niels Peter Sorensen," 158.

40 *New York Sun,* 29 March 1911. See also MacNeil, *Highland Heart,* 179-80.

41 Judge Chambers received additional information from his two sons, "one of whom was registrar of titles, and the other generally heard everything that was going on." The flogging story came from them. In this version, they pulled into a bay "in the almost uninhabited island of Bougainville, took Sorensen ashore and tied him to a cocca palm. Then they flayed him with whips until he was unconscious and sailed away, leaving him there." *New York Sun,* 29 March 1911; Laracy, "Niels Peter Sorensen," 158.

42 Robinson, "The 'Sea Wolf,'" 49.

43 "A sample of green mineral, apparently malachite, from another locality in the Protectorate was submitted by me to the assayer, and found to contain 46.94 per cent. of pure copper." Woodford thought that locality should be explored further. Great Britain, British Solomon Islands, Colonial Reports, *Annual Report for 1897-98,* v. 251, 8: "No further attempt has been made during the year to prospect for minerals, the ill success of the American expedition in 1897 having apparently choked off all further enterprise for the present." Great Britain, British Solomon Islands, Colonial Reports, *Annual Report for 1898-99,* v. 275, 11.

44 The version London heard had the crew dying of "scratch-scratch," a skin irritation. A. Grove Day, *Jack London in the South Seas* (New York, 1971), 146; Jack London, "The Terrible Solomons," in Jack London, *South Sea Tales* (New York, 1911), 199.

45 Alex's testimony, *New York Sun,* 29 March 1911.

46 Ibid.

47 Robinson, "The 'Sea Wolf,'" 49. See also Robert D. Foulke, "Life in the Dying World of Sail, 1870-1910," *Journal of British Studies* 3, 1 (1963), 112-13.

48 "Later I got the schooner safely back to 'Frisco.'" Robinson, "Real Sea Wolf," 13; NYSCA, *Nels P. Sorenson v. Sun Printing and Publishing Association,* Alex MacLean's testimony, 46-49; *San Francisco Chronicle,* 1 September 1898, 5. In an interview with Noel Robinson in 1912, MacLean said he buried eighteen of his crew, seventeen at sea. Noel Robinson, "The Story of My Life," *Vancouver News-Advertiser,* 1 January 1913, magazine section, 7.

49 D'Arcy Marsh, "London's 'Sea Wolf' in Scot's Clothing," *Vancouver Province,* 31 May 1958, 15; According to Neil MacNeil, when Alex reached Apia again on 11 May 1898, "he had

only four living men aboard and they were all sick." MacNeil, *Highland Heart,* 180; Laracy, "Niels Peter Sorensen," 158.

50 Charles Lillard, "Dining with a Sea Wolf," *Victoria Daily Colonist,* 11 June 1978, 12.

51 MacLean arrived back at Apia "haggard and worn out as much by lack of sleep and anxiety as by the physical strain required to sail his craft, an effort which, towards the end of the voyage when he was compelled to keep awake at night for fear of encountering in the dark other vessels that might be making for the port or leaving it, left its mark for a long time upon even his iron frame and constitution." Robinson, "The 'Sea Wolf,'" 49. Some of the surviving crew were shipped off to Sydney, Australia, to recuperate. A contemporary San Francisco newspaper account had four of the crew buried at sea. *San Francisco Chronicle,* 1 September 1898.

52 "The 'Sea Wolf' thought it best to make a clean breast to the consul about the marooning and its cause, and the latter, his sympathy for the skipper of the brigantine evidently awakened by the tragedy through which he had passed and the hardihood he had displayed, overlooked the marooning, made any peace that may have been necessary with the authorities on the island, and did all he could to help McLean." *New York Sun,* 29 March 1911. See NYSCA, *Nels P. Sorenson v. Sun Printing and Publishing Association,* Alex MacLean's testimony, 50-51.

53 Laracy, "Niels Peter Sorensen," 159; Robinson, "The 'Sea Wolf,'" 50; *San Francisco Chronicle,* 1 September 1898, 5; NYSCA, *Nels P. Sorenson v. Sun Printing and Publishing Association,* Alex MacLean's testimony, 78-79.

54 LAC, Department of Marine and Fisheries, L.H. Davies to Privy Council, 7 December 1897, enclosure S. 2612, 55th Congress, 2nd session, v. 152, file 425, pt. 11; James T. Gay, "Bering Sea Controversy: Harrison, Blaine and Cronyism," *Alaska Journal* 3 (1973), 13; Jozo Tomasevich, *International Agreements on Conservation of Marine Resources with Special Reference to the North Pacific* (Stanford, 1943), 88.

55 Kurkpatrick Dorsey, *The Dawn of Conservation Diplomacy: U.S.-Canadian Wildlife Protection Treaties in the Progressive Era* (Seattle, 1998), 127-29.

56 *New York Times,* 31 October 1897, 13.

57 The Japanese subsidy did not end until 1909. A.Y. Roppel and S.P. Davey, "Evolution of Fur Seal Management on the Pribilof Islands," *Journal of Wildlife Management* 29, 3 (1965), 455; D.G. Paterson, "The North Pacific Seal Hunt, 1886-1910: Rights and Regulations," in W. Peter Ward and Robert A.J. McDonald, eds., *British Columbia: Historical Readings* (Vancouver, 1981), 350; D.G. Paterson and J. Wilen, "Depletion and Diplomacy: The North Pacific Seal Hunt, 1886-1910," in P. Uselding, ed., *Research in Economic History,* vol. 2 (Greenwich, CT, 1977), 93-94; Leonhard Stejneger, "Fur-Seal Industry of the Commander Islands, 1897 to 1922," *Bulletin of the United States Bureau of Fisheries 1925* 41 (1927), 302. David Starr Jordan later explained there was no bounty, but there was a custom of a company or a vessel's owner paying hunters about ten yen ($5.00) for each seal skin. National Archives and Records Administration, Records of the U.S. Fish and Wildlife Service, Jordan to George H. Bowers, 16 February 1910, RG 22, sec. 91, file 110, pt. 1.

58 Walter A. McDougall, *Let the Sea Make a Noise: A History of the North Pacific from Magellan to MacArthur* (New York, 1993), 394-97; Thomas A. Bailey, *A Diplomatic History of the American People* (New York, 1964), 434-35 and 468-74.

59 E.W. Wright, ed., *Lewis and Dryden's Marine History of the Pacific Northwest* (Portland, 1895), 454-55.

60 LAC, Department of Marine and Fisheries, Fred Peters to L.H. Davies, 10 January 1898, v. 320, file 2691, pt. 1; Peter Murray, *The Vagabond Fleet: A Chronicle of the North Pacific Sealing Schooner Trade* (Victoria, 1988), 172.

61 LAC, Department of Marine and Fisheries, Fred Peters to L.H. Davies, 10 January 1898, v. 320, file 2691, pt. 1; Murray, *Vagabond Fleet,* 170. Back in August 1894, the Americans had offered $425,000 in full settlement. It had been accepted at that time, but Congress had refused to pass the appropriation.

62 LAC, Department of Marine and Fisheries, Julien Pauncefote to Marquess of Salisbury, 17 June 1898, v. 320, file 2691, pt. 1.

63 LAC, Department of Marine and Fisheries, Fred Peters to L.H. Davies, 23 September 1898; Bodwell and Peters, *Report on Seizure of the Onward,* 1880; copy of Peters and Bodwell's report regarding the schooner *Triumph,* v. 320, file 2691, pt. 1; Canada, Bering Sea Claims Commission, *Argument on Behalf of Great Britain* (Ottawa, 1896), 107; United States, Congress, Department of Foreign Relations, *Whaling and Sealing Claims against Russia,* report prepared by Herbert H.D. Peirce, Appendix 1, 1902, Doc. 1, 57th Congress, 2nd session, 93.

64 Peters' partner was Sir Charles Hibbert Tupper. W. Stewart Wallace, *The Macmillan Dictionary of Canadian Biography* (Toronto, 1978), 661-62; C.W. Parker, ed., *Who's Who and Why* (Vancouver, 1914), 95.

65 "The Master [Alex], however, did not leave, but continued sealing until 1 September, and made a very good catch, [and as] the claim was based on the fact that she was supposed to have changed her ground on account of the warning, the award was certainly very handsome considering the small injury done." LAC, Department of Marine and Fisheries, copy of Peters and Bodwell's report regarding the schooner *Triumph,* v. 320, file 2691, pt. 1.

66

Illegal boarding and search of the vessel	$2,000
Legal and other expenses	$250
Time and expense of owner	$200
Estimated catch (8 hunting boats and stern boat from 11 July to 1 October), 3,500 skins at $11 each	$38,500

Bering Sea Claims Commission, *Argument on Behalf of Great Britain,* 147-48. Another claim for the same incident had 2,428 skins at $8 per skin for $19,424 and legal fees of $250. It assumed a catch of 2,500 for the full season. United States, Senate, *Fur Seal Arbitration: Proceedings of the Tribunal of Arbitration at Paris, 1893,* 53rd Congress, 2nd session (Washington, 1895), v. 5, 422. It could also be noted that Baker had entered a contract with Liebes and Company to sell the catch at $6.25 per skin. LAC, Department of Marine and Fisheries, copy of Peters and Bodwell's report regarding the schooner *Triumph,* v. 320, file 2691, pt. 1.

67 LAC, Department of Marine and Fisheries, L.H. Davies to Fred Peters 13 September 1898, v. 320, file 2691, pt. 1. Captain J.C. Blackett, a Cape Bretoner, arrived on the Pacific in the early 1880s and was involved in the *Triumph* since 1887. Wright, *Lewis and Dryden,* 460.

68 LAC, Department of Marine and Fisheries, Fred Peters to L.H. Davies, telegram, 23 September 1898, v. 320, file 2691, pt. 1.

69 BCA, E.C. Baker Diaries, 21 and 26 September 1898, Add. MSS. 707, v. 37; LAC, Department of Marine and Fisheries, Fred Peters to L.H. Davies, 21 September 1898, v. 320, file 2691, pt. 1.

70 G.W.S. Brooks, "Edgar Crow Baker: An Entrepreneur in Early British Columbia," *BC Studies* 31 (1976), 42. See also Robert A.J. McDonald, "Victoria, Vancouver, and the Economic Development of British Columbia, 1886-1914," in W. Peter Ward and Robert A.J. McDonald, eds., *British Columbia: Historical Readings* (Vancouver, 1981), 369-95; Norbert MacDonald, "Seattle, Vancouver, and the Klondike," *Canadian Historical Review* 49, 3 (1968), 234-46.

71 When Baker died in 1920, the net value of his estate was $297,554.36. Brooks, "Edgar Crow Baker," 42; BCA, E.C. Baker Diaries, 5-7 October 1898; Brooks, "Edgar Crow Baker: An Entrepreneur in Early British Columbia" (MA thesis, University of British Columbia, 1976), 289; G.W. Taylor, *Builders of British Columbia: An Industrial History* (Victoria, 1982), 107; LAC, Department of Marine and Fisheries, copy of Peters' and Bodwell's report regarding the schooner *Triumph,* v. 320, file 2691.

72 Dorsey, *Conservation Diplomacy,* 128-29; Tomasevich, *International Agreements,* 87-88; United States, House of Representatives, *Letter from the Secretary of Commerce and Labor Transmitting in Response to House Resolution No. 73, Information Relating to Seal Islands of Alaska, 19 July 1911,* House Doc. 93, 62nd Congress, 1st session, 335; Alvin C. Gluek Jr., "Canada's Splendid Bargain: The North Pacific Fur Seal Convention of 1911," *Canadian Historical Review* 63, 2 (1982), 184.

Chapter 9: The Klondike, 1898-1903

1 It is unclear whether Rusty Campbell refers to dance hall queen Kitty Rockwell or New Brunswick native Kate Ryan, although his mention of the Dawson dance halls suggests the

former. Both passed through Victoria. Ursula Jupp, ed., *Home Port Victoria* (Victoria, 1985), 122; T. Ann Brennan, *The Real Klondike Kate* (Fredericton, 1990).

2 Edwin Tappan Adney, *The Klondike Stampede of 1897-1898* (New York, 1968), 11-12. See also Pierre Berton, *Klondike: The Last Great Gold Rush, 1896-1899* (Toronto, 1992), 102-3; Douglas Fetherling, *The Gold Crusades: A Social History of Gold Rushes, 1849-1929* (Toronto, 1997), 133-34; S.D. Clark, "Mining Society in British Columbia and the Yukon," in W. Peter Ward and Robert A.J. McDonald, eds., *British Columbia: Historical Readings* (Vancouver, 1981), 215-31.

3 Fetherling, *Gold Crusades,* 4.

4 *San Francisco Examiner,* 30 July 1899, 4.

5 *Victoria Daily Colonist,* 3 August 1899.

6 Noel Robinson, "The 'Sea Wolf': Story of a Tragic Treasure Hunt," *The Shoulder Strap* 10 (1943), 47; Ian MacDonald, "Pirate of High Seas Ends in False Creek," *Vancouver Sun,* 15 October 1966, clipping in British Columbia Archives (BCA), Alex McLean, vertical file; J.B. Cook, on the back of a picture of *Minnie, Mary Ellen* in California Historical Society Library, San Francisco. Charles Lillard has him dying in Victoria in August 1899, "Dining with the Sea Wolf," *Victoria Daily Colonist,* 11 June 1978, 12, while Ronald Gillis, "The MacLeans of Cape Breton and Scotland," *Sydney Post-Record,* 17 November 1936, 4, has his death occurring in Cape Nome in 1900.

7 *San Francisco Call,* 8 October 1899, 18; *San Francisco Examiner,* 8 October 1899, 6; *San Francisco Chronicle,* 8 October 1899, 30.

8 Los Gatos California Profile and Resource Guide, http://www.usacitiesonline.com/cacountylosgatos.htm.

9 *San Francisco City Directories, 1894-1903; San Francisco Examiner,* 15 June 1905.

10 Berton, *Klondike.*

11 Richard J. Friesen, *The Chilkoot Pass and the Great Gold Rush of 1898* (Ottawa, 1981), 34 and 42-48; Pierre Berton, *The Klondike Fever* (New York, 1958), 268; Berton, *Klondike,* 251; Samuel B. Steele, *Forty Years in Canada* (New York, 1972), 300; David Neufeld and Frank Norris, *Chilkoot Trail: Heritage Route to the Klondike* (Whitehorse, 1996), 64; Murray Morgan, *One Man's Gold Rush: A Klondike Album,* photographs by E.A. Hegg, (Seattle, 1995), 69-70; Fetherling, *Gold Crusades,* 145.

12 Steele, *Forty Years,* 295-96.

13 Neufeld and Norris, *Chilkoot Trail,* 7 and 65-67; Steele, *Forty Years,* 295-96.

14 Friesen, *Chilkoot Pass,* 48, 78, 92, and 102; Berton, *Klondike Fever,* 269.

15 Steele, *Forty Years,* 310; Neufeld and Norris, *Chilkoot Trail,* 115; Charlene Porsild, *Gamblers and Dreamers: Women, Men, and Community in the Klondike* (Vancouver, 1998), 18 and 201-4.

16 Captain Henry Henderson, *Robert Henderson's Discovery of the Klondike* (Pictou County, NS, 1998), 18.

17 Adney, *Klondike Stampede,* 249, 277, and 420-21; Friesen, *Chilkoot Pass,* 119n12; Benjamin Franklin Gilbert, "Economic Developments in Alaska, 1867-1910," *Journal of the West* 4 (1965), 510; L.H. Carlson, "The Discovery of Gold at Nome, Alaska," in Morgan B. Sherwood, ed., *Alaska and Its History* (Seattle, 1967), 354-55; Berton, *Klondike,* 56-57 and 98-100; Fetherling, *Gold Crusades,* 129-30; Lewis Green, *The Gold Hustlers* (Anchorage, 1977), 9-10; Henderson, *Robert Henderson,* 14-17.

18 Neufeld and Norris, *Chilkoot Trail,* 104 and 113.

19 Steele, *Forty Years,* 309-12, 319, and 329-30; Morris Zaslow, *The Opening of the Canadian North, 1870-1914* (Toronto, 1971), 104-5; Harwood Steele, *Policing the Arctic* (Toronto, 1925), 46.

20 Neufeld and Norris, *Chilkoot Trail,* 112; Canada, North West Mounted Police, Yukon Territory, *Report of the North-West Mounted Police 1899,* 1899, Sessional Paper no. 15, Part 2, 10.

21 Neil MacNeil, *The Highland Heart of Nova Scotia* (Toronto, 1971), 170; Neil MacNeil to writer, 6 November 1986 [on file with author]; "Questions on Cousin Alec's Duel with Bullet Brown," enclosure, Neil MacNeil to writer, 17 September 1987 [on file with author].

22 MacNeil, *Highland Heart,* 171. While the family connection between Neil F. MacNeil and Alex MacLean is unclear, there are MacLeans on Neil F.'s father's and mother's side. Two of Johnnie A.'s brothers were Captain Alex and Captain Michael. See S.R. MacNeil, *All Call Iona Home* (Antigonish, 1979), 262-66.

23 Neil MacNeil to writer, 6 November 1986 [on file with author]; *Bennett Sun,* 5 August 1899.
24 Thomas Stone, *Miners' Justice: Migration, Law and Order on the Alaska-Yukon Frontier, 1873-1902* (New York, 1988), 174; William R. Morrison, "Policing the Boomtown: The Mounted Police as a Social Force in the Klondike," *Northern Review* 6 (1990), 89; Roderick Charles Macleod, "Sir Samuel Benfield Steele," *Dictionary of Canadian Biography,* vol. 14 (Toronto, 1998), 967-72.
25 The scows were numbered 170-75 and the boats 176-79. The database for this information is an amalgamation of the Chilkoot Pass and Lake Bennett archival records. See North West Mounted Police, Chilkoot, http://www.goldrush.org/pan/vol06.htm, 2. They were H.A. Ferguson (Dawson), Archie McHillok (Scotland), T.W. Doyle (Tacoma), Michael McNeil (Cape Breton), John A. McNeil (Cape Breton), E.M. Arich (Eureka, CA), E.J. Donovan (Tacoma), Colin Graur (Nova Scotia), J. Liddell (Airdrie), W.H. Horlee (Medford, OR), Dan Grant (Nova Scotia), R.C. Smucker (Seattle), H. Ohman (California), A. Copeland (Arcata, CA), J.A. Grant (Molden, MA), J.C. Mcrae (Nova Scotia), Archibald A. Macdonald (Nova Scotia), Alexander McLean (San Francisco), Chas Brown (San Francisco), Alva C. Hodges (Ellensburg, WA), Dan A. Micholson (Baddeck, Cape Breton, NS), Joe Bradwich (Seattle), A.F. Whipple (Tacoma), Charles L. Veat (Vonoma, CA), William Henderson (Glasgow, Scotland), and Charles Smith (Duluth, MN). See also Helene Dobrowolsky, *Law of the Yukon* (Whitehorse, 1995), 26; Neufeld and Norris, *Chilkoot Trail,* 129; Arthur Treadwell Walden, *A Dog-Puncher on the Yukon* (Boston, 1931), 196.
26 *Bennett Sun,* 5 August 1899.
27 Neufeld and Norris, *Chilkoot Trail,* 112.
28 Murray Lundberg, "Northern Roadhouses: An Introduction," http://www.explorenorth.com/library/yafeatures/bl-roadhouse.htm.
29 *Bennett Sun,* 31 May 1899.
30 Ibid., 9 December 1899.
31 *Yukon Sun,* 17 April 1900, cited in Neufeld and Norris, *Chilkoot Trail,* 118-19.
32 *Bennett Sun,* 9 December 1899; Murray Lundberg, Roadhouse database, 706; North West Mounted Police, *Report of the North-West Mounted Police 1899,* 1901, Sessional Paper no. 28a, Part 3, 54.
33 Neufeld and Norris, *Chilkoot Trail,* 117-20; Clarence C. Hulley, *Alaska: Past and Present* (Westport, CT, 1981), 259-60.
34 Neil MacNeil to writer, 6 November 1986 and 17 September 1987 [on file with author]; *St. F.X. Alumni News* (spring 1993), 8.
35 Gillis, "MacLeans of Cape Breton and Scotland"; MacNeil, *Highland Heart,* 173-77.
36 W.D. McBride, "Saga of Famed Packets and Other Steamboats of Mighty Yukon River," *Cariboo and Northwest Digest* 5, 1 (1949), 114; Berton, *Klondike,* 396; Stan Cohen, *Yukon River Steamboats* (Missoula 1982), 115.
37 North West Mounted Police, *Report of the North-West Mounted Police 1899,* 1900, Sessional Paper no. 15, Part 2, 2 and 46.
38 Art Downs, *British Columbia-Yukon Sternwheel Days* (Surrey, 1992), 18-19.
39 Kenneth J. Kutz, *Klondike Gold: The Philatelic History of the Klondike Gold Rush* (Darwin, 1995), 138. See also North West Mounted Police, *Report of the North-West Mounted Police 1899,* 1900, Sessional Paper no. 15, 36 and 54; *Dawson Daily News,* 10 November 1899; Edward L. Affleck, compiler, *Affleck's List of Sternwheelers Plying the Inland Waters of British Columbia, 1858-1980* (Vancouver, 1992), 41.
40 *Dawson Daily News,* 7-8 November 1899.
41 *Klondike Nugget,* 11 November 1899.
42 Jack London, *The Sea-Wolf,* edited and introduced by John Sutherland (Oxford, 1992), 43-44.
43 *Klondike Nugget,* 11 November 1899.
44 Jonathan Auerback, *Male Call: Becoming Jack London* (Durham, 1996), 16-17; T. Stone, "Atomistic Order and Frontier Violence: Miners and Whalemen in the Nineteenth Century Yukon," *Ethnology* 22 (1983), 331.
45 *Klondike Nugget,* 11 November 1899; *Dawson Daily News,* 10 November 1899; Kutz, *Klondike Gold,* 138; Fetherling, *Gold Crusades,* 153.
46 *Dawson Daily News,* 28 October 1899 and 1, 6, 7, and 10 November 1899.

47 "There is nothing which has so established the high reputation which the force has among the inhabitants of this territory as the assistance invariably given to any person in distress, from accident, sickness or want of food. No case is ever neglected." North West Mounted Police, *Report of the North-West Mounted Police 1899,* 1900, Sessional Paper no. 15, Part 2, 4.
48 Ibid., 54.
49 Library and Archives Canada (LAC), Northwest Mounted Police Records, SF 2792: Herbert Gregory, RG 18, file 3396.
50 MacNeil, *Highland Heart,* 171-73.
51 Stone, "Atomistic Order," 337.
52 Neil MacNeil to writer, 17 September 1987 [on file with author]. The interview in the letter refers to three typed pages, "Questions on Cousin Alec's Duel with Bullet Brown," which Mr. MacNeil kindly enclosed.
53 North West Mounted Police, *Report of the North-West Mounted Police 1899,* 1900, Sessional Paper no. 15, 3; Fetherling, *Gold Crusades,* 155; Robert Stewart, *Sam Steele: Lion of the Frontier* (Toronto, 1979), 216.
54 A census of Dawson by the North West Mounted Police in 1898 had 3,205 Americans out of a total population of 4,445; Canadians, the second largest group, numbered 645. North West Mounted Police, *Report of the North-West Mounted Police 1899,* 1900, Sessional Paper no. 15, 54; Fetherling, *Gold Crusades,* 125; Porsild, *Gamblers and Dreamers,* 3-23 and 201-4.
55 *Dawson Daily News,* 8 November 1899.
56 Ibid., 10 November 1899; *Klondike Nugget,* 11 November 1899; North West Mounted Police, *Report of the North-West Mounted Police 1899,* 1901, Sessional Paper no. 28a, 37-43.
57 North West Mounted Police, *Report of the North-West Mounted Police 1899,* 1900, Sessional Paper no. 15, Part 2, 44,
58 MacNeil, *Highland Heart,* 173.
59 LAC, Records of the Yukon Territory, Alphabetical Death Register, 1898-1903, RG 91, v. 225; *San Francisco Examiner,* 24 September 1899, 3.
60 Andrea R.C. Helms and Mary Childers Mangusso, "The Nome Gold Conspiracy," *Pacific Northwest Quarterly* 73, 1 (1982), 10-12; L.H. Carlson, "Nome: From Mining Camp to Civilized Community," *Pacific Northwest Quarterly* 38 (1947), 233; Benjamin F. Gilbert, "Economic Developments in Alaska, 1867-1910," *Journal of the West* 4 (1965), 512.
61 MacNeil, *Highland Heart,* 174-75. "He was sheriff of Nome around the turn of the century." City of Vancouver Archives (CVA), George J. McInnis, "Alexander MacLean," manuscript. McInnis uses Neil MacNeil as his source.
62 Berton, *Klondike Fever,* 439-45.
63 William R. Hunt, *North of 53: The Wild Days of the Alaska-Yukon Mining Frontier 1870-1914* (New York, 1974), 201.
64 William R. Hunt, *Distant Justice: Policing the Alaskan Frontier* (Norman, 1987), 84.
65 North West Mounted Police, *Report of the North-West Mounted Police 1899,* 1900, Sessional Paper no. 15, Part 8, 55; Canada, Mr. William Ogilvie, Commissioner of the Yukon Territory, *Report of Mr. William Ogilvie, 20 September 1899,* 1900, Sessional Paper no. 33u, 27.
66 L.H. Carlson, "The First Mining Season at Nome, Alaska, 1899," *Pacific Historical Review* 16 (1947), 165.
67 For a partial list of those sent south by the American authorities from Nome, see Hunt, *Distant Justice,* 78, 87-90, 141, and 348n2, and his *North of 53,* 100-2 and 117. For the "blue ticket" practice, see Morrison, "Policing the Boomtown," 94.
68 Eddy was fired from his job as a United States deputy marshal in 1905. Stone, *Miners' Justice,* 253.
69 Hunt, *North of 53,* 105.
70 Hunt, *Distant Justice,* 70 and 82; Robert K. DeArment, "A Look at Two Professional Lawmen: George A. Scarborough and Frank M. Canton," *Journal of the West* 34, 1 (1995), 8-12; Edward Everett Dale, ed., *Frontier Trails: The Autobiography of Frank M. Canton* (Norman, OK, 1966).
71 Hunt, *Distant Justice,* 328-29.
72 Carl J. Lomen, *Fifty Years in Alaska* (New York, 1954), 17-18 and 39-40. See also Helms and Mangusso, "The Nome Gold Conspiracy," 12-16.

73 Morrison, "Policing the Boomtown," 88. See also Stone, *Miners' Justice,* 276-77.

74 Hunt, *North of 53,* 248.

75 *Klondike Nugget,* 24 May 1902.

76 *Klondike Nugget,* 7 October 1901; McBride, "Saga of Famed Packets," 104; Cohen, *Yukon River Steamboats,* 111.

77 Gillis, "McLeans of Cape Breton and Scotland."

78 McBride, "Saga of Famed Packets," 104; Cohen, *Yukon River Steamboats,* 111; *Klondike Nugget,* 24 May 1902; Downs, *British Columbia-Yukon: Sternwheel Days,* 145; *Dawson Daily News,* 23 May 1902; Murray Lundberg, "Yukon River Sternboats," www.explorenorth.com/library/yafeatures/bl-boats.htm; North West Mounted Police, *Report of the North-West Mounted Police 1899,* 1900, Sessional Paper no. 15, 13; and 1901, Sessional Paper no. 28a, 6. Robert Miller has a copy of the transfer of ownership from his great-grandfather, C.E. Miller, dated 31 October 1900, which lists Alex MacLean as having an interest in the vessel [copy on file with author].

79 McBride, "Saga of Famed Packets," 104.

80 Murray Lundberg, "Yukon River Sternboats," www.explorenorth.com/library/yafeatures/bl-boats.htm, 175; McBride, "Sage of Famed Packets," 104.

81 Noel Robinson, "The Story of My Life," *Vancouver News-Advertiser,* 1 January 1913, 7.

82 The *San Francisco City Directory, 1903* has Alex as master of the steamer *City of Sydney* and residing at 1420 Webster. See also James Hitchman, *A Maritime History of the Pacific Coast, 1540-1980* (New York, 1990), 19-20; *Record of American and Foreign Shipping,* 1900, 362; CVA, George J. McInnis, "Alexander MacLean," manuscript.

83 *Victoria Daily Times,* 14 July 1902; *Victoria Daily Colonist,* 15 and 17 July, 1902; Victoria, BC, Ross Bay Cemetery Records, Parks Department.

84 *San Francisco City Directory,* 1900-04; *San Francisco Examiner,* 15 June 1905.

85 Prices at the London sale were 80 percent above those of the previous year. *San Francisco Examiner,* 15 December 1899, 12; 16 December 1899, 4; 18 December 1899, 7; 10 January 1900, 7.

86 The arbitrator dealt with four Russian seizures; the other three, *Cape Horn Pigeon, C.H. White,* and *Kate and Anna,* had all been seized in 1892. United States, Congress, Department of Foreign Relations, *Whaling and Sealing Claims against Russia,* report prepared by Herbert H.D. Peirce, Appendix 1, 1902, Doc. 1, 57th Congress, 2nd session, 453-63; J.B. Moore, *A Digest of International Law* (Washington, 1906), v. 1, 924-29.

87 Peirce was secretary of the American embassy in St. Petersburg in 1900. Congress, Department of Foreign Relations, *Whaling and Sealing Claims,* 7 and 197; National Archives and Records Administration, Records of the U.S. Fish and Wildlife Service, *Fur Trade Review,* March 1907 (enclosure), RG 22, sec. 91, file 430, 190-92.

88 Congress, Department of Foreign Relations, *Whaling and Sealing Claims,* 101-16.

89 Ibid., 7, 117-20, 171, 185, 348, 456, and 463; Moore, *A Digest of International Law,* v. 1, 1927-29; United States, Congress, Behring Sea Claims Commission, *Record of Evidence Taken at Victoria, British Columbia by the Commissioners under the Convention of 8 February 1896, between Great Britain and the United States* (Washington, 1897), v. 2, 1264; United States, House of Representatives, Department of Commerce and Labor, *A Statement Submitted in Re the Fur-Seal Herd of Alaska to the House Committee on Expenditures in the Department of Commerce,* compiled by H.W. Elliott (Washington, 1913), 124.

90 Thomas Seaman has Alex receiving the $28,588. "The Adventures of 'Sea Wolf' McLean," *Victoria Daily Colonist,* 21 June 1953, magazine section, 11. One source has Alex MacLean and Max Weisman receiving some of the award. United States, House of Representatives, Department of Commerce and Labor, *Report from Committee on Expenditures in the Department of Commerce and Labor, in Relation to Fur-Seal Industry of Alaska, 31 January 1913,* House Report 1425, 62nd Congress, 3rd session, 4; House of Representatives, Department of Commerce and Labor, *A Statement Submitted in Re the Fur-Seal Herd,* 122-23.

91 The source is Henry Elliott. *New York Times,* 18 January 1914, 2. See also Elliott's statement in House of Representatives, Department of Commerce and Labor, *A Statement Submitted in Re the Fur-Seal Herd,* 123-24 and 132.

92 United States, House of Representatives, Seal Islands of Alaska. *Letter from the Secretary of Commerce and Labor Transmitting in Response to House Resolution No. 73, Information Relating to Seal Islands of Alaska, 19 July 1911.* House Doc. 93, 62nd Congress, 1st session, 555-56; *Victoria Daily Colonist,* 20 September 1907.

93 Charles Lillard, *Seven Shillings a Year: The History of Vancouver Island* (Ganges, 1986), 177; NARA, Records of the U.S. Fish and Wildlife Service, file 430 (bound section titled "Elliott data").

94 H.W. Elliott, "Thirty Years of Japanese Seal Piracy in Alaskan Waters," *New York Herald,* 8 September 1907, magazine section, 5.

95 United States, Senate, *Report from Committee on Foreign Relations, Amending S. 3410, to Authorize and Provide for Hearing and Trial of Suits by Citizens of United States for Compensation for Losses and Damages Occasioned by Seizure of Certain Vessels Engaged in Pelagic Fur Sealing, 13 April 1904,* report prepared by J.T. Morgan, Senate Report 2128, 58th Congress, 2nd session, 1-6.

96 United States House of Representatives, Judicial Committee, *Unlawful Seizures of Vessels in Bering Sea, Report to Accompany S. 1192 ... Submitted by Mr. Graham, 1 March 1924,* House Report 253, 68th Congress, 1st session, 2.

97 United States, House of Representatives, *Report from Committee on Ways and Means, Amending H. 13387, 2 June 1902,* report prepared by J.A. Tawney, House Report 2303, pt. 1, 57th Congress, 1st session, 2.

98 Ibid., 6-7.

99 Ibid., pt. 2.

100 Kurkpatrick Dorsey, *The Dawn of Conservation Diplomacy: U.S.-Canadian Wildlife Protection Treaties in the Progressive Era* (Seattle, 1998), 134.

Chapter 10: Poaching with the *Carmencita*, 1904-05

1 *San Francisco City Directory,* 1900-04; *San Francisco Examiner,* 15 June 1905, 1.

2 D.G. Paterson and J. Wilen, "Depletion and Diplomacy: The North Pacific Seal Hunt, 1886-1910," in P. Uselding, ed., *Research in Economic History,* vol. 2 (Greenwich, CT, 1977), 96-98.

3 Robben Island, in the Okhotsk Sea, would be ceded to Japan after the Russian-Japanese war. Walter A. McDougall, *Let the Sea Make a Noise: A History of the North Pacific from Magellan to MacArthur* (New York, 1993), 444-47; Leonhard Stejneger, "Fur-Seal Industry of the Commander Islands, 1897 to 1922," *Bulletin of the United States Bureau of Fisheries 1925* 41 (1927), 293.

4 Library and Archives Canada (LAC), Royal Commission to Investigate and Report upon Claims of Certain Canadian Pelagic Sealers, 1913-15, RG 33, series 107, v. 1, 1343-54.

5 Gordon Newell, ed., *The H.W. McCurdy Marine History of the Pacific Northwest* (Seattle, 1966), 104. See also Briton Cooper Busch, *The War against the Seals: A History of the North American Seal Fishery* (Montreal and Kingston, 1985), 292-93n64.

6 British Columbia Archives (BCA), Stuart Thompson, "Five Months with the Sea Wolf," interview by Salvatore Billeci, San Francisco, c. 1952, Add. MSS. E/E/M221T.

7 *Marine Digest,* 8 May 1971, 17.

8 *San Francisco Chronicle,* 15 June 1905; *San Francisco Examiner,* 15 June 1905 and 31 January 1906, 7. John Lyman, "Letter to Editor," *Marine Digest,* 7 August 1971, 26-27; *Oakland Tribune,* 15 June 1905; National Archives and Records Administration (NARA), Pacific Sierra Region, *United States v. Robert J. Tyson et al.,* Case 4307(3), Criminal Case Files 1851-1912 (United States District Court, Northern District of California), S.E.R. de Smidt, W.J. Wood, and W.J. Woodside, 9 June 1905, RG 21, Box 336.

9 *San Francisco Chronicle,* 15 June 1905. See also Lyman, "Letter to Editor," 26-27; *San Francisco Examiner,* 31 January 1906, 7.

10 Thompson, "Five Months," 1-3; *San Francisco Examiner,* 15 June 1905.

11 *San Francisco Examiner,* 15 June 1905.

12 NARA, Records of the U.S. Fish and Wildlife Service, agent's report, 12 October 1904, enclosed in Acting Attorney General to Secretary of Commerce and Labor, 10 January 1905, RG 22, sec. 91, file 114, sub-file *Carmencita.*

13 *San Francisco Chronicle,* 15 June 1905.
14 Gordon Ireland, "The North Pacific Fisheries," *American Journal of International Law* 36 (1942), 400-24.
15 Thompson, "Five Months," 2.
16 Ibid., 2; *San Francisco Chronicle,* 14 June 1905.
17 Thompson, "Five Months," 3-4.
18 *San Francisco Chronicle,* 15 June 1905; Robert O'Brien, "Alex McLean, the Sea Wolf," *San Francisco Chronicle,* 25 June 1952.
19 Thompson, "Five Months," 3-6.
20 LAC, Department of Marine and Fisheries, Commander Nugent to Vice Admiral Sir G. Noel, 8 October 1904; Sir Claude MacDonald to Marquess of Lansdowne, November 1904; Newbury to McDougall, 27 September 1905, RG 23, v. 359, file 3136; *San Francisco Chronicle,* 15 June 1905.
21 Thomas Seaman, "The Adventures of 'Sea Wolf' McLean," *Victoria Daily Colonist,* 21 June 1953, magazine section, 11.
22 Cecil Clark, "Seawolf McLean Tweaked Russia's Beard," *Victoria Daily Colonist,* 5 April 1959.
23 *San Francisco Chronicle,* 15 June 1905.
24 Ibid., 14 June 1905. See also Thompson, "Five Months," 4; NARA, Records of the U.S. Fish and Wildlife Service, agent's report, 12 October 1904, file 114.
25 Thompson, "Five Months," 4.
26 *San Francisco Examiner,* 14 June 1905; *San Francisco Chronicle,* 15 June 1905.
27 Thompson, "Five Months," 4.
28 *San Francisco Chronicle,* 14 June 1905; LAC, Department of Marine and Fisheries, Newbury to McDougall, 27 September 1905, v. 359, file 3136; NARA, Records of the U.S. Fish and Wildlife Service, agent's report, 12 October 1904, file 114; Thompson, "Five Months," 4.
29 See enclosures in NARA, Records of the U.S. Fish and Wildlife Service, agent's report, 12 October 1904, file 114, including clipping from *Victoria Daily Colonist,* 26 August 1904.
30 Thompson, "Five Months," 8.
31 Ibid., 7-8. See also Lyman, "Letter to Editor," 26-27; Elmer Green, ed., *Adventures of Carl Rydell: The Autobiography of a Seafaring Man* (London, 1924), 70.
32 The operative's reports, dated 11, 12, and 14 October 1904 are enclosed in NARA, Records of the U.S. Fish and Wildlife Service, Acting Attorney General to Secretary of Commerce and Labor, 16 January 1905, file 114, sub-file *Carmencita.*
33 Eric Hobsbawm, *Primitive Rebels: Studies in Archaic Forms of Social Movement in the Nineteenth and Twentieth Centuries* (Manchester, 1959), 15-17.
34 The registration, according to Stratton, had been forfeited on 24 September. NARA, Records of the U.S. Fish and Wildlife Service, F.S. Stratton to Washington, 27 February 1905, and Secretary of Commerce and Labor to Attorney-General, 9 January 1905, file 114, sub-file *Carmencita.* See also *San Francisco Examiner,* 14 June 1905; *San Francisco Chronicle,* 14 June 1905; LAC, Department of Marine and Fisheries, Sir Wilfrid Laurier to Governor General-in-Council, 27 December 1905, v. 359, file 3136.
35 *San Francisco Examiner,* 15 June 1905; Lyman, "Letter to Editor," 26-27. Norman Hacking, "The Victoria Sealing Fleet," *The Sea Chest* (Spring 1982), 99.
36 Busch, *War against the Seals,* 143.
37 A.E. Smith to State, 6 January 1905, cited in Alvin C. Gluek Jr., "Canada's Splendid Bargain: The North Pacific Fur Seal Convention of 1911," *Canadian Historical Review* 63, 2 (1982), 183.
38 Philip S. Foner, ed., *The Social Writings of Jack London* (Secaucus, 1964), 61.
39 Ambrose Bierce to George Sterling, 18 February 1905, cited in ibid., 60-61.
40 Earle Labor and Jeanne Campbell Reesman, *Jack London,* revised edition (New York, 1994), 58.
41 Russ Kingman, *A Pictorial Life of Jack London* (New York, 1979), 47-140. While in high school, London wrote a series of short stories for the student paper, based on his sealing experiences in 1893. James Sissons III, ed., *Jack London's Articles and Short Stories in the Ægis* (Oakland, 1981).
42 Tony Williams, "From Novel to Film," in Rocco Fumento and Tony Williams, eds., *Jack London's 'The Sea Wolf': A Screenplay by Robert Rossen* (Carbondale, IL, 2001), xviii.

43 Labor and Reesman, *Jack London,* xiii; Dale Walker, compiler, *The Fiction of Jack London: A Chronological Bibliography* (El Paso, 1972), 33.
44 Robert O'Brien, "Alex McLean, the Sea Wolf," *San Francisco Chronicle,* 27 June 1952.
45 NARA, Records of the U.S. Fish and Wildlife Service, Acting Attorney General to Secretary of Commerce and Labor, 16 January 1905, enclosures, file 114; *Victoria Daily Colonist,* 8 September 1905.
46 United States, House of Representatives, Seal Islands of Alaska, *Letter from the Secretary of Commerce and Labor Transmitting in Response to House Resolution No. 73, Information Relating to Seal Islands of Alaska, 19 July 1911,* Taylor to Charles J. Faulkner, 23 February 1905, House Doc. 93, 62nd Congress, 1st session, 218.
47 NARA, Records of the U.S. Fish and Wildlife Service, F.W. Villiers to Foreign Office, enclosure, 20 March 1905, file 114.
48 LAC, Department of Marine and Fisheries, Statement of Robert Mullins, San Francisco, 25 February 1905, enclosure from P. Ornelas to Newbury, 23 September 1905, v. 359, file 3136. As for Sanchez, "little is known of him but it is said by those now here that he became in debt." *Victoria Daily Colonist,* 15 September 1905.
49 LAC, Department of Marine and Fisheries, P. Ornelas to Newbury, 23 September 1905 (statements by Sanchez and Mullins enclosed), v. 359, file 3136.
50 *Victoria Daily Colonist,* 8 September 1905.
51 LAC, Department of Marine and Fisheries, Newbury to McDougald, 27 September 1905, v. 359, file 3136.
52 "I, Robt Mullins, Master Carpenter of Victoria, B.C. do certify that the schooner, named the *Acapulco,* was built at Victoria for Jose Sanchez, a citizen of Mexico, and that said schooner is of wood build, has one deck, two masts, is 92 feet in length, 29 feet in breadth, 8 feet in depth, of 138 net tons burden." LAC, Department of Marine and Fisheries, P. Ornelas to Newbury, 23 September 1905, v. 359, file 3136. The *Jennie Thelin* was ninety-one feet with a 29.5 foot beam and weighed 146 gross tons. *Marine Digest,* 8 May 1971, 17-21.
53 LAC, Department of Marine and Fisheries, Ornelas to Newbury, 23 September 1905, v. 359, file 3136.
54 *San Francisco Examiner,* 14 June 1905.
55 LAC, Department of Marine and Fisheries, Newbury to John McDougald, Commissioner of Customs, 27 September 1905, v. 359, file 3136.
56 Ibid.; LAC, Department of Marine and Fisheries, Report Outwards, Victoria, 2 March 1905, No. 840, v. 359, file 3136.
57 *Victoria Daily Colonist,* 7 September 1905.
58 *Vancouver Province,* 6 September 1905.
59 *San Francisco Examiner,* 15 June 1905.
60 *San Francisco Chronicle,* 14 June 1905. See also *Victoria Daily Colonist,* 17 June 1905.
61 *San Francisco Examiner,* 14 June 1905.
62 House of Representatives, Seal Islands of Alaska, *Response to House Resolution No. 73,* Communications Relative to Revenue-Cutter Patrol, 11 March 1905, 217-18.
63 LAC, Department of Marine and Fisheries, Newbury to McDougald, 28 September 1905, v. 359, file 3136; *Victoria Daily Colonist,* 27 August 1905.
64 *San Francisco Chronicle,* 15 June 1905.
65 Green, ed., *Adventures of Carl Rydell,* 70.
66 BCA, Max Lohbrunner, "Reminiscences," Add. MSS. E/D/L83, 7-8.
67 LAC, Department of Marine and Fisheries, Newbury to McDougald, 28 September 1905, v. 359, file 3136.
68 *San Francisco Chronicle,* 14-15 June 1905.
69 LAC, Department of Marine and Fisheries, Newbury to McDougald, 28 September 1905, v. 359, file 3136.
70 *San Francisco Chronicle,* 15 June 1905.
71 LAC, Department of Marine and Fisheries, Newbury to McDougald, 28 September 1905, v. 359, file 3136.
72 *Victoria Daily Colonist,* 7 September 1905. See also LAC, Department of Marine and Fisheries, Newbury to McDougald, 28 September 1905, v. 359, file 3136.

73 NARA, Pacific Sierra Region, *United States v. Robert J. Tyson et al.*

74 US Revised Statutes, section 5440, U.S. Comp. Stat. 1901, 3676: "If two or more persons conspire either to commit any offence against the United States, or to defraud the United States in any manner or for any purpose." *San Francisco Chronicle,* 14 June 1905; NARA, Pacific Sierra Region, *United States v. Robert J. Tyson et al.*

75 *San Francisco Examiner,* 14 June 1905; Busch, *War against the Seals,* 124.

76 *San Francisco Examiner,* 14 June 1905. Dennis Hensley, "Jack London's Use of Maritime History in the Seawolf," *Pacific Historian* 23, 2 (1979), 6, described de Smidt as a hooligan who surrendered in Tahiti. One should use Hensley with caution.

77 *San Francisco Chronicle,* 14 June 1905.

78 Cited in *Victoria Daily Colonist,* 17 June 1905, which noted it was a "characteristic comment" from that paper.

79 Hobsbawm, *Primitive Rebels,* 15.

80 *San Francisco Chronicle,* 15 June 1905.

81 Ibid., 14 June 1905.

82 Ibid., 15 June 1905. Witnesses before the grand jury included Daniel Clausson, S.E.R. de Smidt, Henry Sterling, Johnson MacCormac, E.F. Scott, Stewart Thompson, P.S. Tellar, W.M. Housner, H.B. Madison, E.H. Rix, James Sharkey, W.J. Shreve, H.M. Moffatt, and Henry E. Farmer. NARA, Pacific Sierra Region, *United States v. Robert J. Tyson et al.*

83 Clarise Stasz, *Jack London's Women* (Amherst, 2001), 65.

84 Robert A.J. McDonald, "'He Thought He Was the Boss of Everything;' Masculinity and Power in a Vancouver Family" (fifth annual Seagram Lecture, McGill Institute for the Study of Canada, Montreal, 17 January 2001), 3.

85 Tina Loo, "Of Moose and Men: Hunting for Masculinities in British Columbia, 1880-1939," *Western Historical Quarterly* 32, 3 (2001), 300.

86 T.J. Jackson Lears, *No Place of Grace: Antimodernism and the Transformation of American Culture, 1880-1920* (Chicago, 1981), xv.

87 Ibid., xv, 5, and 303.

88 Ibid., 112.

89 Anne-Marie Harvey, "Sons of the Sun: Making White, Middle-Class Manhood in Jack London's David Grief Stories and the *Saturday Evening Post,*" *American Studies* 39, 3 (1998), 39.

90 Amy Kaplan, "Romancing the Empire: The Embodiment of American Masculinity in the Popular Historical Novel of the 1890s," *American Literary History* 2, 4 (1990), 662 and 659.

91 Lears, *No Place of Grace,* 103; Kaplan, "Romancing the Empire," 660.

92 Kaplan, "Romancing the Empire," 662.

93 Labor and Reesman, *Jack London,* 60.

94 Jonathan Auerbach, *Male Call: Becoming Jack London* (Durham, 1996), 178. "*The Sea-Wolf* is about *social* mastery politics represented in rather raw terms. Accepting as a given the equation between masculinity and aggression, femininity and submission, London turns these perfectly traditional cultural associations inside out, relocating in relation to shifting identities marked by social class, vocation, and, most important, bodies that can both give and take intimate expressions of power" (194).

95 *San Francisco Chronicle,* 15 June 1905; *Oakland Tribune,* 14 June 1905.

96 *Oakland Tribune,* 14 June 1905; *San Francisco Chronicle,* 15 June 1905.

97 *San Francisco Chronicle,* 14 June 1905.

98 Ibid., 15-16 June 1905.

99 Ibid., 15-16 June 1905. Liquor smuggling in Alaska was profitable and easy. See Roland L. DeLorme, "Liquor Smuggling in Alaska, 1867-1899," *Pacific Northwest Quarterly* 66, 4 (1975), 145-52; Hobsbawm, *Primitive Rebels,* 15-17.

100 *San Francisco Examiner,* 15 June 1905.

101 *San Francisco Chronicle,* 14-15 June 1905.

102 *San Francisco Examiner,* 15 June 1905. See also Henry E. Huntington Library, San Marino, CA, Jack London Collection, Jack London to *New York Times,* 18 August 1905, and to Emma F. MacLean, Battle Ground, Washington, 12 December 1914: "I never personally laid eyes upon Capt. Alex McLean in my life but I was seal hunting off the coast of Japan and crossed the trail of his schooner many times in 1893. At that time, on the steamer *Alexander,*

another seal hunter, was his brother Captain Dan McLean. Somewhere in a newspaper clipping eight or ten years ago I read that Captain McLean's wife and daughter, or daughters, lived in Oakland, California. I imagine a letter addressed to Mrs. Captain Alex McLean, Oakland, Alameda County, California, would reach her." (Emma McLean had seen a note in the *Oregonian* on 4 September concerning his death and believed he was "my uncle in Vancouver, B.C. that I have heard nothing of for so long.") McLean to London, 10 November 1914.

103 *Victoria Daily Colonist,* 18 June 1905. Thomas Seaman later wrote that London "grasped opportunity for publicity by claiming Alex McLean as the prototype for his Wolf Larsen of the novel. Their characters were widely different, but London never knew." Seamen, "Adventures of 'Sea Wolf' McLean." This would be echoed by Cecil Clark: "As a publicity stunt, London – or his publisher – promptly claimed that the book's principal character, Wolf Larsen, was modeled after Alex MacLean. In reality there was no similarity; Wolf Larsen was a bucko who inspired terror in his men. MacLean wasn't that type at all." Cecil Clark, "Victoria Was a Smuggler's Hide-Away," *Victoria Daily Colonist,* 15 January 1961.

104 *Victoria Daily Colonist,* 18 June 1905.

105 Ibid., 20 June 1905.

106 For examples, see Hensley, "Jack London's Use of Maritime History," 1-2. See also Joseph Noel, *Footloose in Arcadia: A Personal Record of Jack London, George Sterling, Ambrose Bierce* (New York, 1940), 235: "'The South Sea Pearler' was the original source of 'The Sea Wolf' ... George Sterling also knew that I had contributed the original suggestion for the central character of 'The Sea Wolf.'" Charles Watson has argued that while Kipling's influence was significant for the creation of Larsen, the "shaping influence seems to have been London's rereading of *Moby-Dick,* for as others have noticed, Larsen bears a strong resemblance to Captain Ahab." *The Novels of Jack London: A Reappraisal* (Madison, 1983), 57-59.

107 This was the cook, "the coal-black Celt with the second-sight." This fictional character was based on George Maxwell. His father had come north as a young boy, and he as well as his children were raised in Cape Breton Gaelic communities. Rudyard Kipling, *Captains Courageous: A Story of the Grand Banks* (London, 1908), 48, 140, and 282; Charles W. Dunn, *Highland Settler: A Portrait of the Scottish Gael in Cape Breton and Eastern Nova Scotia* (Toronto, 1968), 139-40; Clara Dennis, *Cape Breton Over* (Toronto, 1942), 31-33.

108 Hensley, "Jack London's Use of Maritime History," 1-8.

109 Ibid., 1-5; *Marine Digest,* 8 May 1971, 20-21. Charles Watson notes that the MacLean rivalry was the basis for an episode in "An Odyssey of the North." Watson, *Novels of Jack London,* 53-78.

110 H.C. Woodbridge, J. London, and G.H. Tweney, compilers, *Jack London: A Bibliography* (Georgetown, 1966), 53.

111 Hensley, "Jack London's Use of Maritime History," 6.

112 *San Francisco Examiner,* 16 June 1905.

113 Ibid.

114 *San Francisco Chronicle,* 14-15 June 1905; *San Francisco Examiner,* 15 June 1905; *Victoria Daily Colonist,* 17 June 1905.

115 *San Francisco Examiner,* 15 June 1905.

116 The *San Francisco Chronicle,* on 17 June, had a three-column ad for London's new work, *The Game,* with *The Sea-Wolf* also prominent.

117 *San Francisco Examiner,* 15 June 1905.

118 *Oakland Tribune,* 15 June 1905.

119 *San Francisco Examiner,* 15 June 1905.

120 *Sydney Record,* 28 June 1905.

Chapter 11: The *Carmencita* Returns to Victoria, 1905

1 *Victoria Daily Colonist,* 7 September 1905.

2 United States, House of Representatives, Seal Islands of Alaska, *Letter from the Secretary of Commerce and Labor Transmitting in Response to House Resolution No. 73, Information Relating to Seal Islands of Alaska, 19 July 1911,* House Doc. 93, 62nd Congress, 1st session, 156. See also *Seattle Post-Intelligencer,* 9 October 1905.

3 *Victoria Daily Colonist*, 6 September 1905, reported that there were 114 skins. W.I. Lembkey, the agent in charge of the seal islands, was informed that the *Shearwater* search discovered 250 skins. House of Representatives, Seal Islands of Alaska, *Response to House Resolution No. 73*, 156. See also Cecil Clark, "Victoria Was Smuggler's Hide-Away," *Victoria Daily Colonist*, 15 January 1961, 8.
4 *San Francisco Examiner*, 25 August 1905; *Vancouver Province*, 12 October 1905.
5 *San Francisco Examiner*, 25 August 1905. See also National Archives and Records Administration (NARA), Records of the U.S. Fish and Wildlife Service, "Seizure of Pelagic Sealers, 1904-12," RG 22, sec. 91, file 114.
6 British Columbia Archives (BCA), Imbert Orchard, "Days of the Sealing Fleet: People in Landscape," interview with Jimmy Newman, Max Lohbrunner, Noel Robinson, 1970, No. 2466. See also Eric Hobsbawm, *Primitive Rebels: Studies in Archaic Forms of Social Movement in the Nineteenth and Twentieth Centuries* (Manchester, 1959), 19-20.
7 *Victoria Daily Colonist*, 7 September 1905.
8 United States, Congress, Behring Sea Claims Commission, *Record of Evidence Taken at Victoria, British Columbia by the Commissioners under the Convention of 8 February 1896, between Great Britain and the United States* (Washington, 1897), v. 1, 440.
9 BCA, Orchard, "Days of the Sealing Fleet."
10 Library and Archives Canada (LAC), Department of Marine and Fisheries, J.C. Newbury to John McDougald, 28 September 1905, RG 23, v. 359, file 3136.
11 *Victoria Daily Colonist*, 27 August 1905. The seal limit on the rookeries was now 15,000 yearly. Usually, this level was reached by 1 August and few remained on the islands after that. *San Francisco Examiner*, 25 August 1905. The *Vancouver Province*, 21 September 1905, also noted a raid around this time.
12 House of Representatives, Seal Islands of Alaska, *Response to House Resolution No. 73*, 156.
13 *Victoria Daily Colonist*, 6 September 1905.
14 House of Representatives, Seal Islands of Alaska, *Response to House Resolution No. 73*, Captain Chas. C. Fengar to Secretary of the Treasury, 20 September 1905, 223-24.
15 United States, House of Representatives, Department of Commerce and Labor, *Report on Alaska fur-seal fisheries, 31 August 1906*, submitted by Edwin W. Sims, Solicitor of Department of Commerce and Labor, House Doc. 251, 59th Congress, 2nd session, 31 August 1906, 20 and 25.
16 The quote is from A.A. Hurst, *The Call of High Canvas* (London, 1958), 250. See also Robert D. Foulke, "Life in the Dying World of Sail, 1870-1910," *Journal of British Studies* 3, 1 (1963), 110.
17 *Victoria Daily Colonist*, 6-7 September 1905; *Vancouver Province*, 6 September 1905; LAC, Department of Marine and Fisheries, Newbury to F. Gourdeau, 23 December 1905, and Newbury to McDougald, 28 September 1905, v. 359, file 3136.
18 Marcus Rediker, *Between the Devil and the Deep Blue Sea: Merchant Seamen, Pirates, and the Anglo-American Maritime World, 1700-1750* (New York, 1993), 261-62. See also Diana and Michael Preston, *A Pirate of Exquisite Mind. Explorer, Naturalist, and Buccaneer: The Life of William Dampier* (Toronto, 2004), 76-77.
19 *Victoria Daily Colonist*, 27 August 1905; *San Francisco Examiner*, 25 August 1905.
20 *San Francisco Call*, cited in *Victoria Daily Colonist*, 31 August 1905.
21 *Victoria Daily Colonist*, 31 August 1905.
22 LAC, Department of Marine and Fisheries, Newbury to McDougald, 28 September 1905, v. 359, file 3136. Newbury added that regarding the American cutter, "I have however no official information on this point." *Vancouver Province*, 5 September 1905.
23 LAC, Department of Marine and Fisheries, Newbury to McDougald, 28 September 1905, v. 359, file 3136.
24 *Vancouver Province*, 6 September 1905.
25 *Victoria Daily Colonist*, 6 September 1905; Clark, "Victoria Was a Smuggler's Hide-Away"; *Seattle Post-Intelligencer*, 6 September 1905, 10.
26 E.H. Harriman, "San Francisco," *Sunset Magazine* 17, 1 (1906), 1, http://shell3.ba.best.com/~sfmuseum/1906/pardee,html.
27 *Victoria Daily Colonist*, 6 and 8 September 1905; *Seattle Post-Intelligencer*, 6 September 1905; LAC, Department of Marine and Fisheries, Newbury to P. Ornelas, Consul General of Mexico,

San Francisco, 19 September 1905, and Newbury to McDougald, 28 September 1905, v. 359, file 3136.

28 The total pelagic catch for 1905 was 25,320 skins. *Victoria Daily Colonist*, 6-8 September 1905; House of Representatives, Department of Commerce and Labor, *Report on Alaska Fur-Seal Fisheries*, 8.

29 *Victoria Daily Colonist*, 6 September 1905; *Vancouver Province*, 6 September 1905; *Seattle Post-Intelligencer*, 6 September 1905.

30 *Victoria Daily Colonist*, 7 September 1905; LAC, Department of Marine and Fisheries, Newbury to McDougald, 28 September 1905, v. 359, file 3136; *Vancouver Province*, 6 September 1905; *Seattle Post-Intelligencer*, 7 September 1905.

31 *Victoria Daily Colonist*, 12 September 1905; *San Francisco Chronicle*, cited in *Victoria Daily Colonist*, 12 September 1905.

32 Newbury wrote the "wild conjecture" assessment on the clipping he sent to McDougald, 28 September 1905. Clipping A is from *Victoria Daily Colonist*, 17 June 1905, "which got into the hands of the crew." Clipping B is from 19 June 1905 issue. LAC, Department of Marine and Fisheries, Newbury to F. Gourdeau, 23 December 1905, v. 359, file 3136; *San Francisco Chronicle*, cited in *Victoria Daily Colonist*, 12 September 1905.

33 Noel Robinson, "The Real Sea Wolf," *Maclean's* 35 (1 January 1922), 13; Ian Macdonald, "Pirate of High Seas Ends in False Creek," *Vancouver Sun*, 15 October 1966, clipping in BCA, Alex McLean, vertical file.

34 *Victoria Daily Colonist*, 13 September 1905; LAC, Department of Marine and Fisheries, Newbury to McDougald, 28 September 1905, v. 359, file 3136.

35 Clark, "Victoria Was a Smuggler's Hide-Away."

36 F. Wilson, San Francisco, had power of attorney from R. de Smidt. There was a suggestion that the latter was sole owner. *Victoria Daily Colonist*, 13-14 September 1905.

37 *Victoria Daily Colonist*, 13 September 1905.

38 LAC, Department of Marine and Fisheries, Newbury to McDougald, 28 September 1905, v. 359, file 3136; R.S.C. 1886, c. 32.

39 LAC, Department of Marine and Fisheries, Newbury to P. Ornelas, 19 and 27 September 1905, and Ornelas to Newbury, 2 October 1905, v. 359, file 3136.

40 LAC, Department of Marine and Fisheries, Newbury to Ornelas, 6 October 1905, v. 359, file 3136. In enclosing copies to Ottawa, Newbury hastened to add: "It will be seen from this that the Provisional Certification was procured from the Consul-General through misrepresentation and fraud on the part of parties in San Francisco owning or operating the vessel and that as soon as the Consul-General had evidence of the facts he promptly reported to his Government who instructed him to cancel the Certificate of Registry which he had issued." LAC, Department of Marine and Fisheries, Newbury to McDougald, 15 November 1905, v. 359, file 3136.

41 LAC, Department of Marine and Fisheries, Ornelas to Newbury, 31 October 1905, v. 359, file 3136.

42 *Vancouver Province*, 14 September 1905.

43 Cited in *Victoria Daily Colonist*, 16 September 1905.

44 *Victoria Daily Colonist*, 14 and 16 September 1905; Tom MacInnes, *Klengenberg of the Arctic: An Autobiography* (London, 1932), 142.

45 William F. Benedict, "Death Downs the 'Sea Wolf,'" *San Francisco Chronicle*, 4 October 1914, magazine section, 2.

46 Clark, "Victoria Was a Smuggler's Hide-Away."

47 *Victoria Daily Colonist*, 14 September 1905. The story had appeared in the *San Francisco Examiner* on the previous Monday.

48 *Victoria Daily Colonist*, 14 September 1905; LAC, Department of Marine and Fisheries, Newbury to McDougald, 28 September 1905, v. 359, file 3136, which includes the story with his assessment written across it. For information on the $30,000, see Clark, "Victoria Was a Smuggler's Hide-Away."

49 *Sydney Record*, 18 September 1905.

50 *Victoria Daily Colonist*, 15 September 1905; LAC, Department of Marine and Fisheries, Newbury to McDougald, 27 and 28 September 1905, v. 359, file 3136.

51 *Victoria Daily Times*, 14 September 1905.
52 LAC, Department of Marine and Fisheries, Newbury to McDougald, 28 September 1905, v. 359, file 3136. Newbury later explained to F. Gourdeau: "I could not see my way clear to prosecute under imperial Bering Sea act as vessel carried the Mexican flag. The case is complicated and involved" (on 20 December 1905).
53 LAC, Department of Marine and Fisheries, Newbury to P. Ornelas, Consul General of Mexico, San Francisco, 19 September 1905, and Newbury to McDougald, 28 September 1905, v. 359, file 3136; *Victoria Daily Colonist*, 15 September 1905.
54 *Victoria Daily Times*, 14 September 1905; *Victoria Daily Colonist*, 15 September 1905.
55 The individuals involved in the action were Charles Croft, C. Walker, Peter Bishop, George Baker, F. Clausen [sic], and Samuel Smith. *Victoria Daily Colonist*, 16, 19, and 24 September 1905. The *Seattle Post-Intelligencer* reported that Fred Wilson maintained that de Smidt was the "sole owner." 15 September 1905.
56 If registered as a British schooner in Victoria, the duty would be around $250; if registered in the United States, the duty would be avoided. Gordon Newell, ed., *The H.W. McCurdy Marine History of the Pacific Northwest* (Seattle, 1966), 212; *Marine Digest*, 8 May, 3 July, and 7-14 August 1971.
57 NARA, Records of the U.S. Fish and Wildlife Service, Moffatt to John E. Wilkie, 15 September 1905, and Sims memo, 16 September 1905, file 114.
58 *Vancouver Province*, 21 September 1905; *Seattle Post-Intelligencer*, 15 September 1905.
59 *Seattle Post-Intelligencer*, 21 September 1905. See also *Vancouver Province*, 21 September 1905.
60 *Victoria Daily Colonist*, 22 September 1905.
61 Robert O'Brien, "Alex McLean, the Sea Wolf," *San Francisco Chronicle*, 30 June 1952; *Fur Trade Review* (March 1907), 190-92, contained in NARA, Records of the U.S. Fish and Wildlife Service, file 430; United States, House of Representatives, Department of Commerce and Labor, *A Statement Submitted in Re the Fur-Seal Herd of Alaska to the House Committee on Expenditures in the Department of Commerce,* compiled by H.W. Elliott (Washington, 1913), 117-18.
62 There is a renewal of his certificate as master of ocean steam vessels and as a San Francisco pilot, dated 20 February 1907. BCA, Alex McLean, vertical file. See also O'Brien, "Alex McLean, the Sea Wolf."
63 Customs Act, R.S.C. 1886, c. 32.
64 Cited in *Sydney Record*, 26 September 1905.
65 *Vancouver Province*, 12 October 1905.
66 "Cape Breton Man a Noted Poacher" was the front-page heading. *Sydney Post*, 19 September 1905 and 27 September 1905. The writer was not identified in the newspaper.
67 Don MacGillivray, "Henry Melville Whitney Comes to Cape Breton: The Saga of a Guilded Age Entrepreneur," *Acadiensis* 9, 1 (1979), 44-70; Ron Crawley, "Class Conflict and the Establishment of the Sydney Steel Industry 1899-1904," in Ken Donovan, ed., *The Island: New Perspectives on Cape Breton History, 1713-1990* (Fredericton, 1990), 145-64; David Frank, "The Cape Breton Coal Industry and the Rise and Fall of the British Empire Steel Corporation," *Acadiensis* 7, 1 (1977), 3-34.
68 Charles W. Dunn, *Highland Settler: A Portrait of the Scottish Gael in Cape Breton and Eastern Nova Scotia* (Toronto, 1968), 131-32.

Chapter 12: Setting the Record Straight

1 *San Francisco Examiner*, 29 January 1906, 7. By 1908, he was at 815 Burrard Street in Vancouver. City of Vancouver Archives (CVA), George J. McInnis, "Alexander McLean," manuscript.
2 *Vancouver Province*, 30 November 1905.
3 *Victoria Daily Colonist*, 7 August 1906.
4 Ibid., 28 January 1906. Fred Forrest and Alex MacLean and a Mr. Winch of Victoria had an interest in the *Ella G.* Percy Kent Winch was Alex's nephew, the son of Frank Winch and Marie Dauphin Winch. CVA, George J. McInnis, "Alexander McLean," manuscript, citing *Seattle Post-Intelligencer*, 29 January 1906.
5 The semi-weekly *Victoria Daily Times*, 30 January 1906, 4; *San Francisco Examiner*, 30 January 1906, 1.

6 *San Francisco Examiner,* 30 January 1906, 1.
7 It was a major maritime tragedy, with over 100 lives lost and some serious questions raised about the rescue attempts. *Victoria Daily Colonist,* 9 March 1906 and 14 February 1908, 13; *San Francisco Examiner,* 23 January-10 February 1906; Michael C. Neitzel, *The Valentia Tragedy* (Surrey, 1995).
8 *Victoria Daily Colonist,* 28 January 1906.
9 *San Francisco Examiner,* 30 January 1906, 1. See also *Victoria Daily Colonist,* 28-30 January 1906; *San Francisco Examiner,* 29 January 1906.
10 *Seattle Post-Intelligencer, San Francisco Chronicle,* and *San Francisco Examiner,* 29 January 1906.
11 *Halifax Herald* and *Sydney Record,* 1 February 1906.
12 *San Francisco Examiner,* 30 January 1906, 1.
13 *Victoria Daily Colonist,* 30 January 1906, 12; *San Francisco Examiner,* 30 January 1906, 1. Twain's cable read: "The reports of my death are greatly exaggerated" and was sent to the Associated Press in 1897. Emily Morison Beck, ed., *Bartlett's Familiar Quotations* (Boston, 1980), 625.
14 National Archives and Records Administration (NARA), Pacific Sierra Region, *United States v. Robert J. Tyson et al.,* Case 4307(3), Criminal Case Files 1851-1912 (United States District Court, Northern District of California), RG 21, Box 336; *San Francisco Chronicle,* 26 January 1906, 2, and 6 February 1906; *San Francisco Examiner,* 27 January 1906, 6, 31 January 1906, 7, and 1 February 1906, 3; John Lyman, "Letter to Editor," *Marine Digest,* 7 August 1971, 26-27. Cecil Clark, "Victoria Was a Smuggler's Hide-Away," *Victoria Daily Colonist,* 15 January 1961, 8. Special thanks to Lisa Miller, an archivist at NARA, San Bruno, CA.
15 NARA, Pacific Sierra Region, *United States v. Robert J. Tyson et al.* On 12 May 1916, a *nolle prosequi* was entered and the charge was withdrawn. P.G. Osborn, *A Concise Law Dictionary* (London, 1964), 221-22. Thanks to Blaise MacDonald (deceased) for legal clarification.
16 *Victoria Daily Colonist,* 9 March 1906.
17 United States, Senate, *Unlawful Seizure of Vessels in Bering Sea, 21 February 1906,* Senate Report 1201, 59th Congress, 1st session, 2-3; United States, House of Representatives, *Unlawful Seizure of Vessels in Bering Sea, 28 March 1906,* House Report 2674, 59th Congress, 1st session, 3-4.
18 *Victoria Daily Colonist,* 7 August 1906.
19 Ibid., 10 August 1906.
20 Robert Dunn, "Alaska, the Seal-Warder, and the Japanese Raiders," *Harper's Weekly* 50 (15 September 1906), 1310-11; *Sydney Record,* 11 August 1906.
21 *Sydney Record,* 11 August 1906. Robert DeArmond, a careful researcher, noted "it was reported" that MacLean was involved in the 1906 raid. "The Men behind the Sea Wolf," *Alaska Life* (May 1946), 44.
22 United States, House of Representatives, Seal Islands of Alaska, *Letter from the Secretary of Commerce and Labor Transmitting in Response to House Resolution No. 73, Information Relating to Seal Islands of Alaska, 19 July 1911,* Henry Wood Elliott to Wm. Loeb Jr., 4 September 1906, House Doc. 93, 62nd Congress, 1st session, 454; United States, House of Representatives, Department of Commerce and Labor, *A Statement Submitted in Re the Fur-Seal Herd of Alaska to the House Committee on Expenditures in the Department of Commerce,* compiled by H.W. Elliott (Washington, 1913), 119 and 201.
23 *Victoria Daily Colonist,* 7 and 10 August 1906, 28 June 1907, and 20 September 1907; House of Representatives, Seal Islands of Alaska, *Response to House Resolution No. 73,* 554-55 and 677.
24 House of Representatives, Seal Islands of Alaska, *Response to House Resolution No. 73,* 274-76; Leonhard Stejneger, "Fur-Seal Industry of the Commander Islands, 1897 to 1922," *Bulletin of the United States Bureau of Fisheries 1925* 41 (1927), 293 and 315-18.
25 F. Martin, *Sea Bears: The Story of the Fur Seal* (Philadelphia, 1960), 135.
26 G.O. Williams, *The Bering Sea Fur Seal Dispute: A Monograph on the Marine History of Alaska* (Juneau, 1984), 50-60. See also Martin, *Sea Bears,* 138; Alvin C. Gluek Jr., "Canada's Splendid Bargain: The North Pacific Fur Seal Convention of 1911," *Canadian Historical Review* 63, 2 (1982), 186-87.
27 United States, Senate, Alaskan Fisheries Division, *Reports Relating to Alaskan Seal Fisheries, 1906 and 1907, 11 March 1908,* report prepared by W.I. Lembkey, 1908, Senate Doc. No.

376, 60th Congress, 1st session, 9-12; House of Representatives, Seal Islands of Alaska, *Response to House Resolution No. 73,* 447.

28 The twelve were sentenced to three months at the jail in Valdez and then deported to Japan. For details, see Lembkey's report of 15 October 1906 in House of Representatives, Seal Islands of Alaska, *Response to House Resolution No. 73,* 249-52 and 391; Senate, Alaska Fisheries Division, *Reports Relating to Alaskan Seal Fisheries,* 12-15; Gordon Newell, ed., *The H.W. McCurdy Marine History of the Pacific Northwest* (Seattle, 1966), 129; Martin, *Sea Bears,* 135-42; *Seattle Post-Intelligencer,* 9 August 1906, 1-2.

29 Senate, Alaska Fisheries Division, *Reports Relating to Alaskan Seal Fisheries,* Agent Lembkey's preliminary report, 15 October 1906, 10-11.

30 Ibid., 27-28.

31 Ibid., 30.

32 House of Representatives, Seal Islands of Alaska, *Response to House Resolution No. 73,* Judge to Lembkey, 10 September 1906, 248.

33 Ibid., Elliott to Wm. Loeb Jr., Secretary to the President, 4 September 1906; Elliott to the President, 3 October 1906; Elliott to Hon. V.H. Metcalf, Secretary, Commerce and Labor, 3 October 1906, 454-57.

34 Senate, Alaska Fisheries Division, *Reports Relating to Alaskan Seal Fisheries,* 12. Sims was on the *McCulloch* when it conveyed the Japanese prisoners captured on St. Paul Island to Alaska. *New York Times,* 10 August 1906. House of Representatives, Seal Islands of Alaska, *Response to House Resolution No. 73,* Sims to Charles Earl, 22 September 1906, 248 and 455-56. Sims also wrote that he was disregarding Elliott's "acreage measurements" made in 1872-74 and 1890 because the method was "proven unreliable." United States, House of Representatives, Department of Commerce and Labor, *Report on Alaskan Fur-Seal Fisheries, 31 August 1906,* submitted by Edwin W. Sims, Solicitor of Department of Commerce and Labor, House Doc. 251, 59th Congress, 2nd session, 36.

35 House of Representatives, Seal Islands of Alaska, *Response to House Resolution No. 73,* 448-53 and 1159.

36 *Victoria Daily Colonist,* 20 September 1907. The passage from Bering Sea to Cape Flattery usually took between twelve to fifteen days, so it would just be possible for MacLean to raid in mid-July and get back to operate a tug out of Vancouver in early August, but one tends to side with the *Victoria Daily Colonist* over Elliott. See also British Columbia Archives, Max Lohbrunner, "Reminiscences," Add. MSS. E/D/L83, 6.

37 Williams has Alex in command of a sealer in 1906 with both Peruvian and Japanese registry. Williams, *Bering Sea,* 77n119. He does not cite a reference for 1906. Gordon Newell, ed., *The H.W. McCurdy Marine History of the Pacific Northwest* (Seattle, 1966), 248-49.

38 *Fur Trade Review,* March 1907, 190-92, cited in House of Representatives, Seal Islands of Alaska, *Response to House Resolution No. 73,* 1154.

39 United States, House of Representatives, Department of Commerce and Labor, *Expenditures in Commerce Department Committee, Fur Seal Industry ... submitted by McGuire of Oklahoma, 27 July 1914.* House Report 500, pt. 2, 63rd Congress, 2nd session, 13.

40 Henry Elliott, "The Loot and Ruin of the Fur-Seal Herd of Alaska," *North American Review* 185 (1907), 427-28.

41 Henry Elliott, "Thirty Years of Japanese Seal Piracy in Alaskan Waters," *New York Herald,* 8 September 1907, magazine section, 5.

42 The *Victoria Daily Colonist* version, 20 September 1907, which is rather abbreviated, identified Elliott as the author. The *Sydney Record,* 14 September 1907, was more comprehensive but gave no byline.

43 *Sydney Record,* 14 September 1907; House of Representatives, Department of Commerce and Labor, *Report on Alaskan Fur-Seal Fisheries,* 40. The average pelagic fur seal price at the London auction in 1890 was $15.25 per pelt. D.G. Paterson and J. Wilen, "Depletion and Diplomacy: The North Pacific Seal Hunt, 1886-1910," in P. Uselding, ed., *Research in Economic History,* vol. 2 (Greenwich, CT, 1977), 97.

44 Elliott, "Thirty Years of Japanese Seal Piracy."

45 Ibid.; *Fur Trade Review,* March 1907, in NARA, Records of the U.S. Fish and Wildlife Service, "Elliott data," file 430; Department of Commerce and Labor, *A Statement Submitted in Re the*

Fur-Seal Herd, 119 and 201; United States, Senate, *Report from Committee on Foreign Relations, amending S. 3410, to Authorize and Provide for Hearing and Trial of Suits by Citizens of United States for Compensation for Losses and Damages Occasioned by Seizure of Certain Vessels Engaged in Pelagic Fur Sealing, 13 April 1904,* report prepared by J.T. Morgan, Senate Report 2128, 58th Congress, 2nd session, 3-6.

46 NARA, Records of the United States Circuit Court of Boston, petition for naturalization, 1 December 1882, RG 21, sec. 146, file 156.

47 *Victoria Daily Colonist,* 14-15 September 1905, 29 December 1896, and 20 June 1905; Library of Canada (LAC), Department of Marine and Fisheries, Newbury to McDougald, 27-28 September 1905, RG 23, v. 359, file 3136; United States, Senate, *Fur Seal Arbitration: Proceedings of the Tribunal of Arbitration at Paris, 1893,* 53rd Congress, 2nd session (Washington, 1895), v. 3, 436 and 443.

48 *Victoria Daily Colonist,* 20 September 1907; *Sydney Record,* 14 September 1907; United States, Congress, Department of Foreign Relations, *Whaling and Sealing Claims against Russia,* report prepared by Herbert H.D. Peirce, Appendix 1, 1902, Doc. 1, 57th Congress, 2nd session, 93.

49 The Canadian contingent acquired most of their skins from the St. George herd that season. LAC, Department of Marine and Fisheries, Joseph Boscowitz et al. to Minister of Marine and Fisheries, 28 July 1908, v. 153, file 425, pt. 12; House of Representatives, Seal Islands of Alaska, *Response to House Resolution No. 73,* 541.

50 House of Representatives, Seal Islands of Alaska, *Response to House Resolution No. 73,* 504-6. See also Senate, Alaska Fisheries Division, *Reports Relating to Alaskan Seal Fisheries,* 81.

51 *New York Herald,* 17 August 1907, 2.

52 Senate, Alaska Fisheries Division, *Reports Relating to Alaskan Seal Fisheries,* 66, 70, and 89-92; House of Representatives, Seal Islands of Alaska, *Response to House Resolution No. 73,* 543.

53 Newell, *McCurdy Marine History,* 129n13; Martin, *Sea Bears,* 135.

54 *New York Times,* 10 August 1906.

55 House of Representatives, Seal Islands of Alaska, *Response to House Resolution No. 73,* Taylor to Elihu Root, 9 December 1907, 537 and 605.

56 House of Representatives, Department of Commerce and Labor, *Report on Alaskan Fur-Seal Fisheries,* 25.

57 Senate, Alaska Fisheries Division, *Reports Relating to Alaskan Seal Fisheries,* 92-95; House of Representatives, Seal Islands of Alaska, *Response to House Resolution No. 73,* 506.

58 Williams, *Bering Sea,* 60.

59 *Victoria Daily Colonist,* 28 June 1907.

60 Newell, *McCurdy Marine History,* 248-49; Williams, *Bering Sea,* 60-61.

61 Semi-weekly *Victoria Daily Colonist,* 4 September 1908, 16 and 20 October 1908, and 10 November 1908. *Victoria Daily Colonist,* 8 and 13 November 1908.

62 House of Representatives, Seal Islands of Alaska, *Response to House Resolution No. 73,* 694.

63 Semi-weekly *Victoria Daily Colonist,* 17 November 1908.

64 House of Representatives, Seal Islands of Alaska, *Response to House Resolution No. 73,* 590 and 605-8.

65 Ibid., 605-6, 677-78, and 692. See also LAC, Royal Commission to Investigate and Report upon Claims of Certain Canadian Pelagic Sealers, 1913-15, RG 33, v. 1, pt. 3, 348.

66 House of Representatives, Seal Islands of Alaska, *Response to House Resolution No. 73,* Munger to Secretary of the Treasury, 19 July 1908, 590, 674-75, 681-85, and 692.

67 Ibid., 30 July 1908, and Lembkey's annual report, 15 September 1908, 605-8, 685-86, and 692.

68 The memorandum dealing with the case was dated 9 March 1909. House of Representatives, Seal Islands of Alaska, *Response to House Resolution No. 73,* 691-95.

69 Williams, *Bering Sea,* 60-61 and 81. Williams' references are a bit confusing. Most of his sources here are congressional documents and none specifically mention MacLean in the context of the 1908 raid and the *Kensei Maru.* See House of Representatives, Seal Islands of Alaska, *Response to House Resolution No. 73,* 691-94.

70 Sims travelled on the cutter taking the seized sealers to Valdez. See House of Representatives, Seal Islands of Alaska, *Response to House Resolution No. 73,* 605-8, 674-75, and 685-86.

71 The "infamous" captain of *Winifred* fame was another legendary sealer, Gus Hansen, known as the Flying Dutchman, who had been nailed by "Fighting Bob" Evans in 1892. In his references, Williams also notes "Captain McLean of course was well known to the Revenue Marine in Alaska having formerly been the skipper of the *Winifred* and other vessels which had made incursions into the rookeries on both sides of Bering Sea." However, in 1892, the *Winifred* had been skippered by Gus Hansen, as Williams himself pointed out. Williams, *Bering Sea,* 36 and 81n184.
72 Semi-weekly *Victoria Daily Colonist,* 29 September 1908, 4, 30 October 1908, and 27 November 1908.
73 NARA, Alaska Region, *United States v. Schooner No. 2 Kensai Maru,* Civil Case Files 1902-39, file 355 (United States District Court, 3rd Division, Valdez, Alaska), RG 21; Semi-weekly *Victoria Daily Colonist,* 27 November 1908 and 1 December 1908; *Victoria Daily Colonist,* 6 September 1908, which also notes that the majority of the crew were Bonin Islands men. See also NARA, Records of the U.S. Fish and Wildlife Service, "Fur Seal Papers from files of Secretary Nagel," file 110, "Seizure of Pelagic Sealers, 1904-12," file 114, and "*Kensai Maru* Seizure," file 118.
74 Semi-weekly *Victoria Daily Colonist,* 27 November 1908.
75 *Vancouver Province,* 20 May 1908.
76 *Victoria Daily Colonist,* 16 April 1908. See also *Vancouver Province,* 15 April 1908; *Sydney Record,* 30 April 1908.
77 Art Downs, *British Columbia-Yukon Sternwheel Days* (Surrey, 1992), 69 and 75-77; R.G. Large, *The Skeena: River of Destiny* (Surrey, 1996), 119 and 137; Canada, Department of Marine and Fisheries, *Annual Reports,* 1908, Sessional Paper no. 21b, 140.
78 The pelagic catch that season was 15,000, with Victoria sealers accounting for 4,440 of them. The North American Commercial Company harvested 22,409. Semi-weekly *Victoria Daily Colonist,* 18 December 1908.
79 Williams' sources are Gordon Newell's *Sea Rogues' Gallery* (Seattle, 1971), 38-47; and Dennis E. Hensley's "Jack London's Use of Maritime History in the Seawolf," *Pacific Historian* 23, 2 (1979), 1-6. Newell's pertinent chapter, "Way of the Sea Wolf," lists many of the unsubstantiated accusations levelled against the MacLeans throughout their careers. Newell also notes that the *Kensai Maru* became the *Carmencita.* This chapter first appeared in *Adventure Magazine* (June 1955). Newell's *McCurdy Marine History,* 212 and 248-49, repeats many of these claims.
80 *Victoria Daily Colonist,* 26 October 1908, citing *Shipping Illustrated.* See also Jack London, *The Sea-Wolf,* edited and introduced by John Sutherland (Oxford, 1992), 43.
81 *Victoria Daily Colonist,* 28 October 1908.
82 Charles Madsen, with John Scott Douglas, *Arctic Trader* (New York, 1957), 185.

Chapter 13: The Final Years

1 Hugh Laracy, "Niels Peter Sorensen: The Story of a Criminal Adventure," *Journal of Pacific History* 35, 2 (2000), 159; *New York Sun,* 16 July 1908 and 29 March 1911; Robert D. Foulke, "Life in the Dying World of Sail, 1870-1910," *Journal of British Studies* 3, 1 (1963), 118.
2 *New York Sun,* 29 March 1911. When asked if his nickname was Sandy McLean, he replied: "Some used to call me Sandy." New York Supreme Court Archives (NYSCA), *Nels P. Sorensen v. Sun Printing and Publishing Association,* 1911, Alex McLean's testimony, 6.
3 *New York Sun,* 16 July 1908; Laracy, "Niels Peter Sorensen," 159.
4 *New York Sun,* 16 July 1908 and 29 March 1911; NYSCA, *Nels P. Sorensen v. Sun Printing and Publishing Association,* Alex McLean's testimony, 1.
5 Noel Robinson, "The Story of My Life," *Vancouver News-Advertiser,* 1 January 1913, magazine section, 7.
6 NYSCA, *Nels P. Sorensen v. Sun Printing and Publishing Association,* Alex McLean's testimony, 14; *New York Sun,* 29 March 1911.
7 NYSCA, *Nels P. Sorensen v. Sun Printing and Publishing Association,* Alex McLean's testimony, 52.
8 *New York Sun,* 29 March 1911.
9 NYSCA, *Nels P. Sorensen v. Sun Printing and Publishing Association,* Alex McLean's testimony, 86.

10 *New York Sun,* 29 March 1911.
11 NYSCA, *Nels P. Sorensen v. Sun Printing and Publishing Association,* Alex McLean's testimony, 6.
12 Ibid., 131 and 134.
13 Ibid., 53-54.
14 Ibid., 54-56.
15 Ibid., 57-59.
16 Jack London, *The Sea-Wolf,* edited and introduced by John Sutherland (Oxford, 1992), 103-4 and 180-83; Clarice Stasz, "The Social Construction of Biography," *Modern Fiction Studies* 22, 1 (1976), 55-56.
17 Russ Kingman, *A Pictorial Life of Jack London* (New York, 1979), 271-72; Clarice Stasz, *Jack London's Women* (Amherst, 2001), 208.
18 *New York Sun,* 29 March 1911.
19 Laracy, "Niels Peter Sorenson," 159-60.
20 Robinson, "Story of My Life."
21 Milton S. Eisenhower Library, Johns Hopkins University, William Churchill Collection, "Sorensen of the South Seas," Alex McLean to William Churchill, 23 April 1911, Scrapbook, Ms. 225.
22 D'Arcy Marsh, "London's 'Sea Wolf" in Scot's Clothing," *Vancouver Province,* 31 May 1958, 15; J. Gordon Smith, "Romance of the Pacific Coast Sealing Trade," *Toronto Globe,* 18 February 1911, 5. See *Henderson's Vancouver Directory,* 1910-14.
23 Beaton Institute of Cape Breton Studies, Cape Breton University, William "Billy Senator" MacDonald Papers, MG 12, file 88, A2a-g; *Vancouver News-Advertiser,* 5 September 1914; British Columbia Archives (BCA), Coroner's Report, Alex MacLean, 5 September 1914, Add. MSS. 383, v. 14, 6, GR 1327; City of Vancouver Archives (CVA), George J. McInnis, "Captain Alexander McLean," manuscript.
24 Robinson, "Story of My Life."
25 Noel Robinson, "The 'Sea Wolf': Story of a Tragic Treasure Hunt." *The Shoulder Strap* 10 (1943), 47.
26 Noel Robinson. "The Real Sea Wolf," *Maclean's* 35 (1 January 1922), 13.
27 Ibid., 12.
28 Ibid.; Robinson, "Story of My Life"; Noel Robinson, "Original of 'Sea Wolf' Resented Jack London's Book," *Vancouver Province,* 19 June 1943, magazine section, 3.
29 Lois Rather, *Jack London, 1905* (Oakland, 1974); Russ Kingman, *A Pictorial Life of Jack London* (New York, 1979), 152-54.
30 Robinson, "Story of My Life."
31 Robinson, "The 'Sea Wolf,'" 47. For William Hunt, "London's interest in the two-brother theme probably came from his friendship with Daniel and Alexander MacLean." *Arctic Passage: The Turbulent History of the Land and People of the Bering Sea* (New York, 1975), 249.
32 Robinson, "Story of My Life."
33 Tom MacInnes, *Klengenberg of the Arctic: An Autobiography* (London, 1932), 10.
34 NYSCA, *Nels P. Sorensen v. Sun Printing and Publishing Association,* Alex McLean's testimony, 65 and 72; *New York Sun,* 29 March 1911.
35 Kingman, *Pictorial Life,* 71 and 82; Otha Donner Wearin, *Johnny Heinold's First and Last Chance Saloon* (no place, 1974), 31-33.
36 Ronald Gillis, "The McLeans of Cape Breton and Scotland," *Sydney Post-Record,* 17 November 1936, 4.
37 CVA, George J. McInnis, "Captain Alexander McLean," manuscript.
38 NYSCA, *Nels P. Sorensen v. Sun Printing and Publishing Association,* Alex McLean's testimony, 53 and 61-63.
39 *New York Sun,* 29 March 1911.
40 Tom MacInnes, *Chinook Days* (Vancouver, 1926), 154.
41 Maxwell Geismar, ed., *Jack London: Short Stories* (New York, 1960), x; Charles N. Watson, *The Novels of Jack London: A Reappraisal* (Madison, 1983), 59.
42 "Tom MacInnes confirmed this view." Neil MacNeil, *The Highland Heart of Nova Scotia* (Toronto, 1971), 187-88.

43 London suggested that Mrs. McLean, who lived in Battle Ground, Washington, write a letter to Captain McLean's wife in Oakland. Emma F. McLean to Jack London, 10 November 1914; Jack London to Emma F. McLean, 12 December 1914, both contained in Henry E. Huntington Library, Jack London Collection, nos. 14412 and 12561. There is the possibility that they had crossed paths, but London was too drunk to remember. See Jack London, *John Barleycorn* (Santa Cruz, 1981). Also, Sam S. Baskett cautions that this source "cannot be trusted as autobiography." "Jack London on the Oakland Waterfront," *American Literature* 27, 3 (1955), 371.

44 Robinson, "Real Sea Wolf," 12.

45 "I did not know Alexander McLean intimately – few people did – though I foregathered with him upon a number of occasions during the years when I was covering the waterfront for one or other of the Vancouver newspapers." Robinson, "The 'Sea Wolf,'" 50.

46 Library and Archives Canada (LAC), Royal Commission to Investigate and Report upon Claims of Certain Canadian Pelagic Sealers, 1913-15, RG 33, series 107, v. 4, pt. 16, 1255. See also H.J. Morgan, *The Canadian Men and Women of the Time* (Toronto, 1912), 288.

47 *Marine Digest,* 36 (August 1958), 27.

48 Kurkpatrick Dorsey, *The Dawn of Conservation Diplomacy: U.S.-Canadian Wildlife Protection treaties in the Progressive Era* (Seattle, 1998), 134 and 134-39.

49 It included Edwin W. Sims and Charles H. Townsend. United States, House of Representatives, Seal Islands of Alaska, *Letter from the Secretary of Commerce and Labor Transmitting in Response to House Resolution No. 73, Information Relating to Seal Islands of Alaska, 19 July 1911,* House Doc. 93, 62nd Congress, 1st session, 811-12.

50 LAC, Department of Marine and Fisheries, *Annual Reports from Collector of Customs, Victoria, to Deputy Minister of Marine and Fisheries,* 22 December 1906, 17 December 1907, 18 December 1908, 20 December 1909, 20 December 1910, and 18 December 1911, RG 23, v. 262, file 1750. Price in 1909 was $30 per skin. United States, Congress, Department of Commerce and Labor, Bureau of Fisheries, *Special Investigation of the Alaska Fur Seal Rookeries, 1910,* report prepared by Harold Heath (Washington, 1911), 15.

51 In 1910, "pelagic sealing, on the part of the Japanese, continued with unabated vigor." Congress, Department of Commerce and Labor, *Special Investigation of the Alaska Fur Seal Rookeries, 1910,* 17; NARA, Records of the U.S. Fish and Wildlife Service, George Bowers to Charles Nagel, 17 November 1909, RG 22, sec. 91, file 110, pts. 1-2. See also Jozo Tomasevich, *International Agreements on Conservation of Marine Resources with Special Reference to the North Pacific* (Stanford, 1943), 90.

52 NARA, Records of the U.S. Fish and Wildlife Service, John S. Webb to Charles Nagel, regarding draft of lease proposed by the Bureau of Fisheries, 12 February 1910, file 110, pts. 1-12.

53 Alvin C. Gluek Jr., "Canada's Splendid Bargain: The North Pacific Fur Seal Convention of 1911," *Canadian Historical Review* 63, 2 (1982), 188.

54 House of Representatives, Seal Islands of Alaska, *Response to House Resolution No. 73,* 928; D.G. Paterson and J. Wilen, "Depletion and Diplomacy: The North Pacific Seal Hunt, 1886-1910," in P. Uselding, ed., *Research in Economic History,* vol. 2 (Greenwich, CT, 1977), 94-95.

55 Many sealers had originally been halibut schooners. E.W. Wright, ed., *Lewis and Dryden's Marine History of the Pacific Northwest* (Portland, 1895), 434. The halibut industry had been expanding continually from 1890. Paterson and Wilen, "Depletion," 127.

56 C. Fox Smith, *Sailor Town Days* (Boston, 1923), 178.

57 Gordon Newell, ed., *The H.W. McCurdy Marine History of the Pacific Northwest* (Seattle, 1966), 232.

58 Dorsey, *Conservation Diplomacy,* 145-62.

59 Ibid., 4 and 242.

60 Tomasevich, *International Agreements,* 91; Gluek, "Canada's Splendid Bargain," 179.

61 The report, from Commissioner L.A. Audette, was presented on 10 January 1916. Canada, *Pelagic Sealing Commission,* 1916, Sessional Paper no. 79.

62 Canada, Pelagic Sealing Commission, *Commissioner's Report,* 1916, Sessional Paper no. 79, 27-29 and see also Schedule B, 15.

63 F.W. Wallace, "B.C. Sealers Claims Revive Memories of Old Days," *Canadian Fisherman* 21, 8 (1934), 19. See also C.C. Tansill, *Canadian-American Relations, 1875-1911* (New Haven, 1943), 371.
64 Frank Kelley, "Descendants of Victoria Sealing Fleet Pioneers Still Hope for Settlement of Due Compensation," *Victoria Daily Colonist,* 16 November 1947, magazine section, 1; *Victoria Daily Colonist,* 19 November 1947; Peter Murray, *The Vagabond Fleet: A Chronicle of the North Pacific Sealing Schooner Trade* (Victoria, 1988), 236.
65 Gluek, "Canada's Splendid Bargain," 199.
66 NARA, Records of the U.S. Fish and Wildlife Service, T.W. True to George Bowers, 15 June 1911; Bowers to Charles Walcott, 10 July 1911; and Walcott to Bowers, 19 July 1911, all contained in file 430; Marshall McLean, "An Effort to Protect Fur Seal," *Field and Stream* 15 (1910), 722-76.
67 NARA, Records of the U.S. Fish and Wildlife Service, Nagel to Dr. Henry Osborn, 12 July 1911; Bowers to Rothermel, 4 August 1911; and Memo on Elliott and Hornaday Charges, all contained in file 130.
68 United States, House of Representatives, Department of Commerce and Labor. *Report from Committee on Expenditures in Department of Commerce and Labor, in Relation to Fur-Seal Industry of Alaska, 31 January 1913,* report prepared by J.H. Rothermel, House Report 1425, 62nd Congress, 3rd session; United States, House of Representatives, Department of Commerce and Labor. *Expenditures in Commerce Department Committee, Fur Seal Industry ... submitted by Mr. Rothermel, 4 April 1914.* House Report 500, pt. 1, 63rd Congress, 2nd session. See also *New York Times,* 30 January 1913, 1 and 3; 1 February 1913, 7; 18-19 January 1914.
69 Briton Cooper Busch, *The War against the Seals: A History of the North American Seal Fishery* (Montreal and Kingston, 1985), 156; United States, House of Representatives, Department of Commerce and Labor, *Expenditures in Commerce Department Committee, Fur Seal Industry ... submitted by McGuire of Oklahoma, 27 July 1914.* House Report 500, pt. 2, 63rd Congress, 2nd session; NARA, Records of the U.S. Fish and Wildlife Service, H.M Smith to Secretary of Commerce, 28 September 1916; and memo, 30 June 1917, both contained in file 130; United States, Senate, Commerce Committee, *Alaska Fur Seals Hearing on S. 3679, to Amend Act to Prevent Extermination of Fur-Bearing Animals in Alaska, 10 June 1926,* 69th Congress, 1st session, 2-6.
70 Canada, Department of Marine and Fisheries, *Annual Reports,* 1913, Sessional Paper no. 21b, 63; 1914, Sessional Paper no. 21b, 37; *Vancouver News-Advertiser,* 5 September 1914.
71 Albert Foote, "The Old Fashioned 'Bars and Brass Rails,'" *Vancouver Sun,* 12 August 1939, magazine section, 4.
72 *Vancouver Province,* 4 September 1914. According to Albert Foote, "Jake never got over this matter, thinking, perhaps, that his excessive hospitality might have [had] something to do with it." "Old Fashioned 'Bars and Brass Rails.'"
73 BCA, Coroner's Report, Alexander McLean, 5 September 1914, 9-10.
74 Ibid., 7.
75 Ibid., 7-10.
76 Ibid., 4.
77 *Vancouver News-Advertiser,* 5 September 1905.
78 Dr. George Frederick Curtis did the post mortem, estimating the body was six feet tall, around 190 pounds, and about forty-eight years in age. BCA, Coroner's Report, Alexander McLean, 5 September 1914, 3.
79 *San Francisco Chronicle,* 5 September 1914.
80 *Vancouver News-Advertiser,* 5 September 1914. See also CVA, Major Matthew Collection, Captain Alexander McLean, Add. MSS. 54.
81 *Vancouver News-Advertiser,* 6 September 1914.
82 MacInnes, *Chinook Days,* 149-50. See *Sydney Record,* 5 September 1914.
83 Robinson, "The 'Sea Wolf,'" 51. Captain George Marchant, one-time skipper of the *Beaver,* was one of the mariners who acted as pallbearers at Alex's funeral. Robinson, "Real Sea Wolf," 13.

84 Jones 2, Block 42, Plot 14, Lot 12. Lots 11 and 12 were purchased by a McLean. Lot 11 remains vacant. Mountain View Cemetery Records, Fraser St., Vancouver; W. Smith to M. Reiman, 21 April 1986 (enclosed), Vital Statistics, Ministry of Health, British Columbia, 13 April 1986 [copy of correspondence on file with author].

85 William Benedict, "Death Downs the Sea Wolf," *San Francisco Chronicle,* 4 October 1914, magazine section, 2.

86 Andrew Walker Roy, "'Sea Wolf' Was Nova Scotian," *Halifax Herald,* 8 February 1958, 5.

87 *Victoria Daily Colonist,* 5 April 1915, 3; *Victoria Daily Times,* 3 April 1915; Victoria, BC, Ross Bay Cemetery Records, Parks Department.

88 BCA, Death Registration, 1926-09-363178.

89 Robinson, "Story of My Life."

90 Lisa Norling, "Ahab's Wife: Women and the American Whaling Industry, 1820-1870," in Margaret S. Creighton and Lisa Norling, eds., *Iron Men, Wooden Women: Gender and Seafaring in the Atlantic World, 1700-1920* (Baltimore, 1996), 70-91.

91 The pallbearers were T. McCosh, Captain R.B. Bennett, Captain J.M. Hewitson, and Captain C.I. Harris. Charlie Harris, a sealer and harbour pilot, was originally from Gabarus Bay, Cape Breton. *Victoria Daily Times,* 18 and 20 January 1926; *Victoria Daily Colonist,* 19 and 21 January 1926; *Victoria Daily Times,* 13 March 1943. Her daughter Marie Winch died 10 January 1941 at the age of eighty-two. There is a small stone with the engraving: "In Loving Memory of Josephine Dauphin (1840-1915)/Lucy McLean (1862-1926)/Marie Winch (1859-1941)" in the graveyard. Victoria, BC, Ross Bay Cemetery Records, M72 E3/ M73 E2/M74.

92 The Division of Vital Statistics in British Columbia was unable to locate either individual in that province. Peter Bazowski to writer, 1 November 1984 [on file with author]. Nor is there any record of her in the Yukon. D. Darbyshire to writer, 12 August 1994 [on file with author]. Catherine fits into "the possibility that many young women in late nineteenth-century Victoria openly sought independent career goals." Peter A. Baskerville, "'She Has Already Hinted at Board': Enterprising Urban Women in British Columbia, 1863-1896," *Social History* 24, 2 (1993), 225.

93 D'Arcy Marsh, "London's 'Sea Wolf' in Scot's Clothing," *Vancouver Province,* 31 May 1958, 15. Attempts to establish a marriage or death certificate for Catherine were unsuccessful. Special thanks to Father Tim Coonen, St. Mary's Catholic Church, Dawson City; Cheryl Thompson, Dawson City Museum and Historical Society, and Ed and Star Jones, Santa Fe, New Mexico for their efforts.

94 United States, Senate, *Report from Committee on Foreign Relations, Amending S. 3410, to Authorize and Provide for Hearing and Trial of Suits by Citizens of United States for Compensation for Losses and Damages Occasioned by Seizure of Certain Vessels Engaged in Pelagic Fur Sealing, 13 April 1904,* report prepared by J.T. Morgan, Senate Report 2128, 58th Congress, 2nd session, 2.

95 Senate, *Report from Committee on Foreign Relations, Amending S. 3410,* 5.

96 John J. Underwood, *Alaska: An Empire in the Making* (London, 1913), 270. See United States, Senate, *Report from Committee on Foreign Relations, on S. 390, to Confer Jurisdiction Upon Circuit Court of United States for 9th Circuit to Determine in Equity Rights of American Citizens under Award of Bering Sea Arbitration of Paris; with Views of Minority, 29 January 1908,* report prepared by J.B. McCreary, Senate Report 140, 60th Congress, 1st session; United States, Senate, *Report from Committee on Foreign Relations favoring S. 391, 12 January 1910,* report prepared by H.D. Money, Senate Report 45, 61st Congress, 2nd session; United States, House of Representatives, Judiciary Committee, *Unlawful Seizures of Vessels in Bering Sea, Report to Accompany S. 2235 [to Confer Jurisdiction Upon Court of Claims to Adjudicate Claims of American Citizens Who Suffered Damages or Loss Resulting from Seizure, Detention, Sale, or Interference by United States of Vessels Charged with Unlawful Sealing in Bering Sea during Years 1875-96], submitted by Mr. Classon, 9 March 1922,* House Report 784, 67th Congress, 2nd session.

97 The favourable report came out of United States, House, Judicial Committee, *Unlawful Seizures of Vessels in Bering Sea, Report to Accompany S. 1192 ... submitted by Mr. Graham, 1 March 1924,* House Report 253, 68th Congress, 1st session. See also *Victoria Daily Times,* 25

January 1910; G.O. Williams, *The Bering Sea Fur Seal Dispute: A Monograph on the Maritime History of Alaska* (Juneau, 1984), 58; James Thomas Gay, "Bering Sea Controversy: Harrison, Blaine and Cronyism," *Alaska Journal* 3 (1973), 13.

98 See LexisNexis® Academic, *Bird et al. v. United States and Twenty-three Other Cases,* Nos. 5067-5090 inclusive, 24 F.2d 933 (12 March 1928) (Circuit Court of Appeals, Ninth Circuit); *San Francisco Chronicle,* 28 February 1928, 7.

99 LexisNexis® Academic, *Whitelaw v. United States,* No. 17114, 9 F.2d. 103 (16 September 1925) (District Court, N.D. Cal., First Division). See also LexisNexis® Academic, *The La Ninfa; United States v. The La Ninfa,* 49 F. 575 (1 October 1891) (District Court, District of Alaska); LexisNexis® Academic, *La Ninfa; Whitelaw v. United States,* 75 F. 513 No. 24 (29 June 1896) (Circuit Court of Appeals, Ninth Circuit).

100 LexisNexis® Academic, *Bird et al. v. United States and Twenty-three Other Cases.*

101 Ibid.

102 NARA, Pacific Sierra Region, *M.J. Lyon et al. v. United States,* United States District Court, Northern Division of California, San Francisco, 22 August 1928, Case No. 17543, Notes of Payment of Judgment, RG 21, Doc. 26,.

103 Elizabeth Faue, *Writing the Wrongs: Eva Valesh and the Rise of Labor Journalism* (Ithaca, 2002), 12; BCA, Coroner's Report, Alexander McLean, 6-8.

Chapter 14: The Legend of Alex MacLean

1 Richard Dorson, *America in Legend: Folklore from the Colonial Period to the Present* (New York, 1973), 76.

2 Ibid., 62.

3 Ibid., xv.

4 William A. Wilson, "Folklore and History: Fact Amid the Legends," in Jan Harold Brunvand, ed., *Readings in American Folklore* (New York, 1979), 456.

5 Richard Dorson, *American Folklore and the Historian* (Chicago, 1971), 161 and 159.

6 Ibid., 61.

7 Ibid., 158.

8 Charles Lillard, "Dining with a Sea Wolf," *Victoria Daily Colonist,* 11 June 1978, 12; Charles Lillard, *Seven Shillings a Year: The History of Vancouver Island* (Ganges, 1986), 176.

9 Dorson, *American Folklore,* 139.

10 Horace Beck, *Folklore and the Sea* (Middleton, CT, 1973), 369.

11 Keith Walden, "The Great March of the Mounted Police in Popular Literature, 1873-1973," Canadian Historical Association *Historical Papers* (1980), 41 and 54.

12 *Victoria Daily Colonist,* 26 October 1908.

13 Eric Sager, "Memory, Oral History and Seafaring Labour in Canada's Age of Steam," in Colin Howell and Richard Twomey, eds., *Jack Tar in History: Essays in the History of Maritime Life and Labour* (Fredericton, 1991), 245. For Klondike examples of faulty memories, see William R. Hunt, *North of 53: The Wild Days of the Alaska-Yukon Mining Frontier, 1870-1914* (New York, 1974), 201 and Pierre Berton, *The Klondike Fever* (New York, 1958), 439-45.

14 Walden, "Great March," 56.

15 Wilson, "Folklore and History," 462.

16 F.M. Kelley, "Sealing with the Sea Wolf," *Victoria Daily Colonist,* 18 June 1933, magazine section, 1.

17 Sager, "Memory, Oral History and Seafaring Labour," 237-38.

18 Robert D. Foulke, "Life in the Dying World of Sail, 1870-1910," *Journal of British Studies* 3, 1 (1963), 105-36.

19 Eric Sager, *Seafaring Labour: The Merchant Marine of Atlantic Canada, 1820-1914* (Montreal and Kingston, 1989), 201-21.

20 Sager, *Seafaring Labour,* 245-65.

21 Beck, *Folklore and the Sea,* 355.

22 *Halifax Herald,* 16 December 1994; Marcus Rediker, *Between the Devil and the Deep Blue Sea: Merchant Seamen, Pirates, and the Anglo-American Maritime World, 1700-1750* (New York, 1993), 185.

23 Beck, *Folklore and the Sea,* 356-57.

24 Horace P. Beck, "The Making of the Popular Legendary Hero," in Wayland D. Hand, ed., *American Folk Legend: A Symposium* (Berkeley, 1971), 121.
25 Dorson, *American Folklore,* 167.
26 Charles Madsden, with John Scott Douglas, *Arctic Trader* (New York, 1957), 185; Neil MacNeil, *The Highland Heart of Nova Scotia* (Toronto, 1971), 170-88. In 1914, Charles Spring described Dan MacLean as "a brother of the Sea Wolf." Library and Archives Canada (LAC), Royal Commission to Investigate and Report upon Claims of Certain Canadian Pelagic Sealers, RG 33, series 107, v. 3, pt. 13, 347.
27 Beck, "Making of the Popular Legendary Hero," 122-31.
28 Land transfer documents from 1883 have Alex's mother and sisters making their mark. Sydney, Registry of Deeds, Book QQ, 204-12; Jack London, *The Sea-Wolf,* edited and introduced by John Sutherland (Oxford, 1992), 88.
29 Dorson, *America in Legend,* 61; 75; Dorson, *American Folklore,* 91.
30 Beck, *Folklore and the Sea,* 122; Beck, "Making of the Popular Legendary Hero," 128.
31 Noel Robinson, "The 'Sea Wolf': Story of a Tragic Treasure Hunt, *The Shoulder Strap* 10 (1943), 47.
32 D'Arcy Marsh, "London's 'Sea Wolf' in Scot's Clothing," *Vancouver Province,* 31 May 1958, 15.
33 Noel Robinson, "The Story of My Life;" *Vancouver News-Advertiser* 1 January 1913, magazine section, 7; Ronald Gillis, "The MacLeans of Cape Breton and Scotland," *Sydney Post-Record,* 17 November 1936, 4. George Cessford described them as "a pair of steel blue eyes." Cecil Clark, "Seawolf McLean Tweaked Russia's Beard," *Victoria Daily Colonist,* 5 April 1959; London, *The Sea-Wolf,* 21, 143, 192, and 221.
34 William F. Benedict, "Death Downs the 'Sea Wolf,'" *San Francisco Chronicle,* 4 October 1914, magazine section, 2.
35 Beck, "Making of the Popular Legendary Hero," 130.
36 Robinson, "Story of My Life."
37 British Columbia Archives (BCA), Imbert Orchard, "Days of the Sealing Fleet; People in Landscape," interview with Jimmy Newman, Max Lohbrunner, Noel Robinson, 1970, No. 2466.
38 Beck, "Making of the Popular Legendary Hero," 130.
39 Dorson, *American Folklore,* 101; Dorson, *America in Legend,* 61.
40 Thomas Seaman, "The Adventures of 'Sea Wolf' McLean," *Victoria Daily Colonist,* 21 June 1953, magazine section, 11.
41 Clark, "'Seawolf' McLean Tweaked Russia's Beard."
42 Norman Hacking, "Freebooter of Sealing Recalled," *Vancouver Province,* 28 August 1971, 15.
43 Clark, "'Seawolf' McLean Tweaked Russia's Beard."
44 Marsh, "London's 'Sea Wolf' in Scot's Clothing."
45 *New York Sun,* 29 March 1911.
46 London, *The Sea-Wolf,* 70.
47 Agnes Rothery, *The Ports of British Columbia* (New York, 1943), 31-32.
48 MacNeil, *Highland Heart,* 184. See also Noel Robinson, "The Real Sea Wolf," *Maclean's* 35 (1 January 1922), 41; London, *The Sea-Wolf,* 43 and 191.
49 Robinson, "Real Sea Wolf," 41.
50 Rothery, *Ports of British Columbia,* 31-32.
51 MacNeil, *Highland Heart,* 175, 178.
52 Ibid., 184.
53 Ibid., 184. For a similar version, see Beaton Institute of Cape Breton Studies (BI), Cape Breton University, Joseph Lawrence MacDonald, interview, Tape 326. See London, *The Sea-Wolf,* 165-69.
54 W.G. Emery, "With the Fur-Seal Hunters," *National Magazine* 6, 2 (1897), 99-109; *San Francisco Coast Seamen's Journal,* 9 and 16 October 1895; New York Supreme Court Archives, *Nels P. Sorensen v. Sun Printing and Publishing Association,* 1911, Alex MacLean's testimony, 13, 48, and 98; Robinson, "Story of My Life."
55 R.N. DeArmond, "The Men behind the Sea Wolf," *Alaska Life* (May 1946), 44.
56 Robinson, "The 'Sea Wolf,'" 47.

57 Stephen Tatum, *Inventing Billy the Kid: Visions of the Outlaw in America, 1881-1981* (Albuquerque, 1982), 122.
58 *Sydney Post,* 27 September 1905.
59 See Tatum, *Inventing Billy the Kid,* 188.
60 Frank Luther Mott, *A History of American Magazines, IV 1885-1905* (Cambridge, 1957), 636.
61 Amy Kaplan, "Romancing the Empire: The Embodiment of American Masculinity in the Popular Historical Novel of the 1890s," *American Literary History* 2, 4 (1990), 659-90; T.J. Jackson Lears, *No Place of Grace: Antimodernism and the Transformation of American Culture, 1880-1920* (Chicago, 1981).
62 Emmett Dalton, in collaboration with Jack Jungmeyer, *When the Daltons Rode* (Garden City, 1931), 199; Tatum, *Inventing Billy the Kid,* 195.
63 *Sydney Record,* 14 and 24 September 1907. See also London, *The Sea-Wolf,* 343; Tony Williams, *Jack London, The Movies: An Historical Survey* (Los Angeles, 1992), 223.
64 Hobart Bosworth, "My Jack London," *Mark Twain Quarterly* 5, (1943), 2-5 and 24. The first public showing was in San Francisco on 5 October 1913. Williams, *Jack London, The Movies,* 26-28. For some of the background difficulties, see Clarise Stasz, *American Dreamers: Charmian and Jack London* (New York, 1988), 267-77.
65 Jack London to Hughes Massie, 16 December 1916, contained in King Hendricks and Irving Shepard, eds., *Letters from Jack London* (London, 1965), 411.
66 MacNeil, *Highland Heart,* 187-88. MacLean might have been mollified had he known that Edward G. Robinson would be Wolf Larsen in the classic film treatment in 1941.
67 Aside from the early unofficial versions, the movies include:

- *The Sea Wolf,* 3 reels, 1913;
- *The Sea Wolf* (with Hobart Bosworth and Viola Barry), 1913;
- *The Sea Wolf* (Paramount-Artcraft, with Noah Berry, Mabel Julienne Scott, and Tom Forman), 1920;
- *The Sea Wolf,* 1926;
- *The Sea Wolf* (with Milton Sills, Raymond Hackett, and Jane Keith), 1930;
- *The Sea Wolf* (Warner Brothers, with Edward G. Robinson, Ida Lupino, John Garfield, and Barry Fitzgerald), March 1941;
- *Barricade* (with Raymond Massey and Robert Douglas), 1950 (this one is in a cowboy setting);
- *Wolf Larsen* (Allied Artists, with Barry Sullivan, Peter Graves, Gita Hall, Thayer David, and John Alderson), October 1958; and
- *Wolf Larsen* (with Chuck Connors), 1975.

H.C. Woodbridge, J. London, and G.H. Tweney, compiler, *Jack London: A Bibliography* (Georgetown, CA, 1966), 282-86; John Sutherland's notes in London, *The Sea-Wolf,* 342-46. *Halifax Sunday News,* April 1993, http://204.202.128/archive/news/Todays_Stories/980625/cage062598.html.

68 MacNeil, *Highland Heart,* 170. Neil's father "had known both brothers from youth, [and] maintained contact of some sort" with Alex for years, as did Neil's older uncle, Captain Alexander MacNeil. Neil MacNeil to writer, 6 November 1986 [on file with author].
69 Michael to Mary Ellen, 12 April 1966 (copy received from Bill Norin, Claremont, CA) [on file with author].
70 BI, William "Billy Senator" MacDonald Papers, MG 12, file 88, A2b.
71 "Billy Senator" MacDonald died in 1959. Noel Robinson, "Real Sea Wolf"; Robert Morgan, *Perseverance: The Story of Cape Breton's University College 1952-2002* (Sydney, 2004), 33-34 and 52.
72 Earle Labor and Jeanne Campbell Reesman, *Jack London* (New York, 1994), 8-9.
73 Allan Smith, "The Myth of the Self-Made Man in English Canada, 1850-1914," *Canadian Historical Review* 59, 2 (1978), 211-12.
74 Smith, "Myth of the Self-Made Man," 189-90.
75 Susan Ward, "Social Philosophy as Best-Seller: Jack London's 'The Sea-Wolf,'" *Western American Literature* 17, 4 (1983), 329.

76 H.J. Snow, *In Forbidden Seas: Recollections of Sea-Otter Hunting in the Kurils* (London, 1910), 264.
77 Eric Hobsbawm, *Primitive Rebels: Studies in Archaic Forms of Social Movement in the Nineteenth and Twentieth Centuries* (Manchester, 1959), 15-25.
78 *San Francisco Examiner,* 15 June 1905; *San Francisco Chronicle,* 14-15 June 1905.
79 Dorson, *American Folklore,* 91-92.
80 Tatum, *Inventing Billy the Kid,* 197.
81 Dorson, *America in Legend,* xiv.
82 Kevin Franklin, "In Search of Sophia," *Tucson Weekly,* 11-18 December 1997, http://www.tucsonweekly.com/tw/12-18-97/outthere.htm.
83 Jonathan Auerbach, *Male Call: Becoming Jack London* (Durham, 1996), 1.
84 B.A. McKelvie, "Victoria Mariner Tells Story of 'Sea Wolf' Alex MacLean," *Vancouver Province,* 8 May 1943, magazine section, 3; Noel Robinson, "Original of 'Sea Wolf' Resented Jack London's Book," *Vancouver Province,* 19 June 1943, magazine section, 3; Gillis, "MacLeans of Cape Breton and Scotland."
85 Frank Kelley, "Descendants of Victoria Sealing Fleet Pioneers Still Hope for Settlement of Due Compensation," *Victoria Daily Colonist,* 16 November 1947, 20; *Victoria Daily Colonist,* 19 November 1947; Ron Kenyrn, "Over the Forearm," *Vancouver Province,* 8 December 1936, 4; F.W. Wallace, "B.C. Sealers Claim Revive Memories of Old Days," *Canadian Fisherman* 21, 8 (1934), 19.
86 *Vancouver Province,* 19 September 1949, 11.
87 *Marine Digest,* 8 May 1971, 17-21; 3 July 1971, 22; 7 August 1971, 26-27; 14 August 1971, 22-23.
88 George Bowering, *Shoot!* (Toronto, 1994), 59.
89 Edward Butts, "The McLean Gang," *Canadian Encyclopedia,* vol. 2 (Edmonton, 1985), 1062-63.
90 George Bowering, *Bowering's B.C.: A Swashbuckling History* (Toronto, 1996).
91 J.I. Little, "Popular Resistance to Legal Authority in the Upper St. Francis District of Quebec: The Megantic Outlaw Affair of 1888-89," *Labour/Le Travail* 33 (Spring 1994), 97-124. See also E.P. Thompson, "The Moral Economy of the English Crown," *Past and Present* 50 (1971), 76-136.
92 George Donaldson, letter to the editor, *Vancouver Sun,* 22 September 1966.
93 Charles Lillard, "The Silent Voices of the Past," *Victoria Times Colonist,* 12 September 1987.
94 London, *The Sea-Wolf,* 140.
95 Raymond Davis, "The Fur Seal Killers," *Defenders,* 50 (1975), 374-80.
96 Gustav W. Verderber, "In the Presence of Seals," Sojourns in Nature, http://www.sojournsinnature.com/essayseals.php; and "Of Seals and Sealing," http://www.native-net.org/archive/nl/9502/0251.html.
97 Seal Pups Being Skinned Alive, http://www.cbc.ca/stories/print/2004/04/14/canada/seals_20040414; and, About the Canadian Seal Hunt, http://www.hsus.org/marine_mammals/protect_seals/about_the_canadian_seal_hunt/?prin.
98 Cecil Adams, "Is Paul Bunyan a Fraud?" The Straight Dope, http://www.straightdope.com/columns/020510.html.
99 Otha Donner Wearin, *Johnny Heinold's First and Last Chance* (no publisher, 1974), 32-33, http://www.heinoldsfirstandlastchance.com.
100 Benedict, "Death Downs the 'Sea Wolf,'" 2.
101 Allan E. Marble, *Nova Scotians at Home and Abroad* (Windsor, 1977).
102 Conversations with Michael MacPhee, Big Pond, 6 July 1995; Donald MacEachern, Sydney, 7 March 1994; Johnny Macintyre, East Bay, 27 September 1994.
103 Conversation with Donnie MacLellan, Sydney, 5 May 1997.
104 T.W. Paterson, "Alex McLean Was Much Bigger Than Life," *Nanaimo Daily News,* 15 October 1999, C2.
105 Tatum, *Inventing Billy the Kid,* 173.
106 Rosemary Langhout, "Alternative Opportunities: The Development of Shipping at Sydney Harbour 1842-1889," in K. Donovan, ed., *Cape Breton at 200: Historical Essays in Honour of the Island's Bicentennial 1785-1985* (Sydney, 1985), 53-69; Eric Sager, with Gerald Panting,

Maritime Capital: The Shipping Industry in Atlantic Canada, 1820-1914 (Montreal and Kingston, 1990).

107 John Shaw, "Observations on the Cape Breton Gàidhealtachd and Its Relevance to Present-Day Celtic Studies," in Gordon MacLennan, ed., *Proceedings of the First North American Congress of Celtic Studies* (Ottawa, 1988), 75-87; Ian McKay, *The Quest of the Folk: Antimodernism and Cultural Selection in Twentieth-Century Nova Scotia* (Montreal and Kingston, 1994); Michael Kennedy, *Gaelic Nova Scotia: An Economic, Cultural, and Social Impact Study* (Halifax, 2002).

108 David Frank, *J.B. McLachlan: A Biography* (Toronto, 1999), 7.

109 Rex Murphy, "Yesterday's Hero, Tomorrow's Hypocrite," *Toronto Globe and Mail,* 4 March 2006, A19.

110 *Toronto Globe and Mail,* 4 March 2006, A3.

111 Halifax Herald, *13 September 2006, B3.*

112 Ibid., 16 March 2007, A4.

113 Associated Press, 3 February 2007, http://www.ctv.ca/servlet/ArticleNews/print/CTVNews/20070202/fur_seal_070302/2007.

Bibliography

Archival Collections

Beaton Institute of Cape Breton Studies, Cape Breton University. Ronald Gillis Papers, MG 12, file 87.

–. G. Fred MacDonald Collection, MG 15, file 41.

–. Joseph Lawrence MacDonald, Tape 326.

–. William "Billy Senator" MacDonald Papers, MG 12, file 88.

–. Captain John Parker Collection, MG 12, file 50.

British Columbia Archives. E.C. Baker Diaries, Add. MSS. 707.

–. James Baker, vertical file.

–. Alf Bissett, vertical file.

–. Coroner's Report, Death Registration, Alexander McLean, Add. MSS. 383/14, GR 1327, Attorney General (1872-1937).

–. Max Lohbrunner, "Reminiscences," Add. MSS. E/D/L83.

–. B.A. McKelvie, "Saga of Sealing." Manuscript from the recollections of Captain Ernest F. Jordan, Add. MSS. 5.

–. Captain Alex McLean, vertical file.

–. Imbert Orchard, "Days of the Sealing Fleet: People in Landscape." Interview with Jimmy Newman, Max Lohbrunner, Noel Robinson, 1970, No. 2466.

–. R.H. Roy Collection, Add. MSS. 995.

–. J. Gordon Smith, Add. MSS. 383.

–. Charles Spring, "Origins of Pelagic Sealing in British Columbia and Its Progress," manuscript.

–. Eva Marie Sweeney, Add. MSS. 792.

–. Stuart Thompson, "Five Months with the 'Sea Wolf.'" Interview by Salvatore Billeci, San Francisco, ca. 1952, Add. MSS. E/E/M221T.

–. Victoria Sealing Company, Add. MSS. 16.

California Academy of Sciences, Anthropology Department. Liebes Collection, notes.

Cape Breton. St. Mary's Church, East Bay, Parish Records.

City of Vancouver Archives. Herbert Lindsay Cadieux Collection, vol. 38, 241-45.

–. George J. McInnis, "Alexander MacLean." Manuscript.

–. Major Matthew Collection, Captain Alexander McLean, Add. MSS. 54.

Halifax, NS. Greg McDonald Private Collection. James McNeil correspondence

Henry E. Huntington Library, San Marino, CA. Jack London Collection.

Library and Archives Canada (LAC). Department of Marine and Fisheries, RG 23.

–. Dominion Police Records, 1872-1919, RG 18.

–. Great Britain, Admiralty, Pacific Station Records, RG 8.

–. North West Mounted Police Records, RG 18.

–. Records of the Yukon Territory, RG 91.

–. Royal Commission to Investigate and Report upon Claims of Certain Canadian Pelagic Sealers, 1913-15, RG 33.
–. Sir Arthur Percy Sherwood Papers, MG 29/C/103.
Milton S. Eisenhower Library, Johns Hopkins University, Baltimore, MD. William Churchill Collection, Ms. 225.
National Archives and Records Administration (NARA), College Park, MD. Records of the United States Circuit Court of Boston, Petition for Naturalization, RG 21.
–. Records of the U.S. Fish and Wildlife Service, RG 22, Sec. 91.
Nova Scotia Archives and Records Management, Halifax. City Prison Register, Halifax, RG 35.
–. Stipendiary Magistrate's Court, RG 42.
Sydney. Registry of Deeds.
Vancouver, BC. Mountain View Cemetery Records.
Victoria, BC. Parish Records, St. Andrew's Cathedral, Victoria.
Victoria, BC. Ross Bay Cemetery Records, Parks Department.

Government Reports

Canada. Behring Sea Claims Commission. *Argument on Behalf of Great Britain.* 1896.
–. *Correspondence Relative to the Seizure of British American Vessels in 1886.* Ottawa, 1897.
–. Department of Fisheries. *Annual Reports.* 1885–89. Sessional Papers.
–. Department of Marine and Fisheries. *Annual Reports.* 1882–84 and 1907–16. Sessional Papers.
–. House of Commons. *Parliamentary Debates.* 1887-89.
–. Minister of Public Works. *Annual Reports.* 1881–84. Sessional Papers.
–. North West Mounted Police, Yukon Territory. *Reports.* 1900–02. Sessional Papers.
–. Mr. William Ogilvie, Commissioner of the Yukon Territory. *Report.* 1900. Sessional Papers.
–. Pelagic Sealing Commission. *Commissioner's Report.* 1916. Sessional Papers.
Great Britain. *British Solomon Islands, Colonial Reports. Annual Reports.* 1897-99.
–. Colonial Office. Original Correspondence, Western Pacific, 1878-1914. CO 225.
United States. Congress. Behring Sea Claims Commission. *Record of Evidence Taken at Victoria, British Columbia by the Commissioners under the Convention of 8 February 1896, between Great Britain and the United States.* Washington: Government Printing Office (GPO), 1897.
–. Department of Commerce and Labor, Bureau of Fisheries. *Special Investigation of the Alaska Fur-Seal Arbitration: The Counter Case of the United States before the Tribunal of Arbitration to Convene at Paris.* Washington: GPO, 1893.
–. Department of Foreign Relations. *Whaling and Sealing Claims against Russia.* Report prepared by Herbert H.D. Peirce. Appendix 1, 1902, Doc. 1, 57th Congress, 2nd session.
–. Department of the Treasury. Commission on Fur-Seal Investigations. *The Fur Seals and Fur Seal Islands of the North Pacific Ocean.* Compiled by Henry W. Elliott. 3 volumes. Washington: GPO, 1898.
–. Department of the Treasury. *Seals and Salmon Fisheries and General Resources of Alaska.* 4 volumes. Washington: GPO, 1898.
–. *Report on the Condition of the Fur-Seal Fisheries of the Pribilof Islands in 1890.* Compiled by H.W. Elliott. Paris, 1893.
–. *Seal Rookeries, 1910.* Report prepared by Harold Heath. Washington: GPO, 1911.
United States. House of Representatives. Seal Islands of Alaska. *Letter from the Secretary of Commerce and Labor Transmitting in Response to House Resolution No. 73, Information Relating to Seal Islands of Alaska, 19 July 1911.* House Doc. 93, 62nd Congress, 1st session.
–. Department of Commerce and Labor. *Expenditures in Commerce Department Committee, Fur Seal Industry ... Submitted by McGuire of Oklahoma, 27 July 1914.* House Report 500, pt. 2, 63rd Congress, 2nd session.
–. Department of Commerce and Labor. *Report on Alaskan Fur-Seal Fisheries, 31 August 1906.* Submitted by Edwin W. Sims, Solicitor of Department of Commerce and Labor. House Doc. 251, 59th Congress, 2nd session.

–. Department of Commerce and Labor. *Report from Committee on Expenditures in Department of Commerce and Labor, in Relation to Fur-Seal Industry of Alaska, 31 January 1913.* Report prepared by J.H. Rothermel. House Report 1425, 62nd Congress, 3rd session.
–. Department of Commerce and Labor. *Expenditures in Commerce Department Committee, Fur Seal Industry ... Submitted by Mr. Rothermel, 4 April 1914.* House Report 500, pt. 1, 63rd Congress, 2nd session.
–. Department of Commerce and Labor. *A Statement Submitted in Re the Fur-Seal Herd of Alaska to the House Committee on Expenditures in the Department of Commerce.* Compiled by H.W. Elliott. Washington: GPO, 1913.
–. Judicial Committee. *Unlawful Seizures of Vessels in Bering Sea, Report to Accompany S. 1192 ... Submitted by Mr. Graham, 1 March 1924.* House Report 253. 68th Congress, 1st session.
–. Judiciary Committee. *Unlawful Seizures of Vessels in Bering Sea, Report to Accompany S. 2235 [to Confer Jurisdiction Upon Court of Claims to Adjudicate Claims of American Citizens Who Suffered Damages or Loss Resulting from Seizure, Detention, Sale, or Interference by United States of Vessels Charged with Unlawful Sealing in Bering Sea during Years 1875-96], Submitted by Mr. Classon, 9 March 1922.* House Report 784, 67th Congress, 2nd session.
–. *Report from Committee on Ways and Means, amending H. 13387, 2 June 1902.* Report prepared by J.A. Tawney. House Report 2303, pt. 1, 57th Congress, 1st session.
–. *Unlawful Seizure of Vessels in Bering Sea, 28 March 1906.* House Report 2674, 59th Congress, 1st session.
United States. Senate. *Alaskan Fisheries Division. Reports Relating to Alaskan Seal Fisheries, 1906 and 1907, 11 March 1908.* Report prepared by W.I. Lembkey. 1908. Senate Doc. 376, 60th Congress, 1st session.
–. Commerce Committee. *Alaska Fur Seals Hearing on S. 3679, to Amend Act to Prevent Extermination of Fur-Bearing Animals in Alaska, 10 June 1926.* 69th Congress, 1st session.
–. *Fur Seal Arbitration: Proceedings of the Tribunal of Arbitration at Paris, 1893.* 15 volumes. 53rd Congress, 2nd session. Washington: 1895.
–. *Report from Committee on Foreign Relations, on S. 390, to Confer Jurisdiction upon Circuit Court of United States for 9th Circuit to Determine in Equity Rights of American Citizens under Award of Bering Sea Arbitration of Paris; with Views of Minority, 29 January 1908.* Report prepared by J.B. McCreary. Senate Report 140, 60th Congress, 1st session.
–. *Report from Committee on Foreign Relations Favoring S. 391, 12 January 1910.* Report prepared by H.D. Money. Senate Report 45, 61st Congress, 2nd session.
–. *Report from Committee on Foreign Relations, Favoring S. 2286, to Confer Jurisdiction upon Circuit Court of United States for 9th Circuit to Determine in Equity Rights of American Citizens under Award of Bering Sea Arbitration of Paris, 21 February 1906.* Report prepared by J.T. Morgan. Senate Report 1201, 59th Congress, 1st session.
–. *Report from Committee on Foreign Relations, Amending S. 3410, to Authorize and Provide for Hearing and Trial of Suits by Citizens of United States for Compensation for Losses and Damages Occasioned by Seizure of Certain Vessels Engaged in Pelagic Fur Sealing, 13 April 1904.* Report prepared by J.T. Morgan. Senate Report 2128, 58th Congress, 2nd session.
–. *Unlawful Seizure of Vessels in Bering Sea, 21 February 1906.* Senate Report 1201, 59th Congress, 1st session.

Court Documents

La Ninfa. Federal Reporter 75 (September-October 1896).
National Archives and Records Administration (NARA), Pacific Sierra Region. *Martinez v. U.S.*, No. 5083, RG 276, 48, Transcript of Record.
–. *M.J. Lyon et al. v. United States*, No. 17543 (US District Court, Northern District of California), RG 21, Doc. 19, Reporter's Transcript, 26-27 April 1927; Doc. 26, Notice of Payment of Judgment.
–. *M.J. Lyon et al. v. U.S. District Court*, No. 17540 (US District Court, Northern District of California), RG 21, Doc. 18, Assignment of Errors, 10 August 1927.
–. *Rose Sparks Martinez v. United States*, No. 5083 (US District Court, Northern District of California, Court of Criminal Appeal, Ninth Circuit), RG 276, Transcript of Record, 11 April 1927.

–. *Stewart Norrie et al v. Schooner Edward E. Webster,* Case 10264 (US District Court, Northern District of California), Admiralty Case Files 1851-1934, RG 21, Box 520.

–. *United States v. Robert J. Tyson et al.,* Case 4307(3) (US District Court, Northern District of California), Criminal Case Files 1851-1912, RG 21, Box 336.

NARA, Alaska Region. *United States v. Schooner No. 2 Kensai Maru* (US District Court, 3rd Division, Valdez, Alaska), Civil Case Files 1902-39, RG 21, file 355.

New York Supreme Court Archives, NY. *Nels P. Sorensen v. Sun Printing and Publishing Association, 1911.*

LexisNexis® Academic. *Bird et al. v. United States and Twenty-three Other Cases,* Nos. 5067-5090 inclusive, 24 F.2d 933 (12 March 1928) (Circuit Court of Appeals, Ninth Circuit).

–. *The Coquitlam; Earle et al. v. United States,* No. 200, 77 F. 744 (16 November 1896) (Circuit Court of Appeals, Ninth Circuit).

–. *The La Ninfa; United States v. The La Ninfa,* 49 F. 575 (1 October 1891) (District Court, District of Alaska).

–. *La Ninfa; Whitelaw v. United States,* No. 24, 75 F. 513 (29 June 1896) (Circuit Court of Appeals, Ninth Circuit).

–. *H. Liebes & Co. v. Commissioner of Internal Revenue,* No. 14501, 15 B.T.A. 149 (30 January 1929) (US Board of Tax Appeals).

–. *H. Liebes & Co. v. Commissioner of Internal Revenue,* No. 68231, 34 B.T.A. 677 (5 June 1936) (US Board of Tax Appeals).

–. *N.A.C.C. v. U.S.,* No. 337, 81 F. 748 (7 June 1897) (Circuit Court of Appeals, Ninth Circuit).

–. *Steamer Coquitlam v. United States,* No. 804, 163 U.S. 346; 41 L. Ed. 184; 165 Ct. 1117 (18 May 1896) (US Supreme Court).

–. *United States v. The Coquitlam,* 57 F. 706 (18 September 1893) (District Court, District of Alaska).

–. *U.S. v. Louis Olsen,* No. 4004, 74 F. 246 (28 April 1896) (District Court, District of Oregon).

–. *U.S. v. N.A.C.C.; N.A.C.C. v. U.S.,* No. 431, 74 F. 145 (27 April 1896) (US Supreme Court).

–. *Whitelaw v. United States,* No. 17114, 9 F.2d. 103 (16 September 1925) (District Court, Northern District of California, First Division).

Secondary Sources

"A Never Old Story of the North Pacific." *Canadian Merchant Service Guide* (1923): 44-45.

Adams, Cecil. "Is Paul Bunyan a Fraud?" The Straight Dope, http://www.straightdope.com/columns/020510.html.

Adney, Tappan. *The Klondike Stampede of 1897-98.* New York: Ye Galleon Press, 1968 [1900]. Reprint, Vancouver: UBC Press, 1994.

Affleck, Edward L., compiler. *Affleck's List of Sternwheelers Plying the Inland Waters of British Columbia, 1858-1980.* Vancouver: Alexander Nicolls Press, 1992 [1924].

Alverstone, Right Honourable Viscount. *Recollections of Bar and Bench.* London: E. Arnold, 1914.

Ashbury, Herbert. *The Barbary Coast: An Informal History of the San Francisco Underworld.* New York: Garden City Publishing, 1933.

–. *The French Quarter: An Informal History of the New Orleans Underworld.* New York: Garden City Publishing, 1938.

Auerbach, Jonathan. *Male Call: Becoming Jack London.* Durham: Duke University Press, 1996.

Bailey, Thomas A. *A Diplomatic History of the American People.* New York: Appleton-Century-Crofts, 1964.

Baker, William Avery. *A Maritime History of Bath, Maine and the Kennebec River Region.* Bath, ME: Marine Research Society of Bath, 1973.

Baskerville, Peter A. "'She Has Already Hinted at Board': Enterprising Urban Women in British Columbia, 1863-1896." *Social History* 24, 2 (1993): 205-28.

Baskett, Sam S. "Jack London on the Oakland Waterfront." *American Literature* 27, 3 (1955): 363-71.

Beck, Emily Morison, ed. *Bartlett's Familiar Quotations.* Boston: Little, Brown, 1980 [1882].

Beck, Horace. *Folklore and the Sea.* Middleton, CT: Wesleyan University Press, 1973.

–. "The Making of the Popular Legendary Hero." In Wayland D. Hand, ed. *American Folk Legend: A Symposium,* 122-31. Berkeley: University of California Press, 1971.

Begg, Alexander. *History of British Columbia*. Toronto: McGraw-Hill Ryerson, 1972 [1894].

Bemis, Samuel F. *A Diplomatic History of the United States*. New York: Henry Holt and Company, 1942.

Benedict, William F. "Death Downs the 'Sea Wolf.'" *San Francisco Chronicle,* 4 October 1914, magazine section, 2.

Berton, Pierre. *Klondike: The Last Great Gold Rush 1896-1899*. Toronto: Penguin, 1992 [1958].

–. *The Klondike Fever*. New York: Alfred A. Knopf, 1958.

–. *The Klondike Quest: A Photographic Essay, 1897-1899*. Toronto: McClelland and Stewart, 1983.

Bittermann, Rusty. "Agrarian Protest and Cultural Transfer: Irish Immigrants and the Escheat Movement on Prince Edward Island." In Thomas P. Power, ed., *The Irish in Atlantic Canada,* 96-106. Fredericton: New Ireland Press, 1991.

–. "Farm Households and Wage Labour in the Northeastern Maritimes in the Early Nineteenth Century." *Labour/Le Travail* 31, 1 (1993): 13-45.

–. "The Hierarchy of the Soil: Land and Labour in a Nineteenth-Century Cape Breton Community." *Acadiensis* 18, 1 (1988): 33-55.

Bosworth, Hobart. "My Jack London." *Mark Twain Quarterly* 5 (1943): 2-5 and 24.

Bowering, George. *Bowering's B.C.: A Swashbuckling History*. Toronto: Viking, 1996.

–. *Shoot!* Toronto: Key Porter Books, 1994.

Brennan, Ann. *The Real Klondike Kate*. Fredericton: Goose Lane, 1990.

Brooks, G.W.S. "Edgar Crow Baker: An Entrepreneur in Early British Columbia." *BC Studies* 31 (1976): 23-43.

–. "Edgar Crow Baker: An Entrepreneur in Early British Columbia." MA thesis, University of British Columbia, 1976.

Brown, Robert Craig. *Canada's National Policy, 1883-1900: A Study in Canadian-American Relations*. Princeton: Princeton University Press, 1964.

Burnham, John. *The Rim of Mystery: A Hunter's Wanderings in Unknown Siberian Asia*. New York: G.P. Putnam's Sons, 1929.

Busch, Briton Cooper. *The War against the Seals: A History of the North American Seal Fishery*. Montreal and Kingston: McGill-Queen's University Press, 1985.

Butts, Edward. "The McLean Gang." *Canadian Encyclopedia,* volume 2. Edmonton: Hurtig Publishers, 1985.

Cameron, James. *For the People: A History of St. Francis Xavier University*. Montreal and Kingston: McGill-Queen's University Press, 1996.

Campbell, Charles S. Jr. "The Anglo-American Crisis in the Bering Sea, 1890-1891." *Mississippi Valley Historical Review* 48 (1961-62): 393-414.

–. "The Bering Sea Settlements of 1912." *Pacific Historical Review* 32 (1963): 347-67.

Careless, J.M.S. "The Business Community in the Early Development of Victoria, British Columbia." In D.S. Macmillan, ed. *Canadian Business History: Selected Studies, 1497-1971,* 104-23. Toronto: McClelland and Stewart, 1972.

Carlson, L.H. "The First Mining Season at Nome, Alaska, 1899." *Pacific Historical Review* 16 (1947): 163-75.

–. "Nome: From Mining Camp to Civilized Community." *Pacific Northwest Quarterly* 38 (1947): 233-42.

–. "The Discovery of Gold at Nome, Alaska." In Morgan B. Sherwood, ed. *Alaska and Its History,* 353-80. Seattle: University of Washington Press, 1967.

Chaikin, Ira. "James Douglas Warren." *Dictionary of Canadian Biography,* volume 14. Toronto: University of Toronto Press, 1998.

Chapelle, Howard I. *The American Fishing Schooners 1825-1935*. New York: W.W. Norton and Company, 1973.

Clark, Cecil. "Seawolf McLean Tweaked Russia's Beard." *Victoria Daily Colonist,* 5 April 1959, 8-9.

–. "Victoria Was a Smuggler's Hide-Away." *Victoria Daily Colonist,* 15 January 1961, 8-9.

Clark, S.D. "Mining Society in British Columbia and the Yukon." In W. Peter Ward and Robert A.J. McDonald, eds. *British Columbia: Historical Readings,* 215-31. Vancouver: Douglas and McIntyre, 1981.

Cocke, Mary and Albert. "Hell Roaring Mike: A Fall from Grace in the Frozen North." *Smithsonian* 13, 11 (1983): 119-37.

Cohen, Stan. *Yukon River Steamboats*. Missoula, MT: Pictorial Histories Publishing Company, 1982.

Crawley, Ron. "Class Conflict and the Establishment of the Sydney Steel Industry 1899-1904." In Ken Donovan, ed. *The Island: New Perspectives on Cape Breton History, 1713-1990,* 145-64. Fredericton: Acadiensis/University College of Cape Breton Press, 1990.

Creighton, Margaret S., and Lisa Norling, eds. *Iron Men, Wooden Women: Gender and Seafaring in the Atlantic World, 1700-1920*. Baltimore: Johns Hopkins University Press, 1996.

Crockford, Cairn Elizabeth. "Nuu-Chah-Nulth Labour Relations in the Pelagic Sealing Industry, 1868-1911." MA thesis, University of Victoria, Victoria, 1996.

Davis, Raymond. "The Fur Seal Killers." *Defenders* 50 (1975): 374-80.

Dale, Edward Everett, ed. *Frontier Trails: The Autobiography of Frank M. Canton*. Norman, OK: University of Oklahoma Press, 1966 [1930].

Dalton, Emmett. *When the Daltons Rode*. Garden City: Doubleday, Doran and Company, 1931.

Day, A. Grove. *Jack London in the South Seas*. New York: Four Winds Press, 1971.

DeArment, Robert K. "A Look at Two Professional Lawmen: George A. Scarborough and Frank M. Canton." *Journal of the West* 34, 1 (1995): 8-12.

DeArmond, R.N. "Letter to Editor." *Marine Digest,* 3 July 1971.

–. "The Men behind the Sea Wolf." *Alaska Life* (May 1946): 7, 40, and 44.

DeArmond, R.N., and John Lyman. "The Sealing Fleet." *Marine Digest* 35, 6 (4 May 1957-15 February 1958).

de Bertrand Lugrin, N. "Epic of the Seal Hunters." *Canadian Geographical Journal* 4 (1932): 295-304.

Decker, Peter R. "Jewish Merchants in San Francisco: Social Mobility on the Urban Frontier." In Moses Rischin, ed. *The Jews of the West: The Metropolitan Years,* 11-29. Berkeley: American Jewish Historical Society, 1979.

DeLorme, Roland L. "The Alaska Commercial Company and the U.S. Customs Bureau in Alaska." In *The Sea in Alaska's Past: Conference Proceedings,* 155–79. Anchorage: publisher unknown, 1974.

–. "Liquor Smuggling in Alaska, 1867-1899." *Pacific Northwest Quarterly* 66, 4 (1975): 145-52.

Devine, T.M. "The Flight of the Poor: Highland Emigration to Canada in the Mid-Nineteenth Century." In Cyril Byrne et al., eds. *Celtic Languages and Celtic Peoples,* 645-60. Halifax: D'Arcy McGee, Chair of Irish Studies, 1992.

Dobrowolsky, Helene. *Law of the Yukon: A Pictorial History of the Mounted Police in the Yukon*. Whitehorse: Lost Moose, 1995.

Doig, Ivan. *Winter Brothers: A Season at the Edge of America*. New York: Harcourt Brace Jovanovich, 1980.

Domville-Fife, Charles, ed. *Epics of the Square-Rigged Ships*. London: Seeley Service, 1958.

Dorsey, Kurkpatrick. *The Dawn of Conservation Diplomacy: U.S.-Canadian Wildlife Protection Treaties in the Progressive Era*. Seattle: University of Washington Press, 1998.

Dorson, Richard M. *American Folklore and the Historian*. Chicago: University of Chicago Press, 1971.

–. *America in Legend: Folklore from the Colonial Period to the Present*. New York: Pantheon Books, 1973.

Downs, Art. *British Columbia-Yukon Sternwheel Days*. Surrey, BC: Heritage House, 1992.

Duncan, B. "A Letter on the Fur-Seal in Canadian-American Diplomacy." *Canadian Historical Review* 43, 1 (1962): 42-47.

Dunn, Charles W. *Highland Settler: A Portrait of the Scottish Gael in Cape Breton and Eastern Nova Scotia*. Toronto: University of Toronto Press, 1968 [1953].

Dunn, Robert. "Alaska, the Seal-Wardens and the Japanese Raiders." *Harper's Weekly* 50 (15 September 1906): 1310-11.

Elliott, H.W. "The Loot and the Ruin of the Fur-Seal Herd of Alaska." *North American Review* 185 (1907): 426-36.

–. "Thirty Years of Japanese Seal Piracy in Alaskan Waters." *New York Herald,* 8 September 1907, magazine section, 5.

Emery, W.G. "With the Fur-Seal Hunters." *National Magazine* 6, 2 (1897): 99-109.
–. "Hunting the Fur Seal." *Outing* 31 (1898): 536-48.
Evans, Robley D. *A Sailor's Log: Recollections of Forty Years of Naval Life*. New York: Smith, Elder, 1901.
Ewart, John S. *British Protection: Behring Sea Seizures*. Ottawa: J.S. Ewart, 1913.
Fergusson, C. Bruce. *Place-Names and Places of Nova Scotia*. Halifax: Public Archives of Nova Scotia, 1967.
–, ed. *Uniacke's Sketches of Cape Breton and Other Papers Relating to Cape Breton Island*. Halifax: Public Archives of Nova Scotia, 1958.
Faue, Elizabeth. *Writing the Wrongs: Eva Valesh and the Rise of Labor Journalism*. Ithaca: Cornell University Press, 2002.
Fetherling, Douglas. *The Gold Crusades: A Social History of Gold Rushes, 1849-1929*. Toronto: University of Toronto Press, 1997 [1988].
Fingard, Judith. *Jack in Port: Sailortowns of Eastern Canada*. Toronto: University of Toronto Press, 1982.
–. "The Winter's Tale: The Seasonal Contour of Pre-Industrial Poverty in British North America, 1815-1860." Journal of the Canadian Historical Association *Historical Papers* (1974): 65-94.
Fisher, Robin. *Contact and Conflict: Indian-European Relations in British Columbia, 1774-1890*. Vancouver: UBC Press, 1977.
Fitzgerald, William G. "The Romance of Seal Hunting." *Wide World Magazine* 1, 1 (1898): 4-11.
Foner, Philip S. *The Social Writings of Jack London*. Secaucus, NJ: Citadel Press, 1964.
Foote, Albert. "The Old Fashioned 'Bars and Brass Rails.'" *Vancouver Sun*, 12 August 1939, magazine section, 4.
Ford, Clellan S. *Smoke from Their Fires: The Life of a Kwakiutl Chief*. New Haven: Yale University Press, 1941.
Foulke, Robert D. "Life in the Dying World of Sail, 1870-1910." *Journal of British Studies* 3, 1 (1963): 105-36.
Frank, David. "The Cape Breton Coal Industry and the Rise and Fall of the British Empire Steel Corporation." *Acadiensis* 7, 1 (1977): 3-34.
–. *J.B. McLachlan: A Biography*. Toronto: James Lorimer and Company, 1999.
Franklin, Kevin, "In Search of Sophia," *Tucson Weekly*, 11-18 December 1997.
Friesen, Richard J. *The Chilkoot Pass and the Great Gold Rush of 1898*. Ottawa: Parks Canada, 1981.
Fumento, Rocco, and Tony Williams, eds. *Jack London's 'The Sea Wolf': A Screenplay by Robert Rossen*. Carbondale, IL: Southern Illinois University Press, 2001.
Garland, Joseph E. *Down to the Sea: The Fishing Schooners of Gloucester*. Boston: David R. Godine, 1983.
–. *Gloucester on the Wind: America's Greatest Fishing Port in the Days of Sail*. Dover: Arcadia Publishing, 1995.
Garraty, John A. *Henry Cabot Lodge: A Biography*. New York: Knopf, 1953.
Gay, James Thomas. *American Fur Seal Diplomacy: The Alaskan Fur Seal Controversy*. New York: P. Lang, 1987.
–. "Bering Sea Controversy: Harrison, Blaine and Cronyism." *Alaska Journal* 3 (1973): 12-19.
–. "Henry W. Elliott: Crusading Conservationist." *Alaska Journal* 3 (1973): 211-16.
Geiger, Glenn A. "The Saga of the Alaskan Fur Seals." *The Explorer* 17 (1975): 5.
Geismar, Maxwell, ed. *Jack London: Short Stories*. New York: Hill and Wang, 1960.
Gibb, Paul. "Selling Out Canada? The Role of Sir Julian Pauncefote in the Bering Sea Dispute, 1889-1902." *International History Review* 24, 4 (2002): 817-44.
Gilbert, Benjamin F. "Economic Developments in Alaska, 1867-1910." *Journal of the West* 4 (1965): 504-21.
Gillis, Ronald. "The McLeans of Cape Breton and Scotland." *Sydney Post-Record*, 17 November 1936, 4.
Glanz, Rudolf. "From Fur Rush to Gold Rush: Alaskan Jewry from the Late Nineteenth to the Early Twentieth Centuries." *Western States Jewish Historical Quarterly* 14 (January 1975): 95-107.

Glavin, Terry. *The Last Great Sea*. Vancouver and Toronto: Douglas and McIntyre, 2000.

Gluek, Alvin C. Jr. "Canada's Splendid Bargain: The North Pacific Fur Seal Convention of 1911." *Canadian Historical Review* 63, 2 (1982): 179-201.

Gough, Barry M. *The Royal Navy and the Northwest Coast of North America, 1810-1914*. Vancouver: UBC Press, 1971.

Graham, Gerald S. "The Ascendancy of the Sailing Ship, 1850-85." *Economic History Review* 9, 1 (1956): 74-88.

Green, Elmer, ed. *Adventures of Carl Rydell: The Autobiography of a Seafaring Man*. London: Edward Arnold and Company, 1924.

–. *Captain Carl Rydell: On Pacific Frontiers – A Story of Life at Sea and in Outlying Possessions of the United States*. Chicago: World Book Company, 1926.

Green, Lewis. *The Gold Hustlers*. Anchorage: Northwest Publishing Company, 1977.

Hacking, Norman. "British Columbia Steamboat Days, 1870-1883." *British Columbia Historical Quarterly* 11, 2 (1947): 82.

–. "Freebooter of Sealing Recalled," *Vancouver Province*, 28 August 1971, 15.

–. "Ship and Shore." *Vancouver Province*, 29 November, 13 December 1956, and 28 August 1971.

–. "The Victoria Sealing Fleet." *The Sea Chest* (Spring 1982): 97-101.

Hamilton, C.I. "Seamen and Crime at the Cape, ca. 1860-1880." *International Journal of Maritime History* 1, 2 (1989): 1-35.

Harriman, E.H., "San Francisco," *Sunset Magazine* 17, 1 (1906): 1–3.

Harris, Cole. *The Resettlement of British Columbia: Essays on Colonialism and Geographical Change*. Vancouver: UBC Press, 1997.

Harvey, Anne-Marie. "Sons of the Sun: Making White, Middle-Class Manhood in Jack London's David Grief Stories and the *Saturday Evening Post*." *American Studies* 39, 3 (1998): 37-68.

Heath, Ian. "Charles Morris Woodford: Adventurer, Naturalist, Administrator." In Deryck Scarr, ed. *More Pacific Islands Portraits*, 193-210. Canberra: Australian National University Press, 1978.

Helms, Andrea R.C., and Mary Childers Mangusso. "The Nome Gold Conspiracy." *Pacific Northwest Quarterly* 73, 1 (1982): 10-19.

Henderson, Captain Henry. *Robert Henderson's Discovery of the Klondike*. Pictou County, NS: E.L. Baudoux, 1998.

Hendricks, King, and Irving Shepard, eds. *Letters from Jack London*. London: MacGibbon and Kee, 1965.

Hendrickson, Robert. *The Ocean Almanac*. Garden City: Doubleday, 1984.

Hensley, Dennis. "Jack London's Use of Maritime History in The Seawolf." *Pacific Historian* 23, 2 (1979): 1-8.

Hinckley, Ted C. *The Americanization of Alaska, 1867-1897*. Palo Alto: Pacific Books, 1972.

–. "Rustlers of the North Pacific." *Journal of the West* 2 (1963): 22-30.

Hitchman, James H. *A Maritime History of the Pacific Coast, 1540-1980*. New York: Lanham, 1990.

Hoare, J.E. *Japan's Treaty Ports and Foreign Settlements: The Uninvited Guests 1858-1899*. Folkestowe: Japan Library, 1994.

Hobsbawm, Eric. *Primitive Rebels: Studies in Archaic Forms of Social Movement in the Nineteenth and Twentieth Centuries*. Manchester: Norton, 1959.

Hornsby, Stephen J. "Migration and Settlement: The Scots of Cape Breton." In D. Day, ed. *Geographical Perspectives on the Maritime Provinces*, 15-24. Halifax: St. Mary's University Press, 1988.

–. *Nineteenth Century Cape Breton: A Historical Geography*. Montreal and Kingston: McGill-Queen's University Press, 1992.

Howay, F.W., and E.O.S. Scholefield. *British Columbia from the Earliest Times to the Present*, 4 volumes. Vancouver: S.J. Clarke, 1914.

Howay, F.W., W.H. Sage, and H.F. Angus. *British Columbia and the United States*. Toronto: Ryerson, 1942.

Hulley, Clarence C. *Alaska: Past and Present*. Westport, CT: Greenwood Press, 1981 [1970].

Hunt, William R. *Arctic Passage: The Turbulent History of the Land and People of the Bering Sea, 1697-1975*. New York: Scribner, 1975.

–. *Distant Justice: Policing the Alaskan Frontier*. Norman, OK: University of Oklahoma Press, 1987.

–. *North of 53: The Wild Days of the Alaska-Yukon Mining Frontier 1870-1914*. New York: Macmillan, 1974.

–. *STEF: A Biography of Vilhjalmur Stefansson, Canadian Arctic Explorer*. Vancouver: UBC Press, 1986.

Hurst, A.A. *The Call of High Canvas*. London: Cassell, 1958.

Ireland, Gordon. "The North Pacific Fisheries." *American Journal of International Law* 36 (1942): 400-24.

Jackson, Elva E. *Cape Breton and the Jackson Kith and Kin*. Windsor, NS: Lancelot, 1971.

–. *North Sydney, Nova Scotia: Window on the Past*. Belleville, ON: Mika Publishing, 1982 [1974].

Johnston, Rev. A.A. *A History of the Catholic Church in Eastern Nova Scotia*, 2 volumes. Antigonish, NS: St. Francis Xavier University Press, 1971.

Johnston, Hugh. "Native People, Settlers and Sojourners, 1871-1916." In Hugh J.M. Johnston, ed. *The Pacific Province: A History of British Columbia*, 165-204. Vancouver: Douglas and McIntyre, 1996.

Johnston, Samuel P., ed. *Alaska Commercial Company, 1868-1940*. San Francisco: E.E. Wachter, 1940.

Jones, Dorothy Knee. *A Century of Servitude: Pribilof Aleuts under U.S. Rule*. Washington: University Press of America, 1980.

Jones, Laurie. *Nootka Sound Explored: A Westcoast History*. Campbell River, BC: Ptarmigan Press, 1991.

Jordan, David Starr. *The Days of a Man*, 2 volumes. New York: World Book Company, 1922.

Josephson, Matthew. *The Robber Barons*. New York: Harcourt, Brace and Company, 1934.

Junger, Sebastian. *The Perfect Storm: A True Story of Men against the Sea*. New York: Norton, 1997.

Jupp, Ursula, ed. *Deep Sea Stories from the Thermopylae Club*. Victoria: Morris Printing, 1986 [1971].

–, ed. *Home Port Victoria*. Victoria: Morris Printing, 1985 [1967].

Kaplan, Amy. "Romancing the Empire: The Embodiment of American Masculinity in the Popular Historical Novel of the 1890s." *American Literary History* 2, 4 (1990): 660-90.

Kelley, Frank. "Descendants of Victoria Sealing Fleet Pioneers Still Hope for Settlement of Due Compensation." *Victoria Daily Colonist*, 16 November 1947, 20.

–. "Sealing with the Sea Wolf." *Victoria Daily Colonist*, 18 June 1933, magazine section, 1.

Kennedy, Michael. *Gaelic Nova Scotia: An Economic, Cultural, and Social Impact Study*. Halifax: Nova Scotia Museum, 2002.

–. "'Lochaber no more': A Critical Examination of Highland Emigration Mythology." In Marjory Harper and Michael Vance, eds. *Myth, Migration and the Making of Memory: Scotia and Nova Scotia, ca. 1700-1990*, 267-97. Halifax: Fernwood/John Donald, 1999.

Kenyrn, Ron. "Over the Forearm." *Vancouver Province*, 8 December 1936, 4.

Kingman, Russ. *A Pictorial Life of Jack London*. New York: Crown Publishers, 1979.

Kipling, Rudyard. *Captains Courageous: A Story of the Grand Banks*. London: Macmillan, 1908.

–. *Collected Verse of Rudyard Kipling*. London: Hodder and Stoughton, 1912.

Kitchener, L.D. *Flag over the North: The Story of the Northern Commercial Company*. Seattle: Superior Publishing Company, 1954.

Knight, Rolf. *Indians at Work: An Informal History of Native Indian Labour in British Columbia, 1858-1930*. Vancouver: New Star Books, 1978.

Knuckle, Robert. *In the Line of Duty*. Burnstown, ON: General Store Publishing House, 1994.

Kutz, Kenneth J. *Klondike Gold: The Philatelic History of the Klondike Gold Rush*. Darwin, CT: Gold Fever Publishing, 1995.

Labor, Earle, and Jeanne Campbell Reesman. *Jack London*, revised edition. New York: Twayne Publishers, 1994.

Labor, Earle, Robert C. Leitz III, and I. Milo Shepard, eds. *The Complete Short Stories of Jack London*, 3 volumes. Stanford, CA: Stanford University Press, 1993.

Lane, Patrick. "The Great Pacific Seal Hunt." *Raincoast Chronicles* 1, 4 (1974): 44-47.
Langhout, Rosemary. "Alternative Opportunities: The Development of Shipping at Sydney Harbour 1842-1889." In K. Donovan, ed. *Cape Breton at 200: Historical Essays in Honour of the Island's Bicentennial 1785-1985,* 53-69. Sydney: University College of Cape Breton Press, 1985.
Laracy, Hugh. "Niels Peter Sorensen: The Story of a Criminal Adventurer." *Journal of Pacific History* 35, 2 (2000): 147-62.
–. "'Quixotic and Utopian': American Adventures in the Southwest Pacific, 1897-98." *Pacific Studies* 24, 1-2 (2001): 39-62.
Large, R.G. *The Skeena: River of Destiny*. Surrey: Heritage House, 1996 [1951].
Lears, T.J. Jackson. *No Place of Grace: Antimodernism and the Transformation of American Culture, 1880-1920.* Chicago: University of Chicago Press, 1981.
Lillard, Charles, ed. "Dining with a Sea Wolf." *Victoria Daily Colonist,* 11 June 1978.
–. *Mission to Nootka, 1874-1900*. Sidney, BC: Gray's Publishing, 1977.
–. *Seven Shillings a Year: The History of Vancouver Island*. Ganges, BC: Horsdal and Schubart, 1986.
–. "The Silent Voices of the Past." *Victoria Times Colonist,* 12 September 1987.
Little, J.I. "Popular Resistance to Legal Authority in the Upper St. Francis District of Quebec: The Megantic Outlaw Affair of 1888-89." *Labour/Le Travail* 33 (1994): 97-124.
Lomen, Carl. *Fifty Years in Alaska*. New York: David McKay Company, 1954.
London, Charmian. *The Book of Jack London,* 2 volumes. New York: Century, 1921.
London, Jack. *John Barleycorn*. Santa Cruz: Western Tanager Press, 1981 [1913].
–. *The Sea-Wolf.* Edited and introduced by John Sutherland. Oxford: Penguin, 1992.
–. *South Sea Tales*. New York: Macmillan Company, 1911.
Loo, Tina. "Of Moose and Men: Hunting for Masculinities in British Columbia, 1880-1939." *Western Historical Quarterly* 32, 3 (2001): 296-320.
Lovell, John. *Canadian Dominion Directory, 1871*. Montreal: John Lovell, 1871.
"Lt.-Col. The Hon. James Baker." *Western World* 5, 58 (1894): 245-46.
Lubbock, Basil. *The Down Easters: American Deep-Water Sailing Ships, 1869-1929.* Glasgow: Brown, Son and Ferguson, 1971 [1929].
–. *Round the Horn before the Mast.* Glasgow: Brown, Son and Ferguson, 1986 [1902].
Lugrin, N. de Bertrand. "Epic of the Seal Hunters," *Canadian Geographical Journal* 4, 5 (May 1932).
Lutz, John. "After the Fur Trade: The Aboriginal Labouring Class of British Columbia, 1849-1890." Journal of the Canadian Historical Association *Historical Papers* 3 (1992): 69-93.
–. *Makúk: A New History of Aboriginal-White Relations.* Vancouver: UBC Press, 2008.
–. "Work, Wages and Welfare in Aboriginal–Non-Aboriginal Relations, British Columbia, 1849-1970." PhD dissertation, University of Ottawa, Ottawa, 1994.
Lyman, John. "Letter to Editor." *Marine Digest* 7 (1971): 26-27.
MacDonald, Ian. "Pirate of High Seas Ends in False Creek." *Vancouver Sun,* 15 October 1966.
MacDonald, Norbert. "Seattle, Vancouver, and the Klondike." *Canadian Historical Review* 49, 3 (1968): 234-46.
MacDonnell, Margaret. *The Emigrant Experience: Songs of Highland Emigrants in North America.* Toronto: University of Toronto Press, 1982.
MacGillivray, Don. "Henry Melville Whitney Comes to Cape Breton: The Saga of a Gilded Age Entrepreneur." *Acadiensis* 9, 1 (1979): 44-70.
MacInnes, Tom. *Chinook Days*. Vancouver: Sun Publishing Company, 1926.
–. *Klengenberg of the Arctic: An Autobiography*. London: Jonathan Cape, 1932.
Mack, Gerstle. *Lewis and Hannah Gerstle*. New York: publisher unknown, 1953.
MacKenzie, Michael. *Memories Recalled*. Sydney, NS: City Printers, 1992.
MacMillan, A.J. *To the Hill of Boisdale*. Sydney, NS: City Printers, 1986.
–. *A West Wind to East Bay*. Antigonish, NS: Casket Printing and Publishing, 2001.
MacNeil, Neil. *The Highland Heart of Nova Scotia*. Toronto: Saunders, 1971 [1948].
MacNeil, S.R. *All Call Iona Home*. Antigonish: Formac Publishing, 1979.
Madsen, Charles, with John Scott Douglas. *Arctic Trader*. New York: Dodd, Mead, 1957.
Marble, Allan E. *Nova Scotians at Home and Abroad*. Windsor: Lancelot Press, 1977.

Marsh, D'Arcy. "London's 'Sea Wolf' in Scot's Clothing." *Vancouver Province,* 31 May 1958, 15.
Marsh, M.C. "Fur Seals and the Fur Seal Question." *Alaska-Yukon Magazine* 3, 6 (1907): 457-69.
Marshall, Don B. *California Shipwrecks*. Seattle: Superior Publishing, 1978.
Martin, Fredericka I. *The Hunting of the Silver Fleece*. New York: Greenberg, 1946.
–. *Sea Bears: The Story of the Fur Seal*. Philadelphia: Chilton Company, Book Division, 1960.
Matthews, Frederick C. *American Merchant Ships 1850-1900,* series I. New York: Dover, 1987 [1930]; Series II. New York: Dover, 1987 [1931].
McBride, W.D. "Saga of Famed Packets and Other Steamboats of Mighty Yukon River." *Cariboo and Northwest Digest* 4, 4 (1948): 97-112 and 5, 1 (1949): 94-115.
McCann, Leonard. "Clarence Nelson Cox." *Dictionary of Canadian Biography,* volume 13. Toronto: University of Toronto Press, 1994.
–. *The Honourable Company's* Beaver. Vancouver: Vancouver Museums and Planetarium Association, 1980.
McCharles, Aeneas. *Bemocked of Destiny*. Toronto: William Briggs, 1908.
McDonald, Robert A.J. "Victoria, Vancouver, and the Economic Development of British Columbia, 1886-1914." In W. Peter Ward and Robert A.J. McDonald, eds. *British Columbia: Historical Readings,* 369-95. Vancouver: Douglas and McIntyre, 1981.
–. "'He Thought He Was the Boss of Everything': Masculinity and Power in a Vancouver Family." Fifth Annual Seagram Lecture, McGill Institute for the Study of Canada, Montreal, 17 January 2001.
McDougall, Walter A. *Let the Sea Make a Noise: A History of the North Pacific from Magellan to MacArthur*. New York: Basic Books, 1993.
McKay, Ian. "Colin McKay's Alternative Vision of the Age of Sail." In Lewis Jackson and Ian McKay, eds. *Windjammers and Bluenose Sailors: Stories of the Sea by Colin McKay,* 21-32. Lockport, NS: Roseway, 1993.
–. *"The Crisis of Dependent Development: Class Conflict in the Nova Scotia Coalfields, 1872-1876."* In Greg Kealey, ed. *Class, Gender, and Region: Essays in Canadian Historical Sociology,* 30-34. St. John's: Committee on Canadian Labour History, 1988.
–. *The Quest of the Folk: Antimodernism and Cultural Selection in Twentieth-Century Nova Scotia*. Montreal and Kingston: McGill-Queen's University Press, 1994.
McKelvie, B.A. "Victoria Mariner Tells Story of 'Sea Wolf' Alex McLean." *Vancouver Province,* 8 May 1943, magazine section, 3.
McLean, Marshall. "An Effort to Protect Fur Seal." *Field and Stream* 15 (1910): 722-26.
McLeod, David A. *Cape Breton Captain: Reminiscences from Fifty Years Afloat and Ashore*. Edited by Ron Caplan. Wreck Cove NS: Breton Books, 1992.
Mills, D.O. "Our Fur Seal Fisheries." *North American Review* 151 (1890): 300-6.
Moore, J.B. *A Digest of International Law,* 8 volumes. Washington: Government Printing Office, 1906.
Morgan, H.J. *The Canadian Men and Women of the Time*. Toronto: William Briggs, 1912.
Morgan, H. Wayne, ed. *The Gilded Age*. Syracuse: Syracuse University Press, 1970.
Morgan, Murray, with photographs by E.A. Hegg. *One Man's Gold Rush: A Klondike Album*. Seattle: University of Washington Press, 1995 [1967].
Morgan, Robert. *Perseverance: The Story of Cape Breton's University College 1952-2002*. Sydney: University College of Cape Breton Press, 2004.
–. "'Poverty, Wretchedness, and Misery': The Great Famine in Cape Breton, 1845-1851." *Nova Scotia Historical Review* 6,1 (1986): 88-104.
Morrison, William R. "Policing the Boomtown: The Mounted Police as a Social Force on the Klondike." *Northern Review* 6 (1990): 83-97.
Mott, Frank Luther. *A History of American Magazines, 1885-1905,* volume 4. Cambridge, MA: Harvard University Press, 1957.
Murphy, Rex. "Yesterday's Hero, Tomorrow's Hypocrite," *Globe and Mail,* 4 March 2006, A19.
Murray, Peter. *The Vagabond Fleet: A Chronicle of the North Pacific Sealing Schooner Trade*. Victoria: Sono Nis Press, 1988.
Muscatine, Doris. *Old San Francisco: The Biography of a City*. New York: G.P. Putman's Sons, 1975.
Narell, Irena. *Our City: The Jews of San Francisco*. San Diego, CA: Howell-North Books, 1981.

"Neil MacNeil." *St. Francis Xavier University Alumni News* (Spring 1993).

Neitzel, Michael C. *The Valencia Tragedy*. Surrey, BC: Heritage House Publishing, 1995.

Neufeld, David, and Frank Norris. *Chilkoot Trail: Heritage Route to the Klondike*. Whitehorse: Lost Moose, 1996.

Newell, Dianne. *Tangled Webs of History: Indians and the Law in Canada's Pacific Coast Fisheries*. Toronto: University of Toronto Press, 1993.

Newell, Gordon, ed. *The H.W. McCurdy Marine History of the Pacific Northwest*. Seattle: Superior Publishing Company, 1966.

–. *Pacific Steamboats*. Seattle: Superior Publishing, 1958.

–. *Sea Rogues' Gallery*. Seattle: Superior Publishing, 1971.

Nichols, Robert H. "Seal Hunters of the North Pacific." In R.E. Watters, ed. *British Columbia: A Centennial Anthology,* 123-28. Toronto: McClelland and Stewart, 1958.

Noble, Dennis L. "Fog, Reindeer, and the Bering Sea Patrol, 1867-1964." In *The Sea in Alaska's Past,* 112-54. Anchorage: Alaska Historical Society Conference Proceedings, 1979.

Noble, Dennis L., and Truman R. Stobridge. "Early Cuttermen in Alaskan Waters." *Pacific Northwest Quarterly* 78, 3 (1987): 74-82.

Noel, Joseph. *Footloose in Arcadia: A Personal Record of Jack London, George Sterling, Ambrose Bierce*. New York: Carrick and Evans, 1940.

Norling, Lisa. "Ahab's Wife: Women and the American Whaling Industry, 1820-1870." In Margaret S. Creighton and Lisa Norling, eds. *Iron Men, Wooden Women: Gender and Seafaring in the Atlantic World, 1700-1920,* 70-91. Baltimore: Johns Hopkins University Press, 1996.

O'Brien, Robert. "Alex McLean, the Sea Wolf." *San Francisco Chronicle,* 23 June 1952, 13; 25 June 1952, 17; 27 June 1952, 13; 30 June 1952, 19.

–. *This Is San Francisco*. San Francisco: Whittlesey House, 1948.

Osborn, P.G. *A Concise Law Dictionary,* 5th edition. London: Sweet and Maxwell, 1964.

Parker, Captain John. *Cape Breton Ships and Men*. Aylesbury: Hazell Watson and Viney, 1967.

Parker, C.W., ed. *Who's Who and Why*. Vancouver: publisher unknown, 1914.

–, ed. *Who's Who and Why, 1917-1918*. Toronto: publisher unknown, 1918.

Partridge, Eric. *The Penguin Dictionary of Historical Slang*. Abridged by Jacqueline Simpson. Middlesex: Penguin, 1980.

Paterson, D.G. "The North Pacific Seal Hunt, 1886-1910: Rights and Regulations." In W. Peter Ward and Robert A.J. McDonald, eds. *British Columbia: Historical Readings,* 343-66. Vancouver: Douglas and McIntyre, 1981.

Paterson, D.G., and J. Wilen. "Depletion and Diplomacy: The North Pacific Seal Hunt, 1886-1910." In P. Uselding, ed. *Research in Economic History,* 81-140. Greenwich, CT: JAI Press, 1977.

Paterson, T.W. "Alex McLean Was Much Bigger Than Life." *Nanaimo Daily News,* 15 October 1999, C2.

–. "Northwest Pirate." *Victoria Daily Colonist,* 19 May 1968, magazine section, 12-13.

–. "Victoria's Own Sea Wolf." *Victoria Daily Colonist,* 25 February 1973, 10.

Pethick, Derek. *S.S.* Beaver: *The Ship That Saved the West*. Vancouver: Mitchell Press, 1970.

Pickelhaupt, Bill. *Shanghaied in San Francisco*. San Francisco: Flyblister Press, 1996.

Porsild, Charlene. *Gamblers and Dreamers: Women, Men, and Community in the Klondike*. Vancouver: UBC Press, 1998.

Powers, Madelon. *Faces along the Bar: Lore and Order in the Workingman's Saloon, 1870-1920*. Chicago: University of Chicago Press, 1998.

Preston, Diana and Michael. *A Pirate of Exquisite Mind. Explorer, Naturalist, and Buccaneer: The Life of William Dampier*. Toronto: Penguin, 2004.

Rankin, Effie. *As a' Bhraighe/Beyond the Braes: The Gaelic Songs of Allan the Ridge MacDonald, 1794-1868*. Sydney: University College of Cape Breton Press, 2004.

Rather, Lois. *Jack London, 1905*. Oakland: Rather Press, 1974.

Record of American and Foreign Shipping. New York: American Shipmasters' Association, 1877, 1878, 1897, 1900, and 1915.

Rediker, Marcus. *Between the Devil and the Deep Blue Sea: Merchant Seamen, Pirates, and the Anglo-American Maritime World, 1700-1750*. New York: Canto, 1993 [1987].

Reiger, G. "Song of the Seal." *Audubon* 77, 5 (1975): 6-27.
Reksten, Terry. *More English Than the English: A Very Social History of Victoria*. Victoria: Orca Book Publishers, 1986.
Rhoda, Jean. "Fur Seal in Alaskan Waters." *Overland* 62, 3 (1913): 225-32.
Roberts, Charles G.D., and Arthur L. Tunnell, eds. *A Standard Dictionary of Canadian Biography,* volume 1. Toronto: Murray Print Company, 1934.
Robinson, Noel. "Original of 'Sea Wolf' Resented Jack London's Book." *Vancouver Province,* 19 June 1943, magazine section, 3.
–. "The Real Sea Wolf." *Maclean's* 35 (1 January 1922): 12-13 and 41. Reprinted in *Cape Breton Mirror* 2, 2 (1953): 12-13 and 20; and in *Cape Breton Mirror* 2, 3 (1953): 21-22.
–. "The 'Sea Wolf': Story of a Tragic Treasure Hunt." *The Shoulder Strap* 10 (1943): 47-51.
–. "The Story of My Life." *Vancouver News-Advertiser,* 1 January 1913, magazine section, 7.
Roppel, A.Y., and S.P. Davey. "Evolution of Fur Seal Management on the Pribilof Islands." *Journal of Wildlife Management* 29, 3 (1965): 448-63.
Rothery, Agnes. *The Ports of British Columbia*. New York: Doubleday, 1943.
Rowe, William Hutchinson. *The Maritime History of Maine*. Gardiner, ME: Harpswell Press, 1989 [1948].
Roy, Andrew Walter. "Life and Death of the Sea Wolf." *Atlantic Advocate* 98 (1958): 77-81 and 83-84.
–. "'Sea Wolf' Was Nova Scotian." *Halifax Chronicle-Herald,* 8 February 1958, 5.
Roy, Patricia E. *A White Man's Province: British Columbia Politicians and Chinese and Japanese Immigrants, 1858-1914*. Vancouver: UBC Press, 1989.
Sager, Eric. "Memory, Oral History and Seafaring Labour in Canada's Age of Steam." In Colin Howell and Richard Twomey, eds. *Jack Tar in History: Essays in the History of Maritime Life and Labour,* 236-45. Fredericton: Acadiensis Press, 1991.
–. *Seafaring Labour: The Merchant Marine of Atlantic Canada, 1820-1914*. Montreal and Kingston: McGill-Queen's University Press, 1989.
Sager, Eric, with Gerald Panting. *Maritime Capital: The Shipping Industry in Atlantic Canada, 1820-1914*. Montreal and Kingston: McGill-Queen's University Press, 1990.
Saunders, E.M., ed. *The Life and Letters of the Rt. Hon. Sir Charles Tupper*. Toronto: Cassell, 1916.
Scheffer, Victor B., C.H. Fiscus, and E.I. Todd. *History of Scientific Study and Management of the Alaskan Fur Seal, Callorhinus Ursinus, 1786-1964*. Washington: National Marine Fisheries Service, 1984.
Seager, Allen. "The Resource Economy, 1871-1921." In Hugh J.M. Johnson, ed. *The Pacific Province: A History of British Columbia,* 165-204. Vancouver: Douglas and McIntyre, 1996.
"Sealing." *Canadian Gazette* (London), 17 December 1891.
Seaman, Thomas. "The Adventures of 'Sea Wolf' McLean." *Victoria Daily Colonist,* 21 June 1953.
Shalkop, Robert L. *Henry Wood Elliott, 1846-1930: A Retrospective Exhibition*. Anchorage: Anchorage Historical and Fine Arts Museum, 1982.
Shaw, John. "Brief Beginnings: Nova Scotian and Old World Bards Compared." In Donald MacAulay, James Gleasure, and Colum Obaoill, eds. *Festchrift for Professor D.S. Thomson,* Scottish Gaelic Studies, volume 17, 342-55. Aberdeen: University of Aberdeen, 1996.
–. "Observations on the Cape Breton Gàidhealtachd and Its Relevance to Present-Day Celtic Studies." In Gordon MacLennan, ed. *Proceedings of the First North American Congress of Celtic Studies,* 75-87. Ottawa: University of Ottawa, 1988.
Shepard, Isabel S. *The Cruise of the U.S. Steamer* "Rush" *in Behring Sea*. San Francisco: Bancroft, 1889.
Sherwood, Morgan B. *Exploration of Alaska, 1865-1900*. New Haven: Yale University Press, 1965.
Sissons, James, III, ed. *Jack London's Articles and Short Stories in the Ægis*. Oakland: Star Rover House, 1981.
Slocum, Joshua. *Sailing Alone around the World*. Edited by Walter Magnus Teller. New York: Collier Books, 1962 [1958].

Sloss, Frank H. "Who Owned the Alaska Commercial Company?" *Pacific Northwest Quarterly* 69 (1977): 120-30.

Smith, Allan. "The Myth of the Self-Made Man in English Canada, 1850-1914." *Canadian Historical Review* 59, 2 (1978): 189-218.

Smith, C. Fox. *Sailor Town Days*. Boston: Houghton Mifflin, 1923.

Smith, J. Gordon. "Romance of the Pacific Coast Sealing Trade." *Toronto Globe,* 18 February 1911, 5.

–. "The Romance of Sealing." *Canadian Magazine* 21 (1903): 393-401.

Snow, H.J. *In Forbidden Seas: Recollections of Sea-Otter Hunting in the Kurils*. London: E. Arnold, 1910.

Sprague, Lynn T. "Exterminating the Fur Seal." *Overland Monthly* 62 (1903): 435-39.

Stasz, Clarise. *American Dreamers: Charmian and Jack London*. New York: St. Martin's Press, 1988.

–. *Jack London's Women*. Amherst: University of Massachusetts, 2001.

–. "The Social Construction of Biography: The Case of Jack London." *Modern Fiction Studies* 22, 1 (1976): 51-71.

Steele, Harwood. *Policing the Arctic*. Toronto: Ryerson, 1925.

Steele, Samuel B. *Forty Years in Canada*. Toronto: McGraw-Hill Ryerson, 1972 [1915].

Stejneger, Leonhard. "Fur-Seal Industry of the Commander Islands, 1897 to 1922." *Bulletin of the United States Bureau of Fisheries 1925* 41 (1927): 289-332.

Stewart, Robert. *Sam Steele: Lion of the Frontier*. Toronto: Doubleday Canada, 1979.

Stone, T. "Atomistic Order and Frontier Violence: Miners and Whalemen in the Nineteenth Century Yukon." *Ethnology* 22 (1983): 327-40.

–. *Miners' Justice: Migration, Law and Order on the Alaska-Yukon Frontier, 1873-1902*. New York: Peter Lang, 1988.

Story, Norah. *The Oxford Companion to Canadian History and Literature*. Toronto: Oxford University Press, 1967.

Sutherland, David. "Wooden Ships and Iron Men Revisited." *Acadiensis* 7, 1 (1978): 101-6.

Sweeney, E.M. "Rescue on the Sealing Grounds." *Victoria Daily Colonist,* 1 January 1972, 6.

Tansill, C.C. *Canadian-American Relations, 1875-1911*. New Haven: Yale University Press, 1943.

–. "The Fur Seal Fisheries and the Doctrine of the Freedom of the Seas." *Canadian Historical Association Report* (1942): 71-81.

Tatum, Stephen. *Inventing Billy the Kid: Visions of the Outlaw in America, 1881-1981*. Albuquerque: University of New Mexico Press, 1982.

Taylor, G.W. *Builders of British Columbia: An Industrial History*. Victoria: Morris Publishing, 1982.

"The Serious Outlook in Bering Sea." *The Nation* 52, 1347 (1891): 52 and 332-33.

Theroux, Joseph. "William Churchill: A Fractured Life." *Hawaiian Journal of History* 29 (1995): 97-123.

"Thomas Ross, Veteran of Coast Guard, Dies." *Marine Digest* 50, 27 (1958): 36.

Thompson, E.P. "The Moral Economy of the English Crowd." *Past and Present* 50 (1971): 76-136.

Thompson, John Herd, and Stephen J. Randall. *Canada and the United States: Ambivalent Allies*. Montreal and Kingston: McGill-Queen's University Press, 1994.

Thornton, Patricia. "The Problem of Out-Migration from Atlantic Canada, 1871-1931: A New Look." *Acadiensis* 15, 1 (1985): 3-34.

Tomasevich, Jozo. *International Agreements on Conservation of Marine Resources with Special Reference to the North Pacific*. Stanford, CA: Stanford University Press, 1943.

Tupper, C.H. "Crocodile Tears and Fur Seals." *National Review* 23 (1896): 87-92.

Underwood, John J. *Alaska: An Empire in the Making*. London: T. Fisher Unwin, 1913.

Van Nostrand, Jeanne. "The Seals Are about Gone" *American Heritage* 14, 4 (1963): 11-16 and 78-80.

Voss, J.C. *Venturesome Voyages*. London: Grafton Books, 1989 [1913].

Walden, Arthur Treadwell. *A Dog-Puncher on the Yukon*. Boston: Houghton Mifflin, 1931.

Walden, Keith. "The Great March of the Mounted Police in Popular Literature, 1873-1973." *Canadian Historical Review Historical Papers* (1980): 33-56.

Walker, Dale L., compiler. *The Fiction of Jack London: A Chronological Bibliography*. El Paso, TX: Texas Western Press, 1972.

Walker, Franklin. *Jack London and the Klondike*. San Marino, CA: Huntington Library, 1966.

Wallace, Frederick William. "B.C. Sealers Claim Revive Memories of Old Days." *Canadian Fisherman* 21, 8 (1934) 19.

–. *Roving Fisherman: An Autobiography*. Gardenvale, QC: Canadian Fisherman, 1955.

–. *Wooden Ships and Iron Men*. London: White Lion, 1973 [1924].

Wallace, W. Steward. *The Macmillan Dictionary of Canadian Biography*. Toronto: Macmillan, 1978.

Ward, Susan. "Social Philosophy as Best-Seller: Jack London's 'The Sea-Wolf.'" *Western American Literature* 17, 4 (1983): 321-33.

Watson, Charles N. Jr., ed. *The Novels of Jack London: A Reappraisal*. Madison: University of Wisconsin Press, 1983.

Wearin, Otha Donner. *Heinold's First and Last Chance*. No publisher, 1974.

Wells, Harry L. "Hunting the Fur Seal." *The West Shore* 14, 10 (1888): 547-58.

Wilcox, R. Turner. *The Mode in Furs: The History of Furred Costume of the World from the Earliest Times to the Present*. New York: Charles Scribner's Sons, 1951.

Williams, Gerald O. *The Bering Sea Fur Seal Dispute: A Monograph on the Maritime History of Alaska*. Juneau: Alaska Maritime Publications, 1984.

–. "Michael J. Healy and the Alaska Maritime Frontier, 1880-1902." MA thesis, University of Oregon, Eugene, 1987.

Williams, Tony. "From Novel to Film." In Rocco Fumento and Tony Williams, eds. *Jack London's The Sea Wolf: A Screenplay by Robert Rossen*, xvii-xxvi. Carbondale, IL: Southern Illinois University Press, 2001.

–. *Jack London, The Movies: An Historical Survey*. Los Angeles: David Reyl, 1992.

Willis, Archie. "In the Days of Sealing." *Victoria Daily Colonist*, 28 June 1970, magazine section, 4.

–. "Victoria Sealers Defied High-Handed Americans." *Victoria Daily Colonist*, 24 May 1970, 4–5, 11.

Wilson, William A. "Folklore and History: Fact amid the Legends." In Jan Harold Brunvand, ed. *Readings in American Folklore*, 449–66. New York: W.W. Norton and Company, 1979.

Woodbridge, H.C., J. London, and G.H. Tweney, compilers. *Jack London: A Bibliography*. Georgetown, CA: Talisman Press, 1966.

Wright, E.W., ed. *Lewis and Dryden's Marine History of the Pacific Northwest*. Portland: Lewis and Dryden Printing Company, 1895.

Zaslow, Morris. *The Opening of the Canadian North, 1870-1914*. Toronto: McClelland and Stewart, 1971.

Index

Note: ACC refers to Alaska Commercial Company; AM, to Alex MacLean; BJ, to Baker, James; BJC, to Blackett, John C.; BJG, to Blaine, James G.; BSCC to Bering Sea Claims Commission; BT, to Burnes, Tommy; CCN, to Cox, Clarence Nelson; DJL, to Dauphin, Josephine Licour; NACC, to North American Commercial Company; NWMP, to North West Mounted Police

Printed and bound in Canada by Friesens

Set in Stone by Artegraphica Design Co. Ltd.

Copy editor: Stacy Belden

Proofreader: Stephanie VanderMeulen

Indexer: Anne Fisher